WRITING IN THE WORKS

WRITING IN THE WORKS

Susan Blau
Boston University

Kathryn Burak
Boston University

Fourth Edition

WADSWORTH
CENGAGE Learning·

Australia · Brazil · Japan · Korea · Mexico · Singapore · Spain · United Kingdom · United States

WADSWORTH
CENGAGE Learning·

Writing in the Works, **Fourth Edition**
Susan Blau, Kathryn Burak

Product Director: Monica Eckman

Product Team Manager: Nicole Morinon

Product Manager: Laura Ross

Content Developer: Kathy Sands-Boehmer

Associate Content Developer: Rachel Smith

Product Assistant: Claire Branman

Media Developer: Janine Tangney

Marketing Manager: Erin Parkins

Senior Content Project Manager:
   Rosemary Winfield

Art Director: Marissa Falco

Manufacturing Planner: Betsy Donaghey

IP Analyst: Ann Hoffman

IP Project Manager: Betsy Hathaway

Production Service: Bruce Hobart, SPI Global

Compositor: SPI Global

Text Designer: Ke Design

Cover Designer: Ke Design

Cover Image: Sky Noir Photography by Bill
   Dickinson/Getty Images

For product information and technology assistance, contact us at
Cengage Learning Customer & Sales Support, 1-800-354-9706.

For permission to use material from this text or product,
submit all requests online at **www.cengage.com/permissions**.

Further permissions questions can be emailed to
permissionrequest@cengage.com.

Library of Congress Control Number: 201594996

ISBN: 978-1-305-08716-3

Cengage Learning
20 Channel Center Street
Boston MA 02210
USA

Cengage Learning is a leading provider of customized learning solutions with employees residing in nearly 40 different countries and sales in more than 125 countries around the world. Find your local representative at **www.cengage.com**.

Cengage Learning products are represented in Canada by Nelson Education, Ltd.

To learn more about Cengage Learning Solutions, visit **www.cengage.com**.

Purchase any of our products at your local college store or at our preferred online store **www.cengagebrain.com**.

Printed in the United States of America
Print Number: 01   Print Year: 2015

BRIEF CONTENTS

Segretain/Getty Images

Bikeriderlondon/Shutterstock.com

Yavuzsariyildiz/iStockphoto.com

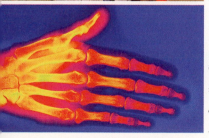

Image Source/Aurora Photos

v

©mj007/Shutterstock.com

Tony Law/Redux

©John Lock/Shutterstock.com

Part 5: Writing to Argue

Part 6: Research and Documentation

Part 7: Grammar Handbook

DETAILED CONTENTS

Part 1: The Writer's Craft

Chapter 3: Collaboration, Peer Review, and Writing as a Public Act   44

Chapter 4: Reading, Thinking, and Writing Critically   60

Part 2: Writing to Explore

Chapter 5: Writing a Narrative: Memoirs   89

Chapter 6: Writing about Others: Profiles   125

Chapter 7: Synthesizing Information:
The Essay of Ideas   **165**

Part 3: Writing to Inform

Chapter 8: Writing Short Articles: The Explainer   193

Part 4: Writing to Analyze

Chapter 10: Writing an Evaluation:
Reviews **245**

Chapter 11: Writing a Causal Analysis: Long Researched Articles **271**

Chapter 13: Creating a Visual Argument:
Public Service Messages   **339**

Chapter 14: Writing for Your Community: Proposals   367

Part 6: Research and Documentation

Chapter 15: Research   399

Chapter 16: Documentation 423

Part 7: Grammar Handbook

Chapter 17: Grammar Refresher   487

Chapter 20: Trouble Spots for Nonnative Speakers of English (available in MindTap edition only)

WRITING PROJECTS

Chapter 1   **Write about the Rhetorical Situation.** Book Review: *Difficult Men* by Brett Martin. Summarize the article and comment on the writer's choices and how they relate to the specific genre of a book review. In your analysis, include your observations about how carefully the writer considers the audience and the choices the writer makes that reflect an understanding of who the readers are and why they are reading.

Chapter 2   **Write a Literacy Narrative.** Tell your reader about the process of your becoming a writer. Recount a pivotal moment in your reading or writing life—a moment of realization that came from frustration, accomplishment, or experimentation.

Chapter 4   **Write a Rhetorical Analysis.** Choose a text and write your own rhetorical analysis using the lists of questions in this chapter to guide you through reading and formulating ideas, summarizing, and writing an analytical thesis that explains a pattern you observed or a decision you made about the text.

Chapter 5   **Write a Memoir.** Write a true story about some part of your life, relating a single event or a series of closely linked events. Show a change of mind or heart, a discovery, a confirmation or contradiction of a belief, a disappointment, or a decision.

Chapter 6   **Write a Profile.** At their best, profiles invite the reader into the subject's world. In your profile of a person or group, focus on some specific aspect that is noteworthy. You do not have to admire the people you write about, but you should find their accomplishments, lifestyles, or philosophies interesting and maybe even fascinating to explore.

Chapter 7 **Write an Essay of Ideas.** Choose an idea that you connect with personally—something that you can illustrate (show) in action through your own life experience. The concept should be a big idea, one that will take some exploration, such as *gratitude*. Find an outside source or two from literature, film, music, science, comedy, or recent or historical events that gives the reader another perspective on the meaning of the concept. Blend and synthesize the sources to discover a new way of thinking about the concept.

Chapter 8 **Write a Short Article, an Explainer.** Write an explainer that answers a question raised by some recent event, or write a short article about something most people do not know about—a new discovery or trend, or a bit of insider's knowledge of a subject. Bust a myth, or confirm one, dig into something commonplace, or something overlooked, and show your readers what they've been missing.

Chapter 9 **Write a Report.** Report on recent events or a trend that has significance for your community—school, town, group—and publish your story in a newspaper, newsletter, blog, or on a website. Write a story with a good headline that focuses and summarizes the news.

Chapter 10 **Write a Review.** Choose a field you like and feel knowledgeable about—for example, film, literature, music, websites, video games, food, and so on. Then select a subject readers would want to read an evaluation of and write a review. You might choose a product, a service, a piece of art, or even a destination.

Chapter 11 **Write a Causal Analysis.** Identify a pattern or trend. Find proof the trend exists in statistics and anecdotes from practitioners and other experts. Those same sources may lead you toward your speculation about why the trend came about and/or what significant effects have been the result. Create a well-reasoned analysis defending your conclusions about what are the causes and/or effects of the trend.

Chapter 12   **Write an Argument.** Choose an issue that is current and debatable, one that could be argued from different perspectives. Define your position on the issue, and then find a good opportunity to add to the debate. Your argument should include an informed perspective, moving beyond personal preference and into a logical argument that demonstrates you understand the issue fully by including all sides, not just the position you are defending.

Chapter 13   **Create a Visual Argument.** In most advertisements, public service messages included, visuals work in conjunction with words. Find a nonprofit group or organization in your community that offers information or services that could benefit the public. Choose a medium (print, video, alternative). Research accurate and useful information, create images to support that information, and have the words and images work in concert. Your aim is to serve your community by raising awareness of an issue, initiating a new behavior or attitude, or changing a behavior or attitude.

Chapter 14   **Write a Proposal.** A fresh way to help solve a local, community, or global public problem is to write a proposal. Identify a problem, suggest a feasible solution, and present the benefits of the solution. The purpose of any proposal is to persuade readers to take some action: to donate time or money or to create a program, plan, or public service campaign.

Chapter 15   **Create an Annotated Bibliography.** Create an annotated bibliography, an alphabetized list of sources, put into one of the documentation styles (MLA, APA, or another) that you then notate with summary, evaluation, and/or commentary.

DIY (DO IT YOURSELF) MEDIA AND DESIGN

DIYs offer a variation on the assignment that explores issues of media and design for a variety of microgenres.

THEMATIC CONTENTS

Personal Experience

Science and Technology

Social Change

PREFACE

When we started writing this book, we were kind of "out there," suggesting that students think of the writing they do in school as important, not just in their academic lives but also important in the so-called real world—their lives as workers and as citizens. Back then, our assumption was, as it still is now, that we are all writers for life.

Are you a writer? Most people would decidedly say no.

Oh, maybe I wrote some school papers, and the occasional letter of application.

That's all? You don't write reports, letters of complaint, recommendations? You don't speak out at public forums or respond to blogs and message boards? Most professional, college-educated people would actually be surprised to find how much they do write.

So, are you a writer?

Well, I write, but I'm not a writer.

Our goal in writing this book is twofold. First, our aim is to demystify the writing most people are exposed to every day—the kind of writing that informs and teaches and entertains and enlightens. And second, we aim to help train confident, worldly writers—students who see themselves as fluent, capable, and well prepared to ride the global communication wave: Students who say yes, I am a writer.

We hope, through our approach to writing, that students see not just the relevance of the skills, but also their practicality, that writing is a valuable personal tool. We do want them to understand that it takes effort, but we also allow them to ask why it is worth the effort—why should they want to be writers? To answer that, we make two pacts with our students. The first is that writing well will have value in their lives, particularly as they develop distinct voices through their studies and later in their professional lives. The second pact is that their writing will have readers.

An Emphasis on Student Writing for Real-World Audiences: The Classroom and Beyond

The classroom is the first real-world audience a student experiences, but we make the point that students can write for audiences beyond the classroom. We start by choosing readings that are high quality and current, writing that people turn to in order to become informed, educated, entertained, and enlightened. We make these choices because the writing we ask students to do is part of the world they inhabit—or aspire to inhabit—a world where they imagine themselves as players. *Writing in the Works* will help them learn to write reports, blogs, memoirs, news stories, reviews, editorials, and researched magazine articles. They will learn the tried-and-true academic writing skills—narration, exposition, analysis, and persuasion—in a context that makes sense and has meaning to them. We reinforce those skills with practice exercises seeded throughout the book, practice exercises that say to the student-writer, bring what you already know about writing and build on that knowledge. The end results are students who enter the stream of ideas with the ability to think critically and creatively, have a healthy skepticism and confidence, and most importantly be flexible writers who can adapt the messages to many different audiences.

Teachers who have used this book have seen their students publish their writing in print publications and on websites. Students have often been paid for their work (movie reviews, profiles, and news stories, to name a few), and sometimes they have donated their writing to advocacy groups for use in public service. Many of our students have contributed their pieces to this book and can see their classroom work enter the world as worthy examples of student writing in a particular genre. In the end, students have left the course with a portfolio of writing samples—and of accomplishments that have a connection to a bigger, more diverse world that includes—but also goes beyond—the classroom.

An Organization That Reflects a Real-World Writing Process

We have organized each assignment chapter in this book in a way that allows students to gain mastery on their own if they are so inclined. Each writing assignment is broken down into distinct skills that are reinforced by practices placed throughout the chapters. The practices build the skills that students need to complete the longer chapter assignment. Contemporary professional and student writing provide examples for students to read and assimilate. The process plans help students organize priorities for each genre.

As teachers guide students through skills and then ask them to put their skills together, students gain a sense of mastery. The goal is to put writing into a process that involves reading, critical thinking, researching, drafting, revising, and peer reviewing and then to let students take charge of their own writing. This kind of process prepares them for writing beyond the classroom in the workplace and in civic life. We stress that the study of writing has its roots in the academic world but that its branches reach well into the world of politics, entertainment, and commerce. And along those lines, the assignments of this book look to the future of writing for a digital world where verbal and visual messages are inseparable. Students of real-world writing must have analytical skills to read images as well as text.

Research Integrated as Part of a Real-World Approach to Writing

The "worldly" approach of *Writing in the Works* also means thinking in a new way about research skills and the ways that research has usually been isolated to one or two assignments in writing classes. Professional writing involves research in all writing, and each of the assignment chapters integrates research into the writing task. Students learn what kind of research they need to do even before they can write a memoir or an essay, and they learn how to research in print, online, and in person.

We offer students all the traditional information about finding, evaluating, and documenting their sources in print media, but we also help them fine-tune their skills in evaluating and documenting new media, including blogs and social media, for their research. This edition has a new emphasis on the spoken word (podcasts and speeches), a skill that is more and more in demand in the digital world. We include the most recent documentation guidelines, so students can cite their sources accurately and avoid even the whiff of plagiarism. Plagiarism has become a pressing problem in the digital age, and we help students understand the parameters of intellectual property theft so they can avoid committing an act of unintentional plagiarism.

NEW TO THIS EDITION

In this fourth edition of *Writing in the Works*, we have kept a dual focus of writing as both academic and practical. At the same time, we have updated the content and the spirit of the book for the contemporary writing environment. Students learn to write for the digital world but do so as exploration of serious ideas that will engage a real-world audience.

Throughout the book, and in three new chapters, we emphasize critical thinking skills with an emphasis on synthesizing, defining, and evaluating. These skills are central to the development of good academic writing and good real-world writing. After all, what school allows students to do—take chances and think big thoughts—has much more impact when it finds a reader.

- ■ **NEW!** A chapter on the Essay of Ideas, an innovative genre that teaches synthesis by combining personal narrative with research to come up with a new way of defining a word or concept.
- ■ **NEW!** A chapter on the Explainer, a short article (popularized by *Slate Magazine*) that provides answers to questions such as: "Why were animals so big in the past?" or "How do you fake your own death?" The answers include larger implications that reveal patterns in behavior, historical context, or scientific phenomenon.
- ■ **NEW!** A focus on spoken word and social media. Updated DIY Media and Design feature in each assignment chapter now includes microgenres such as the graphic memoir, a spoken word project and the podcast, and PechaKucha, the art of concise presentations.
- ■ **NEW!** The chapter on reviews now covers film, restaurant, music, and video game reviews.
- ■ **ENHANCED!** This new edition includes an added emphasis on critical thinking skills. Critical thinking and critical reading are introduced in Chapter 4 and each assignment chapter includes critical thinking questions based on the readings as well as a prompt to model some aspect of the style or technique used in the reading.
- ■ **EXPANDED!** This new edition includes more about visual literacy. Exercises focus on analyzing bold images in each chapter. Each assignment chapter features a visual literacy exercise which helps students hone their ability to create and analyze images including infographics.

SPECIAL FEATURES

✓ **Comprehensive coverage of the Thesis Statement (the Big Idea).** Each chapter includes extensive coverage of composing a thesis statement, noting that the focus of a thesis statement can change depending on the genre. For example, the thesis statement can be argumentative, explanatory, or interpretive. This coverage is highlighted in a section called The Big Idea.

✓ **Emphasis on the Rhetorical Situation** Chapter 1 on The Rhetorical Situation (including audience, purpose, genre, design, visual literacy, and media concerns) features an assignment on analyzing the rhetorical situation of a book review. Each writing assignment includes a section on that genre's rhetorical situation and poses questions for considering the rhetorical situation after each reading.

✓ **Process Plan**—a graphic organizer for key elements in each assignment.

✓ **Streamlined Chapter** structure that begins with Chapter Objectives, a Process Plan, the assignment, a model of the genre, and a condensed description of the rhetorical situation for that genre.

✓ **The Rhetorical Situation** for each chapter includes a brief description of that genre's purpose, audience, voice, and media or design.

✓ **Literacy Narrative** assignment with walk-through of student paper in Chapter 2, including coverage of the rhetorical strategies.

✓ **Chapter 3, Collaboration, Peer Review, and Writing as a Public Act,** includes the popular walk-through of one student's writing process.

✓ **Rhetorical Analysis** assignment in Chapter 4, Reading, Thinking, and Writing Critically, with an annotated sample from an inspiring reading, "Hardscrabble Salvation," plus a student's rhetorical analysis.

✓ **Social media coverage** in Chapter 9, Writing a Report: News for Print, Web, and Social Media focuses on the important role social media now plays in research and reporting. This chapter also emphasizes the critical skill of summary with special coverage of creating an Abstract.

✓ **Comprehensive coverage of written and visual arguments and logical appeals** in Chapter 12, Writing an Argument: Editorials, Commentaries and Blogs and in Chapter 13, Creating a Visual Argument: Public Service Messages.

✓ **Coverage of the annotated bibliography** in Chapter 15, Research. The instruction includes an annotated model and an assignment.

HALLMARK FEATURES

✓ **Real-world approach** emphasizes the genre of each assignment and publication possibilities that further connect writing inside and outside the classroom.

✓ **Student writing** is included in each chapter in the readings section and often as the model essay.

✓ **Research paths** are included in each chapter to make research part of every writing project.

✓ **The Writer's Notebook, Peer Review Logs, and Revision Checklists** provide additional prompts to aid in invention, revision, and proofreading.

✓ **Practices** are provided that coach students through skills related to each genre.

✓ **Writer's Notebook** offers a selection of exercises that teachers can use as collaborative and journal writing.

✓ **Four-in-one value** text includes rhetoric, reader, research, and handbook.

ONLINE RESOURCES

MindTap® English for Blau/Burak's *Writing in the Works* 2nd edition engages your students to become better thinkers, communicators, and writers by blending your course materials with content that supports every aspect of the writing process.

- Interactive activities on grammar and mechanics promote application in student writing.
- Easy-to-use paper management system helps prevent plagiarism and allows for electronic submission, grading, and peer review.
- A vast database of scholarly sources with video tutorials and examples supports every step of the research process.
- Professional tutoring guides students from rough drafts to polished writing.
- Visual analytics track student progress and engagement.
- Seamless integration into your campus learning management system keeps all your course materials in one place.
- MindTap lets you compose your course, your way.

For additional instructor support materials, including PowerPoint slides, the instructor's manual, and a guide to using this book to meet WPA outcomes, go to login.cengage.com.

- The **instructor's manual** provides teaching suggestions, suggested answers to exercises, and a sample course syllabus to assist instructors in teaching the course.
- Using *Writing in the Works* **to Meet WPA Outcomes: An Instructor's Guide**, which can also be found in the instructor's edition of the book, clearly specifies the ways *Writing in the Works* supports the four primary outcomes of the Council of Writing Program Administrators' (WPA) Outcomes Statement for First-Year Composition.

ACKNOWLEDGMENTS

First, our thanks go to our students who bring their enthusiasm to our classrooms, providing insights, criticisms, and ideas about how to make writing instruction useful and interesting. Without them, we would never know what works. We thank our colleagues in the CO201 Writing Program at Boston University, who helped us test our ideas and have generously shared their own ideas for inclusion in this book. We extend gratitude to the teachers who have used the earlier editions of *Writing in the Works* and who have shared our excitement about the material while offering their encouragement and suggestions. Our families continue to inspire us and support us. And finally, we thank the editorial staff at Cengage Learning: our diligent editor, Kathy Sands-Boehmer, who miraculously kept so many balls in the air; Rosemary Winfield, our Project Manager; Marissa Falco, our Art Director; and the permissions folks who went the extra mile to help us secure the readings and images that make this fourth edition of *Writing in the Works* so fresh and engaging.

We also owe a debt of gratitude to all our reviewers and particularly to Jared Abraham at Weatherford College and Allyson Jones at Stevens-Haneger College for the early and formative guidance on the new organization of the text as well as for seeing us through every stage of development. In addition, the research section and the addition of the annotated bibliography was improved by their comments and by those of Mark Bagget, Samford University; Dana Brewer, Weatherford College; Michael Lueker, Our Lady of the Lake University; and Dylan Parkhurst, Stephen F. Austin University. The advice of Stephen Amidon, Indiana Purdue University, Fort Wayne; Shauna Gobbel, Northampton Community College; and Amy Stolley, Saint Xavier University was instrumental in creating the final organization for each chapter early on in the book's development.

In addition, we thank the many colleagues all over the country who wrote such thoughtful and useful comments as they reviewed this book, during the development of the first edition, the revisions of the second and third editions, and now for this new fourth edition:

Fred Bayles, *Boston University*; Andrea L. Beaudin, *Southern Connecticut State University*; Amanda Bemer, *Southwest Minnesota State University*; Sheri Benton, *University of Toledo*; Jose M. Blanco, *Miami Dade College*; Mary Ann Bretzlauf, *College of Lake County*; Dana Brewer, *Weatherford College*; Greg Brister, *Valley City State University*; Ron Brooks, *Oklahoma State University*; Mark Browning, *Johnson County Community College*; Jo Ann Buck, *Guilford Technical Community College*; Melissa Vosen Callens, *North Dakota State University*; Susan Carlton, *Boston University*; Thomas Chester, *Ivy Tech Community College*; Aaron Clark, *Brookhaven College*; Nelda Contreras, *Brookhaven College*; Avon Crismore, *Indiana University–Purdue University, Fort Wayne*; Rachel Darabi, *Indiana University–Purdue University, Fort Wayne*; Cherie Post Dargan, *Hawkeye Community College*; Adenike Davidson, *University of Central Florida*; Susan Shibe Davis, *Arizona State University*; Brock Dethier, *Utah State University*; Julia K. Ferganchick, *University of Arkansas at Little Rock*; Susan Garrett, *Goucher College*; Gregory R. Glau, *Arizona State University*; Leslie Goldberg, *Tufts University*; Roy Neil Graves, *University of Tennessee, Martin*; Jo-Sandra B. Greenberg, *Brookhaven College*; John Hall, *Boston University*; Ghazala Hasmi, *J. Sargeant Reynolds Community College*; Robert Heaton, *Utah State University*; Vicki Hendricks, *Broward, South Campus*; Scarlett Hill, *Brookhaven College*; Jack Jacobs, *Auburn University*; Meredith James, *Eastern Connecticut State University*; Allyson Jones, *Stevens-Henager College*; Tatiana Keeling, *Central Arizona College*; Millie M. Kidd, *Mount St. Mary's College*; Paul Lehman, *University of Central Oklahoma*; Mitchell R. Lewis, *Elmira College*; JoAnne Liebman Matson, *University of Arkansas at Little Rock*; Alfred J. López, *Florida International University*; Peter Lovenheim, *Rochester Institute of Technology*; James J. McKeown, Jr., *McLennan Community College*; T. Gerard McNamee, *Eastern Oregon University*; Constantina Michalos, *Houston Baptist University*; Kate Mohler, *Mesa Community College*; Cindy Moore, *St. Cloud University*; Ed Moritz, *Indiana University–Purdue University, Fort Wayne*; Heather Moulton, *Central Arizona College*; Marti L. Mundell, *Washington State University*; Charles Naccarato, *Ohio University*; Scott Oates, *University of Wisconsin, Eau Claire*; R. J. Osborne, *Grossmont College*; Victoria Ramirez, *Weber State*

University; Peter Rand, *Boston University*; Dick Ravin, *Boston University*; Gordon Reynolds, *Ferris State University*; Lawrence Roderer, *J. Sargeant Reynolds Community College*; Connie G. Rothwell, *University of North Carolina at Charlotte*; Karin Russell, *Keiser University*; Mark Schaub, *Grand Valley State University*; Steven P. Schneider, *University of Texas, Pan-American*; Ingrid Schreck, *College of Marin*; Joseph M. Schuster, *Webster University*; Arvis Scott, *McLennan Community College*; Rhonda L. Smith, *Jacksonville College*; Howard Tinberg, *Bristol Community College*; Pay Tyrer, *West Texas A&M University*; Kendra Vaglienti, *Brookhaven College*; Taline Voskeritchian, *Boston University*; Xiao Wang, *Broward Community College*; and Charles Warnberg, *Brookhaven College*.

Susan Blau
Kathryn Burak

THE WRITER'S CRAFT

THE RHETORICAL SITUATION
WRITERS' CHOICES

Prose is architecture, not interior decoration.
—ERNEST HEMINGWAY

Never before has information been so immediate and so accessible. Thanks to wireless and digital technology, information about the world, our friends, the weather, and more is always at our fingertips. Practically every day Facebook offers members new applications that allow them to connect with each other in new ways—through pokes, virtual hugs, and vampire bites. Once the domain of the under-21 crowd, Facebook now includes political candidates whose pages are loaded with up-to-the-minute information and pictures, so we can see the gaffes and grimaces of world leaders broadcast 24/7 on YouTube.

The Internet has opened the globe to libraries and museums as well as coffee shop conversations. A sixth-grader in Des Moines, Iowa, might have access to as much information as a university student at Oxford. We have so much information and so many facts and opinions that at times trying to get an understanding of an issue can be like trying to get a drink of water from a hose turned on full blast. But information alone has little value. Being able to see beyond the packaging, pictures, and music videos that are the companions to most of our daily messages is vital to becoming successful in academics as well as in careers. Those people who navigate the raging stream of information skillfully will be those who can think critically and read discriminately—those able to tell the treachery from the treasure. They will be writers who understand the significance of words and the connections between the words and images of messages.

They will also be the people who understand the myriad of choices writers face each time they sit down to compose. Assume that some bureaucratic mix-up gets you riled. You want to set things right or at the very least vent your pent-up anger. Do you fire off a quick e-mail? Write a 500-word op-ed for the local paper? Send a formal letter of complaint to the head of the company? To decide, you have to consider the rhetorical situation you are in—that is, what you want to communicate and to whom. Maybe the e-mail will suffice to diffuse your anger, but the thought-provoking letter of complaint might get you a more considered response. The op-ed will do the best job of broadcasting your concerns to the most people, but it will not necessarily reach the individual who could do something about the problem.

Every time you sit down to write, you have to make these kinds of choices. Each rhetorical situation includes choices about

- genre: what type of text you are writing
- purpose: what you are trying to accomplish
- audience: whom you are writing for
- voice: how you want to sound
- media and design: how you want your writing to look

Choosing the Right Genre

A genre is a type of writing—from an informative report to a blog posting—and each type of writing requires particular rhetorical moves. Usually, the genre for your classroom writing assignments is already chosen for you. You may be asked to write a memoir or an essay, perhaps a report or a review. Each of these genres follows a general pattern and comes with a set of readers' expectations. Readers pick up a film review, for example, to find out a critic's analysis and evaluation of a film—and maybe to get some news about the stars. Within the confines of any genre is room to experiment, to take some risks, to surprise, and even to delight your reader.

But before the delight can happen, you have to do some thinking about the best genre for your purpose. If you have a story to tell about something that happened to you, you could write a memoir or you could choose to write a personal essay. To figure out which is best suited for your purposes, you have to figure out what each offers you as a writer. Both genres, in this case, are nonfiction and autobiographical, but the memoir is narrative in structure. It tells a story that offers insight into some slice of your life. The personal essay is interpretive. You may tell a story but then you expand on it; you philosophize and draw connections and conclusions. Which genre is the right one for the story you want to tell?

PRACTICE 1.1

Collaborative Activity: Identifying Genres and Patterns

1. Choose an area of interest among these three: books, music, and films.

2. For your chosen area, generate as many genres as you can think of for that area. Make the genres as specific as you can, so instead of "fiction" as a genre for books, divide that category into mysteries, romances, science fiction, and so forth.

3. Select three or four of the genres you have identified, and make a list of your expectations for that genre. What patterns do you expect to find in a mystery novel, for example, or a science fiction one?

When left to your own devices, you make the choice of genre by analyzing the rhetorical situation. Each of the elements—genre, purpose, audience, voice, design—are interrelated. If you care a great deal about the importance of eating local and organic food, for example, and you want to write about that topic, you have to decide what you are trying to accomplish. If it is to persuade others to your way of thinking, you have to figure out your audience. Whom do you want to persuade? If your intended audience is the fast-food–loving college student, then how do you best reach that audience? What kind of evidence do you have to amass? What kind of voice will help change students' minds? What is the best genre for your purpose and your audience? There is no one right answer. Perhaps you should write an argumentative essay and publish it on your college's website. Or perhaps you should write a spoof or a parody for a website that spoofs the news, like *The Onion*, knowing that many unpersuaded students would be better convinced through humor.

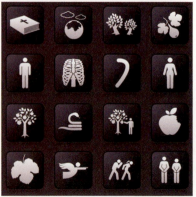

Different ways to tell the story of Adam and Eve—From classic to memes.

You also need to keep up-to-date on how the purpose or audience of genres sometimes change or shift. Blogs, for example, began as informal genres, almost as website logs (as the name suggests) or diary entries, read by a handful of friends or like-minded people. In time, journalists and experts in a variety of fields began blogging and some blogs morphed into more substantial writing with a much wider readership. Today, most writers and many students keep blogs, and they are becoming part of an aspiring writer's portfolio.

In the following chapters you will learn to write in a variety of genres: essays, memoirs, news stories, reviews, editorials, blogs, proposals, public service messages, websites, and magazine articles. You will learn the usual patterns of that genre, and you will learn how to make a smart choice about which genre best suits your purpose.

Identifying Your Purpose

Let's figure out the *purpose* for this typical writing assignment:

> Choose a local issue on your college campus or in your community, or select a global issue that is in the news and that interests you. Decide what your position is on this issue and argue persuasively for your position in a letter to the editor, a column, a blog, or a guest editorial for a specific newspaper or online news site.

This assignment gives you a great deal of information about the rhetorical situation. Four genres—a letter to the editor, a column, a blog, or a guest editorial—are suggested and each has somewhat different requirements and audiences. But the general purpose of the assignment is clear: you are to "argue persuasively" on a position in the news. After you identify your topic and your position, you can use that information to figure out what is meaningful to you in that topic and what your specific purpose will be.

Let's say you have chosen to write about texting and driving—a hot-button topic on your campus. One possible thesis for an editorial that supports a bill outlawing texting while driving might be "Texting while driving endangers the lives of drivers, passengers, and pedestrians and must be outlawed." Your general purpose is "to argue"; your specific purpose is to prove the point that texting while driving endangers people's lives.

The General Purpose

We have all had the experience of not really knowing what we want to say and doodling around on paper, trying out one idea or sentence after another, attempting to figure out what on earth we want to say about a topic. How do you determine your

purpose for an academic assignment or one in the workplace or in your community? Are you going to

- *tell* a story (Writing to Explore)
- *report* on an event (Writing to Inform)
- *review* a book or *analyze* a poem (Writing to Analyze)
- *argue* for building bicycle lanes in city streets or *lobby* for an internship (Writing to Argue)

Keep in mind that these purposes are not mutually exclusive. You could certainly write an essay that tells a story about your ability to keep cool under pressure while at the same time analyze the pressurized situation—all to persuade your reader that you would be the perfect intern in a busy public relations firm. Under the general headings of exploring, informing, analyzing, and persuading, you can break down your purpose into smaller categories, such as educating, explaining, expressing an emotion—really anything at all that you want to accomplish through your writing.

You can often figure out the purpose of a classroom assignment by looking at its language. Many essay assignments have the purpose embedded in the topic or question asked. If the topic asks you to "support" or "justify," or "argue," you can be certain that the purpose of the paper is for you to take a position on a controversial topic and support it with evidence. If you are asked to "describe," or "illustrate," or "report," your purpose is most likely to inform your reader about a topic. "Explicate" or "review" suggests that you analyze, and "tell a story" or "give an example" often suggests that you explore a situation in more depth.

The Specific Purpose: The Big Idea

Writing can be exploratory or experimental, but if you are writing for a public audience (a teacher, an editor, a producer), take this process of identifying your purpose one step further. You can think of your specific purpose in a piece of writing as the point—or the *big idea*—you are trying to communicate. Every piece of writing, no matter how long or complicated, is organized around one big idea that is your perspective on your topic—the point you are making in your writing.

Whatever your purpose, though, you have to know what idea you are trying to communicate. The big idea behind your writing provides the focus of your paper. After you figure out your big idea, you can then narrow your focus to the specific point you want to make in your writing.

Different genres have different terminology for the big idea. In academic essays, the big idea is called a *thesis*. In stories, it is called the *theme*. In an advertisement,

Tips about the BIG IDEA

Each piece of writing has one main big idea.

1. The big idea is not an obvious fact.
2. Because #1 is true, the big idea needs help: explanation, support, and defense.
3. Stick to the big idea until the very last word of your writing.

the big idea is called a *concept*, and in an editorial or other argumentative essay, it is referred to as a *claim*. The big idea in analysis or review writing is your *interpretation*. Journalists call the big idea in a feature article the *nut graf* or the *bridge graf* (*graf* being shorthand for *paragraph*).

FAQS about the BIG IDEA

Q: Is it always a single sentence?
A: No, sometimes your big idea takes a paragraph or two. This is especially true in profiles and trend analyses.

Q: Is it always an opinion?
A: No, in a short essay, the big idea is factual, but it is a fact that needs some explanation, not something obvious like grass is green.

Q: Do narratives really have a single big idea?
A: Well, depending on your interpretation, yes. But keep in mind that 10 people could watch the same movie and come up with 10 interpretations. When you are writing a narrative, chances are likely that you have a predominant message or a reason to tell the story—a point that goes beyond the events and into what the events say.

Q: How could a news story have a big idea?
A: News stories have angles, or ways to decipher the importance of the events. In the angle, the reader will find the big idea. Interestingly, though, since news stories are stories, they share this ability to mean several things, depending on the audience. So, a single news event could have, and often does have, several different angles once it is reported, but each of those angles will come in a separate story. One big idea per customer, please!

PRACTICE 1.3
Engaging Your Audience

Create a reader profile for the following writing assignments:

- A film review for an online general-interest magazine
- An essay for the "Modern Love" section of the *New York Times*
- A book review for your campus newspaper
- A literary analysis for your American Literature class
- A public service print advertisement for MADD (Mothers Against Drunk Driving)
- An analysis of an online game for a gaming website, such as IGN ■

Engaging Your Audience

In today's world we are closer to our "audience" than ever before. Facebook posts, blogs, and tweets all let our readers follow our daily lives, read our musings, and get to know us well. But how do we go through that virtual looking glass and get a sense of who the readers are?

Your readers can be easily bored and distractible. If the blog is not engaging, the next one is only a click away. Magazines can be put down, letters crumpled, or reports put in the "circular file." Your job as a writer is to engage your reader, but first you have to know something about this elusive being.

Understandably, students often write for their professors. After all, the professor will be the first-line reader and evaluator of the work. The problem, of course, is imagining your professor as your only reader limits your range. Consider a broader readership: a world full of potential readers. Who are they? What will draw them to your message? What will make them come back for more?

Think of your audience as readers familiar with the genre. News readers want their information delivered in clear, direct language with all the pertinent information summarized quickly in the first paragraph or two. You can think of this reader gulping morning coffee and surfing the Internet. On the other hand, a reader who picks up a memoir or reads a personal essay expects to be riveted by the story of your life and has probably set aside some leisure time to do so. Maybe this reader is tucked in bed with her e-reader.

You can create this kind of profile of your reader for any assignment you tackle. Keeping in mind the expectations of the genre and the purpose of your writing will help guide you to a sense of your audience. A useful rule of thumb is to think of your reader as "intelligent but ignorant." What this means is that your reader is smart but does not yet know your take on the topic. Explaining your ideas to this reader keeps you focused and on your toes.

Creating Your Voice

As you make choices about genre, purpose, and audience, you also have to consider your writer's *voice*. You create a voice as you write—a voice that speaks directly to your reader and discloses something about who you are. When you talk, you reveal your personality by the words you choose to use and by your tone of voice, volume, and inflections. You can also use expressions and gestures—body language—to make your points. A raised eyebrow or a dismissive shrug can convey irony or negativity, even if your words are full of praise.

Tone: Formal, Personal, Lyrical, or Plainspoken

When you write, you have fewer tools with which to work than when you are talking. You are limited to expressing your attitude through your choice of words and sentence structure—maybe even through punctuation and graphics. Nevertheless, you can still create writing that falls anywhere on the spectrum between sounding formal to sounding chatty, and you can also create a desired *tone*. You can make your writing sound, among other ways, ironic, droll, funny, cutting, serious, cynical, lively, lyrical, dull, or flippant.

Creating your voice is part of the craft of writing. Whenever you write an academic essay, an application for a study-abroad program, or a letter of appeal to raise money for a charity, you make decisions about how you want to sound and how you want your reader to respond to you. You develop an inner ear—a sense of what sounds right and what sounds discordant—as you gain experience in writing and reading.

Of course, a writer does not have just one voice. You have multiple voices that you use in writing, just as you do in speech, for different audiences. Just as you would probably not curse in the classroom, you would usually not use slang or sloppy writing in an academic essay or a scholarship application.

More to the point, you fit your voice to the assignment's purpose and the conventions of your chosen genre. When writing a music review for your college newspaper, you might appropriately use a humorous voice, one filled with wordplay and puns. On the other hand, when writing an essay or editorial expressing your views on the death penalty, you would probably use a serious, even impassioned, voice.

All of these voices are authentic. They are all part of who you are and how you express yourself in different situations. No matter what choices you make as a writer—to use a formal or personal tone, lyrical or plainspoken language—you create your voice through the words you use and the way you structure your sentences. Keep in mind that you control your language; you make conscious choices to use *this* word rather than *that* one, a long sentence rather than a short one.

How do you make those decisions? All writers confront these questions of voice. Some genres and some audiences require a certain style, but more often than not, style is more of a writer's choice. You might use a common word like *house* or its more fussy cousin *edifice*. Maybe you will write a simple sentence to cement a point, or perhaps you will use a lengthy one to create an unbroken series of images. The end product of all these stylistic choices becomes your writer's voice, your personality emerging from the page.

Stylistic Choices and the Writer's Voice

Even when writing about seemingly dry topics, good writers try to engage their readers. The following passage comes from a book called *The Lives of a Cell* by science writer Lewis Thomas.

> We live in a dancing matrix of viruses; they dart, rather like bees, from organism to organism, from plant to insect to mammal to me and back again, and into the sea, tugging along pieces of this genome, strings of genes from that, transplanting grafts of DNA, passing around heredity as though at a great party.

PRACTICE 1.4
Defining Voice

Define the voices in the following passages. Support your definition by citing specific examples of vocabulary, sentence structure, or punctuation. If you can, make a guess about the writer's occupation and intended audience. On what evidence do you base your guess? In what kind of publication would you expect to find each of the passages?

1. Like a sweeter *Ugly Betty*, *Jane the Virgin* is a telenovela, but one with a sense of irony and wit, simultaneously winking at and embracing its own format. It is easily the most charming new TV series of the fall line-up for 2014, a highly stylized, big-hearted, zippy Technicolor dramedy that is also, uncloyingly, another example of network TV's growing—at least for the moment—diversity.

2. The African American contribution to composition studies—an enormous one—flows from various confluences inside African American intellectual and rhetorical traditions. Free black churches, culturally specific jeremiads, slave
(continued)

Thomas is having fun with this writing. He begins with a short, simple assertion but chooses a surprising adjective—*dancing*—to describe the matrix of viruses in which we live. Then, by stringing together the long series of phrases, Thomas makes his sentence seem to dance as well. He plays with language as he plays with sentence length by returning to the dance image at the end of the sentence. He shows the viruses passing around heredity as one might pass around canapés: *as though at a great party*. Here is a writer who has put a great deal of effort into his writing, but the result seems effortless. His style is lively, and his voice is engaging. Above all, his writing is crystal clear.

(continued)

narratives, secret schools, black women's clubs, and black colleges all represent an enriching merger of African American intellectual and activist concern with writing instruction initiatives.

3. Knit in a breathable pique-stitch from smooth Peruvian combed cotton, these shirts have a weathered softness and a comfortable, broken-in feel you will enjoy right away. Gently sandwashed to mellow the colors and minimize shrinkage. ■

Deciding on Media and Design: Packaging Your Message

As a writer, you also have to consider how to package, or deliver, your message—in what medium and with what design elements. Writing is rarely black words in 12-point type on a white page nowadays. Words often come with music and images that move or stay still, and that sometimes can be delivered immediately to a cell phone. You definitely have to contemplate *how* your message will be read, whether it is on paper or on a screen. Imagine a two-story billboard. Then think about the tiny screen of your cell phone. What is possible to write on each of these spaces is just one part of your thinking about how a message might be delivered to your audience. You must consider what is customary as well as what is appropriate.

Considering Your Media

In writing for the business world, as in dressing for the professional world, certain choices are predetermined. You will present information onscreen, perhaps using PowerPoint. You will augment your presentations with film. You will need to think

Universal Uclick

1 THE RHETORICAL SITUATION

about the size of the words, the typeface or font, the amount of words anyone would want to read on a screen. These are not arbitrary decisions. These elements are not decorations.

The way your message is read will help you choose what you write. There is no escaping the interconnected nature of how a message looks and what it says to specifically targeted readers.

FAQS about Packages for Messages

Q: What if my message takes several forms—a speech that also will appear on the Internet?

A: In most cases, determine what the main delivery system is. For example, if your main delivery is a YouTube video of a speaker, your writing should conform to the rules for the spoken word: writing short, concrete sentences that work with the breath of the speaker.

Q: How will I know the best package for my message?

A: Most of the time, the answer to this is tied up with the outcome you would like to achieve. If you are writing a blog, you want to engage your readers and you want them to come back later and read more. You will keep brevity in mind, remembering how onscreen readers do not like to scroll too much, for example.

Q: Should I think about how to incorporate other kinds of media—sound and photographs?

A: Yes and no. The reality of being a working writer means you enter the stream of writing and the stream is crowded with messages, each one competing with all the others. But your message should not include media for the sake of it. Remember, this is not about decoration. These choices help carry your message and help make it stronger, but ultimately it is your big idea, the clarity of your message, and the style of your message that will make or break it. It is important to remember: sometimes a message can simply be words on a page, billboard, or phone screen.

Ten Tips for a Clear Writing Style

Writers, whether in the professional or academic world, put a premium on a crisp, direct writing style that communicates ideas clearly, economically, and precisely.

(continued)

Ten Tips for a Clear Writing Style *(continued)*

1. **Cut Clutter** Cluttered writing hides your good ideas under unnecessary padding and robs your sentences of their power. You can express the most complex ideas in clear language that helps your reader understand your thinking.

   Wordy: *The students who won the prizes will meet the judges at the conference on the day when they hold the dinner to commemorate their work.*

   Clear: *The prize-winning students will meet the judges at the conference's commemorative dinner.*

2. **Avoid Redundancy** Be alert to the meanings of the words you select. For example, many people misuse the word *unique*. If you know that *unique* means one of a kind, unrivaled, and incomparable, you will not make the common error of qualifying it with *very*.

   Other redundant expressions:

   Refer ~~back~~   ~~Tall~~ skyscraper

   Repeat ~~again~~   ~~End~~ result

   Free ~~complimentary~~ dinner   Cooperate ~~together~~

   Smiled ~~happily~~   ~~Basic~~ fundamentals

3. **Limit Qualifiers** Qualifiers (adjectives and adverbs) limit or modify other words; they also add color and texture to writing. However, some qualifiers—such as *many, somewhat, very, relatively,* and *rather*—do the opposite; they make writing dull. Try reading the following sentence from E. B. White's *The Elements of Style* without the qualifiers *particularly, little, very, rather,* and *pretty,* and see if you agree that these words sap the sentence of its strength.

   > The constant use of the adjective *little* (except to indicate size) is particularly debilitating; we should all try to do a little better, we should all be very watchful of this rule, for it is a rather important one, and we are pretty sure to violate it now and then.

4. **Cut *It is* and *There are* from Your Writing** When possible, take extra care to avoid writing or to rewrite sentences beginning with *It is* or *There are*. Known as expletive constructions, these phrases commit two writing sins: they add unnecessary

language, and they keep your reader from getting to the point of the sentence.

Original: *There are two cats sleeping in the bay window.*

Rewrite: *Two cats sleep in the bay window.*

5. **Use Your Natural Vocabulary** Sometimes writers are tempted to pump some air into flabby prose by inflating their language. Almost always, the result sounds awkward, unnatural, and even confusing. When you use your natural vocabulary, words that have meaning and nuance for you, you can communicate more precisely, more clearly, and with more authority.

Pumped up: *The deleterious result of prolixity in writing results in obfuscatory textual material.*

Natural: *Wordiness results in confusing writing.*

6. **Limit Jargon** The business world is notoriously infested with jargon—"I appreciate this opportunity to input that concept from a business effectiveness viewpoint"—but doctors, economists, grammarians, and others also speak to each other in a kind of specialized language. It is tempting for those of us who wish to sound knowledgeable to try out "insider" language, especially when writing a paper for a class in literature, sociology, or psychology—fields that have a specialized vocabulary. Whenever possible, avoid that temptation.

7. **Avoid Euphemism** *Euphemism* is language that covers up the truth either out of prudery (using *powder room* instead of *bathroom* or *bathroom* instead of *toilet*); sensitivity (using *passed on* instead of *died*); or the desire to sound more respectful or elevated (using *waste disposal personnel* instead of *garbage collectors*). Euphemisms can make your writing sound wordy and pretentious.

8. **Use the Active Voice (Most of the Time)** A sentence is in the active or passive voice, depending on whether the subject of the sentence performs or receives the action. In the active voice, the subject is the actor. In the passive voice, the subject receives the action.

Passive voice: *The president was elected by the voters in a landslide victory.*

Active voice: *Voters elected the president in a landslide victory.*

(continued)

Ten Tips for a Clear Writing Style *(continued)*

Certain genres also call for the passive voice.

Lab report: *"Liquid was poured into the test tube"* and *"Incisions were made." (passive)*

Readers of lab reports focus on what happened, what actions occurred. Knowing exactly who poured the liquid into the test tube is not important.

Newspaper article: *Three people were injured last night in a house fire. (passive)*

This sentence places emphasis on the injured people rather than on the fire itself.

9. **Use Concrete Nouns** Concrete nouns refer to objects, persons, or places that you can perceive with your five senses. (Abstract nouns refer to ideas or concepts—such as *forgiveness*, *trust*, and *love*.) Readers remember specifics, not generalities. If a person you are describing sits under a tree, let your readers know if the tree is a redwood or a pine, if it is old and gnarled or a sapling.

A really tall building	A skyscraper
An extremely cheap person	A miser
A lot of good food	A feast

10. **Use Strong Verbs** The verb packs the most punch in a sentence. Strong verbs describe or express action, giving a sentence its energy and power. Weak verbs do the opposite; they deaden sentences.

    Forms of the verb *to be* appear more than any other verb in English sentences. All of the forms of *to be* (*am*, *is*, *are*, *was*, *were*, *being*, *been*), called *state-of-being* or *linking verbs*, show no action.

    Any time you can substitute an active verb for a form of *to be*, you can infuse some liveliness into your sentence.

Weak: *There was a thief robbing my building.*

Stronger: *A thief robbed my building.*

    The more precisely you can choose a verb, the clearer your meaning becomes. You can eliminate modifiers if you select a verb with the precise meaning you seek.

Original: *I looked at the book very carefully.*

More precise: *I scrutinized the book.*

Identifying Active and Passive Voices

Test your understanding of the active and passive voice by identifying the following sentences as active or passive and by rewriting any passive-voice sentences in the active voice.

1. *Lincoln* was viewed by my entire history class.

2. Super Bowl ads are watched more avidly than the game itself.

3. The New Year's Eve party was attended by the rich and famous.

4. The band played its final set to the audience's loud approval.

5. World War II was won in 1945.

6. World War II ended in 1945. ■

Designing Your Message

The nonverbal parts of messages—illustrations and photographs—shape our understanding of a message in the same way that words do. These messages can be completely nonverbal and, if they are well designed, we can "read" them as we would read written language. Nonverbal communication—facial expressions and body language—reveals how much information we understand without language. Even as babies, before we understood language, our earliest attempts at "reading" were figuring out what to make of the world around us. Babies cry when they look at angry faces but smile when they look at happy faces. Just the drawings of faces can elicit these responses from an infant.

Our understanding of nonverbal messages is as much learned as it is instinctive, and this understanding seems deeply imbedded in our perception of information—so deeply imbedded that we do not always understand why we are persuaded by the things we see. But if we slow down the process of perceiving messages—looking and reading—we can understand why some images are so very powerful. Keep in mind that learning to look critically is a skill much like learning to read critically.

Think about an angry note you might write by hand with underlining and all capital letters. (*"I DON'T EVER WANT TO SEE YOU AGAIN!"*) The medium you use to convey your anger might be a thick Sharpie-brand marker—a good choice for delivering a strong (not to mention waterproof) message.

Now consider the same message written in pink crayon. The words would say one thing literally, but the appearance of the words on paper might connote something else. Small alterations in the way the message looks can add up to big changes in what the message means. Most of the messages you receive daily—and many of the ones you create—are packaged with visual imagery: photographs, illustrations, and even streaming video. As you read through the chapters of this book, you will learn how to decode many types of visual messages and learn to *look critically*. To become better at critical "seeing," you will examine many of the choices designers and artists have made—from the font or typeface choices to the cropping or placement of images on the page or screen. To get started, look at two examples of visual elements in messages: layout and color.

LAYOUT   One important visual element is the way words are placed on the page, also called *layout*. Changing the font or size or orientation of the letters in a word or on the page changes the meaning and creates nuance. Think about how you might write in all caps to get attention or show anger or string a word vertically down a page, as some poets do, using the blank page as a canvas for their thoughts.

COLOR   Color, another important design element, has great influence on emotion and, in turn, on perceived meaning. As with all things visual, our associations with color are as instinctive as they are culturally learned. The image of a bride

PRACTICE 1.6
Editing for Clarity and Brevity

Revise this passage, changing vague nouns to specific ones and substituting strong verbs for weak ones. Try to eliminate every use of a form of *to be*, even if it means rewriting the sentences.

There are a lot of people doing research today who are conducting an investigation into how the things in our heads work. The question they are looking to answer is how our brains store stuff. One woman in psychology is focusing on animal studies. Dr. Phyllis Johnson is doing experiments with rats who are running around in confusing places. She is looking to find out how neurological impulses work as these rodents are going through the mazes. A man who is also in psychology, Dr. Louis Young, is working with human subjects who are students at the local college. These subjects will be doing things inside magnetic resonance imaging machines. It is hoped that these things that they do will be providing answers to long-standing questions about stuff we remember. ■

Using Layout to Emphasize Meaning

Use the following sentence to explore how layout could enhance or change the written meaning of the words. Limit yourself to layout choices only. Choose Times Roman or Arial font, up to 20 points in size. Limit your space to an 8½ by 11-inch sheet of white paper.

We used to play a game in which we would hold our breaths for as long as we could. ■

PRACTICE 1.8

Using Color to Emphasize Meaning

How might this image be used to make a point?

RED

1. First, list all the meanings of the word *red*.

2. Next, list all the meanings associated with the color *green*.

3. Now, think of one product that might be advertised with this image. ■

dressed in all white would not have the same meaning if viewed in the Far East, where brides have traditionally worn red. Can you imagine what the neighbors would say in the United States if a person in mourning wore purple? However, in Thailand, wearing purple would be completely appropriate at a time of mourning. Because color takes on its own character depending on where the viewer lives, web designers are warned that they need to be aware of the intensity of meaning colors can carry. Shades and hues of colors can convey different emotions to different viewers. As you begin to look at messages in a more critical way, also consider the importance of color.

DESIGN CHECKLIST The significance of the nonverbal parts of messages is more important than ever now that so much of our communication takes place on video screens. To become an astute reader of the visual, you first need to break down the nonverbal parts of a message into separate elements. Knowing what to look for is key. The following list is a good way to begin "looking" critically.

1. **Look at the individual elements. Without trying to interpret the significance of the visual elements, describe what you see.** You might describe the drawing by Saul Steinberg, on the opposite page, in these words.

   This is a line drawing of a little girl and a grown-up man. The characters face one another in profile. The drawing is very simple. Coming from the man's mouth is a dark, jagged line. The line starts at his mouth and makes some angular turns and then ends in the air near the girl. The line starting at the girl's mouth is curlicued and forms childish drawings of dogs and houses and flowers, all connected. The man's line is drawn over the girl's. The drawing has a cartoonish look to it.

2. **Look for patterns and make connections.** Carefully observing the details of the drawing might result in this type of description.

   This simple and amusing line drawing shows an adult and a child talking to each other. Your eye is drawn first to the heavy, bold line that represents the words coming out of the adult's mouth. The man seems to speak in a loud, assertive voice, and the subject of his words seems to be abstract, especially when compared with the little girl's words. She talks about all kinds of things—puppies and houses and flowers—all of which seem concrete and playful.

3. **Form an opinion or theory.** You might come to this conclusion.

   The adult attempts to impress or instruct the child by speaking loudly. Since his line cancels hers out, he has the upper hand. Steinberg's mes-

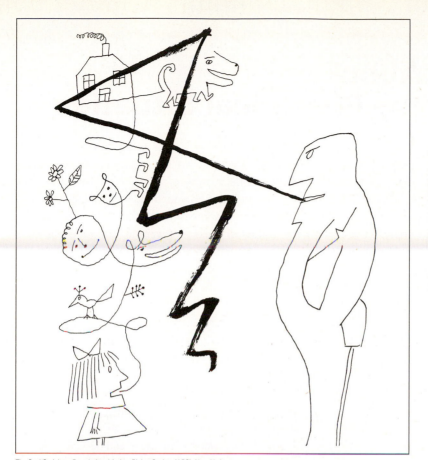

The Saul Steinberg Foundation / Artists Rights Society (ARS), New York

sage may be that children have interesting—if not always perfectly logical—things to say, but adults speak with more authority. Steinberg's drawing comments on the puffed-up egos of some adults and their inability to listen to children.

Writing About the Rhetorical Situation

As you now know, all these decisions a writer makes about genre, purpose, audience, voice, media, and design are interrelated and interdependent. Even choices about your title, structure, organization, tone, sentence length, and word choice depend on who your readers are and why they are reading. To apply your understanding of these choices as you begin to analyze the rhetorical situation of a piece of writing, first read this book review about television's current crop of antiheros: "difficult men."

Walter White from *Breaking Bad*

NO MORE MR. NICE GUYS

"Difficult Men" by Brett Martin*

Lisa Schwarzbaum

MANY YEARS ago, in an era when the phrases "boob tube," "idiot box" and "vast wasteland" went unchallenged as television descriptors among the Discerning Classes, I sat in a pool of prospective jurors on a case involving a fancy jeweler. Aiming, apparently, to assess whether we were likely to confuse the actions of real-life rich people with those on "Dynasty," the defense lawyer asked each of us, "Do you watch TV?" "Nah," swore a majority of my exceptionally discriminating citizen peers. "Just a little." "Maybe some 'Nova' from PBS on a black-and-white TV."

Had counsel tried that line of questioning today, odds are she would have gotten a very different earful, including enthusiastic recitations of dialogue from "The Sopranos"; sophisticated analyses of Don Draper's character flaws on "Mad Men"; and celebrations of "Six Feet Under," "Deadwood," "The Wire" and the violent, amoral mayhem that drives "Breaking Bad." Today, those same potential jurors are more likely to say they don't go to many movies (see above re "boobs" and "idiots"), because they're home watching good television, much of it on cable rather than network TV. We're in a fascinating moment in the creative cycles of popular culture, when television—O.K., fine, the best of television—is embracing complexity, subtlety and innovation in storytelling with an exciting maturity. We're in a moment when the intricate structure and deep character development in long-form dramas can stand up to comparison with great literature.

We're in a time when going to work for what the brilliant British television writer Dennis Potter once called "the medium of the occupying power" is a high calling. (Except maybe for David Chase, the cranky-genius creator of "The Sopranos." Hold that thought.)

Following what the journalist Brett Martin identifies as a first burst of literary energy in the 1950s (when the medium was young) and a second in the 1980s (when the forward-thinking television executive Grant Tinker's MTM Enterprises begat the groundbreaking "Hill Street Blues"), this moment of ascendancy has become television's "Third Golden Age." And in "Difficult Men," Martin maps a wonderfully smart, lively and culturally astute survey of this recent revolution—starting with a great title that does double duty. Because for starters, the antiheroic protagonists in what the author calls "the signature American art form of the first decade of the 21st century, the equivalent of what the films of Scorsese, Altman, Coppola and others had been to the 1970s or the novels of Updike, Roth and Mailer had been to the 1960s," are indeed difficult men. (And they are all men.) The best-loved fellows in the Third Golden Age include suburban mobsters ("The Sopranos"), compromised cops ("The Shield"), touchy drug dealers ("The Wire"), lying ad execs ("Mad Men"), outrageous brothel keepers ("Deadwood") and even a relatable serial killer ("Dexter"). Not a nice guy in the bunch.

But the men (and they are all men) who created these works of TV art and have presided over them as show runners are difficult men, too—many of them S.O.B. pieces of work, it turns out, with sharp edges that contribute to their characteristic storytelling styles. David Simon, the itchy *Baltimore Sun* journalist who put his mark on "Homicide: Life on the Street," "The Corner,"

"Treme" and his masterpiece of Baltimore-as-cosmos, "The Wire," reveals himself to be a perpetually dissatisfied ranter who once chastised "Wire" fans for, essentially, liking his series the wrong way (i.e., talking about favorite characters rather than the show's larger political message). The "Hill Street Blues" writer David Milch, the "wildly unpredictable" creator of "Deadwood," set in the rich muck of late-19th-century gold-rush South Dakota and ripe with gorgeous, florid, filthy dialogue, is a mess of autocratic perversity and struggles with addiction. "If there was a method to this madness," Martin writes with a psychological insight that enhances his nimble reporting, "it seemed to be that of a fireman setting blazes only he is capable of putting out, thus ensuring his own heroic indispensability."

As for Matthew Weiner, who graduated from "The Sopranos" and went on to create that magnificent period-piece dirge to gray flannel suits we know as "Mad Men," Martin astutely notes, "Certainly it was not a unique question in the history of the arts: how someone capable of seeming insensitive and out of emotional touch in the real world could also produce work of exquisite emotional intelligence and empathy."

Not every boss man in "Difficult Men" is as maddening. Under the guidance of the show runner Alan Ball, the writers' room for "Six Feet Under"—the one about the dysfunctional family of funeral directors—"could lay plausible claim to being the happiest in TV." And Vince Gilligan, the creator and show runner of "Breaking Bad"—the one about the high school teacher with the meth lab—gets a warm shout-out as "someone who managed to balance the vision and microscopic control of the most autocratic show runner with the open and supportive spirit of the most relaxed."

But it is to David Chase of "The Sopranos" that Martin gives his fullest attention, his juiciest writing. This is no doubt in part a result of the generous access the author had to the show's production team and almost all the actors in connection with writing "The Sopranos: The Complete Book," an official companion tied to the unsettling conclusion of the series in 2007. (One exception: James Gandolfini, whose recent, sudden death now casts a shadow on these pages.) But also, clearly, something in Chase's complexity—I believe the Freudian (or is it mob?) term for that condition of perpetual discontent and agita is *meshugge*—provides an insight into everything that has come together to make ours such a rewarding moment in television storytelling. At least about men.

"David Chase's long, unfortunate slide upward into success" is how Martin archly describes Chase's progress during the not-so-golden ages of the medium, writing for "Kolchak: The Night Stalker" and "The Rockford Files," among other productions, while dreaming of becoming a New Jersey-bred Fellini or Godard. A screenwriter was what he had always wanted to be and still wants to be, a filmmaker, an artist. (He did release a feature-length movie in 2012, the autobiographical drama "Not Fade Away," which felt strikingly episodic, like … a TV series.) In the years since "The Sopranos" first went on the air in January 1999, many profiles have been written about this Dyspeptic Man Who Prefers Movies, with exaggerated attention paid to the haunting effect of his deceased mother, Norma, on her son's creation of Tony Soprano's fictional (monstrous) mother, Livia, as well as to all the other not-to-be-trusted women in the "Sopranos" universe.

But "Difficult Men" is the first time Chaseness takes on a larger meaning, as one man's urge to tell stories that matter within the medium of the occupying power becomes emblematic of a whole cadre of buck-the-system storytellers doing the same. Yes, they're all men; someone else will have to write the Difficult Women book about "Girls," or the uncharted, outrageous political stuff the creator and show runner Shonda Rhimes is doing with "Scandal." On network TV, no less. (Someone else who's not a man had better get a shot at making some great television, so there's enough material to fill that book.) Meanwhile, I look forward to the day the creator of "The Sopranos" is called for jury duty. And some D.A. asks about his viewing habits. And the guy who invented one of the masterpieces of the medium says he doesn't care for the stuff, thus adding to his résumé: Difficult Juror.

Lisa Schwarzbaum, a former critic at Entertainment Weekly, is a freelance writer.

Questions about the Rhetorical Situation

1. **Considering Genre** What information does this review include? What features cue you in to the fact that this is a review of a book?

2. **Considering Audience** Why would someone read this article? Where was it published? Who would be the typical reader? Does the reader need any special knowledge, vocabulary, or background to understand this review?

3. **Considering Purpose** What is the writer's goal in this review? How much information about the book does the writer provide? What other information does the writer include that suggests her purpose in writing this review?

4. **Considering Voice** How would you describe the reviewer's voice? How does the voice reflect both the subject matter and the reasons someone would want to read about this book?

5. **Considering Media and Design** Research images for the show "Mad Men." Find the opening title's image of the silhouette of a man with his arm stretched over the back of a sofa. What does this image reveal or imply about the show's era and the role of men? About the main character of the series?

Writing about the Rhetorical Situation

In three to four paragraphs, summarize the article and comment on the writer's choices and how they relate to the specific genre of a book review. In your analysis, include your observations about how carefully the writer considers the audience who will read the review. Consider the choices the writer makes that reflect an understanding of who the readers are and why they are reading.

THE WRITER'S PROCESS

You can't wait for inspiration. You have to go after it with a club.
—JACK LONDON

The Writing Process

For most people, writing is a messy business—not straightforward at all. If you watch a video of a writer at work (which writing researchers actually do), you will see more seemingly random activity—and more emotion—than you might expect. Most writers, once they begin to write, jump from task to task. Some might start writing and then back up and make a list. Others might order their notes and then write a conclusion before writing the paper itself. And still others might spend an hour on a single paragraph or get the whole paper done in that hour. Writers also stretch, yell, grimace, pace the room, and laugh aloud.

Research also reveals that some writers move in a straight line from stage to stage in the writing process, but many authors do not first brainstorm, then draft, then revise, and then proofread. Instead, writers often move both forward and backward among stages, often revisiting earlier stages before advancing. This process, known as *recursive*, looks more like a circle than a straight line.

As the diagram on page 24 suggests, to move forward, you sometimes have to back up and reconsider a key idea, do a little more research, or think for a while about the meaning of a word. You can brainstorm at any part of the process, not just before you write; and while you are brainstorming, you are often also revising by editing out the workable ideas from the impractical ones. (*Dumb idea. . . . That won't work. . . . Maybe I could go in this direction. . . . That won't support the argument, but I might be able to use it later.*) During revision, ideas can surface that redirect the whole paper or generate whole new sections.

Kate Burak

Getting Started

Sometimes the hardest part of writing is getting started. Most of us have concocted a hundred ways to delay that moment. One person has to clean the room in which she writes; another has to have all his research done, notes organized, and virtual pencils sharpened; and yet another works out of chaos, needing a cluttered desk to get started. Once the writing actually begins, other behaviors click in. One person cannot finish a sentence unless every word is spelled correctly and the sentence is grammatically perfect; another types madly, almost randomly, discovering what she means as she writes.

PRACTICE 2.1
Writing Rituals

1. Describe your own writing rituals. What do you do to get yourself primed for writing?

2. Interview a classmate about his or her writing rituals. Compare your rituals with your classmate's rituals.

3. Observe the writing ritual of someone you know—a friend, family member, or roommate, for example. Watch this person get ready to write. Take notes on your observations. Then interview the person and see if his or her perception matches yours. ■

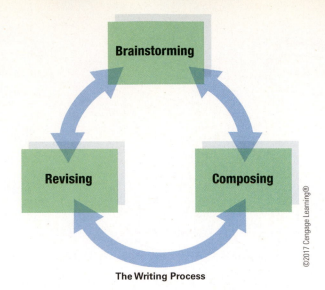

Brainstorming

Revising

Composing

©2017 Cengage Learning®

The Writing Process

Finding Your Own Writing Process

Ways of jump-starting the writing process are as individual as each writer. A friend tells this story about discovering her own writing process. Sara, a teacher and writer, took a six-month leave from teaching to research and write a series of articles. She woke up on Morning One, feeling enormous relief that she did not have to put on work clothes, gulp down breakfast, and drive twenty miles to her office through rush-hour traffic. A cup of coffee in hand, and still wearing sweats and a T-shirt, she sat down in front of her computer. Nothing. She got up, paced, sat down again. Panic set in. She decided to take the day off and not rush herself.

Day Two mirrored Day One. So did Day Three. By Day Four, Sara dreaded getting up, so she lay in bed, trying to figure out the problem. It came to her that she had interrupted her lifelong habit of thinking and planning her day's writing as she showered, dressed, and drove. So she did just that. She showered, dressed, drove for twenty minutes around her neighborhood, got out of her car, reentered her house, took off her coat, sat down at the computer, and began writing.

Driving randomly around your neighborhood or campus may not be the best way for you to start a writing assignment, but most writers have their own rituals, whether they are as simple as having that second cup of coffee or as elaborate as Sara's. Discovering what works for you may be one of the most important first steps to becoming a comfortable and confident writer.

Keeping a Writer's Notebook

One way to help you get started is to have a place to record random thoughts, overheard dialogue, and ideas that come unbidden in the midst of your daily life. Whether it is a tablet, a black-and-white composition notebook, a reporter's spiral notepad, or napkins held together with paper clips, almost all writers keep this kind of notebook, also known as a *daybook* or *journal*. Blogs also serve as public places to share writing, ideas, insights, and tidbits of interesting information.

One student described his writing ritual in this way:

> I react with a few instinctive ideas (oh, this, that, the other thing) and then forget about it for a few days. Probably in the back of my mind, some little neuron-slash-hamster is running inside the wheel of idea generation, churning out plethoric subconscious thoughts. Eventually one of those thoughts will be something Neanderthalic—I'm not too smart— like "Paper. Thursday. Due," and off like a maniac I run to my computer. Although I claim to write nonstop till it's done, I really do take my fair share of breaks. "Oh, this comma is a good excuse to eat a cookie," or "Oh, that letter Z represents the time to check my e-mail," or "Ah, this prose is so poetic I'll play guitar for half an hour." So things take a lot longer than expected, but this keeps my little hamster from getting too tired.
>
> —Nathan Welton, Reprinted by permission of the author.

When you first get an assignment, read it carefully. Record it in your journal. When you have a writing assignment, the assignment itself may retreat to the back of your mind as you go about your daily life. Being aware of what your assignment is can help you on a subconscious level. As you jog or shower, or even as you talk with friends or attend a class, you may find yourself thinking about the topic or coming up with an approach or an idea for the assignment. As you come up with ideas, jot them down.

Similarly, you might wake up in the morning with a solution to a knotty writing problem that you were trying to untangle when you went to bed, or perhaps that you were not even consciously thinking about. By giving the matter a rest while you do, you can gain a new perspective. If you keep a notebook by your bedside, you can write a few notes while the ideas are fresh.

Writing an idea inscribes it not only on the paper but also in your mind. Your ideas can incubate in a notebook. When it is time to write, you may find your words flowing more clearly than you had imagined they would because of the activity of your subconscious mind. Writing can also help you retrieve memories of other words you have written, ideas you have formed, passages you have read, or experiences you have had. One idea leads to another. You will discover that the very act of writing can get your creativity flowing. Bringing forth one idea stimulates a series of other ideas, even pulling long-forgotten details from your memory.

PRACTICE 2.3

Keeping a Notebook

1. Keep a writer's notebook for two days. Jot down ideas.
   - Dreams or snippets of dreams you remember when you wake
   - Funny or insightful comments made by friends or professors
   - Clever advertisements or tag lines
   - Quotations from your reading
   - Overheard conversations
   - Unusual events from the news or from your own observations
   - Controversies that you hear or read about
   - Original writing: descriptions of people, places, and events that interest you

2. Write about anything that might work well in a piece of writing, but do not use your notebook as merely a log of your activities. Think of it as a collecting place for images, quotations, ideas, and bits of dialogue. Fill at least two pages each day.

3. Write a few paragraphs evaluating the experience of keeping a notebook for these two days. ■

Techniques for Getting Unstuck, Getting Started, and Getting Refreshed

If you become blocked, you may want to think about using some brainstorming techniques to get started. Brainstorming is useful when you begin to cast about for topics or ideas about topics, when you want to develop an idea, when you are reading about and researching a topic, and when you need to refresh your thinking.

BRAINSTORMING When you brainstorm, you let all your ideas rush out unimpeded, bringing with them the flotsam and jetsam that get carried along. Brainstorming opens your mind. Later, you can consider which ideas to keep and which to reject. Be careful not to edit yourself in content or in form. Let the ideas flow.

Freewriting is the practice of writing without limitations and without a clear destination, using free association. It is writing to discover meaning. Write freely for a set period of time, such as 10 minutes, and write everything you can think of about your topic.

Clustering, also known as *word webbing* or *branching*, can be a powerful brainstorming technique. Writers who are visual thinkers discover that clustering helps them find relationships among ideas, allowing them to generate a complex interrelationship of ideas. When you create a word web, you write a keyword in the center of a page, circle the word, and in quick succession write a series of associated words or phrases radiating out from it. Circle each word or phrase, and connect it with a line to the previous and successive one. When you run that string as far as it will go, return to the center, and begin again in another direction. (See the example of a cluster map.)

PRACTICE 2.4

Getting Unstuck: Freewriting

1. Try your hand at freewriting as it is described in the list of terms above and on the next page. If you do not have a topic in mind or an assignment to work with, write about anything you know about: basketball, colonial America, music, global warming, cooking, chaos theory, or civil liberties, perhaps.

2. Read your freewrite. Circle any interesting ideas that might be useful to develop for later writings. Put a box around any phrases or sentences that might be keepers.

3. What was your response to the freewriting? Is it a technique you might find useful? Why or why not? ■

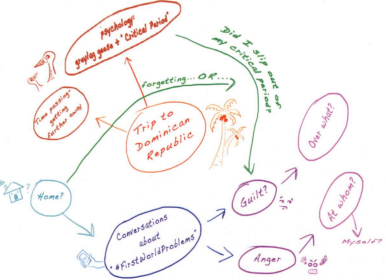

Cluster Mapping of #FirstWorldProblems from Chapter 7

Listing and Outlining are good, quick ways to get your ideas on paper for safekeeping and consideration. Once your ideas are on paper, you can rearrange, reorder, and develop them. The structure of the list or outline allows you to see the difference between equal main points and subordinate, less important points or between your general ideas and the specific supporting information.

Collaborating with a partner or in a group can also be helpful because you can build on each other's knowledge and backgrounds. When you collaborate with others, you have to find language to articulate your ideas, and the feedback you get provides you with fresh perspectives.

Planning and Shaping

No matter what type of writing assignment, part of the process is doing some research, developing a working thesis, finding a focus, and organizing your material.

Creating a Research Path

You put your foot on the research path when you begin asking questions about your topic and then start finding the answers, which, of course, often leads to more questions. As you continue researching, you may find new avenues to travel, different directions to take, and, in the best of situations, surprising discoveries to make.

There are many ways to begin your research. You can talk to people who know the subject or to friends and classmates, just to start airing your thoughts. You can go online to find information, and you can go to the library and find books and articles on your subject. Read for information and inspiration. Whether you are writing a short or long researched article, a blog, a film script, or a memoir, you can jump-start your thinking by reading widely and deeply. (For more guidance on a variety of primary and secondary research techniques from conducting an interview to conducting an effective Web search, see Chapter 15, "Research.")

Remember to take careful notes on the ideas, quotations, and sources you consult as you gather your information. You can think of your sources as the signposts on your journey. You will need to remember who sent you in what direction, and you do that by giving credit to those whose words you have read, absorbed, or been inspired by. (See Chapter 16 for more on documentation and avoiding plagiarism.) Part of the fun of research lies in becoming knowledgeable about a topic and familiar with the experts, the theories, and the controversies.

You continue on that research path throughout the writing process. You can consult sources as you brainstorm, as you write your first draft, and as you revise. The more you learn about a topic, the more interesting it becomes to you, and the better you can communicate that interest—even intellectual excitement—to your readers.

Developing a Working Thesis

The term *big idea* refers to the overarching concept in a piece of writing. It is the first step in developing your thesis. For example, the big idea of an editorial you might write could be to persuade your administration to use green technology in new buildings on campus.

The Specific Focus of Your Big Idea

After you identify this big idea, you can then refine it and narrow it down to form the specific point you are making. As stated in Chapter 1, this specific point of a piece of writing goes by many names. In a news story it can be the *angle*; in a proposal it can be a *plan*; and in a memoir it is referred to as a *theme*. Also, it can be called an *evaluative thesis* in a review, or an *analytical thesis* in a researched article, or an *argumentative thesis* in an editorial.

Here is an example of how you might narrow your big idea and develop your thesis:

THE **BIG IDEA** **Persuade the Administration to Use Green Technology in New Buildings**

Argumentative Thesis: Green technology is not only good for our planet but it also will be a cost-effective way to heat and cool the new lecture halls.

No matter what it is called, your specific focus helps you organize your ideas and communicate your thinking to your audience. Your specific focus should be

- Substantive (not self-evident)
- Neither too broad nor too narrow for the scope of the paper
- Supported by evidence (facts, statistics, expert opinion, anecdotes, examples) in the body of your paper
- Engaging to your audience

Often, your thinking will shift as you develop your topic. You may not even discover your true focus until you have explored some side paths. Stay flexible as you draft your paper, and refine or redefine your big idea.

Organizing Your Material

After you have identified your big idea and homed in on your thesis, consider how best to develop the ideas and support the thesis. An informal list is all some writers need, especially for a short piece of writing. Outlines are useful with more complex subjects. Here, for example, is an outline for an editorial arguing to increase the budget for the student escort service on a college campus.

Sample Student Outline

I.   Thesis: Student escort service is underfunded, a situation that compromises student safety.

II. Other student activities have much larger budgets
   A. Sports
   B. Outdoor club
   C. Debate society

III. The escort service budget is too small
   A. $800 for advertising and staffing
   B. No money to purchase a van or pay for gas
   C. Statement from head of escort service about lack of money

IV. Student safety is compromised
   A. Anecdote about sophomore girl who reported a stalker
   B. Statement of Chief of Police Perez: "If even one student is frightened on this campus, we have to beef up security." (Personal interview 2/19/15)

V.   Call for action: We have to get more funding for the student escort service.
   A. Petition administration
   B. Elect new student government

Outlining also makes good sense and is a powerful organizational strategy *after* you have written your first draft—as a springboard into revision. Once you have a draft in hand, putting your ideas into outline form allows you to get an overview of how the paper has taken shape so far and to see where you might need to revise. As you line up your main and subordinate points, you can easily see if your points are parallel, if your support is sufficient, and if your ideas proceed logically.

Whether you outline at the beginning, middle, or end of your writing process, make sure you think of the resulting structure as flexible. The outline should open up your thinking, not limit it.

Writing the First Draft

Your first draft can be messy and experimental, free-form and rough. Get your ideas on paper, and keep the ideas flowing. Try not to edit yourself or think of your worst writing critic peering over your shoulder. The first draft is not the place to worry about grammar, spelling, and style—yet. You will have plenty of time later to revise and edit your paper.

Developing Paragraphs

Every piece of writing needs an introduction, body, and conclusion as well as an organizing principle—a reason why this paragraph follows that one. A clear organization sets up expectations, even a sense of anticipation, for readers. Your job as a writer is

to keep readers interested and moving forward. Ideally, readers should be drawn into your writing by your introduction, and they should keep reading because they are on a well-lit path that leads inevitably to your conclusions.

- **Introduction:** The introductory section of a piece of writing should engage the reader and announce the topic. Invite your reader into your piece of writing with a lively voice and a clear focus on your paper's big idea. Expository introductions often explain a topic and can begin with a compelling analogy or metaphor, or offer a fact or statistic. Narrative introductions can create a scene, describe a setting, quote a character in the story, or tell a short anecdote.
- **Body:** The body of your paper is the meaty part. Depending on the genre, this is where you inform, explore, analyze, or argue. Just as the thesis statement announces the topic and focus of your paper, the topic sentence announces, in general terms, the subject of your paragraph. Most paragraphs begin with a clear topic sentence that provides overviews but often needs to be supported by specifics. Lists and outlines are useful at this stage to help you sort your big topic into main points and subordinate points and to make sure you have put your points into the best possible order.
- **Conclusion:** The conclusion should not be an afterthought. Its function is to complete your argument or story and to remind the reader of your big idea. The best conclusions present an image, a quotation, or an idea that lingers in the readers' minds. Leave your reader with something to ponder.

Using Rhetorical Strategies to Develop Your Writing

You have some choices to make when it comes time to develop the body of your paper. You can tell a story, describe a scene, give examples, explain a process or a term, compare and contrast or explore reasons why something happened, or, of course, you can combine these strategies to suit your purpose. Each part of the rhetorical situation—the genre, your purpose, the audience, your voice, the media and design—will affect how you choose to develop your ideas.

If you were writing about the Grand Canyon, for example, for a science class or a science publication, you might want to explain the *process* of the formation of canyons. For a travel article, you might decide instead to *tell the story* of your trip to the Grand Canyon, explaining the canyon from a visitor's perspective.

You may also combine a number of strategies in a single piece of writing. For an article about the history of jazz, you might define the musical genre in the first paragraph, tell the story of the first jazz performance in the second paragraph, and then compare jazz with other musical genres—such as the blues, for example—in the third paragraph. What is important is not which pattern you choose but that you build a strong structure for your piece of writing.

PRACTICE 2.5

Using Rhetorical Strategies

Practice some of the strategies that you will find starting on page 30 for developing a short article by writing several sentences on one or more of the following topics.

1. Give an example of how it feels to have a learning disability. Illustrate what the person experiences.

2. Write a short description of an unusual ethnic food that most people have not tried.

3. Write a concise narrative of a historical event in your community. Include character, conflict, and drama.

4. Define a term that many people have heard but do not fully understand, such as *encryption*, the *infield fly rule*, or *postmodernism*.

5. Explain the process you go through when you dispute a traffic ticket.

6. Compare and/or contrast two college campuses. ■

Descriptions and examples of some effective rhetorical strategies follow. As you examine each development strategy, think of the strategy as a possible way to develop an entire article as well as a way to develop an individual paragraph:

- Narration — Telling a story
- Description — Creating a picture with words
- Examples — Using specifics to make a point
- Process analysis — Explaining how something is done
- Comparison and/or contrast — Showing similarities and differences
- Classification — Breaking down into parts
- Causes and/or effects — Exploring the reasons why something occurred and/or discussing its aftereffects
- Definition — Explaining what something is

NARRATION 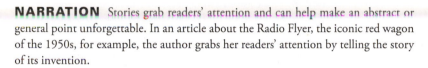 Stories grab readers' attention and can help make an abstract or general point unforgettable. In an article about the Radio Flyer, the iconic red wagon of the 1950s, for example, the author grabs her readers' attention by telling the story of its invention.

> It's hard to imagine a 1950s suburb without a little red wagon on the corner, filled with a pile of kids who would mentally transform it into a spaceship or stagecoach. Radio Flyer, based in Chicago, has sold more than 100 million wagons since its founding nearly a century ago. These little wagons were the creation of Antonio Pasin, who came to the U.S. from Italy in 1914, at 16. Pasin, the son of a cabinetmaker, settled in Chicago and started a business building cabinets for phonographs. But the wooden wagon he built to cart around his tools proved to be his most popular creation. Customers kept requesting one for their children.
>
> —Resma Memom Yaqub, "Backstory: Radio Flyer." Retrieved from http://www.inc.com. Reproduced with permission of Goldhirsh Group in the format Republish in other published product via Copyright Clearance Center.

DESCRIPTION Description requires close attention to sensory details: sights, sounds, scents, and textures. This description of Marion Pritchard is from a profile of a Holocaust rescuer. Pritchard was 81 years old when the profile was written, and she was living quietly in Vermont.

> Standing in her garden, not much taller than her sweet peas and daylilies, Pritchard doesn't look like the intrepid rescuer who defied the Third Reich. Sitting in her book-lined living room, speaking in a thin voice that crackles like a fire, she gives no hint of the cunning rebel who risked her life for strangers.
>
> —J. R. Moehringer, "A Hidden and Solitary Solider," *Los Angeles Times*, January 20, 2002

PRACTICE 2.6

Using Narration

Choose one of the following topics, and write a narrative paragraph using a brief story from your own or someone else's life to support the topic. Be sure to help your reader by providing clear transitions.

- Allergies
- Books
- Music
- Learning to drive
- Exercise

PRACTICE 2.7

Using Description

Choose one of the following topics. Brainstorm a list of descriptive details using some of your senses: sight, touch, smell, and sound.

- A comfortable room in your home
- An object you can see from where you are now sitting
- A swimming pool
- A computer keyboard
- A teacher, a coach, or a boss

EXAMPLES Examples allow you to make your meaning clear and also force you to refine your own thinking. This paragraph about bar codes gives readers a number of examples about why bar codes are versatile and important.

> The bar code is one of the killer apps of the digital economy. More than a million companies worldwide use the familiar UPC (Universal Product Code) symbol to identify consumer products. But the UPC symbol is just a subset of a much wider world of bar codes that are used for all kinds of identification and inventory control. FedEx, UPS, and the U.S. Postal Service use proprietary bar codes to move mail and parcels. NASA uses bar codes on the back of the heat-resistant tiles of its space shuttles to make sure the right tiles get in the right places. Researchers use tiny bar codes to track bees in and out of hives.
>
> —Charles Fishman, "Bar None" from "Agenda Items,"
> *Fast Company*, June 2001, p. 147.

PROCESS ANALYSIS Process analysis explains how something works (a computer, a grading system, the electoral college), how something was accomplished (the Russian Revolution, the formulation of the AIDS cocktail), or how to do something (organize a walkathon, solve an algebraic equation, dissect a frog or a poem). Gruesome though they may be, autopsies fascinate many people, and in this paragraph, the author describes the process of starting a forensic autopsy.

> The first step is to photograph the body. Trace evidence such as hair samples and nail scrapings (preserved by paper bags on the hands) are collected, and fingerprints taken. Descriptions of clothing and jewelry are recorded, then the items are removed. The body is laid out on its back on the steel autopsy table, X-rays are taken and then the body is cleaned. The next step is to weigh and measure the body, and note any identifying marks (such as tattoos and scars).
>
> —Noreen P. Browne, "Anatomy of an Autopsy," *Biography Magazine*
> (August 2002): 76.

COMPARISON AND/OR CONTRAST Showing similarities between and among ideas, people, places, or objects can help readers gain a context or framework in which to learn about the subject. Similarly, by showing how things differ, you can help readers understand a new or an unfamiliar idea.

The two standard ways to organize comparison or contrast are the block format and the point-by-point format. In the *block format*, you present all information about the first item, then move on to the second. In the *point-by-point format*, you alternate discussion of one item with discussion of the second item. In either case, be sure you do not just point out similarities and differences; you also have to interpret them.

In the following excerpt from a short article about impressionist painters in the United States, the comparison and contrast of French and American artists give the reader a deeper understanding and appreciation of the techniques and philosophy of impressionism, showing how each group of artists interpreted the form from its own national perspective:

> American impressionists such as John H. Twachtman, Childe Hassam, Theodore Robinson, and Mary Cassatt were influenced by the French painters in the 1890s and into the early 20th century. Like their French counterparts, they were interested in recreating the sensation of light in nature and used intense colors and a similar dab or fleck brushstroke, but they parted with the French painters' *avant garde* approach to form. The French artists rejected painting as a pictorial record of images and made the details of their subjects dissolve into the painting, leaving the impression of an image rather than a record of an image. American impressionists, on the other hand, took a more conservative approach to representing the details of figures and form. The American artists were interested in capturing the specific subject, not just in representing the idea of a subject.
>
> —Kate Burak, "American Impressionists"

CLASSIFICATION When you develop your ideas through classification, you divide your information into mutually exclusive classes. The simplest classification system breaks information down into two categories—for example, animals that eat meat and those that do not eat meat. More complex topics break these categories into smaller subdivisions.

Classification is a useful way to organize large amounts of information and provide an overview of what will follow. For example, in the introduction to *The Fourth Genre*, the writers divide and classify literature into the usual three genres: poetry, drama, and fiction. But their purpose is not to explain these three genres; instead, they use this classification to define a new "fourth genre": creative nonfiction.

> Creative nonfiction is the fourth genre. This assumption, declared in the title of this book, needs a little explaining. Usually literature has been divided into three major genres or types: poetry, drama, and fiction. Poets, dramatists, and novelists might arrange this trio in a different order, but the idea of three literary genres has, until very recently, dominated introductory courses in literature, generic divisions in literature textbooks, and categories of literature in bookstores. Everything that couldn't be classified in one of these genres or some subgenre belonging to them (epic poetry, horror novels) was classified as "nonfiction," even though, as Jocelyn Bartkevicius points out elsewhere in this collection, they could be classified as "nonpoetry" just as well. Unfortunately, this

PRACTICE 2.10
Using Comparison and/or Contrast

Assume that you are writing an article explaining the educational system in the United States to someone from another country. Focus on the difference between high school and college or between elementary school and junior high school.

1. List three or four points of similarity and dissimilarity.

2. Develop one paragraph of comparison and/or contrast. ■

classification system suggests that everything that is nonfiction should also be considered nonliterature, a suggestion that is, well, nonsense.

—Robert L. Root Jr. and Michael Steinberg, *The Fourth Genre*

PRACTICE 2.11
Using Classification

1. Working with a partner, divide the following subjects into mutually exclusive categories: study-abroad programs, computers, films, gyms, relatives, and college classes.

2. Make a list of categories you would use when writing about college classes for the following purposes:
   a. A registration pamphlet
   b. A letter home
   c. An article on grade inflation
   d. A source guide written by students to give helpful advice to other students
   e. A humorous editorial for your school or community newspaper ■

CAUSES AND/OR EFFECTS Another way to explain and develop concepts is to explore the reasons why an event or a trend occurred or to discuss its after-effects. In writing, exploring causes means finding out why something happened; exploring effects means finding out—or sometimes speculating about—what the results will be. This excerpt from a historical article about the Great Depression focuses mostly on two causes of the Depression: the unequal distribution of wealth and speculation in the stock market.

The Great Depression was the worst economic slump ever in U.S. history, and one which spread to virtually all of the industrialized world. The depression began in late 1929 and lasted for about a decade. Many factors played a role in bringing about the depression; however, the main cause for the Great Depression was the combination of the greatly unequal distribution of wealth throughout the 1920s, and the extensive stock market speculation that took place during the latter part of that same decade. The maldistribution of wealth in the 1920s existed on many levels. Money was distributed disparately between the rich and the middle-class, between industry and agriculture within the United States, and between the U.S. and Europe. This imbalance of wealth created an unstable economy. The excessive speculation in the late 1920s kept the stock market artificially high, but eventually led to large market crashes. These market crashes, combined with the maldistribution of wealth, caused the American economy to capsize.

—Paul A. Gusmorino III, "Main Causes of the Great Depression"

DEFINITION A basic definition puts a word or an idea into a recognizable category and then explains how it is like or different from all others in that category. For example, the writer of this editorial defines the term *microcredit* in the first paragraph by putting the term in the category of "a small loan" and showing how it is different from all other small loans by saying it goes specifically to poor women.

These small loans, as little as $25, go to the poorest people, mostly women living on $1 a day or less. These loans could protect against terrorism by undermining the poverty that feeds social decay and destruction.

—"Microprogress," from *The Boston Globe*

Linking Ideas Clearly with Effective Transitions

Coherent paragraphs link ideas clearly, from one paragraph's main point to the next. *Transitions* are words that link ideas within paragraphs and that link paragraphs to one another. Transitional words and phrases such as *first of all*, *then*, *next*, *on the other hand*, *interestingly*, and *however* signal your intentions and keep readers moving smoothly from idea to idea. You can think of transitions as having three main functions—to show changes in time, in space, and in logic.

- Time transitions such as *then*, *after*, and *meanwhile* are used when the piece is reporting a process or another series of linked events. Time transitions link elements in a timeline.
- Space transitions such as *under*, *above*, *behind*, and *near* act as directions. Usually found in articles that describe places or objects, they show connections between the component parts. Space transitions help move readers around in a space the way a camera would control and move the audience's point of view in a film.
- Logical transitions such as *on the other hand*, *however*, *therefore*, and *likewise* emphasize the logical connection between ideas. For example, when you are comparing opposing ideas, you would explain one theory, then indicate that you are moving on to an opposing point of view with the phrase *on the other hand*. In writing an extended definition, you might conclude your article with a sentence that begins with *therefore*.

Good transitions act as road signs and guide readers through the article. Even in a brief piece of writing, readers can lose their way. Transitions provide the links that keep readers alert to sudden turns or connecting paths the writer might take. If *you* get lost while writing your first draft, consider the rhetorical situation: Who are you writing for and why? Asking yourself these questions can help you get back on track.

PRACTICE 2.12
Using Cause and Effect

1. Choose one of these topics, and make a list of its possible causes.
   - The breakdown of the traditional nuclear family
   - The popularity of a specific musical style
   - The popularity of cell phones

2. Choose one of these topics, and make a list of its possible effects.
   - Cloning humans
   - Prohibiting alcohol on all public college campuses
   - Establishing an effective rapid-transit system for large cities ■

Asking Questions about the Rhetorical Situation

- What is the purpose of this writing? Is it going to *tell* a story or *report* on an event, *review* a book or *analyze* a poem, *argue* for building bicycle lanes in city streets or *lobby* for an internship?

(continued)

PRACTICE 2.13

Using Definition

In one or two sentences, write your own definition of one of the following words, putting it in its appropriate category and then showing how it is different from all others in that category.

- Techno music
- Cyberspace
- Terrorism
- Indie films ■

Asking Questions about the Rhetorical Situation *(continued)*

■ What development strategies will best support my points? Some development strategies are examples, stories, definitions, analysis of causes and effects, facts, details, and comparisons.

■ Who is my targeted audience? You may be writing for a teacher or for a scholarship committee. If you are writing a news report, for example, it may be helpful to think of people reading it over morning coffee or on a bus or train on their way to work. Always think of your readers as intelligent and interesting people.

Revising

> When I see a paragraph shrinking under my eyes like a strip of bacon on a skillet, I know I'm on the right track.
>
> —Peter DeVries

Revision consists of more than finding and fixing surface errors such as typos or finding livelier synonyms for dull words. Changing words, checking spelling, and cleaning up grammatical and mechanical errors are all important end-stage writing activities, but they are not the essence of revision. Successful revision consists of truly rethinking your draft. You have to be willing to change your focus, reorder your thinking, lop off whole sections, and develop others.

You might need some time and distance between writing the first and second drafts to do this. Most writers depend on taking some kind of break between writing and include a reader in the revision process. Your reader can be a teacher or a classmate who understands that your aim is to find the places where your writing is both on and off key, where you need more and where you need less. You can also read your draft out loud to yourself. Both these activities allow you to gain new perspectives and see your writing with fresh eyes, especially if you have just finished a marathon writing session. Ideally, leave a day or two for end-stage revising. Collaborating on a final draft—"peer review"—is covered in more depth in the next chapter.

Five Steps of Revision

■ **Refocusing**

Did your big idea hold up over the course of your writing? If not, a good way to start your revision is to rewrite that one-sentence statement. Answer the question "What is the main point (or thesis) of this paper now?"

■ **Reordering**

Do your organizational skills pull your readers in and keep them reading? Sometimes moving the elements of a piece of writing to another place can change the meaning, pacing, and logic. Outlining what you have written can be extremely useful at this point.

■ **Adding**

Is your writing specific? Can you give an example? *Can you explain that in more detail? What is your evidence?* Do not let yourself get away with sloppy thinking, unexplained ideas, and unsupported generalizations.

■ **Cutting**

Do you need all these words? Despite what most beginning writers believe, extra words can cut back on clarity, losing the point. Cutting can be a painful but necessary part of revising. "Murder your darlings," as writer Arthur Quiller-Couch advises.

■ **Editing and Proofreading**

Have you caught all the spelling and grammar errors? Nothing destroys a writer's credibility like a simple typo.

Revising for Style

Enhancing style does not mean adding flourishes to your writing but rather improving its sound, rhythm, flow, originality, and impact. Style is not an add-on to a piece of writing—it is an integral part of it—the sum of all the choices you have made about words, sentence length, and paragraph structure. For most writers, sentence crafting occurs during revision, not during the initial rush to commit ideas to paper. It makes sense to wait until your ideas are focused and fully developed before you work on style because many of the passages you might need to work on may not appear in the first draft. The more you pay attention to the details of good style, however, the more it will become second nature, and the more you will find yourself making deliberate choices even as you begin writing your first draft.

An X-ray of his painting, *Breezing Up*, by Winslow Homer reveals details of his earlier craft. In his revision, Homer eliminated an additional passenger near the mast and two extra boats that he had originally placed on the horizon.

THE RHYTHM OF SENTENCES As you write, pay attention to the rhythms you can create with language, but, as with all creative techniques, be careful not to overdo it. Too many overly long sentences can create confusion, just as too many short sentences in a row can be tedious to read. Too much parallelism or too many triplets (defined below) sound silly and may distract or annoy your reader. Used thoughtfully, though, the rhythms of your sentences can make your writing powerful and memorable.

- **Sentence Variety** Generally speaking, short sentences are dramatic and punchy. They add emphasis and variety to a passage. In "The Endless Hunt," Gretchen Ehrlich, chronicling an arduous hunting journey that she took with an Inuit family in Greenland, writes,

  When the sun slips behind the mountains, the temperature plummets to 18 degrees below zero. All six of us crowd into the tent. Shoulder to shoulder, leg to leg, we are bodies seeking other bodies for warmth. With our feet on the ice floor, we sip tea and eat cookies and go to bed with no dinner. When we live on the ice, we eat what we hunt—in the spring that means ringed seals, walrus, or polar bears. But we did not hunt today.

All of Ehrlich's language is clear in this short passage, but she varies her sentence structure, using two short, simple sentences for emphasis.

Other rhythmical techniques create a sense of balance or harmony in your writing.

- **Parallel Construction** *Parallel construction* uses two or more words, phrases, or clauses with the same grammatical construction.

  We shall fight on the beaches; we shall fight on the landing grounds; we shall fight in the fields and in the streets; we shall fight in the hills; we shall never surrender.

  —Winston Churchill

- **Items in a Series** *Triplets* present items in a series of three: three words in a list, three parallel phrases or clauses, or three sections in a paper:

  The outdoor play area contains picnic tables, chairs, and swings; indoors, two-story playrooms are packed with toys, blankets, and more swings.

THE SOUND OF WORDS When you speak words aloud, you can hear that some sounds are pleasing whereas others are harsh. Some letters and combinations of letters—such as *s*, *sh*, *l*, *oo*, and *m*—make soothing sounds. *Smooth, shush, lull,* and *momma* use the sounds of those soothing letters to augment the meaning of the words. Conversely, some letters sound harsh; usually those are called *plosives*. Plosives are made with a small explosion of air, as in the letters *k*, *p*, *t*, and *b*. (You can test to determine

whether a letter is a true plosive by saying it aloud in front of a burning match. A well-articulated plosive can extinguish the match.) The word *cacophonous* uses the *k* sound to create a harsh sound for a word that means "noisy, harsh, or disharmonious."

Playing with sound techniques is not only for poets and creative writers. Good writers in all fields pay attention to the sound as well as the sense of language. They use *alliteration*, the repetition of consonant sounds at the beginning of a string of words, and *onomatopoeia*, words that "speak" their meanings, like *click*, *snap*, and *buzz*.

In a paragraph filled with alliteration and onomatopoeia, writer Philip Gourevitch describes Ralph Bass, the talent scout who first discovered James Brown, "the godfather of soul":

> So Ralph Bass knew the repertoire; he'd heard more gravel-voiced shouters, high-pitched keeners, hopped-up rockers, churchy belters, burlesque barkers, doo-wop crooners, and sweet, soft moaners—more lovers, leavers, losers, loners, lady-killers, lambasters, lounge lizards, lemme-show-you men, and lawdy-be boys—than any dozen jukeboxes could contain.

FIGURES OF SPEECH Poets often use figures of speech: "fog creeps on little cat feet"; "love is like a red, red rose"; a life choice is a "road less traveled." Personification, similes, and metaphors can liven up any writing, not just poetry. Copywriters, journalists, corporate executives, scientists, and students often use figurative language to extend the literal meaning of their words.

These figures of speech add nuance and depth to writing. When you personify a nonhuman object, you give it human qualities: *the wind shrieked*, for example. Metaphors and similes compare unlike things. Metaphors imply the comparison (*the wind was an angry ghost*) and similes state the comparison by using the words *like* or *as* (*the wind was like an angry ghost*).

In *The Good Doctor*, his *New Yorker* profile of Dr. Paul Farmer, an American doctor who has been treating AIDS patients in Haiti for twenty years, writer Tracy Kidder uses a metaphor to create a visual image of Farmer:

> Farmer is an inch or two over six feet and thin, unusually long-legged and long-armed, and he has an agile way of folding himself into a chair and arranging himself around a patient he is examining that made me think of a grasshopper.

This grasshopper metaphor enhances the visual image of an agile, long-limbed man. You can also be playful and use puns or other kinds of wordplay, when appropriate, to emphasize serious themes. One public service campaign for a homeless shelter shows a picture of a bedraggled man sleeping on a steam grate on a city sidewalk. The copy reads, "Imagine waking up and feeling this grate." Although the message is serious, the writer's play on the words *grate* and *great* makes the reader stop, think about, and perhaps pay more attention to the problem of homelessness. (See Chapter 13 for more on using literary techniques in writing.)

(continued)

2. Churchill once said that to encounter Franklin Roosevelt, with all his buoyant sparkle, his iridescent personality, and his inner élan, was like opening your first bottle of champagne. Roosevelt genuinely liked people, he enjoyed taking responsibility, and he adored being president.
    —*Doris Kearns Goodwin*, No Ordinary Time

3. The Maui surfer girls love one another's hair. It is awesome hair, long and bleached by the sun, and it falls over their shoulders straight, like water, or in squiggles, like seaweed, or in waves. They are forever playing with it—yanking it up into ponytails, or twisting handfuls and securing them with chopsticks or pencils, or dividing it as carefully as you would divide a pile of coins, and then weaving it into tight yellow plaits.
    —*Susan Orlean*, "The Maui Surfer Girls" ■

2 THE WRITER'S PROCESS

Writing the
Literacy Narrative

A short step away from thinking about your writing process is thinking about when you first became aware of yourself as a literate person, someone who could read and write. The literacy narrative, a form of memoir (see Chapter 6 for more on the memoir), reveals these moments and relies on the elements of storytelling: scenes constructed with characters, conflict, and setting. Told in first person, the literacy narrative allows a glimpse into how a writer got started, the struggles of writing, or the process of discovering the power of words. In *On Writing*, Stephen King—best-selling author of books such as *Misery*, *The Shining*, *It*, and *The Stand*, among many others—reflects on his beginnings as a writer.

STEPHEN KING

On Writing*

Stephen King's writing memoir, On Writing: A Memoir of the Craft*, combines personal narrative with advice to writers. In the following excerpt, King tells how he made a sickly childhood year bearable by reading and eventually writing.*

THAT YEAR my brother David jumped ahead to the fourth grade and I was pulled out of school entirely. I had missed too much of the first grade, my mother and the school agreed; I could start it fresh in the fall of the year, if my health was good.

Most of that year I spent either in bed or housebound. I read my way through approximately six tons of comic books, progressed to Tom Swift and Dave Dawson (a heroic World War II pilot whose various planes were always "prop-clawing for altitude"), then moved on to Jack London's bloodcurdling animal tales. At some point I began to write my own stories. Imitation preceded creation; I would copy *Combat Casey* comics word for word in my Blue Horse tablet, sometimes adding my own descriptions where they seemed appropriate. "They were camped in a big dratty farmhouse room," I might write; it was another year or two before I discovered that *drat* and *draft* were different words. During that same period I remember believing that *details* were *dentals* and that a bitch was an extremely tall woman. A son

> *"I read my way through six tons of comic books"*

of a bitch was apt to be a basketball player. When you're six, most of your Bingo balls are still floating around in the draw-tank.

Eventually I showed one of these copycat hybrids to my mother, and she was charmed—I remember her slightly amazed smile, as if she was unable to believe a kid of hers could be so smart—practically a damned prodigy, for God's sake. I had never seen that look on her face before—not on my account, anyway—and I absolutely loved it.

She asked me if I had made the story up myself, and I was forced to admit that I had copied most of it out of a funnybook. She seemed disappointed, and that drained away much of my pleasure. At last she handed back my tablet. "Write one of your own, Stevie," she said. "Those *Combat Casey* funnybooks are just junk—he's always knocking someone's teeth out. I bet you could do better. Write one of your own."

I remember an immense feeling of *possibility* at the idea, as if I had been ushered into a vast building filled with closed doors and had been given leave to open any I liked. There were more doors than one person could ever open in a lifetime, I thought (and still think).

I eventually wrote a story about four magic animals who rode around in an old car, helping out little kids. Their leader was a large white bunny named Mr. Rabbit Trick. He got to drive the car. The story was four pages long, laboriously printed in pencil. No one in it, so far as I can remember, jumped from the roof of the Graymore Hotel. When I finished, I gave it to my mother, who sat down in the living room, put her pocketbook on the floor beside her, and read it all at once. I could tell she liked it—she laughed in all the right places—but I couldn't tell if that was because she liked me and wanted me to feel good or because it really *was* good.

"You didn't copy this one?" she asked when she had finished. I said no, I hadn't. She said it was good enough to be in a book. Nothing anyone has said to me since has made me feel any happier. I wrote four more stories about Mr. Rabbit Trick and his friends. She gave me a quarter apiece for them and sent them around to her four sisters, who pitied her a little, I think. *They* were all still married, after all; their men had stuck. It was true that Uncle Fred didn't have much sense of humor and was stubborn about keeping the top of his convertible up, it was also true that Uncle Oren drank quite a bit and had dark theories about how the Jews were running the world, but they were *there*. Ruth, on the other hand, had been left holding the baby when Don ran out. She wanted them to see that he was a talented baby, at least.

Four stories. A quarter apiece. That was the first buck I made in this business.

Analyzing a Literary Narrative

Write an analysis of Stephen King's *On Writing*. Include (1) a one-sentence summary of the story, (2) an overview of your impression of the piece, (3) a description of King's style and voice, and (4) a few examples from the text as illustrations.

Critical Thinking Questions

1. Summarize the story King tells in a sentence or two.
2. What are the main development strategies King uses in this piece?
3. How would you describe King's voice in this piece? Give an example or two of lines you find particularly engaging.
4. In the first paragraph, why does King mention his brother David? How does that mention help us understand Stephen King's character, and how does that understanding play into the bigger picture of the story?
5. King uses many images and figures of speech as he relates his story. Find a few lines that you think are particularly well written. Analyze his techniques (for example, exaggeration, metaphor, wordplay) and explain your response.
6. What is King's main point in this literacy narrative?
7. Why would someone be motivated to read about how Stephen King got started writing? Does he have an advantage that another writer of a literacy narrative or a memoir might not have?

Writing Your Own Literacy Narrative

Tell your reader about the process of your becoming a writer. Recount a pivotal moment in your reading or writing life—a moment of realization that came from frustration, accomplishment, or experimentation. Refer to Chapter 6 for more details on how to create scenes, characters, conflict, and setting.

COLLABORATION, PEER REVIEW, AND WRITING AS A PUBLIC ACT

Everyone needs an editor.
—TIM FOOTE

Most of your writing happens in private—just you and your empty sheet of paper or blank screen. But in the real world, the world of college classes and the workplace beyond, writing becomes a public act. You write for an audience: a professor or an editor or the people who sign on to your Twitter account or read your blogs. Authors of books and articles work with editors; proposal or report writers in community or workplace situations often write collaboratively, freely sharing ideas and criticism. A good reader can give you some perspective on your writing and help you find out how well you have communicated your ideas. Your peers can give especially useful feedback because they have tackled the same writing assignment and may have confronted the same writing problems.

Peer Review

Revision is the heart of the writing process; it is an opportunity to look anew at what you have written. Of course, you are revising during the entire writing process, not just at the end. You revise as you plan and write, as you choose one idea or word rather than another. The most significant revision, however, usually occurs as you move from an early draft to a final one.

Between drafts is a good time to have a friend or someone from your college's writing center look over your writing with you. You can also read your draft out loud

akindo/iStockphoto.com

to yourself. Both these activities allow you to gain new perspective and look at your writing with fresh eyes, especially if you have just finished a marathon writing session. Ideally, leave a day or two for end-stage revising.

Even if you have enough time between writing an early draft and a final draft to gain some perspective, editing your own writing can be difficult. Your ideas may be clear to you, but are they clear to a reader? In the real world of writing and publishing, writers have trusted colleagues and editors to give them "notes" or feedback on their writing before they tackle the final draft. The peer-review process in college prepares you for these real-world writing situations. Many writing classes use the workshop method, having students read and critique each other's writing. As many writers have discovered, the peer-review process can be extremely useful if the collaboration stays focused on

- helping the writer strengthen the piece of writing
- helping the peer reviewer strengthen his or her critical thinking

Your criticism should always be in the service of helping the writer improve. To make the peer-review process work, and work well, you should understand the process and the roles of the writer and the peer reviewer.

The Process

Writing classes approach peer review in different ways. Some, for example, use peer review groups of three or four students; others use peer review pairs. Some students e-mail drafts to peer reviewers; others bring hard copies to distribute in class. Some students write comments directly on the papers they are critiquing; others use separate peer review logs; and still others just talk, letting the writer take notes. Regardless of the form, the peer-review process allows each writer to have a set period of time in which to get specific feedback on a piece of writing.

The Writer

Bring in (or e-mail) enough copies of your paper so that each peer reviewer has a copy.

1. Read the piece aloud, or let someone else read it aloud. Reading or listening to your own writing is an extremely useful technique. You can pick up problems in logic, word choice, structure, grammar, and voice that you did not "hear" when you read your writing silently. Reading aloud also allows peer reviewers to hear the cadences of your writing while they read along.

2. Identify areas on which you would like to receive feedback. You can do this by jotting down questions before the session or by asking questions during the session.

3. Listen carefully to the feedback you get. Be open to new ideas about how to develop your paper or support your points.

4. Be selective in the advice you accept. Not all that you hear may be useful. Filter the advice through your intentions for that piece of writing. If the advice conflicts with what you want to do—or with what other readers have said—you can decide not to follow it.

The Peer Reviewer

When you serve as a peer reviewer, respond as a reader, not as a teacher. Some students feel uncomfortable in the role of peer reviewer (*"I'm not a teacher!"*), so don't respond as an expert in writing but as the intelligent reader you are. Tell the writer where the writing engaged you and where it lost you, where you were riveted by it and where your interest flagged. Point to sentences or images that worked well and those that seemed vague or confusing. This kind of reader response gives useful information to the writer.

Respond kindly and honestly. It should go without saying that criticism is meant to help, not to inflict pain on the writer. Caustic comments undercut the process, and so does being dishonest. If you find a piece of writing weak or undeveloped, say so. Conversely, if the writing is strong and effective, let the writer know.

Be as specific as possible. "I loved it" and "It was boring" are not useful comments. "I felt as though I could see the mountains you describe in the third paragraph" tells the writer why you loved the writing. "You repeated the same point several times in the first three paragraphs" tells the writer exactly why you were bored. The more specific you can be, the more useful the writer will find your comments, and the stronger your own critical thinking will become.

Focus on specific aspects of the writing. All the assignment chapters in this book include peer-review logs that pose questions for your consideration. Copy these logs or download them from the website, and then use them to write responses to the writer or as guides for discussion. You can also use the Ten Questions for Peer Review to give useful responses to a classmate's writing and as a guide for discussion.

The Power of Collaboration

Ten Questions for Peer Review

1. **Introduction** What technique does the writer use to open the paper? Does it engage your interest? Could you suggest a better place for the paper to begin?

2. **Body** Where does the body of the paper begin? Is there a good transition from the introduction to the body?

3. **Thesis or Big Idea** What do you think is the paper's theme or thesis? Where is this theme/thesis stated explicitly? Where is it implied through images, language, or events?

4. **Title** Does the title also direct the reader's attention to the theme? If the title is weak, can you suggest an alternative?

5. **Organization** What structure holds up this piece of writing? Is the line of argument or the story line clear?

6. **Evidence** Is there enough specific support for the argument or scenes that move the story forward? What else might the writer add or develop?

7. **Conclusion** Does the conclusion provide a sense of completeness? Does it leave the reader thinking about the topic in new ways?

8. **Style** Are all the sentences clear, concise, and economical? Is there clutter or redundancy that can be cut, or passive voice that should be active?

(continued)

One Student's Writing Process

Justin Lin was assigned a memoir—a story about an important event in his life. The drafts presented here show how he developed his memoir from an initial freewriting exercise, through peer reviewing, to the final draft. Note the significant changes and improvements Justin made as he received feedback and as his thinking about the topic deepened.

SAMPLE FREEWRITE In brainstorming for the memoir assignment, Justin did a freewrite on the following topic: "Write about a moment you remember particularly vividly. Include weather, a gesture, dialogue, sound, a scent, and a color."

A cold aura loomed through the night. As it grew stronger, it engulfed me like a tidal wave. I voraciously devoured the air as my eyes shot wide-open. Their eyes moved left to right . . . right to left. I caught my breath in complete blackness and scanned the bunk above to collect my thoughts. Light footsteps from around the hammocks surfaced. I heard squeaky mice-like chatter get closer. The odor of sweat, vomit, and mud from the older boys soon filled my nostrils. Their eyes focused in on the target. Crack! In an instant, a barrage of socks filled with rocks crashed from above—Whack! Thump!

"Stop it," he shouted. As I listened to this beating, I slithered into my covers. I shut my eyes and held my breath. Gritting my teeth together, I waited for it to end. Sweat on my forehead formed when I thought to myself, "What if I'm next?" "Stop it! I'm sorry . . . !" Felix cried. The pounding stopped just like that; I could not make out the perpetrators—four, five, or six of them fled back to their bunks. In sheer flashes, all the damage was done. The deafening silence in this cold . . . cold summer night that entwined with puppy-whimpers from above, kept me awake. "He was just a little kid . . . he was just a little kid," I repeated quietly.

THE PEER REVIEWER annotated the first draft following the direction provided by the peer-review questions on pages 47–48. For a completed peer review log, see pages 52–54.

I Was Just a Little Kid

Justin Lin

The ninety-degree sun beat on his tan face. He had a scar across his right upper lip, most likely caused by a fight, that seemed to stretch more and more every time he barked at us. "You imbeciles, get down and give me push-ups," he commanded. Down-up "sir one sir," down-up "sir two sir," we screamed back the count in unison until the hundredth push-up was completed. Sergeant Haines was not a very nice man—he just seemed bitter with his life. "Get up, dammit. Get up," he screamed. "Sir yes sir," we screamed back while falling into formation. Sergeant Haines began lecturing us about life while we were enduring the desert heat in the peak of summer. "What does he know about life," I mumbled quietly while trying to catch my breath from the push-ups. This was the eighth day out of this grueling ten-day ordeal.

[margin note: puts you in the middle of the scene]

[margin note: detail]

[margin note: conflict]

While he yapped on and on, I drifted off into a daydream and tried to remember how I got myself into this predicament. My right brow lifted and I grinned as I recalled how stupid I was to let my Dad persuade me to endure boot camp. He made this Devil Pups Military Program sound fun, and convincingly he told me that it was a chance to become a man. Ever since I was ten he would say, "Justin, you will amount to nothing if you don't grow up." Repeatedly saying this to me, I naturally began to believe him—I was scared of growing up, but in actuality I was more scared of not growing up.

[margin note: internal monologue (IM)]

[margin note: too much IM]

I jumped trains of thought to when he dropped me off. He was so proud. I do not believe I have ever seen my Dad stand as proud as he did on that day. I remembered his proud grin as he grabbed me to hug me. He whispered, "When you are done with this, you will be a man." Then he stepped into his Lexus and drove away. I saw the car whip a cloud of dust from the dirt roads. In moments he had stranded me at Camp Pendleton, imprisoned with malevolent juvenile delinquents and evil Drill Sergeants. I was thirteen years old, my dad's decision to send me to Devil Pups was just as wrong as my willingness to come.

[margin note: conflict]

[margin note: end of setup? I'm not sure]

continues next page

"What the hell are you grinning for?" Sergeant Haines' beady eyes pierced mine. My pre-pubescent voice managed to squeal out, "Sir, nothing, sir." The older boys in my platoon snickered in the background, but I was too afraid to look. Sergeant Haines walked away, but I knew he was keeping his eye on me. I stood like a statue; my feet together making a forty-five degree V, my hands clenched together at pocket side, my head up with my eyes looking straight forward. We had been drilled on staying in this form since the first day. My legs had gotten tired the first couple days because each muscle had to be tensed up, but I got used to it. I could not even wipe the sweat running down to my eyebrows, but worse yet was a little dime-sized itch in the middle of my back. I could not scratch lest he would catch me and make the platoon do something horrible. I no longer could abstain from scratching. Just as I went to scratch, Sergeant Haines caught someone up the line sway back and stumble. The platoon was going to pay for making another mistake.

narrative detail

Surprisingly, Sergeant Haines did not scream at us, but we all knew he had just about had it with our crap. He told us to face right and march on. The four rows of ten turned in accord and began to march. He took us to the track. "Two-hundred meter sprints, up and back . . . until I get tired," Haines said as he signaled us to begin. "Until I get tired . . . until I . . . get tired," rang through my ears as I paced myself. There was no doubt we would keep running until we vomited. I knew I would wear out fast, and I did not want to be the first one to stop. The day got hotter reaching well past a hundred. Sweat drops from my face hit the pavement and evaporated as I ran. "Left . . . right . . . left . . . right," I thought as I sucked in air. I finished three lines and then my mouth dried up—I started getting dizzy—I stopped—I leaned over and threw up all my breakfast.

Sergeant Haines ordered me to keep on running. I could not move. He signaled me to come to him. I hunched over and slowly dragged my legs to him. I reached him and I barely could stand in correct form—feet by my side, and hands clenched at my pocketside. "You must be kidding me . . . you ran half ass like that and couldn't even finish four . . . Why?" he screamed at me. I was afraid of this man. I just wanted to crawl into a hole and never see his face again. I cleared my throat and said, "Sir, I'm just a little kid, Sir." He scoffed back at me and said, "Little baby, if you want to be a man in this world, you need to suck it up."

"Sir, Yes, Sir!" I yelled.

3 COLLABORATION, PEER REVIEW, AND WRITING AS A PUBLIC ACT

He spat on the pavement and ordered me to do a hundred push-ups. I saw his spit sizzle and fry on the hot pavement, and I knew the pavement would burn my hands. I bit my lip. I knelt down. Feeling my hand melt on the pavement, my eyes stung a little as they started to water. The heat was unbearable—down-up . . . "Sir one Sir"—down-up . . . "Sir two Sir." Each tear ran down the bridge of my nose and splattered on the pavement and hissed away. I was too weak to do this . . . couldn't he see? I struggled for the third push-up. I felt his boot nudge me on the right side just before he kicked me. I fell down. My back burned on the pavement, so I began to get up. I stopped as he neared me. I had cried so much that I could only see Sergeant Haines's silhouette along with the bright beams of sun that outlined his figure. "You might as well stay down there," as he kicked me back down and walked away.

good detail

Cuts, bruises, and burns can only hurt for so long. They at least heal.

summary

I cried a little longer, but everyone was done vomiting, and Sergeant Haines called us to form together and march to the classroom. As we prepared for the graduation of the Devil Pups Program, the older kids that sat by me were whispering to each other about what had happened this afternoon. Later, I found out all this running was caused by my bunkmate, Felix. Felix was just as young as I, but shorter in height. I knew the older kids were upset about this and I knew something horrible would happen to Felix.

The day was a blur because I was lightheaded from all the vomiting I had done from the running. I cried myself to sleep, and wished for the couple next days to come quickly.

A cold aura loomed through the night. As it grew stronger, it engulfed me like a tidal wave. I voraciously devoured the air as my eyes shot wide-open. Their eyes moved left to right . . . right to left. I caught my breath in complete blackness and scanned the bunk above to collect my thoughts. Light footsteps from around the hammocks surfaced. I heard squeaky mice-like chatter get closer. The odor of sweat, vomit, and mud from the older boys soon filled my nostrils. Their eyes focused in on the target. Crack! In an instant, a barrage of socks filled with rocks crashed from above—Whack! Thump!

good detail

vivid

"Stop it," he shouted. As I listened to this beating, I slithered into my covers. I shut my eyes and held my breath. Gritting my teeth together, I waited for it to end. Sweat on my forehead formed when I thought to myself, "What if I'm next?"

continues next page

"Stop it! I'm sorry . . . !" Felix cried. The pounding stopped just like that; I could not make out the perpetrators—four, five, or six of them fled back to their bunks. In sheer flashes all the damage was done. The deafening silence in this cold . . . cold summer night was entwined with puppy-whimpers from above and kept me awake. "He was just a little kid . . . he was just a little kid," I repeated quietly.

PEER REVIEW LOG

As you work with a writing partner or in a peer-editing group, you can use these questions to give useful responses to a classmate's memoir and as a guide for discussion.

Writer's Name: **Justin Lin**

Date: **February 8**

1. Bracket the introduction of the memoir. What technique does the writer use to open the story? Do you find it effective, or could you suggest a better place for the story to begin?

   The writer is putting us in the middle of a scene, but the scene is interrupted by lots of telling—he seemed to be bitter with his life. This slows down the action of the scene. But the description of the sergeant—what he looks like, etc.—it's easy to picture him.

2. Put a line under the last paragraph of the set-up. How effectively has the writer set up the story? What other information or sensory details might help you better understand the events that follow?

   Not sure I can do this—the whole thing seems like set-up. I think the focus of the story is the night-time beating and how this might have affected the writer, so everything that leads up to that scene seems like set-up, but it's hard to tell.

3. Box a section that presents the setting of the story. What details might make the setting stronger, more vivid, or more specific?

   The paragraph that starts "He spat on the pavement . . ." seems to give setting, but the whole description of the sergeant and what the "pups" were asked to do also seems to be setting for the violent scene at night. It's a place that's tough to be in. The spit sizzling seems exaggerated, almost like something you would see in a cartoon. Is that what you wanted? You might think about adding some more details of things you can see while you feel sick, how the yellow dust seemed sickly yellow, or what you stare at as you try not to think about your pain. You might be looking at the mountains way off in the distance or the shade trees that are really far away from the place you are standing.

4. Write a sentence that expresses the theme of the story as you understand it. What images, language, and events point to that theme? Does the title also direct the reader's attention to the theme? If the title is weak, can you suggest an alternative?

> The father says, "When you are done with this, you will be a man." This seems like part of the writer's theme—that he is just thirteen but looking for some kind of big change. He seems ready for a change. The title "I Was Just a Little Kid" shows me that some kind of change will take place, but I don't see it (the change) in the rough draft. Part of the theme seems to be the writer's definition of what makes a "man," what being a "man" will mean to him after this experience.

5. Put a check mark next to the first place you notice the conflict beginning to emerge. What is the conflict? What are the obstacles for the central character? What is at stake?

> I see two conflicts here: surviving the camp and the sergeant, and impressing dad. The writer seems to want to make his father proud of him, and he has to get through the camp in order to do that. The conflict becomes really clear when the writer says the father was wrong and so was he. What is at stake for the writer is his chance to become a man, at least in his father's eyes, and also staying physically strong throughout the ordeal. He is physically threatened, too, and part of what makes this story interesting is the question of whether he will hold up through the pain. Will he get really hurt—injured by the other "pups" or by the training somehow?

6. What is your impression of the main character(s)? Suggest places where the characters' actions and dialogue could be strengthened to develop them more fully.

> The main character is a mixture of frightened and willing. The writer says, "My right brow lifted" when he thinks back on how he got to the camp. It seems more like something somebody could see him doing, not something he could see. The main character could have some things he does when he's nervous, like cracking his knuckles or biting his tongue really hard when he wants to talk back but shouldn't.

7. Look at the narrative techniques the writer uses in the memoir. Identify places where the writer uses summary and places where the writer creates a scene through narrative detail. Identify places where the writer uses dialogue with a D and places where the writer uses internal monologue with IM. Which sections might be strengthened by *showing* through narration and dialogue rather than *telling* through summary and internal monologue?

> I like the part where he drifts into the IM of saying how he got to the camp in the first place, but it seems like too much at one time, and there might be more dialogue or description here. It seems like a lot of telling about the background, too much IM.

8. What kind of voice does the writer use to tell the story? Is it appropriate and consistent with the narrator's age and circumstance? How might the voice better reflect the narrator's character?

> The voice is good in the story. It seems like the right age, especially the things he notices in the night scene when he can't see anything. These things seem childlike—the way the main character is on the inside even though he seems tough on the outside. Some sentences seem more like the adult talking—"desert heat in the peak of summer"—this is not a 13-year-old talking, obviously. It's the more grown-up writer talking here. The voice is a good mixture of the two perspectives.

9. Draw a box around the conclusion. What technique does the writer use? Is the conclusion effective in leaving a last impression that fortifies the theme? Does the last paragraph add anything necessary to the story? Would the story be injured by cutting it?

> This is hard to do because the last paragraph seems less like a conclusion and more like the climax of the story. "He was just a little kid" is the conclusion somehow. It is the moment the main character sees how stupid it is to put these boys through all this just so they can be taught a lesson. He seems to realize something here, but there is too much packed into the image, and it doesn't seem to relate back to the theme of becoming a man in his father's eyes, which is the main conflict. The ending doesn't seem like an ending.

10. Comment briefly on the writing style. Write "vivid" next to a passage you think is particularly well written.

> I like the way the story is written. I was interested in finding out what happened to him, and it kept me reading. I don't see any major problems with the style.

FINAL DRAFT Using the peer reviewer's comments and his own sense of where he wanted his story to go, Justin Lin wrote this final draft.

READING

When I Was Just a Little Kid
Justin Lin

I REMEMBERED HIS confident grin as he went to hug me. He whispered, "When you are done with this, you will be a man." Glancing down, I watched the summer sun hit his shiny leather shoes as he glided across the rocky path back to his Lexus. As he went to open the door, his new clean-cut hairstyle and facial features reflected off the window. Standing at the car door in his black suit, my dad turned to check on me one more time. In hindsight, there was nothing he could do to prepare me for the terror I would face in the last three days of Boot Camp. Then, he swiftly took his black coat off, placed his right leg into the car first and then maneuvered into the seat. He closed the door and drove away. I saw the Lexus whip a cloud of dust from the dirt roads. In an instant, he had stranded me at Camp Pendleton for the next ten days—imprisoned with juvenile delinquents and Drill Sergeants. I had once believed that I would be scared to grow up, but in actuality I was more scared of not growing up. I was thirteen years old, one of the youngest at the Devil Pups Military Program, and my dad's decision to send me here was just as wrong as my willingness to come.

"What the hell are you grinning for?" said Sergeant Haines, with his beady brown eyes piercing mine. I snapped out of my daydream to notice the scar across his right upper lip. My prepubescent voice managed to squeak out, "Sir, nothing, Sir." The older boys in my platoon snickered in the background, but I was told never to fidget. I stood like a statue. My feet were together making a forty-five degree angle, and my hands were clenched together at my side pocket. My head did not drop, and my eyes were focused straight ahead into space. We were drilled to stand in attention since the first day.

Sergeant Haines' six-foot frame towered over me, and the momentary shade he created disappeared as he walked away. I knew he was keeping his eye on me. He was a lanky Caucasian, and if he wanted to hurt somebody with his shiny black boots, he would. Having already been seven days into boot camp, I knew better than to be caught off-guard. Just as I thought this, a cadet two rows in front of me fell to the black pavement. The cadet was disoriented, and as he turned around to jump back into formation, I discovered it was my bunkmate, Felix. Felix was from South American descent. He was just as young as I, but shorter. He stood about five feet tall, where I was five feet, two inches. Like me, he had come to Devil Pups to be a man but was falling short of the mark. Although he was my bunkmate, there was no time for me to get to know him.

Surprisingly, Sergeant Haines did not scream at us, but I knew he was irritated. He told us to face right and march on. The four rows of ten turned in accord and began to march. He took us to the track. "Two-hundred meter sprints, up and back . . . until I get tired," Haines said as he signaled us to begin. "Until I get tired . . . until

> "Cuts, bruises, and burns can only hurt for so long. At least they heal."

I . . . get tired," rang through my ears as I paced myself. There was no doubt we would keep running until we vomited. The day got hotter, reaching well past a hundred degrees. As I ran, sweat drops from my face fell . . . skipped from my wet shirt to my dirty jeans and hit the track only to be evaporated. "Left . . . right . . . left . . . right," I thought as I gasped for air. Just as I turned the corner to finish the fourth line, my mouth dried up. I started getting dizzy—I stopped—I leaned over—I let the stomach acids leave my burning abdomen to pour onto the track.

From the side of the track, Sergeant Haines ordered me to keep running. I could not move. He signaled for me to come to him. I hunched over and slowly huffed-and-puffed my way towards him. When I reached him, I barely could stand in attention—feet by my side—hands clenched by my pocket-side.

"You must be kidding me . . . you ran half ass like that and couldn't even finish four . . . Why?" he screamed into my left ear. My heart raced a little faster.

I cleared my throat and said, "Sir, I'm just a little kid, Sir."

He scoffed at me and replied, "Little baby, if you want to be a man in this world, you need to suck it up."

"Sir, yes, Sir!" I yelled.

He spat on the pavement and ordered me to do a hundred push-ups. Watching his spit sizzle and fry on the hot pavement, I knew the pavement would burn my hands. I bit my lip. I knelt down. I felt my hands melt on the pavement, and my eyes stung a little as they started to water. Down-up . . . "Sir, one, Sir," down-up . . . "Sir, two, Sir." Each tear ran down the bridge of my nose—splattered on the pavement and hissed away. I was too weak to do this . . . Couldn't he see? I struggled and shook for the third push-up. I felt his black boot nudge my right side just before he kicked me. I fell down. My back cooked on the pavement, so I began to get up. I stopped as he neared me. With my swollen eyes, I could only make out Sergeant Haines' silhouette against the bright sun. "You might as well stay down there," he said, and with that, he kicked me back down and walked away.

I cried a little longer, but everyone had finished vomiting, and Sergeant Haines called us to form together. We marched to the classroom so we could prepare for the graduation of the Devil Pups Program. While in class, the older kids who sat by me were whispering to each other. I listened closely as they talked about being upset with Felix for making us run. Intuitively, I knew something horrible would happen to Felix.

The rest of the day was a blur because I was lightheaded from all the vomiting I had done. I cried myself to sleep and wished for the next couple days to pass quickly.

An eerie sensation loomed through the night. As it grew stronger, it engulfed me like a tidal wave. In a panic I voraciously devoured the air as my eyes shot wide-open. My eyes flickered anxiously—left . . . right . . . right . . . left. I caught my breath in the blackness and scanned the bunk above to collect my thoughts. My ears perked up to hear light footsteps surface around the hammocks. The squeaky mice-like chatter got closer. The odor of sweat, vomit, and mud from the older boys soon filled my nostrils. I saw their eyes narrow and focus in on their target. Crack! In an instant, a barrage of socks filled with rocks crashed from above. Whack! Thump!

"Stop it!" he pleaded, as the rocks pounded his flesh. As I listened to this beating, I slithered into my covers. I shut my eyes and held my breath. Gritting my teeth together, I asked God in a silent prayer to make it end quickly. With each swing, I felt my innocence slip away. I had never seen anything like this before. Sweat formed on my forehead when I thought to myself, "What if I'm next?"

"Stop it! I'm sorry . . . !" Felix cried. The pounding stopped just like that; I could not make out the perpetrators—four, five, or six of them fled back to their bunks. In an instant, all the damage was done. The deafening silence in this cold . . . cold summer night was entwined with puppy-whimpers from above that kept me awake. "He was just a little kid . . . he was just a little kid," I repeated quietly.

The sun's rays peeked through the little opening under the door. At any moment Sergeant Haines' boots would crunch on the gravel outside the door, and he would barge in screaming crude lines, flipping on the lights as he had done in the past mornings. I lay in bed for a moment and then I sat up. Indeed, it was a new day.

The door handle rattled a little and Sergeant Haines stomped in. This time I was ready for him. I stood in attention next to my already made bed. The sheets wrapped around the bed so tightly that even quarters could bounce off of them.

The last day was relatively simple. We marched for most of the day in preparation for the ceremony, "Left . . . right . . . left . . . right . . . skip step . . . halt . . . attention." We were prepared for the graduation. The American Flag, the Marine Corp Flag, and beside it the Devil Pups Flag, which the color guard held, danced and fluttered like butterflies in the wind. Before I knew it, I was seeing the same flags fly high during our graduation.

The day I had prayed for since I stepped into Camp Pendleton had come. I should have been filled with joy, but I wasn't. I should have felt as if I had conquered something, but I didn't. I should have become a real man, but I wasn't.

After the ceremony, my mom with her reassuring smiles and kisses came to retrieve what remained of the Justin she had left behind ten days earlier. Behind her, my dad stood in his three-piece suit and leather shoes. As if he were a military cadet, he stood at attention, feet together making a forty-five degree V, hands clenched together at pocket side, head up with eyes locked into space. He extended his hand to congratulate me and saw everything he had wanted to see—himself. In the car ride out of Camp Pendleton, my dad, like a curious child, asked me questions about Devil Pups. I answered concisely, trying not to reveal the trauma I had endured. He asked the one question that has stuck out these past seven years, "How does it feel to be a man?"

I thought about what I wanted to say: "Dad, I'm thirteen years old. I was just a little kid."

Awake from the fleeting daydream, I wet my chapped lips and gave him a fake half-smile. That day, I told him what he had wanted to hear. "Dad, it's just a great feeling." The Lexus got onto the on-ramp of the freeway and drove home.

Questions for Critical Thinking

What connections can you see between the freewrite and the final draft?

1. Did the peer reviewer give any advice that you disagree with? If so, what advice would you have given instead?
2. What specific advice that the peer reviewer gave did Lin successfully integrate into the final draft?
3. Compare the introductions to the first draft and the final draft. In the first draft Lin begins the story with a scene at the Devil Pups Military Program. In the final draft he begins earlier, in the car with his dad. What did Lin gain by changing the introductory scene? What did he lose? Which do you like better, and why?
4. The peer reviewer comments that, in the first draft, he doesn't see the writer's change from being a kid to understanding what it means to be a man. Does Lin make this change more apparent in the final draft? If so, how does he make it more apparent?
5. The peer reviewer comments that the ending does not seem conclusive enough. Compare the endings of the first and final drafts. Which do you think is more successful, and why?

Writing Portfolios

Building a portfolio of your writing and your writing process creates a record of your progress as a writer. Electronic or paper, portfolios allow you to collect your writing in one place, reflect on your growth as a writer, and eventually select pieces that you might want to develop further or even send off for publication. In the Peer Review section, Justin Lin's freewrite, first draft, the peer reviewer's comments, his final draft, and eventually the professor's evaluation would provide good material to file in a portfolio. Together they provide an overview of his writing process and interesting material for him to reflect on and to evaluate.

Tips for Building a Writing Portfolio

1. File all your freewriting, research, notes, drafts, peer responses, and teacher evaluations for each piece of writing.

2. Label each stage of this process carefully.

3. Write notes about your process as you proceed through each piece of writing. Note places that you might develop further or where you got stuck and need some advice.

4. At certain intervals (maybe mid-semester and toward the end of term), read through your portfolio.

5. Write a short reflection on how you see your development as a writer. What was your writing process? How would you assess your overall performance?

If you build an online portfolio, you can also upload photos, music, or videos to complement your writing.

A writing portfolio can be useful beyond your writing class. You can use your portfolio to store pieces you may eventually use to apply for internships, jobs, or graduate school. Professional writers create portfolios of their published writing to submit to editors and often pick and choose the pieces most appropriate for the publication. However you use your portfolio, it is an important record of your work and your progress as a writer.

Publishing

Writing matters in college. Whether you are writing an explication of an essay for your literature class, a poem for your creative writing class, a research paper for sociology, or a lab report for biology, you will be evaluated not just on your ideas but also on how well you express them. Your writing will be held to the same high standards in your community and in your workplace. In education, in business, and in the arts and sciences, employers' biggest complaint is the unclear writing produced by their new hires. You will be ahead of the game if you learn how to write your cover letters, grant applications, blogs, reports, memos, analyses, and evaluations clearly and compellingly.

One of the goals of this book is the publication of student writing. Internet technology has made it easier for you to get your writing published. In blogs and in Facebook or MySpace pages, you can, in effect, become the publisher of your own writing. For many, it has become almost second nature to post thoughts and feelings in some public space on the Web. College magazines, newspapers, and websites are perfect places to publish your writing beyond your circle of friends. You can also find professional—and maybe paid—possibilities for publication.

Newspapers, magazines, and websites look for fresh voices on topics that you may be writing about for your writing class: your views on politics, popular culture, films, books; your stories about personal moments that others your age could relate to; or your stories about people who intrigue you.

READING, THINKING, AND WRITING CRITICALLY

*When you start reading in a certain way, that's
already the beginning of your writing.*

—TESS GALLAGHER

Typically, our paths to literacy began with having picture books read to us, progressing to reading "chapter" books and comic books on our own. In these childhood books, words and images play off each other, each giving meaning and resonance to the other. Try thinking about *Where the Wild Things Are*; if this book was part of your childhood, images of Maurice Sendak's monsters probably leap to mind, maybe even before you remember Max shouting, "Let the wild rumpus start."

Even as children, the way we engaged with a text started with questions: Where will the story lead? Who is telling me about this? How does it make me feel? Why would I believe in wild things? Consciously, as well as subconsciously, the questions we ask open or close the gates to what we read.

As college students, you are bombarded with words and images in books, articles, and websites. Sometimes a text simply speaks directly to you. Something about the way it is written or something about its subject matter takes hold. Other times what we read seems foreign to us—even if it is written in our native tongue. It might have specialized language, or be written about a topic that requires some insider knowledge. We cannot seem to cut our way through the thicket of it. The message is wordy, convoluted, or illogical.

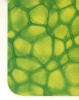

David Pearson/Alamy

The Salvadore Dali Museum illustrates the importance of looking at both the entire picture as well as the component pieces.

Knowing how messages take form and what effect they have on us as readers is what it means to read, think, and write critically. When we are "critical" in this way, we do not necessarily criticize or find fault. Rather, we develop a healthy skepticism about the messages we read in textbooks, trade books, advertising, classroom presentations, television news broadcasts, YouTube, and so on. We start to understand the connection between the words in a message and the way that message appears: the design of the message and the visual images that accompany it.

Or so we should.

It all begins with the kinds of questions we ask. This chapter gives you a method for reading and thinking—a method that offers

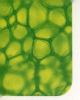

questions to guide your inquiry. The importance of questions cannot be overstated, because that is really where understanding a text lies. Without asking questions, you are a passive receiver, neither intercepting tricks nor helping yourself to the good stuff. You are on the outside, looking through a window.

Questions get you inside.

Ten Questions for Critical Thinking and Reading

These 10 general questions provide an overview of critical thinking and reading skills. You can use these questions to begin thinking critically about any text you are reading.

1. What genre (type of text) are you reading? Is it a story, a review, an argument, or a factual article? Does it conform to the expectations and conventions of its genre or vary from them?

2. Who is the intended audience? How do you know?

3. What is the topic of the piece of writing? Is it something you know about, or is the information new to you?

4. How credible is the writer? Is the writer an expert, a scholar, or an authority? Is the writer exploring ideas or authoritatively presenting information?

5. What is the writer's overall point (thesis)? What kind of evidence does the writer use to support this point? Is the evidence taken from credible sources?

6. What are the main points of each paragraph or section? Do they further support the thesis or digress from it?

7. What is the writer's conclusion? Does the conclusion flow logically from the evidence?

8. What kind of language does the writer use? Is some of the language nuanced, having more than one meaning?

9. What kind of voice does the writer use? Can you locate any irony, sarcasm, anger, passion, or pomposity?

10. Do you agree or disagree with the writer's ideas? How do you respond to the overall thrust of the piece of writing?

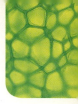

Developing a Healthy Skepticism: Believing and Doubting

Being a healthy skeptic means holding off complete acceptance of something until you have really thought it through. Sometimes a piece of writing might seem difficult because it is actually written without much regard for readers and their ease at understanding and following the logic. Many times, messages can be intentional traps or well-designed lures. The packaging of these messages is aimed directly at attracting readers. Promotion and arguments can be disguised as information and even entertainment in order to gain entry through the gates. Too often we wholly accept writing that we do not completely understand.

On the other hand, you can miss out on a deep understanding of a text if you only doubt. Holding off acceptance until you have looked closely can also mean you use your power as a reader to relate some part of your experience to the text you are reading: something you have read or lived through, a movie you have seen, a piece of music you have heard, or a story you remember being told. In these cases, you believe. Not only do you accept the text, you also allow it to expand what you have already stored in your mind. It is for you to decide—using a healthy skepticism—whether ultimately to doubt or to believe. You will have to decide whether the value of the writing and the message is worth your trouble, worth what will be necessary to wade through the text, and worth what you can learn from the

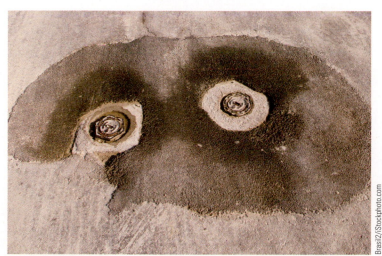

Brasil2/iStockphoto.com

Topography? An animal's face? What evidence leads you to doubt or believe it is one of these?

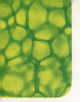

message the text is trying to convey. Three ways to become a more skeptical (and critical) reader are:

- Ask questions about the text.
- Determine the bias of the sources.
- Distinguish facts from opinions.

Ask Questions about the Text

Looking beneath the surface to analyze words and images helps you decode subtle messages in all that you read and observe. Your critical thinking, reading, and observation skills make you an informed and educated person, one who can think independently and not be swayed by deceptive or false information. First, you have to actively engage with the text, whether it is a Facebook page, a blog, or an article in a scholarly journal. Then you have to begin to decode its meaning.

- Question the text's authority.
- Challenge, or show a healthy skepticism about, the ideas presented.
- Look for patterns of meaning.
- Determine the context of the text.
- Make connections between the text and other works or between the text's words and its images.
- Read for explicit and implicit meanings—what is said, what is implied, and what is intentionally left unsaid.

Use the Ten Questions for Critical Thinking and Reading shown earlier in this chapter to help you decode meaning, understand nuance, and uncover authors' intentions. Make those questions personal with the starting-point questions that follow. Together, these sets of questions will help you form a clear opinion about a text.

- Do I believe what I am reading?
- Do I have any doubts?
- Do I understand the point?
- Who is writing the message? What is the purpose behind the message?
- Is the message aimed at my doing something afterward? Is that "something" desirable to me?
- Is the message trying to convince me of something? Is that "something" I am open to?
- Do I find myself agreeing or disagreeing?
- Does the message surprise me or confuse me in any way?
- Is the writing—organization, word choice, sentence structure, style—unusual or unexpected? Does it remind me of other writing I have read?
- How does the message make me feel?

When you ask yourself some starting-point questions, you can take charge and call the shots. What's more, these questions point out the connection between your reading

and your writing. When you start to master the art of reading with healthy skepticism, and you become the writer, the tables get turned: as a writer, you understand how to have the control over the reader *because* you can anticipate the questions. Imagine—no, make that *expect*—a reader is asking the exact same things about your writing.

Determine the Bias of Sources

A great deal of your reading requires you to extract information from sources. Not all sources are credible or reliable, however; some are biased, expressing only one side of an issue. Some information is misleading, some is just plain wrong, and some writers have agendas and want to convince you to believe as they do.

How do you know whether sources are credible and provide a balanced view or whether they are trying to manipulate you to believe their perspective? Sometimes it is obvious. A writer who represents a national tire company is going to have a different slant on tire safety than a writer representing a consumer advocacy group. At other times bias is more difficult to detect. For example, political campaigns often produce videos that look and sound like news reports, although the issues are clearly slanted toward the political views of the candidate. In this and in all cases, it is important to be skeptical and consider the source.

You can go a long way toward determining whether a source is distorted by bias by researching the writer's background and the type of publication in which the writing appears.

PRACTICE 4.1

Detecting a Source's Bias

Read any two editorials from your favorite news site and answer the following questions:

1. What facts or details establish each writer's credibility? What research could you do to find out more?

2. What are each writer's biases? How do you know?

3. How fairly does each writer present his or her point of view?

4. What, if anything, detracts from the fairness of either piece? ■

Ask Questions about the Writer's Background and Publication Type

- Can you assess the writer's expertise by looking at the writer's degrees or affiliations? What is the writer's profession? What else has the writer published?

- Can you tell whether the writer has a vested interest in this topic? Does the writer work for an organization that has a vested interest in the topic?

- Who published this information? Does it appear in a well-known journal, magazine, website, or newspaper? Is a book published by a mainstream publishing house or university press? Is it self-published on a website?

- When was this information published? Is it recent?

(continued)

> ## Ask Questions about the Writer's Background and Publication Type *(continued)*
>
> - Is the work a classic in its field? Have any significant knowledge, discoveries, and theories been added to the field since the work was published? (You can figure out the answer to these questions, in part, by reading other bibliographies in the same field and noting how often the source is cited and which other sources are most often cited.)
> - What sources does this work cite? What is listed in its bibliography? Are these sources ones you have read about in other works?

> ## Ask Questions about the Way the Material Is Written
>
> - Does the writer disclose a particular bias?
> - Does the writer fairly present other viewpoints or conflicting information?
> - Does the writer ridicule other points of view or attack people who disagree with him or her?
> - Is the writer's thinking illogical or careless? (See Chapter 12 for a more in-depth discussion of logical fallacies.)
> - Does the writer furnish clear explanations and supporting evidence for his or her bias?

You can always use a writer's bias to understand one side of an issue so long as you understand where that writer is coming from—what assumptions and values the writer expresses.

Distinguish Fact from Opinion

When someone begins a sentence with "It is a fact that . . ." often what follows is an opinion, not a fact at all. "It is a fact that Dino's is the hottest club in town" is a fact only if you are talking about room temperature and have literally checked the temperature of every nightspot in the area.

- *Facts* provide information that can be checked and definitively proved to be true—not just once but repeatedly. That Saddam Hussein, the former leader of Iraq, was found hiding in a spider hole on December 14, 2003, is a fact. That the boiling point of water is 212 degrees Fahrenheit is a fact. That the planets revolve around the sun is a fact.

- *Opinions* are subjective. They present a person's perspective, and they can vary from person to person. That Saddam Hussein was the most evil despot in history is an opinion. That you should drink green tea made only with freshly boiled water is an opinion. That a person's astrological sign can control his or her personality and destiny on a day-to-day basis is an opinion as well. For example, if you wrote, "Saddam Hussein, the most evil despot in history, was found in a spider hole on December 14, 2003," you would be combining fact and opinion.

Understanding the difference between fact and opinion allows you to see when opinion masquerades as fact and to hold writers accountable for clear and logical thinking. In your own writing, be careful not to blur the line between opinion and fact. Report writing (observation reports, lab reports, news reports, business reports) requires you to maintain as much objectivity as possible. You have to present facts—what you can verify through your own observations or through research—and present opinions only in quotations from experts, participants, or observers. Distinguishing fact from opinion is not as easy as it may seem, in part because writers often intermix the two, blurring the line between what is an indisputable fact and what is a subjective opinion.

Reading Actively

Active reading exercises your mind and should also exercise your hand. When you read with a healthy skepticism, plan to underline, box, or star passages, and to write notes in the margins. Use the annotation tools on e-books to annotate the text. Look for key ideas, subordinate points, evidence that supports the points, and the writer's conclusion. Also be alert for "loaded language"—in other words, for what is unsaid as well as what is said.

Active reading, by definition, disallows mental passivity. You have to be aware of the questions you have, as well as the feelings, ideas, and connections the text provokes within you. Remember, you are in control of the text—the text does not control you. Question what you are reading. Do not accept what you read as gospel or dismiss it out of hand. Weigh it against your own opinions and knowledge. Allow yourself to be convinced by a well-reasoned argument, but make sure the argument is bolstered by clear and convincing evidence. The following activities will help fine-tune your critical reading skills.

- Underlining key points
- Annotating and making marginal notes
- Outlining or clustering
- Paraphrasing and summarizing

PRACTICE 4.2

Distinguishing Fact from Opinion

Decide which of the following sentences present facts (F), which present opinions (O), and which intermix facts and opinions (F & O). Choose two sentences that intermix facts and opinions, and rewrite them to make them completely factual.

1. The price to attend, a $10 donation, was not a problem for supporters.

2. More than 200 college women attended sorority rush this year.

3. Jamnesty is a yearly event that raises money for an Amnesty International letter-writing campaign.

4. After last night's hockey game, which the team lost 0–6, senior captain Scott Gomes argued with head coach Don Webster.

5. "Gomes told Coach that he should tell the players to keep their heads up," said teammate Joe Friendly, who witnessed the exchange.

6. The argument dealt a serious blow to the team's ongoing struggle for unity and improved morale. ■

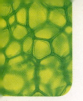

Underlining Key Points

Underlining key words and ideas as you read helps you concentrate on what you are reading and store information in your long-term memory. When you review the material, your underlining serves as a shortcut to key points. Be selective in what you underline. Weed out the essential from the nonessential; do not underline every word—only the words that convey important points.

While reading the explanatory essay, "The Claim: Exercising on an Empty Stomach Burns More Fat" by Anahad O'Conner, one student underlined the following points. The underlining shows one way to highlight the essential information in these paragraphs.

> Working out while hungry may fly in the face of conventional wisdom, but many athletes and gym-goers push themselves on empty stomachs in the belief they'll burn more fat.
>
> The idea, advocated in popular fitness books over the past decade, is that exercising on an empty stomach forces the body to dip into fat stores for fuel instead of the carbohydrates quickly available from a pre-workout meal or snack. But while it seems to make sense, research shows that exercising in this way doesn't offer any benefit and may even work against you.

Too much more underlining would make the strategy less useful since it would require rereading almost all the original text. You should be able to understand the essence of the two paragraphs by reading only the underlined words.

Annotating and Making Marginal Notes

Annotations are the marks you make on a piece of writing: underlining, highlighting, bracketing, boxing, starring, numbering, drawing arrows between points, or putting check marks in the margin. As you read, annotating aids your comprehension of the material and it saves you time when you review the material later. You can productively annotate most texts by creating your own set of lines, boxes, or stars. Here is one system of marks:

✳ Star the overall point (thesis) of the piece.

Underline the topic sentence (main point) of each paragraph.

Next to each paragraph, summarize its main point in a phrase or two. | Summarize

Box the evidence that supports each topic sentence.

Put a wavy line under the conclusion.

Some readers use colored pencils, marking different elements in different colors. Online textbooks allow you to use a whole range of colors, fonts, and symbols right on the text. You can annotate at any time in your reading and research, but annotating as you first read a text has the advantage of recording immediate impressions and keeping you alert and interactive. You cannot fall asleep—or at least nodding off is more difficult—when your mind is engaged and you are marking the text in a systematic way. It is also useful to go back to a text and look for different elements on a second or third reading. For example, the first time through you might underline unfamiliar words or put question marks next to confusing passages. The second time you might mark main and supporting points to highlight the writer's argument and organization.

As you annotate, also make notes in the margins, calling attention to and defining the points that the annotations mark. Interact with the text by writing questions, comments, and other responses. A "Huh?" in the margin will remind you to go back and re-read a confusing passage. Have a conversation, even if it is one-sided, with the writer.

The reading that follows, "Hardscrabble Salvation," is annotated, so you can see how someone might have this kind of conversation with the text. In this piece, Joel Preston Smith offers homage to his mother. How you bring your readers into agreement that your mother is worthy of homage requires you to step outside your feelings about your most basic, and arguably most significant, relationship and yet be deeply embedded in those emotions at the same time. What is even more difficult is knowing how to cast the picture you might see in a mirror—the self you rarely see, but must portray for a reader. Joel Preston Smith has fashioned a hybrid homage/memoir/literacy narrative.

Outlining or Clustering

After you have read and annotated a text, *outlining*, which you probably learned as a way to organize your thoughts before or during the writing process, can be used as a reading strategy for creating a map of the writer's thinking. An outline helps you understand the main points and notice any detours or dead ends in the writer's thinking. More importantly, an outline reveals the writer's principles of division—that is, how the writer breaks down the topic into categories.

An alternate way to understand a writer's thinking is to create a visual map: a *cluster* or a *word web*. Put the writer's main point in the middle of a page, circle it, and as you read, take notes that radiate out from this central idea. After you draw lines to show the relationships of the ideas to one another, you have created a visual map of the key ideas in a text. People who are visual thinkers often favor this strategy over outlining. (Clustering is explained and illustrated in more detail in the section titled "Techniques for Getting Unstuck, Getting Started, and Getting Refreshed" in Chapter 2.)

- Outlines of readings tend to be informal, quick sketches. Even if you do not produce an outline with Roman numerals and capital and lowercase letters, be sure to organize the outline or word web so that you can visualize the relationships among the ideas.

- Put bibliographic information (author, title, place of publication, publisher, date) at the top of your outline so that you will be able to find the original source.
- Begin the outline with the main point or thesis statement. If you cannot find a sentence in the text that presents the specific point, use your own words to summarize the main point.
- Link elements of the same importance (main points, supporting points) visually by aligning them in similar ways. Use numbers, bullet points, or indentations to show which ideas have similar weight.
- Be selective. Reduce a great deal of information to its essential points. You are creating an outline or a sketch, not an oil painting.

ANATOMY OF A READING*

Hardscrabble Salvation

Joel Preston Smith

In 1974 my mother, my father, and I moved from a trailer park in Cleveland to a 97-acre farm in Liberty, West Virginia. I was 13, a city brat, an only child, and I thought I'd died and gone to hell. The world I left was coated in concrete, which led to shopping centers and movie theaters. The world to which I was banished was covered in corn, beans, potatoes, and squash, which led to blisters.

Courtesy of Joel Preston Smith

word choice reveals his point of view

typical story of moving to the country. Predictable change of heart coming by the end?

A wise child would have been grateful. He would have seen that so much land, so much freedom, is worth a little blood. He would have thanked his mother for this second birth, and his father for teaching him how to care for land.

What child would do that?

*Joel Preston Smith, "Hardscrabble Salvation," from *In Good Tilth* – November-December 2010. Reprinted with permission.

4 READING, THINKING, AND WRITING CRITICALLY

I was not that child. I fought against the land, against the work. I doubt that I passed up many opportunities to complain to my mother, and I'm sure all my grievances could be summed up as "You did this to me. You're working me to death. You're killing me."

My father, who was once a tree surgeon, died of a heart attack four months after we moved, age 40, sitting in his Chevy pickup in the parking lot of an auto-repair shop, waiting to fill out a job application. My mother's voice was hoarse when she told me. I'd woken to the sound of crying to find strangers from the funeral home sitting in our living room. She assured me that everything would be all right.

It was not all right. With winter on our doorstep, we had no running water, no heat, no electricity, no money. She did what many people in small towns in West Virginia do—she found work at a plant, and drove two hours a day, round trip from the boonies to South Charleston, which bills itself as the "Chemical Capital of the World," to earn enough money to afford the privilege of owning and tending land.

In the evenings she came home and worked with me on the hillsides, hobbling over stumps on her one strong leg, swinging an ax, helping me clear land. She'd contracted polio at age 2, and her left leg, from the thigh down, was mostly bone.

She was relentless. She shamed me. Standing under 5 feet 2 inches, she weighed less than 100 pounds. She was a crippled widow, young and frail. Everything was against her. Yet every day she came home and worked me into the ground.

I don't remember her ever telling me "You have to do this." I learned my work ethic from watching her refuse to quit, refuse to succumb to poverty, refuse to allow grief to crush her and take her home and her land.

Now I measure all my work by whether it would live up to her standards. I learned from my mother that pride in one's work is a better reward than comfort. I learned tenacity. What courage I have is rooted in her, in my memories of how hard she worked to keep us clothed, sheltered, fed. There have been times in my life—

Courtesy of Joel Preston Smith

sounds like a typical kid

detail that shows the sense of sadness

he says these two things, that her voice is hoarse and that she's trying to reassure at the same time she is suffering

detail that shows her work is gritty, dangerous, unappealing—implied

sad detail, shows her, physically

we wouldn't have believed this without seeing all the earlier detail

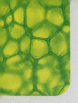

divorce, two trips to Iraq, the bitter loss of people I have loved—when I have nearly given up, but each time I turn to these memories of my mother, and I keep going. When I was 23, still working on the farm, I stopped having normal dreams. My dreams were sightless and soundless, yet I saw stories. Words on paper, line after line after line . . . neatly typed. The stories were beautiful, and I would wake up with the last lines echoing, happy at first, then worried. Normal people—especially farm kids—shouldn't be dreaming in Courier 12-point type.

Twenty-five years have passed since then. I'm 48, a journalist, and my work as a writer and photographer has led me 2,500 miles away from my mother and our farm in Liberty. I write about agriculture for *In Good Tilth* and *Sound Consumer*, and about the environment for other publications. I wish I could say that the words that once came to me in dreams now just pour themselves effortlessly onto paper. They don't. Every story I write feels like five acres of corn, shot through with crab-grass, in the hot sun.

What I lack in talent, I try to make up for with tenacity. Each day I write, I try to find something that resembles the beautiful words I once dreamed. I would have given up long ago were it not for the memories of my mother's courage. When I feel impoverished—in spirit or intellect or ability—I call to mind an image of her propping herself up with a double-bladed ax on a hillside, her face smeared with dirt, beautiful, weary, but relentless. That image has sustained me. I hear myself saying, often, "You are not killing me. You are saving me."

I was wondering how to write this story. I was worried about what I could possibly say that would honor my mother in so few words. I dreamed I was standing inside some kind of rock shelter. There was a cleft in the stone, and outside stood a forest bathed in light. The forest is real. I've seen it many times, hiking through our woods in Liberty, where the trees are as familiar to me as old friends. I felt as though the light and the warmth of the forest were an invitation. I was being welcomed.

Margin notes:

this is what he did with his hardship

stories hurt him—why write?

writes because that's what he dreams of—making his own dreams come true

the writer's main point—to honor his mother

The ending takes us back to the opening image—rural, natural—but his feelings about the land have changed.

Photo credit: Courtesy of Joel Preston Smith

Paraphrasing

When you *paraphrase*, you put material that you have read into your own words. By paraphrasing passages as you read, you reinforce your understanding of the material.

- Look up unfamiliar words so that you have a thorough understanding of the writer's points.
- Put the main ideas in your own language *and your own sentence structure*, making sure not to simply substitute a few words in the sentence but to actually rewrite it without distorting the meaning or adding any details not in the original text.
- Put quotation marks around words or phrases you take from the original.
- Cite material you quote and material you paraphrase in your bibliography and in-text citations.

As you read new material, finding your own words to explain concepts helps you understand and "own" them. As you integrate quotations from print, electronic, or expert sources into your writing, you will often want to paraphrase them, saving direct quotations for especially articulate passages or original ideas.

Summarizing

Summarizing shows your understanding of a text. As you distill the main point in your own words, you might note the important highlights, but you will not include examples, anecdotes, digressions, or elaborations that enliven or illustrate the writing. Most summaries are significantly shorter than the originals, perhaps a third or a fourth of the original article's length.

To write a good summary, you have to distinguish between the essential points and the nonessential points. Underlining or highlighting the topic sentence of each paragraph is a good way to begin writing a summary.

Put any material taken directly from the original text in quotation marks. Maintain the integrity of the original text. Do not change the intended meaning, interpret the text, or add your own opinions to a summary.

Analyzing and Synthesizing

Analysis and synthesis, in general, can help you understand a piece of writing on a deeper level. When you analyze a text, you break it down into its component parts, which you can then examine more closely. Synthesis helps you connect the parts with other information to form generalizations or conclusions about the work.

Analysis

Different kinds of materials require different criteria for analysis. You might analyze a memoir, for example, by looking at the narrative elements of character, setting, conflict, plot, and theme. You would analyze an editorial or argumentative essay by

PRACTICE 4.3
Outlining and Paraphrasing

Using "Hardscrabble Salvation" as your text:

- Create a reading outline that includes
    Source:

    Main Point:

    Brief Outline of Text:

- Paraphrase this quotation from the story:
    I fought against the . . . work. I doubt that I passed up many opportunities to complain to my mother, and I'm sure all my grievances could be summed up as "You did this to me. You're working me to death. You're killing me."

- Summarize the story in two or three sentences. ■

focusing on the individual points that support the argument and the kinds of evidence (facts, statistics, anecdotes, and examples) used to illustrate each point. You might analyze a photograph, a painting, or an ad in purely visual terms: How do the colors, shapes, or images create meaning?

The purpose of analysis is to gain a clearer understanding of the individual parts so that you better understand the composition and meaning of the whole. Often, analysis leads you to make connections and uncover assumptions you might not understand or see on a first reading or a first viewing.

One way to analyze text is to take a close look at the language the writer uses. As you decode meaning, understand nuance, and uncover authors' intentions, you learn to identify language and images that are full of truth and wisdom as well as language and images that may be filled with half-truths and deception. As a reader, you can better understand a writer's meaning by detecting and interpreting irony and figurative language. Writers use irony and figures of speech such as metaphors, similes, personification, and hyperbole to create mood, tone, and nuance in order to add layers of meaning to their writing. Understanding how writers use these techniques will help you determine the writer's purpose, detect bias, and think critically about the subtexts of works you are reading.

INTERPRETING FIGURES OF SPEECH A *metaphor* is a figure of speech in which dissimilar things are compared to or substituted for one another. What is important in metaphorical language is not the comparison itself but rather the qualities that are implied in the comparison. As with irony, if you miss the implied meaning, you misread the writer's intention. Writers use metaphors to write with economy while enhancing meaning. If you understand the nuance suggested by figures of speech, you are better able to detect the writer's mood or bias.

> Metaphor (from "Hardscrabble Salvation"): "*I felt as though the light and the warmth of the forest were an invitation.*"

Writers use various other types of figures of speech to imply meaning. A *simile* is an explicit comparison between two unlike things using *as* or *like*.

> Simile: "*Every story I write feels like five acres of corn, shot through with crabgrass, in the hot sun.*"

Other common figures of speech are *personification*, which gives human qualities to nonhuman things: The mountains glowered in the distance. *Hyperbole* is intentional overstatement: It would take us *a lifetime* to climb the peak.

IRONY Writers often create or point out situations that are *ironic*, those in which there is conflict between what is said and what is meant, or between what one

PRACTICE 4.4
Deciding on Principles of Division for Analysis

Decide on a principle you might use to divide each of the following topics for analysis. For example, to analyze a photograph, you might divide it into technical elements (composition), aesthetic elements (balance and harmony), and narrative elements (story and theme).

1. A cartoon

2. A novel

3. An advertisement

4. A textbook

5. A painting

expects to happen and what actually happens. It would be ironic, for example, if a company that promoted itself as family friendly cut its day-care and family-leave programs at the first budget crisis. An example of irony comes from an editorial in the *Chicago Tribune* about surgeons who take out the wrong organ or perform the wrong procedure on a patient. The writer's outrage is magnified by her discovery that the Joint Commission on Accreditation of Healthcare Organizations has decided that patients, not surgeons, are responsible for making sure the correct surgery is performed.

> As a result the commission is suggesting that the patient take matters into her own, uh, two hands. So carry a Magic Marker or a waterproof laundry pen with you to the hospital, not to fill out all those interminable haven't-I-answered-this-five-times-before printed forms, but so you can draw a dotted line around the part requiring work and write in bold letters "CUT ALONG DOTTED LINE."

> —Dianne Donavan, "Hipbone's Connected to . . . ," *Chicago Tribune*

Irony is a wink from the writer to the reader. The astute reader sees the wink and understands the writer's true intention. The danger comes when the irony—or the wink—misses the mark, and the reader winds up believing the opposite of the intended meaning. Certainly, this barb would hit the wrong target if the reader took seriously the writer's suggestion to write "cut along dotted line" on a body part before undergoing surgery. As a reader, you have to be alert to the cues that signal irony. Often, a writer employs irony to point out the absurdity or illogical nature of a situation or to express anger or outrage.

Synthesis

Synthesis helps you pull together information from different sources and integrate previously learned information with new information. This combination of old and new material may lead to original insights into the work. For example, have you read other pieces that are similar to "Hardscrabble Salvation"—other memoirs or stories about the influence of mentors and parents? What elements of those stories remind you of the writing seen in "Hardscrabble Salvation"?

Synthesis also occurs when you read many sources on the same topic, perhaps as research for an argumentative essay or editorial. As you read different views, you begin to notice patterns of thinking. By synthesizing the information you read, you build an understanding of the relationships among the ideas, deciding which you agree with, which you might challenge, which you might use to support your arguments, and which you will refute. Here are some questions to ask as you pull together ideas from different sources:

PRACTICE 4.5
Irony

Try writing an ironic comment or two to suggest the absurdity of the following situations.

1. You discover that a course you need to graduate is offered only once every three years.

2. You find out that the entry-level job you applied for went to someone who has five years of experience in the field.

3. You read that health benefits were denied a family because it had too many seriously ill members.

4. Your dog gets a credit card offer in the mail. ■

PRACTICE 4.6
Metaphor

Create a metaphor or simile for a person you see often: a bus driver, a cafeteria worker, a security guard, a dog walker, or a professor. Use the metaphor to reveal your bias toward this person.

Example: My boss scuttled across the floor, his antennae alert for any fun we might be having. ■

- Where are the points of similarity? What main points about the topic appear in all or most of the readings?
- Where are the points of dissimilarity? Where do the writers disagree about the topic?
- What kind of interpretations do different writers present? For example, is one writer exploring a topic from a psychological angle and another from a historical or literary point of view?
- What aspects of the topic do different writers focus on? Is one writer looking at causes and another at effects? Is the writer identifying a problem, proposing a solution, or both?

Understanding patterns and their organization, generalizing from given facts, relating knowledge from various sources, and predicting and drawing conclusions are all part of synthesizing information. In synthesizing, you connect different pieces of information to make the material more memorable and manageable and to prompt original thinking.

Visual Literacy: Analyzing Images That Come with Text

PEOPLE MAIL their "secrets" anonymously on one side of a postcard and the results are collected on postsecret.com. Some questions will help you analyze the connection between image and text. Use the two PostSecret examples to practice analyzing how images connect to text by answering the following:

- What kind of image is it—a photograph, painting, portrait, or computer-designed image?
- What tone or mood is created by the image? What elements in the image (line, color, shape, texture) create this mood?
- How does the image relate to the text? Is it a literal illustration or does it take the topic in a new direction?
- Does the image add information to the text?
- How do the text and image work together?

I was just

to you

another tourist destination

Harper Collins Publishers

People anonymously reveal their secrets through messages that are made up of words + pictures on the PostSecret website and books.

THERE WILL BE A DREAM THAT COMES TO EACH AND EVERY PERSON IN WHAT EVER SHAPE OR FORM THEY BEST UNDERSTAND AND...

This Dre

Harper Collins Publishers

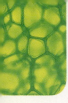

John Shane

You can see things differently if you look close or from afar, as in this close-up shot of a poppy.

PRACTICE 4.7

Analyzing Words and Images

1. Choose any short essay in Chapter 8 for analysis. Read it carefully, and answer the general questions on page 62 about analyzing readings.

2. Write a sentence that draws a conclusion about the essay's meaning.

3. Choose any image in this chapter. Look at it carefully, and answer the general questions about analyzing images on this page.

4. Write a sentence that draws a conclusion about the meaning of the image you chose to analyze.

5. Find your own "image + text" example from the Web or from print (advertising and children's books make great subjects for this), and write an analysis of how the images work with the text. ■

A good test of your ability to synthesize material from different sources is writing a *synthesis sentence* that pulls together and summarizes the material in broad terms. Read two or more sources carefully. Underline, annotate, and make notes in the margins that help you understand the meanings. Then write a sentence combining this information. For example, Joel Preston Smith, author of "Hardscrabble Salvation," is also a photojournalist who published a book of images of ordinary Iraqis. If you looked through his photography and read his memoir, you might synthesize the two by writing:

> In his new book of photojournalism, *Night of a Thousand Stars*, Smith puts a human face on the everyday struggles of Iraqis much the way he portrays his mother's battle to work the land after her husband's death in his literacy narrative "Hardscrabble Salvation."

Understanding Logical Appeals

Writers want to keep you connected, even riveted, to their stories and ideas. They want to convince you that their writing is worth the time and energy you spend reading it. Appealing to their readers' logic and emotions and establishing themselves as trustworthy are ways writers have connected to their readers since ancient Greek thinkers identified these appeals. Classical thinking breaks logical appeals down into *pathos*, *logos*, and *ethos*. These might appear to be distant, ancient concepts, but you

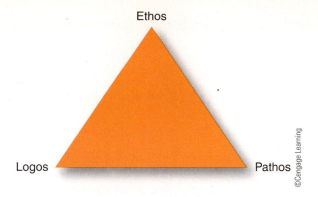

Ethos

Logos   Pathos

©Cengage Learning

might be surprised by how thoroughly they address almost every writing situation you could find yourself in. Learning to identify these appeals in others' writing is yet another part of thinking and reading critically.

Pathos refers to how you connect to your reader's emotions. Joel Preston Smith, for example, had to walk that fine line between evoking his reader's emotions and being overly sentimental as he remembered his hard-working mother. His careful description of her, complete with the details of her polio, does indeed create emotion.

Other kinds of writing rely much more on *logos*, or appealing to the mind. The yearly State of the Union address needs to include some of this kind of logic, perhaps a few statistics that tell us the country is sound and safe. Yet, presidents often begin their assessments of the state of the union on an emotional note by honoring audience members who have overcome obstacles or demonstrated courage. Almost every state of the union address will include both an appeal to the head and to the heart.

The most abstract of these appeals is *ethos*, which is attached to the writer's trustworthiness. How qualified is the writer to state this opinion or tell this story? Most people have some area of expertise, a reputation, and credentials that make their statements credible. Their "wisdom" gives their statements that seal of approval. Think about how Joel Preston Smith creates *ethos* by including these details about himself.

> *I'm 48, a journalist, and my work as a writer and photographer has led me 2,500 miles away from my mother and our farm in Liberty. I write about agriculture for* In Good Tilth *and* Sound Consumer, *and about the environment for other publications.*

PRACTICE 4.8

Writing a Synthesis Sentence

Read two reviews of any currently released film. Choose one of these reviews to consider in relation to the other.

1. Read the reviews carefully, underlining and annotating their main points.

2. Write a sentence for each review that summarizes its main points.

3. Write a sentence that synthesizes the two reviews.

4. If you have seen this film, add a sentence that draws a conclusion about the film from your own perspective. ■

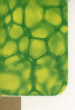

Writing a
Rhetorical Analysis

The word "rhetoric" does not mean anything goes, as in "That is just rhetoric." This word is used in the sense that it was used by Aristotle, who wrote the first guidebook to effective persuasion, *The Art of Rhetoric*. The goal of a rhetorical analysis is to explore why a text is (or is not) effective and/or persuasive. As with any textual analysis, the key features of a genre will determine what will be analyzed. For a short story, you might review the elements of fiction: character, plot, setting, point of view. For an argument, you might examine the logic of its structure.

In a rhetorical analysis, you will identify the elements that will be the focus of your writing and analyze their significance for the overall effectiveness of the piece. The trick to writing an analysis is following the steps of asking questions, making observations about the text, and organizing your own response.

- Break the text down so you have control over it. This step helps you see what your thinking is as you read—notes you make in the margins and right in the text—*inside* the writing. You really have to "interact" with the writing—get the page dirty.
- Formulate your ideas about a message, making notes about what you read and making sense of how your ideas spring from the text you have read.
- Write an analysis that shows *your* command of the text and that offers your insights based on your response. It is important to remember the "your" in that last sentence: All readers bring their own experiences to a text, and yours has as much to offer as anyone's.

ASSIGNMENT Choose a text and write your own rhetorical analysis using the lists of questions in this chapter to guide you through reading, formulating ideas, and summarizing. Write an analytical thesis that explains a pattern you observed or a decision you made about the text.

A step-by-step guide follows, along with a sample of the notes and a rhetorical analysis by Elizabeth Ramsey-Vidales.

STEPS IN WRITING A RHETORICAL ANALYSIS

Step One: Consider the rhetorical situation, in particular the purpose and the audience of the text you are analyzing.

- What genre is the piece?
- How is the writing going to be used in the world?

Step Two: Think about the components of the genre in general.

- Does the piece I am analyzing fit neatly into that genre or is it exceptional?
- Among others in its genre, what personality does this piece of writing have? Which words, phrases, or organizational structure make it fit in? Which devices make it stand out?

Step Three: Make some judgments.

- What is outstanding (good, bad, outrageous, noteworthy, unusual) about the piece of writing?
- What do I remember when I have finished reading?
- What is engaging? Boring? Fascinating?

Step Four: Write your rhetorical analysis. Include:

- An analytical thesis that gives an overview of a pattern you observe or a decision you have made about the text.
- Summary of the text.
- Examples that support your thesis.

Student Elizabeth Ramsey-Vidales went through these steps as she wrote her rhetorical analysis of "Hardscrabble Salvation."

Step One: Consider the rhetorical situation, in particular the purpose and the audience of the text you are analyzing. What genre is the piece? How is the writing going to be used in the world?

> The genre is literacy narrative. This is an essay of ideas about how or why someone writes. I do not know how it will be used, except to tell people that it is always hard to write—or do anything, and Joel Preston Smith finds inspiration in his mother. People might enjoy reading this, but it is not a very specific genre.

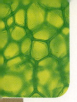

Step Two: Think about the components of the genre in general. Does the piece you are analyzing fit neatly into that genre or is it exceptional?

> It does tell me about how Joel Preston Smith started to write and how he keeps going, even though it is hard. He uses his mother's work with her hands, working the land, and compares his work to hers. If she would not give up, he will not.

Among others in its genre, what personality does this piece of writing have? Does it sound like the others? Which words, phrases, or organizational structure make it fit in? Which devices make it stand out?

> I could really see this piece of writing as a graduation speech, something that makes people motivated, inspired. It is a typical story of hardship, but I do not remember her ever telling her son "You have to do this." What makes it different from other overcoming-hardship stories is the lack of preaching or moralizing. I notice he uses a lot of repetition of sentence structures—like speech writers might. It sounds Biblical a little. I can hear Martin Luther King in the rhythm of the sentences. He uses direct quotation, descriptive details—very specific detail. He also leaves things implied. When he says "Chemical Capital of the World," we get an impression without the writer having to explain. It fits into the pattern. This story could seem very pitiful, but the writer holds back and does not allow it to go there. He is not pitying; he is showing what she overcame, how brave his mother was.

Step Three: Make some judgments: What is outstanding (good, bad, outrageous, noteworthy, unusual) about the piece of writing? What do I remember when I have finished reading? What is engaging? Boring? Fascinating?

> I was interested in the story he told. I notice he never mentioned writing until very late in the piece. The story starts when he is 13 and they are poor. He tells about how hard his mother worked. He really does not talk about himself too much, except to say what he did not do—he did not appreciate things. And then about half-way through he states his thesis: "Now I measure all my work by whether it would live up to her standards."

Step Four: Write your rhetorical analysis.

Craft an analytical thesis that identifies the pattern you observe or a decision you have made about the text.

> In "Hardscrabble Salvation," Joel Preston Smith tells the story of his mother's struggle to survive and work the land. His narrative uses the same style as a Southern Revival preacher might, expressing the complexity of suffering while offering inspiration.

STUDENT RHETORICAL ANALYSIS

A Rhetorical Analysis of "Hardscrabble Salvation"

Elizabeth Ramsey-Vidales

From the first few lines of his literacy narrative, you suspect the writer, Joel Preston Smith, is going to fall in love with the countryside his parents have moved him to from his home in Cleveland with its "concrete, which led to shopping centers and movie theatres." It's not hard to imagine he might fall in love with the land that is covered in "corn, beans, tomatoes, and squash," even it if it does lead to "blisters."

Discussion of first impression, where the writer intentionally begins

But what he reveals to his reader is not just another Hallmark movie about a 13-year-old brat who comes to appreciate nature. Instead, he focuses on his mother. She is the star of the story. And with just the sound of a preacher's cadences, but absolutely no preaching, he shows us his mother's struggle to survive, "a crippled widow, young and frail," and her determination to work the land. He uses a Southern Revival preacher's speaking style in his narrative about hardship and "salvation."

Summary

Thesis: this is the main point: a pattern in the writing. It needs defending but also fleshing out. In what ways is his narrative like a preacher's?

That very word, "Salvation" in the title, in fact, establishes the religious overtones in the narrative. In the first few sentences the writer mentions "hell," but it's only a "lite" version of hell he sees during his first four months of moving to Liberty, West Virginia. After his father dies suddenly, leaving his mother and him with "winter on our doorstep, we had no running water, no heat, no electricity, no money," his picture of hell changes. Joel Preston Smith immediately turns our attention to his mother, "a crippled widow, young and frail," as she struggles to work a factory job, driving two hours a day "to afford the privilege of owning and tending the land."

The first way it is like a kind of preaching: word choice. The writer uses preaching words

Summary

Though the structure of the narrative takes on a "testimonial" feel of an inspirational revival story, the sentence structures remind us of the sound of a Southern preacher's rhythms and cadences, particularly in the repetition of sentence structures:

The structure of sentences

> A wise child would have been grateful. He would have seen that so much land, so much freedom, is worth a little blood. He would have thanked his mother for this second birth, and his father for teaching him how to care for land.

continues next page

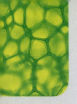

I was not that child. I fought against the land, against the work.

And another example a bit later in the piece:

In the evenings she came home and worked with me on the hillsides, hobbling over stumps on her one strong leg, swinging an ax, helping me clear land. She'd contracted polio at age 2, and her left leg, from the thigh down, was mostly bone.

She was relentless. She shamed me. Standing under 5 feet 2 inches, she weighed less than 100 pounds. She was a crippled widow, young and frail. Everything was against her. Yet every day she came home and worked me into the ground.

The author weaves powerful details of his personal story into the language and rhythms, avoiding almost all mention of abstraction. Instead he says simply that his mother worked at the "Chemical Capital of the World," allowing the reader to fill in the blanks of what that might have meant to her spirits and her already compromised health.

<!-- annotation: Comment on how the writer uses specifics -->

When he says "Normal people—especially farm kids—shouldn't be dreaming in Courier 12-point type," we get another taste of how powerfully his specificity defines the characters of the story. And through this example, Joel Preston Smith shows a way of hinting at religion without being religious, and likewise when he turns to his own writing, he has a way of shaking off self-importance. He makes a little joke.

<!-- annotation: A tie-in to the thesis -->

His metaphor for farming—"Every story I write feels like five acres of corn, shot through with crabgrass, in the hot sun"—might seem trite considering his mother's struggles, but Joel Preston Smith makes it seem honest and forthright and self-effacing. "What I lack in talent, I try to make up for with tenacity. . . . When I feel impoverished—in spirit or intellect or ability—I call to mind an image of her propping herself up with a double-bladed ax on a hillside, her face smeared with dirt, beautiful, weary, but relentless. That image has sustained me. I hear myself saying, often, 'You are not killing me. You are saving me.'"

<!-- annotation: Figurative language -->

And when the story concludes with him finding the trees in the woods of Liberty are as "familiar as friends," the readers find themselves where they expected they might end up—with the speaker finding a home in the country. Because Joel Preston Smith so expertly led the readers through his mother's struggle, the end transcends predictable and moves into salvation—through writing.

<!-- annotation: Something mentioned in the opening that comes back into focus -->

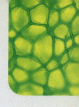

Questions for Rhetorical Analysis

1. What is the writer's (Elizabeth Ramsey-Vidales) first impression of "Hardscrabble Salvation"?
2. Identify the sentence or two where the writer summarizes the story.
3. What does the writer choose to focus on in her analysis? What is her main point or thesis?
4. What evidence does the writer use to support her thesis? What specific words or phrases does she cite?
5. How does the writer conclude her analysis? How does she connect the conclusion with the opening paragraph?

PART 2

WRITING TO EXPLORE

Bikeriderlondon/Shutterstock.com

THE STORY COASTER

WRITING A NARRATIVE

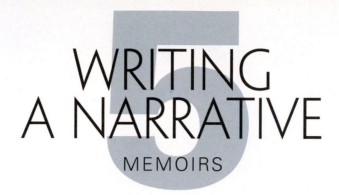

MEMOIRS

Everybody needs his memories.
They keep the wolf of insignificance from the door.
—SAUL BELLOW

When you write a memoir, a true story from your life, you will, of course, be the main character. This means you're about to get on the "story coaster." And this might come as a surprise to you, but you're not alone on this ride. Someone else is coming along: your readers. The most important thing for any storyteller is when readers get so engaged they actually forget they're reading. That's your goal—to get into your readers' imaginations, to make sure they are in the scene with you, taking your footsteps, feeling the breeze through your open car window. But how can a true story—something that actually happened to you—be told in such a way that your readers will step inside your story and enjoy the coaster? Most of us are pretty savvy about what makes a story good, but there are some common elements to help you lure an audience to a story. Sure, as readers we eschew cookie-cutter plots and stereotypical characters. Still, every writer who has attempted to craft a narrative has thought about what goes into storytelling—elements such as rising action and exposition. The things that are universal about the way we tell stories might even subliminally appeal to why we intentionally seek out stories in books and in films. It's a desire to get strapped into the seat and take off on the ride.

> ## Chapter Objectives
>
> **build your story around a central theme or big idea**
> 94
>
> **find details that bring your story to life**
> 96
>
> **craft your story by showing *and* telling**
> 100
>
> **use the narrative elements of setting, conflict, character, and point of view**
> 101
>
> **plot your story along a narrative arc**
> 105

PROCESS PLAN

Prepare

- Choose a true story with personal meaning, maybe about a transformational moment or series of events.

- Figure out the best structure: chronology, flashback, flashforward, another?

- Choose key scenes to render in detail. Do some research about when the story took place. What else was happening in the world?

Draft

- Introduction: Create scenes through detail and description. Introduce characters, create the conflict.

- Body: Develop the plot logically and incrementally. Bring the story to some high point of tension, the climax.

- Conclusion: Resolve the conflict subtly with an image or a line of dialogue that resonates and reinforces the theme.

Revise

- Clarify your theme. What is the bigger picture? Seed in the theme.

- Add details or images that reinforce the theme.

- Be sure your title points your reader toward your theme.

Understanding
the Writing Project

YOUR MEMOIR has a special appeal because it's a true story. People read to be entertained and informed, but with memoirs, people are especially interested in the fact that the story really happened. Part of the appeal is the knowledge that the same thing could happen to them—or that maybe in some way, on some level, it already has. This thematic connection with the reader gives memoirs their universal appeal.

Because narratives are both engaging and personal, you can use them in many ways—to persuade people, to move them to action, to entertain them. Narratives about you or about someone else can enlighten readers, revealing a particular perspective on the past or providing an insight into culture and lifestyle. You might write a personal narrative to explore identity, to illustrate trends, to bring a human face to statistics.

ASSIGNMENT Write a memoir—a true story—about some part of your life. Your story can relate a single event or a series of closely linked events. Show a change of mind or heart, a discovery, a confirmation or contradiction of a belief, a disappointment, or a decision. Include the following narrative elements:

- Scenes full of detail and imagery
- Characters with motivation and depth
- Incremental, logical development of the plot
- Conflict and theme

Another possible way to tell your story is to use both words and images as you might see in a graphic novel. The DIY section of this chapter (page 109) will give you some pointers.

Memoir

DAVID GOLDENBERG

Hunting a Chimp on a Killing Spree

I RAISED the gun as the chimpanzee inspected a bunch of bananas, close enough that I could hear him softly grunting. Taking aim, I leaned back against a tree to control my trembling. My weight made the giant banana leaves rustle overhead, and he turned to face the noise. He walked unsteadily a few feet in my direction at first, clutching a bunch of bananas to his broad chest. Then he dropped the fruit and broke into a four-limbed run straight at me.

In the mid-1990s, that chimp, named Saddam, started to attack and kill children in the villages near Uganda's Kibale National Park. Groups of wild chimps, including those I came to study, sometimes hunted red colobus monkeys and other animals, but Saddam was the only one in the area known to prey on humans, which is why he was named for the dictator. One victim was grabbed from a blanket as her mother was picking millet nearby. Saddam later pulled a small child off the back of a woman digging in a cassava field. He grew bolder, and by the summer of 1998, he had attacked seven children, killing at least two of them. (Though it is difficult to be absolutely sure, he is believed to have been solely responsible for the spate of attacks.)

Horrified by the violence and fearful that their harmless study chimps would become targeted by angry villagers, Kibale's primatologists sent a trained tracker named Kateeba Deo to find Saddam. Deo could examine a piece of dung and tell you the size of the chimp who produced it. But he had no experience with guns, so he needed an armed companion.

That was me: a college freshman crazy about monkeys and anything to do with them. I was in Uganda taking a summer course in wildlife management. One of the researchers taught me to use his Telazol-loaded dart gun, which would incapacitate the chimp from a distance, so a villager could then dispatch him with a machete.

As we entered the bush on the first day of the hunt, Deo told me that, unlike most chimps, Saddam was a loner. It was very likely that the rest of his group was decimated by deforestation and poaching. Saddam, though, had adapted to life in what remained of the forest around the village of Ruteete. He had learned to avoid humans when possible but became a skilled raider of their crops. When there were no suitable trees, he made nests on the ground.

Saddam's home range was vast, and the forest was dense (where it hadn't been cleared). After each

5 WRITING A NARRATIVE

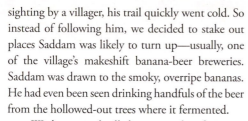

sighting by a villager, his trail quickly went cold. So instead of following him, we decided to stake out places Saddam was likely to turn up—usually, one of the village's makeshift banana-beer breweries. Saddam was drawn to the smoky, overripe bananas. He had even been seen drinking handfuls of the beer from the hollowed-out trees where it fermented.

We kept watch all day, every day, for more than a month, sweating in the shade of banana trees and passing time by chewing sugarcane and whittling sticks into toothpicks. Finally, on one Thursday afternoon in late July, Deo touched my shoulder and pointed to the trees in the back of the banana grove. They had started to shake. A chimp's black shape came in and out of view as he slowly moved toward us. At last he emerged—Saddam, without a doubt—knuckle-walking toward a huge stack of fermenting bananas. When I practiced with the gun, I was able to hit targets

smaller than his torso from the same distance. But then he started to charge.

Through the sight of the rifle, I watched Saddam come at me. All I had to do was squeeze the trigger. But I stood frozen as he advanced to within a few feet. I braced myself, but suddenly Saddam pivoted right and stormed noisily into the forest. That was the last time I saw him.

I returned to college for my sophomore year, happy to get back to a place where most problems could be solved with a well-crafted excuse. A few months later, just before a midterm that seemed so incredibly important to me, I received a letter from Deo informing me that Saddam had finally been stopped: a group of local hunters armed with spears, and a ranger with a rifle, surrounded him in a marsh and killed him. They tracked him there from the scene of his last violent act: the slaying of an 18-month-old girl.

Questions for Critical Thinking

1. Why do you think the author starts the narrative with something that happens near the end of the story? What might be the effect on the reader of telling a story out of order?

2. Red Colobus monkeys and cassava and millet fields might be exotic for most readers. Does the writer take a risk using these special names? How might a reader respond to details that might be outside his or her life experiences or knowledge? What are the benefits of taking risks like this?

3. Consider the character of this chimpanzee, Saddam. What do you know about him? What does the writer leave out?

4. Why does the writer include this statement from paragraph 2: "Though it is difficult to be absolutely sure, he is believed to have been solely responsible for the spate of attacks." Why include the uncertainty?

5. Does the speaker's action—or rather, lack of action—make sense with what you know about him as a character? Does the writer give you any clues about who he is at the time—his mindset?

THE  BIG IDEA Theme

Unlike a traditional essay where the thesis is explicitly stated in the first paragraph and the rest of the paper emerges out of that thesis (see Chapter 2, The Writer's Process), exploratory writing such as the memoir often does not have an explicit thesis. A story's theme often reveals itself to the writer at the end of the essay as a cumulative result of the story that has been told—as part of the process of exploration. Simply put, the theme is what your story is about: its point and its larger significance.

The theme you choose to reveal in your memoir depends on what actually happened, how it affected you, and what it helped you understand. Stories about significant events in childhood, for example, often have to do with coming of age or experiencing a rite of passage as you leave some part of your childhood behind. It does not matter what theme you reveal in your story, so long as you make a point that has meaning for you as well as for your readers. Readers want to take something away with them and gain a greater understanding about the world, about people, and about life experiences.

Finding out what a story means—moving the story beyond simply the basic facts of the events—can be a challenge. Sometimes you need to write the story several times before you see the meaning. Often you will find clues in your language and the imagery you intuitively use. For example, one student drafted a story about her embarrassment while dancing on the stage in middle school. The

5 WRITING A NARRATIVE

other students were talking, laughing, and making fun of her. It was a pivotal moment for her, but she could not figure out what the story was really about on a thematic level. When she reread her own language about her "flesh-colored leotard" and her "naked feet," she realized that she was writing about being metaphorically naked, stripped of her dignity. With that insight, she was able to deepen her story, add language that emphasized her sense of exposure, and find more universal themes about vulnerability and violation.

Thematically, for example, a story about moving to a new place could be about how you reinvented or transformed yourself. The theme of a story about winning over a difficult stepparent could be about gaining control, being out of control, being rejected, or being accepted. A story about meeting your Internet friend face to face could have the themes of trust and taking chances. The theme comes from your story, but it also reveals a more universal truth that you and your readers share, even though you have not had duplicate experiences.

Once you discover your theme, you can use it to help sharpen the focus of your memoir. Make sure to "seed" it into your story—leaving hints about the theme in details and language. One caution: do not confuse *theme* with *moral*. A moral reduces the entire meaning of your story to a cliché, such as "and what I learned is that you can't tell a book by its cover" or "easy come, easy go." Most memorable stories are about something deeper, more meaningful, and less clichéd. Surprising or unexpected twists, complex responses, and expectations turned upside down make for interesting and realistic themes.

Kate Burak

Research Paths: Finding Details That Bring Your Story to Life

Recalling something that depicts the culture or time period that is the setting for your story can enrich the experience for your reader. Vivid details can also help create a sense of place—not just a physical place but also a place in time. Time markers can provide a larger context for your story and help deepen your theme—the central insight you embed in your story. One writer, recalling the November her parents separated, remembered watching a dazed Barack Obama, his wife, and two young daughters walk onto the stage following the presidential election. She observed how uncertain the family seemed, how tentative. The election itself wasn't a part of the story—it just happened to be playing out in parallel time—but the image had resonance and connection to the themes of the story: family, change, history, an uncertain future.

Visual Literacy: Snapshots

THE PHOTOS in this chapter tell stories. Most are personal photos—the kind that people keep on their refrigerator doors and in little frames on their desks or nightstands.

Choose one of these photos and imagine what the story might be. From what point of view is the story told? Who is the main character? What is the setting? What happened right before the photo was taken? Right after? Write about the moment that the photo freezes. Write in the present tense.

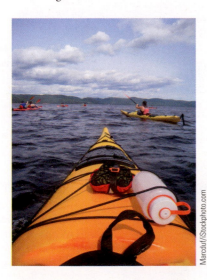

Marcduf/iStockphoto.com

Ferrantraite/iStockphoto.com

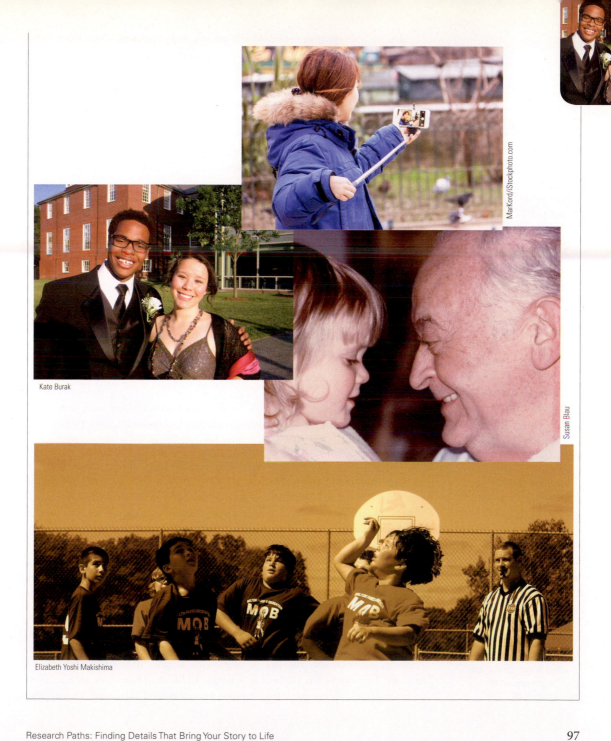

Kate Burak

Susan Blau

MarKord/iStockphoto.com

Elizabeth Yoshi Makishima

This exercise is based on a game called "Taboo," in which certain words are banned. The object of the exercise is to write descriptions without using taboo words. Here are some practice examples using the five senses:

- Describe the feeling of jumping into water on a hot summer day. Do not use the words *cool, cold, refreshing, icy,* or *numbing.*

- Describe the sounds of a restaurant. Do not use the words *clinking, voices,* or *laughter.*

- Describe the smell of a library. Do not use the words *books, dust,* or *disinfectant.*

- Describe the look of a disappointed person. Do not use the words *frown, worry lines,* or *stooped shoulders.*

- Describe the taste of coffee. Do not use the words *bitter, chocolate,* or *delicious.*

In pairs or groups, create challenges such as this for another group. Exchange challenges and write descriptions. ■

Details from sporting events, advertisements, and popular television shows from the year(s) or period you are writing about can add irony or humor and can help the reader understand characters in your story. Consult websites, searching for the year or using keywords such as "clothes from (the year)" or "what was in your lunch box in (the year)?" Find out which films were being reviewed, which books were on the bestseller list, which news stories were in the headlines, and which songs were popular. This research can help you gather details for your story and jog your memory about long-forgotten details. An interviewer once asked Pete Hamill, author of the memoir *A Drinking Life,* how he captured the Brooklyn of his childhood. His response:

> You can get help with memory. You can look at old newspapers. You can listen to the music that was played. In my case, I got the Billboard lists for the different years I was writing about and made tapes. I went to oldies record shops like Colony Records on Broadway. I would be driving with the tape player on, and it would create whole rooms, you know? I think if you get the details right, if you get the thing very specific, it inadvertently becomes universal. There's always some detail that someone says, "Damn, the author knows what he or she is talking about. That was the kind of candy that was in the second row of the candy store in New York in a given year." Whether you are in New York or Tokyo, the sense of the specific makes it available and understandable. It feels true. You can't as a writer be wrong on those things. Otherwise, you'll get letters saying, "What do *you* know?"

> —Carolyn T. Hughes, "A Thinking Life: A Conversation with Pete Hamill," *Poets & Writers Magazine,* September/October 1999. Poets & Writers Inc., 90 Broad Street, Suite 2100, New York, NY 10004. www.pw.org.

Pay attention to all the details you can gather from a source published on the date of your memoir. If you can, get a local newspaper or check the headlines on a "This Day in History" website for the place where your story was set, and look at the weather for that day and the forecast for the next day. A brewing storm and an unusually warm February day can be authentic details and can possibly add thematic significance to your story.

Talk to your friends about what they remember about the time period. What were the trends? The gossip of the time? What music would have been playing on the radio?

Creating Narrative Scenes

Although memoirs are true stories, memoirists borrow techniques from fiction to make their stories feel personal to a public audience. They create scenes full of narrative detail—scenes that leave footprints in their readers' memories. They explore themes that connect to their readers' lives. Some inexplicable chemistry of the elements in a story gives it the power to get and keep readers' attention and to make an impression. Compare these two versions of the same story.

■ **Narrative A** Ironically, it was a beautiful day, and I felt quite relaxed as I rode the train from upper Manhattan, and we passed by the more run-down buildings. Suddenly we came upon a gruesome scene. A little boy had been hit by the train. A crowd of people stood around, as well as police and other rescue workers. Near me two men were playing a game of cards. This game of chance reminded me of the danger in the world: life is a game of chance. As I thought about it, I noticed the men pay attention to the poor dead boy for just a second and then turn right back to their bridge game.

■ **Narrative B** One afternoon in late August, as the summer's sun streamed into the car and made little jumping shadows on the windows, I sat gazing out at the tenement-dwellers, who were themselves looking out of their windows from the gray crumbling buildings along the tracks of upper Manhattan.

As we crossed into the Bronx, the train unexpectedly slowed down for a few miles. Suddenly from out my window I saw a large crowd near the track, held back by two policemen. Then, on the other side from my window I saw a scene I would never be able to forget: a little boy almost severed in halves, lying at an incredible angle near the track. The ground was covered with blood, and the boy's eyes were opened wide, strained and disbelieving in his sudden oblivion. A policeman stood next to him, his arms folded, staring straight ahead at the windows of our train. In the orange glow of late afternoon the policemen, the crowd, [and] the corpse of the boy were for a brief moment immobile, motionless, a small tableau to violence and death in the city.

Behind me, in the next row of seats, there was a game of bridge. I heard one of the four men say as he looked at the sight, "God, that's horrible." Another said, in a whisper, "Terrible, terrible." There was a momentary silence, punctuated only by the clicking of the wheels on the track. Then, after the pause, I heard the first man say: "Two hearts."

—Willie Morris, *North Toward Home*

Narrative A provides information about an incident but does not invite you into its world. The writing does not create a sense of place, nor does it put you in the middle of a scene. Though explaining can be important in making a vague point clear, when you write a narrative, you want to *show*, rather than tell, all you can. You want to roll the tape, run the movie.

On the other hand, in Narrative B writer Willie Morris uses description to invite you into a scene and create a mood. The opening takes you to a specific moment,

place, and mood, a late August afternoon on a train moving through the tenements of the Bronx. From this setting the story can progress.

People inhabit this setting. The narrator introduces himself as a train-rider, an observer of the scene about to unfold. Through his eyes you can see the tenement-dwellers and the tableau of the boy, the policemen, and the crowd. Then the writer shifts his and your attention to the four card players on the train. Morris creates many characters for such a brief story, but each plays a part in building the scene.

If you think of narratives as movies rather than as still photos, you can see why something must happen in order for a story to develop. Even though the story is very short, Morris allows the images to create a specific picture: an unforgettable scene of the tragic death of a small boy. Vivid pictures like this create the footprints.

Morris creates a setting and moves characters into it. Something happens there: a story filled with tension unfolds. He begins developing the theme in the first sentence as he is looking out at tenement-dwellers who in turn are looking back at him. The idea that people look at each other without really seeing each other—a theme that is hinted at in the first sentence—is seeded in. It germinates and ripens throughout the story.

When you begin, you might have a theme in mind for your memoir. It should provide an insight into who you are, but at the same time reveal something universal. Even in a scene as brief as this one, you can see the elements of story: setting, character, conflict, and the way the theme is a cumulative result of the story that has been told, a part of the process of exploration.

Showing and Telling: Creating a Vivid Picture

Storytelling invites your reader to enter a world that you create. A memoir should allow your reader to experience your story as it happens, as you, the narrator, may have experienced it in real life. Mark Twain advised writers, "Don't say the old lady screamed. Bring her on and let her scream." However, "show; don't tell" is one of those rules that may be easier to understand than to do. Writing your memoir is a prime time to practice this skill.

If you want to evoke a feeling, description and well chosen detail should lead your reader to that feeling. But not every moment in a memoir needs to be created in such detail. Sometimes you might need to get from one time period to another with a quick explanation rather than a descriptive scene, and so you might summarize or use internal monologue to clue your reader into what you are thinking. "Showing" can emphasize a moment, whereas "telling" allows you to fast-forward over unimportant details.

PRACTICE 5.3

Show and Tell

Read the following scenario:

Fifteen-year-old Angela is arguing with her mother. She wants to wear a tight, short purple t-shirt to school. Her mother has forbidden her to wear revealing clothing and will not let Angela out of the house until she changes.

Write a short scene. Use description and dialogue to show, and then use summary and internal monologue to tell. Choose one point of view to write from—Angela's, her mother's, her father's, her sibling's, or that of her best friend, who is waiting to walk with her to school. ■

Summary: Tells

Summary can give you a chance to advance the story to an episode or scene that you want to focus on. Summary will not offer pictures for your reader to remember, so you should keep it to a minimum, using it as a transitional device to connect moments and to help your story flow.

> Later that night I called each member of my mother's family. I assured them that the accident was minor. At that point, nobody could know what would happen one month later.

Narrative Description: Shows

Narrative description puts you into a scene the way a camera would. Every detail you mention becomes significant to your reader. Detail slows down the movement of the story, focusing carefully on the moment. Use narrative description to emphasize dramatic and important moments.

> Sophie stood shivering on the porch. Her eyeliner was smeared, and her hair was slicked back by the rain. Her light jacket clung to her sharp, bony shoulders. As she started to speak, the thunder roared. I could see her mouth moving, but I could not make out the words.

Internal Monologue: Tells

Internal monologue is like the voice-over in a film. It is the script of what is going on in your head. Use it sparingly to add drama or to help clarify a scene. Remember that this type of explaining will not create pictures your reader can remember.

> I wondered why my father would be up so late. Did he know about the argument? I wished I had one of those dads who works all the time and never pays attention to what is going on in the house.

Dialogue: Shows

Use dialogue to reveal character, not to provide information. You can combine full dialogue with summary to advance the dialogue. Write conversations or parts of conversations rather than speeches.

> "Where's the car key?" I asked, opening the door.
> "In the ignition," she said.
> "You keep the key in the ignition?"
> "No, of course not," she answered. "I wouldn't keep the key in the ignition. It's stuck."

Narrative Elements: Setting, Character, Conflict, Point of View

Every story happens in a specific place, is inhabited by characters who have to overcome some kind of obstacle, and is told from a particular vantage point. These essential elements of narrative are setting, character, conflict, and point of view.

Setting

The setting is the time, place, and social or cultural context of a story. Most memoir writers establish the setting early in the piece to bring the reader more fully into the remembered place. In the excerpt from *North Toward Home* (as on p. 99), Willie Morris sets the mood for his commuter train ride with a sense of late summer and the hypnotic shadows of the train. The larger elements of the city and the impersonal way people sometimes treat each other in cities also are essential in understanding the meaning of the story.

Consider the setting of a run-down horse stable. Stables in general might make you think of the daily chores of farm life or the privileges of the wealthy. But the following description of the horse stable at the Diamond D Ranch creates an air of neglect.

> No one at Diamond D knew how to properly care for horses. Most of the animals were kept outside in three small, grassless corrals. The barn was on the verge of collapse; our every entry was accompanied by the fluttering sounds of startled rats. The "staff" consisted of a bunch of junior high and high school kids willing to work in exchange for riding privileges. And the main source of income, apart from the pony parties, was hacking—renting out the horses for ten dollars an hour to anyone willing to pay. Mrs. Daniels bought the horses at an auction whose main customer was the meat dealer for a dog-food company; Diamond D, more often than not, was merely a way station. The general air of neglect surrounding the stable was the result more of ignorance than of apathy. It's not as if we didn't care about the horses—we simply didn't know any better.
> —Lucy Greely, *Autobiography of a Face*

A story can also be set at a particular time. In the following example, a brutal winter becomes the setting for a story about finding shelter—in a literal and a figurative sense.

> Winter was like a dark and endless tunnel I entered when I left the house for school. The clouds pulled themselves down around me, reducing clear sky to a place just above my head. I could almost touch those gray clouds that blotted out the sun for weeks and weeks on end. The cold was sometimes so intense that my nostrils would freeze, sticking together, and the coldness could transform the snow. There were

days when it did not melt, or adhere to anything, but lasted as a fine powder that squeaked under my boots. The prowling winds skulked through the maze of buildings of the housing project where I lived, waiting behind corners to attack, to shoot icy blasts up my nose, down my throat. And then there was inside.

—Connie Porter, "GirlGirlGirl"

Character: Creating Character through Dialogue

You are the narrator of your memoir, and in telling your story, you communicate how the experience affected you, how it mattered to you, and how it changed you. You introduce the other characters and show their actions and their personalities.

The people in your memoir are characters with needs, motivations, and choices. They can act and react, change or refuse to change. In Willie Morris's scene, the main characters are the card players who are as anonymous as the boy who is killed by the train. This anonymity helps express the theme of the story—namely, how impersonal tragedy can be. The true center of Morris's tale, though, is the speaker, the person who observes the action and understands the irony of the bridge player's comment, "Two hearts."

As a narrator, you need not explain your feelings or explain at length about the characters. Instead, you are a lens for the action. Your goal is to show, not tell. Rather than tell the reader what you are thinking through internal monologue or explain what a character is like, you reveal character through details or incidents. Rather than explaining, imagine how you would film such material. Keep asking, "What is my movie showing now?"

Not every character in your story has to be fully developed. Some minor characters will be in the story simply to move the plot along. The police officer with the big sunglasses that made him look like a bug—the one who gave you the speeding ticket on the fateful day when you also got caught running a red light—will appear only for a moment. Still, all characters require careful attention. They should be clearly drawn and have clear motivation. What they do develops logically from *who* they are.

Dialogue allows the reader to hear the characters' voices, letting the writer reveal characters effectively through their own words. The challenge of using dialogue in a memoir is trying to stay true to your memory while selecting just the right language to reveal character. The reader will not expect you to remember the exact words you uttered five or ten years ago or even a month ago, but the reader will expect you to re-create conversations as accurately as possible.

People have "signatures" in their speech—words, gestures, pauses, or subject matter that reveal who they are. Think about how people actually speak. One character might say "like" a lot or ramble from one subject to another. Another might pause often, be evasive, answer questions with few words, or repeat questions. Dialogue can highlight personality and emotion and can create drama.

1. To understand how dialogue reveals character, go to a public place—a café, a dining hall, a bus, a subway car, a lecture hall—and eavesdrop on a conversation. Write down as much of the conversation as you can in 10 or 15 minutes.

2. As soon as possible, rewrite the conversation, adding all the details about setting, appearance, gestures, and tone of voice that you can remember.

3. Read over this version of the conversation, and write a paragraph about what the speakers' language reveals about them. Focus less on content and more on who dominates the conversation, how colorful or dull their words are, how expressive or monotonous their voices are, and what their verbal idiosyncrasies are.

   a. What can you tell about each speaker's character from this dialogue?

   b. Which pieces of dialogue would you choose to reveal a specific personality?

   c. Which sections of dialogue would you eliminate? ■

Punctuating Dialogue

Here are a few tips on the technical aspects of writing dialogue:

■ Begin a new paragraph with each new speaker.

■ Put quotation marks around each speaker's words.

■ Place periods and commas inside the quotation marks.

"All right," I said, "I will walk with you."

■ Place a question mark and an exclamation mark inside quotation marks if the quotation is itself a question or an exclamation. Place the question mark or exclamation mark outside the quotation marks if the sentence around the quotation poses the question or makes an exclamation.

"When can we start walking?" she asked.
When did you say, "I would rather drive"?
"I want to go now!" he said.

■ Use *said* or *says* for most attributions.

Conflict

The struggle, search, or mystery that drives your story forward comes from internal or external conflict. Conflicts can originate from inside (such as when you begin to outgrow a friend) or from outside (such as when your parents say that they are getting a divorce and that you must decide with whom you will live). After it has been introduced, conflict advances through scenes. The conflict gets more complicated as the main character encounters obstacles along the way. This development of conflict is the backbone of a narrative, and it must develop incrementally and logically.

A character requires motivation to grapple with a conflict and also needs to have a stake in the outcome. Think about telling a story about becoming so fed up with a frustrating boss that you quit your job. The story could center on your personal conflict: Should you quit the job and suffer the consequences of unemployment? What is your motivation to quit? You may have been harassed or felt intimidated. The stakes also need to be clear. If you quit, you have to change your lifestyle, live on less, or perhaps move home. Readers want to know why the conflict is important. The motivation and stakes create the tension and reveal the significance of the conflict.

Point of View

Art students will tell you that the most difficult assignment—and they are almost always given this assignment in a beginning drawing class—is to draw a self-portrait. Drawing yourself is complicated not only because drawing and studying the shape and shadows of your own face are very difficult but also because objectifying yourself compounds the challenge. You are not used to looking at yourself from an emotional distance. Writing about yourself as a character is the same sort of challenge.

Writing a memoir requires a first-person point of view, a way of looking at things limited to only what you can see or feel or know. For example, when writing about how you rolled down the car window to see why the police officer was stopping you, you cannot say your face was crimson red. How could you know that? You could say that you felt the heat pulsing in your cheeks. Or you possibly could have seen your face reflected in the mirrored sunglasses the officer was wearing, but this point needs to be clear to your reader.

Your point of view might be limited to your knowledge and understanding at the time of the story: "I am looking at the officer for some signal that he is not mad. All I see is me, my red face, all guilty-looking, staring back at myself in his big, mirrored sunglasses."

You might also write in the first-person point of view that expresses an understanding of an event that has ripened with time:

> I looked at the police officer's face for some signal that he was not mad at me. I would not find out until later that the officer was my mom's high-school sweetheart and a really nice guy. At that moment all I saw was me, my red face, all guilty-looking, staring back at myself in his big, mirrored sunglasses.

You cannot know what the officer is seeing (unless you see it, too) or thinking. "He thought I was a stupid kid" is expressed from a third-person point of view—*he*, not *I*, thought. You should use one point of view throughout a story unless you are experimenting with a special effect.

The Narrative Arc (Plot): Set-Up, Rising Action, Climax, Resolution

All stories have to start somewhere and end somewhere else. As a writer, you have choices to make about where the story should begin and what the best structure would be to move the events to a satisfying conclusion. Whatever choices you make, the basic requirement of narrative order remains the same: the story progresses incrementally, in steps.

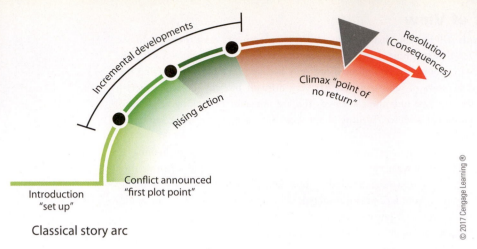

Classical story arc

A typical narrative structure has a beginning, a middle, and an end, making up a *narrative arc*. A narrative arc provides a visual map of a story, showing how writers typically build up tension to a climactic moment and then allow the tension to decrease to the story's resolution. A classical story arc looks like the arc above.

Some writers emphasize different parts of the story and may make their readers wait to begin the climb. In the opening memoir in this chapter (page 92), "Hunting a Chimp on a Killing Spree," author David Goldenberg starts the story with an event that happens near the end of the story.

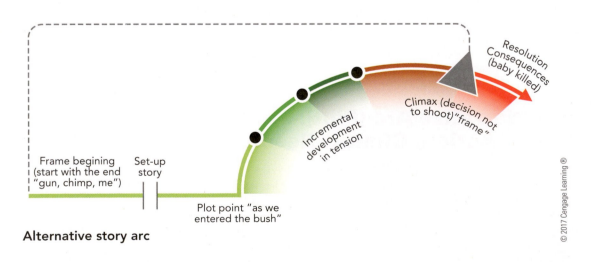

Alternative story arc

You can structure your story in a number of ways. The most common is straight chronology, starting at the beginning and working your way through an event as it occurred. You can also organize sections of your story by using flashbacks and flashforwards. You might even begin the story at the end, as David Goldenberg does, flashing forward and then moving back to the beginning. If you use this technique, be sure to provide clear transitions. Another writer who also begins at the end is Bernard Cooper, who tells his readers directly: "But none of this had happened yet." In effect, he restarts the story, using straight chronology this time.

> My mother and father and brother were asleep. It was quiet except for the ticks and groans of our Spanish house contracting in the cold. Degree by degree the temperature had dropped; November deepened. Undertones of orange were gone from the sky, the threat of rain sustained for weeks. What was to come was held in suspension, waited to happen: the blast of pain in my brother's chest, sensation drained from his fingers and toes, the blood in his body freed from its boundaries, leaving his lips, the ambulance attendants surging through our door, strangers in white who flanked a gurney, my father begging them not to use the siren—whatever you do, don't use the siren—afraid the sound would frighten his son.
>
> But none of this had happened yet. It was just after dawn. A pale light filled the hall. I stood in the doorway and stared at my parents sprawled in sleep. Their limbs were flung at improbable angles. Their mouths were slack. Beneath closed lids, eyes followed the course of dreams whose theme I tried to guess. But their faces—sunken in a stack of pillows, released from the tension of fear and hope—were emptied of all expression.
>
> —From Bernard Cooper, "Dream House,"
> *Harper's Magazine*, July 1990.

Tips for Building a Narrative Arc in Your Story

Introduction and Set-Up

- Hook the readers by tempting them to read the story.
- Set the readers on the path that leads to the conflict.
- Build the narrative using one, two, or more paragraphs.
- Give readers essential information or context for the story.
- Announce or suggest the story's conflict.

(continued)

Tips for Building a Narrative Arc in Your Story

(continued)

Rising Action

- Create a series of events that heighten the conflict.
- Make events occur incrementally, one step at a time.
- Use one, two, or several events.
- Do not include every step along the way; use just the essential ones.

Climax

- Make the climax the moment of highest tension.
- Be sure the climax brings the conflict into high relief.
- Create the climax as the "point of no return," when things can never be the same.

Resolution

- Do not feel you must tie up all the loose ends.
- Point the reader back to the theme.
- Do not make the conclusion a summary of a "lesson learned."
- Reveal how you have—or in some cases have not—resolved the conflict.

DIY MEDIA AND DESIGN

The Graphic Memoir

A graphic novel is an excellent example of how to tell a story more by "showing" than "telling." Graphic novels use the conventions of comic-book design. Each page is segmented into panels, often six or eight. The illustration can reveal many small details that you might not be able to capture in language. Although their images are static, graphic novels are similar in some ways to films. They can both "show" through images and dialogue and "tell" through voice-over narration. To create a graphic memoir out of a scene of your memoir, or to create a scene from scratch, you will have to consider how to show through illustration, tell through narration, and reveal internal monologue and dialogue through speech and thought bubbles. Tips for creating a graphic memoir follow:

- Limit narration to concepts not easily drawn or to time transitions.
- Let the images speak for themselves.
- Remember that captions interrupt and slow down the action.
- Reveal character through carefully crafted dialogue.
- Limit the speech and thought balloons to two or three in a panel.
- Show the characters in action in the panels.

Captions appear in boxes in the corners or on the top or bottom of the panel for narration. Usually captions indicate a change in setting or time—the fast-forward or backward kind of time-travel more easily accomplished in verbal narrative. Dialogue appears in speech balloons or thought balloons (a series of small balloons leading to the speech balloons).

As an example, look at how this excerpt from Marjane Satrapi's memoir of coming of age in Iran in the 1980s, the graphic novel *Persepolis*, defies the limits of "written" stories because it is able to "show" through illustrations. To further explore the difference between a narrative and a visual genre, take the graphic representation and translate it into narrative prose. Using only words (no pictures), evoke the scene on page 111. Begin with the sentence, "I turned around to see them one last time," and end with the sentence, "It would have been better to just go."

PERSEPOLIS: The Story of a Childhood by Marjane Satrapi, translated by Mattias Ripa & Blake Ferris, translation Copyright © 2003 by L'Association, Paris, France. Used by permission of Pantheon Books, a division of Random House, Inc. page 3

Note how Satrapi reveals three things in her first drawing: The main character is a girl; she is one of many girls wearing veils; and she is in a segregated school. The illustrations also establish point of view; Satrapi, for example, captures a child's perspective in her drawings. (This is the beginning page of the story.)

Note how Satrapi ends with a powerful visual image. The last words of your memoir should be a distinct statement, a bit of poetry, an unforgettable image that lingers long after the reader has finished.

READINGS

Memoirs can be funny, sad, contemplative, unsettling. You may know you want your reader to relate to the experience, but sometimes the experience is outside your reader's own personal experiences. That might require some extra balance between showing and telling. The following memoirs show some typical and atypical rites of passage from playground dares, through first jobs and unlikely friendship.

Fainting
Hailey Markman

Hailey Markman was a student when she wrote this piece. It is a story that has universal resonance despite its unconventional circumstances.

"WHAT DO YOU think they're doing?" I asked Michael, my best friend and lunch yard companion.

He followed my gaze to a group of popular kids from our grade. They were in a tight circle and looked pretty serious for a bunch of 6th graders talking during lunch.

"I dunno, probably gossiping. Maybe making fun of some 5th graders. The usual," he said, grinning at me. I smiled back, but I wasn't convinced.

"They don't look like they're just gossiping," I said.

Michael and I had been best friends since the second day of kindergarten. Both of us had started one day late, so our teacher made us seat buddies. I remember being struck by how kind he was, and how easily he helped others. At five, of course, my thought process was more along the lines of, "He's nice; let's be friends," but even then I knew how to pick 'em.

I was a pretty awkward and nerdy kid, not necessarily a loner, but I never had more than a few friends at a time. The popular kids rarely spoke to me, and I didn't really want them to. I never liked the way they acted, or the way they treated my friends and me. I was more than happy to have a few close friends, rather than be part of a group that I didn't like.

We watched the group of kids from our spot under a shady tree out on the far end of the field. After a few minutes, the group broke apart, and a few of them walked away, toward the other side of the school. The rest stood awkwardly in the middle of the blacktop, not speaking to each other.

"It's probably nothing important. It never is," said Michael, rolling his eyes at them.

The next day, I was having lunch with my friend Anne when Victoria, a popular girl who had spoken to me once in six years, walked up to us.

"Hey guys," said the body-snatcher that must have taken over Victoria's body.

"Um. Hi," I said. *Why was she talking to us?*

"So, do you guys wanna hang out with me today?"

Reprinted by permission of Hailey Markman.

5 WRITING A NARRATIVE

I stared at her for an awkwardly long time, confusion building up inside me. I didn't want to hang out with Victoria, and I was startled by the invitation. It didn't make sense.

"Yeah, totally!" Anne chimed in. I gave her a look. Her eagerness was a little sickening.

"Cool, come on," said Victoria, grabbing Anne's hand and pulling her along. Anne looked back at me and gestured for me to follow. I waited for a second, but my curiosity got the better of me, and I hurried to catch up to them.

We walked to the other side of the school, past a few classroom buildings and the cafeteria, and ended up at the library.

"Oh, we're going to the library?" I said, relief washing over me. As a true bookworm, the prospect of hanging out at the library calmed my nerves about Victoria's sudden urge to be our new best friend.

"No," Victoria said with a smirk. "We're going *near* the library."

She led us to the library's rear doors, but then steered us to the left, to an alcove I'd never been in. There were a couple kids standing there, chatting excitedly. They looked up when she walked over, and stopped talking. Clearly, Victoria was in charge of this meet-up.

"Okay guys, let's start. Anne, you're gonna go first."

Anne looked at Victoria in surprise, her eyes wide.

"Uh . . . what are we doing?" Anne asked.

"Well, we've been calling it 'fainting.' I'm not really sure what it's actually called. But it's amazing. You'll see."

The next few minutes seemed to take one thousand years to pass. My vision blurred, and my whole body tensed as I watched my friend take a paper bag from Victoria, who instructed Anne to breathe into it. I watched as Anne breathed faster and faster and cut herself off from oxygen. I watched her fall to the ground. I watched her twitch and seize. And I watched her eyes roll backward until only the whites were visible. Eventually, she stopped seizing and sat up. After a few seconds, or possibly a few years, she looked up at Victoria, smiled, and said, "Yeah . . . that *was* amazing."

I couldn't talk. I couldn't see. I couldn't breathe. I felt as though I was the one who had passed out. The silence in my head was deafening. I felt nothing, and I felt everything. It was a completely new feeling, one that I couldn't describe or explain.

"Hailey, it's your turn," Victoria said.

"Um, no. No. No, thanks," I said, struggling to form words.

"What, are you scared?"

I decided that honesty was the best way to go at this point. "Yes. I'm scared. This . . . this isn't safe, right? Like, I don't—"

"It's fine, whatever, just do it," Victoria snapped. She was irritated. She didn't like that I was wasting her time. Or maybe she didn't like that I was saying no to her.

"No," I said as I started to turn away. "I can't. No."

I walked away from the alcove alone, lost in thought. I passed kids playing foursquare, laughing and cheering for their friends. I passed chalk drawings of suns with glasses and wide smiles. I passed little ones dressed up as superheroes and princesses. I longed to be those kids. I wanted to erase my memory, to go back to drawing my own chalk pictures on the blacktop with

> "I stared at her for an awkwardly long time, confusion building up inside me. I didn't want to hang out with Victoria, and I was startled by the invitation. It didn't make sense."

my little group of friends. I needed time to go backward.

When lunch was over, I was the first to go into the classroom. I sat down and stared at my hands, waiting for the day to be over. Kids were just starting to return to their seats when I heard my name.

"Yeah, she's probably gonna tell on everyone and get the whole 6th grade in trouble," said someone to my left.

"She is way too chicken to tell on us. She wouldn't even try the fainting thing!" said another voice.

"She's crazy. It's so much fun. I can't wait to go again after school."

The voices all blended together as the kids around me continued their whispered conversation. I tried to block out the world, to not hear anything, but their words slithered into my ears like snakes, snapping and biting at me.

I had no idea what to do. I wanted to tell someone. I knew that was the right thing to do—all of the afterschool specials said so. I didn't want anyone to get hurt, especially my friends, but I didn't want to be hated. Despite never having been one of the popular kids, I had never been *hated*.

I wouldn't have to say names, I thought. *I'd just have to tell someone that something bad was happening. Then they could make it go away. And everyone would be safe. And everything could be normal again . . .*

I made it through the rest of the day, and as soon as the final bell rang, I hurried out of my classroom to find Michael. I scanned the sea of grade-schoolers for my best friend's face. After a minute, I saw him. My heart swelled with relief. He would understand. He would listen to my story and he would be there for me. I started to walk toward him, but I stopped when I saw him being beckoned by a group of popular students from our class. I saw him make his way toward them. I saw them usher him toward the library. And before I could see anything else, I ran.

I ran as only children do, with my shoes smacking against the blacktop and my arms and legs flailing behind me. I pushed people aside and I sidestepped through a minefield of backpacks. I reached the main office in seconds, and I thrust the door open.

Questions for Rhetorical Analysis

1. The narrator's persona in this memoir is her sixth-grade self. How successful is she in creating the voice and sensibilities of a sixth-grader? What choices of language and detail contribute to this effect?
2. How well does the opening paragraph set the story in motion? What does the dialogue set up or foreshadow about the story to come?
3. At what point are you aware of the conflict? What is the conflict?
4. Three characters, aside from the narrator, inhabit this story. What characteristics define Michael, Anne, and Victoria? Are they fully realized characters or types?
5. How well does the writer capture the grade-school setting? Find some specific details to support your answer.
6. Without resorting to clichés, explain the theme of this memoir.
7. The writer concludes with a scene that implies what she decided to do. Do you find this a satisfying ending to the story? Explain.

5 WRITING A NARRATIVE

Questions for Critical Thinking

1. Victoria is a recognizable character—a mean girl, perhaps. What other characters from literature or film does she bring to mind?
2. What motivates the narrator to "tell"? Is her decision consistent with her character? What would you have done in this situation when you were in sixth grade?

Style Practice: Imitation

Keeping the narrator's sixth-grade persona in mind, write some internal monologue for her that might show her conflict before she thrusts open the door in the final scene.

All Washed Up

Antonya Nelson

Writer Antonya Nelson remembers the time she was fired from her waitressing job.

MY BOSS that summer prided himself on having kissed all the waitresses. According to others, he had made them all cry. I swore that he would neither kiss me nor make me cry.

This was a busy restaurant-bar in tourist-laden Telluride, Colorado. My job was to bus tables and wash dishes. I also played first base for the restaurant's softball team. At eighteen, I wasn't old enough to wait tables and serve drinks; at eighteen, I was still living in my parents' summer house, so my work felt casual. I had another job, at the local historical museum, where the crazy curator was constantly giving me pieces of the exhibits, like double-headed railroad spikes or articles of a prostitute's clothing. I would take the gifts home, then sneak them back the next day. At night, I worked at the restaurant.

Like the waitresses, I divided my time between the public front and the private kitchen. Like the waitresses, I was a girl. But, unlike them, I didn't feel superior to the bartenders (front) or the cooks (kitchen), nor did I receive tips. I was not only the worst-paid but also the youngest staff member, which encouraged avuncular treatment from the men—the bartenders would send me shots of tequila, which I tossed down in between sending loads of steins through the Hobart. The waitresses liked to bestow advice—depilatory, pharmacological, chauvinistic. They thought I was pretty good at softball, and I didn't present a threat in the restaurant, stuck as I was elbow-deep in sludgy black water.

That busy kitchen combination of steam, grease, and tequila was heady and golden. The cooks fought with one another, dashed outside to get stoned, retreated to the walk-in to feed their munchies, and argued volubly about skiing or women or spices; about the bluegrass festival at the town park; about our boss, who was universally disliked but not universally understood. Some of these people intended to remain in the restaurant business. My status as temporary drudge made me stand out—that and a lack of humility. I was a college student; I had places to go when the summer ended.

On the night that I was fired, James Taylor was singing in the park. He'd seen fire and he'd

seen rain. . . . My back was quacked from softball—a torqued swing had sent me into a cataclysmic spasm—and I couldn't haul the pony keg up from the basement. So I got one of the cooks to help, along with the drug-addled brother of my boss's silent partner; I recruited my own brother, two years younger, to haul the trays of beer steins to me from the front. I was still running the dishwasher. And I was still slamming shots. When the boss—nicknamed the Fireplug, two inches shorter than I, a dead cigar always between his lips—took me to task, I pointed out that I'd covered for myself rather than phoning in injured. Who cared if my brother wasn't on the payroll, or that No Man, the cook, had temporarily been away from his burners? But the Fireplug didn't see it that way.

> "My status as temporary drudge made me stand out—that and a lack of humility. I was a college student; I had places to go when the summer ended."

I should have told him what I knew about the damage his vengeful staff had done behind his back. They'd contaminated pots of soup and tubs of dressing, thrown away dozens of plates and sets of cutlery, played bombs away with brandy snifters. They swindled and overcharged, sneaked in after hours to eat and steal, refused to wash their hands or scour the cutting surfaces, had sex in the walk-in. Flabbergasted and tongue-tied, attempting to say "I quit" before he said "You're fired," I didn't have the chance to rat on the others. I did, however, let him know that, as far as I was concerned, earning a college degree meant never having to work for someone like him again.

We'd been having this conversation at the sink. He turned to the busy kitchen and whistled it quiet. "Hey," he yelled. "How many of you went to college?" Everyone there raised a hand— even the dimwit brother of the silent partner.

"We're gonna miss you, First Base," my boss announced as he rocked forward and delivered a liver-lipped, ashtray-flavored kiss to my chin. Then he disappeared into the dining room. That's how he brought me to tears.

My own brother merely shrugged when I called to him from the back door. Already, he was rolling up his sleeves, eying my tequila nuggets. He'd been hired on the spot to replace me. Up the hill I stormed, back to our house, where my family sat around the kitchen table playing bridge and drinking gin, the front door closed against the "caterwauling" coming from the festival grounds— James Taylor's encore. My little sister was pleased to see me; she was terrible at bridge, and got dragged in only when no one else was available. A visiting cousin, between semesters at Baylor, was her partner. He's the one who started the pitying refrain that has become part of family lore: "Nobody gets fired washing dishes."

Questions for Rhetorical Analysis

1. How does the writer help the reader understand who the main character is at the beginning of the story? What "showing details" do you extract a read-between-the-lines impression from?
2. What is the major conflict of her story?
3. What are some details that create this conflict? Which ones "show" and which ones "tell"?
4. Do the behind-the-scenes details seem realistic? Did any surprise you? Was the conclusion satisfying? What does it suggest about this experience for the narrator?

Questions for Critical Thinking

1. When was this story set? What details in the story define the era? If this were set today, what would you substitute for those details?
2. On one level this story is about the narrator's feeling that she's going places that the other kitchen workers are not. What do you think she feels about her younger self as she relates this story of being fired? How do you relate to her?

Style Practice and Imitation

Write the last scene of a story and then write another scene starting from the beginning.

Impression
Melissa Hochman

Melissa Hochman's memoir "Impression" was selected for a reading at her college. The memoir was also published in the writing program's online magazine. Read it and see why.

I HATED TERRY. He sat next to me in Creative Writing and plucked keys off the keyboard to serve as his own personal set of Scrabble pieces. He'd form various words from curses to body parts, SAT vocabulary to interjections. He'd make a ruckus by both stripping and then replacing the entire components of the keyboard as I struggled to write a story or a poem on the computer beside him. He took great pleasure in restarting my computer while I was on page four of an unsaved document (I could never grab his dirty fingers in time to stop him from pressing the button). He wore the same outfit every day: green flannel button-down with an Allman Brother's Peach album t-shirt underneath, faded blue jeans, brown oversized belt (oversized so that the leather after the buckle swung low to his knee) and brown combat boots. He carried a distinct odor with him that smelled of tuna fish and peanut butter and intensified from the tips of his shaggy hair to the soles of his clunky combat boots. When he wasn't destroying the computers, he was sleeping. When he wasn't sleeping, he was roaming the halls looking for trouble.

When I first met him, I had attempted to talk to him, befriend him even. I brought up an Allman Brothers' concert I had gone to over the summer and how I had seen him working at Auntie Anne's in the mall. He took one look and scoffed at me; he would have none of my company. I decided I didn't like him. For the rest of the four years, he kept to himself, drew cartoons, and created random objects from long pencil shavings. But the thing about Terry was that he was a genius, and everyone in the class knew it.

My intensive creative writing class consisted of 12 people and spanned my entire high school career. We shared our most intimate thoughts, our most private work and our most absurd ideas, as well as a passion for creating beauty from 26 letters. Although our small family all shared talent, we did not all share an appreciation for it.

Reprinted by permission of Melissa Hochman.

While we all worked, Terry goofed off. While we all spent time and exerted will power for a contest piece, Terry slept. When we read our own pieces aloud and engaged in constructive criticism, Terry remained silent.

When he did write, which was only during times of mandatory in-class story development and workshops, it was flawless. He drafted screenplays I could envision on the feature screen. He crafted characters and defined not just what they did for a living, but how their morning coffee order included two espresso shots, soy milk, and the plop, plop of three sugar cubes, which set off a series of waves whose waters rose and broke against the interior of a recycled cup—every detail, every grimace, and every conversation came full circle. When he tried, he made allusions of the rarest form, had impeccable word choice, and wrung sentences with syntax so right it made you want to call a publishing company and exclaim, "Yes it was I; I discovered him and I want half the profits." A film of jealousy clung to my body like thick sea foam when he read his pieces aloud because I knew I was not as gifted as he was and that his potential far exceeded my own. I couldn't help but wish that I could capture dialogue as he did; understand and describe distinct movements as he did; set up a solitary scene with comedic, horrific, romantic and dramatic elements as he did.

However, outside of the creative writing classroom Terry was not viewed as brilliant. Consistently in the principal's office for various acts of vandalism, setting off the fire alarm and cursing at a teacher, Terry spent his weekends smoking marijuana alone outside of the 7-11.

During the September of senior year, Terry decided to bring a BB gun to school. He brought it to lunch, drew it from his backpack while he was outside, and pretended to fire the pellets at his surroundings. Though he never aimed it at another person, the administration dealt with the matter seriously. Considering Terry's record, they decided to search his locker. They found Shakespeare plays, textbooks that did not belong to him, and a poster of Sigmund Freud.

Behind the poster of Freud was a half-filled Ziploc bag of marijuana and a separate bag containing three LSD tabs. Terry was expelled and placed in a juvenile detention facility 20 minutes away from the high school.

After the news surfaced, there was a shift in our creative writing class. I looked over at the keyboard that had all of its keys intact. I looked at the electric pencil sharpener that had all of its shards still entangled within its clear plastic base. Gone were the intermittent grunts, gone were the strumming sounds of five fingertips on the desk next to mine. In some strange way, I sincerely missed that smelly genius.

Three months after Terry left, my creative writing teacher carried two manila envelopes into the classroom. Her normally pale complexion was rosy and bright. She proudly laid the envelopes on the table and allowed everyone to take note of the return address: The Scholastic Art and Writing Awards. An award from

> "When he tried, he made allusions of the rarest form, had impeccable word choice, and wrung sentences with syntax so right it made you want to call a publishing company and exclaim, 'Yes it was I; I discovered him and I want half the profits.'"

Scholastic meant you had it. It meant a certificate; it meant an awards ceremony; it meant a cash prize, and it meant that someone besides your mother saw a spark in something you had written. My name was on one envelope, and Terry's name was on the other.

After the excitement settled, my teacher wondered what to do with Terry's envelope. She didn't want to send it to him at his new school, and she didn't trust his family to recognize the significance of the award. No one had Terry's phone number or had kept in contact with him since he had left, but we couldn't allow it to just sit there. I assumed that Terry still worked at Auntie Anne's, so I volunteered to deliver the envelope.

As I walked up the mall staircase to the second floor, I could hear his familiar, raspy voice chanting, "Roll, twist, pat." As I hid out of sight behind a tall beam, I watched him continue to roll, twist, and pat pretzel dough for a few more minutes before someone came over to him and told him he could go on a break. Terry threw off his hat and apron and jumped over the side of the counter, heading for the staircase. I stepped to the side of the beam so that he could see me and he made his way over to where I stood. As he came closer he extended his arm and pointed at the envelope clutched in my hand.

"That my X-Mas gift?"

I handed him the envelope. After a moment, he lifted his long, shaggy hair to reveal a large forehead with a furrowed brow.

"No fuckin' way," he said, before opening the envelope. He took out a small gold key, a certificate with his name on it, and a copy of his science fiction short story.

"This was the only thing I typed up all year. It was a first fuckin' draft."

It was the first emotion I had ever seen him display: he was surprised, humbled, and in disbelief.

"Yeah, winning that's a pretty big deal," I told him, ignorantly assuming that he hadn't realized the significance of what he was holding.

"No shit," he said. "You win regionals and then you're eligible to go to nationals. You get to nationals and it means you get to go to D.C. for free. Get out of here for a little while." He ran his fingers over the raised seal on his certificate and traced the letters of his name.

"Well, uh, congratulations," I said. "Maybe I'll see you around."

He held up his hand and told me to wait a minute. He went back to Auntie Ann's and came out with a notebook that had doodles and holes on the front cover with loose paper sticking out of the sides. He rolled the notebook, making a twisting motion with his two palms before patting the notebook flat again.

"I've been workin' on some stuff, nothin' great. But I want you to take this back and have everyone look at it. You know, just a couple pieces, if you guys have time."

I was in shock. I couldn't believe that he still wrote, let alone had enough work to fill a notebook. I couldn't believe that he cared about the opinions of his fellow classmates, or that he hoped to improve. I couldn't believe that he was capable of saying so many words at once.

I nodded and walked away. As I placed the notebook in my bag, a card fell out. It was an Auntie Ann's frequent buyer card, with six pretzel punches already stamped through. According to the card, I had purchased six pretzels and was due for a free one.

I turned around and Terry said, "That's to make sure you come back."

Questions for Rhetorical Analysis

1. Hochman doesn't allow her reader to hear Terry's voice until the final scene of the story, until after she paints a portrait of a disaffected "genius." Reread the dialogue in the final scene. How does that dialogue reveal Terry's character? What does it reveal about the narrator?
2. Where does the writer first engage the reader and introduce the story's conflict?
3. This story has a long set-up before the story actually begins. Identify the place where the story is set in motion. Why do you think Hochman has such a long set-up? Is it effective?
4. The narrator seems to be on the sidelines of this story, but it is her character and her character arc that is of central interest. What change does she experience? Cite evidence from the story to support your answer.
5. In what way do pretzels and pretzel-making serve as metaphors in this story?
6. The final scene at the mall is rendered in great detail. Is it an effective conclusion to the story? Why or why not?

Questions for Critical Thinking

1. Terry is a recognizable character—a kind of disaffected student who has great intellectual promise. What other characters from literature or film have these qualities? Do you find Terry a sympathetic character? Why?
2. What motivates the narrator to reach out to Terry? Would you have done the same?

Style Practice: Imitation

Begin a paragraph with the sentence, "I hate (fill in the blank)." Then, as Hochman does in the first paragraph, explain what is hateful, but also intriguing, about this person.

WRITING & REVISION STRATEGIES

Gathered here are three interactive sections for you to use as you write and revise your memoir.

- Writer's Notebook Suggestions
- Peer Review Log
- Revision Checklist

Writer's Notebook Suggestions

You can use these exercises to do some start-up thinking and writing for your memoir.

1. Write about a moment that you remember well. Include all of the following: weather, a gesture, dialogue, music, color, and a smell. Do not exceed 250 words.

2. Using the writing you did for the first question (or some other memory), change the voice. Use one of the examples in the chapter as a model.

3. Using the writing you did for the first question (or some other memory), draw your memoir in graphic novel form, telling your story in images with a few lines of explanation or dialogue.

4. Take any paragraph of memory writing and change the verbs to the present tense.

5. Write two different openings for a story about your first day at school or your first day on a job. Choose from the following types of openings:

   a. Start in the middle of action.
   b. Start by describing a photograph of that day (real or imagined).
   c. Start by seeing your reflection in a mirror or window.
   d. Start at the end.
   e. Start with dialogue.

6. Choose a day from your life that you remember well, not necessarily because it was dramatic or important but because you can recall many of the details. Write a diary entry as if the day were yesterday.

7. Write a paragraph that combines internal monologue, dialogue, summary, and descriptive narrative.

8. Write about yourself in the third person.

9. Describe the weather on a day that was important to you.

10. Remember a phone call that was hard for you to make. Write the dialogue.

11. Describe someone who has left an impression on you by describing a place in which that person belongs. How does the place represent the person?

12. Use the letter-to-a-friend technique: Write a letter explaining an event to someone you know well.

Peer Review Log

As you work with a writing partner or in a peer-review group, you can use these questions to give helpful responses to a classmate's memoir and to guide your discussion.

Writer's Name: _____

Date: _____

1. Bracket the introduction of the memoir. What technique does the writer use to open the story? Do you find it effective, or could you suggest a better place for the story to begin?

2. Put a line under the last paragraph of the set-up. How effectively has the writer set up the story? What other information or sensory details might help you better understand the events that follow?

3. Box a section that presents the setting of the story. What details might make the setting stronger, more vivid, or more specific?

4. Write a sentence that expresses the theme of the story as you understand it. What images, language, and events point to that theme? Does the title also direct the reader's attention to the theme? If the title is weak, can you suggest an alternative?

5. Put a check mark next to the first place where you notice the conflict beginning to emerge. What is the conflict? What are the obstacles for the central character? What is at stake?

6. What is your impression of the main character(s)? Suggest places where the characters' actions and dialogue could be strengthened to develop the characters more fully.

7. Examine the narrative techniques that the writer uses in the memoir. Identify places where the writer uses summary and places where the writer creates a scene through narrative detail. Label places where the writer uses dialogue with D and places where the writer uses internal monologue with IM. Which sections might be strengthened by showing through narration and dialogue rather than by telling through summary and internal monologue?

8. What kind of voice does the writer use to tell the story? Is it appropriate for and consistent with the narrator's age and circumstance? How might the voice better reflect the narrator's character?

9. Bracket the conclusion. What technique does the writer use here? Is the conclusion effective in leaving a last impression that fortifies the theme? Does the last paragraph add anything necessary to the story? Would the story be injured if this paragraph were cut?

10. Comment briefly on the writing style. Write V where the writing could be strengthened by substituting active verbs for "to be" verbs and T where the writer could use a better transition. Put an asterisk (*) next to places where the writer uses interesting verbs and good transitions.

Revision Checklist

As you do your final revision for your memoir, check to make sure that you

- used an interesting, attention-getting opening
- set up the story
- created a setting that helps develop the mood of the story
- presented a clear conflict
- developed the conflict incrementally, in steps
- presented a climax
- described your characters
- made your main character's motivation clear
- explored a theme that has significance for you and your reader.

Andy Warhol's interpretation of Marilyn Monroe.

WARHOL, ANDY/Art Resource, NY

WRITING ABOUT OTHERS

PROFILES

An ordinary life examined closely reveals itself to be exquisite and complicated, somehow managing to be both heroic and plain.
—SUSAN ORLEAN

In painting a portrait, an artist sets out to create a likeness of a person, a recognizable image. The artist's aim, however, is only in small part to record the details of the subject: color of hair, slope of nose, or smile. The real art of portrait painting lies in the way the artist interprets and reveals the subject. In a good portrait, through some combination of light and shadow, expression, and detail, the essence of the subject emerges, not just the likeness but also the character of the subject.

A profile is a portrait in words. It provides an in-depth look at a person or sometimes a group of people from a specific perspective or angle. This angle makes the portrait very different from a general picture of a person, what might amount to a simple "driver's license" description: height, weight, and date of birth, for example. As we look at the more in-depth issues of character—the struggles, commitments, and decisions of others—we may even recognize ourselves. Along the way, we also learn about the professions, passions, and lifestyles of famous, infamous, and even ordinary people, and perhaps extend the boundaries of our own lives.

*Chapter
Objectives*

PROCESS PLAN

Prepare

- Find a profile subject you can interview who represents a career, a trend, a movement in history, a philosophy, or a lifestyle.

- Become an expert: Research the subject's area, read similar profiles, read about the issues the subject represents.

- Write interview questions: Ask for stories, examples, experiences that will concretely illustrate the ideas your subject represents.

Draft

- Introduction: Hook your reader with a scene, anecdote, or statistic.

- Body: Develop the "big idea," the interpretive thesis of your profile. Organize the profile to explain this thesis.

- Include physical description, moments where the reader sees the subject in action, and comments from others who know the subject or the ideas represented.

- Conclusion: End with an image or a memorable quotation.

Revise

- Remind your reader of your thesis at strategic points to stay focused.

- Cut references to the interview itself. For example, avoid saying, "Next I asked. . . . " Focus on the subject, not on yourself.

- Check for two types of transitions: (1) those that connect paragraphs and (2) those that remind us of the big idea.

Understanding the Writing Project

PROFILES ARE word portraits. They are not biographies, filled with facts about when someone was born, where the person grew up and went to school, or if the person got married and had kids, and so on. Instead, profiles paint a picture of some piece of a person's life, leading to an interpretation of what is interesting or important about that person and that person's world.

Look at this biographical entry about a writer whose books you are likely to know, but you may not recognize from the facts about his life.

> He was born in Springfield, Massachusetts, on March 2, 1904, and graduated from Dartmouth College in 1925. At Oxford University, he studied toward a doctorate in literature. There he met Helen Palmer, the woman he eventually married. After returning to the United States, he worked for a humor magazine. Later, he joined the army during World War II and was sent to Hollywood, where he won several Oscars for his documentaries about Adolph Hitler, and one for a cartoon called *Gerald McBoing-Boing*.

These dryly listed facts do not give a clue about who this man really is. Instead of a portrait, which reveals some basic element of character, we get a snapshot—information without interpretation.

The following paragraph, which interprets this person's character, provides a perspective, and it helps reveal the writer, whom you will now most likely recognize.

> He used to doodle in school, strange little drawings. His high school art teacher told him never to plan a career in art. Likewise, his writing teacher at Dartmouth College discouraged him from becoming a writer. Even his fraternity brothers voted him least likely to succeed. Being misunderstood, though, would not get in his way. This writer's first children's book was rejected 43 times. Then a friend agreed to publish it. The writer went on to win an Oscar for a cartoon, but even more importantly, he kept trying new things. At the encouragement of his publisher, he set out on a campaign against boring children's books, hoping to make learning to read more interesting than Dick and Jane had. And, in 1954, using a list of 220 words he thought a first grader could learn, he wrote an instantly successful book. It was called *The Cat in the Hat*.
>
> —Adapted from Outpost 10F, *Poetry Guild*, and *Stories for a Teen's Heart*

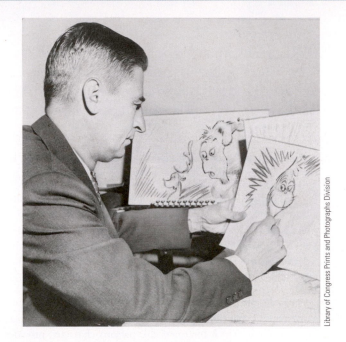

Library of Congress Prints and Photographs Division

The writer, of course, is Theodor Geisel, known all over the world as Dr. Seuss, author of *How the Grinch Stole Christmas, Green Eggs and Ham*, and more than 40 other children's books. The second paragraph, rather than just listing biographical facts, creates a portrait of this unique artist, focusing on his quirky sensibilities, his "misunderstood" character, and his early conflicts.

At their best, profiles invite the reader into the subject's world. Malcolm Gladwell, author of many *New Yorker* profiles, says that profiles should be more sociological than psychological. He claims no interest in a profile subject's childhood or even the intimate details of that person's life. What interests him is the subculture in which the subject belongs. He writes that "the individual is a means to examine another world—the world in which that person lives."

ASSIGNMENT Write a profile of a person or a group. Focus on some specific aspect that is noteworthy. You do not have to admire the people you write about, but you should find their accomplishments, lifestyles, or philosophies interesting and maybe even fascinating to explore. (Oral history is another avenue to explore for recording fascinating people's lives. See the DIY on page 144 for some pointers.) You also do not have to choose someone who is rich and famous. Sometimes the most interesting profiles are about ordinary people.

Profile

Jack Falla was a writer, teacher, and sports journalist. This profile spotlights the teacher who really taught him how to write.

JACK FALLA

The Top Drill Instructor in Boot Camp 101

THE BULLWHIP lay on the bookcase, coiled around its wooden handle like a snake around its rattle.

I was in the second-floor office of associate professor Gerald Powers at Boston University's College of Communication. A student carrying a sheaf of papers had slunk away from Powers's desk as I entered, "REWRITE" scrawled across the top paper in red pencil. The whip had struck again.

"Not my day to be popular," said Powers, rising from his chair to shake hands. He is a slight man, perhaps 5 feet 9, with close-cropped graying hair, and a reserved, somewhat bemused manner.

"At least you spared him the stamp," I said, nodding toward the open door. We could hear the retreating student's footsteps in the hall.

"Oh, I still have it," said Powers, smiling for the first time and opening his desk drawer to take out a rubber stamp that says REWRITE in block letters. "And I have the other one at home."

The other stamp is even more succinct; it simply reads BULLSHIT.

The stamps and Powers's willingness to use them on students' papers are two of the reasons he carries the reputation that inevitably falls upon one faculty member at every college in the world: toughest sumbitch on campus. Powers is one of those professors from whom hordes of students recoil at preregistration, choosing instead to slink over to the "twinkies" courses. Yet somehow the sumbitches manage to endure.

For 20 years, Powers has taught various writing courses within BU's Public Relations Department. And for 20 years he has ritualistically slain compromise in the first minute of the first class. His usual greeting:

"Deadlines are immovable. Meet them if it kills you. The only excuse for failing to turn in a paper on time is a death in the family. In which case," he adds, "I prefer that the death be yours."

Neal Boudette, a recent survivor of a Powers class, recalls another intimidating tactic: "One day Powers opened his briefcase in class and took out that whip. He said, 'This is a gift from former students. They thought it symbolized the way I work.' I said to myself, 'This man is a lunatic. He uses terror to teach.'"

"I try to set the tone early," says Powers, describing his First-Day-of-Class Grand-Entrance Fantasy. "I think I should enter the class ahead of a train of graduate assistants carrying my briefcase and books, backed up by an orchestra playing the march from Verdi's *Aida*."

Adapted from Campus Voice, August/September 194. Reprinted with permission.

That would certainly get the class's attention, I agreed.

It is also a day-one ritual for Powers to tell his students that almost every assignment will have to be rewritten—twice. At which point some unfortunate will inevitably raise his hand and ask, "What if you do it right the first time?"

"Humor me," he will say.

"I think students take his classes as some kind of self-flagellation," says BU grad Denise Graveline. "They know Powers's reputation, and they want to see if they can meet the challenge."

Meeting the challenge takes a strong self-image on the students' part because Powers, like many professors of the hard-line persuasion, can be brutal in class.

For example, one student began an editorial with "In this modern world of ours today . . ."

Powers read it aloud. "Nice lead," he said, then commented, "if we don't count its being dull, pointless, and triply redundant."

Then there was the now-famous classroom argument between Powers and a student who tried playing hardball in defense of his use of the alleged word *irregardless*.

"Not a proper word," said Powers.

"It's in the dictionary," yelled the student, who then had the temerity and monumental bad judgment to charge to the front of the room and bang his Webster's down on the table.

"My dear boy," said Powers, picking up the dictionary and sliding into what he calls his full William F. Buckley, "let us read the definition. '*Irregardless:* illiterate use of the word *regardless*.'"

Powers's students routinely receive graded papers bearing so much red penciling that it looks as though Powers has bled on them.

"Nice typing. Horrible writing" is a frequent comment in the river of red. And to a student who once argued that good layout photos would help "carry his story," Powers replied, "Illustrating that story would be like perfuming a pig."

"He demeaned us," says former Powers student Bob Hughes, "until most of us rose above ourselves in the effort to prove we were better than he gave us credit for being." No one escapes Powers's sarcasm. A graduate assistant once gave a lecture while Powers observed from the back of the room. The students were less than animated, prompting the grad assistant to say with forced good humor, "Professor Powers, is there something you can do to wake up the class?"

"Begging your pardon," replied Powers, "I wasn't the one who put them to sleep."

And to a student who was considering a freelance writing career, Powers advised, "An excellent idea, particularly if you had the foresight to be born the daughter of a railway magnate."

Three or four weeks into each term, the school's advising center begins to resemble a refugee processing station with students in dazed or indignant retreat from Powers's thermonuclear teaching.

"Students would come in crying 'mental abuse' or 'I can't take it in there,'" says BU grad Maryellen Kennedy, who observed these semiannual crises during four years of working in the advising center. "A lot of people transfer to other courses, but all that does is add to the Powers mystique."

"Students genuinely fear him," adds Graveline.

But, like other sumbitches from the football field to the physics lab, Powers claims he doesn't care.

"I'm an elitist," he says, pointing out that his teaching methods derive from the classical private-school tradition as he experienced it at Boston Latin, St. Sebastian's, and Harvard.

"I divide students into four categories," he says. "First are those I actively detest. The brown-nosers, grade grubbers, and B.S. artists. Then there are what I call the Rimless Ciphers. They're neuter. They occupy space. I'm neither for them nor against them. The largest group is made up of pleasant, nice people. I have great empathy for students in this group who try hard. Finally, there is a small group—the select and gifted few—the ones you never forget."

Powers may be harder on his protégés, however, than on any of his other students. I recall one of the chosen, a senior who had done well in two of Powers's courses and who was suddenly doing poorly after going through that most painful of undergraduate crises: Breaking Up with the Girlfriend. There were some of us who feared for the young man's emotional stability. Powers was not among us.

"Do you know what Robert Frost once said was all he knew about life?" Powers said to the student. "'It goes on.' When you come into this class, you leave your personal problems outside."

Yet Powers has a single overwhelmingly redeeming feature that he probably shares with a good many other campus SOBs. He will go to the mat for his students.

Kennedy describes a typical scene at the student advising center: "The reception room would be crowded with students waiting to see advisers, and suddenly Powers would burst in with a student in tow. Immediately, Powers's student would become the best kid with the most pressing problem in the entire university. Powers would have to get him into this course or out of that course, and it would have to be done that minute. Sometimes Powers would just bypass everyone and go charging into a dean's office."

"When alumni return to school, the one name you hear most often is Powers," says Graveline. "The message is usually 'If you can get through Powers's courses—and put up with him telling you to straighten your tie and shine the back of your shoes—you can probably survive the transition from campus to the world of work.'"

Powers readily admits that he is more concerned with his students' job search than with their paper chase. Each year he places dozens of students in high-paying internships with such corporate giants as Ford, Alcoa, and General Electric. He sends these former waitresses and lifeguards away in May with the admonition "Screw up and you'll answer to your boss this summer and to me next fall."

But Powers's students—those who survive, that is—don't often screw up. And as much as they may curse his name as they're plowing through yet another endless rewrite, a large percentage will someday look back and realize that he was the one professor who made a difference in their lives.

I lifted the bullwhip off the bookcase and let it uncoil on the floor.

"So why do you keep teaching?" I asked.

"Same reason most of the other SOBs in this profession do it," he said, leaning back in his chair. "I do it for the money."

I put the bullwhip back on the shelf. We went to lunch. I bought.

||||||||||||||||||||||||||||||||||||||||||||||||||||||||||||||

Questions for Critical Thinking

1. Falla adds to the mythology of the enduring value of a "tough" teacher. Do you agree that "tough" teachers are the most effective ones? Explain your answer.
2. The bullwhip and the rubber stamps define Powers's teaching style. Think about a teacher who affected you in some way—positively or negatively. What symbols would you use to define that teacher? Why?

1. Go out to a public place: a restaurant, park, or lobby, for example. Choose one person to observe for as long as 10 minutes. Make note of the person's gestures, body language, clothing, and hairstyle. If you can catch a few words of dialogue, write them down.

2. Decide what impression that person made on you.

3. Without telling your reader what you think about the person, describe, in one paragraph, what you observed. Select and arrange details and choose words that will help shape your reader's impression.

4. When you return to the classroom, read your paragraphs out loud. Have classmates tell you what impression they get from your writing. ■

The Rhetorical Situation

Purpose: To paint a word portrait of a person or group, to reveal something important or interesting about the world that person or group inhabits.

Voice: Your voice should call attention to the profile subject, not to yourself. Keep your subject in the foreground and yourself in the background.

Audience: Your reader wants to learn about the person or group but also about the culture or lifestyle that the subject represents. Readers want to discover something in your profile subject's life that reflects on their lives as well.

Media and Design: Published profiles appear just about everywhere in community, workplace, and professional settings. In college, you might compose oral histories or historical profiles that shed light on a social movement, discovery, medical breakthrough, or phenomenon.

Choosing a Good Profile Subject

The media are starting to heed the old axiom that everybody has a story. The ordinary-person genre has become a professional crusade for one reporter. David Johnson, at the Lewiston, Idaho, *Morning Tribune*, selects a name randomly out of the phone book for his features about people not normally considered newsmakers. Johnson has been writing his column "Everyone Has a Story" for over 20 years and has written more than 1,000 pieces about ordinary people.

Finding Your Topic

The following list demonstrates the range of topics students have written about. Student writers discovered these topics at their colleges, in their neighborhoods, in their family's circle of acquaintances, and by word of mouth.

- An 89-year-old Russian immigrant who has lived through "World War II, Communism, Stalin, Brezhnev, Gorbachev, and the breakup of the Soviet Union"
- High school chess players who challenge the "chess nerd" stereotype as well as one another
- A local band that combines punk rock with Irish sentimentality

Portrait overtaken by graffiti.

Frederic Lezmi/laif/Redux

- A college woman who wears the college mascot suit and views college sports from this unique perspective
- A director of a summer arts camp for inner-city kids who believes that the arts teach essential cognitive skills

Finding Your Focus

Finding the story in your subject's life that resonates and will have meaning for your reader is just as important as choosing a good profile topic. You can often locate this meaning in a point of tension or conflict. If you were writing a profile of a professional wrestler, for example, a point of conflict might be whether professional wrestling is above board and how this particular wrestler deals with the perception of fakery in the sport. A profile about a student athlete might explore the tension between the demands of academic work and athletic training.

Five Questions to Help Focus Your Profile

1. Is your subject in some way related to a news story or a current trend or idea?
2. Is your subject in some way unusual, odd, or offbeat?

PRACTICE 6.2

Finding a Good Profile Topic

1. List five possible profile topics. Think of people you know or people you have heard about who have had interesting experiences, do interesting work (perhaps in a field you might want to enter), have interesting or unusual hobbies or interests, or espouse interesting philosophies.

2. Choose one person from your list and freewrite for 5 minutes about that person. What are possible points of tension or conflict in the person's story? What would you want to find out about him or her? What questions would you ask? ■

3. Can you link your subject to a noteworthy achievement, an innovation, a contribution, or a discovery?

4. If your subject is not unique, how does he or she fit in? Does your subject represent what is typical about a profession, interest, lifestyle, or conflict? Can your subject reveal something found in others with the same profession, interest, lifestyle, or conflict?

5. Why would readers be interested in this person? What is the payoff for readers?

PRACTICE 6.3

Identifying the Nut Graf or Interpretive Thesis

Find three profiles published in newspapers, magazines, or websites. For each, identify and underline the nut graf, the spot where the writer reveals the interpretive thesis or theory about the subject. This is usually a sentence or two. If you do not find a nut graf directly after the lead paragraph(s), see if it has been pulled out and used as a subhead after the title. For each nut graf you identify, comment on how well you think it presents the profile's focus. Explain your reasoning. ■

THE BIG IDEA **The Nut Graf or Intepretive Thesis**

A profile usually explicitly states its thesis directly after the lead, the introductory paragraph or paragraphs. This thesis is often embedded in a paragraph that journalists call the *nut graf*. *Nut* means the kernel of the idea; *graf* is journalistic shorthand for "paragraph." Some call this paragraph the "bridge"; another way to understand its function is to understand that it bridges the lead and the body of the paper.

When you write your profile, you might not find your focus until you have completed your research. Research often uncovers a new insight as you explore your subject, and it may help you unearth a compelling, previously untold story. Peter Scanlan, in *The Quill*, a publication of the Society of Professional Journalists, gives this advice for finding or developing a profile focus: look for conflicts, questions, obstacles, or "pivotal moments" in someone's story:

- When things have changed
- When things will never be the same
- When things have fallen apart
- When you do not know how things will turn out

The nut graf announces your focus—that is, your interpretation of your subject—and it stems from your exploration of your subject. If you are having trouble finding your own focus for a profile, sometimes it is helpful to use this template to help figure out your thesis:

(Name of your profile subject) is a _____ who _____ .

For example, for the profile of Theodor Geisel (Dr. Seuss), you could fill in the blanks in a number of ways.

Theodor Geisel was *a writer and artist* who *changed the way children read.*
Theodor Geisel was *a visionary* who *never let fate govern him.*

A word of caution here: remember that an interpretive thesis is never a factual statement about the person (for example, *Theodor Geisel was the author of* Green Eggs and Ham) but rather stems from your interpretation of your profile subject, an interpretation that you then have to support through your research.

Key Elements in Effective Profiles

- **Physical description:** Physical description should be brief and relevant. Give your reader a glimpse of some defining characteristics that reflect your interpretation but not a feature-by-feature portrait.

- **Quotations from the subject:** Quotations are the lifeblood of profiles. Quotations from your subject allow your reader to actually hear your subject's voice and to bring that person to life.

- **Quotations about the subject:** Quotations from others allow for multiple perspectives and allow you to draw a complex character, who, like all of us, has many layers.

- **Examples:** Your profile needs proof—in other words, examples that illustrate how or when your subject did something noteworthy or revealing of character.

- **Anecdotes:** Some of the best examples come in the form of anecdotes, or small stories. Your source can be your subject or people who know your subject well.

- **Factual information (background and context):** Embedded in your profile should be factual information that deepens your reader's understanding of the subject. Explanatory, or expository, passages explain everything from background information on the subject's life to concepts needed to understand the world in which the subject lives.

PRACTICE 6.4
Identifying Profile Elements

1. Find a published profile you like (from a recent publication, website, or from the readings in this chapter). Get a handful of highlighters or use the color highlighter on your computer's toolbar. As you read the profile, use different colors to highlight all the following elements you can find:

- Physical description
- Quotations from the subject
- Quotations about the subject
- Examples
- Anecdotes
- Factual information

2. By looking at the color patterns, make an assessment of the kinds of elements the writer used. Which elements did the writer rely on most? ■

Next, figure out a logical pattern of development that stems from your nut graf. Select quotations, anecdotes, and facts that support your interpretation. For example, in "The Top Drill Instructor in Boot Camp 101" (page 129), the nut graf comes after the introductory scene where the writer visits his former professor's office. The seventh paragraph begins with the interpretive thesis, "The stamps and Powers's willingness to use them on students' papers are two of the reasons he carries the reputation that inevitably falls upon one faculty member at every college in the world: toughest sumbitch on campus." The rest of the profile flows from this point; the reader gets example after example of Powers's toughness but also clearly understands how and why he "manages to endure."

Visual Literacy: Analyzing Portraits

Examine the Two Portraits of Andy Warhol

1. Look at each portrait carefully. Pay attention to

   ■ the background (context)
   ■ the focal point of the portrait (where the artist directs your attention first)
   ■ the pose of the subject, his body language
   ■ the positioning of the subject in the frame—his size and presence
   ■ the colors and design of the clothing and the background images

Portrait of Andy Warhol, by Jamie Wyeth (1976).

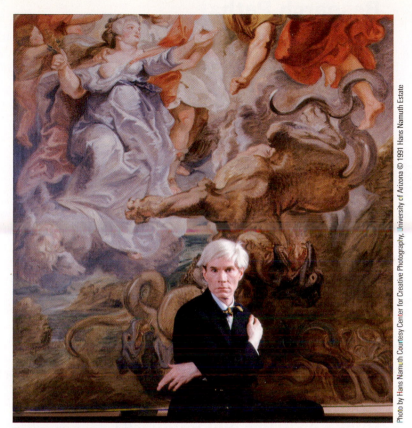

Portrait of Andy Warhol, by Hans Namuth (1981).

2. What impression do you get about the character in each painting or photograph?
3. Does the artist refer to other paintings or images in the style or design?
4. Does the author refer to other characters—from literature, popular culture, mythology, or stereotypes?
5. What specific details contribute to your interpretation?

- Write an interpretive thesis using the steps under The Big Idea, pages 134–135.
- Answer these questions for the other portraits in this chapter.

Research Paths

How interesting your reader finds your story hinges on what you discover and uncover in your research. The more you learn, the stronger and more credible your voice becomes, and the more you will enliven and focus your writing. A well-researched profile includes these elements:

- Print and electronic sources, including social networking sites such as Facebook as well as sources about the subject's field of interest
- Direct observation of the person in a place that has relevance for him or her
- Interviews with many people (multiple sources)

Social Media

Social media sites are quickly becoming ways to get in touch with people whom you might not have met any other way. Facebook, LinkedIn, and other social networking sites provide good entry points for learning details about your subject's interests, getting some contact information, or finding out some basic information about your subject's biography. Message boards and forums as well as Twitter can lead you to people who might know about the field your subject represents, and lead you to possible outside interviews to help contextualize your subject. Be careful, though, to assess your source's credentials for acting as an "expert" whose comments have worth in your work. Be certain to verify your source's identity and claims. The rule of thumb for writers is to make sure you can find a second source that offers similar information. Statistics, documents, and other people can help verify claims.

Online Searches and Databases

Other useful contextual information—facts and statistics—are available on databases. Through online searches, you can find the names and contact information for authors or members of groups. Often you will find links or lists of sources that lead you to people who might be willing to offer an expert opinion on your subject or topics.

Direct Observation

Novelist Eudora Welty said, "Stories don't happen nowhere." She was talking about the significance of setting in creating an impression. Characters in profiles, as in fiction, inhabit places, and the places they inhabit reveal something about who they are.

One student, writing a profile of a nutritionist, visited her office. The student begins her profile this way:

PRACTICE 6.5
Search for Sources

1. Possible profile subjects include the following:
   - A high school teacher who has just been named Math Teacher of the Year
   - A college student who is a professional skater
   - An inventor who is working on creating a nonpolluting combustion engine
   - A marathon runner

Choose one of these subjects, or one from the "Finding Your Topic" on page 132, and do a search for print and electronic sources that you could read for background information. List at least three sources. Use correct bibliographical citation, as shown in Chapter 16. ■

Bright red Coca-Cola bottles intermix with Special K cereal boxes on the top of her food pyramid shelf. Tiny sugar cubes, used to illustrate how much sugar is in different sizes of soda, form geometric shapes from the size of a three-ounce piece of steak to an extra-large pancake. On the shelf below, [a] vitamin C–dense Tropicana orange juice box mingles with the fiber-rich Quaker Oats box, decked out in its reds, whites, and blues. Every flavored water drink out on the market from pineapple to strawberry line[s] the third shelf like a row of soldiers.

—Yoonie Park, "Hold the Line in Body Fat"

The description of the office shelves brings the reader into the subject's nutrition-savvy world and leads to the writer's assessment that the subject "does not offer the quick fix; instead, she brings us a pinch of fun and enjoyment with eating healthfully." If you can shadow your profile subject for a day or an afternoon and observe him or her in daily life—teaching nutrition, racing dirt bikes, or painting a picture—you will find revealing details and establish a solid narrative base for your profile.

Interviews

Interviews are the mainstay of field research. Through interviewing sources, you gather firsthand information from experts as well as opinions, responses, and thoughts from anyone familiar with the subject. (For more information on interviewing, see the box on Tips for Good Interviews on the next page as well as page 140 in Chapter 15.)

Charles Fishman, whose short article about Disney's laundry service you can read in Chapter 8, is an award-winning journalist who has also written articles and books about Tupperware, bomb-making factories, NASA, and Wal-Mart. We asked him about his reputation for gaining unusually good access to sources. His response follows:

I have gotten into some amazing places. I talked my way into the nation's only bomb factory—the factory where the U.S. military makes every non-nuclear bomb dropped in Afghanistan and Iraq, a facility six times the size of Manhattan. I spent two weeks on the busiest maternity ward in the U.S.; I actually attended the births of something like 40 babies. I not only got to write about the creation of the largest cruise ship in history—I spent four days in the shipyard where it was being constructed. I have stood at the top of the launch pad from which the space shuttles are launched.

You don't get invited into any of these places. You have to ask.

Choosing Good Quotations

Following is a list of quotations gathered for a profile written about Damian DiPaola, the owner and chef (or as he prefers it, "cook") at an Italian restaurant. Journalist David Maloof gathered these quotations from interviews with DiPaola and from observing DiPaola in conversation with coworkers. Decide which quotations you would (1) quote fully, (2) quote partially, (3) paraphrase, or (4) omit. Explain why you made these decisions.

- "I've been making cappuccinos since I was four years old in my Dad's café."

- "My mother had a knack for making the greatest dinners with the least ingredients. She used lots of vegetables and fish and pasta. My father would make the elaborate meals, such as lobster *fra diavlo* and rack of lamb."

- "A chef is someone who runs around with a clipboard and a pen and then goes out in the dining room and takes credit for everything."

Tips for Good Interviews

Although conducting an interview might seem as simple as having a conversation, planning ahead and being well prepared will help you get the best material possible.

- **Start Early.** Leave plenty of time for phone or e-mail tag.

- **Set Up the Interview.** Arrange to meet at a specific time and place, preferably in the subject's workplace or home.

- **Make a Contact List.** Compile a list of people who know your subject and the issues discussed in the profile. As you interview your subject and the secondary sources, ask for names of other people knowledgeable about the subject or the subject's field.

- **Do Your Homework.** Go into the interview informed. Enter your source's name—and the topic's name—into an Internet search engine and check out the results before you sit down to talk.

- **Prepare for the Interview.** Write at least 10 questions. Make them open-ended, not ones that can be answered by *yes* or *no*. Ask, "How do you think the Internet will be used in the future?" rather than "Do you think the Internet will be used only for shopping?"

- **Conduct the Interview.** If you find it hard to start, ask some general questions to warm up. "What are you doing when you are not working (or in school)?" often opens up an interesting path of inquiry.

- **Be a Careful Observer.** Pay attention to small details. A small detail of dress or an idiosyncratic gesture can bring your subject to life for your reader.

- **Transcribe Your Notes.** Add any details of physical appearance or setting that might be useful to remember later.

- **Read Your Notes Critically.** Annotate your notes as you read through them. Underline important information. Make stars next to or highlight good quotations.

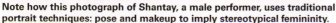

Peter Doyle

Note how this photograph of Shantay, a male performer, uses traditional portrait techniques: pose and makeup to imply stereotypical femininity.

(Continued)

- "I did have a house, but when I bought my [business] partner out, I had to sell the house."

- "About a year ago, I weighed 205. I lost 35 pounds. I ate a lot of angel hair pasta with escarole in chicken broth."

- "We're not 'chefs' here. We prefer to be called 'cooks.' *Chef* is a French word. It means 'chief' or 'commander of the kitchen.'"

    Profile published in the Hampshire Life Magazine section of the *Daily Hampshire Gazette*, June 27, 1997. ■

Multiple Points of View

If you just tell a story from your subject's perspective, you have not written a profile as much as an as-told-to story—a story told from only your subject's point of view as he or she tells it to you. Your reader gets only your subject's point of view. To develop a more balanced and more complex perspective (even a contradictory or negative one), provide your reader with multiple points of view about your subject. These secondary sources can be coworkers, relatives, neighbors, or competitors, to name a few.

If you are writing about the owner of the first Vietnamese noodle shop in town, for example, interviewing nearby restaurant owners might give you an interesting perspective on the business. Interviewing the owner's spouse, children, chef, and servers adds other, more personal layers to the story. Phoning the restaurant reviewer who gave the new restaurant four stars might reveal even more about the owner's abilities.

Beginnings and Endings

How to start and how to end are often the trickiest parts of writing a profile. You want to capture your reader's attention from the very first line of your piece, and you want to end gracefully, giving a sense that your exploration of the subject is complete and satisfying.

Portrait, Girl with Pearl Earring, by Jan Vermeer (1632–1675).

Beginnings

Of all the types of introductions (leads) available, three are the most common and most useful: the setting, the anecdote, and the generalization.

SETTING LEAD The scene-setting lead can use description, detail, and direct quotations to bring the reader directly into a scene that introduces the profile subject in his or her milieu:

> The bullwhip lay on the bookcase, coiled around its wooden handle like a snake around its rattle.
>
> I was in the second-floor office of associate professor Gerald Powers at Boston University's College of Communication. A student carrying a sheaf of papers had slunk away from Powers's desk as I entered, "REWRITE" scrawled across the top paper in red pencil. The whip had struck again.
>
> —Jack Falla, "The Top Drill Instructor in Boot Camp 101"

ANECDOTAL LEAD An anecdotal lead hooks the reader by telling a brief but complete story that gives the reader some insight into the person's character:

China's Cultural Revolution was in full force in 1968, when Shen Tong was born. His grandparents had been among its first victims; when his grandfather openly criticized the village mayor, he and his wife became targets for the Red Guards.

The day before they were to be paraded through their village in dunce caps, they hanged themselves from their bamboo bed frame.

—Midge Raymond, "The Long Journey Home"

GENERALIZATION LEAD A generalization lead begins with a broad, umbrella statement, then narrows down to the specific point, or person, of the profile:

Tonight, an artist in Allston will eat tripe. On Newbury Street, a weary shopper will eat beef tendon. And in Harvard Square, students and parents and the odd out-of-towner will slurp their way through a selection of intensely flavored and very inexpensive noodle soups they'd probably never heard of just two years ago.

These parallel dining adventures come courtesy of Duyen Le, the accidental noodlemonger from Vietnam whose Pho Pasteur restaurants have taken pho, the steaming soul food of northern Vietnam, from Formica tabletops in Chinatown and Dorchester to higher-rent neighborhoods where, not so long ago, the prevailing notion of ethnic food featured spaghetti carbonara.

Le may be the quietest titan of the Boston food scene.

—Kelly Horan, "The Quietest Mogul"

Endings

The best kind of conclusion in a profile presents an image or a quotation that leaves a final impression on readers, reminding them of your focus.

Good quotations can be irreverent, eccentric, funny, witty, wry, angry, or emotional. What they should not be is boring, self-evident, or confusing. Quotations can reveal character; sum up a point; create an image; or provide irony, insight, or tension for the piece. Quotations should be articulate, clear, and accessible, unless what they are intended to reveal is a person's nervousness or perhaps evasiveness.

Often profile writers return to the introductory scene to create a sense of coming full circle. In Jack Falla's "Top Drill Instructor in Boot Camp 101," notice how he returns to Professor Powers's office at the conclusion of his profile. The final line, "I put the bullwhip back on the shelf. We went to lunch. I bought." brings the twin thematic strands of the profile together. Professor Powers is uncompromisingly tough but he also has a lasting effect on—and admiration from—his ex-students.

DIY MEDIA AND DESIGN

Oral History: A Spoken Word Project

Telling another's story through the spoken word is the core of oral history projects. The most interesting subjects are people who have lived through an era or experience that has historical significance but, just as with written profiles, everyday people living ordinary lives have memories worth adding to the historical record.

You might want to think about parents, grandparents, or friends of the family who might have been in World War II, Vietnam, Iraq, or Afghanistan. Or think of people who have been on the cutting edge of social or political movements.

One important caveat about oral history is that it must be an accurate account of your subject's story and not include rumor or hearsay. Since oral history depends on the spoken word and your subject's memory, it is important to record the story accurately, whether you take notes by hand or use audio or video recordings. When conducting interviews for an oral history:

- Be sure your subject understands that the conversation is not private but will become part of a historical record.
- At the beginning of each recording session, state the name of the interviewee, the place, and date of the session.
- Keep the tone conversational.
- Allow your subject to tell the story in his or her own time and manner.
- Do not try to fill in dead spaces in the interview. Silence allows your subject to recall events.
- End the interview after an hour, two at most.
- Have your subject sign a release form that simply includes the subject's name, your name, the date, and the subject's permission to use the interview for a school project.
- Transcribe your notes soon after the interview.
- Analyze the interview. What other information do you need? What new questions come to mind? Are all the facts and dates correct?

One nonprofit group, StoryCorps, began recording and collecting interviews between parents and their children, siblings, or friends in 2003. Since then it has archived tens of thousands of interviews, which you can listen to on its website.

READINGS

One student writer, Thanos Matthai, explores the life of a Muslim teen. Journalist J. R. Moehringer visits a Vermont farm to explore the former life of a Holocaust rescuer. And student Alyssa Parisi profiles a wrestler whose life has been changed by the sport.

A Fine Balance: The Life of a Muslim Teenager

Thanos Matthai

Thanos Matthai wrote this profile of his fellow student, Mohamed Ahmed, for his writing class. Matthai examines the tension between Mohamed's Islamic faith and his college culture.

MOHAMED AHMED arrives at the frat party with several of his friends. After putting his coat away, he talks to his friends for a little before going to the bar to get a drink.

"Can I get a Coke?" he asks the guy behind the bar. The bartender tells him that the Jack Daniels is running out, but that there's still some left for another rum and Coke.

"No, I only want Coke," says Mohamed. The bartender gives him a puzzled look, but obligingly pours him a Coke. Mohamed rejoins his friends, who are all embracing their plastic cups of Bud Light. He decides to go watch the "Beirut" game in the next room and passes several couples grinding to Sisqo's "Thong Song." The "Beirut" game becomes boring, and he goes back to find his friends completely drunk.

A month later Mohamed returns home during a break from college and its party life and catches up with all his high school friends. While hanging out at a friend's house, they all talk about the people whom they've met at college. Some of

> "Mohammed has had to make tough choices, sometimes forcing him to almost lead two separate lives."

Mohamed's friends are in relationships while the rest have "hooked up" with people.

"Hey, Mohamed, how many girls have you hooked up with?" asks one friend chuckling.

Mohamed blushes a little and laughs quietly along with his friends.

"You know I'm not allowed to do that," he replies, stating what his friends already know.

Islam is the reason that Mohamed doesn't behave in the same manner as his friends. His parents emigrated from India in 1980; his is the only Muslim family in a wealthy suburban town outside of Boston of which only 196 out of 10,000 residents are not white. Always surrounded by people who held beliefs almost directly contrary to his own, Mohamed has had to make tough choices, sometimes forcing him to almost lead two separate lives.

As a Muslim, Mohamed is forbidden from many things that his friends take for granted, such as drinking alcohol, having sex outside of marriage, and even eating pork. If Mohamed eats out with his friends, he usually has to order vegetarian dishes because the meat in most restaurants isn't *zabiha:* slaughtered in a manner that the Koran, the holy book of Islam, deems *halal*, or fit for a Muslim to eat. "The nearest *halal* restaurant to me is a 25-mile drive to either Boston or Providence," he says. When offered a Starburst candy, he declines it, saying that it is *haram*, or completely forbidden by the Koran, because it contains enzymes and emulsifiers that could have been obtained from pigs.

"Starting from middle school, I was raised to hang out only with Muslims because they were good influences," says Mohamed. "I had no friends in school, but I did a lot of stuff with my cousins and people I knew from the mosque." Walking around his room at home, he points to the old history and biology books that he used to read in his free time. "I was a real geek," he says, laughing as he flips through *The World's Greatest Cities*.

Although initially quiet and not very social, Mohamed became heavily involved with school activities during his junior and senior years. "Mohamed's mother really pushed him to take part in things and to succeed," says his cousin Kareem Ahmed.

According to Mohamed, football and student council were the two activities that really changed him. "The football team wanted me to hang out with them and made me hang out with them," he says as he picks up a football and tosses it in the air. With a husky 6 foot 3 inch frame, dark complexion, thick eyebrows, and close-cropped black hair, he was a fierce-looking outside linebacker. "Their popularity and the fact I was vice president of the student council really helped me get to know people," he adds. Mohamed was also valedictorian and a member of many service-oriented groups like the National Honor Society and the Leo Club, which helped him meet more people.

"Many kids found him interesting because he was so naïve and different from them," says his friend Jim Dorsey. "As they spent more time with him, they began to like him and become friends."

Many people find Mohamed to be a welcome change from the average teenager. "He's so different from my other guy friends because he's not caught up with material things and not obsessed with beer," says Shannon Riley, one of Mohamed's closest friends. "He's more interested in other things like religion and politics."

"In the beginning of high school, no one had any idea what Islam was," says Mohamed. "Even though nothing bad happened to me after 9/11, I really made it a point to talk about Islam because all people knew about it was what they saw on television."

"Mohamed was much more aware of things outside America because he was a religious minority," says Jim. According to Jim, very few of Mohamed's friends were knowledgeable enough to be concerned about such things and discuss them, so they usually avoided discussions about politics and religion with him.

"I talked about Islam and politics so much that people got sick of it, but I felt I had to give them an accurate picture of what was going on," says Mohamed as he scrolls through the BBC website.

> "Even though nothing bad happened to me after 9/11, I really made it a point to talk about Islam because all people knew about it was what they saw on television."

As Mohamed became more social and more involved in school activities, the differences between him and his friends became more apparent. "He had no idea about things that we thought were common knowledge," says Todd Shuman, a friend who also became Mohamed's roommate at college. Mohamed was not exposed to the same TV shows, jokes and experiences as his friends, and often found it hard to relate to them. *Sheltered*, *innocent*, *inexperienced* and *gullible* are some adjectives his friends use to describe him.

"It's almost as if things he couldn't do intrigued him, so he always asked questions about things like sex and being drunk," adds Todd.

More than reveal cultural differences, greater interaction with his friends forced Mohamed to walk a fine line. "He was always motivated to be in the public eye, but this kind of backfired because he became almost too social," says Kareem. Kareem has a good understanding of Muslim teenagers because he studied at a school in Pakistan for one and a half years. According to him, most first generation American Muslims are raised much more strictly than those living in predominantly Muslim countries like Pakistan or Egypt. "Parents are often scared that their kids are going to lose touch with their cultural roots, so they give them much less freedom," says Kareem. Many of his friends in Pakistan went to dance clubs, stayed out late, and socialized with girls.

"My dad didn't want me to hang out with anyone except Muslims because they could be a bad influence," says Mohamed. "I was raised to never be friends with girls or even to talk to them unless they were family," he adds.

While the Koran does not explicitly state that interaction with the opposite sex is wrong, it does state that men should not have impure thoughts about women other than their wives. At family functions, men and women are segregated and eat separately. Many traditional Muslims also encourage their children not to be friends with members of the opposite sex, says Kareem.

When asked about simply being friends with girls, Mohamed hesitantly replies that it's okay to be friends. "But I still kind of believe what I was raised to believe," he says. "I don't really know," he adds quickly, a pained expression on his face as he looks away.

> "Most first generation American Muslims are raised much more strictly than those living in predominantly Muslim countries like Pakistan or Egypt."

Group projects for his classes were the initial excuses for staying out late. Then it was hanging out with the guys. "I kind of got used to people drinking at parties, so I went to them sometimes," he says. But according to his friends, at parties he would only stop by for five minutes to say hello to people.

Mohamed eventually told his mother that he spent time with girls. "She was ticked off at first, but then she became okay with it because she knew that I wouldn't do anything like date or have sex, which would violate Islamic principles," he says.

"I don't even know if my dad knows," he says with a faraway expression. "I didn't say anything to him because he's very traditional."

Then there was the one party that changed everything. "I stopped by this one party and Michelle, one of my best friends, was really drunk," says Mohamed as he remembers the evening. Michelle insisted that he have a sip from her cup, saying that it was only Sprite. Mohamed spit

it out when he realized that the cup also had some alcohol (he would later find out it was vodka) in it.

"He got so angry that he started yelling at Michelle and pushed her over," says Shannon. "Michelle's boyfriend wanted to start a fight with Mohamed, but people broke it up."

"That really changed my outlook on things," says Mohamed. "That one of my best friends could do something like that knowing full well that I couldn't drink alcohol." Michelle apologized repeatedly, but it took almost a year and a half for Mohamed to finally forgive her.

"When I look back at things now, I kind of regret a lot of things," says Mohamed as he looks around his dorm room. "I feel like in some ways it was a waste of time because I angered my parents for being out all the time and grew kind of distant from my cousins and other Muslim friends."

Sitting on his bed, he quietly contemplates his situation. "Sometimes I feel I've done wrong by even going to parties and stuff and it really depresses me," he says slowly and softly as he looks at a copy of the Koran on his desk.

Shannon, on the other hand, thinks otherwise. "Sometimes something bad needs to happen to shake you up so you realize how things really are," she says.

Mohamed will sometimes go to college parties with his friends because he wants to meet new people and because "the dorm gets boring when nobody is around." Instead of remaining on campus during the weekend, he often goes home; however, he knows that he can't keep returning home for the rest of his life.

"Sometimes I feel that there are two different voices or sides to me," he says. "One side is Islam and its principles and the other . . . well, I don't know what it is."

Mohamed reads a lot of Nietzsche, Aristotle and Plato in his college classes. "I like reading their books because their thoughts and ideas are so logical and make so much sense to me," he says while looking through Aristotle's *Nicomachean Ethics*.

He looks again at the copy of the Koran on his shelf. "But it's totally different from anything in Islam," he says with a sigh.

Questions for Rhetorical Analysis

1. The writer does not appear at all in this profile but stays in the background. What effect does this have on the reader? Look particularly at the scenes that the writer must have observed.

2. What impression do you have of Mohamed Ahmed in the opening scene at the frat party? What details contribute to your impression?

3. Identify the nut graf in this profile. What phrase in this paragraph encapsulates the writer's thesis? Where else can you find language or details that express the tension in this profile?

4. How does Matthai develop his profile? What elements—physical description, quotations from and about the subject, examples, anecdotes, factual information—does he weave into the portrait? Which are most memorable?

5. What research has Matthai done for this profile? Are there places where you think the profile needs more information?

6. The concluding scene is set in Mohamed's dorm room. What details in the conclusion reveal Mohamed's character and the quality of his life? In what ways has your impression of him changed or deepened from the opening scene?
7. How effective is the title of this profile in summing up its central points?

Questions for Critical Thinking

1. This profile is one of many stories told about cultural differences; this one is specifically about a Muslim teen. Does Mohamed Ahmed's story change your understanding of Islam? In what way?
2. Where do your values conflict with mainstream culture in your community?

Style Practice: Imitation

This profile concludes with a contrast between the secular books Mohamed reads and the Koran. The profile ends with this quotation:

> "I like reading their books because their thoughts and ideas are so logical and make so much sense to me," he says while looking through Aristotle's *Nicomachean Ethics*.
>
> He looks again at the copy of the Koran on his shelf. "But it's totally different from anything in Islam," he says with a sigh.

Choose a quotation from your subject that might end your profile and that would reveal your profile subject's conflict. Conclude the sentence with a gesture, like a sigh.

A Hidden and Solitary Soldier

J. R. Moehringer

Pulitzer-prize winner J. R. Moehringer was the Atlanta bureau chief of the Los Angeles Times. *In addition to his many profiles, he has published a memoir,* The Tender Bar, *and collaborated with Andre Agassi on his memoir titled* Open. *The following "profile in courage" is about Marion Pritchard, a grandmother living quietly in Vermont who, while living in Holland during World War II, rescued people from the Holocaust, shot a Nazi policeman, and survived imprisonment. The profile was published in the* Los Angeles Times.

AS THE SUN dips behind the Vermont tree line, the family sits down to dinner and the talk goes in a thousand directions—books, politics, the Red Sox. Eventually the conversation turns to Grandma, and the Nazi she gunned down.

Grandma looks into her lap, shyly. The adults discuss the story in low voices while the children strain to hear from the far end of the table. "What are you talking about?" says Marion Pritchard's 12-year-old granddaughter, Molly.

Silence. "Grandma and the policeman," someone says.

"Oh," Molly says—not shocked, but bored. She's heard that story a million times.

It often happens this way. Pritchard's family doesn't get too excited about her daring past.

J. R. Moehringer, "Hidden and Solitary Soldier," *LA Times,* January 20, 2002. Reprinted with permission.

They glide over the fact that she rescued scores of children from the Holocaust, survived seven months in a Nazi prison and killed one Nazi who got in her way. They take for granted that Grandma is a war hero—or else they can't quite believe it. The stories of extraordinary bravery don't fit with the aproned woman they see before them, who is frightened of squirrels and public speaking and who feels guilty when she swats a fly.

Strangers tend to be less casual about Pritchard's past. Psychologists study her, biographers woo her, governments fete her and invite her to speak. Visitors occasionally appear at her door, unannounced, to meet her, shake her hand, thank her.

Lately interest in Pritchard has grown even more avid. People want to be around her, now more than ever, because they know she's been here before: a nation under attack, a constant state of fear, a fanatic enemy bent on killing innocent civilians, especially Jews. The last time, Europe was ground zero, and Pritchard was one of those who ran into the fire.

But for a profile in courage, she keeps a fairly low profile. She lives at the end of a dirt road, in the middle of a sparse woods, on the outskirts of a town—Vershire, Vt.—that doesn't appear on many maps. She spends her days reading, teaching, seeing patients—she's been a psychoanalyst most of her working life—and listening to her beloved Verdi. You might hear "Chorus of the Hebrew Slaves" wafting from the open windows of her big white farmhouse when you turn off the dirt road.

> "The stories of extraordinary bravery don't fit with the aproned woman they see before them, who is frightened of squirrels and public speaking and who feels guilty when she swats a fly."

As history does its ominous U-turn, she watches quietly from a safe distance. This isn't her fight. And yet, when hatred hits closer to home, she reverts instantly from recluse to rescuer. When anti-Semitism and homophobia flared in her corner of Vermont not long ago, Pritchard fought back with everything she had.

People want to know where this 81-year-old woman gets her grit. She eludes the question the way she once eluded her pursuers. "There's nothing you can tell somebody that's going to make them less fearful," she says in her faint Dutch accent. "I was scared stiff all the time during the war."

She prefers to let her life speak for itself. And its lessons are clear:

You can't always hide from hate.

Or from history.

And sometimes it's best not to try.

Standing in her garden, not much taller than her sweet peas and daylilies, Pritchard doesn't look like the intrepid rescuer who defied the Third Reich. Sitting in her book-lined living room, speaking in a thin voice that crackles like a fire, she gives no hint of the cunning rebel who risked her life for strangers.

She hides the hero somewhere inside.

When the memory of an injustice comes up, though, her blue eyes darken, her voice takes on a ragged quality, like a gypsy violin, and there she is, in plain sight, Marion van Binsbergen, the young girl who tried to save the world one child at a time. It happens when she remembers Hitler's shock troops devouring Europe in 1940, smashing into Amsterdam, where she was living with her younger brother and her parents. Overnight, the streets were filled with Nazis, "all 6 feet tall" and smug, she says.

She heard stories. Mass arrests. Night trains. Camps. She knew what was happening, but she didn't really know, until one day: She was 20 years old, riding her new bicycle near the school of social work where she was a graduate student, when she saw a truck double-parked outside a Jewish children's center. Some Nazi soldiers were rousting the children—all between 2 and 8 years old—and rushing them onto the truck. The children were sobbing. The soldiers were pitiless and efficient.

"It didn't take long," she says.

One soldier grabbed a little girl by her pigtails and hurled her onto the truck.

"I couldn't believe what I was seeing," Pritchard says. "Two women came from the other side of the street to try to stop them, and [the Nazis] threw them in with the kids."

She seems to be watching the 60-year-old scene play out in the middle of her living room, each detail as clear as the books and rugs and pot-bellied stove, and she becomes angry all over again. "That," she says, "was indeed the moment when I decided what was the most important thing to do."

Pritchard decided to rescue Jews—hide them, smuggle them, help them however she could. Though not Jewish herself, she made rescuing Jews her mission, for no reason other than that it was right.

People who make such decisions are the products of extraordinary parents, says Eva Fogelman, who has studied Holocaust rescuers, including Pritchard, for years. Most rescuers,

> "She heard stories. Mass arrests. Night trains. Camps. She knew what was happening, but she didn't really know, until one day"

Fogelman has found, were given an exquisite sense of justice as children, along with an unwavering self-confidence, "so they could withstand fears."

Pritchard remembers, for example, an exchange between her mother and the Germans. "The Nazis were looking for able-bodied men," she says. "They came and made my brother get out of bed. He was 14 at the time. Fortunately, he was still small and skinny, and they told him he could go back to bed. Then they said to my mother, 'What are you doing with all that bunting?' My mother had all this red, white and blue material out on the kitchen table. My mother was a lady. She never swore. But she said, 'I'm making a Union Jack—to hang out the window when you sons of bitches get kicked out of here!'"

Pritchard coughs and covers her mouth. She looks away, and her eyes fill with tears. "It's funny," she says. "You can tell a tale a lot of times, and then suddenly, for some reason, it gets harder."

Pritchard estimates that she helped 150 Jews, nearly all of them children. She doesn't know the precise number. She didn't keep track, in case she was caught. "The less you knew, the better."

Nor does she know how many of the children she helped were able to survive the war. She would hide a child for a day, an hour, then pass the child along, into the night, into the woods, into history. She only knows that most of Holland's 140,000 Jews were killed, so it's likely that most of the children she met didn't make it. She gave them, at best, a few more days, or hours. Hers may have been the last kind face they saw.

Every rescue was different. She'd bring a child home, or simply to the next rescuer. She'd

guide a child in the night to a safe house, or a clearing in the woods. She'd place a Jewish newborn with a non-Jewish couple. Occasionally, she'd walk a child in the light of day right past a group of Nazi soldiers.

In 1981, Pritchard was honored by Yad Vashem, Israel's official Holocaust authority, as one of the "Righteous Among the Nations." Her name was placed in the pantheon of Israel's national heroes, alongside Holocaust rescuers such as Oskar Schindler. She was recognized as one of the great moral exemplars of the century, from whom, the writer Cynthia Ozick wrote, "we can learn the full resonance of civilization."

And still she regrets not doing more. She's haunted by the children she couldn't save, the countless Anne Franks. She knew Anne Frank, in fact. And Anne's older sister, Margot. She met them once at a birthday party. Years later, a mutual friend met the Frank sisters at Bergen-Belsen, and saw them die.

Besides the children who passed briefly through Pritchard's hands, she hid one Jewish family for the duration of the war. She took Fred Polak and his three children—Lex, 7, Tom, 4, and Erica, an infant— to a farmhouse on the outskirts of the city and cared for them as though they were her own while their mother fought with the Dutch Resistance.

By day, Pritchard and the family kept to a routine, playing and walking in public, pretending to be non-Jews. At night, when the Nazis came around and demanded everyone's papers, Pritchard hid the family in a pit beneath the living room floor. Whenever Pritchard heard a motor coming up the road, she hurried the Polak family into the pit. "Regular people didn't have motors," she says. "Only Germans. So when you heard a motor, you knew."

> "Every rescue was different."

Even when the Nazis weren't coming, she made the Polaks practice sliding away the coffee table, pulling up the floorboards, diving into the pit. Survival hinged on doing the drill faster and faster. "We got it down to 30 seconds," she says, still proud.

Pritchard was arrested during the war, but not for rescuing Jews. She was simply studying with friends who were part of the Dutch Resistance, and when the Nazis raided the apartment, everyone was taken, Pritchard included.

Memories of prison return to her, unbidden, at odd moments. In an elevator or a strange bathroom, if the door doesn't open right away, she feels trapped. Having a manicure, she recalls the way she filed her nails in prison, by rubbing them against her cell walls.

Every detail of prison remains vivid, but she doesn't share them. "I never have told, and I don't know whether I ever will tell, about the relatively minor torture I underwent."

She does describe, with a self-mocking smile, her sudden surge of religion. "It came naturally. 'Dear God, if you let me out of here, I'll be good forever after.'"

She was better than her word. When the Nazis set her free after seven months, she went back to rescuing Jews and took even greater risks, helping to pull off a daring kidnap in which she stormed a house and snatched a 2-year-old girl whom the Nazis were about to torture—their way of making her parents name members of the Dutch Resistance.

Then there was the Nazi she killed, a sadistic Dutch policeman she'd known all her life. He surprised her one night at the farmhouse, no sound of a motor to warn her, no time to hide the Polaks in the pit. Acting on a tip, the policeman crept up to the farmhouse on foot and burst in the door. "Somebody must've betrayed us," Pritchard says.

In that terrible moment, Pritchard says, there was no choice. Behind some books on a shelf was a gun given to her by a friend. She grabbed the gun and fired. "One shot," she says. "Dead as a doornail."

She doesn't remember pulling the trigger. She doesn't remember feeling anger or regret. "I remember the exhilaration when he was lying on the floor," she says. After covering the policeman with a sheet, she phoned a friend, Karel Poons. He arranged for the body to be smuggled to an undertaker, to be buried secretly with a recently deceased resident of the town. "Oh," she says, in the ragged violin voice, "Karel was wonderful."

She thought of him often in 2000, when Vermont legislators voted to let gay couples "marry," plunging the state into a yearlong political crisis. Poons was gay, and it couldn't have mattered less to Pritchard. She loved him, trusted him with her life. So when the debate over gay rights in Vermont turned ugly, she took it personally.

But she kept quiet for the sake of her patients. "If someone comes to me who is an ardent Republican," she says, "I want them to be able to tell me anything."

Eventually, as she feared, the anti-gay rhetoric spawned something darker. Swastikas began to appear all around her, on lawns and mailboxes and the elementary school across the street from her office. She couldn't keep quiet any longer.

In a letter to the local newspaper, Pritchard gave Vermonters a stern history lesson, reminding them that Hitler began by persecuting everyone "different." Then she hammered signs into her front yard, supporting candidates friendly to gay rights.

One night her phone rang. A menacing voice told Pritchard to take down her signs "or you'll be sorry."

The signs stayed.

The voice called again.

The signs stayed.

Finally, someone crept up to Pritchard's farmhouse in the middle of the night, no sound of a motor to warn her, and stole the signs. It felt, she says, as if the past itself had crept out of the shadows. "I never thought," she says, "in Vermont of all places."

> "Pritchard gave Vermonters a stern history lesson, reminding them that Hitler began by persecuting everyone 'different.'"

Meeting Pritchard many years after the war, Erica Polak had trouble believing that this small, dignified grandmother was once all that stood between her and the camps. "She's such a tiny woman," Erica says by phone from her home in Holland. "She came from a very sophisticated family. And then, to go underground, to do such brave things? It's unbelievable."

Erica's mother never discussed the war. And with Pritchard, Erica feels the same reticence. Revealing means reliving.

"She lets go of a tiny piece at a time," Erica says, "and most things she doesn't let loose at all."

The honor from Yad Vashem seemed to loosen Pritchard a bit. She began to accept speaking invitations. Last fall she even helped teach a seminar at Clark University in Worcester, Mass., the only college in the nation to offer an advanced degree in Holocaust Studies. Despite cataracts and heavy traffic on the interstate, Pritchard sometimes drove herself to the school, four hours each way.

Deborah Dwork, who heads the center for Holocaust Studies at Clark and taught the seminar with Pritchard, says the students would fall perfectly silent whenever Pritchard spoke. One young woman confided to Dwork: "I never thought in my life I'd have the opportunity to be at the same table as a saint." Dwork feels the same way. "Just being with her makes me calmer," she says.

Each class began with Pritchard sharing a wartime memory. Then there would be a discussion of the week's assigned reading. The final hour of class was given over to the latest news. The students asked Pritchard for her take, and she gave it, unvarnished. One day she spoke about walking the razor's edge, about living each day in danger. She told the students that terrorism is yet another of life's perils, no more lethal than all the others. Evil didn't end with World War II, she said.

You can't always hide from hate. Or from history.

It was as close as she comes to giving advice. "The notion that someday everything in the world is going to be lovely, I haven't had that for a long, long time," Pritchard says. "I guess I hoped that right after World War II. But humans don't change, it seems."

In those heady days after the war, there were many reasons for optimism, but the main reason was U.S. Army Lt. Tony Pritchard, who did what the Nazis couldn't. He found Marion van Binsbergen.

He spotted her at a Paris rail station, where they were both bound for the refugee camps—he with the Army, she with the United Nations. They got into an argument immediately. She scolded him for complaining to a fellow soldier about all the "awful Dutch girls." He told her that he was simply remarking, "What an awful lot of Dutch girls."

She laughed, and so it began.

"It's summer, it's peace," she says. "After years of deprivation, of no food and no fun, suddenly you're on the French coast. We got American officer Army rations, which included liquor and wine. I'd never had hard liquor before."

They married in 1947, her wedding dress sewn by concentration camp survivors. A few months later, they came to the U.S., first to Cambridge, Mass., where they started their family, eventually to Vermont, in 1967. It was Tony who found the Vermont house, part of an old dairy farm, with 120 acres of white birches and sugar maples, set in the middle of raw wilderness.

Rebuilding the house was Tony's passion until he died 10 years ago. Now keeping the house is Pritchard's mission. It takes daily courage. Besides intruders in the shadows, she must contend with the brutal cold, the isolation, the temperamental septic tank and the steep staircase, down which she recently took a bad fall.

She deems it a small price to pay for staying connected to Tony, her fellow hero, who fought with Patton at the Battle of the Bulge and went with the first troops into the nightmare of Buchenwald. She and Tony could talk about anything, Pritchard says, which was vital, because they often couldn't talk to anyone else. At dinner parties and other social events, they were discouraged from describing the horrors they witnessed. Too depressing, friends said. Move on.

Over time, their silence included their children. Pritchard's three sons—52-year-old Arnie and the 49-year-old twins, Ivor and Brian—didn't know much about their mother's past until 1981, when Israeli officials phoned to say that Pritchard would soon receive one of their nation's most sacred honors.

In Israel, Brian watched as his mother received the thanks of a nation. She was showered with praise, he says, and blinded by flashbulbs. Then the ceremony ended and everyone started for the doors—except for a group of sad-faced men and women. They moved closer to his mother, their hands extended, and he wondered who they could be.

Then he realized. They were survivors of the camps.

"That," he says, his voice unsteady, "was when I knew . . ."

Once, at a school, Brian heard his mother reveal the thing she never reveals, the details of her time in prison. A boy in the audience asked politely and Pritchard wasn't able to deny him a straight answer. She told how the guards pressed a knife in her arm, demanding information. When she wouldn't talk, they pressed harder.

It was the first time Brian had heard the story, and it explained the scar on his mother's left forearm. It also made him wonder how many other stories and scars will remain hidden forever.

"We'll never know all there is to know," Arnie says. But he quickly adds: "I think I know enough."

> "It was the first time Brian had heard the story. . . . It made him wonder how many other stories and scars will remain hidden forever."

What the brothers do know is always hard to reconcile with the woman their children call Grandma. "It challenges the imagination," says Ivor. "To put these two things next to each other—these extraordinary heroic things and the very ordinary experience of your mother, who's afraid of some things and doesn't like to do some things, and is shy and uncomfortable in front of people—it's incongruous."

And so, after dinner, it may be the incongruity that causes Pritchard's granddaughter to brush off the story of Grandma and the Nazi. Instead, Molly wants to hear the birds.

"Please, can we hear the birds?" she pleads.

Inside the cage are two birds made of luminous paper, and underneath is a key, which Pritchard now winds tight. When she releases it, the birds spin to face each other, and their beaks fly open. The room suddenly fills with bird song.

The children stare in awe. The adults tilt their heads and smile. The sound is beautiful but also haunting. Like voices from a vanished world. It's not possible to know what they are saying. But it's clear that they are somewhere other than this delicate hiding place above Pritchard's kitchen, and that they are happy and free.

Questions for Rhetorical Analysis

1. It is clear from the narrative portion of this profile that the writer visited and observed Marian Pritchard at her Vermont farm, yet his first-person voice is absent from this profile. What effect does this have on the reader?
2. Identify the portion of the profile that is the lead. In what ways do the dialogue and setting in the lead introduce Marian Pritchard to the reader?
3. What is the dominant impression of Pritchard that Moehringer creates in this profile? Support your answer with a few details from the profile.

4. Identify places in this profile where Moehringer used

    direct observation

    print or electronic sources

    interviews with the subject

    interviews with secondary sources

    What kind of research did he use most heavily? What do these multiple sources of research add to the profile?

5. Does the scene between Pritchard and her granddaughter provide an effective conclusion to the profile? Why or why not?

Questions for Critical Thinking

1. Moehringer writes, "You can't always hide from hate. Or from history." In your experience, is this statement true? Explain.

2. Taking action against intolerance, as Pritchard did on a grand scale in Nazi Europe and on a smaller scale in rural Vermont, takes conviction and courage. Do you agree? What other stories—from your life or the life of others—could illustrate this statement?

Style Practice: Imitation

Find an instance where Moehringer uses metaphorical language, a balanced sentence, a telling detail, or a vivid description. Then, imitate that technique using your own material from your profile.

What Makes Cauliflower Ear So Enticing

Alyssa Parisi

By Parisi making her subject representative of the sacrifices and habits a college wrestler must endure, we get a glimpse at both the individual and the sport. Why does a college student spend so much time on a sport others seem to misunderstand?

IT'S A SUNDAY in early March. The air in Binghamton, New York is clean and brisk, still holding the winter chill that seems to last through May. But inside Binghamton University's gym, the atmosphere is warm and tense as Boston University's John Hall prepares for his match in the Colonial Athletic Association conference championships. His stomach rumbles as he jogs and stretches behind the mat, but his lack of food for the past several hours is the last thing on his mind.

"I had a fractured neck, slightly bulging disk, and a second nerve in my shoulder that didn't work," Hall says, reflecting on the way he felt before that match. "And then I had back spasms. So going into the match, I was feeling shitty to begin with."

But the three-time captain of BU's wrestling team and previous CAA champion was ready to fight for a win. "It was all I could do to overcome my injuries," says Hall.

Unfortunately, that day was the last time Hall would take the mat for BU's wrestling team. The injuries he had fought to overcome throughout the season had finally pushed his body over the edge in this last match.

"I didn't lose during regular season, even with these injuries that all came on that year," Hall reflects. "That was just the last straw my body could take."

Since he was a freshman in high school, Hall had dedicated himself to the sport of wrestling. According to Hall, that kind of dedication to this sport is not something you can just stop on a dime. "Once you've involved wrestling in your life, it will never leave you, whether you wrestled for a year in middle school or from when you were five to an Olympian," says Hall.

Like many other collegiate athletes whose sports lack a professional league they can continue on to, Hall was not ready to give up just yet; his love of the sport was simply too strong. Even though his collegiate career may have been over, wrestling had become a part of who he was and always would be.

In fact, Hall admits that he already knew he wanted to become a wrestling coach. At that point in his career, the University of Pennsylvania had contacted him about a coaching position for their wrestling team. He was also considering coaching at his home gym, Wrestling Prep, in San Jose, California.

"I had a fractured neck, slightly bulging disk, and a second nerve in my shoulder that didn't work," Hall says, reflecting on the way he felt before that match. "And then I had back spasms."

But why wrestling? Why not football, or basketball?

"Actually, I was pretty good at basketball. And I had played football longer than I had wrestled," says Hall. "But I was so in love with wrestling. Football didn't have the same challenge. I wanted something that would impact me as a person."

Hall got what he wished for when he came to BU to wrestle five years ago. Hall joined the team in the bottom five of his freshman class of ten. He had very little experience compared to his peers, most of which (whom) had been wrestling since middle school or earlier. After not being expected to achieve much as a freshman, Hall ended up getting the second best record on the team that year, earning him the award for Most Outstanding Freshman. But even after this success, the rest of his collegiate career as a wrestler remained an uphill battle. During his junior year, Hall suffered severe nerve damage in his shoulder and neck.

"That was when the doctors were pretty convinced that I wasn't going to wrestle ever again," says Hall as his head drops. "It was a pretty rough time for me." He ended up redshirting that season due to injury and was able to stay for a fifth year, adding another year of competitive wrestling to his career.

Hall dealt with injuries throughout college. But he strongly believes that wrestling truly transformed him into a confident, strong individual. "Other sports will never demand the same physical requirements that wrestling does," he says.

And he may be right. Wrestlers must undergo skin checks and weigh in at 8 a.m.

the morning of every single match and cannot compete if they are even half a pound over their weight class. They starve themselves for several days, working out in full sweats on nearly empty stomachs, and neglecting to replenish their bodies afterwards in order to make weight. Most other athletes could not even dream of performing under such conditions.

"If I don't eat before practice, I feel like I'm going to pass out," says Katherine Lim, a sophomore on BU's women's soccer team and a member of the Philippines' National Team. "I've seen the wrestlers here lose a ton of weight now that they're in season. They're my friends, and it's weird seeing them like this. Their faces are where it's most noticeable, especially their sunken cheeks."

If starving themselves was not enough, the intensity at which wrestlers must compete would be enough to drive any sane athlete away from the sport in seconds. Wrestlers must use every ounce of their strength, skill, and mental discipline to compete for three two-minute periods. During tournaments, they may even have two or three matches a day. That means battling as hard as they can with another person—who weighs exactly the same as they do and is just as determined to win as they are—not just once, but up to three times in a day.

But Hall believes that this aspect of the sport is both the most difficult and the most empowering. "Because it requires more mental toughness than most people are willing to give and because there's no potential for a professional league," he says, "you learn the value of working for something because it's worth working for, not because you'll get the glorification for it."

This belief Hall holds—that wrestling changes a person's life for the better—seems to be common among other wrestlers as well. In a *New York Times* article by Gbenga Akinnagbe, the actor who appeared in *The Wire*, writes that wrestling saved his life.

Akinnagbe had spent most of his school years in programs for troubled youth. "I was fast on my way to becoming a thug," he admits in his article. But during his junior year at Magruder High School in Rockville, Maryland, he finally got his chance to change his course of life. Although he was nervous and intimidated, he made it to his first wrestling practice. "That first day of practice, my life changed," Akinnagbe writes.

Akinnagbe writes that the sport of wrestling taught him how to tame the "internal chaos" he felt and use it constructively—instead of letting it take control of him and get him kicked out of multiple schools. Several aspects of his life improved after he began wrestling, from the way others greeted him to his ability to make friends, and even to his chances of getting into college.

"Wrestling taught me discipline," he writes. "Most important, it taught me that I was the master of my own destiny. Bad things did and would continue to happen to me, but I no longer had to be a victim."

And just like Hall, it appears Akinnagbe also found it difficult to give up wrestling. Though his acting career takes priority in his life now, he admits that wrestling has not completely disappeared from his life. "Although it drives my manager and agent crazy, I still wrestle when I can," he writes.

Fortunately for Hall, he does not have to worry about juggling both acting and wrestling. After Hall finished his fifth year at BU this May, he returned home to Palo Alto, CA and has been fulfilling his dream of coaching ever since. Hall is also in the middle of training to compete again.

But, wait a minute; I thought wrestling didn't have a professional league?

True, but there is another option.

According to Hall, MMA, or Mixed Martial Arts, is the most viable option for wrestlers who want to continue to fight after their college careers have ended. "MMA is the best transition for wrestlers, and wrestlers transition best into MMA," says Hall.

Hall now trains once a week with a small group of UFC (Ultimate Fighting Championship) fighters, including Cain Valasquez—a former UFC Heavyweight Champion and the currently ranked number two heavyweight in the world. To Hall, this transition for him seemed perfectly logical. He even believes that wrestling is such a physically and mentally demanding sport that it allows for transitions into other sports, such as football. One athlete who made this transition is Steven Neal who wrestled through college, won an Olympic medal for wrestling, and was then drafted to the New England Patriots even though he had never played a game of college football. "I don't think there is any other sport in the world that would allow that to happen," says Hall.

Hall and Akinnagbe are just two examples of how the sport of wrestling has transformed a person's life for the better. But one can argue that wrestling is more than that. "Wrestlers are a different breed," adds Lim. "My teammates and I are very close with them, and I've gotten to know a lot of them pretty well over the last year. There's definitely something about them that sets them apart from the rest."

While Lim cannot quite pinpoint exactly what sets wrestlers apart from other athletes, Hall appears to have an explanation. "What wrestling does is find that one part of you that defines you and separates you from others; it pulls that out of you and requires you to use that," Hall explains, adding that wrestling "takes that special thing in you that makes you want to be great and forces it out of you."

"And they all kind of look alike too, partly because of the cauliflower ear," adds Lim.

It is clear from these examples that wrestling impacts athletes in an extremely powerful way. It requires that participants be willing to completely devote themselves to their sport and give everything they possibly can to it—regardless of pain and injury.

"We all finish competing one day in our lives, but that mentality never leaves," says Hall. "Whether or not I'm a wrestling coach for the rest of my life, I will always be a wrestler."

Sources

Interview Part 1 with John: Sunday, November 25, 5pm via Skype

Interview Part 2 with John: Tuesday, December 4, 8pm via Skype

Interview with Katherine: Thursday, December 6, 7pm

John Hall's Wrestling Prep Biography

http://www.wrestlingprep.com/john-hall-joins-wrestling-prep-staff/

New York Times article: "A Metamorphosis on the Wrestling Mat," by Gbenga Akinnagbe

http://www.nytimes.com/2012/03/04/sports/forgbenga-akinnagbe-a-metamorphosis-on-the-wrestling-mat.html?_r=0

Questions for Rhetorical Analysis

1. The subject of the profile makes the claim, "Other sports will never demand the same physical requirements that wrestling does." Has the writer provided enough details about the subject to give him the "authority" to make that claim?
2. What do you learn about wrestling as a culture by reading John Hall's story?
3. How much of what you learn about the culture of wrestling is the writer's interpretation, her opinion, or fact?
4. How does the writer include another perspective on Hall's experience? What are some additional ways the author might include sources to help Hall's perspective seem typical or atypical in the larger world of wrestling?

Questions for Critical Thinking

1. How would a profile about a college soccer (basketball, football, tennis) player require a different approach?
2. How does your prior knowledge about wrestling affect your reading of this profile? Does a reader require some background knowledge to really understand this profile?
3. When you finish reading the profile, which words or ideas come to mind?
4. Condense the main point from the profile to a single sentence.

Style Practice: Imitation

Write a brief opening scene from a profile about someone. Show the person in the middle of some action.

WRITING & REVISION STRATEGIES

Gathered here are three interactive sections for you to use as you write and revise your profile.

- Writer's Notebook Suggestions
- Peer Review Log
- Revision Checklist

Writer's Notebook Suggestions

These short exercises are intended to jump-start your thinking as you begin to write your profile. They also might provide some useful topic suggestions.

1. Choose a person to describe, perhaps a classmate. Describe the subject's clothing in three sentences that also give your reader a strong impression of character. Here is an example.

   > He's clad in wrinkled khakis and a long-sleeved shirt adorned with a fine patina of fuzz, and his steel wool-colored hair hasn't recently encountered a comb. If Fay looks like hell, he feels even worse. While on the trip, he contracted filaria, a blood-borne infestation of tiny, threadlike worms that, if left untreated, can block the flow of lymph inside a victim's body and cause the extremities to swell to a grotesque size. . . . Fay grimaces and peers through Coke-bottle glasses—he's had trouble with his eyesight since childhood—into a forest of Brooks Brothers suits and elegant dresses.
   > —Patrick J. Kiger, "Grand March of an American Misfit"

2. Listen in on a conversation—in a café, in a bookstore, or on public transportation. Take notes, and then write one page of your overheard conversation. Use spoken and unspoken communication: include all gestures, facial expressions, pauses, and inflections (when voices rise or fall, become whispers, and so on).

3. Identify some off-beat businesses in your area (petting zoos, tattoo parlors, used book stores). Make a list of five businesses you want to know more about.

4. Write a brief portrait introducing your best friend. Focus on a single aspect of his or her life or a single character trait.

5. Watch a profile documentary film (type: profile documentary into YouTube for some options). Make notes about how many quotations from the subject you hear. What sources are quoted, and what do they have to say? How many anecdotes do you hear? How does the filmmaker move the story from one time period to another?

6. Attend a sporting event and observe one player during play, on the bench, and after the game. Record all gestures, signs of emotion, and actions. Afterwards, write a descriptive lead for a profile on the player.

7. Observe someone with a technical skill, such as a bread baker, an interpreter for the deaf, a dentist, or a plumber. Write a one-paragraph description of the process you observed, making it easy to understand.

8. The following description is from a profile of Lieutenant Colonel Robert O. Sinclair, commander of the 13th Marine Expeditionary Unit of Camp Pendleton, California. Look at the way the writer uses the present tense to pull readers into the scene. Note how he uses repetitive sentence structure, verb choice, and sensory detail and emphasizes the details of the description with explanation.

> His pale-blue eyes are bloodshot from lack of sleep. His face is camouflaged with stripes and splotches of greasepaint—green, brown, and black to match his woodland-style utilities, fifty-six dollars a set, worn in the field without skivvies underneath, a personal wardrobe preference known as going commando. Atop his Kevlar helmet rides a pair of goggles sheathed in an old sock.
>
> —Mike Sager, "The Marine" Esquire 136, no. 6 (December 2001). Reprinted by permission of the author.

Choose someone to describe. Write a one-paragraph description, imitating Sager's style. Use similar sentence structures, details, and combination of description with explanation.

9. Choose one of the paintings or photographs that create visual profiles in this chapter, and write a paragraph translating what you see into descriptive language.

Peer Review Log

As you work with a writing partner or in a peer-editing group, you can use these questions to give helpful responses to a classmate's profile or as a guide for discussion.

Writer's Name: _____

Date: _____

1. Bracket the lead of this profile. What kind of lead is it? Could the profile start with a more interesting scene, anecdote, or generalization, perhaps one found later in the piece?

2. Underline the nut graf. Does the nut come too early or late in the profile? Judge this by asking whether the lead has set up the nut sufficiently. Does the focus seem like a natural extension of the opening? Does it seem artificially tacked on? Can the wording be more specific?

3. Is the nut graf a good overview of the story? Does it deliver everything it promises? Point out places where the writer refers to the idea in the nut, reinforcing and developing the thesis as the profile progresses. Locate any missed opportunities to remind the reader of the focus of the profile.

4. Look at the way the profile is organized. Make a quick outline of the profile's structure. What might strengthen the organization?

5. Circle major transitions between sections. Do the sections have good transitions? Do the narrative sections tie in with the factual, expository ones?

6. Does the story show and tell? Identify places where the writer uses description, anecdotes, examples, and facts. Does the profile need more of these elements to illustrate the generalizations made in the paragraphs?

7. What is the major impression you get of the profile subject? What details lead you to this impression? Could the writer insert more description, anecdotes, or character-in-action scenes to reveal character?

8. Annotate the sources the writer integrates into the profile by marking the places where the writer uses direct observation (DO), interviews from the subject and about the subject (I), and print or electronic sources (PS or ES). Could the profile use another source or two? Are there good quotations from reliable sources? Is the attribution clear?

9. Does the profile achieve a sense of balance? Does it have quotations from enough sources to create multiple perspectives of the subject? If the subject is being praised, are there enough illustrations, quotations, and evidence to support this praise?

10. Bracket the conclusion. Does the profile end with a memorable image? Is there a way to strengthen the conclusion?

Revision Checklist

As you do your final revision, check to make sure that you

- wrote an engaging lead
- announced your thesis in a clear nut graf or in the deck
- created a major impression of your profile subject
- used some or all of the typical profile elements to add color, interest, and depth:

  - Physical description
  - Quotations from the subject
  - Quotations about the subject
  - Examples
  - Anecdotes
  - Factual information

- Created a multifaceted portrait by using different perspectives from your sources
- Clearly attributed research from direct observation, interviews, and print and electronic sources
- Limited or eliminated the use of the first person (I)
- Provided clear transitions for your reader
- Concluded memorably, perhaps with a lingering image of your subject

SYNTHESIZING INFORMATION

THE ESSAY OF IDEAS

Learning how to think really means learning how to exercise some control over how and what you think. It means being conscious and aware enough to choose what you pay attention to and to choose meaning from experience because if you cannot exercise this kind of choice in adult life you will be totally hosed.

—DAVID FOSTER WALLACE, "THIS IS WATER"
COMMENCEMENT ADDRESS AT KENYON COLLEGE, 2005

It is easy enough to say what a word means. For example, what is an hour? You can measure an hour like this: an hour is 60 minutes—right? Or one-twenty-fourth of a day. But what does an hour mean when you are waiting for the sun to rise after a sleepless night? What is an hour when you have been waiting for someone special—and that person is an hour late? Or what is an hour when you have been dreading something and only an hour is left until it happens? Then the word *hour* means something else, something it could take a while to explain. And that explanation requires you to put the word in the context of that sleepless night, in the context of your plans to meet that special person, in the context of why you dread what you know will inevitably happen.

Some concepts defy definition in the first place. What does one mean, for example, when one says *beauty, gender, race, justice,* or *entitlement?* Putting each of those words in a context and showing them in action can help. When have you observed or experienced an example of beauty, gender, race, justice, or entitlement? What did you see, hear, feel, smell?

By synthesizing, your "inner" reflection and "outer" evidence, you reveal the broader meaning of a concept in a new way. This synthesis blends together your ideas with ideas outside yourself to form a new definition, not one you'll find in the dictionary.

Chapter Objectives

write a definition thesis
171

find outside sources to extend your definition
174

brainstorm for a concept
176

synthesize personal experience and outside sources
177

use induction and deduction to organize your essay
178

transform your written essay to the spoken word
179

PROCESS PLAN

Prepare

- Choose a concept you want to examine—one that has personal resonance and will allow you to speak in the first person, as an authority.

- Look at the concept from a number of different perspectives using the brainstorming guides later in this chapter.

Draft

- Choose one or two personal experiences that show the meaning of a concept through an action.

- Find one or two sources outside your experience that bring in another perspective on the concept: for example, something from current events, history, philosophy, science, art and literature, popular culture and technology.

- Synthesize: Combine several of your sources into a new perspective defining the concept. Write a thesis that expresses the perspective concisely. You may use this thesis at the beginning of your essay as the main claim, followed by examples (deductive reason) or lead up to it through your examples (inductive reason).

- Write an introduction that hooks the reader with a scene, anecdote, or example.

- Organize your thinking, moving from source to source. The sources might contrast or complement each other.

- Write a conclusion that reveals the significance of your perspective on the concept.

Revise

- Make sure your reader can follow you as you move through different ways of looking at the concept. Check for clear transitions.

- Check your obligation to your reader: Do you have enough explanation to show how you are connecting the different views?

- Cut any extra words. Combine sentences and check all adjectives and adverbs for clarity and precision.

Understanding
the Writing Project

Personal Experience + Outside Sources = Synthesis

THE ESSAY of ideas gives you the chance to explore an idea or a concept from several perspectives—yours as well as others'. Your unique way of looking at a word or concept will incorporate a variety of sources.

Using some personal narrative in your essay can help show the concept in action—as it played out in the context of real life. The narrative helps add layers to the meaning. The personal narrative part of the essay illustrates the concept in action and adds a layer of meaning. The outside sources bring other perspectives to your reflections about the meaning of a concept, confirming or expanding the meaning so that you can reach a conclusion that is both complete and convincing. In this way, your essay of ideas provides a persuasive answer to the question:

What does _____ mean?

ASSIGNMENT: Choose an idea that you connect with personally, something that you can illustrate or show in action through your own life experience. The concept should be a big idea, one that will take some exploration, such as "gratitude," as student Jolaina Jessler does in the essay that follows.
   Write the personal narrative section in a way that the reader will also experience it—with good, concrete detail and description. Then, find an outside source or two from literature, film, music, science, comedy, recent or historical events that might give the reader another perspective on the meaning of the concept. Or work in the reverse, starting with the outside source and bringing in a personal experience that enriches the meaning of the source. As you blend and synthesize the sources, you will discover a new way of thinking about the concept.

   The synthesis of ideas essay can be found everywhere in daily life; newspapers and magazines often include these essays. They can also come in the form of blogs or speeches. Blogs commonly combine personal anecdote with news or facts. In fact, personal and news websites are especially good sources for this genre of writing. Also, since the form allows the writer to combine an intimate perspective with a larger context, spoken word is a good delivery method. Speech writers use the essay of ideas to synthesize material from multiple sources and show how one person's experiences fit into a larger picture. You might hear an essay of ideas as a radio feature, for example, or as a TED (technology, entertainment, and design) talk. Often, this kind of speech will be delivered at an occasion—a graduation, an anniversary of an event, or the launch of a new project.

Essay of Ideas

Student Jolaina Jessler used her experience doing community service in Haiti combined with a theory she learned in her developmental psychology class to create a new, personal definition of gratitude.

JOLAINA JESSLER

#First-World-Problems

ON JUNE 25, 2011, I felt a bead of sweat roll down my neck and join the sticky layer of perspiration that coated my skin. I ducked under the low-hung doorway and stepped into the dark, crowded room. Though the low hum of flies was muted for a brief moment of relief, the solid, impenetrable heat remained. "This is my home," my new friend Manes announced proudly, his Haitian accent coloring each word with warmth. "God has blessed us with a bed." As I looked around the small, 10×10 hut, I saw a small cot in the corner and four other faces beaming in agreement. "We are lucky."

On January 11, 2012, I lounged comfortably in a beanbag chair, surrounded by friends sipping hot chocolate as warm air poured from the heater and chased away the remnants of the cold from the doorway of the dorm room. The hum of voices on the TV blended with the voices of my friends, laughing easily and recalling the best parts of the movie we'd just watched. We stood up from the bunk beds and stretched out our backs that had grown stiff from leaning against the wall. "Sorry there's no couch," my friend said to me from his bed, "We didn't have room for one once we brought in the TV. Hash

tag first-world-problems." The room erupted in laughter as we all tried to out-do each other with versions of the joke that had spread like wildfire over the Internet in the previous months. Quietly, another friend added, "Water contaminated with diphtheria. Hash tag third-world-problems."

The summer of 2011, I traveled to Hato Mayor, Dominican Republic, with a team of people from my church. During our visit, we worked with a group called Meeting God in Missions to reach a village of impoverished Haitian refugees. Through the course of the week we provided medical and dental care, food, and vacation bible school for the people of the village. Though the level of poverty in the village stunned me, perhaps more surprising was the joy with which each of the villagers lived, and the gratitude that each of them exuded at receiving the most basic of things. Every bag of rice given was a precious blessing, every tooth pulled was a miraculous cure, and every balloon animal blown up was a beautiful gift that would without fail be displayed as a prominent decoration in the huts the next day.

Upon my return to the United States, I couldn't see my world the same way. My once

Reprinted with permission by Jolaina Jessler.

comfortable, air-conditioned house felt like an excessive indulgence; my own bedroom a gross theft of unnecessary space. I felt bitter contempt when I turned on the television and saw reality stars sobbing over the crisis of a drunken argument and disgust at advertisements that each boasted their products as the "one thing you really *need* to finally be happy." But nothing was stronger than the sickening torment I felt when I heard myself, a mere week after returning home, complain to a friend how annoying it was that my sister had taken the car, which just the two of us shared, out for the night. "Can't I just get my own car already?" I asked. I realized that I was already slipping back into the sense of entitlement that was so characteristic of the world I was used to. How was it that I could be discontent about anything in my world of abundance when the Haitians and Dominicans, who lived with so little, experienced such joy?

I recently learned about a theory in developmental psychology that says there are certain phases in an organism's life in which an event must occur in order for development to precede normally. During these phases, referred to as critical periods, graylag geese become attached to their mothers to learn how to behave; certain birds must hear an adult singing before they themselves can sexually mature; and human infants develop their sense of binocular vision. Closely related to critical periods are sensitive periods, which are time periods that are optimal, but not necessary for certain development to take place.

Originally, I frequently thought about my time returning to the United States as a critical period. I was burdened by a need to be more and more grateful faster, and to live with less. Certainly if I enjoyed my life it meant necessarily that I was forgetting about the sufferings of my Haitian friends. If my friends or I complained about an inconvenience or problem, I assumed that we were being entitled and spoiled. The problem with this outlook was that no matter how much contempt I had for material goods, nothing I could do would solve the problems in the Dominican Republic. No amount of gratitude would change the infrastructure of a country whose immigrants were so rapidly falling behind. My new perspective from my short trip that had showed me how lucky I was to have so much was fusing with everything that I had been taught through first-world media that said I could never have enough. My pre-existing conventions battled against my newly found convictions, and the guilt that I felt because of it was unsustainable. Entitlement battled gratitude, and wrought with the guilt I felt at not being able to solve the problems, I began to lose hope. Slowly, and with the counsel of some of the people that I went on the trip with, I began to gain a better understanding of what it means to be grateful.

I now believe that gratitude is not something we need to feel "enough" of in order to keep ourselves from being entitled or spoiled, nor do I think it is feeling guilty about what you have. Instead, I have come to see gratitude as the gift of open eyes that let you see that you have enough. I believe that gratitude is necessary for contentment, because it is only when you realize how blessed you are that you can stop the endless search for something more fulfilling. My Dominican and Haitian friends seem to be happier than I am— happier than a lot of people I know. Perhaps they have grasped this. They certainly seem to me to be grateful every day for their friends, families, and loving God.

It has now been nine months since my trip to the Dominican Republic. My life before and after the Dominican has not changed very much. I am currently attending one of the most expensive universities in the country, and I would be a hypocrite if I suggested that I have in some way eschewed the conveniences and opportunities of society. I occasionally laugh when I read "first-world-problems" on Twitter, and must even confess to using the popular hash tag to describe conditions as sobering as running out of *Grey's Anatomy* episodes to watch on Hulu and not knowing which of the hundreds of instant-stream shows to turn to. Despite these facts, one thing has changed in me. I now try to be conscious of looking at each day as if it were a sensitive period, one in which I can continue to learn how to be grateful for what I have. I would like to look at each day like a gift, and when things seem hard, I remember the Dominican and remember that I have enough. Through the eyes of gratitude, the world becomes hopeful. One day I hope to be as grateful as my friends, despite smothering heat or bitter cold, 10×10 hut or palace.

Questions for Critical Thinking

1. Jessler opens her essay by contrasting her environment in Haiti with the environment in her college dorm. What does she imply by the contrast? Make a similar comparison between two very different environments you have experienced.
2. Describe the culture shock Jessler experienced when she returned to the United States. What would you list under #First-World-Problems?
3. How was Jessler's trip to Haiti a critical period in her life? A sensitive period? Can you make the critical/sensitive period analogy to some times in your life?
4. By synthesizing her experience in Haiti with a theory in developmental psychology and with a popular Internet meme, Jessler creates a personal definition of gratitude. How would you explain this concept of gratitude? How does it resonate with your thinking about gratitude?

THE  The Synthesis Thesis

The surprise element—probably what makes essays of ideas most intriguing to an audience—is the synthesis, the combining of your personal experience with ideas from others into a fresh or original BIG IDEA. Essentially, the essay of ideas boils down to defining a concept by answering this question:

What does _____ mean?

But the definition you arrive at is one that you have constructed from your research, not one you would find in a dictionary. Because you are synthesizing different perspectives on the term or concept, the answer requires an extended explanation, an argument that demonstrates your conclusion is valid. In the essay "# First-World-Problems," Jolaina Jessler leads her reader inductively through her experience in Haiti and her understanding of a theory in psychology to define gratitude "as the gift of open eyes that let you see that you have enough."

Jonanthan Franzen, in "Pain Won't Kill You" (in the Readings section), takes the two terms *like* and *love* and shows us how each contrasts with the other. He leads us inductively to his thesis:

> *The simple fact of the matter is that trying to be perfectly likable is incompatible with loving relationships.*

Our understanding of what Franzen means when he says "likable" and what he means when he says "love" is essential to our acceptance of his main claim, which is something along the lines of "to thine own self be true."

Visual Literacy

Try *visual brainstorming* to help connect your topic to personal experiences and outside sources. Even if you don't consider yourself a visual person, tapping into a new method of generating ideas will work different parts of your brain and can help you make unexpected connections. Remember, the essay of ideas is all about synthesizing.

First, create an online collage. Use the social networking site Pinterest to collect and post images you can associate with your subject. Browse through other pins and do an image search on google to help you curate your collection. Be creative with your key words and see what you can find to unlock ideas and connect to unexpected sources. Look for quotations as well as photos and drawings that link to your topic. Your pins might help you if you get stuck during a later stage of the writing process. Taking a look back at your Pinterest page after the first draft, for example, can help you think of things you left out, or even ways to connect seemingly disconnected ideas.

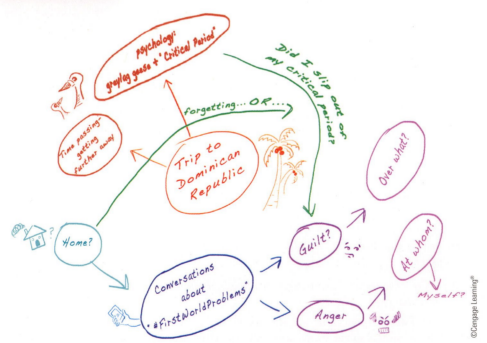

The author of #First-World-Problems created a mind map for her brainstorming.

7 SYNTHESIZING INFORMATION

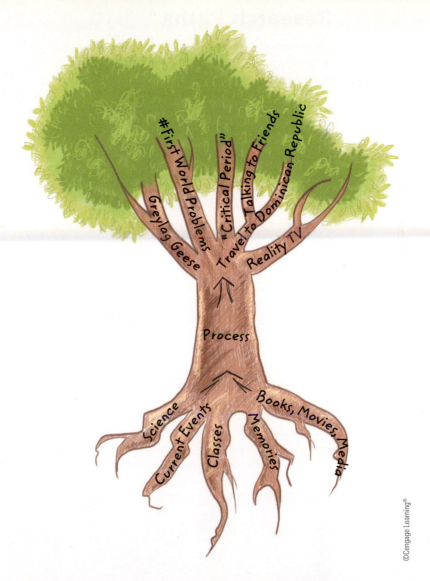

Labels on the tree (branches, top to bottom): Greylag Geese, #First World Problems, "Critical Period", Talking to Friends, Travel to Dominican Republic, Reality TV

Trunk: Process

Roots: Science, Current Events, Classes, Memories, Books, Movies, Media

Second, creating a mind map can help free up ideas. Try using software from a site such as wise-mapping.com to help you visualize ideas. Or go free-hand. Use colors. Make notes. Draw arrows, think of sub-ideas that spring from bigger points. Allow yourself to go off on digressions. The beauty of mind mapping is that you can actually see the branches of your thinking, and how you leapt from one idea to the next. See the mind map on page 172 that Jolaina Jesser used when she was writing #First-World-Problems.

Research Paths

The alchemy of combining sources in the essay of ideas is the path to fresh, imaginative writing your reader will pay attention to and remember—in other words, writing that has an impact.

How do you go about finding material that will provide a range of perspectives? First, use your own experiences. Personal memories are useful in providing concrete narrative detail and showing a concept in action. Put your reader into the moment by creating a scene with detail.

One way to deepen your thinking is to read. The research for your essay of ideas can be as creative as the writing. Spend some time on the Internet, experimenting with different kinds of Google searches using your concept as the keyword. Check out the academic databases and see how various fields of study interpret your concept. Go to online bookstores as well as a bricks and mortar bookstore and leaf through titles. If your concept is timely or current, chances are you will easily find cultural references—music, movies, books—that are also considering it. But wade into deeper waters, too, looking for unlikely connections. Ancient Greek philosophers, politicians, environmentalists, and poets all have interesting things to say about "gratitude," for example. What happened in the past that might surface in your story and create some interesting or controversial sparks?

Connect to popular culture, movies, music, television, and more. One student, in writing about the concept of "war," started with a card game she and her brother used to play that once became so intense the two of them shredded the deck of cards. She linked this story to something from the news that week about a bombing attack on Libya and linked again to a remark Jon Stewart made on *The Daily Show* about the bombing. By combining all the material, she explored the use of the term *war* and how purposefully it has been avoided in recent years, with politicians choosing to use *conflict* instead. Her research was reading the news and watching a television show, but yours might include reading biographies or going back to a poem you remember from childhood.

Susan Blau

Looking at a writer's bulletin board is like looking into her mind.

No matter how you find your sources, be sure to seek out the primary source rather than relying on references to it. It is easy enough to review a film or a television show on YouTube or other Internet sources, but you should also read newspapers or journal articles, access databases, and talk to people with experience in or knowledge about your concept. The more you know about and understand the topic—whether it is about first-world-problems, pinball, or bird-watching—the more sure and authoritative your voice will be.

You will want to create a Works Cited page, which you can review in Chapter 16, "Documentation." Be sure to keep accurate and thorough notes of all your sources whether they are books, articles, websites, television shows, music, films, or speeches. You can find specific information on how to cite all of these sources in Chapter 16, but the most essential point to remember about citations is that you must give credit to the creator of any intellectual property (see also "Avoiding Plagiarism" on page 424).

Steps in Writing Your Essay

Find a Topic

Sometimes a personal experience is so memorable that thinking about it leads you to insights about your values or identity or relationships—all things that help you define who you are or what you believe. Bumping into an old friend just when you were thinking about her might make you think about fate or coincidence. Later that day in psych class you might hear a lecture on Carl Jung's theory of synchronicity, which is defined as a meaningful coincidence. What a coincidence, you might think! (Maybe it's even worth exploring.) In your research you might even come across a reference to the 80s band The Police and their Synchronicity tour. How does that fit together? Or does it? How would you define this kind of coincidence? Do you believe in fate?

Other times, you may find that an event in the world, a film, or a piece of writing triggers a response in you, reminding you of an experience or a moment in your life. Maybe you read about Jung's theories of synchronicity in psych class and it started this whole stream of thought: the time you were thinking about an old friend, the role of fate in your life.

Either way—starting with the personal experience or starting with the outside source—can lead you to find a topic for your essay of ideas. It helps sometimes to categorize the possibilities into timely or current events, controversial issues, and "evergreen" topic ideas that are always interesting to explore. These few ideas may help prompt your thinking:

Timely or Current: Binge Watching, Local Food, Fear of Missing out (FoMo), The "Share" Economy

Controversial: Affirmative Action, Ze: The Gender-Free Pronoun, Genetically Modified Foods

Evergreen: Piracy, Truth, Beauty, Bargains, Happiness, Addiction

Brainstorm Ideas

Here's a secret known by professional writers: brainstorming is where the real excitement of writing lies. And here's another secret: most people have no idea how to brainstorm. You might have heard about clustering and mapping and freewriting. These are great ways to get writing flowing, but figuring out what you want to say after you decide on a topic might work better if you use *directed freewriting*. This is a method of brainstorming that is contained, or that uses some guides to help you generate fresh ideas. Following are several methods: the Aristotelian method, the measurement method, and the analogy method.

THE ARISTOTELIAN METHOD This method, borrowed from the teachings of the Greek philosopher Aristotle, asks you to put the concept into a general category, and think about how it might be different from other terms in the same category. For example, you might begin a directed freewrite about the idea of "piracy." Start generating ideas by putting "piracy" into a category. Remember there is no right or wrong answer to this. You might choose "kinds of theft." Then ask how acquiring music or books online without paying for them is different from other types of stealing. You might begin your definition by saying, "Music piracy is a kind of theft that has no real victim." Conversely, you might define music piracy as "a kind of theft that impoverishes the very artists we revere." As you develop your freewrite, more ideas might come to you. One writer's process of the brainstorming phase may be seen on page 172.

THE MEASUREMENT METHOD This method is best used when measuring something that might be difficult to quanitfy. At the beginning of the chapter, the example of "what is an hour" exemplifies this method. It is easy to quantify an hour literally, but more difficult metaphorically. It's not as easy to measure happiness or truth, but it could be interesting to try. Keep in mind that the word *measure* is used loosely here. We can quantify wealth, but when we do so, do we also quantify *happiness*?

Example: Can we use a quantifiable approach to define *marriage*? For example, a couple is "married" by common law standards through a specific time spent living together, but marriage also has a host of other meanings that may be spiritual, romantic, legal, or controversial. Can we consider cohabitating couples married and people who don't live together as not married? Is physical distance a way to measure marriage? The old definition of *marriage* (one man, one woman) is changing, legally, so is marriage now more significantly quantified by a number—as in, "Only 2 *people* may be married to each other at any one time"?

THE ANALOGY METHOD A good way to help a reader relate to a new concept is to compare it to a familiar concept. To make its point, a group arguing

PRACTICE 7.2

Defining by Measuring or Quantifying

Write a short definition for one of the following by using two different methods of quantifying or measuring. For example: "Adult"—measured in age: someone is considered to be a legal adult at the age of 18. Another way to measure "adult" is to decide whether a person is fully grown—or to use an X-ray of a femur bone.

Define these words using the measurement method:

woman/man	mother/father
viral	Democrat
Republican	organic ■

PRACTICE 7.3

Defining by Comparison or Analogy

Think of an analogy for the following concepts:

- Leaving home
- Cheating on a test
- Suffering from chronic depression
- Being a shopaholic ■

against affirmative action gave away free candy, for example, but only to people who "qualified" by merit of their race. The group compared the entitlement to candy to entitlement to college acceptance. It was a controversial way to illustrate a concept by comparing it to something else. In your writing, you can make comparison in many ways. One student, writing about the dissolution of her parents' marriage, after a series of breakups and reconciliations, used the plot from *50 First Dates* as an analogy. The couple in the movie had to re-create their relationship every day because of the woman's memory problem. The student compared the plot of that movie to her parents' continued reconciliations—"re-creations" of their marriage.

The Importance of SHOWING

An essay of ideas requires more than just explaining abstract concepts. The very best writers of these essays borrow from techniques of fiction to help keep readers interested and to develop the characteristics of personality and an individual's voice. Remember that this writing is based on personal insight, and the "person" will emerge through the details.

Ways to SHOW

- Use specific scenes to illustrate personal experience. (Instead of saying what would usually happen, say what happened this one particular time.)

- Evoke sensory detail—pinpoint things you can see that set a place and time.

- Remember to combine senses—what you can hear, smell, touch, and see.

- Consider the point of view: If you are young in the story, focus on those things a young person would notice. If you are an outsider, what is strange to you that might be ordinary to others?

- Don't forget how interesting it is to hear a little dialogue.

- Create signatures for characters. You will not have lots of characters, but each one should still have a distinct feature that sets him or her apart—a physical feature such as a piece of clothing or a hairstyle or gesture.

- Use internal thoughts and summary sparingly, but do use them a way to help the story progress.

PRACTICE 7.4
Synthesizing

Practice blending in two seemingly distinctly different ideas.

- Write two paragraphs in which you use a fact from sociology, science, or technology with a scene, character, or theme from a current movie.

- Write one paragraph in which you combine the elements of a current event with something you saw on *The Simpsons* or another television show.

- Write about love and food in the same paragraph.

- Write three paragraphs in which you (1) describe a personal experience with fear and (2) summarize a suspenseful film and (3) show how one idea from both elements has led you to a conclusion about what fear is, how it works, or its causes and/or effects. ■

Organize Your Ideas

Since there is no set-in-stone format for the essay of ideas, writers can be either totally liberated or totally frustrated by the structure. You can avoid total frustration by keeping several things in mind.

The essay requires at least three parts:

- A personal experience
- At least two outside sources that may seem unrelated at first glance
- A conclusion that brings the personal experience and the outside sources together and shows their relevance in enlarging the meaning of the concept.

INDUCTION OR DEDUCTION? Some writers prefer to use inductive reasoning, listing the material in chunks, and even using a white space between sections so these chunks are self-contained. As one chunk of material follows another, we start to see the ideas add up, like an equation:

$$A + B + C + = \text{My Thesis or Big Idea} \ldots$$

The conclusion, then, reveals how the elements add up, or what the sum of the pieces is.

Other writers like to start with the main point, or thesis, and work their way through the logic. The essay begins with your "definition" thesis, proceeds to the pieces of evidence, and wraps up with a more detailed restatement of the main point. You can think of deductive structure as working through the equation backwards, with the sum up front:

$$\text{My Thesis} = A + B + C + \ldots$$

Anthya Cohen/Lebrecht

Self-portrait by Anthya Cohen

PRACTICE 7.5
The Art of Showing, Not Telling

Describe a place that was important to you. Include details from all five senses. Make sure the meaning of the place is clear, but don't tell the reader what it means to you. Read your description to the class and have them "read between the lines" and tell you what they think the place meant to you. ■

PRACTICE 7.6
Inductive and Deductive Organization

- Answer this question in a sentence: What do I mean when I say "failure"?
- Write an opening paragraph for an essay of ideas that begins with that sentence.
- Write an opening paragraph for an essay of ideas that ends with that sentence. ■

PRACTICE 7.7
Write a Speech

Write a three-minute speech you can deliver to your classmates. As a group, agree on the occasion for this speech you are about to compose—a particular season, a holiday, an anniversary, a special moment in history—whatever the class decides is a good context. ■

DIY MEDIA AND DESIGN

Speech and Podcast

The essay of ideas lends itself to speaking, since it springs from personal insights. If your intention is to present the ideas in the form of the spoken word, keep this at the forefront of your mind: imagine you are speaking to just one other person. This is the key to inviting each listener into your words. Using the material from your essay of ideas, record yourself reading on an MP3 file and post the recording on any site that offers free podcast hosting or on YouTube.

Writer David Sedaris says that he makes conscious choices when building sentences for the human breath. Since he is as much a performer as a writer, and since people are as likely to listen to his personal stories and essays as they are to read them, the decisions he makes about his writing are shaped by how he will encounter his audience. Preparing your personal essay for reading aloud may require you to make adjustments to sentence length and pacing. Rehearse your reading. Revise accordingly, and then make a recording.

You can hear examples of personal essays on *This American Life* (NPR) or *The Moth Radio Hour* for further ideas about presentation of your essay in an audio file.

Reinventing Your Essay of Ideas as a Special Occasion Speech

In the Readings section, Jonathan Franzen's commencement address to Kenyon College, which was edited for print, shows you how compatible the skills of writing an essay of ideas are to writing a special occasion speech, such as a graduation talk. A remarkable commencement address by the writer David Foster Wallace, called "This Is Water," might also help you see how a big idea gets developed and then relayed to an audience through the spoken word.

Both Franzen's and Wallace's addresses were delivered on the occasions of graduation, but speeches can be delivered at other important moments, as well. You may be called on to give advice or impart your ideas as part of different occasions, celebrations, or commemorations: your grandparents' 50th anniversary, your sister's wedding, your favorite charity's fundraiser. As you take on a speech for any of these occasions, the advice in this chapter about combining personal experience and outside sources to explore the meaning of a concept will help you. But it is important to give your audience special consideration for these speeches.

Remember to include the audience in your speech in an intimate way. The personal experience part of the writing is especially good at helping you relate to a gathered audience on a special day.

Here are some tips that help speakers connect to an audience:

- Address your audience specifically.
- Call out a few specific details you know about the people in the audience.
- Refer to some recent shared experience or a person important to the group.
- Tailor your comments to the shared moment, and make connections between the occasion and your points.

READINGS

Student Jake Shauli takes on the daunting task of defining *happiness* by connecting the concept of happiness to playing pinball. In his graduation address to students at Kenyon College, novelist Jonathan Franzen challenges the "techno-consumer" culture and its particular way of defining *liking* and *loving*.

Pinball and Happiness

Jake Shauli

Student writer Jake Shauli makes a compelling argument that connects his passion for pinball to the pursuit of happiness.

IN MY house we used to have a pinball machine. It was old and had problems that were too costly to have repaired, but it still worked. For example, there was a malfunction in the mechanism that moves the ball from the gutter back to the launch area. Every time I lost I would have to manually open the front of the machine and move the ball over myself with a small blue plastic toy screwdriver. I was so young that to play it I used to have to stand on a stool or chair. But in a way it was the perfect training machine. Having to go through the ordeal of resetting the ball every time I lost

Reprinted with permission by Jake Shauli.

forced me to play longer games. The machine's layout was rudimentary with three large bumpers, slingshots, targets and a "u" shaped track in the back that to make the ball go through you had to time your shot just right. Every pinball machine has these elements in more sophisticated arrangements. It was at home where I practiced, but at foreign machines where the real fun was.

I play pinball any chance I get. Hotels, restaurants, bowling alleys, Dave and Busters', even ski lodges. If it's there, you can bet I will go and play it. Off the top of my head I can remember playing Terminator, Simpsons, South Park, Adams Family, Harley Davidson, Road Show, and Back to the Future themed pinball machines. When I was with my parents, anytime I saw a pinball machine they knew I was going to ask. But no, I didn't clean out their pockets. With skill you can play for almost a half hour or even longer on a single credit. Replay scores, extra-ball, multiball, you name it I have gotten it.

You might say that what has me hooked is a combination of flashing lights and busy sounds, like a video game, but that's not how I see it. When you play pinball, there's something physical about it that you can't replicate virtually; it just isn't the same. There is something about standing in front of a machine bigger than you, trying to beat it with only two buttons that is different from fighting against artificial intelligence or chance as in other games. Pinball is about fighting gravity, velocity and time with concentration, skill and timing. When you play pinball you can feel the force of the flipper launching the metal sphere away from the gutter. You can feel the excitement when the bumpers bounce the ball back and forth racking up countless points with each clink. When I encounter a pinball machine, I feel compelled to give it my game and see how many millions of points I can score and if I can make it to the high score charts, a nearly impossible task.

Playing pinball is an experience and challenge. A few times I have even had spectators watch me and root me on, their eyes peeled under the glass on the ball as they stood on the side of the table. I think what drew them over was the sheer time I spent in front of that machine playing without stopping. Sure, some of them were family friends but they seemed just as captivated by the game as I was by just watching. It was as if the machine were my stage, and I was the performer.

> "When you play pinball, there's something physical about it that you can't replicate virtually . . ."

But pinball is slowly fading away. Stern, a Chicago based manufacturing company, is now the only company making the machines. Venue owners see them as low-profit earning entertainment machines that require expensive maintenance and are thus mostly being purchased by private individuals. Pinball museums have started to spring up in cities such as Las Vegas and Seattle. The last machine I saw was at a family friend's house in Utah. It was a themed machine I've never played before so it was a no-brainer asking him if I could play. To my dismay he said I could try but it was usually broken. He said you have to play often to keep it from breaking, which was shocking to me. It was then that the sad reality became clear to me that the reason pinball machines are fading away is because people just aren't playing them.

◆ ◆ ◆

There are many mysteries about happiness that humans do not understand but that have been slowly explored by social scientists and individuals. The reason long-term happiness is impossible to find is one of them that according to Jeff Zira is an evolutionary adaptation. Happiness is only fleeting. The rationale behind why humans cannot be happy for long is simple. In an explanation of this fact, he explained at a TEDxBU conference, "evolution is at odds with our goal of happiness." The second year MIT MBA student went on to say that to be permanently happy is to stop surviving. If a human is happy, he no longer wants to go on and keep creating and exploring. He cannot be happy for long if he wants to survive. In other words, long-term happiness keeps us from being productive so evolution has made it impossible for us to attain it.

Another mystery is why buying things only temporarily makes one happy even if the purchase is an expensive or long-term purchase. There are some purchases that people believe will be life changing and make them forever a happier person. For example buying one's dream car may make one happy for a few months, but after this period the car becomes just a part of normal life and it is no longer special. In his book *The Upside of Irrationality* (Harpers, 2010), Dan Ariely, Professor of Psychology and Behavioral Economics at Duke University, called this phenomenon the "hedonic treadmill" because no matter how happy one is from a purchase, one will soon return to the happiness level one was at before buying the item. Some people try to defy this phenomenon by buying experiences rather than things but the phenomenon still occurs. If you consider gaming, the same thing occurs. The feeling of beating a video game is fleeting and leaves one left to find another game and again work one's way to the

top of the treadmill. It's in playing the game that people get the most pleasure.

We will never be indefinitely happy, but always in the pursuit of happiness. It is why we suffer from the hedonic treadmill. We assume that our lives will be better with a new thing, but we slowly realize things are just the same. Ironically it is in the pursuit of happiness that people are closest to finding long-term happiness. I believe humans derive the most pleasure from the things they cannot have because it's the closest thing we have to long-term happiness. In math you can get infinitely close to an axis with an asymptote, but you will never actually reach it.

Playing a game of Pinball to me represents happiness in the same way. Pinball isn't subject to the hedonic treadmill because you can't win. The goal is to win, but it will never happen. The better you get, the closer you get to winning, but you can't win. The longer I play a game of pinball, the more fun I have. It is the pursuit of that everlasting happiness, the battle to conquer the pinball machine that makes playing so enjoyable. Winning itself isn't.

But this is also the reason pinball isn't being played as often. People like to win. Winning a game of Halo may make you happy for only a minute or so, but it doesn't matter because you can just play again or get a new game. If you think you will be happier with a new pair of shoes you can buy them and be happy for a while and then be subjected to the hedonic treadmill. But why play pinball if you can't feel the satisfaction of the win? How can I still be excited to play pinball when I know I can't win while I at least have a shot if I play *Call of Duty*? While it could just be that I grew up with a fascination for the game, it could also be that I'm okay with not winning because at the end of the day, life isn't about winning. And if life is like pinball, then you can't win. How can you win in life? Do you win if you have the nice car, trophy wife, and million-dollar house? Winning in life is an illusion. If the goal in life is to somehow become eternally happy, an impossible task, then the closest you can get is in the pursuit of happiness, something I've grown to accept and embrace. I try to keep the game going and keep being happy with skill but eventually the ball will somehow make its way past my two flippers leaving the screen to read GAME OVER. But that doesn't stop me. I keep playing. If pinball is like life, then being happy is just about getting better at it.

Questions for Rhetorical Analysis

1. How would you describe Shauli's voice in this essay? What techniques does he use that help create that voice?
2. In describing his personal experience with pinball, what qualities of the game does Shauli emphasize? How do these qualities foreshadow his connection of pinball to happiness?
3. Identify the thesis of this essay of ideas. Does the writer lead you to this thesis inductively or deductively?
4. What are the outside sources Shauli references in this essay? Are they credible sources?
5. How well does Shauli connect the personal experience to the outside sources in the conclusion? What, in essence, is this essay about?

Questions for Critical Thinking

1. What is Shauli's argument about the value of playing a game such as pinball as opposed to playing video games? Do you agree?
2. What aspects of real life, as opposed to virtual life, could be used as similar examples of being in the *pursuit* of happiness?
3. When have you been on the "hedonic treadmill"?

Style Practice: Imitation

Describe an activity that you are passionate about. Begin, as Shauli does, by showing how you first came to do this activity.

Pain Won't Kill You

Jonathan Franzen

Author Jonathan Franzen is famous for his best-selling novels, The Corrections *and* Freedom. *When he was invited to deliver the commencement address at Kenyon College in 2011, he relied on some of the conventions such occasions require: a combination of intimacy and big ideas as he worked his way from his new cell phone to his love of birds. The piece that follows is a version of that speech, turned essay of ideas published in the* New York Times.

A COUPLE OF weeks ago, I replaced my three-year-old BlackBerry Pearl with a much more powerful BlackBerry Bold. Needless to say, I was impressed with how far the technology had advanced in three years. Even when I didn't have anybody to call or text or e-mail, I wanted to keep fondling my new Bold and experiencing the marvelous clarity of its screen, the silky action of its track pad, the shocking speed of its responses, the beguiling elegance of its graphics.

I was, in short, infatuated with my new device. I'd been similarly infatuated with my old device, of course; but over the years the bloom had faded from our relationship. I'd developed trust issues with my Pearl, accountability issues, compatibility issues and even, toward the end, some doubts about my Pearl's very sanity, until I'd finally had to admit to myself that I'd outgrown the relationship.

Do I need to point out that—absent some wild, anthropomorphizing projection in which my old BlackBerry felt sad about the waning of my love for it—our relationship was entirely one-sided? Let me point it out anyway.

Let me further point out how ubiquitously the word "sexy" is used to describe late-model gadgets; and how the extremely cool things that we can do now with these gadgets—like impelling them to action with voice commands, or doing that spreading-the-fingers iPhone thing that makes images get bigger—would have looked, to people a hundred years ago, like a magician's incantations, a magician's hand gestures; and how, when we want to describe an erotic relationship that's working perfectly, we speak, indeed, of magic.

Let me toss out the idea that, as our markets discover and respond to what consumers most want, our technology has become extremely adept at creating products that correspond to our fantasy ideal of an erotic relationship, in which the beloved object asks for nothing and gives everything, instantly, and makes us feel all powerful, and doesn't throw terrible scenes when it's replaced by an even sexier object and is consigned to a drawer.

To speak more generally, the ultimate goal of technology, the telos of techne, is to replace a natural world that's indifferent to our wishes—a world of hurricanes and hardships and breakable hearts, a world of resistance—with a world so responsive to our wishes as to be, effectively, a mere extension of the self.

Let me suggest, finally, that the world of techno-consumerism is therefore troubled by real love, and that it has no choice but to trouble love in turn.

Its first line of defense is to commodify its enemy. You can all supply your own favorite, most nauseating examples of the commodification of love. Mine include the wedding industry, TV ads that feature cute young children or the giving of automobiles as Christmas presents, and the particularly grotesque equation of diamond jewelry with everlasting devotion. The message, in each case, is that if you love somebody you should buy stuff.

A related phenomenon is the transformation, courtesy of Facebook, of the verb "to like" from a state of mind to an action that you perform with your computer mouse, from a feeling to an assertion of consumer choice. And liking, in general, is commercial culture's substitute for loving. The striking thing about all consumer products—and none more so than electronic devices and applications—is that they're designed to be immensely likable. This is, in fact, the definition of a consumer product, in contrast to the product that is simply itself and whose makers aren't fixated on your liking it. (I'm thinking here of jet engines, laboratory equipment, serious art and literature.)

But if you consider this in human terms, and you imagine a person defined by a desperation to be liked, what do you see? You see a person without integrity, without a center. In more pathological cases, you see a narcissist—a person who can't tolerate the tarnishing of his or her self-image that not being liked represents, and who therefore either withdraws from human contact or goes to extreme, integrity-sacrificing lengths to be likable.

If you dedicate your existence to being likable, however, and if you adopt whatever cool persona is necessary to make it happen, it suggests that you've despaired of being loved for who you really are. And if you succeed in manipulating other people into liking you, it will be hard not to feel, at some level, contempt for those people, because they've fallen for your shtick. You may find yourself becoming depressed, or alcoholic, or, if you're Donald Trump, running for president (and then quitting).

Consumer technology products would never do anything this unattractive, because they aren't people. They are, however, great allies and enablers of narcissism. Alongside their built-in eagerness to be liked is a built-in eagerness to reflect well on us. Our lives look a lot more interesting when they're filtered through the sexy Facebook interface. We star in our own movies, we photograph ourselves incessantly, we click the mouse and a machine confirms our sense of mastery.

And, since our technology is really just an extension of ourselves, we don't have to have contempt for its manipulability in the way we might with actual people. It's all one big endless loop. We like the mirror and the mirror likes us. To friend a person is merely to include the person in our private hall of flattering mirrors.

I may be overstating the case, a little bit. Very probably, you're sick to death of hearing social media disrespected by cranky 51-year-olds. My aim here is mainly to set up a contrast between the narcissistic tendencies of technology and the problem of actual love. My friend Alice Sebold likes to talk about "getting down in the pit and loving somebody." She has in mind the dirt that love inevitably splatters on the mirror of our self-regard.

The simple fact of the matter is that trying to be perfectly likable is incompatible with loving relationships. Sooner or later, for example, you're going to find yourself in a hideous, screaming fight, and you'll hear coming out of your mouth things that you yourself don't like at all, things that shatter your self-image as a fair, kind, cool, attractive, in-control, funny, likable person. Something realer than likability has come out in you, and suddenly you're having an actual life.

Suddenly there's a real choice to be made, not a fake consumer choice between a BlackBerry and an iPhone, but a question: Do I love this person? And, for the other person, does this person love me?

There is no such thing as a person whose real self you like every particle of. This is why a world of liking is ultimately a lie. But there is such a thing as a person whose real self you love every particle of. And this is why love is such an existential threat to the techno-consumerist order: it exposes the lie.

This is not to say that love is only about fighting. Love is about bottomless empathy, born out of the heart's revelation that another person is every bit as real as you are. And this is why love, as I understand it, is always specific. Trying to love all of humanity may be a worthy endeavor, but, in a funny way, it keeps the focus on the self, on the self's own moral or spiritual well-being. Whereas to love a specific person, and to identify with his or her struggles and joys as if they were your own, you have to surrender some of your self.

The big risk here, of course, is rejection. We can all handle being disliked now and then, because there's such an infinitely big pool of potential likers. But to expose your whole self, not just the likable surface, and to have it rejected, can be catastrophically painful. The prospect of pain generally, the pain of loss, of breakup, of death, is what makes it so tempting to avoid love and stay safely in the world of liking.

"The simple fact of the matter is that trying to be perfectly likable is incompatible with loving relationships."

And yet pain hurts but it doesn't kill. When you consider the alternative—an anesthetized dream of self-sufficiency, abetted by technology—pain emerges as the natural product and natural indicator of being alive in a resistant world. To go through a life painlessly is to have not lived. Even just to say to yourself, "Oh, I'll get to that love and pain stuff later, maybe in my 30s" is to consign yourself to 10 years of merely taking up space on the planet and burning up its resources. Of being (and I mean this in the most damning sense of the word) a consumer.

When I was in college, and for many years after, I liked the natural world. Didn't love it, but definitely liked it. It can be very pretty, nature. And since I was looking for things to find wrong with the world, I naturally gravitated to environmentalism, because there were certainly plenty of things wrong with the environment. And the more I looked at what was wrong—an exploding world population, exploding levels of resource consumption, rising global temperatures, the trashing of the oceans, the logging of our last old-growth forests—the angrier I became.

Finally, in the mid-1990s, I made a conscious decision to stop worrying about the environment. There was nothing meaningful that I personally could do to save the planet, and I wanted to get on with devoting myself to the things I loved. I still tried to keep my carbon footprint small, but that was as far as I could go without falling back into rage and despair.

BUT then a funny thing happened to me. It's a long story, but basically I fell in love with birds. I did this not without significant resistance, because it's very uncool to be a birdwatcher, because anything that betrays real passion is by definition uncool. But little by little, in spite of myself, I developed this passion, and although one-half of a passion is obsession, the other half is love.

And so, yes, I kept a meticulous list of the birds I'd seen, and, yes, I went to inordinate lengths to see new species. But, no less important, whenever I looked at a bird, any bird, even a pigeon or a robin, I could feel my heart overflow with love. And love, as I've been trying to say today, is where our troubles begin.

Because now, not merely liking nature but loving a specific and vital part of it, I had no choice but to start worrying about the environment again. The news on that front was no better than when I'd decided to quit worrying about it—was considerably worse, in fact—but now those threatened forests and wetlands and oceans weren't just pretty scenes for me to enjoy. They were the home of animals I loved.

And here's where a curious paradox emerged. My anger and pain and despair about the planet were only increased by my concern for wild birds, and yet, as I began to get involved in bird conservation and learned more about the many threats that birds face, it became easier, not harder, to live with my anger and despair and pain.

How does this happen? I think, for one thing, that my love of birds became a portal to an important, less self-centered part of myself that I'd never even known existed. Instead of continuing to drift forward through my life as a global citizen, liking and disliking and withholding my commitment for some later date, I was forced to confront a self that I had to either straight-up accept or flat-out reject.

Which is what love will do to a person. Because the fundamental fact about all of us is that we're alive for a while but will die before long. This fact is the real root cause of all our anger and pain and despair. And you can either run from this fact or, by way of love, you can embrace it.

When you stay in your room and rage or sneer or shrug your shoulders, as I did for many years, the world and its problems are impossibly daunting. But when you go out and put yourself in real relation to real people, or even just real animals, there's a very real danger that you might love some of them.

And who knows what might happen to you then?

Questions for Rhetorical Analysis

1. Franzen wrote this piece as a commencement speech. Could you tell this by reading it? Why or Why not?
2. Find the original speech and compare the elements that are omitted from the printed essay. Why leave out these parts? How does delivering a talk that has both personal material and notions from the world, at large, differ from writing for print?
3. Consider the structure of this essay. Make a brief outline of the topics the writer covers.
4. What is Franzen's thesis? What exactly is he defining?
5. How does Franzen link the pieces of this essay together? What type of transitional devices does he use?
6. Franzen starts with cell phones and ends with birds. Comment on the ending—is it effective?

Questions for Critical Thnking

1. Do you disagree or agree with Franzen's statement that techno-consumerism tells people that if you love someone you will buy stuff?
2. What sort of person does Franzen make himself out to be? How does that persona help/hurt his message about love?
3. Is Franzen taking the Facebook definition for *liking* something the wrong way? How do you see the Facebook definition of *like*?

Style Practice: Imitation

Write a paragraph with your definition of *like*, *love*, or *friendship*. Use Franzen's technique of finding the word defined outside yourself first—in advertising, media, science, or literature.

WRITING & REVISION STRATEGIES

Three interactive sections will help as you write, revise, and think about the design of your essay of ideas.

- Writer's Notebook Suggestions
- Peer Editing Log
- Revision Checklist

Writer's Notebook Suggestions

These short exercises are intended to jump-start your thinking as you begin to write your essay of ideas.

1. Write a paragraph about a regional or ethnic food most people don't know about. Describe the meaning of the food to the region or culture where you find it.

2. Explain the meaning of a family ritual that is important to you. Describe the ritual in a way that implies its importance in your family.

3. Describe a process that most people know about (how to brush your teeth, brew tea, change a lightbulb) to a space alien.

4. Explain the symbolic meaning of a piece of clothing.

5. Define the term *rite of passage* as it might apply to your life.

6. Write a scene that reveals a new way of thinking about something—a reversal that comes from disappointment or betrayal.

7. Write a scene that reveals a small truth you realized.

8. Take a term most people take for granted (for example, *mother, father, girlfriend, boyfriend, baseball, hockey*) and redefine it in your own personal way.

9. Explain a scientific concept to a group of fourth-graders (for example, why some of them have blue eyes when their parents don't).

10. Find a concept that has recently changed in meaning and discuss how you think the change came about.

11. Write about an expression that's taboo to you. Why is it so?

12. Choose a word from a profession, hobby, or other particular field of interest to you—a term most people will not know—and explain its meaning.

Peer Editing Log

As you work with a writing partner or in a peer editing group, you can use these questions to give helpful responses to a classmate's essay of ideas and as a guide for discussion.

Writer's Name: _____

Date: _____

1. Underline the essay's "synthesis" thesis. Make suggestions to strengthen it by rewording it or placing it elsewhere. If you think it might be improved, make suggestions.

2. Identify the paragraphs that present the personal experience portion of the definition. Are there ways the writer can strengthen these scenes with techniques from fiction writing, such as dialogue, description, or sensory details?

3. Identify the places where the writer brings in outside sources. Are these sources credible? Do they need more attribution?

4. Does the writer synthesize or show how the sources are linked by using effective transitions? Can you suggest places where the transitions could be strengthened?

5. Put brackets around the conclusion. Is it successful in linking the personal experience to the outside sources? If not, can you suggest ways the writer might clarify the connection?

6. Underline any language that seems awkward or confusing. Put check marks next to any language you find particularly fresh and appealing.

Revision Checklist

As you do your final revision for your essay, check to make sure that you

- answered the question, What do I mean when I say_____?
- incorporated the answer in a clearly stated definition thesis
- wrote an engaging and focused section on your personal experience
- used narrative techniques of dialogue and sensory detail to add color and interest to the personal experience
- used outside sources—readings, films, expert opinions, and so on—to extend your definition
- attributed your sources clearly
- blended the "showing" and the "telling" with clear transitions that synthesized the sources and ideas
- wrote in a personal yet not informal voice
- concluded by clarifying the connections between your personal experience and the outside sources

WRITING TO INFORM

Tolga Akmen/Anadolu Agenc/Getty Images

WRITING SHORT ARTICLES

THE EXPLAINER

I have made this letter longer than usual, only because I have not had the time to make it shorter.

—BLAISE PASCAL, LETTRES PROVINCIALES (1657)

A fact about human nature—that people are inherently curious about details—explains the popularity of a regular feature called "Explainer" on the online magazine *Slate*. People ask questions (How do you fake your own death?), and the Explainer provides basic answers (*First, buy a boat*), along with larger implications, such as revealing patterns in behavior or historical context or scientific phenomenon. These posts essentially take a magnifying glass to the tiny subject and fill in the details, answering *how* or *when* or *why*. The answers might move the questions beyond trivia (*Why do we drink lemonade in hot weather?*) and into explaining chemistry (*Acidity has a role in quenching thirst.*). Sometimes looking at what seems like a random question (*Which is safer—prison or the streets? Prison.*) opens a window to larger implications about society, ethics, power, gender, or commerce.

Explainers are one version of a type of short article that is the bread and butter of magazines and websites. Sidebars accompany news stories and act as an *aside* would in a play, giving some insight into a topic that is a fragment of the news subject. The announcement of a new, pernicious disease might direct us to the details of the contagion, but a sidebar might tell us *"Who gets to name new diseases?"* Likewise, when a series of destructive tornadoes might be the subject of the news, a curious writer might ask *"How did people describe the sound of a tornado before the advent of trains?"* (*A peculiar moaning sound*), while explaining something about our language that enables us to discuss fear and danger.

193

PROCESS PLAN

Prepare

- Read widely to see what's in the news, or what questions need some answers.

- Choose a topic and pose it as a question. Ask: "Why? How? When?" and "So What?"

- Write your explanatory thesis: the answer to your question.

- Collect "sticky stuff": interesting material that sticks in your reader's mind and defends your thesis.

Draft

- Introduction.
- Pose the question.
- Begin with your explanatory thesis (deductive organization) or lead the reader to it (inductive organization).
- Body.
- Explain the answer to your question.
- Provide your reader with context for this topic.
- Integrate your sources into the body of the article.
- Conclusion: Write an ending that restates or makes a comment on the main subject. Be sure you have answered the question you posed.

Revise

- Add good transitions.

- Check your obligation to your reader: Do you have enough evidence to back up your thesis?

- Cut any extra words: Combine sentences and make sure all adjectives and adverbs are necessary.

Understanding
the Writing Project

SHORT WRITING is deceptively difficult. You don't want to bore your reader with too much detail, but you want your short article to answer the question fully. Having a unique idea—one that hasn't been covered already—will help you gain the attention of readers on the Web or in print.

Your style also counts: you just don't have the luxury of extra words or repetition to make your points. Your writing should be as authoritative as it is reader-friendly. Curious readers are looking for a little entertainment with their information—facts, but without the stuffiness of an encyclopedia or dictionary. Always think you are one person explaining something to one other person. Allow your own voice to shine through.

ASSIGNMENT Write an explainer answering a question raised by some recent event or write a short article about something most people do not know about—a new discovery or trend, or perhaps a bit of insider's knowledge of a subject. Bust a myth or confirm one, dig into something commonplace, reveal something overlooked, and show your readers what they've been missing.

As you begin to think about subjects, consider your purpose. Imagine that your article puts a magnifying glass on a little-known piece of the world. The view you offer should be tightly focused and intensely detailed. Using multiple sources—print, online, and observation and interview when you can—helps you develop original articles. Compressing and combining the details from your research provides a brief but still rich view of this small slice of life.

Your first task in writing an explainer is something akin to "turning over the closest stone" to see what's underneath, to look at the commonplace, or do the opposite, dive into something that's unique or new, take another tack and try myth busting—or myth confirming. In short, explore. At first, don't rule out any topics. Begin by asking questions: *Why do dolphins beach themselves? Was Dracula real?* At the end of your research and writing, you will take your reader into small, previously unexplored corners of the world. There, you'll be able to explain something larger by looking closely at something "tiny."

Short Article

BRIAN PALMER

Why Is There So Much Salt in Processed Foods? Because Salt Is Delicious

THE INSTITUTE of Medicine concluded this week that there is no reason for people to keep their sodium consumption below 1,500 milligrams per day, as had been previously recommended for most adults. The panel's approved level of 2,300 milligrams per day, however, is still far below the average of 3,400 milligrams of sodium that Americans consume per person per day, much of it from processed foods. Why do processed foods have so much salt?

Because salt tastes great. Salt is often lumped together with fat and sugar, two other ingredients that humans find irresistible. (Michael Moss' recent best-seller, *Salt Sugar Fat: How the Food Giants Hooked Us*, has an excellent discussion of the power of salt.) But one of those things is clearly not like the others. Sugar and fat are indicators of high caloric content, something that would have helped our ancestors survive. Salt is required only in small amounts, so it's not entirely clear why we love it so much, or why we love so much of it. But we clearly do. Young people love salt. Old people love salt even more. Infants crave salt. It's not surprising that food manufacturers pile salt into their products.

Commercial food-makers, indisputably, use more salt than we do at home. Almost all of the top sources of sodium in the American diet—including meat pizza, white bread, cheese, hot dogs, ham, ketchup, white rolls, and flour tortillas—come from foods typically purchased in prepared form. There are several possible explanations for this. After years of nagging from public health experts, home cooks may hold back on salt for dietary reasons. Some commentators believe that packaged foods have higher salt content because they are otherwise bland, perhaps due to a lack of freshness. That's possible, but the Explainer is skeptical. There's little evidence that salt-free processed foods would be otherwise flavorless, and, besides, restaurants that use fresh foods also salt their foods well above home-cooking levels.

The more likely explanation is the quasi-addictive effect of high salt consumption. Food sellers don't just want you to like their products, they want you to crave them in increasing quantities. The more salt a person eats, the more salt he or she wants. In 2011 researchers at Philadelphia's Monell Chemical Senses Center, the source of many salt consumption studies, found that

Slate.com, May 15, 2013.

8 WRITING SHORT ARTICLES

babies who eat salty, starchy foods almost immediately begin to crave salt at higher levels than their salt-naive peers. There are even indications from rodent studies that a mother's salt intake, transmitted to her baby in her breast milk, can affect its salt cravings later in life. Perhaps even more importantly for the processed food industry, people who lower their sodium intake for just two to three months experience a measurable decrease in salt cravings. (Jonathan Swift was aware of this effect: After a prolonged period of salt deprivation, the main character in *Gulliver's Travels* becomes convinced that salty foods are merely a way to sell alcohol.)

In 1937 Irish-born physician Robert Alexander McCance convinced several colleagues to join him on a salt fast and to further reduce their internal sodium levels with heavy exercise and sweating. After several days, they had very little appetite and their experience of flavor completely changed. McCance claimed that rinsing his mouth with sodium restored the taste of food, suggesting that salt is an important contributor to our interest in any foods, not just those with high salt levels.

Questions for Critical Thinking

1. How does the headline attract attention for this short article? Does the writer fulfill the promise in the headline?
2. What are the most interesting pieces of information that you take from this explainer? How would you explain the gist of this piece to a friend?
3. "Food sellers don't just want you to like their products, they want you to crave them in increasing quantities." Write a response to post on this explainer's comment section.
4. What does this writer do to engage you? To gain your trust?
5. Which sources does the writer use to explain the claim?

THE **BIG IDEA**   **Writing an Explanatory Thesis**

Short expository articles should surprise as much as they inform. Their point, or thesis, should be interesting and fresh. If you hold your topic selection to the criteria that the subject should explain some little-known phenomenon or place that is new to readers, you need to prove to your readers that the subject is worthy of their time.

In making your writing appeal to readers, the first steps are to make sure

1. your article has a thesis statement worthy of proof
2. you have enough detail to back up your thesis

This detail comes from research in print and online sources and from people you interview—practitioners and experts. The detail might be statistics, facts, or quotations that reveal opinions or recount experiences.

Your subject might be new or unfamiliar to your reader, but you should have command of it. It is important that you understand it inside and out, so that your explanation is easy to understand. You need to examine the context for the subject— where it fits in with others, how it works, what its significance is. After you do that kind of thinking, you can form a theory that helps you explain the relevance of the subject. The theory does not have to be original, but it does need some defending. A good thesis is one that—only through a body of evidence—will seem reasonable and convincing to a reader.

THE BIG IDEA in an explanatory article reveals **WHAT** and a **SO WHAT** in a single sentence.

The **WHAT** of the Salt article: Processed food has a great deal of salt.

The **SO WHAT**: Salt is quasi-addictive.

The *thesis*, or the concise statement that sums up the WHAT and the SO WHAT is:

> Food sellers don't just want you to like their products; they want you to crave them in increasing quantities.

This is a *theory*, or a *claim*, because, although it may be true, it is not a fact that is self-evident, such as saying that the chemical makeup of salt is NaCl(sodium chloride.) A *thesis*, instead, is big enough to bear the questions: What do you mean? How is what you're saying reasonable, believable, credible?

In a short article or an explainer, the thesis needs to be focused tightly enough to have those questions answered in just a few paragraphs.

What Should I Write About? Ways of Looking at a Subject

With any writing, the most difficult part is getting started. But the old maxim, "How do I know what I think until I see what I say?" can direct your writing process toward generating ideas. Several "systems" for looking at a topic can help you examine where your subject fits in the world—its context. Asking questions about the subject will help you see its significance and relevance to a reader, and will also help direct your research.

METHOD OF INQUIRY: QUESTIONS TO ASK ABOUT YOUR SUBJECT

1. Separate the subject into parts. What are its individual parts?
2. Put the subject into a category. How is your subject different from the others in the category?
3. Has your subject changed over time?
4. How can the subject be "measured" or "calculated"?
5. What is a metaphor for your subject?
6. Can you describe a process involved with your subject?
7. Describe it. How can you look at your subject from different points of view—magnified, cut into cross sections, from far away, from an outsider's viewpoint?

PRACTICE 8.2

Using Methods of Inquiry Questions

Choose a topic you might write about and use questions about your subject to generate interesting ways to write about your topic. ■

Research Paths: Use Primary and Secondary Sources

To begin your search for facts, and even as a part of your brainstorming, you will probably do a keyword search on the Internet. Of course, you should take care in evaluating sources, and be diligent in taking good notes along the way. (For more on

evaluating sources and taking good notes, see Chapter 15, "Research.") Most importantly, do not limit yourself to one source. Using only a dictionary or an encyclopedia for the question about whether a tomato is a fruit or a vegetable, you might miss some interesting information. For example, the Supreme Court ruling in 1893 that declared tomatoes would be classified as fruits can be found on a website. On the other hand, you might find a website that offers information that contradicts authoritative sources and would therefore not be a good source. With Web material, it is best to find at least two sources that agree on information.

When you use sources in your article, be sure to provide clear and accurate attribution. For a short article, you might integrate the source material and the attribution into the text of the article. For example, you might write, "The *Encyclopaedia Britannica* defines *tomato* as 'any fruit of the numerous cultivated varieties of *Lycopersicon esculentum*, a plant of the nightshade family (Solanaceae); also, the fruit of *L. pimpinelli folium*, the tiny currant tomato.'"

Remember to keep track of your sources as you find them. (Academic essays call for a complete citation of sources on a Works Cited page. This source from a Works Cited page uses *Modern Language Association (MLA)* style. For more on ways to keep track of your sources, see Chapter 15, "Research," and Chapter 16, "Documentation," for guidelines on citing and documenting your sources.). If you can, talk to people with experience in or knowledge about the subject area. These primary sources can provide examples and illustrations that you will not get anywhere else.

PRACTICE 8.3

Finding Sources and Integrating Research

Choose one of the following topics, then list at least one website, one print source, and one expert whom you might consult to get information.

- Pencils
- Hashtags
- Synthesizers
- The gold standard
- Matchbooks
- Lightning strikes

Sticky Stuff and Your Obligation To Your Reader

Charles Fishman, author of "The Scoop on Disney's Dirty Laundry," on page 204, offers two bits of advice about writing good short articles:

> Writing short is harder for a simple, basic reason. Every piece of writing needs a beginning, middle and end. It needs a point. It needs expository information. That's the basic bones of any story. In a short space, though, it can be hard to get in the color, fun, telling detail, a good anecdote, humor, drama. My goal is always to make sure a piece has as much of that kind of material in it— what I think of as the "sticky stuff," the bits people might remember, might tell a friend, while also fulfilling whatever obligation the piece must fulfill for readers.

Visual Literacy: Finding a Thesis in a Photo Essay

PHOTO ESSAYS "show different aspects of a topic visually." The photos here imply notions about Comic Con and the Cosplay phenomenon. Do some research about the history and development of Cosplay and Comic Cons that occur throughout the world. Look for details about the culture, the practitioners, or any developments or changes in the phenomenon over time or in different places.

- Write a caption that might accompany this photo essay.
- Make a statement that reveals a bigger picture about a trend, an underlying pattern, or the role of "role-playing" in entertainment or a lifestyle.
- Create your own photo essay (with five to seven photographs) that explores and reveals several noteworthy aspects of a place, an organization, or an event. Think about something local—for example, write about an attraction that might be well known to you but not well known nationally—a music festival that has its own spin or flavor, or perhaps an organization that serves a specific purpose. Use your photographs to expand your viewer's impression of the "character" of the topic, its causes or effects, its tone and importance to individuals participating.
- Write the thesis that would accompany your photo essay.

Tania/A3/contrasto/Redux

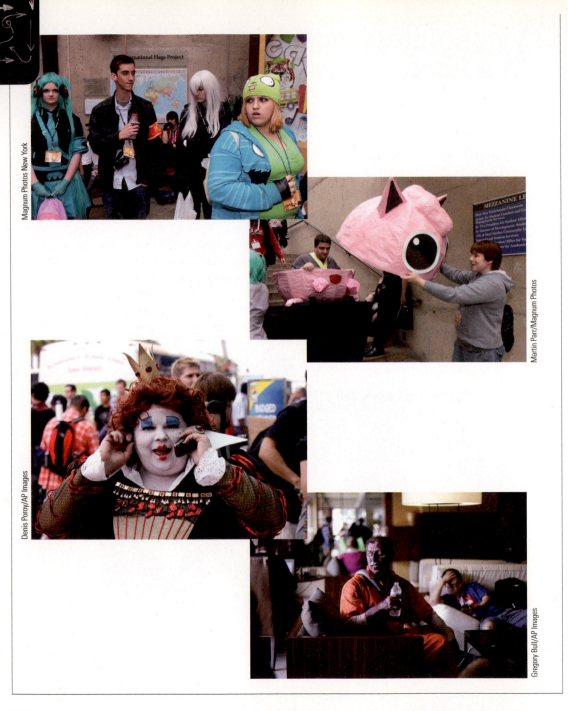

Magnum Photos New York

Martin Parr/Magnum Photos

Denis Poroy/AP Images

Gregory Bull/AP Images

Organize Your Thinking: Structure Your Writing

After you have done your brainstorming and researched your topic for good details and accuracy, it is time to start organizing your points. Two possible ways to organize your writing are deduction and induction.

Deduction or Induction?

A common way to organize your points is to include your thesis early in the article, shortly after introducing the general subject, and then to follow it with proof that it is a reasonable theory. This is *deductive* organization. Beginning with the thesis can be useful for grabbing the readers' attention. In the article about salt that opens this chapter the author states upfront that adding salt to food makes people crave more: "Food sellers don't just want you to like their products, they want you to crave them in increasing quantities." If you continue to read, you will find out the reasons this theory is valid.

Charles Fishman, on the other hand, uses *inductive* organization in his article about Disney's laundry (page 204), laying out his collection of facts and then announcing what they add up to: his thesis or theory about how all of Disney is at the mercy of the laundry.

Mystery drives inductive reasoning, with the reader following along like a partner in detecting the point to the pattern.

The Introduction

Keep in mind your obligations to your readers. The beginning, or introduction, of a short article should announce the general topic and provide something "sticky"—an unusual fact, a telling detail, or vivid description—to hook the readers. This "sticky" material, as Charles Fishman describes it, is something that stays with your readers—something your readers might mention later to a friend. You promise your readers more of that, if they continue, and that is why they do.

The Body

The body of your short article contains the substance of your piece: the explanation, evidence, or support for your thesis or main claim.

The Conclusion

The conclusion for most writing restates the main subject, but in a short article, you do not have words to waste. Often the writer looks for an interesting way to remind the readers of the subject, or relates an anecdote—or a fact—that may extend the readers' thinking about the topic. In concluding his answer to why there is so much salt in processed food, Palmer relates an experiment done in 1937 that suggests that salt raises people's interest in all food, adding some interesting information beyond the specific question he is answering.

PRACTICE 8.4

Strategies for Conclusions

Look at the concluding paragraph in any of the essays in this chapter.

- Identify the strategy the writer uses in the conclusion.

- Write an alternative ending to the essay using a different strategy. ■

DIY MEDIA AND DESIGN

PechaKucha (20 × 20)

PechaKucha nights give ordinary people an opportunity to explain something they do, create, or study to their neighbors and friends, often in restaurants, bars, town halls—even public parks. PechaKucha (translated from Japanese as "chit-chat") began in 2003 in Tokyo for beginning architects to show their work to the public. Soon the format went viral. Now you can find PechaKucha nights in cities and towns all over the world, some of which you can see online. A PechaKucha event is a fun way to practice the art of concise presentations.

Create your own PechaKucha presentation with 20 PowerPoint slides and a script that includes 20 seconds of talk for each slide. (The whole presentation should take 6 minutes and 40 seconds.) Explain something you do or know well in a way that your audience will find fresh and fascinating.

READINGS

Short articles help readers understand a topic they find useful, new, surprising, related to something in current thinking or in the news—or just plain interesting. The three readings that follow demonstrate the range of topics—and approaches—you can find in short articles. They reveal the surprising and unglamorous world of Disney's laundry operation, explore the possibility that dolphins commit suicide, and debunk the contemporary image of vampires being "attractive, tormented and misunderstood."

The Scoop on Disney's Dirty Laundry
Charles Fishman

Charles Fishman wrote this short article for the Orlando Sentinel's *Sunday magazine. He implies as much as he "tells" in this article about the inner workings of Disney World.*

THERE ARE no illusions in Ed Fox's shop at Walt Disney World. There are no animatrons, no goofy, grinning characters, no artificial cheer. Ed Fox's shop is where Disney comes clean—the laundry.

There's not much magic to it, just a lot of work: 400 people on duty 365 days a year, two full shifts a day, with a little linen left over for a third shift.

Disney's dirty linen gets done in a nondescript, two-story building the size of a city block. Labeled "Laundry and Dry Cleaning," it has a logo that looks at first like just a group of bubbles, but on reflection resolves itself into a soapy Mickey head.

Inside, the place looks truly un-Disneyesque—industrial, in fact. There is no air conditioning, no one wears a uniform, the staff contains a good measure of immigrants and many of the signs on the walls contain instructions in Spanish.

The machines look vaguely familiar, except for their size. The clothes dryers are the size of dump trucks. The machine that irons and folds 915 queen-sized sheets an hour looks like a printing press. The washers hold 900 pounds of laundry at a time, computers control the mix of detergents.

The laundry uses 400,000 cubic feet of natural gas a day and 350,000 gallons of water. It is one of the biggest facilities in the country.

Every towel, napkin, bed sheet, table cloth, pillow case, bath mat—every piece of linen used in any Disney hotel or restaurant, every uniform or costume used in the Magic Kingdom or Epcot or Pleasure Island—they all come here.

Every sheet in every occupied room is changed every day; every employee gets a freshly dry-cleaned uniform. Designed, as Fox says, for the 1,500 hotel rooms and "one little Magic Kingdom" that existed when Disney first opened in 1971, "we're just bursting at the seams now."

His people clean up after 6,100 hotel rooms and three big parks, plus a couple of smaller ones. When Disney planners talk of new facilities, all Fox sees is more linen and no more capacity.

The operation is full service. Drivers pick up dirty laundry and return clean laundry to 260 locations at Disney on 13 pick-up routes.

The facility is divided roughly in half—laundry on one side, dry-cleaning on the other.

During a holiday week, the facility did 818,000 pounds of laundry. Incoming laundry is dumped onto a conveyor belt, which takes it to a second floor sorting room. It returns to the first-floor washing area through stainless-steel chutes that dump dirty linens directly into washing machines. Eventually, closet-sized carts filled with pristine linens wait to be trucked out.

"The clothes dryers are the size of dump trucks."

Dry cleaning is also sorted first, according to color and pattern and the kind of attention it needs. The dry-cleaning ranges from ball gowns and full-dress tuxedos to chefs' hats and emergency medical technician uniforms to Mickey Mouse costumes. Much of it makes its way through the laundry on hangers dangling from elaborate moving conveyors, about 25,000 pieces a day.

All of Disney is at the mercy of the laundry. According to Fox, most hotels, restaurants and parks have no more than a four-day supply of their laundry. To forestall disaster, three maintenance men work full-time each shift.

Last summer, when a machine that provided heat to dry and iron sheets broke down, Fox says, "I just started calling every laundry guy I knew on the phone, and the first one who said yes got

all my business." He ended up trucking Disney's sheets to Space Coast Hospital in Rockledge.

Among the secrets revealed amid Disney's dirty laundry is that the sheets you sleep on and towel off with in your suite at the new, luxe Grand Floridian may have last done duty in the most ordinary room at the Contemporary.

At Disney, all linens are created equal.

Questions for Rhetorical Analysis

1. What is the writer's larger purpose in explaining Disney's laundry operation? What's his "big idea"?
2. Identify the thesis statement in this essay. What details support this thesis?
3. Earlier in the chapter, Fishman talked about the "sticky stuff," the details that stick in the reader's mind. Give some examples of details that have sticking power.
4. The research for this essay is from primary sources, direct observation, and secondary sources. Find examples of each kind of research. Is any kind of research more interesting to you as the reader? Why do you think Fishman cites so many numbers?
5. Reread the last two paragraphs. What techniques does the author use in the conclusion? Is it an effective ending?

Questions for Critical Thinking

1. How is this essay a "scoop"? What do you find out that is surprising or newsworthy?
2. The opening paragraph shows the reality behind the illusion created at the "Magic Kingdom." What other topics might lend themselves to this kind of exploration?
3. "At Disney, all linens are created equal." What else is created equal at Disney? What isn't?

Style Practice: Imitation

Describe a behind-the-scene view from some event you attended—a circus, a concert, a dance, a lecture. Show the contrast between the audience's experience of the event and your insider knowledge.

Do Dolphins Commit Suicide?

Matthew Hardcastle

Matthew Hardcastle wrote this explainer in his graduate Science Journalism class. The explainer was later published by BUNews.

THIS SUMMER, hundreds of dolphins beached themselves along the coast of New England. The National Oceanic and Atmospheric Administration (NOAA) has tentatively pegged the cause of this particular dolphin die-off as a viral outbreak. Yet even in normal years, dozens of dolphins around the country become stranded in shallow water or beach themselves on shorelines. Are these often

BU News Service, September 22, 2013.

sickened or injured animals simply disoriented, or are they making a conscious decision to leave their tightly-knit social groups and die on the beaches? In other words, do dolphins commit suicide?

Quite possibly.

From what we know of dolphin intelligence, they certainly have the capability of choosing to die. According to Lori Marino, a researcher who studies the brains and behaviors of animals, we know that dolphin intelligence has a lot in common with human intelligence. By administering tests to captive dolphins using mirrors, props, and memorized tasks, researchers have proved that the marine mammals are self-aware, remember their past actions, and can even think about their own thoughts.

However, compared to humans a dolphin's sense of self-identity is more tightly tied up to its social identity. In the wild, this dolphin groupthink can result in one sick leader beaching its entire pod. To swim away from the shore and defy the will of the group would go against their core instincts. If rescuers push healthy dolphins back to sea while their leader remains on shore, the dolphins will usually just re-strand themselves.

Dolphin neurology also differs significantly from humans. The sophisticated echolocation system that dolphins use to hunt also serves as a constant form of communication, transferring personal information at a greater rate than do our sluggish human voices. A dolphin's limbic system, the part of the brain that controls emotions, is also highly developed. Marino describes dolphins as hyper emotional; when they are hunted by fishermen, simple panic can send dolphins into cardiac or neurological shock.

A dolphin's mix of intelligence, strong social bonds, and hyper-emotionality can backfire in the form of destructive behavior. Dolphins in captivity, even those born into it, are deprived of social interaction with their own kind, resulting in high levels of stress. Captive dolphins may ram their heads into the sides of their tank or aggressively lash out at other dolphins.

> "From what we know of dolphin intelligence, they certainly have the capability of choosing to die."

When a stressed dolphin jumps out of its tank, is it making a decision to end its life? When a sick dolphin beaches itself, is it a selfless act made for the good of its social group? It's hard to say. A test has not yet been developed to show whether dolphins understand the permanence of death or their own actions.

However, Marino said, dolphins can and do lose the will to live. If two dolphins in captivity become close companions, the removal or death of one will cause the other to spiral into despondency. The abandoned animal will stop eating and spend more and more time floating lethargically at the surface. At that point, it is only a matter of time before the dolphin dies of a broken heart.

Questions for Rhetorical Analysis

1. Does Hardcastle succeed in creating a voice that is both authoritative and reader-friendly? Support your judgment with a few examples.
2. What does the writer do in the introduction to engage his reader and raise interest in his topic?
3. What kind of sources does the writer integrate into this explainer? Are they credible sources?
4. Find the explanatory thesis, the big idea, in this piece. Is the piece organized inductively or deductively?
5. At the end, has Hardcastle supported his thesis? Is the conclusion convincing?

Questions for Critical Thinking

1. After reading this explainer, what would you tell a friend about whether or not dolphins commit suicide? What questions do you anticipate your friend might have? What other information would you need to convince your friend of your point of view?
2. Dolphins are often credited with having "a lot in common with human intelligence." What do you know about other animals that are seen this way?
3. Name other examples of "groupthink"—either in the animal or human world.

Style Practice: Imitation

Write a question or two about topics that you might want to explore that could be answered with "Quite possibly" as Hardcastle does in the opening of this explainer.

Dracula Was the Original Thug

Douglas Starr

Douglas Starr co-directs the Science Journalism Program at Boston University and writes about science, medicine and the environment. This article, published in the online magazine Slate, *followed the publication of his book* The Killer of Little Shepherds: A True Crime Story and the Birth of Forensic Science.

VAMPIRE MOVIES and TV shows are the rage nowadays—perhaps because their heroes are attractive, tormented, and misunderstood, which is how many young viewers see themselves. But the original Dracula was not quite so attractive. In fact, he was the very model of a thug.

When Bram Stoker wrote the novel *Dracula* in 1897, people were in a panic about crime. They had difficulty understanding why—in an era blessed with prosperous empires, flourishing arts and sciences, and a burgeoning consumer culture—crime rates were rising throughout Europe and the United States. For answers they turned to science, itself one of the glories of the Victorian age.

One popular theory, devised by the Italian psychologist Cesare Lombroso, was that criminals were born that way. Lombroso spent his career searching for the roots of criminal behavior, interviewing and examining thousands of living criminals and dissecting the brains of thousands who had been executed. One gloomy day in December 1871, he found what he was looking for. He was conducting an autopsy of the notorious robber Giuseppe Villella when he noticed an unusual malformation: a small hollow at the base of the skull under which was an enlarged portion of the spinal cord. He had never seen this before in human beings, only lower animals and certain "inferior races."

The inspiration struck him like lightning: Criminal behavior was not something people learned but a malformation they were born with.

Lombroso dissected hundreds more brains and claimed to find the defect in most of them. Lombroso's observations and statistics were notoriously sloppy, but to his mind his theory fit perfectly with the most advanced science of the day. Only a decade earlier, Paul Broca, the father of neurology, had discovered that damage to a particular part of the brain caused an inability to form words. Wouldn't it also stand to reason that a malformation of a different part of the brain could lead to criminal behavior? He borrowed from Darwin's theory as well, or at least as interpreted in the late 19th century. If people evolved from primitive beings, could there not be the remnants of a primitive being in each of us? Some scientists proposed that in some people those primitive traits not only survived but thrived, magnified by generations of defective blood lines.

All this led Lombroso to suggest the existence of a kind of a subspecies of human, which he called "Criminal Man." Possessed of congenitally criminal brains, these creatures roamed the modern world like savages misplaced in time, lacking any sense of civilized morality. "Theoretical ethics passes over these diseased brains as oil does over marble, without penetrating it," wrote Lombroso.

Criminal Men bore traits that went along with the more primitive brain, including insensitivity to pain and the inability to blush or feel shame. They also bore telltale physical characteristics—which Lombroso called stigmata—including lantern jaws, jug ears, and unibrows. Such people, ruled by their primitive instincts, had poor impulse control and a tendency toward violence.

Lombroso's theory became immediately popular, for it played into the era's mania for measurement and its fascination with the dark side of human nature. He served as an expert witness at trials, determining guilt not by the evidence from the crime scene but by analyzing the defendant's appearance. In one case, two brothers were accused of murdering their stepmother. After examining the defendants, Lombroso testified that one of them was "clearly the criminal type, exhibiting huge jaws, swollen sinuses, extremely pronounced cheek bones, a thin upper lip, large incisors . . . and left-handedness." The man was convicted.

Not everyone agreed. The French criminologist Alexandre Lacassagne felt that social conditions, not heredity, led to most criminal behavior. His group, called the French School or Lyon School (for the location of his institute), saw the criminal as a product of his environment, including factors such as family, education, and poverty. Someone might have a propensity to crime but the "social milieu" could either magnify or repress it. The two schools of thought waged battle for decades, a rivalry that marked the beginnings of the nature-nurture debate.

Yet it was much more convenient to blame criminals, not society. So for decades the field of "criminal anthropology" flourished among scientists and crime-fighters alike. Darwin's cousin, Francis Galton, who coined the term "eugenics" and introduced fingerprinting to Great Britain, used Lombroso's theories to create a crime-fighting manual. He collected dozens of photos of criminals, sorted them according to the crimes they had committed, and then used photo overlays to create composite prototypes of thieves, con artists, and murderers. It was a field guide to the identification of born criminals.

> "Criminal behavior was not something people learned but a malformation they were born with."

Lombroso's theory also fired the imaginations of philosophers and writers. The Hungarian philosopher Max Nordau, who in his landmark book *Degeneracy* condemned modern art and culture as retrograde, was a pal of Lombroso's and dedicated the book to him. Nordau felt that not only had certain individuals slid back on the evolutionary scale, but so had society, with its carnal pleasures and bohemian lifestyles. The characters in *The Strange Case of Dr. Jekyll and Mr. Hyde* exemplified the contrast between the civilized man and his primitive counterpart, albeit within the same body.

Which brings us to Dracula. While we can't say for certain whether Bram Stoker read any of Lombroso's 30 books or more than 1,000 papers, it's clear from the text that he was influenced by Lombroso's thinking. Consider this cluster of behavioral characteristics: "excessive idleness, love of orgies . . . craving of evil for its own sake, the desire not only to extinguish life in the victim, but to . . . drink its blood."

Sounds like a description of Count Dracula? It's actually from Lombroso's book *Criminal Man*.

Or consider this passage from *Dracula*, in which Van Helsing, the fictional Dutch professor who pursues the Count, asks the book's heroine, Mina Harker, to describe the villain. Harker has been bitten by the vampire and is gradually falling under his sway.

> "Tell us . . . dry men of science what you see with those so bright eyes," asks Van Helsing.
>
> "The Count is a criminal and of the criminal type," says Harker. "Nordau and Lombroso would so classify him."

In a 1975 annotated version of the novel, the scholar Leonard Wolf juxtaposes Harker's full description of Dracula with Lombroso's portrait of the criminal man:

> Harker: "His face was . . . aquiline, with a high bridge of the thin nose and peculiarly arched nostrils."
> Lombroso: "[The criminal's] nose on the contrary . . . is often aquiline like the beak of a bird of prey."
> Harker: "His eyebrows were very massive, almost meeting over the nose."
> Lombroso: "The eyebrows are bushy and tend to meet across the nose."
> Harker: " . . . his ears were pale and at the tops extremely pointed."
> Lombroso: " . . . with a protuberance on the upper part of the posterior margin . . . a relic of the pointed ear."

Given the evidence, maybe it's time for a fact-check on the vampire's image as presented to the TV-watchers of today. Tormented? Yes. Misunderstood? Maybe. Attractive? Not at all. The original Dracula was the embodiment of brute evil—much like his literary contemporary, Mr. Hyde.

But there's a lesson to be learned from today's pretty vampires. After all, aren't the real blood-suckers of today those nicely coiffed corporate types who wrecked our economy from their aeries on Wall Street? They don't look at all thuggish. It almost makes us long for the old Dracula, with his pointy ears and unibrow. What a relief it must have been to be able to recognize evil and run from it.

Questions for Rhetorical Analysis

1. The article was originally published on the online magazine *Slate*. Can you find any telltale signs that the author was thinking of an online readership?
2. Who would be searching on the Web for an article like this one? Describe who you believe is the intended reader.
3. Which key words might that reader use to find this article?
4. How does the writer connect his sources? Find the transitions.

Questions for Critical Thinking

1. Do some research and try to figure out when vampires got attractive.
2. The writer connects science and literature from the same time period. Can you connect something currently being discussed in science, sociology, psychology, or politics with a film or book or video game?
3. Do you find any evidence that directors still rely on physical characteristics that have origins in the kind of thinking Starr discusses here? If you think so, which films or movies might you point to as examples?

Style Practice: Imitation

Create your own parallel examples from two different sources to show their similarities, the way Starr does with the quotations from Harker and Lombroso.

WRITING & REVISION STRATEGIES

Gathered here are three interactive sections for you to use as you write and revise your short article.

- Writer's Notebook Suggestions
- Peer Review Log
- Revision Checklist

Writer's Notebook Suggestions

You can use these exercises to do some start-up thinking and writing for your short article.

1. Explain a process you are familiar with, or choose one of the following:

    - Ordering coffee at Starbucks
    - Finding the right seat at the movies
    - Composing a Facebook post

- Shopping for textbooks
- Taking a multiple-choice exam

2. Research the origin of the three-ring circus, and write a paragraph about it, using narration.

3. In three concise sentences, explain the historical background of any issue in the news today.

4. Explain an unusual way of making money that most people do not know about.

5. Compare bottled water with tap water in several paragraphs. Write for a general interest publication.

6. Report on a small but remarkable episode in your school's history.

7. Write several paragraphs about a particular video game.

8. Write the beginning of a short article related to sports. Choose your topic, or use one of the following:

- Explain the shape of a football.
- Describe the different tennis court surfaces.
- Report on the origin of mixed martial arts or parkour.

Peer Review Log

As you work with a writing partner or in a peer review group, you can use these questions to give useful responses to a classmate's short article and as a guide for discussion.

Writer's Name: _____

Date: _____

1. Identify the explanatory thesis (underline it). Does it reveal the focus clearly? Why? What might make it stronger?

2. What are the writer's obligations to the reader? What promises has the writer made in the opening of this piece?

3. Identify any development strategies the writer uses by making a note in the margin.

4. Who do you think is the audience for this article? In what ways are the strategies appropriate or inappropriate for this audience?

5. Do you understand the writer's explanation of the idea, process, event, person, or place? Put a question mark next to any point that you find confusing or that needs more explanation. What other information might you need?

6. List the main points of the article. Can you suggest other points the article might cover?

7. Where is the "sticky stuff"?

8. Does the writer have a sense of the purpose of the article—as a school assignment, an article, or a website? Identify any places that seem too formal or too informal for the purpose. Put a check mark next to any material that seems at odds with the formal or informal approach, and make a note.

9. How well does the author use transitions? Write T where the writer could use a transition or might change a transition. Write a brief note to the writer.

10. Does the article come to a satisfactory conclusion? How would you suggest that the writer improve the conclusion?

Revision Checklist

As you do your final revision of your short article, check to make sure that you

- wrote an engaging opening sentence
- stated your thesis clearly and accurately
- explained your point with "sticky stuff," details, descriptions, and quotations.
- used clear transitions keyed to the development strategies you used
- wrapped up your explanation in a clear concluding sentence or two
- acknowledged your sources

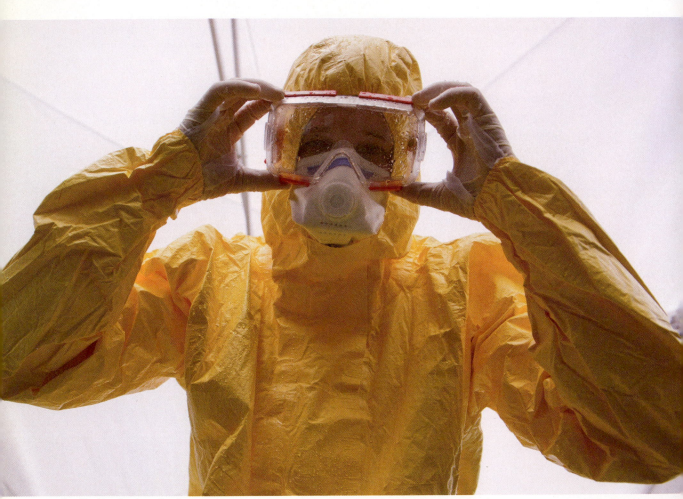

Timm Schamberger/Getty Images News/Getty Images

WRITING A REPORT

NEWS FOR PRINT, WEB, AND SOCIAL MEDIA

Journalism is literature in a hurry.
—MATTHEW ARNOLD

You might be casually looking at Facebook when you first get hints that a big story has broken—posts alluding to a toxic oil spill, a bomb scare, a flood, a scandal—some news event that peaks your interest. So, you flick over to Twitter or Instagram to get more details. On your favorite social media source, you find lots of information flying at you, fast and furiously. But what's fact and what's rumor, and what's plain wrong? How long does it take to weed through all the material and distinguish between the "citizen journalists" and the bona fide reporters? How much of what you are reading is misinformation or mistakes or even pranks?

Even less dramatic stories—a controversy over the cancellation of the musical *Spamalot* at your local high school, for example—can attract a readership eager for high-quality, reliable information. You'll find lots of opportunities to provide reliable, trustworthy, and useful information to eager readers online, in community newsletters, newspapers, on websites, and in social media. But, first, what will make your news worthy of a reader's trust?

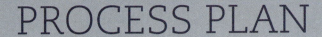

PROCESS PLAN

Prepare

- Choose a current topic and test it for newsworthiness.

- Interview people involved with the story, such as eyewitnesses and experts.

Draft

- Introduction (or lead)

- Write a summary of the main point, answering Who? What? Where? When?

- Incorporate the angle into the summary. How? Why?

- Body

- Arrange quotations so that your story is a kind of conversation about the news—with one quotation logically following another.

- Write sentences that set up each new topic in quotations and function as transitions.

- Conclusion: End with a quotation that offers the "human side" of the issue.

Revise

- Cut back on all unnecessary words—no phrases like "there are" or "it is."

- Make sure paragraphs are brief—limited to one idea and/or one quotation each.

- Check the use of a consistent objective voice: third person, past tense, and none of your own opinions.

Understanding the Writing Project

TODO EVERY second of every day somebody is reporting news: on Facebook, Twitter, and blogs; on television, radio, newspaper, and websites; and on broadcasts and narrowcasts going out over cable, the airwaves, and high-speed phone lines. The way we reach these stories is constantly changing, but what readers ask for in good news reports is not. They want writing that is fair, balanced, well-researched, reliable, and, probably more than anything, concise.

The concise form of newswriting, with a focus on abstracting the main point from a whole collection of information, will provide you with skills that serve you well in school. Often you are asked to provide a very brief overview of reading, write an annotated bibliography, or propose a complicated research project in a few paragraphs. In research papers this kind of overview is called an *abstract*. In summarizing literature, the summary is called the *précis*. This skill of summarizing is the cornerstone of all critical, analytical writing—and also at the heart of news reporting.

ASSIGNMENT Report on recent events or a trend that has significance for your community—school, town, group—and publish your story in a newspaper, newsletter, blog, or website. Write a story with a good headline that focuses and summarizes the news. Your report should include the following key features:

- ■ **The Lead**   Leads should include what happened, who was involved, where, and when.
- ■ **Details**   Details should follow the lead in order of importance.
- ■ **Quotations from Sources**   Eyewitnesses, people involved, and experts should tell the story for you.

Report

Katherine Donnelly

KATHERINE DONNELLY was asked to write a news report about some trend she observed on her campus. As a soccer player at a Division One school, she herself was part of the story. The challenge for her was to report the news without using her opinions. She uses primary sources—players diagnosed with concussions—as well as secondary sources to fill out the details of the story for her readers, and provide a balance of insights and opinions on the issue.

KATHERINE DONNELLY

Concussions: A Hidden, but Potentially Deadly Sports Injury Gets a Closer Look

AFTER BOSTON University researchers proposed, earlier this month, that a depression—inducing illness caused by frequent hits to the head in football games might be to blame for the death of a University of Pennsylvania student, coaches, trainers and students are speaking out against the danger athletes can cause themselves by keeping their concussions quiet.

The autopsy of 21-year-old Owen Thomas revealed that the UPenn student was suffering from Chronic Traumatic Encephalopathy—a brain disorder that has affected a number of NFL players—before his suicide. The disease, which can cause paranoia, aggression and dementia, is typically associated with athletes who have had long careers and experienced multiple concussions. Thomas's diagnosis makes him the youngest and first collegiate athlete on record to have suffered through CTE.

Reprinted by permission of Katherine Donnelly.

This discovery has more recently triggered fears that repeated blows to the head during the physical sport could put young athletes in high school and college at risk. According to a recent story from ESPN.com, every year more than 50,000 high school football players, between 14 and 18 years old, suffer from concussions, especially dangerous at this age because brain tissue is still growing.

BU Women's Soccer Coach Nancy Feldman said athletes commonly experience a concussion and pass off the pain as a headache that will eventually go away. She said she encourages her players to err on the side of caution when it comes to injuries.

Thomas—who would have been one of his team's senior captains this season—hanged himself in his apartment off of UPenn's campus five months ago. His mother told ESPN in a Sept. 14 story that he had never been formally diagnosed with a concussion and that he had not shown any obvious indicators of depression in the time leading up to his death.

"You can't take chances with injuries to the brain," Feldman said. "[Athletes] must seek medical attention right away or it will only get worse."

BU Athletic Trainer Erica Shaya pointed out that athletic departments at BU and beyond have begun to address the issue of head trauma and its consequences more adamantly in recent seasons. She said BU requires athletes to sign a specific concussion waiver before their seasons that makes the reporting of concussion symptoms and corresponding seeking of medical attention mandatory. "Some leagues actually have kids taking pre-season brain scans now," Shaya said. "All concussions are serious and may result in complications including prolonged brain damage and death."

Shaya added that athletes at BU must take and pass a computerized concussion test prior to the season in order to be eligible to play. The "Impact Test" organizes students' medical profiles, asks them questions about their health history and leads them through a series of neurophysiological tests, such as word discrimination, symbol and color matching, and design memory, to clear them for competition.

Some students say the testing is patronizing and needless. Junior Michelle Kielty—a member of the women's soccer team—said student athletes should be able to determine for themselves if their condition is worthy of medical attention.

"To me, it's kind of a waste of time," she said. "I think we can judge for ourselves if we feel the injury is that bad."

College of The Holy Cross senior and soccer player Jessica Pham said she supports the testing, but understands that some athletes have an "invincibility complex."

"I used to think the test was useless too," said Pham, who has experienced seven concussions as a collegiate athlete. "But after I kept getting headaches. I had to report it, and the test showed I had one."

Pham said she is now required to wear a protective headband known as a "Total 90" during practices and games to soften the blow another hit to the head might deal her. She said now that she has taken the steps to keep herself safe, she wants to help other students to understand that owning up to injury is not the end of the world.

"It's easy not to want to let your coaches down—your teammates down," she said. "You think you can overcome it."

"It just isn't worth it not to report it or at least get it checked out," Pham added. "What's missing one practice compared to a whole season? Or your life, for that matter."

Questions for Critical Thinking

1. With so much information available to readers and viewers, how do readers choose which stories they will read? What connects a person to a news story? What draws them to certain stories and not others? Who would be drawn to this story? Why?
2. What identifies a news story to you? Is it the tone? Word choice? How does this piece of writing seem different from other types of writing?
3. Do you trust this story? Why or why not?

The Rhetorical Situation

Purpose: News reports explain recent events or developments to interested communities.

Voice: The formal style of newswriting is authoritative and objective. Readers should not be able to detect personal opinion in the writing.

Audience: Interested readers might have a stake in the story—something to lose or gain from the outcome or cause of the events. Readers might also seek out the novelty of the story, the human interest or celebrity angle.

Media and Design: Social media is a way to spread the word about events or new developments in ongoing stories. Writing for blogs can be a way for writers to find a community that would be interested in their news reports.

THE BIG IDEA Thesis or Angle in a News Story

One of the paradoxes of a news report—like other kinds of reports (see the selection on abstracts on page 229)—is that, yes, it is a story, but, no, it is not written chronologically, at least not from the very beginning. This organization may seem at odds with the way people tell stories to their friends: "I had to go the store for some milk, so I drove over to the 7-Eleven and parked, and after I got my milk and got in line at the counter, I heard the crash outside." Instead, news stories flip right to the outcome: "Five people were seriously injured when a car being pursued by a police cruiser collided with a passenger van pulling out of the parking lot of a convenience store on the outskirts of town last night." So, why would I read the rest? Some readers won't, but others will be intrigued enough to want to find out all the details of the story.

The importance of the *news lead*—which is the journalistic term for the opening paragraph of a news story—is to summarize the whole event (to answer *who*, *what*, *where*, *when*)—but also to provide an angle. As a reporter, you slice into a story and decide what is most significant in these events. And although it seems at odds with the goals of keeping your own opinion out of the news story and remaining objective, the angle does provide a kind of interpretation—a way of understanding the news.

The photographer's comments on this photo: This photo was taken at Galvin Middle School. The assignment desk asked me to go see whether there were any photos of Acia Johnson that we could use because the trial in her death was about to start. The principal said, "Let me get her teacher. You probably want to talk to her." As the teacher opened this case dedicated to Johnson's memory, she was hunched over. Then she turned around and just started crying. At that point, there are two things going through your mind: Are you the human, compassionate person who's going to go over and say, "I'm sorry. Is everything all right?" And then the journalist in me kicks into high gear and says, "That's a great picture." Sometimes one wins over the other. —John Tlumacki

John Tlumacki/Boston Globe/Getty Images

Think about this lead:

> This Fall, Boston University is stepping up precautions for athletes in regard to head injuries.

In this lead, we have the *who, what, where, when* questions answered, in keeping with traditional news form, but we do not yet know why the university is stepping up precautions.

Consider how much this extra information shapes your understanding of the story:

> After Boston University researchers proposed, earlier this month, that a depression-inducing illness caused by frequent hits to the head in football games might be to blame for the death of a University of Pennsylvania student, coaches, trainers, and students are speaking out against the danger athletes can cause themselves by keeping their concussions quiet.

The photograher's comments: It was just a slow day. Oftentimes you're driving around trying to find something, and it can be frustrating because sometimes you just don't. So I headed down to Hull. I was driving down the street, and I noticed two trees moving on the sidewalk. I stopped and I shot [photographed] them. I introduced myself, and it turned out to be two 14-year-old boys trying to cause a commotion. It became clear to me what the picture was going to be when they came upon an unsuspecting person. —Bill Greene

The angle of the news story, the *how* or *why*, helps the reader see the context and significance of the story. With this additional information, we can see that the angle of this story is the danger of athletes keeping quiet about their concussions. Other reporters might choose other angles from which to report this story, perhaps focusing on the depression caused by head injuries. The angle reveals its newsworthiness.

Summary + How or Why = News Angle

So, if the story's lead and angle tell you what happened, why read on? Because the lead still has an element of mystery—it still needs more explaining.

Research Paths: Current, Accurate, and Reliable

Doing the reporting for news stories will be similar, in some ways, to the kind of research you probably have done for term papers, but it will be markedly different in other ways, as it will require you to deal with primary sources as well as secondary ones. In developing the story, you will rely on the observations, knowledge, and

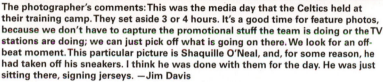

Jim Davis/Globe Staff/Boston Globe/Getty Images

The photographer's comments: This was the media day that the Celtics held at their training camp. They set aside 3 or 4 hours. It's a good time for feature photos, because we don't have to capture the promotional stuff the team is doing or the TV stations are doing; we can just pick off what is going on there. We look for an off-beat moment. This particular picture is Shaquille O'Neal, and, for some reason, he had taken off his sneakers. I think he was done with them for the day. He was just sitting there, signing jerseys. —Jim Davis

insights of experts, analysts, and eyewitnesses. Information from these sources is valuable in helping advance a reader's understanding, not just of what happened but also of its significance and context. Perhaps you will additionally be consulting academic, political, or legal documents, which can help ensure the veracity or accuracy of your report. This kind of direct, raw information is referred to as *primary source* material because it represents original research.

One example of a primary source would be a police report. News writers often have to gather stories from reports that offer a raw form of information: who reported a stolen bicycle, for example, where and when it was stolen, what the circumstances were, and so on. This theft might be part of a trend on college campuses, maybe the third stolen bike that week. If you were examining the police report as a primary source, you would have to decide whom to interview to bring in the human perspective and how to create a summary of the events from the raw data. The police report might look like the one on the next page.

Writers of news reports prefer to do their own research so they can be personally sure of its validity. Rarely do reporters rely solely on other stories, though occasionally looking at previous reports about the same issue can help reveal context. Knowing

Clark City Police

Clark City, Iowa 98765

Type: *Theft 2* **Reported Date/Time:** *October 23, 2015, 5:10 pm*

Reported By: *Browne, Gillian* **DOB:** *3/22/97*

Address: *23 Main Street*

Williams Hall

Clark City, Iowa

General Description: *Blue and white 21-speed road bicycle, bought in 2013*

Value: *$800*

Description of Incident: *Gillian Browne, freshman student at Clark City Community College, stated that on the above date, at the above time and location, she had left class at 1:00 pm on 10/23/15 and found her bicycle gone from the bicycle rack in front of Williams Hall. The bicycle was chained and locked with a kryptonite lock. Browne said that three other bicycles had been stolen from the same area during the past week.*

There are no suspects.

C—Closed

PRACTICE 9.1

Summary

Read this police report and write a summary of what happened. Revise your summary so it has the voice and style of a news story lead. ■

what was reported in the past can give you a sense of whether a recent event seems atypical or a continuation of a larger pattern of events or behaviors. These kinds of published accounts, called *secondary sources*, can be useful in helping you become expert on the topic you are writing about.

Just keep in mind that most of your reporting needs to be original reporting: You will talk to people. You will look for facts in the form of data from studies, books, and reports.

Newsworthiness

In choosing a topic for a news story, the first step is to figure out what makes a story newsworthy—of interest to readers of newspapers, newsletters, or websites. Ask yourself these questions as a first test for story ideas:

1. Is the story timely or about an issue that is currently "in the air"? A story about football is best reported leading up to or during football season, for example. Issues in the news such as concerns about the economy or up-and-coming elections can be timely.
2. How many people have a stake in the topic? Are many people involved? Does the issue have the potential to reach out to a big group?
3. Is the story interesting because it involves people from your community? Even a plane crash that is far away could be newsworthy if someone from your hometown is involved.
4. Is a celebrity involved? This does not just mean Hollywood stars, but your town's state champion wrestler or a well-loved teacher.
5. Is the story offbeat in some way? Report stories that many people would agree are worth reading about, like someone who sells her house to devote a year to community service in Africa. Not everyone does that. People would want to know why she did.

PRACTICE 9.2

Practicing Voice

Choose a fairy tale—*Cinderella, Hansel and Gretel, Little Red Riding Hood,* or *Snow White*—and rewrite it in the voice of newswriting. ■

Objectivity and Balance: Giving Readers an Unbiased Story

Balance is a term journalists use to describe the content of a news story. A close relative of *objectivity*, and certainly an ingredient in the voice of objectivity, balance refers to the inclusion of many points of view. Quotes that reflect opposing opinions help news writers avoid one-sided, biased writing. Showing your readers that you have reported the full spectrum of observations and points of view helps establish the voice of objectivity in your writing. Here are some specific "rules" of news voice and style:

1. Write in third person.
2. Use simple past tense.
3. Include careful citation of sources (names, titles of people, in-text citations of researched material).
4. Use phrases like "according to" and "as reported in" to help establish this voice of objectivity.
5. Never, ever include your opinion. Instead, include the opinion of others.

Since the early days of newspapers, the voice of newswriting has become an identifiable style with the information that readers find useful being reported and

PRACTICE 9.3

Looking for Worthy News

Evaluate the following for newsworthiness. If worthy, identify the place the story would be posted or printed:

1. When the university opened this fall, authorities discovered cracks in the walls of a brand-new dormitory.

2. A restaurant in your town has lost its liquor license.

3. The town little league Snack Shack accidentally burned down.

4. Students at your school are complaining about the student center closing on Sundays at 3 o'clock. ■

written in the same way: with a focus on what the readers want to know. In addition to following the cardinal rules just mentioned for establishing the objective voice, the credibility of your voice depends on addressing the readers' expectations that they will find verifiable information that is organized, succinct, and up-to-date. Accuracy is a high priority in news stories and one of the most significant draws for readers.

PRACTICE 9.4

Looking at the Angle

Choose two stories in today's news. Read them carefully and figure out their angles. See how many other angles you could approach the stories from. Generate at least three other angles for each story. Write a lead sentence for each of the new angles you created. ■

Tips on Sources for News

■ **Interviews** Take good notes and make sure you write down names and phone numbers. Steer the conversation into specifics whenever you can. Instead of asking yes-or-no questions, ask for stories and examples. Follow up on interesting answers by asking for more details. (More on interview tips can be found in Chapter 15, "Research.")

■ **Observations** Testimony from eyewitnesses is useful and interesting, but you can also use your own direct observations. Does that politician sometimes park illegally in a handicapped spot? Did the fire burn the whole house? Were protesters chanting obscenities? Use your observation to help set the scene of news events, noting telling details such as "the sea of green T-shirts at the rally" or the icicles clinging to the building after a fire.

■ **Documents** Marketing studies and governmental statistical reports and surveys are widely available online, but you have to be aware of the source. Increasingly, public legal documents such as deeds, lawsuits, licenses, and court records can also be found on the Web.

Visual Literacy: Eyewitness Accounts

PHOTOGRAPHS—and film and video—make everyone an eyewitness to an event. The best examples of photojournalism capture more than just the landscape of that moment, though. They also tell a story with characters and conflict. They make us all eyewitnesses. Read the captions that accompany these news photos and the other photos in this chapter to get the photographers' insights into what they were thinking.

Bringing Your Reader into the Moment with Photographs That Tell Stories

Create your own photograph to accompany a news event—a rally, a festival, a reading, a significant storm or heat wave, a grand opening are some examples. Write a caption to go along with your photo. Remember to ask the names of anyone in the picture—ask for spelling, age, and hometown.

Agoes Rudianto/Anadolu Agency/Getty Images

Indonesian Muslims offer prayers at a mosque on the first day of the Eid al-Adha in Surakarta, Central Java, Indonesia, on October 4, 2014. Muslims around the world celebrate the Eid al-Adha, also called the Feast of the Sacrifice, to commemorate Prophet Abraham's readiness to sacrifice his son as an act of obedience to God.

Using Any Kind of Camera, Go Out and Take Photos That Reveal Stories

Once you have collected three photos, bring them into class. Ask yourself: Which story does my photograph tell? On a sheet of paper you will keep secret, write down the narrative you intended to convey in the photograph, like the captions with the photos. Ask classmates to write down the story they detect in the photograph. Compare the reactions to your intention, and discuss the elements of the photograph that led your viewers to your intention—or away from it.

Pat Greenhouse/The Boston Globe/Getty Images

The photographer's comments: In this, the Cathedral of the Holy Cross, Cardinal O'Malley was saying a memorial Mass for the victims of the Haitian earthquake. I caught this woman at just the right moment. When I look at it, just the way her hands are held, I get a sense that she's shielding her face from the horrors of everything that happened, but with the rosary in her hands, it's revealing hope at the same time. She was singing a song. —Pat Greenhouse

Clear and Concise: Two Types of Summaries

When you write summaries and abstracts, you condense many words into few. You state the main point—"the bottom line"—in your own words, and leave out the details. To summarize an event, you would want to focus on the outcome and perhaps generalize about the causes and effects. In writing an abstract, which is a summary of a piece of report or analysis, you will state the overall conclusion.

The News Lead

A *news lead* is a concise summary of an event, with a sense of how or why the event has significance. One way to think of this summary is as an overview. Writing a good summary is particularly relevant in writing for the Web and social media where readers, or viewers, are less inclined to kick back and spend a long time with information. "Quick and hot" is one way experts describe digital information.

WRITE A SUMMARY: THE NEWS LEAD To practice your skills at writing a summary lead, read the following Toland Foods press release. Translate the press release into the style of news and write a concise, straightforward news lead that gives an overview of what happened and how Toland Food is reacting. Limit yourself to one to two sentences.

PRACTICE 9.5

Finding an Angle

Write down some possible angles that might come out of the facts of this story:

You go to a book signing at your campus bookstore and the author, who is originally from your hometown, has written a book about his hunting expedition in Africa. Animal rights advocates are picketing outside. People have trouble getting past them and into the store. Inside the store, eight people are waiting to have books signed. ■

RELEASE DATE: 1 NOVEMBER 2015

TOLAND FOODS ANNOUNCE REBATE ON EARTH'S OWN ORGANIC BROCCOLI

TOLAND FOOD DISTRIBUTORS ANNOUNCED today that they are extracting Earth's Own Organic Broccoli from markets, starting immediately. Consumers who had previously purchased Earth's Own Organic Broccoli are welcome to a full refund from vendors.

Broccoli purchased between the dates of October 1 and October 28, 2015, qualify for the refund.

"We are responding in a proactive fashion to the possible connection between our fresh vegetable products and Listeria, and the 47 reported cases of illness in the tri-state area. We always advise consumers to wash their hands before preparing fresh vegetables, to make sure their food preparation areas are sanitized and to cook food thoroughly," said Frederick Grimes, Toland Food spokesperson.

According to FDA standards, a product can be labeled "organic" if it is produced without pesticides and abides by water conservation standards set by the governmental organization.

"Since organic fruits and vegetables are not chemically treated in the same way conventional produce is, the opportunity for bacteria to grow is naturally higher than it might be," said Grimes. "We stand by our food. It's 100% organic, according to FDA requirements."

The Abstract

An *abstract*, similarly, is a summary, but a summary of a research paper. Like news leads, abstracts can function as a freestanding source of information, independent of the context in which they might appear. You can read a news lead and know what happened. You can read an abstract and understand the main claim of a research paper.

The following exercise on abstracts and the preceding one on the news lead will allow you to practice reading material and extracting a concise summary of its information.

WRITE A SUMMARY: THE ABSTRACT Read the following report and summarize the Institute of Medicine Committee's conclusions in a single sentence.

REPORT BRIEF • SEPTEMBER 2009

LOCAL GOVERNMENT ACTIONS TO PREVENT CHILDHOOD OBESITY

IN THE UNITED STATES, 16.3 percent of children and adolescents between the ages of two and 19 are obese. This epidemic has exploded over just three decades. Among children two to five years old, obesity prevalence increased from 5 percent to 12.4 percent; among children six to 11, it increased from 6.5 percent to 17 percent; and among adolescents 12 to 19 years old, it increased from 5 percent to 17.6 percent. . . . The prevalence of obesity is so high that it may reduce the life expectancy of today's generation of children and diminish the overall quality of their lives. Obese children and adolescents are more likely than their lower-weight counterparts to develop hypertension, high cholesterol, and type 2 diabetes when they are young, and they are more likely to be obese as adults.

In 2008, the Institute of Medicine (IOM) Committee on Childhood Obesity Prevention Actions for Local Governments was convened to identify promising ways to address this problem on what may well be the epidemic's frontlines. The good news is that there are numerous actions that show potential for use by local governments. Of course, parents and other adult caregivers play a fundamental role in teaching children about healthy behaviors, in modeling those behaviors, and in making decisions for children when needed. But those positive efforts can be undermined by local environments that are poorly suited to supporting healthy behaviors—and may even promote unhealthy behaviors. For example, many communities lack ready sources of healthy food choices, such as supermarkets and grocery stores. Or they may not provide safe places for children to walk or play. In such communities, even the most motivated child or adolescent may find it difficult to act in healthy ways.

Institute of Medicine, Report Brief of September 2009, "Local Government Actions to Prevent Childhood Obesity." Reprinted with permission.

The Body of the News Story: The Devil in the Details

Although the rules of newswriting are changing as media become more tailored to the desires of readers who sometimes prefer a more narrative approach, the tradition of telling stories without opinion is still valued by readers. No matter their leanings, readers will return to a source that offers original, fully detailed reporting that is fair and intelligent. But readers are after more than just facts or data when they choose to read a news story. They are interested in the characters, conflicts, and themes in those stories. Readers ask news writers to be observant and accurate, as their stories unfold mysteries and uncover important truths.

This is why quotations are a key ingredient in writing for this genre: quotations from people who understand the circumstances can help us understand the story. The quotations in a news story can even be thought of as a conversation about the topic—a kind of back and forth between knowledgeable people. Through eavesdropping on that conversation, our understanding of the story grows deeper. Because the news writer has done a good job gathering, selecting, and compressing information, we learn what the "experts" know. And we learn it quickly.

Using Paraphrase and Quotation

There are three ways to use material from interviews and other sources: full quotations, partial quotations, and paraphrases.

Full Quotations

Full quotations are usually a full sentence or two, transcribed exactly as they were spoken.

Example: "There is no evidence, at this point in time, that the accident was related to alcohol," said Ted Vargen, Wake County district attorney.

Use full quotations especially for well-phrased thoughts, memorable language, and when accuracy is crucial.

Partial Quotations

Selected material from an interview appears in a partial quotation, along with the attribution—the name of the source of the quotation.

Example: People became "hysterical, running out of the lab screaming," according to Marisol Boulanger, an eyewitness to the chemical spill in the chemistry lab on Tuesday.

Use a partial quotation to capture the power of a direct quotation even though the full sentence may be too long, ungrammatical, or confusing.

Both full and partial quotations are most useful when they are clear, provide insight into a character, or help vary the presentation of information in a paragraph.

PRACTICE 9.6
Class Press Conference

Use the following scenario to stage a press conference:

Your town is currently debating a new law that will outlaw text messaging while walking. The proposed penalty for text messaging while walking is $100 for the first offense, $250 for the second, and $500 for the third.

1. Five students from the class will answer questions. The interviewees should represent class members who have texted while walking, those who prefer not to text while walking, those who support the bill, and those who oppose it.

2. After the press conference, formulate a lead that summarizes student opinions of the bill.

3. Write a news story with quotations that reveal the various viewpoints on the issue. ■

Attribution for Quotations

- Always give the name of the source of the quotation, citing the speaker's full name and title.

  Example: "Pollution is causing asthma rates to soar," said Dr. Greg Spiro, head of pediatrics at Faith Hospital.

- Follow a full quotation with the simple verb *said*.

- If you quote the same speaker later, use just the person's last name in the attribution.

  Example: Asthma is a major public health issue, according to Spiro.

- As a rule, do not start quotations with the attribution, as doing this tends to slow the story down. Instead, state the quotation and then cite the speaker's name.

- If you are using a quotation that you found in another source, you must also give attribution to the other source, citing the publication in which it first appeared and identifying the speaker.

  Example: School board member Raisa Perez told the *Sun-Times* last Tuesday that more students would be left out of the free-lunch program if budget cuts continue.

- Use quotations from other printed sources sparingly and only if you absolutely must. If possible, replicate the quotation by calling the source directly or by substituting a similar source and quotation that you have collected.

Paraphrases

Restating a quotation in your own language can help clarify meaning and can be a good way to make information more concise, easier to understand, or more relevant.

Example: Students were instructed in how to handle accidents in the lab, according to Boulanger.

Paraphrase long or wordy quotations or quotations in which the language is fuzzy or vague, grammatically incorrect, or confusing.

Ending the News Story

The structure of the news story evolved because technology has allowed news to be passed around at lightning-fast speeds. For the same reason, news stories do not have "conclusions" that summarize or tie up all the loose ends. Earlier, as news was updated, the tops of stories changed and the bottoms were chopped off, leaving the other stories on a page intact. Instead of changing the whole page, printers were able to change one paragraph of a late-developing story. Since stories were written in descending order of importance, what came last would generally be the least important and the most expendable details. Traditionally, news writers have spent little time thinking about the ends of news stories for this reason. Stories seem to fade out rather than conclude. Nowadays, many news stories end with a quotation, fact, or statistic that shapes the impression of the story.

Tips for Headline and Social Media Writing

- Avoid complex sentence structure.
- Use active verbs.
- Cut back on articles (the, a, an).
- Use concrete language.
- Be specific. Mystery or vagueness won't attract readers.
- Use precise key words that would show up in Internet searches.

DIY MEDIA AND DESIGN

Although many people use social media simply for keeping up with friends, increasingly services such as Twitter and Facebook are becoming important channels for sharing news and information with communities of users who share your interest. For example, if you are a health writer in Louisiana with a special interest in reporting the latest developments in diabetes research, you can quickly and easily connect to a global audience of "followers" or "friends" by tweeting your news or communicating it through a status update on your Facebook page. Your readers are not general-interest browsers, but insiders—possibly doctors, researchers, or patients and their families. They are following you because you are a source of information on a subject they care about.

The best social media writing is taut and concise. Twitter posts—"Tweets"—are limited to 140 characters, which tends to dictate what and how you communicate. Like Twitter, Facebook limits the number of characters permitted in its status updates, but Facebook allows a much more generous 410 characters. Still, brevity and conciseness rule. Think of an extended headline with more detail, but still highly concentrated.

Social media writing is essentially like writing headlines. It must inform and grab the reader. A useful thing to keep in mind is the dictum laid down by old-school newspaper editors. They say when writing a good headline, think about how you would draw the attention of people in a crowded bar if you had to shout out a single sentence. Keep in mind that key words, or specific detail, will draw readers in more than vagueness.

Which of these would be better to shout into the crowd?

- *Four arrested at protest*
- *Plainfield cops arrest four students at tuition-hike protest*

The second is clearly better. It is more concrete, highlighting key details that clearly reveal the content of the story while still being short and to the point.

Let's say you are tweeting or writing a Facebook update on a page for people interested in a controversial plan to arm police in your town with body cameras. Which of these two is more informative?

- *City council will hear proposals on new controversial policing initiative* (65 characters)
- *Body cameras for police will be debated at Tuesday's city council meeting* (64 characters)

The second sentence reveals exactly what might interest them.

READINGS

The articles that follow report news stories that are geared mostly toward college students or administrators. As you read, see if you can imagine a larger, more general audience finding the topics "newsworthy."

Fantasy Football, Real Sanctions

Jake New

Fantasy sports might have real consequences for college athletes, according to this news article.

WITH THE FIRST WEEKEND of the season over, fantasy football fans are either celebrating an early victory or licking their virtual wounds this week—and college athletes are no exception. More than 70 percent of National Collegiate Athletic Association athletes participate in fantasy leagues.

The problem: Many of those athletes violate NCAA rules by doing so.

Twenty percent of NCAA athletes admit to participating in fantasy sports leagues with entry fees and cash prizes, according to a survey conducted last year by the NCAA. All but 1.8 percent of those athletes were men. More than 80 percent of athletes said they didn't realize joining a paid fantasy league was an NCAA violation. The survey's results were based on a representative sample of 23,000 students across 22 sports in all three divisions. If the survey included all NCAA athletes and the percentages held, the number of players violating the rules by entering paid fantasy leagues would be about 90,000.

> "Students can too easily become addicted to gambling, the NCAA states, and can be viewed by 'organized crime and professional gamblers as easy marks for obtaining inside information or affecting a game's outcome.'"

Citing mental, health, and safety issues, the NCAA forbids sports gambling of all types. Students can too easily become addicted to gambling, the NCAA states, and can be viewed by "organized crime and professional gamblers as easy marks for obtaining inside information or affecting a game's outcome." While gambling among college athletes has decreased in recent years, participation in sports wagering and fantasy leagues has gone up.

In 2013, the NCAA described the overall growth of sports wagering as "explosive."

Fantasy sports (a game where players build a virtual team of athletes and compete against each other based on statistics created by how the real athletes perform) have also exploded in popularity. More than 40 million North Americans now play fantasy sports, according to the Fantasy Sports Trade Association. They spend $15 billion per year on league-related expenses. Football is the most popular fantasy sport, and in 2013, $1.6 billion was spent in fantasy football leagues. Four years earlier, that number was just $800 million.

"Fantasy leagues are very popular among college-age students," said Jeffrey Derevensky, co-director of the International Center for Youth Gambling in Canada and a frequent author of NCAA studies about gambling. "The number of fantasy leagues are growing. Americans in particular are very much interested in college sports and athletes in general are really interested in other athletes. A lot of fantasy leagues are done right on campus. They don't have to go to a casino to get involved in a fantasy league. That makes fantasy sports an attractive thing for them."

Though the entry fees for the types of leagues many students join are typically small, the sanctions can be tough.

A college athlete participating in a league involving his own team or university—and there are college fantasy leagues—could permanently lose his eligibility as an NCAA athlete. An athlete participating in any paid league could sit out an entire season.

"The penalties are based on the circumstances of each case and the penalty guidelines set by each division," Emily James, associate director of public relations at the NCAA, said. "Fantasy sports league cases involving student athletes are processed by our student-athlete reinstatement team. Fantasy sports league issues have also been processed as secondary and major violations by our enforcement team."

So why do so many athletes enter paid leagues despite the risk?

Part of the reason is that many athletes don't think of fantasy sports as gambling. And, legally, it's not. Under the Internet Gambling Prohibition and Enforcement Act of 2006, fantasy sports are defined as a game of skill. But James said the NCAA considers fantasy sports to be sports wagering, as it defines sports wagering as "putting something at risk with the opportunity to win something in return." It doesn't matter if the athlete is paying a large fee to join a league on a website or $5 to join a league in his friend's living room: if there's money on the line, it's an NCAA violation.

Even some coaches and administrators don't realize that playing in paid fantasy leagues is against NCAA regulations, Rachel Newman Baker, the NCAA's former managing director of enforcement, said in a statement last year.

"Above almost anything else, a typical student-athlete does not want to negatively impact his or her team," said Newman Baker. "Considering that roughly 40 percent of males think their coaches see sports wagering as acceptable, programmatic efforts to educate need to involve not only student-athletes, but also coaches and administrators."

In 2010, the University of Missouri at St. Louis was placed on two-year probation after the head coach of its men's golf team played in several fantasy leagues with entry fees as high as $1,300. The coach eventually purchased and operated his own fantasy football operation, recruiting a volunteer coach and three of his players to act as commissioners, all while still a golf coach at the institution. Secondary NCAA violations have involved athletic department spokespeople, assistant coaches, and facility managers paying between $30 and $100 to join fantasy leagues.

In the Missouri case, the NCAA cited a lack of education as one of the main drivers of the misconduct. It's a problem, the association says, that extends to many universities and athletic departments.

A quarter of Division I athletes say they have not received information about NCAA gambling rules, according to NCAA surveys. In Divisions II and III, nearly half of the athletes say they haven't been told about the rules. The number of students who have received information about rules concerning fantasy leagues specifically is likely even lower because most officials don't see fantasy sports participation as a student health concern like they do more stereotypical forms of gambling like wagering on sporting events and horse racing, which can more easily lead to addiction, Derevensky said.

"It's against NCAA regulations, but most kids who have gambling problems don't get involved in fantasy leagues," he said. "Most individuals who have gambling problems can't wait that long to find out what the results are going to be. The concern about gambling from a student-athlete perspective involves the health and well-being of the athlete, and the integrity of the game. So the NCAA is trying to educate students about gambling in general."

Questions for Rhetorical Analysis

1. What is the effect of all the numbers and statistics included in paragraph 3?
2. Where does the article prove the trend exists and is problematic?
3. Does the writer spend most of his time explaining causes or effects? Or does he spread his attention across both?

Questions for Critical Thinking

1. Who would find this piece of writing interesting?
2. What would be a good follow-up story to this one? What other angles might a writer develop based on the subjects here—gambling, college athletes, NCAA rules? Make a list of several other articles you might write that would be related to this article.
3. Write a tweet that summarizes this article.
4. Is anything missing from this article that you think would provide good insight?
5. What might be another angle a writer could choose to take with this same information?

Style Practice: Imitation

Rewrite the lead, using the same sentence structure, using a different angle.

Transcript-Free Admissions

Scott Jaschik

This article details an event that might seem relevant only to a small group: applicants to Goucher College. Looking at the way the author has developed the story, however, reveals a bigger picture.

CAN AN APPLICANT explain why he or she would thrive at a given college in two minutes? If the applicant wants to enroll at Goucher College, that is pretty much all it will take under a new admissions option being announced today. Applicants can now submit a two-minute video instead

Scott Jaschik, "Transcript Free Admissions," *Inside Higher Ed*, September 4, 2014. Reprinted by permission.

of all the traditional requirements, such as test scores, transcripts and essays.

"There's a lot of concern that the college application model is broken—I use the word 'insane' sometimes," José Antonio Bowen, Goucher's president, said in an interview.

Asked why the college would make such a radical shift, Bowen spoke of the way scores on the standardized SAT and ACT exams correlate with family wealth, and noted that essays can reflect the ideas of parents or writers for hire. Most colleges that eliminate SAT or ACT requirements cite research that the best predictor of college success is grades in college preparatory courses in high school. So why eliminate the transcript requirement in favor of a two-minute video?

"There are a lot of students out there [for whom] the transcript doesn't look the way they want it to look," Bowen said. "They were totally focused on music or drama or the soccer team, and so for whatever reason, they have a smudge or two on their transcripts." He added that while transcripts may predict academic success in college, that's not all that matters. "They are predictors of how well you will do in school, not how well you will do in life." Bowen said he believes many people are unfairly judged based on less-than-perfect grades and test scores, and sense that they won't be admitted to a good college—despite their many abilities.

Goucher is not being subtle about its willingness to consider students without any transcript. A video the college is releasing on the new option opens with a transcript being ripped up.

Many colleges accept or even encourage applicants to send videos on top of more traditional materials, but Goucher believes it is the first to offer an option based almost entirely on a short video. Applicants will also be required to submit two pieces of work from high school. But the college said that the video alone would make up "the crux" of decisions.

Bowen said applicants will be judged on the substance of their videos, not the production value. He said it would be possible for a student to make a video on a smartphone. "We're going to release the rubric, so there will be no secret way of evaluating these," Bowen said. "We are being very clear. We are looking for authenticity. What's the substance? Are you thoughtful in the way you articulate that story? . . . You will get no points for having fancy lighting or multi-camera angles."

Many open admissions colleges of course may not require standardized tests or transcripts, but Goucher—while not very competitive—is not open admissions. In the last three years it has admitted 72 or 73 percent of applicants. Entering class size at the liberal arts college has been stable in the low 400s.

Scott Sibley, a professor of chemistry and chair of the faculty at Goucher, said via email that the faculty was consulted on the idea and played a role in developing the specifics of the plan. He said that "most faculty here are quite comfortable to have this as an alternative application process."

Some admissions experts—while stressing that they hadn't yet been able to study Goucher's approach—said they were surprised by the idea of going transcript-free.

Jerome A. Lucido, executive director of the University of Southern California Center for

> "There's a lot of concern that the college application model is broken—I use the word 'insane' sometimes," José Antonio Bowen, Goucher's president, said in an interview.

Enrollment Research, Policy, and Practice, said that most admissions officers find the transcript to be key to understanding applicants. "You can see the level of academic work they have taken, the extent to which they have challenged themselves, the curriculum at their high school," he said. Without a transcript, he asked, "How do you know what capabilities a student has?"

Wayne Camara, senior vice president for research at ACT, said that there are many factors beyond academic ability on which colleges may opt to make admissions decisions. "But clearly we know if a college is concerned about the success of students academically, or the success in persistence to graduation, standardized indicators are not only valid but fair, and that includes the transcript." A transcript, he said, is a key way to evaluate the rigor of courses and how a student fared in high school.

"No matter what we say about high school grades, a high school transcript and GPA captures a whole range of courses," Camara said. "Any one course can be unreliable, but a transcript is likely to have four math teachers, four English teachers" and so forth, he said. "You can get a lot of information."

Questions for Rhetorical Analysis

1. Does this story offer the reader a balanced view of the topic? Give examples.
2. Does the writer include any opinion in the story?
3. How many sources does the writer use?
4. Does the writer use transitions? Point to the sentences that help introduce new parts of the discussion.

Questions for Critical Thinking

1. Who is the audience for this piece of writing? Is there some way to broaden the topic to get a larger, more general audience?
2. How might Goucher College benefit from having this story covered by the website insidehighered .com? Can you think of any drawbacks to having the story covered by national media?
3. Is this story controversial? Would you say controversy is always a good ingredient in a news story? Name an example of a story you have recently encountered that has some controversial elements. Would controversy over this policy be beneficial to Goucher? Why or why not?

Style: Imitation

Using this article's lead as a model, write a lead about your own school's admissions policy. The "news" can be whether your school has updated their admissions practices in some way or whether they are maintaining the same practice in spite of pressures to fall in line with more progressive schools. Use the objective voice.

WRITING & REVISION STRATEGIES

Gathered here are three interactive sections for you to use as you write and revise your news story.

- Writer's Notebook Suggestions
- Peer Review Log
- Revision Checklist

Writer's Notebook Suggestions

You can use these exercises to do some start-up thinking and writing for your news story.

1. Read today's news at an online site such as washingtonpost.com or nytimes.com. Make a list of newsworthy topics that are covered in the news stories.

2. Compare the top headlines in two news sources. Can you detect different angles from the headlines alone?

3. If your city or town has two competing newspapers, read the same story in both papers or read the same story in your local paper and on the website of a large, national news organization, including television news sources. Compare the coverage of the stories, looking at the headlines, the leads, the angles, and the writing. Analyze any differences that you find, and note instances of bias or lack of objectivity, if any.

4. Using the topic of a current story in the news—something everybody is talking about—interview two friends and find out their opinions on the topic. Write a 3- to 4-paragraph news story on local reaction to this event, integrating at least two quotations from your friends.

5. Write a short news story about a trend you have observed, and explore its implications, effects, and/or causes by talking to people directly affected by it. (A weather pattern, poor turnout at elections, and parking problems are some examples.)

   a. Report about the trend in the lead.

   b. Get reactions to it and quotations about it from people.

   c. Investigate to determine whether this trend occurs in other places.

   d. Write a lead paragraph for the following story. Set it in the present time, and write it for tomorrow's paper.

In Verona, Italy, the teenage children of two feuding families fall in love. Juliet Capulet and Romeo Montague, with the help of the local friar, Friar Lawrence, escape from their homes and plan to meet at a remote family tomb and then marry secretly. Juliet arrives first. She takes a powerful sleeping potion as she waits for her lover. When Romeo shows up, he mistakenly believes that Juliet has committed suicide, takes out his knife, and kills himself. When Juliet wakes up, she sees her dead lover and, tragically, kills herself with the same knife.

6. Write a letter home or to a faraway friend about your life this week, using news story form and structure. Make sure that your lead summarizes the news, that you have a clear angle, and that you organize your information in order of importance. Do not make anything up.

7. Write an "anniversary" story. Follow up on a story that was happening a year ago. Report any new developments or ongoing issues.

Peer Review Log

As you work with a writing partner or in a peer editing group, you can use these questions to give useful responses to a classmate's news story or as a guide for discussion.

Writer's Name: _____

Date: _____

1. Underline the lead. Put check marks by the *who*, *what*, *where*, *when*, and (if included) *how*. What is missing, if anything? What is the angle?

2. Is the topic of the story newsworthy? Is it interesting to readers? Why would readers find the topic useful?

3. Is the story objective and free of the writer's personal viewpoint? Does the writer seem to be advertising, promoting, or lecturing in the news story? Label any spots that seem biased or promotional with OBJ? (for *objectivity*).

4. Number the sources (1, 2, 3). Do the sources reflect different perspectives on the topic? Could the writer use an opposing or a different view?

5. Are quotations attributed to sources? Note any problems with quotations by writing question marks in the margin. Look for quotations that are too long or too confusing. If you can suggest that the writer paraphrase or use a partial quotation, make a note in the margin.

6. Does the story sound like something you might hear on the evening news? Is the style formal? Circle any words or phrases that jump out as being inconsistent with the voice of news reporting.

7. Does the body of the story reveal enough about the background of the story? Do you have questions about why or how the event happened?

8. Are paragraphs arranged to show order of importance? Draw arrows if you think some paragraphs might be rearranged.

Revision Checklist

As you do your final revision, check to make sure that you

- chose a newsworthy, timely topic
- wrote a concise lead, including *who, what, where, when,* and perhaps *how* or *why*
- included a clear angle
- provided background information to give a full picture
- used correctly attributed quotations from several sources
- organized the story by order of importance
- balanced your reporting to show several sides of an issue and to remain objective
- consulted good sources

PART 4

WRITING TO ANALYZE

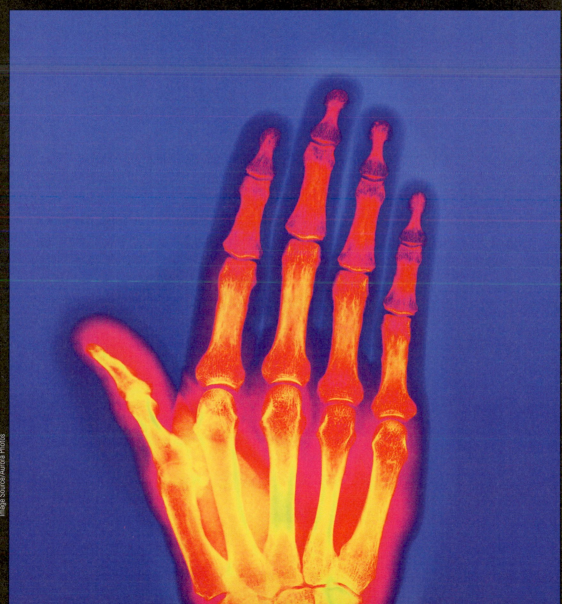

Image Source/Aurora Photos

10 WRITING AN EVALUATION
REVIEWS

I learn more from critics who honestly criticize my pictures than from those who are devout.

—INGMAR BERGMAN

We have become consumers with information always at hand. Consulting Yelp or Trip Advisor or Good Reads or Rotten Tomatoes to figure out whether or not a book, a film, a new restaurant, a performance, a television show or a destination is worth our money or time has become second nature to us. In fact, we can find opinions while we wait in line at a restaurant or at the movies, and often we are swayed by ratings. Registering our own opinions by leaving reviews or comments has also become easier—sometimes as simple as leaving stars or thumbs up or down. Although these quick, consumer-oriented ratings can be useful in getting an impression of something, often we crave deeper analysis—reviews that offer information as well as evaluation of the "worth" of something. Some of us even read reviews to join in the conversation—to see whether others agree with our evaluations, or to ask, "Does anyone else not like this?"

These deeper, more detailed reviews that we seek not only assert opinions, but they also provide information about the subject: How does it fit into the market? What is worthwhile—and what isn't so successful—in the performance or product or film, and why? Should I spend my time and money on this?

> **Chapter Objectives**
>
> **tailor your voice to your subject matter and audience**
> 251
>
> **use background research and context to help defend your evaluation**
> 252
>
> **learn how to write a solid evaluative thesis**
> 254
>
> **form and defend an opinion with illustrations and examples**
> 260

PROCESS PLAN

Prepare

- Find a new film, video game, book, product, service, or recent performance people would be interested in.

- Research the background of the subject.

- Read reviews of similar topics.

- Read reviews on websites where you might publish your own review to get a sense of audience, length, and style.

Draft

- Introduction: Include background information about the subject. Present the evaluative thesis with your overall positive, negative, or mixed opinion. Describe or summarize the subject.

- Body: Select, list, and analyze the most significant attributes of the subject—the "highlight reel," or the elements that helped you form your opinion. Include the positives and the negatives.

- Conclusion: Overall, after considering the merits of the component parts, is the subject worthwhile to consumers or audience members?

Revise

- Check to make sure you have made a clear claim about whether the subject has merit.

- Find more evidence to back up your claim and to defend your thesis.

- Consider how the order of your information works. Can you change the organization to create a better sense of logic?

- Check that your voice is engaging and accessible.

Understanding the Writing Project

MOST REVIEWS start from a visceral response: "I loved it!" "I hated it!" "I don't know what I think." The next step is to figure out why you had that response. What is the author/writer/producer/chef attempting to create? How well does this product work? Should I go on this trip? Your gut feeling is your first response, but maybe you'll change your mind: the film you wrote off as a flop may be, on reflection, more subtle and more successful than you originally thought.

We read reviews because they are useful or because they help us understand something that intrigues us. Well-written reviews are also entertaining and interesting in their own right. Your job, as a reviewer, is to become expert in the subject. You understand where the subject falls in relation to what came before it, what influenced its origins, and how it stacks up to others like it. Readers rely on you to sift through all the material and find the details—the evidence—that support your opinion.

OrangeDukeProductions/iStockphoto.com

ASSIGNMENT Choose a field you like and feel knowledgeable about—for example, film, literature, music, websites, video games, food, and so on. Then select a subject readers would want to read an evaluation of and write a review. You might choose a product, a service, a piece of art, or even a destination. Have a real audience in mind. Choose the website or publication that publishes reviews about your subject. Research your topic by reading other reviews as well as digging into the subject under review.

Review of a Film

YOSHI MAKISHIMA

Divergent Is Just Another Teen Movie

IF A BOOK series based on teens struggling for survival in a dystopian world is wildly successful, then its film adaptation will follow suit—right? Not necessarily. Comparing two of the most popular adaptations of films based on teen fantasy novels, *Divergent* and the juggernaut teen survival romance *The Hunger Games*, proves that translating stories for the screen often comes down to just that—translating—and that a successful teen/romance/survival/dystopian doesn't always create a blueprint for a successful film. It's easy to see where *Divergent* borrowed from other young adult franchises, especially *The Hunger Games*, and it doesn't take much time in the theater to see where *Divergent* falls short, not just in originality but also in creating a believable world for its teen-female-heroine to fight for her survival.

Going down the list, the film *Divergent* can check all the same boxes as *The Hunger Games* novel-to-movie adaptation: Sharp-shooting female protagonist—check. Dystopian North American Fascist regime—check. Culture of ritualized child-on-child violence—check. A Kravitz (Zoë, following her father Lenny's footsteps after his role in *The Hunger Games*)—check.

The Hunger Games comparisons are unavoidable, and frankly, *Divergent* doesn't seem to be making much effort to avoid them.

Divergent, like *The Hunger Games*, opens on our teenage protagonist living in a world of muted colors and shaky cam. Beatrice Prior lives in "Abnegation"—the community service clique, in a post-apocalyptic Chicago restructured into five high school-like groups. We also have the geeks (Erudite), the jocks (Dauntless), the happy hippies (Amity) and the oversharing smartasses (Candor.) If you can't keep track, don't worry—each faction is color-coded for your convenience, outfitted in different monochromatic uniforms.

In this society, every 16-year-old must take an entrance exam involving what appear to be hallucinogenic Jello shots to determine which group they belong to. But when Beatrice is tested, she fits into too many categories. She is Divergent and her test proctor (an imposing Maggie Q) tells her she must hide her condition—or else.

Or else what, you may well ask. And why? We are repeatedly told that "Divergents threaten the system"—but the movie never tells us why (perhaps because the book didn't supply any answers, either), so we're left with a conflict sans any sense of immediate danger. Right there, the audience is left hanging, asking the question, "So what's all this fuss about in the first place?"

In another unexplained-but-seemingly-significant plot point, after the test, we have an ostentatious choosing ceremony, where the teens pick the faction they will belong to. This ceremony should be totally unnecessary, as most of them should already know where they'll end up from the test they just took. Right? But, as in the *The Hunger Games,* this ceremony mostly exists to force the heroine to become a butt-kicking action girl. Accordingly, Beatrice signs up for Dauntless, the tattooed, pierced, leather-clad military faction. (Frankly, it's surprising that more of these 16-year-olds aren't running to join this glamorous crew.)

Once officially assigned to the action-hero crew, Beatrice re-christens herself "Tris" and undergoes the brutal Dauntless initiation training—the violence of which has actually been toned down from the book. In Roth's novel, a peripheral character takes a knife to the eye; the heroine is nearly sexually assaulted; and most of the trainees regularly beat each other into bloody unconsciousness. It's actually a pity they took the rough stuff out. The random, shocking violence in the novel created an atmosphere of peril and urgency that the nearly nonexistent conflict couldn't supply. In *The Hunger Games* film, the constant threat of death and bodily harm (retained from the novel) kept things interesting, even during the more banal moments. The world of *Divergent* feels safer. The movie spends plenty of time letting the characters train for a fight versus some vague danger, without giving them an occasion until a violent inter-faction coup-d'état in the fifth act, which kills off half a dozen supporting characters. But it's too little, too late.

The pacing of *Divergent* is arguably its biggest flaw, but the decision to keep the plodding voiceover from the book also drags down the story. Both *The Hunger Games* and *Divergent* started out as novels that told more than they showed. Both novels are narrated in the present tense by their teenage protagonists. Their voices are humorless, ponderous and sometimes irritatingly petulant. However, when *The Hunger Games* author Suzanne Collins adapted her own novel for the screen, with input from Billy Ray and Director Gary Ross, she made the smart decision to leave Katniss' narrative voice out of the screenplay. In the film version of the *The Hunger Games,* Katniss becomes all wordless action—precisely what we need her to be. The character's silence, combined with the quiet strength of her portrayer, Jennifer Lawrence, made Katniss all the more compelling.

Shailene Woodley, on the other hand—who is just as strong an actress as Lawrence—is undermined by the decision to stay loyal to the first-person narration of the novel—another significant flaw in the screenplay adaptation by Evan Daugherty and Vanessa Taylor. Woodley is forced to deliver stilted lines that seem nearly stupid, when uttered aloud. In the voiceover, for example, Tris tells us, "*They say the war was terrible.*" When she is in conversation with other characters, Tris comes off just as stilted. Her unconvincing language and her lack of clear motivation combine to make it hard for the audience to root for Tris. We can't blame Woodley for not having much of a script to work with. And she's not alone in that. Not even the hunky love interest, Four (yes, even the names are dumb), who is played by Theo James, comes across as overwhelmed with a simple conversation.

Four: My name's Four.

Christina: Four, like the number?

Four: Exactly, like the number.

Christina: What happened, one through three were taken?

Four: What's your name?

Christina: Christina.

Four: The first lesson you learn from me, if you wanna survive here, is keep your mouth shut. Do you understand me?

And we're supposed to believe Four is going to be a worthy ally for Tris? Again, blaming James for a poorly written character seems to be beside the point. In fact, in *Divergent,* not one of the characters wins our sympathy or our understanding. As a result of the anemic development of Tris's character and motivation, the slow and drawn out pacing of the training sequences that offer no real danger, along with the stultifying dialogue, we watch scene after scene, not really caring about who lives and who dies in this world that just happens to be dystopian. At best, Divergent seems like a big, long introduction to a confusing world. Tris, the titular *Divergent,* seems almost bored, as if she, like the audience, is tired of waiting for the story to begin.

Questions for Critical Thinking

1. How does the writer defend her opinion of *Divergent*? What examples help her prove that her opinion has merit?
2. How do the comparisons to *The Hunger Games* help the reader understand the writer's points about *Divergent*?
3. When a movie is an adaptation of a popular book, does the writer always need to compare the movie to the source material? What are the benefits of bringing the novel into the discussion of the film? What are the drawbacks?
4. Who would be interested in reading a review of *Divergent*? Who is the intended audience for the film? Are the two audiences different in any way? How does the writer attempt to speak directly to her imagined reader?
5. Will anyone be offended by this review? Will anyone disagree?

The Rhetorical Situation: The Review

Purpose: The review shows readers how the subject under scrutiny measures up to others like it. The review offers description, analysis, and evaluation.

Voice: Knowing your readers and on which site or in which publication your review will appear on will help you choose the voice and style for your review. If you are reviewing a film, you need to consider the genre of film as well as the place you might see your review posted or published. If you are reviewing a product, you should keep in mind who the consumers are. Technology reviews can be highly technical—or they can be very accessible to the average reader

Audience: Who reads reviews? People who want to use the product or see the film or go to the restaurant. Readers are looking for information as well as evaluation, and they assume that reviews will be fair and honest. Many times the judgment offered in a review helps consumers make decisions. Other times it serves as part of a cultural conversation—a chance for readers to see different viewpoints.

Media and Design: Though most reviews appear in text—on websites and in print—video reviews are quickly becoming a popular way to share opinions with a large audience.

age fotostock/SuperStock

PRACTICE 10.1
Considering Audience

Thinking of this notion of audience, review a coffee shop. Think about the niche the coffee shop occupies. Is it a quirky neighborhood place? Or a slicker, more expensive spot for specialty drinks? Understanding the store's "brand," or how the owner defines its identity, will help you evaluate the atmosphere, the menu, the service, and, of course, the coffee. Write three paragraphs tailored to an audience who is looking for a new coffee shop. ■

Research Paths: Find Out about the Origins of Your Topic

Good reviewers do not simply express an opinion. They reveal the reviewer's knowledge about both the field and how the subject fits into the field. How is the subject of your review different from the other reviews on the same topic? What are the origins of the subject? What are other examples by the same author, director, artist? What was the previous iteration of this product? How does this offering compare to the earlier work? You can find information about the producers of the subject—the artist, company, or organization that is responsible for it and might profit from it. Remember, though, the review is most interesting to your reader because it offers useful information, not just trivia. Sometimes having the information about the history of your subject is more useful in your understanding of it—in firming up your expertise—than it is useful to the review. Doing research about the origins might provide more background.

Where would you go to get this background information? Promotional websites offer information about new products, movies, shows, and so on, but be careful that you do not adopt language that is intended as promotion. Interviews with the creators and performers are usually available on the Internet, too. For deeper background on the topic, you might consult books, journal articles, trade magazines, or perhaps interview experts on the topic.

A concert review for a Taylor Swift performance, for example, illustrates the reviewer's knowledge about her career—the statistics as well as her persona.

> Of course, considering Swift's multi-platinum success—with four albums under her belt in only six years, she's landed a colossal 50 songs on Billboard's Hot 100—she's clearly not in Kansas anymore, but Swift's amazement at seeing a room full of worshippers remains, even though she long ago sold out her first stadium. Indeed, Swift has been working as a professional singer since she was 16, yet she takes the stage with the sort of open-mouthed awe that makes you feel like she's brand new at this. It's an endearing trait to present to the nearly 14,000 fans who packed Staples.
>
> —*The Hollywood Reporter*

An example from *The Boston Globe*'s review of an exhibit of art of the 1980s showcases the writer's expert sense of context—what were the eighties all about?

> The show has plenty to say about a decade many of us mentally cordon off in a bad dream of shoulder pads, Vaseline lens TV dramas, sax-and-synth pop, and hokey, hypocritical "family values" politicians. Bad painting, too.

Molesworth's show tears away the insulation of (completely valid) embarrassment, and makes us face the art of the '80s squarely. Hers is not a dispassionate, inclusive overview of the decade. It is, to cite Charles Baudelaire's call-to-arms for critics, "partial, passionate, and political." It reveals a miscellany of art that was raw, heartfelt, and politically engaged, even if some of it can be seen, from this distance, to have been collapsing too willingly into the arms of the academy, with its zombie talk of deconstruction, male gazes, appropriation, semiotics, and dominant paradigms.

—Sebastian Smee, *Boston Globe*

An album review reveals the background of an artist's developing style:

Where Does This Door Go has a lot going on, and it's clear to see how Hawthorne has built upon the style he was just beginning to cultivate on his last album, 2011's *How Do You Do*, where he infused his retro-soul sound with elements of pop, R&B and even a smattering of hip hop, creating a style that seemed more uniquely his own than his earlier work, although still owing a lot to the soul pioneers before him.

—Michael Garrity, *Paste Magazine* blog

megamix/iStockphoto.com

PRACTICE 10.2

Selecting Criteria

Research a clothing style or trend that has recently become popular. Find the origins of the trend and write the introduction to a review using your research in a lively, conversational way to introduce your reader to the new style. ■

THE  BIG IDEA   Writing the Evaluative Thesis

You can safely assume your readers are seeking out reviews because they are looking for insight into how they might want to spend their time and money. Your readers come with a special interest. So, as you write, imagine you are having a conversation with them and anticipate their reactions to your opinions. What might they want to know more about? What might people who are also knowledgeable about the subject challenge you about? Remember that you could possibly disagree with people who might also know a great deal about a subject. Considering that, what you say has to have more than simple personal preference. Your evaluation must have logic to pull the threads of your evidence together. Logic begins with your evaluative thesis, which often appears in the first paragraph or two of your review.

Analysis of component parts + asserted opinion = evaluative thesis

Warm Bodies (novel)

> A first glance of this novel may leave you with the idea that, although original and perhaps entertaining, it really doesn't have anything to offer in the form of true human insight. But this is not so, as rampant symbolism throughout the novel leaves readers with more than one new perspective on the shape of today's society, and on what really matters in day-to-day life.
>
> —*The Guardian*

Notice how the reviewer begins by anticipating a potential challenge that this young adult novel might not offer insight into the human condition. He counters the challenge by focusing on the novel's symbolism and asserts his thesis that the novel gives the reader "more than one new perspective" on contemporary culture.

Star Trek (video game)

> J.J. Abrams may be Hollywood's most successful imitator. Whether he's paying tribute to Steven Spielberg in his film *Super 8, The X-Files* in *Fringe*, or *Godzilla* films in *Cloverfield*, Abrams knows how to take a pop-culture touchstone and dress it up into something fun—if devoid of originality. The same is true of his *Star Trek* "reboot" film. It's a well-acted and visually attractive special effects bonanza, but it borrows what little emotional impact and gravitas it has from Leonard Nimoy's Spock. Abrams uses *Star Trek's* characters but neglects the themes that made the series great.

The *Star Trek* video game (with which Abrams had no creative involvement) takes that tendency even further, using the series to dress up conventional design.

—Samantha Nelson, Retrieved from the Gameological Society,
http://gameological.com. Reprinted by permission of the author.

The reviewer pans the *Star Trek* video game by comparing it to the same weaknesses found in the *Star Trek* film: lack of originality. This thesis, the reader assumes, will be supported throughout the review.

Visual Literacy: Review a Cover

Select a cover from a video game, an album, a book, or a film. In one paragraph, and in a style that suits the subject matter, write a review that includes a description of the cover and your assessment of how well the cover promotes the material. Consider the following questions:

- Assuming that the reader can't see the cover, what does it look like?
- What is your first impression of the cover?
- Does the cover appropriately convey the book/game/film?
- Is the image accurate in portraying the tone, style, and genre?

NiceMonkey/Superstock

Steps in Evaluation

Identifying Genre or Class

Your readers' expectations stem from their experience with the field in which your subject belongs.

Locating your subject within a specific class, like putting a story within a genre, is a way to start to analyze the subject. You might think of the field it belongs in as a

category or as the smallest group your subject might belong to. In literature or film, this is called a *genre* or *subgenre*. In music or dance, you might think of it as a *style*—hip-hop, classical, jazz, and so on. Some subcategories of hip-hop, for example, might be crunk, nerd core, and Christian rap—each one coming packaged with a unique set of expected characteristics.

These expectations can also be called *criteria*. Criteria are class-specific; they are definitely not one-size-fits-all. For example, in film, you would expect special effects to be a big part of a movie about superheroes, but not even a consideration in a romantic comedy.

Choosing Criteria

Once you begin to define the essential elements of the class your subject belongs in (the genre, style, type), you can sort among those elements to see which ones affected your feelings and helped you form your initial opinion (like, don't like, or mixed).

To start making the list of criteria for forming an evaluation, ask yourself:

- Which elements define the subject as a member of its class to fans or consumers?
- Which elements are least negotiable and most necessary?

IMAGEZOO/Superstock

- Which elements of your subject are unique or innovative?
- Which elements work in favor of a positive opinion?
- Which elements work against a positive opinion?

You will most likely have more criteria than you need. Select the items from your list that help make the clearest case for your overall impression.

Examples of Criteria

Concerts: Performers' abilities to connect to the audience, how live performance compares to recordings, showmanship, pacing

Theatre: Set design, risks the director takes with the setting, costuming, acting, casting

Films: Acting, plot, character, genre expectations, innovations, pacing, special effects, screenwriting (including the idea for the story and the dialogue)

Novels: Premise, genre expectations, character, plot, pacing

Products: Expected features, unique features/new technology, performance, cost

FogStock LLC/Superstock

PRACTICE 10.4
Research Context and Background for a Trend

Choose a piece of technology to review—an application, a new phone or tablet, or a gaming system. Decide which field or category the piece of technology fits into. Create a list of criteria you would use to evaluate items in the same category. What general categories are important to consumers who are perusing the field? ■

Stating Your Opinion

Although some of your readers might be interested in simply finding out what's new, many others want the bottom line: Is this a good way to spend time and money? You should provide your opinion early on. This is where the "big idea" or your evaluative thesis comes into play. The review of *Divergent* that appears earlier in this chapter, for example, clearly states the reviewer's negative evaluation. The writer has also opened up some of her reasons in general terms and allows herself an opening to discuss the film's originality and ability to build a believable world.

> It's easy to see where *Divergent* borrowed from other young adult franchises, especially *The Hunger Games,* and it doesn't take much time in the theater to see where *Divergent* falls short, not just in originality but also in creating a believable world for its teen-female-heroine to fight for her survival.
>
> —Yoshi Makishima

Describing the Subject: The "Highlight Reel"

No review would do its complete job without providing some good description of important elements. Specific detail is key, but so is being choosy. Don't overload your review with a full replay. Think of your review as the highlight reel, showcasing those moments that drive home your reasoning.

To begin, a description of your subject is essential. It helps your reader understand the component parts, what makes your subject different or similar to others like it, and what is noteworthy about it.

In reviews of films, books, and television shows, you can help your reader understand not just genre but also character by selecting good highlights that illustrate hints about plot. In her *New Yorker* review of "Season X, Breaking Bad," writer Emily Nussbaum provides a thorough yet concise overview of the premise of the series. She also provides examples—highlights—that demonstrate how the character of the series has changed.

> When the showrunner Vince Gilligan pitched "Breaking Bad" to AMC, he presented a mission statement, which amounted to a monumental spoiler: he would turn Mr. Chips into Scarface. The show's protagonist was Walter White, a high-school chemistry teacher who had a wife, a disabled teen-age son, and a baby on the way. Given a diagnosis of late-stage lung cancer, Walt took up cooking meth to build a nest egg and, later on, to pay his medical bills. When faced with the dilemma of

whether to kill a menacing thug, he scribbled down a panicked moral calculus. Con: "MURDER IS WRONG!" Pro: "He'll kill your entire family if you let him go."

Ah, those were the days. Nobody could fault Walt when he strangled Krazy-8 with a bicycle lock, only two hours into the series. If television shows have conversion moments that was mine. This was back in the chaotic, improvisatory days of Walt's entry into the drug business, when the acid he'd intended to dissolve a tattooed corpse ended up eating right through a bathtub, so that the "raspberry slushie" of those human remains seemed as though it might leave a stain on the whole world. In a way, it has. Each season, Walt has made far less justifiable choices, each one changing him, with a throb of arrogance here, a swell of egotism there. We're deep in the Scarface stage; the hero of the show is now its villain.

—Emily Nussbaum, *The New Yorker*

A product review, this one for an iPhone, also hits the specific details that define the subject:

To say that Apple's doing things differently would be an understatement. With the 4.7-inch iPhone 6 and the 5.5-inch iPhone 6 Plus, the company introduced two new high-end phones at the same time, both with a complete redesign and a much larger screen size than any iPhone that came before. Gone are the days of 3.5-inch and 4-inch phones that, at one time, seemed to provide more than ample amounts of screen space. Now, the new iPhones make their predecessors look like the tiny handset Ben Stiller used in *Zoolander*. The market has changed, and it was high time Apple did the same.

—Brad Molen

Backing Up Your Opinion with Evidence

Ultimately, your evidence will convince your reader that your opinion is reasonable, believable, and trustworthy. Your evidence answers the question "Why?" Why did you like/dislike the subject? Even if your reader disagrees with your opinion, you can still write a successful review if you make a solid case using good logic and reasoning—in other words, backing up your argument with evidence. Illustrations and examples will help you make that solid case. Think of your argument in a review as flowing from general to specific—from opinions (broad), to slightly more narrow claims, to specific illustrations and examples.

Opinion–Claim–Illustration

In the example that follows, Greg Kot gives Mumford and Sons' "Babel" an unflattering review. His implied opinion is "I didn't like 'Babel.'" This statement is very general—a pure opinion. Naturally, his reader will want to know why. That leads to his claim: he focuses on two criteria—he didn't like the songwriting or the delivery. But that is still general and needs explaining. The question "Why?" is starting to be answered, but is still incomplete, unconvincing. Kot needs to give some examples and illustrations to help make his argument. Specifically, he writes, "The singing veers between a strained roar and a whisper," and the title track, "Hopeless Wanderer," is "overheated." Examples like these make the "Why?" of Kot's argument clear. He continues his critique, using the same kind of specific evidence to support his argument that the album is unsuccessful:

> There's nothing wrong with a rousing sing-along among 25,000 of your closest friends. The real issue with Mumford & Sons is its pedestrian songwriting and predictable delivery. The singing veers between a strained roar and a whisper, and the music shares a similar loud-quiet-loud dynamic that becomes repetitive. They bash away on mandolins, fiddles and dobros like a string band on steroids; you can practically hear the strings snap and the veins pop in the overheated title track, "Hopeless Wanderer," and "I Will Wait." It's almost a relief when the two-minute "Reminder" arrives two-thirds into the album, a short, quiet, late-night respite from the assault.
>
> References to blood, heartbreak, sin and redemption fill the album. They're treated in the abstract, emblems of biblical import that don't really say or reveal much of anything ("Like the city that nurtured my greed and my pride/I stretch my arms into the sky"; "So give me hope in the darkness that I will see the light"; "These days of dust, which we've known/Will blow away with this new sun"). The band pays lip service to the idea of keeping things earthy and organic, and therefore somehow more sincere or heartfelt. But they wash out the gritty details, and their broad, universal images resonate only as fist-pumping bumper-stickers rather than as messy, human vulnerability.
>
> —Greg Kot, *Chicago Tribune*

PRACTICE 10.5
Destination Reviewing

Identify a place that people might want to know more about—a local beach, museum, a place that is important historically, and write a review. Describe the location and give your reader a good sense of whether the trip to visit is worthwhile and why. ■

Depending on your subject, the answer to "why?" you did or did not form a favorable opinion will rely on examples, illustrations, and specific details. Your thinking about criteria will come into play here, as will all your thinking about evaluating a subject.

DIY MEDIA AND DESIGN

Create a Video Product Review for Posting on YouTube

YouTube has become a first stop for consumers who are interested in finding out about products. Effective YouTube video reviews present a range of information. "Unboxing videos" portray all the aspects of literally taking the packaging off a new product and then demonstrating how it's used. Other reviews compare brands of similar products.

You can get a large following and lots of user "hits" if you select a topic people are interested in. Here are some tips for getting started with your video review:

- Watch some reviews and decide on your style. Will you appear in the video or will you show only the product in your video? If you appear, make sure to look at the camera.
- Decide how you will film your review. The easiest way is to use a camera in a phone or other device (laptop, pad, ipod).
- Decide which editing program you will use to combine your clips. (imovie, Windows Movie Maker, and Final Cut are a few options. More free software is also available to download.)

In your product review, consider the following:

- Be fair but honest.
- Use a conversational tone—make your YouTube review sound like you are talking to another person. Also, make notes, but don't read from your notes.
- Open with an introduction—name the product and give background on the company or on the version of the product, cost, size, and so on. Make sure to point out salient information for the consumer.
- Remember, pictures can show only so much. You might need to explain what cannot be seen. How the product feels in your hand and the materials used to construct the product, for example, might not be apparent from video or pictures.
- Demonstrate how the product is meant to be used and narrate the experience. Again, consider the less tangible parts of the experience. Does the product heat up or slip out of your grip? These aren't readily photographed parts of the user experience.
- Include your opinions—criticisms as well as praise.

- Be sure to back your opinions with evidence. The great thing about video reviews is that you can actually show the good and bad parts on the video.
- Use voice-over to help organize your review. Also, use topic sentences as transitions when moving from one part of the review to the next. For example, tell your viewers what you will be showing them next: "Now we'll look at how the screen size of the drawing pad works."
- Make sure you cover each point and don't speed through elements. Give the viewer a chance to listen to your point.
- Keep looping back to general key words, such as "Another of the benefits of buying this brand. . . ."
- Conclude your review by recapping the main points of your review.
- Keep your review to 3 to 6 minutes. If you have a lot to say, separate the review into several videos (introduction to drawing pads and comparison of drawing pads), so your viewer won't have to watch a 15-minute video to get to the comparison of brands.

READINGS

The following selections show three very different kinds of topics for review: video games, music, and fast food.

Warp Drivel

Samantha Nelson

A new Star Trek video game doesn't capture what made the series great.

J.J. ABRAMS may be Hollywood's most successful imitator. Whether he's paying tribute to Steven Spielberg in his film *Super 8, The X-Files* in *Fringe*, or *Godzilla* films in *Cloverfield*, Abrams knows how to take a pop-culture touchstone and dress it up into something fun—if devoid of originality. The same is true of his *Star Trek* "reboot" film. It's a well-acted and visually attractive special effects bonanza, but it borrows what little emotional impact and gravitas it has from Leonard Nimoy's Spock. Abrams uses *Star Trek*'s characters but neglects the themes that made the series great.

The *Star Trek* video game (with which Abrams had no creative involvement) takes that tendency even further, using the series to dress up conventional design. Picking up after the 2009 film, the Vulcans are seeking a replacement for their destroyed world on a planet they've creatively named New Vulcan. The normally logical and patient race apparently can't wait to set up their new home, so they employ an experimental technology that has the unfortunate side effect of opening wormholes. These wormholes, in turn, release ships filled with space dinosaurs—specifically, the Gorn from the original TV series. Now Kirk and Spock have to save the day.

They do that by shooting monsters, chucking grenades, and grabbing weapons off dead foes. They run and duck for cover in a manner highly reminiscent of *Uncharted*. They occasionally do things that you might see in an episode of *Star Trek*, like scanning a sick Vulcan with a tricorder and crawling around a ship's vents to get a jump on an enemy, but more often the developer, Digital Extremes, simply takes familiar pieces of the *Star Trek* universe and uses them with no regard for context or logic.

In *Star Trek: First Contact*, the Enterprise crew uses magnetic boots to explore the outer hull of the spaceship, creating a suspenseful scene as they plod along under constant threat of attack. In this game, you don the boots and are immediately sprinting. In *Star Trek VI: The Undiscovered Country*, Spock uses his psychic mind meld to pry

> "I might have even enjoyed this project if it were an animated film, but with the script slapped on an entirely generic shooter, it just confirmed my worst fears about where the series is heading."

information from the mind of a traitor, and it's an incredibly disturbing rape parallel. Here, Spock does it just to get the code that opens the next door. The game does try to incentivize civilized Starfleet officer behavior—as opposed to shooting everything that moves—by awarding bonuses for avoiding lethal force. To earn the bonus, you set your phasers to "stun," but this is less effective than in the movies or TV shows, as you then have to perform a bare-handed "take down" move before your enemies start attacking you again.

You can play as either Kirk or Spock, with the other always tagging along if another player wants to drop in and take control. With Chris Pine and Zachary Quinto providing the voices, they offer the same amusing banter as they did in the movie. Unfortunately, the game lacks much in the way of stimulating teamwork, instead offering mostly pointless tasks such as having both players press a button repeatedly to pry open a door. The game is also populated with plenty of other lame video game tropes, like doors that have to be opened by tedious hacking minigames, and consoles that you turn on by lugging power sources from other rooms. It's also ugly, buggy, and has a score ripped off from John Williams' work for *Star Wars*.

If you can get past the space dinosaurs, the game does have some decent plot points. An early section where mind-controlled Vulcans beg you for help, even as they attack you, is disquieting. Considering that only 10,000 members of the species remain, I wished I had some version of the population blackboard in *Battlestar Galactica* to keep track of just how screwed the Vulcans are every time I stepped over a pointy-eared corpse. I might have even enjoyed this project if it were an animated film, but with the script slapped on an entirely generic shooter, it just confirmed my worst fears about where the series is heading. Gene Roddenberry imagined a world based on hope, peaceful cooperation, and intellectual exploration, but now the *Star Trek* universe has become a setting for irrelevant violence.

Star Trek

Developer: Digital Extremes

Publisher: Namco Bandai

Platforms: PC, PlayStation 3, Xbox 360

Reviewed on: Xbox 360

Price: PC—$50; PlayStation 3, Xbox 360—$60

Rating: T

Questions for Rhetorical Analysis

1. Consider the audience for this review. Where are places the writer includes insider language that a more general reader might not understand?
2. What are the pros and cons of using this type of language?

Questions for Critical Thinking

1. How does the introduction, which discusses the *Star Trek* reboot film, add or subtract from the video game review? Is it necessary?
2. Locate the paragraph that provides overview or premise of the storyline in the video.
3. What are the criteria the writer points to in order to demonstrate the positive and negative aspects of the game?
4. Discuss the conclusion and the ethics the writer considers in relation to the subject matter—that is, killing Vulcans. Is this aspect of video gaming—ethical thoughts—usually a criterion for evaluating the merit of a particular game?
5. Restate, in your own words, the conclusion of this review.

Style Practice: Imitation

Concisely summarize and explain a process the way the writer does here with the video game, in terms of steps. What happens first, second, third, and so on? Choose the plot of a film, book, or video game to summarize this way.

Album Review: Mumford & Sons, "Babel"

Greg Kot

A music reviewer looks beyond surface criticism and into how the music might be best enjoyed by listeners.

U.K. QUARTET Mumford & Sons emerged from London a few years ago with banjos blazing. Their 2009 debut, "Sigh No More," ended up selling more than 2 million copies and ushered in a hootenanny-style folk-rock wave, which includes bands such as the Head and the Heart and the Lumineers. Last year, they backed Bob Dylan at the Grammy Awards.

The follow-up album, "Babel" (Gentlemen of the Road/Glassnote), is projected to go gold (at least 500,000 sales) in its first week, a rare rock-band commercial success story in an era dominated by pop, R&B and hip-hop. Yet the music of Marcus Mumford, Ben Lovett, Winston Marshall and Ted Dwane has a tendency to drive many music critics nuts; they call the band out for their shallow roots and folkie pretensions. But those criticisms miss the point.

Mumford & Sons aren't really interested in any sort of folk revivalism. They actually have a lot more in common with contemporary arena performers, especially the post-Garth Brooks wave of country artists. Mumford & Sons is to folk music as Kenny Chesney, say, is to honky tonk: They've adopted and adapted some of each genre's signifiers (the vests, rolled-up sleeves and banjos of folk and bluegrass for Mumford, the cowboy hats and steel guitars of country for Chesney), removed some of the darker, grittier subtleties, and put it all into evangelical overdrive so that it sounds uplifting and triumphant in a stadium full of revelers.

> "There's nothing wrong with a rousing sing-along among 25,000 of your closest friends."

There's nothing wrong with a rousing sing-along among 25,000 of your closest friends. The real issue with Mumford & Sons is its pedestrian songwriting and predictable delivery. The singing veers between a strained roar and a whisper, and the music shares a similar loud-quiet-loud dynamic that becomes repetitive. They bash away on mandolins, fiddles and dobros like a string band on steroids; you can practically hear the strings snap and the veins pop in the overheated title track, "Hopeless Wanderer," and "I Will Wait." It's almost a relief when the two-minute "Reminder" arrives two-thirds into the album, a short, quiet, late-night respite from the assault.

References to blood, heartbreak, sin and redemption fill the album. They're treated in the abstract, emblems of biblical import that don't really say or reveal much of anything ("Like the city that nurtured my greed and my pride/I stretch my arms into the sky"; "So give me hope in the darkness that I will see the light"; "These days of dust, which we've known/Will blow away with this new sun"). The band pays lip service to the idea of keeping things earthy and organic, and therefore somehow more sincere or heartfelt. But they wash out the gritty details, and their broad, universal images resonate only as fist-pumping bumper-stickers rather than as messy, human vulnerability.

But then, these aren't songs designed to be appreciated through a cell phone, car speaker or home stereo. They're meant to be heard in the third balcony of a hockey arena.

From the *Chicago Tribune*, September 27, 2012.

Questions for Rhetorical Analysis

1. List the criteria the writer cites for evaluating this album. How might the criteria be different for music from another style?
2. Make a list of criteria for a different album in another genre.

Questions for Critical Thinking

1. How do people use music reviews? How is an album review used differently from a concert review?
2. How does the author of this review reveal his expertise? What makes him seem like a reliable reviewer?
3. How are the lyrics used in the review?
4. Translate this review into a capsule review: say everything the writer says in three sentences.

Style Practice: Imitation

Describe what a song sounds like for readers the way the writer does in paragraph 4: "They bash away on mandolins, fiddles and dobros like a string band on steroids; you can practically hear the strings snap and the veins pop in the overheated title track, 'Hopeless Wanderer,' and 'I Will Wait.'" Make sure to choose words that imply your opinion in your description—words such as *overheated* in this example sentence.

Review: Chipotle's New Vegan Tofu Sofritas
Dana Rengel

Chipotle has a new menu item, tofu sofritas, for all of the vegetarian and vegan customers. Informative food reviews don't have to be about expensive or exotic restaurants, as evidenced in this review about a new dish at the "casual dining" spot, Chipotles.

Last week, a *Huffington Post* blogger proposed that the majority of America will be vegan by 2050. Preposterous? A little. Impossible? You know, maybe not.

Cutting out meat, fish, dairy and eggs is not easy to begin with, but in the past few years it has become easier and easier to switch to a vegan diet thanks to the tremendous boost in popularity. Six months ago, the Eugene Chipotle released their first new menu item, tofu sofritas, for all of its vegetarian and vegan fans.

"The sofritas is extremely popular," said Sarah Lar Rieu, a Chipotle employee. "People come in all the time and say they've heard something cool about the new item we're offering."

In addition to phasing out bacon from their refried beans recipe, the fast-food chain has introduced a spicy crumbled tofu. It's growing in popularity, but still not available in all fifty states. As of now, sofritas are only available in 21 states and a few select cities. The vegetarian in me—which is coincidentally just the normal me—rejoiced! As soon as I heard the good news, I felt a burrito-sized hole in my stomach. And it must be filled.

> "I'm trusting you with this one, Chipotle."

The sofritas is a little unappetizing to look at while it's in front of you at the counter, but as it turns into that amazing, tortilla-wrapped miracle in front of my very eyes, all of my worries disappear. I'm trusting you with this one, Chipotle.

Overall, vegetarians, vegans and omnivores alike seem to enjoy Chipotle's new addition.

"I want to wrap myself up in that burrito," UO psychology senior Bianca Marino said. Marino

By Dana Rengel, University of Oregon Student. From the Daily Emerald.

10 WRITING AN EVALUATION

has been 80% vegan for the last nine months. "But now that I think about it, the Chipotle sofritas isn't the best vegetarian burrito I've had."

Remarkably, Marino claims the best vegetarian burrito is at Hamilton dining hall's Big Mouth Burrito.

Jake Haener, a UO human physiology senior and Marino's omnivore boyfriend, enjoyed the sofritas burrito as well, but agreed that the texture was less than desirable.

Overall, it was delicious, but I see room for improvement. In the spirit of optimism, let's discuss the pros first.

Pros

The tofu is everything you want in a tofu option. Not too squishy or too firm; not at all bland. A lot of people criticize tofu for being bland, but I like to think it's like that friend we all have that's into whatever you're into—it takes on the flavors and seasonings of whatever it's in. Chipotle's webpage dedicated to sofritas says it's seasoned with "chipotle chilis, roasted poblanos, and a blend of aromatic spices."

Chipotle is becoming more and more locally sourced. "Both the meat and the tofu are locally sourced from within the state," said Lar Rieu.

It's not a meat imitator. Personally, this is a pro. It would be easy for Chipotle to go the route of imitation meats such as MorningStar or Boca and use a chicken-flavored seitan, but this is more of a matter of opinion. I dislike "chicken-flavored" things because it tends to make me compare it to the real thing, and to be honest, it's probably not as good.

Cons

Texturally, the tofu falls short. The crumbled tofu gets lost, indistinguishable between the beans and rice. I personally think that it would be pretty successful as tofu cubes rather than crumbled.

As opposed to the vegetables-only vegetarian burrito, guacamole is not a free addition to the sofritas burrito. A tragic loss.

I'm excited that Chipotle is inclusive to the growing demographic of non-meat eaters. It's a smart marketing move and a good way to build a customer loyalty in vegetarians. Let's just see how other fast food chains step up to Chipotle's game.

Questions for Rhetorical Analysis

1. How does using the first-person affect a review? Would this review be just as persuasive without the first person?
2. Rewrite one of the sentences that currently has the first person, "I," and decide which version you prefer. Why is one better to you than another?

Questions for Critical Thinking

1. What effect might the opening sentence have on a reader? Does it help focus this review or is it a distraction?
2. How does the use of quotations function in this review?
3. What kinds of limitations do writers have when reviewing food? Are those limitations different for reviews of fast food as opposed to fine dining? What are essential elements in a review of food?
4. How does the writer go about re-creating the experience of eating sofritas?

Style Practice: Imitation

Describe a new food using the Pros and Cons listing style.

WRITING & REVISING STRATEGIES

Writer's Notebook

1. Write an e-mail to a specific friend, telling him or her about a movie or television show you just watched. Make sure to keep the message conversational—just the way you would speak to each other. How is that different from what you might write in a review? What might you include in a review that you didn't include in the e-mail?

2. Write four-sentence capsule reviews for three meals offered at a dining hall, cafeteria, or café.

3. Make a list of the most clichéd movie review terms you can think of (for example, "Oscar-worthy").

4. Look at the promotional website for a product, service, or performance and analyze the description on the site. Which parts of the description are vague, as opposed to clear and precise? Look at the same product reviewed by consumers. Which elements do the consumers focus on to determine their opinions?

5. On review sites like Booklikes or Amazon or Barnes and Nobel, read reviews of a book you have read. Can you find a theme among the reviews? Do people who have commented on the books share values or opinions about the story, character, or theme?

6. Find two reviews for the same subject: one positive and one negative.

7. Take a poll of 10 people, asking their opinions on a new trend. Note their reasons for liking or not liking the trend. Can you find any patterns? What do people point to as having influenced their opinions? Again, do you see any similarities in the responses?

8. Watch YouTube video reviews of a product you own. Do you agree with the video reviews?

Peer Review Log

As you work with a writing partner or in a peer review group, you can use these questions to give helpful responses to a classmate's review or as a guide for discussion

Writer's Name: _____

Date: _____

1. Bracket the introduction. Does it grab your attention? Why or why not? Suggest one way to strengthen the introduction.

2. What are the keywords in the introduction that help establish the focus?

3. Can you tell by the end of the introduction what the writer's opinion of the subject is? State it in one sentence.

4. Underline all sentences that provide evidence, illustrations, or examples that back up the writer's opinion.

5. Does the writer use the first person "I"? If so, is the first person a help or a distraction?

6. Would the review appeal to a general reader, or does the writer intend the review be published in a place that only very knowledgeable readers will see it? Has the writer made a good assessment of where readers will see the review?

7. Does the writer seem to have enough expertise to review the subject? Is the writer using all the correct terminology without using too much specialty language?

8. Does the writer imply opinion in word choice? Can you point to an effective use of word choice in implying opinion?

9. Does the writer have enough evidence to back up the overall opinion? Can you suggest places to add more detail?

10. Does the writer use a voice, style, and tone that suit the subject matter? Can you point to places the writer is on-target with voice? Can you point to places the tone is too technical?

11. Should the writer compare the subject to others like it?

12. Is the conclusion specific enough?

Revision Checklist

As you do your final revision, check to make sure that you

- wrote an introduction that tips off the reader about your reaction (positive, negative, or a mixture)
- included a sentence that summed up your opinion—an evaluative thesis
- provided background or contextual information
- wrote a good description
- selected criteria that were important to the subject, to your opinion, and to your reader
- provided evidence to back up your opinion
- concluded strongly

Hipster Trek

Celeste Pille (www.celeste-doodleordie.blogspot.com)

WRITING A CAUSAL ANALYSIS

LONG RESEARCHED ARTICLES

It is a capital mistake to theorize before one has data.
—SIR ARTHUR CONAN DOYLE

Why do people bowl alone? It all started with a question, based on an observation from a Harvard researcher named Robert Putnam about the decline of bowling leagues—down 40 percent between 1980 and 1993. Putnam's research, which revealed that people are now less likely to bowl in leagues—or to attend PTA meetings or even go on picnics—led him to argue that people are less connected to their communities and families. During the second half of the twentieth century, he concluded, people were more likely to watch *Friends* on television than make friends.

Putnam's book, *Bowling Alone: The Collapse and Revival of American Community*, became a bestseller as thousands of readers were drawn to his speculation about what happened in the United States to compromise community involvement. His inquiry started with a question. More recently, researchers at the Pew Center have been following other social trends. For example, fewer people are saying they are part of a religious group. Pew research shows that the number of those who declare they are "unaffiliated" with a religion—or "nones" as they have been dubbed—has risen to 20 percent of the population. Pew researchers also found that women who tweet and post photos on social media are less stressed. Maybe you, as a writer, can help answer the question "Why?"

271

PROCESS PLAN

Prepare

- Look for new patterns or trends, or fresh developments in familiar patterns.

- Ask a question: Is the pattern or trend significant?

- Talk to people who are involved in the trend: practitioners/experts.

Draft

- Introduction: Show the trend in action. Write a scene or tell a story that hooks the reader's interest in the first paragraph.

- Body

- State the trend clearly and either place it within a larger context or announce the significance of the pattern.

- Use statistics, testimonials, or surveys to prove the trend exists.

- Anticipate your readers' questions.

- Conclusion: Use a memorable quotation or image that reinforces the thesis.

Revise

- Include reminders of your thesis, restated.

- Check source citations, in text and/or in endnotes.

- Make sure your points have logical transitions.

Understanding
the Writing Project

IF YOU have ever participated in a survey—online, on the phone, even in a short response card that came with a product warranty—you have participated in *causal analysis*, as part of a data group. You have provided information about who you are and most likely what caused you to behave in a certain way: to purchase a product, to view a movie, or to vote for or against something.

Organizations might be interested in your personal information for different reasons: some for purely academic reasons, and some for reasons that are completely self-promotional. Regardless of the intentions, the research all begins with an observation—a theory. As you begin to observe and form theories, you have to ask yourself the question: Is the pattern or trend significant enough to be noteworthy? The best way to answer this question is to look at what might be the causes and/or effects. The word *might* is significant here. Although we can prove a trend exists—with measurements like statistics—our understanding of causes is always speculative. In other words, you have to create a well-reasoned analysis that defends your conclusions about what the causes and/or effects of the trend are.

ASSIGNMENT Identify a pattern or trend—some new development in behavior you have observed—living "off the energy grid," for example. Or you might identify a new twist in an established phenomenon such as marriage among teens. You might be able to come up with a theory if you find the marriage rate is rising or falling among that age group. Write a trend analysis that includes multiple sources and speculation about the causes and/or effects of the pattern or trend you have selected.

Researched Articles

CLAIRE CAIN MILLER

Is Owning Overrated? The Rental Economy Rises

THINGS THAT you can now rent instead of buying: a power drill, a song, a tent, an office for an hour, a Prada handbag, a wedding dress, a painting, a dog, your neighbor's car, a drone.

This new way of consuming—call it the Netflix economy—is being built by Web start-ups that either rent items themselves or serve as middlemen, connecting people who want something with people who own it. They are a growing corner of the broader sharing economy, in which people rent out rooms in their homes on Airbnb or drive people in their cars with Uber or Lyft. Soon, tech entrepreneurs and investors say, we'll be able to rent much of what we always thought we must own.

It is no coincidence that many of these companies—like Rent the Runway for designer dresses and Getaround for private cars—were born during the financial crisis, when people needed new ways to save money, as well as new ways to make it. The ones that have survived and grown during the recovery could herald a cultural shift away from the overconsumption that has driven so much of American culture—not to mention American debt.

The sharing economy is being built by start-ups, including Rent the Runway, which rents out designer fashions.

"It's very counterintuitive from the old individualistic American culture, where what people aspire to has been increasing amounts of privacy, gated communities, owning your own," said Juliet Schor, a sociology professor at Boston College who is studying the sharing economy for a MacArthur Foundation research project. "So it is a real twist on where values, sensibilities and culture have been." Then again, it might just be a new way to fuel conspicuous consumption, albeit in a more financially responsible and potentially less wasteful way. In other words, for some it is less about saving the planet than being seen in the latest, unaffordable Versace gown.

Either way, the entrepreneurs say the rental economy is part of a growing, post-recession movement to value experiences over possessions. Anticipating a new belonging can bring more happiness than actually owning it, studies have shown, and everyone knows how quickly the glow of a new purchase wears off.

"Our value set has changed as a younger generation," said Jennifer Hyman, co-founder and chief executive of Rent the Runway. "We are now in a state of mind where we want to acquire more experiences. The 1990s 'MTV Cribs' show-off-how-much-money-you-have generation is over." (The customer who rents that $1,895 Versace gown for $80 might disagree.)

Even as the economy improves, there is evidence that people might have a chastened

approach to discretionary spending. Though overall consumer spending has returned to pre-crisis levels, it has been rising at a disappointing rate, and the biggest increases are coming from necessities like food and transportation as opposed to small luxuries like apparel and entertainment.

Before the recession and before she was a senator, Elizabeth Warren was a professor at Harvard Law School, and she found that Americans were winding up in debt and without nest eggs not because of spending on clothes, gadgets or restaurants but because of spending on the basics of middle-class life, like homes and cars. So could the answer be to forgo ownership of everything else?

In many ways, renting is just a continuation of what people have always done—borrowing a cup of sugar or a pick-up truck from a neighbor. The difference is that technology has made borrowing possible at a broader scale, and between strangers. Social networking profiles and rating systems offer a level of trust and verification, and mobile phones equipped with GPS take much of the work out of pairing people. Examples are TurningArt for renting artwork, Pley for renting Legos and LiquidSpace for renting an office by the hour.

Still, the services raise questions for consumers—mainly around trust. What happens if someone stains the dress being rented, crashes the car or loses the dog? (The companies have different ways to deal with the risks, including insurance policies, contracts and fees.)

Several such start-ups, like SnapGoods, which was for renting items in your house to neighbors, have been forced to shut down or change their business. Ron J. Williams, the co-founder of SnapGoods, said he learned a lesson about the limits of the rental economy.

"I will not go across town to rent a vacuum cleaner when Amazon can have one on my doorstep tomorrow for only $20 more than it would have cost me to rent it," said Mr. Williams, who now has a start-up called Simplist. "I will, however, go across town to rent a motorcycle that will make indelible memories at a fraction of that bike's full cost."

If the idea persists, these companies could put a dent in retail sales and manufacturing of new products. Some already are. As more people forgo buying songs and stream them using services like Spotify, for instance, music downloads worldwide fell for the first time last year. Uber has tried to make an economic case that sharing cars is more affordable than owning one.

Rent the Runway, which was started in 2009, said that so far this year, new customers and orders were more than double those of last year. Last month, it expanded beyond fancy dresses to accessories like bags and jewelry, which customers can rent for as long as they desire. Ms. Hyman said this service competes with fast-fashion retailers like Zara, from which people buy things to wear for just a few months.

The idea works best for "fallow assets," or expensive items that people rarely use, said Aileen Lee, founder of the venture capital firm Cowboy Ventures, who is on the board of Rent the Runway. That is why the company rents cocktail dresses but not jeans.

As for how much this trend will change consumer culture, consider this: People who rent items often end up buying them. Maybe in this economy, people just need a little hand-holding before making big splurges. And particularly for things that wear out, Ms. Schor said, buying might even be the most ecological and economical choice.

Questions for Critical Thinking

1. Have you observed examples of this trend in your own life? Can you add other examples of the "Netflix economy" from your experience or observation?

2. Comment on the claim that the "rental economy is part of a growing, post-recession movement to value experiences over possessions." Do you agree that this is a trend? Can you cite behavior you have observed (in your life, from news stories, from popular culture) that confirms this movement or that argues against it?

3. Can you point to other trends you have observed that also involved consumer spending—something related to dining out or the amount of money spent on electronics, cell-phone bills, and so on? What do you think causes people to spend on those services or items? Can you speculate about what that type of spending reveals about people and their values? How would you research the causes and effects of consumer spending?

The Rhetorical Situation

Your article will inform readers about some new pattern or something new in a long-standing pattern of behavior.

Purpose: Your article will inform readers about some new pattern or something new in a long-standing pattern of behavior.

Voice: You are a reliable authority on the subject since you've researched it thoroughly. Still, you don't want your writing to be weighed down by statistics and numbers. Write in a style that is both professional and conversational.

Audience: People are perennially curious about discovering new trends and the causes or effects on society, commerce, culture, technology, and the workplace.

Media and Design: Infographics concisely reveal patterns through "visualizing data." You can find free tools online that help you translate your trend analysis into succinct text with images.

THE BIG IDEA

The Analytical Thesis

The analytical thesis—one sentence or several sentences—clearly defines the trend or phenomenon and presents the theory about it. The analytical thesis signals to your readers what they will understand by reading your analysis.

The article about the rental economy, which appeared earlier in this chapter, includes a broad statement:

> [T]he entrepreneurs say the rental economy is part of a growing, postrecession movement to value experiences over possessions. Anticipating a new belonging can bring more happiness than actually owning it, studies have shown, and everyone knows how quickly the glow of a new purchase wears off.

If readers continue—the analytical thesis promises—they will understand what the trend might reveal: that ownership is less of a goal than it used to be. Most important, they will understand, specifically, *why* experience is trumping ownership. This notion, which is the author's theory, needs both explanation and argument. The argument depends on the writer's analysis of data, examples, and illustrations that help make the case. The data reveal the causes and effects of the trend.

Another writer, whose topic is technology, focuses on students' attention spans. He included this analytical thesis:

> Students have always faced distractions and time-wasters. But computers and cellphones, and the constant stream of stimuli they offer, pose a profound new challenge to focusing and learning. Researchers say the lure of these technologies, while it affects adults, too, is particularly powerful for young people. The risk, they say, is that developing brains can become more easily habituated than adult brains to constantly switching tasks—and less able to sustain attention.
>
> —Matt Richtel, "Growing Up Digital, Wired for Distraction"

This writer, whom you will meet later in the chapter, speculates that one effect of having constant access to cell phones and the Internet is losing the ability to concentrate for sustained periods. This resulting shorter attention span is not fact, but a prediction. What follows is an argument defending the theory, citing examples and illustrations, and making a case for why the theory is reasonable.

Research Paths: Organizing Your Investigation of Causes and Effects

To prove that a trend exists and to be able to speculate about its causes, you will be collecting materials online, in the library, and in interviews.

PRACTICE 11.1

Conducting a Survey

Create a list of survey questions related to what type of transportation the students at your college prefer to use. Depending on the location of your school, your questions could include public transportation (if available), carpooling, walking, bicycling, and so on. Include some questions about time spent traveling and cost. Make sure to get responses from a cross section of students, and to ask 20 to 30 students for responses. Write a summary of your findings, focusing on two questions:

1. What was the most common response?

2. Which response was the most surprising? ■

Keeping Track of Your Research

For each source you examine, make note of the following information:

- Author
- Article or chapter title
- Full journal name or book title
- Date and place of publication
- Page number(s)
- For websites, full URL and date

Books

You might not think of books as the first place to begin research, but almost always, one source can lead you to another, and books can be a good way to get to high-quality information as well as additional sources. In current publications, you can get a good understanding of what is new about a topic, even with a quick search of Amazon.com or your library's catalog. (On Amazon.com, you can even read a few pages and browse through the tables of contents for some books.) Books and articles will usually include bibliographies that come in handy in finding more sources. Once you know of an author who has written about your subject, you can do an Internet search to see if more articles are available online or in the library. You can even e-mail the author and ask for an e-mail or personal interview.

Social Media

In your search for practitioners and experts, you might want to consult Twitter, Facebook, and other message boards related to your subject matter. Often you can leave questions on message boards (such as College Confidential Discussions,

Absolute Write) and get answers from people with knowledge of and experiences with your topic. You might even privately e-mail some of the respondents for information they might not want made public. You can send out messages on Twitter that you are looking for information by using the # in front of key words. People who share the special interest could connect with you through that key-wording system. Also, you could put out a call to your friends via Facebook that you are looking for people who can share their experiences regarding your subject.

Internet Search Engines and Directories

You will find some current information by using directories and search engines on the Web, so these sources are good choices for researching current trends. However, not all Web material is equally useful or accurate, so carefully evaluate Web sources. The U.S. government's official website, USA.gov, is a portal that leads you to census data, studies, and other sources of statistical information that can be useful in writing about trends. Any state's department of public health can offer reliable information as well. In general, the most reliable, unbiased sources of statistical information are .gov and .edu sites.

Internet Database

Databases that are available by subscription provide excellent material not usually available on the free Web. LexisNexis, Proquest, and InfoTrac, for example, may be available to you because your library has paid a fee. You gain entry by logging on through your library or by using a password.

Interviews

Ask yourself: Who is involved? Who are the stakeholders? Who is affected? Who is an expert on the topic? Interviewing is an important part of making your trend research original. Through interviews, you gather quotations that give your statistics human faces and real-life stories. Quotations can also enliven your analysis and give it a more engaging style. Two ways to get good quotations are:

1. **Consulting Experts** Experts are people who work in relevant fields and have a deep knowledge of the subject of your trend analysis. Doctors, researchers, and authors of books make good sources and can provide excellent primary source material, making your paper more original than if you relied only on published sources.

2. **Consulting Practitioners** Practitioners are people who have experienced or have observed the trend or who personify it and are also experts. They help make the trend relevant and give it a human side. For some tips on interviewing, refer to page 418 in Chapter 15, "Research."

PRACTICE 11.2
Causes or Effects?

Using the following list of trends:

1. Decide whether you would start exploring the causes or effects of the following trends (or both) and explain why.

2. How would you prove these trends exist?

   Increase in part-time students

   Increase in students studying foreign languages

   Increase in number of women studying science and technology

   Decrease in sports teams at high schools

   Decrease in numbers of children getting vaccinations

   Decrease in number of liberal-arts courses offered at colleges ■

Visual Literacy: Visualizing Information

Analyze the connection between the message and the information in "The Most Dangerous Species in the Boston Harbor."

How do the images draw the reader into the information?

How would you create a metaphorical image that illustrates some factual data—the number of teens who smoke, for example, or the number of songs downloaded from iTunes per day?

THE MOST DANGEROUS SPECIES IN BOSTON HARBOR

Aluminum foil and tin cans
Origin: Trash cans, litter, boaters' debris
Behavior: Once ingested by other harbor dwellers, the metal causes lacerations to internal organs. Smaller creatures can become trapped inside the metal and starve to death
Lifespan: 200-500 years

Plastic bags
Origin: Beaches and trash containers
Behavior: They look a lot like jellyfish, and are eaten by other creatures.
Lifespan: Though they have only been around for 50 years, they will have a 500-1000 year lifespan, potentially, and are made of a polymer that never biodegrades. However, the bags break down and become brittle, scattering into all corners of the harbor and ocean.

Paper Bags
Origin: Beaches, boats
Behavior: Kraft bags degrade quickly, but cause digestive problems in hungry sea life.
Lifespan: 4 weeks

Food wrappers
Origin: Trash cans, careless picnickers
Behavior: They keep the food airtight without leaking grease because they are made from Mylar and plastic, often coated with a chemical that is carcinogenic—bad for humans and fellow harbor inhabitants
Lifespan: 25 years, average

Based on THE MOST DANGEROUS SPECIES IN THE MEDITERRANEAN
Agencia Catalana de l'Aigue
Generalutat de Catalunya
Departament de Medi Ambienti Habitge

Plastic beverage bottles
Origin: Trash containers, boats.
Behavior: Poisons and traps sea life
Lifespan: Average 350-400 years

Cigarette butts
Origin: Toilets, city streets, careless motorists
Behavior: Their toxic blend of soluble chemicals can leach into water within 60 minutes of contact.
Lifespan: Filters—made of cellulose acetate— take three years to break down

Kate Burak

Tips for Establishing Your Ethos

Show That You Understand Your Audience

1. What do your readers already know about the topic? Do not talk down to them.

(continued)

Using the questions for testing topics, evaluate the following observations. Can you detect a possible trend worth investigating?

1. You observed women wearing blue lipstick.

2. The newspaper in your town has decided to publish only three days a week.

3. An elderly neighbor was swindled by a company who took her down payment and never delivered her new windows.

4. Your college has stopped selling bottled water.

5. Your college turned off all wireless Internet connections in classroom buildings. ■

Tips for Establishing Your Ethos *(continued)*

2. Why does your audience not know? Is it because the topic is new? Highly technical? Do not confuse them.

3. Is it a topic some might find controversial? Do not offend your readers.

Show That You Are an Authority

1. Use precise, measurable data, such as statistics, results of polls, and surveys.

2. Interview people who can talk about direct observation and personal experiences or anecdotes (practitioners).

3. Consult secondary sources for anecdotes, illustrations, and examples.

4. Quote experts on the topic (authors of books and articles, experts in the field) who can make generalizations.

Write in an Objective Voice

1. Avoid first person.

2. Do not directly state your opinion. Allow your sources to introduce opinion.

3. Use attribution well: "According to expert sources . . .

Choosing a Good Topic

How do you find a topic that will engage your readers enough that they will want to spend some time reading about it? Two types of patterns make good topics: new patterns or trends, and new developments in familiar patterns and trends.

New patterns can develop along with changes in technology or medicine, laws, or political movements. Looking at the way "generation text" relies on digital communications is a good example of a pattern that is new and is the result of technology. Some patterns in behavior that have been around for thousands of years can still make good subject matter, too. For example, people throughout time and in many cultures have gambled. You can start with gambling as a topic for your initial thinking, and describe some instances you have observed, such as:

1. Aunt Mary buys lottery tickets and plays poker on Tuesday nights.
2. Your state is voting on whether to legalize casino gambling.

3. You have a 13-year-old cousin who really loves online poker.
4. You read about a celebrity athlete who was convicted of gambling on dog fighting.

Use the Questions for Testing Your Topic above for assessing the worth of developing these observations into an analysis.

A Journalist's Tips for Showing the Human Side of Data

To help your writing move beyond becoming a listing of data, consider ways journalists write feature articles that include statistical analysis. (See also the poster on caffeine that brings in facts for interest.)

1. **Find people who have experiences with the trend or pattern—"practitioners" or "observers."** Interview them for realistic details.
2. **When you interview sources who have experiences with the trend, ask questions that lead to "stories."** ("When was the first time?" or "What did you see?")
3. **Begin with a "hook."** A hook might be a piece of someone's story, either in the form of a scene or an anecdote.
4. **Show the trend in action.** Include a demonstration of what your readers might see if they could observe a piece of the picture.
5. **Think of the writing as a conversation.** When you, through a source or statistic, make a point, allow a source (expert or practitioner or statistic) to provide a response—a comment or counterpoint as if your sources were responding to each other.
6. **Do not forget to describe.** When you can, include a detail that shows what the trend looks like, feels like, how much something costs, or how it sounds.
7. **Save a good detail—an image or interesting quotation for the end.** It is the reader's last impression.

The Caffeine Poster

Discovered in 1819 by German chemist Friedrich Ferdinand Runge, caffeine is a crystalline xanthine alkaloid that is a psychoactive stimulant drug.

$C_8H_{10}N_4O_2$
(Caffeine)
1.23 g/cm^3

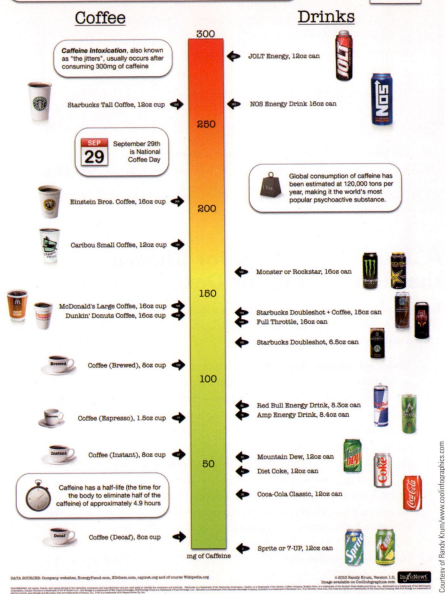

Coffee

Caffeine Intoxication, also known as "the jitters", usually occurs after consuming 300mg of caffeine

Starbucks Tall Coffee, 12oz cup

SEP **29** September 29th is National Coffee Day

Einstein Bros. Coffee, 16oz cup

Caribou Small Coffee, 12oz cup

McDonald's Large Coffee, 16oz cup
Dunkin' Donuts Coffee, 16oz cup

Coffee (Brewed), 8oz cup

Coffee (Espresso), 1.5oz cup

Coffee (Instant), 8oz cup

Caffeine has a half-life (the time for the body to eliminate half of the caffeine) of approximately 4.9 hours

Coffee (Decaf), 8oz cup

Drinks

300

JOLT Energy, 12oz can

NOS Energy Drink 16oz can

250

Global consumption of caffeine has been estimated at 120,000 tons per year, making it the world's most popular psychoactive substance.

200

Monster or Rockstar, 16oz can

150

Starbucks Doubleshot + Coffee, 15oz can
Full Throttle, 16oz can

Starbucks Doubleshot, 6.5oz can

100

Red Bull Energy Drink, 8.3oz can
Amp Energy Drink, 8.4oz can

Mountain Dew, 12oz can

Diet Coke, 12oz can

Coca-Cola Classic, 12oz can

50

Sprite or 7-UP, 12oz can

mg of Caffeine

Courtesy of Randy Krum/www.coolinfographics.com

11 WRITING A CAUSAL ANALYSIS

Using Logic to Analyze Cause and Effect: Avoid Jumping to Conclusions

People sometimes make mistakes when they go looking for what caused something to happen. Two common logical fallacies, as the following discussion describes, demonstrate how faulty reasoning makes for bad logic in causal analyses.

The Post Hoc Fallacy

Walking under a ladder causes bad luck—so do letting a black cat cross your path, breaking a mirror, and spilling salt. Dropping a glass means that company is coming. Finding a four-leaf clover brings good luck. These superstitions are all based on the faulty assumption that because two events happen sequentially, the first has caused the second.

You can see how the superstitions may have arisen: people walk under ladders at a building site and perhaps occasionally bricks fall on their heads, or company seems to arrive just when you have dropped the crystal wine glasses. One coincidence leads to a generalization, but in fact the occurrence of one event does not necessarily mean the second will follow.

Statisticians phrase it this way: correlation does not prove causation. Logicians use the Latin phrase *post hoc, ergo propter hoc*, meaning "after this, therefore because of this," to describe this error in reasoning. When you write about causes and effects, be careful to avoid this fallacy.

The claim in the graph is that general alcohol consumption habits have changed. Can you speculate about how this information might have been gathered? Can you identify any problems with the methods of gathering information about habits like drinking?

Assigning Singular Cause

If you have determined a cause-and-effect relationship between two events, do not assume that any one cause is the only cause. Sometimes a cause can be one of many, and other causes may be hidden or more significant.

For example, if you are looking at the growing problem of obesity among children, you might assume that the cause is the decrease in their physical activity. You know that one reason for weight gain is burning fewer calories, so inactivity could certainly be a cause of obesity.

However, there are enough skinny couch potatoes around to make you look for other causes as well. A slow or malfunctioning metabolism might cause weight gain; calorie-laden fast food can cause weight gain; and genetics may play a part. The causes of obesity are multiple and complex.

Reading Statistics with a Critical Eye

Statistics can be used or misused, depending on how ethical a writer is. Statistics might be distorted to understate or overstate a trend. For example, you might read that 50 percent of the police officers in a small town in Ohio were killed on the job last year. That rate is up 100 percent from the year before. The implication is that this is a dangerous town with a steeply climbing crime rate. The fact of the matter is that the town had two officers, and one was killed while helping a motorist change a tire. Although it is true and unfortunate that one of the two officers was killed last year, it is misleading to say that 50 percent of the force was killed on the job last year.

Statistics, even those that are factual, are not always accurate without a clear context. You must be careful not to use every statistic you find without evaluating it and its source. You must also be careful to use statistics responsibly.

Here is an example of a statistic that needs a full explanation:

> The United States Fire Administration (USFA) announced today that 441 firefighters died while on duty in the United States in 2001. This total, which is more than four and one-half times the average annual number of firefighter deaths for the last decade, includes 343 firefighters lost at the World Trade Center on September 11.

What surprises you about the conclusion you might reach after reading the data presented this way?

> The loss represents the worst total since the USFA began tracking firefighter fatalities in 1977. USFA is a part of the Federal Emergency Management Agency. "2001 was a tragic year for America's fire service," R. David Paulson, United States Fire Administrator, said. "In addition to the many local heroes who died serving their communities nationwide, the eyes of the world turned to New York City on September 11."
>
> —United States Fire Administration, Press Release

PRACTICE 11.5

Evaluating a Chart or Graph

Choose one of the charts or infographics from this chapter and write an evaluation. Use the following criteria: Is the information in the chart or graph clear to a general audience? Can the reader reach multiple conclusions from the data? Write a one-sentence generalization based on the data. ■

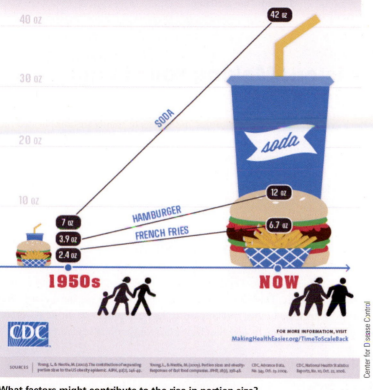

THE NEW (AB)NORMAL

Portion sizes have been growing. So have we. The average restaurant meal today is more than four times larger than in the 1950s. And adults are, on average, 26 pounds heavier. If we want to eat healthy, there are things we can do for ourselves and our community: Order the smaller meals on the menu, split a meal with a friend, or, eat half and take the rest home. We can also ask the managers at our favorite restaurants to offer smaller meals.

40 oz
30 oz
20 oz
10 oz

42 oz

SODA

12 oz

HAMBURGER

6.7 oz

FRENCH FRIES

7 oz
3.9 oz
2.4 oz

1950s   **NOW**

CDC

FOR MORE INFORMATION, VISIT
MakingHealthEasier.org/TimeToScaleBack

SOURCES   Young, L., & Nestle, M. (2002). The contribution of expanding portion sizes to the US obesity epidemic. AJPH, 92(2), 246-49.   Young, L., & Nestle, M. (2003). Portion sizes and obesity: Responses of fast-food companies. JPHP, 28(2), 238-48.   CDC, Advance Data, No. 349, Oct. 25, 2004.   CDC, National Health Statistics Reports, No. 10, Oct. 22, 2008.

Center for Disease Control

What factors might contribute to the rise in portion size?

Numbers can also underplay a trend. It does not seem noteworthy to report that 20 students from the University of Cincinnati will spend spring break building houses with Habitat for Humanity. But if you find out that 600 students from all over Ohio are building houses for the poor, as compared with 200 last year, the numbers start to build a full and reliable picture of a trend.

Numbers can be translated to obscure information or to be more useful to readers. You can say that in 1999 there were 47,895 accounting majors at colleges nationwide. This seems like a lot of prospective accountants. Still, there were 13,325 fewer accounting majors in 1999 than there were in 1995. In context, this statistic can be even more accessible to readers.

Some industry specialists say interest in accounting careers has waned on campuses even though demand remains relatively strong. According to a 2001 study commissioned by the American Institute of Certified Public Accountants, the number of college students choosing an accounting major dropped more than 21 percent from a high of 61,220 in the 1994–95 school year to 47,895 for 1998–99, the most recent year for which figures are available.

—Barbara Claire Kasselmann, "More Than Debits, Credits"

Revision: Making Your Logic Airtight

Research articles that explore the causes and effects of trends are complicated pieces of writing, and asking a reader to follow you through a collection of statistics, quotations, and explanations requires you to be a gentle guide. Transitions, which convince your reader that your analysis is logical and clearly guided in a particular direction, can be divided into three types:

BIG IDEA

1. Big Idea Reminders

You restate your thesis, reminding readers that you have a main point about a pattern. These reminders are like signposts and help you—and your reader—refocus. They say, "Remember, this is the big picture we were thinking about." ("Increased binge drinking on college campuses" might be reworded to remind the reader: "more incidents of heavy drinking among students at parties.")

2. Restatements of Previous Topics

Briefly restate a bit of the previous topic or a phrase from the previous paragraph, then introduce the next point ("Besides being dangerous to the students in an immediate, physical way, these incidents of binge drinking can prove dangerous emotionally, as well. . . .")

3. Single Word Transitions

- Showing chronology (*first, before, later, after*)
- Showing comparisons (*likewise, in this case*)
- Showing contrast (*on the other hand, however, but, although*)
- Showing cause and effect (*because, therefore, as a result*)
- Showing additional thoughts (*also, moreover, and*)
- Showing illustrations (*for example, so you see*)

DIY MEDIA AND DESIGN

Data Storytelling through Infographics

How do you allow the data—the facts, figures, and details—to tell the story?

Like trend stories, infographics give readers researched information about data, but the format relies on visual design to make its case. The idea of "visualizing data" is not a new one—charts and graphs are used in countless ways to condense a big message into an image, with words and numbers to guide the way. Not limited by media, infographics can include interactive websites and videos. Remember that data can tell more than one story. Decide on which one you are telling, and remember you can explain everything. After you make decisions about the "takeaway" for your infographic, consider that trends exist within a time frame and think about how to reveal cause and effect over time. It's your story to tell and your challenge is to tell the story through your selection of data.

Conduct a survey (about health, fitness, consumer behavior, or lifestyle). Ask questions to a diverse sample of at least 20 to 30 people. Design your own infographic or video that makes your collected data visual.

READINGS

The readings in this chapter analyze observable trends among young people—patterns that are shaped by a complex collection of causes.

College Class Tries to Revive the Lost Art of Dating

Heather Cicchese

Is there a solution to the problems that come from the "hookup" culture? A writer looks over the shoulder of a professor who explores the causes and effects of the lost art of dating.

IN A STARBUCKS on the Boston University campus, Dave Griffin sat down with an acquaintance from his hometown of Duxbury [Massachusetts]. Griffin placed two coffees and two croissants on the table.

Griffin and his date caught up on how freshman year had been, the conversation tinged with awkwardness, until they reached the 45-minute time limit. Before they parted ways, he invited her on a second date. He didn't tell her why he'd asked her on the first one.

"I would have asked her out regardless," he said.

Unknown to his companion, Griffin had invited her for coffee as part of an assignment for a Boston College class whose instructor, Kerry Cronin, gives extra credit to any student who will go on a date.

The reason? Because most of them don't know how, Cronin says.

It's not surprising, says Cronin. This is a generation that has grown up with relatively low

> "Cronin describes dating as a 'lost social script.'"

expectations in the realm of happily ever after. Theirs is a world where most embrace group activities, punctuated with the periodic hookup, and communicate largely in digital bursts of 140–250 characters instead of in person.

Cronin says this all came together for her during a lecture she gave about the campus hookup culture eight years ago. She says she was nervously anticipating controversial questions about sex and intimacy, but instead one student asked, "How would you ask someone on a date?"

As she began to answer, the questioner became more specific: "Like, the actual words."

That year, Cronin gave the option of going on a date to students in a seminar she taught to juniors and seniors that examined relationships, spirituality, and personal development.

Only one of the 15 students did. The next semester, she made the assignment mandatory, and some students began choosing the course

Heather Cicchese, "College Class Tries to Revive the Lost Art of Dating," *Boston Globe*, May 16, 2014. Reprinted by permission of the author.

specifically for that reason, saying they had trouble asking people out on dates on their own.

Cronin is associate director of the Lonergan Institute, a philosophy research center at Boston College. She now teaches a philosophy class for freshmen and sophomores that includes discussions of personal ethical and moral choices, and the optional dating assignment is part of the syllabus.

"The idea behind the hookup culture is that these are our 'crazy' and 'independent' years, and dating is too serious or committed," says Meaghan Kelliher, a sophomore who took Cronin's class and went on a "Cronin date." She says the assignment showed her that dating could be "exploratory" rather than a serious commitment.

Cronin describes dating as a "lost social script." Students, she says, don't know where to begin or what to say. Her assignment delineates specific boundaries so students know what to expect. The date has to be 45 to 90 minutes long with a person of legitimate romantic interest.

The student has to pay and has to make the invitation not by text or e-mail but in person, which Griffin did at a BU dance recital he attended with a mutual friend. The date cannot involve alcohol, kissing, and sex.

Dating, Cronin says, has been supplanted on campuses by a hookup culture that can entail anything from kissing to having sex with strangers or acquaintances rather than committed partners. When Cronin gives talks, on the other hand, she plays down the issue of sex and focuses on how dating requires the courage to be vulnerable to another person.

Cronin explains the assignment to her students as "wanting us to do something courageous," says freshman Frank DiMartino, who took the class. "It's easy to hook up with someone you've just met in a dark room after having a few drinks," DiMartino says. "But asking someone out on a date in broad daylight, and when you actually have to know their name, can be really scary."

Professor Kerry Cronin assigns her BC students to go out on a date, with specific requirements for the length, behavior, and use of their interpersonal skills.

Cronin's not expecting students to return to the courting culture of the 1940s or '50s, but she says it would be useful for them to revive and reshape the dating "script." "When my parents and grandparents went on dates they knew what to expect. That's what a social script is, that's why manners work—not because they're truths but because they make things easier," she says.

Students no longer have that script. For them, says Cronin, dating is so rare it feels strange and even creepy. Instead, students use friendships and groups to satisfy social and emotional needs and see hookups as purely physical. But as a result, Cronin says, students don't have a relationship that allows them to address the confusions or expectations that can arise out of hookups.

Relying on groups also prevents students from learning to interact one-on-one. "In a group, you get to know another person as mediated through the group dynamic," Cronin says.

Social media, especially texting, is another way one-on-one conversations are mediated. It provides access to a constructed "virtual self." While it makes students feel connected, Cronin believes it builds habits of "ADD-quality connections" rather than face-to-face relationships.

But students like Griffin, who have taken up the dating assignment, say they enjoyed the experience. "There was a general feeling of awkwardness but also accomplishment," he says.

Another reason students are reluctant to date, says Cronin, is that, "When you ask somebody,

you risk failing, and nobody likes to fail or be vulnerable to rejection."

Especially college students.

"They like to push themselves out of their comfort zone only if the energy and effort will equal success," Cronin says. "But when asking someone out, nothing can ensure the person is going to say yes."

Between 60 and 80 percent of North American college students have had some sort of hookup experience, according to a study published by the American Psychological Association in February 2013. However, a similar percentage, 63 percent of college-age men and 83 percent of college-age women, would prefer a traditional relationship to an uncommitted sexual one, the study found.

"The vast majority of young adults hope to be in a romantic relationship characterized by mutual love and commitment," says Richard McAnulty, an associate professor in psychology at the University of North Carolina at Charlotte, a pattern that hasn't changed despite uncommitted sex becoming more socially acceptable.

"Young adults have not abandoned intimate relationships," McAnulty says. "Those relationships simply look different than in the past." Most students practice "serial monogamy," in which they have consecutive, exclusive relationships involving emotional intimacy and sex.

Though today's young adults are more wary about long-term relationships and settling down, their caution is not unwarranted, considering that about half of American marriages end in divorce.

Critics of the hookup culture fear it will prevent students from being able to form successful long-term relationships later in life. McAnulty says that young adults today are less willing to settle for relationships without sex than their predecessors

were 30 or 40 years ago, but research still has to be done about whether hooking up causes commitment problems later.

Cronin is optimistic about people's ability to "figure things out," and doesn't believe the hookup culture will cause fewer people to get married or lead successful family lives. But for now, the hookup culture, as Cronin puts it, "creates a part of life that is unnecessarily chaotic and lonely."

As for Griffin, he decided he was willing to give dating a try. Outside The Sinclair in Cambridge, he waited to begin his second date.

◆ ◆ ◆

Excerpts from Kerry Cronin's Assignment Rules

- **You must ask someone out in person** (i.e., not in a text message or on Facebook, Snapchat, etc.), **and it must be someone you've never dated.**
- **Arrange the date within three days of asking.** Waiting longer creates unnecessary anxiety, invites drama, and sets the stage for unsolicited (or worse, solicited) opinions and advice.
- **This person must be someone who is a legitimate romantic interest** (i.e., not just a friend). It does not have to be a person you've had a crush on for months or years . . . in fact, it probably shouldn't be that person, since that might be a bit intense.
- **Have a definite and simple plan for the date.** Do not ask the other person to decide what to do on the date. Having a straightforward and simple plan shows care, concern, and takes the pressure off.
- **Pay for the date yourself,** without fuss.

Questions for Rhetorical Analysis

1. What is the "big idea" of this article?
2. What are the causes and effects of the hookup culture, according to the article?
3. What type of opening does the writer choose to use for this piece? How does she attempt to attract the attention of readers?
4. Which trend does this story explain?

Questions for Critical Thinking

1. How do you view the idea of dating as a class assignment? As a social experiment? As a skill someone needs to "practice"?
2. In your opinion, does the writer put a "human face" on the issue of hookup culture?
3. Writers analyze trends in order to explain something new or ever-present. Identify a trend involving social media that you have observed or participated in. Prove it exists by listing examples and describing its component pieces, and discuss the causes and or effects.

Style Practice: Imitation

Write an opening to a trend analysis about a behavior you have observed (at the gym, at a coffee shop, within social media). Use the "human face" approach that the author uses in this article. Include a real person and describe a scene.

Growing Up Digital, Wired for Distraction
Matt Richtel

From the title of this reading you can detect the author's conclusion about the effects of growing up exposed to digital technology, but read carefully to see whether this "distraction" is necessarily a negative outcome of this exposure.

REDWOOD CITY, Calif.—On the eve of a pivotal academic year in Vishal Singh's life, he faces a stark choice on his bedroom desk: book or computer?

By all rights, Vishal, a bright 17-year-old, should already have finished the book, Kurt Vonnegut's "Cat's Cradle," his summer reading assignment. But he has managed 43 pages in two months.

He typically favors Facebook, YouTube and making digital videos. That is the case this August afternoon. Bypassing Vonnegut, he clicks over to YouTube, meaning that tomorrow he will enter his senior year of high school hoping to see an improvement in his grades, but without having completed his only summer homework.

On YouTube, "you can get a whole story in six minutes," he explains. "A book takes so long. I prefer the immediate gratification."

Students have always faced distractions and time-wasters. But computers and cellphones, and the constant stream of stimuli they offer, pose a profound new challenge to focusing and learning.

Researchers say the lure of these technologies, while it affects adults too, is particularly powerful for young people. The risk, they say, is that developing brains can become more easily habituated than adult brains to constantly switching tasks—and less able to sustain attention.

"Their brains are rewarded not for staying on task but for jumping to the next thing," said Michael Rich, an associate professor at Harvard Medical School and executive director of the Center on Media and Child Health in Boston. And the effects could linger: "The worry is we're raising a generation of kids in front of screens whose brains are going to be wired differently."

But even as some parents and educators express unease about students' digital diets, they are intensifying efforts to use technology in the classroom, seeing it as a way to connect with students and give them essential skills. Across the country, schools are equipping themselves with computers, Internet access and mobile devices so they can teach on the students' technological territory.

It is a tension on vivid display at Vishal's school, Woodside High School, on a sprawling campus set against the forested hills of Silicon Valley. Here, as elsewhere, it is not uncommon for students to send hundreds of text messages a day or spend hours playing video games, and virtually everyone is on Facebook.

The principal, David Reilly, 37, a former musician who says he sympathizes when young people feel disenfranchised, is determined to engage these 21st-century students. He has asked teachers to build Web sites to communicate with students, introduced popular classes on using digital tools to record music, secured funding for iPads to teach Mandarin and obtained $3 million in grants for a multimedia center.

He pushed first period back an hour, to 9 a.m., because students were showing up bleary-eyed, at least in part because they were up late on their computers. Unchecked use of digital devices, he says, can create a culture in which students are addicted to the virtual world and lost in it.

"I am trying to take back their attention from their BlackBerrys and video games," he says. "To a degree, I'm using technology to do it."

The same tension surfaces in Vishal, whose ability to be distracted by computers is rivaled by his proficiency with them. At the beginning of his junior year, he discovered a passion for filmmaking and made a name for himself among friends and teachers with his storytelling in videos made with digital cameras and editing software.

He acts as his family's tech-support expert, helping his father, Satendra, a lab manager, retrieve lost documents on the computer, and his mother, Indra, a security manager at the San Francisco airport, build her own Web site.

But he also plays video games 10 hours a week. He regularly sends Facebook status updates at 2 a.m., even on school nights, and has such a reputation for distributing links to videos that his best friend calls him a "YouTube bully."

Several teachers call Vishal one of their brightest students, and they wonder why things are not adding up. Last semester, his grade point average was 2.3 after a D-plus in English and an F in Algebra II. He got an A in film critique.

"He's a kid caught between two worlds," said Mr. Reilly—one that is virtual and one with real-life demands.

> "The worry is we're raising a generation of kids in front of screens whose brains are going to be wired differently."

11 WRITING A CAUSAL ANALYSIS

Vishal, like his mother, says he lacks the self-control to favor schoolwork over the computer. She sat him down a few weeks before school started and told him that, while she respected his passion for film and his technical skills, he had to use them productively.

"This is the year," she says she told him. "This is your senior year and you can't afford not to focus."

It was not always this way. As a child, Vishal had a tendency to procrastinate, but nothing like this. Something changed him.

Growing Up with Gadgets

When he was 3, Vishal moved with his parents and older brother to their current home, a three-bedroom house in the working-class section of Redwood City, a suburb in Silicon Valley that is more diverse than some of its elite neighbors.

Thin and quiet with a shy smile, Vishal passed the admissions test for a prestigious public elementary and middle school. Until sixth grade, he focused on homework, regularly going to the house of a good friend to study with him.

But Vishal and his family say two things changed around the seventh grade: his mother went back to work, and he got a computer. He became increasingly engrossed in games and surfing the Internet, finding an easy outlet for what he describes as an inclination to procrastinate.

"I realized there were choices," Vishal recalls. "Homework wasn't the only option."

Several recent studies show that young people tend to use home computers for entertainment, not learning, and that this can hurt school performance, particularly in low-income families. Jacob L. Vigdor, an economics professor at Duke University who led some of the research, said that when adults were not supervising computer use, children "are left to their own devices, and the impetus isn't to do homework but play around."

Research also shows that students often juggle homework and entertainment. The Kaiser Family Foundation found earlier this year that half of students from 8 to 18 are using the Internet, watching TV or using some other form of media either "most" (31 percent) or "some" (25 percent) of the time that they are doing homework.

At Woodside, as elsewhere, students' use of technology is not uniform. Mr. Reilly, the principal, says their choices tend to reflect their personalities. Social butterflies tend to be heavy texters and Facebook users. Students who are less social might escape into games, while drifters or those prone to procrastination, like Vishal, might surf the Web or watch videos.

The technology has created on campuses a new set of social types—not the thespian and the jock but the texter and gamer, Facebook addict and YouTube potato. "The technology amplifies whoever you are," Mr. Reilly says.

For some, the amplification is intense. Allison Miller, 14, sends and receives 27,000 texts in a month, her fingers clicking at a blistering pace as she carries on as many as seven text conversations at a time. She texts between classes, at the moment soccer practice ends, while being driven to and from school and, often, while studying.

Most of the exchanges are little more than quick greetings, but they can get more in-depth, like "if someone tells you about a drama going on with someone," Allison said. "I can text one person while talking on the phone to someone else."

But this proficiency comes at a cost: she blames multitasking for the three B's on her recent progress report.

"I'll be reading a book for homework and I'll get a text message and pause my reading and put

down the book, pick up the phone to reply to the text message, and then 20 minutes later realize, 'Oh, I forgot to do my homework.'"

Some shyer students do not socialize through technology—they recede into it. Ramon Ochoa-Lopez, 14, an introvert, plays six hours of video games on weekdays and more on weekends, leaving homework to be done in the bathroom before school.

Escaping into games can also salve teenagers' age-old desire for some control in their chaotic lives. "It's a way for me to separate myself," Ramon says. "If there's an argument between my mom and one of my brothers, I'll just go to my room and start playing video games and escape."

With powerful new cellphones, the interactive experience can go everywhere. Between classes at Woodside or at lunch, when use of personal devices is permitted, students gather in clusters, sometimes chatting face to face, sometimes half-involved in a conversation while texting someone across the teeming quad. Others sit alone, watching a video, listening to music or updating Facebook.

Students say that their parents, worried about the distractions, try to police computer time, but that monitoring the use of cellphones is difficult. Parents may also want to be able to call their children at any time, so taking the phone away is not always an option.

Other parents wholly embrace computer use, even when it has no obvious educational benefit.

"If you're not on top of technology, you're not going to be on top of the world," said John McMullen, 56, a retired criminal investigator whose son, Sean, is one of five friends in the group Vishal joins for lunch each day.

Sean's favorite medium is video games; he plays for four hours after school and twice that on weekends. He was playing more but found his habit pulling his grade point average below 3.2, the point at which he felt comfortable. He says he sometimes wishes that his parents would force him to quit playing and study, because he finds it hard to quit when given the choice. Still, he says, video games are not responsible for his lack of focus, asserting that in another era he would have been distracted by TV or something else.

"Video games don't make the hole; they fill it," says Sean, sitting at a picnic table in the quad, where he is surrounded by a multimillion-dollar view: on the nearby hills are the evergreens that tower above the affluent neighborhoods populated by Internet tycoons. Sean, a senior, concedes that video games take a physical toll: "I haven't done exercise since my sophomore year. But that doesn't seem like a big deal. I still look the same."

Sam Crocker, Vishal's closest friend, who has straight A's but lower SAT scores than he would like, blames the Internet's distractions for his inability to finish either of his two summer reading books.

"I know I can read a book, but then I'm up and checking Facebook," he says, adding: "Facebook is amazing because it feels like you're doing something and you're not doing anything. It's the absence of doing something, but you feel gratified anyway."

He concludes: "My attention span is getting worse."

The Lure of Distraction

Some neuroscientists have been studying people like Sam and Vishal. They have begun to understand what happens to the brains of young people who are constantly online and in touch.

In an experiment at the German Sport University in Cologne in 2007, boys from 12 to 14 spent an hour each night playing video games after they finished homework.

On alternate nights, the boys spent an hour watching an exciting movie, like "Harry Potter" or "Star Trek," rather than playing video games. That allowed the researchers to compare the effect of video games and TV.

The researchers looked at how the use of these media affected the boys' brainwave patterns while sleeping and their ability to remember their homework in the subsequent days. They found that playing video games led to markedly lower sleep quality than watching TV, and also led to a "significant decline" in the boys' ability to remember vocabulary words. The findings were published in the journal *Pediatrics*.

Markus Dworak, a researcher who led the study and is now a neuroscientist at Harvard, said it was not clear whether the boys' learning suffered because sleep was disrupted or, as he speculates, also because the intensity of the game experience overrode the brain's recording of the vocabulary.

"When you look at vocabulary and look at huge stimulus after that, your brain has to decide which information to store," he said. "Your brain might favor the emotionally stimulating information over the vocabulary."

At the University of California, San Francisco, scientists have found that when rats have a new experience, like exploring an unfamiliar area, their brains show new patterns of activity. But only when the rats take a break from their exploration do they process those patterns in a way that seems to create a persistent memory.

"Downtime is to the brain what sleep is to the body," said Dr. Rich of Harvard Medical School. "But kids are in a constant mode of stimulation."

> "Downtime is to the brain what sleep is to the body," said Dr. Rich of Harvard Medical School. "But kids are in a constant mode of stimulation."

In that vein, recent imaging studies of people have found that major cross sections of the brain become surprisingly active during downtime. These brain studies suggest to researchers that periods of rest are critical in allowing the brain to synthesize information, make connections between ideas and even develop the sense of self.

Researchers say these studies have particular implications for young people, whose brains have more trouble focusing and setting priorities.

"The headline is: bring back boredom," added Dr. Rich, who last month gave a speech to the American Academy of Pediatrics entitled, "Finding Huck Finn: Reclaiming Childhood from the River of Electronic Screens."

Dr. Rich said in an interview that he was not suggesting young people should toss out their devices, but rather that they embrace a more balanced approach to what he said were powerful tools necessary to compete and succeed in modern life.

The heavy use of devices also worries Daniel Anderson, a professor of psychology at the University of Massachusetts at Amherst, who is known for research showing that children are not as harmed by TV viewing as some researchers have suggested.

Multitasking using ubiquitous, interactive and highly stimulating computers and phones, Professor Anderson says, appears to have a more powerful effect than TV. Like Dr. Rich, he says he believes that young, developing brains are becoming habituated to distraction and to switching tasks, not to focus.

"If you've grown up processing multiple media, that's exactly the mode you're going to fall

into when put in that environment—you develop a need for that stimulation," he said.

Vishal can attest to that.

"I'm doing Facebook, YouTube, having a conversation or two with a friend, listening to music at the same time. I'm doing a million things at once, like a lot of people my age," he says. "Sometimes I'll say: I need to stop this and do my schoolwork, but I can't."

"If it weren't for the Internet, I'd focus more on school and be doing better academically," he says. But thanks to the Internet, he says, he has discovered and pursued his passion: filmmaking. Without the Internet, "I also wouldn't know what I want to do with my life."

Clicking Toward a Future

The woman sits in a cemetery at dusk, sobbing. Behind her, silhouetted and translucent, a man kneels, then fades away, a ghost.

This captivating image appears on Vishal's computer screen. On this Thursday afternoon in late September, he is engrossed in scenes he shot the previous weekend for a music video he is making with his cousin.

The video is based on a song performed by the band Guns N' Roses about a woman whose boyfriend dies. He wants it to be part of the package of work he submits to colleges that emphasize film study, along with a documentary he is making about home-schooled students.

Now comes the editing. Vishal taught himself to use sophisticated editing software in part by watching tutorials on YouTube. He does not leave his chair for more than two hours, sipping Pepsi, his face often inches from the screen, as he perfects the clip from the cemetery. The image of the crying woman was shot separately from the image of the kneeling man, and he is trying to fuse them.

"I'm spending two hours to get a few seconds just right," he says.

He occasionally sends a text message or checks Facebook, but he is focused in a way he rarely is when doing homework. He says the chief difference is that filmmaking feels applicable to his chosen future, and he hopes colleges, like the University of Southern California or the California Institute of the Arts in Los Angeles, will be so impressed by his portfolio that they will overlook his school performance.

"This is going to compensate for the grades," he says. On this day, his homework includes a worksheet for Latin, some reading for English class and an economics essay, but they can wait.

interactivity. As he edits, the windows on the screen come alive; every few seconds, he clicks the mouse to make tiny changes to the lighting and flow of the images, and the software gives him constant feedback.

"I click and something happens," he says, explaining that, by comparison, reading a book or doing homework is less exciting. "I guess it goes back to the immediate gratification thing."

The $2,000 computer Vishal is using is state of the art and only a week old. It represents a concession by his parents. They allowed him to buy it, despite their continuing concerns about his technology habits, because they wanted to support his filmmaking dream. "If we put roadblocks in his way, he's just going to get depressed," his mother says. Besides, she adds, "he's been making an effort to do his homework."

At this point in the semester, it seems she is right. The first schoolwide progress reports come out in late September, and Vishal has mostly A's and B's. He says he has been able to make headway by applying himself, but also by cutting back his workload. Unlike last year, he is not taking advanced placement classes, and he has chosen to retake Algebra II not in the classroom but in an online class that lets him work at his own pace.

His shift to easier classes might not please college admissions officers, according to Woodside's college adviser, Zorina Matavulj. She says they want seniors to intensify their efforts. As it is, she says, even if Vishal improves his performance significantly, someone with his grades faces long odds in applying to the kinds of colleges he aspires to.

Still, Vishal's passion for film reinforces for Mr. Reilly, the principal, that the way to reach these students is on their own terms.

Hands-On Technology

Big Macintosh monitors sit on every desk, and a man with hip glasses and an easygoing style stands at the front of the class. He is Geoff Diesel, 40, a favorite teacher here at Woodside who has taught English and film. Now he teaches one of Mr. Reilly's new classes, audio production. He has a rapt audience of more than 20 students as he shows a video of the band Nirvana mixing their music, then holds up a music keyboard.

"Who knows how to use Pro Tools? We've got it. It's the program used by the best music studios in the world," he says.

In the back of the room, Mr. Reilly watches, thrilled. He introduced the audio course last year and enough students signed up to fill four classes. (He could barely pull together one class when he introduced Mandarin, even though he had secured iPads to help teach the language.)

"Some of these students are our most at-risk kids," he says. He means that they are more likely to tune out school, skip class or not do their homework, and that they may not get healthful meals at home.

They may also do their most enthusiastic writing not for class but in text messages and on Facebook. "They're here, they're in class, they're listening."

Despite Woodside High's affluent setting, about 40 percent of its 1,800 students come from low-income families and receive a reduced-cost or free lunch. The school is 56 percent Latino, 38 percent white and 5 percent African-American, and it sends 93 percent of its students to four-year or community colleges.

Mr. Reilly says that the audio class provides solid vocational training and can get students interested in other subjects.

"Today mixing music, tomorrow sound waves and physics," he says. And he thinks the key is that they love not just the music but getting their hands on the technology. "We're meeting them on their turf."

> "We're meeting them on their turf."

It does not mean he sees technology as a panacea. "I'll always take one great teacher in a cave over a dozen Smart Boards," he says, referring to the high-tech teaching displays used in many schools.

Teachers at Woodside commonly blame technology for students' struggles to concentrate, but they are divided over whether embracing computers is the right solution.

"It's a catastrophe," said Alan Eaton, a charismatic Latin teacher. He says that technology has led to a "balkanization of their focus and duration of stamina," and that schools make the problem worse when they adopt the technology.

"When rock 'n' roll came about, we didn't start using it in classrooms like we're doing with technology," he says. He personally feels the sting, since his advanced classes have one-third as many students as they had a decade ago.

Vishal remains a Latin student, one whom Mr. Eaton describes as particularly bright. But the

teacher wonders if technology might be the reason Vishal seems to lose interest in academics the minute he leaves class.

Mr. Diesel, by contrast, does not think technology is behind the problems of Vishal and his schoolmates—in fact, he thinks it is the key to connecting with them, and an essential tool. "It's in their DNA to look at screens," he asserts. And he offers another analogy to explain his approach: "Frankenstein is in the room and I don't want him to tear me apart. If I'm not using technology, I lose them completely."

Mr. Diesel had Vishal as a student in cinema class and describes him as a "breath of fresh air" with a gift for filmmaking. Mr. Diesel says he wonders if Vishal is a bit like Woody Allen, talented but not interested in being part of the system.

But Mr. Diesel adds: "If Vishal's going to be an independent filmmaker, he's got to read Vonnegut. If you're going to write scripts, you've got to read."

Back to Reading Aloud

Vishal sits near the back of English IV. Marcia Blondel, a veteran teacher, asks the students to open the book they are studying, "The Things They Carried," which is about the Vietnam War.

"Who wants to read starting in the middle of page 137?" she asks. One student begins to read aloud, and the rest follow along.

To Ms. Blondel, the exercise in group reading represents a regression in American education and an indictment of technology. The reason she has to do it, she says, is that students now lack the attention span to read the assignments on their own.

"How can you have a discussion in class?" she complains, arguing that she has seen a considerable change in recent years. In some classes she can count on little more than one-third of the students to read a 30-page homework assignment.

She adds: "You can't become a good writer by watching YouTube, texting and e-mailing a bunch of abbreviations."

As the group-reading effort winds down, she says gently: "I hope this will motivate you to read on your own."

It is a reminder of the choices that have followed the students through the semester: computer or homework? Immediate gratification or investing in the future?

> "His advanced classes have one-third as many students as they had a decade ago."

Mr. Reilly hopes that the two can meet—that computers can be combined with education to better engage students and can give them technical skills without compromising deep analytical thought.

But in Vishal's case, computers and schoolwork seem more and more to be mutually exclusive. Ms. Blondel says that Vishal, after a decent start to the school year, has fallen into bad habits. In October, he turned in weeks late, for example, a short essay based on the first few chapters of "The Things They Carried." His grade at that point, she says, tracks around a D.

For his part, Vishal says he is investing himself more in his filmmaking, accelerating work with his cousin on their music video project. But he is also using Facebook late at night and surfing for videos on YouTube. The evidence of the shift comes in a string of Facebook updates.

Saturday, 11:55 p.m.: "Editing, editing, editing"

Sunday, 3:55 p.m.: "8+ hours of shooting, 8+ hours of editing. All for just a three-minute scene. Mind = Dead."

Sunday, 11:00 p.m.: "Fun day, finally got to spend a day relaxing . . . now about that homework . . ."

Questions for Rhetorical Analysis

1. As a reader, what do you think of having the writer show you this whole issue through the lens of just one person—for instance, Vishal?
2. Is the writer objective, or has he made a decision about how technology is affecting young people?
3. Does the writer seem sympathetic toward Vishal?
4. How does the writer incorporate sources who have never met Vishal?

Questions for Critical Thinking

1. Do you think this article fairly reveals the typical student who is engaged in the digital world?
2. Does the article provide you with a full picture of Vishal or do you sense some things are missing? Does the author seem to withhold some details? Support your answers.
3. Does location have something to do with the kind of involvement this school has with technology, or does region not matter?

Style Practice: Imitation

Find a person who represents a trend (as Vishal does) and write a scene where the person is described in the process of doing something that shows the trend in action.

WRITING & REVISION STRATEGIES

Gathered here are three interactive sections for you to use as you write and revise your trend research article.

- Writer's Notebook Suggestions
- Peer Review Log
- Revision Checklist

Writer's Notebook Suggestions

You can use these exercises to do some start-up thinking and writing for your trend research article.

1. Go to a shopping center and choose a store. Interview sales staff about some new development in the store: a new product or style. Write one paragraph about your findings, incorporating quotations and statistics you have gathered.

2. Observe a high-traffic area for an hour, noting patterns in behavior. Choose one of the following behaviors, or identify your own.

   a. The way people interact with ATMs

   b. The way people use their phones when they are alone in a coffee shop

   c. The way people behave on public transportation

   d. The way people cross a busy intersection

   Write a generalization about behavior within the context. What can you say, in general, about people who ride the bus? Or about the way people behave when using an ATM?

3. Research the nutritional data from a fast-food restaurant. Write a paragraph for an average reader that clearly explains how much fat, sugar, and salt are in the most popular items. Use analogies to help make the facts clear.

4. Survey a group of college students. Ask how many have binge-watched serialized programs on television or streamed on the Web. Which shows are most commonly binge-watched? How many hours are dedicated to the activity? Do they do this alone mostly, or in groups?

5. Do a survey in your writing class. How much time do students spend writing the average paper, how many drafts, and so on. Find out whether each student's practice has changed since high school. Speculate why.

6. Describe a person who illustrates a trend.

7. Find out what are the most popular foods at your college dining hall, cafeteria, or coffee shop. Try one, and then describe the taste and texture. Interview people who have eaten the food (or cooked or served it) and collect quotations. Write a description of the food, incorporating the quotations.

8. Identify a trend at your school or in your community. The following are some examples:

   a. Have you found that more (or fewer) of your friends are interested in food-service careers?

   b. Do you find more interracial or cross-religion dating than there was previously?

   c. Are there more smokers on your campus these days?

Do at least three person-on-the-street interviews, finding out what people think are the causes and/or effects of the trend.

Be sure to get names, approximate or accurate ages, occupations, and places of residence for all the people you interview. Try to get a mix of gender, age, and ethnicity, if possible. After you complete your interviews, write a page on your findings, integrating the quotations as you discuss possible causes and effects of the trend. Be sure to attribute quotations accurately and completely. For example: "Rebecca Wong, an eighteen-year-old freshman at Central College, says, 'Dating a guy on my floor would be like dating my brother.'"

Peer Review Log

As you work with a writing partner or in a peer review group, you can use these questions to give useful responses to a classmate's trend research piece or as a guide for discussion.

Writer's Name: _____

Date: _____

1. Underline the introduction. Did the introduction get your attention? Why or why not? What might make it stronger?

2. Put two lines under the thesis. Does the topic seem noteworthy or interesting to you?

3. Put a star next to the area where the writer provides proof that the trend exists.

4. Note causes in the margins. Note effects in the margins.

5. Number the sources you find.

6. Put a wavy line under transitions, and identify any areas that need transitions with a T.

7. Does the writer explain the causes and/or effects well? Do you see the logic in the argument?

8. Can you think of anything else that the writer might add? More quotations from practitioners or experts? More facts or statistics?

9. Is all research well cited within the text? Do you wonder about the source of any facts or statistics? Note any place where the research needs a source or an attribution.

10. Bracket the conclusion. Does the writer end strongly?

Revision Checklist

As you do your final revision, check to make sure that you

- wrote an engaging introduction
- stated your thesis clearly and accurately
- provided proof that the trend exists
- provided an explanation of causes and/or effects
- cited sources accurately and fully
- used good transitions to show new aspects of your analysis
- included a good ending that leaves the reader with a lasting impression

PART 5

WRITING TO ARGUE

SIPA/Sipa USA

Complot/ Shutterstock.com

WRITING AN ARGUMENT

EDITORIALS, COMMENTARIES, AND BLOGS

An effective editorial has two ingredients . . . a position and a passion.
—RICHARD AREGOOD

Should Grandma spend her declining years with a robot for a caregiver? Looking at advances in robotics and concerned about our aging population, one op-ed writer ruffled a lot of feathers by arguing for robot caregivers for the ill and the elderly. (You can read "The Future of Robot Caregivers" later in this chapter.) Readers chimed in, writing comments that looked at the issue from many different angles and by doing so, enriched the discussion.

Editorials, commentaries, and blogs—and often the comments and letters to the editor that respond to these pieces—are some of the places where you can read, and write, strong opinions about whatever is in the air or on your mind: the continuing crisis in the Middle East, sustainable farming, Internet trolling, or the effects of technological advances in everyday life. Some of these pieces are off-the-top-of-the-head rants; others, and the best of them, offer clear, well-reasoned arguments. The best arguments acknowledge many sides of an issue but promote one with "a position and a passion."

When you take your argument to any public forum, you become a voice in the public debate of an issue. If you choose an issue worth arguing—and you line up solid evidence—you will no doubt find an audience ready to listen, to applaud, or to counter your claims.

PROCESS PLAN

Prepare

- Read newspapers and blogs to detect current issues, controversies, and public debates, and focus on an issue.

- Define the interest groups. Who has something to lose or gain in regard to the issue?

- Research the history of the issue, its origin and its recent developments.

- Decide on a position and identify how you will enter the debate—how to promote your view through publication or comments on blogs, letters to the editor, and so on.

Draft

- Introduction

- Find an illustration, statistic, or story that hooks your reader's interest.

- State the issue and your position in a clear thesis.

- Body: Provide reasons to back up your position.

- Include a refutation that addresses a reasonable aspect of the opponent's argument.

- Conclusion: End with a restatement of the position.

Revise

- Check your word choice and tone, making sure your writing appears to be reasonable and authoritative.

- Consider whether your argument has a logical flow, using transitions.

Understanding
the Writing Project

AN ARGUMENT is not a fight—at least not in the rhetorical realm, where your purpose is to use language well and persuasively. Convincing someone of your position on a controversial topic is an art form, and it requires strategy and solid information.

In college, you will be called on often to illustrate your understanding of history, government, or social issues by taking a side. You might be asked to write about welfare reform for a political science class or the impact of genetically modified food on public health for your biology class. When you write your opinion piece, you will need to demonstrate that you understand the issue fully—including all sides, not just the position you are defending. Your argument should include an informed perspective, moving beyond personal preference and into a logical argument based on research—one that relies on facts, illustrations, statistics.

ASSIGNMENT Choose an issue that is current and debatable, one that could be argued from different perspectives. The topic could be relevant at your school, in your community, or even globally. Define your position on the issue, and then find a good opportunity to add to the debate. You can consider writing a letter to the editor of a newspaper, writing a column for a magazine, or a blog for a website.

Argument

LOUISE ARONSON

The Future of Robot Caregivers

EACH TIME I make a house call, I stay much longer than I should. I can't leave because my patient is holding my hand, or because she's telling me, not for the first time, about when Aunt Mabel cut off all her hair and they called her a boy at school, or how her daddy lost his job and the lights went out and her mother lit pine cones and danced and made everyone laugh. Sometimes I can't leave because she just has to show me one thing, but getting to that thing requires that she rise unsteadily from her chair, negotiate her walker through the narrow hallway, and find whatever it is in the dim light of her bedroom.

I can, and do, write prescriptions for her many medical problems, but I have little to offer for the two conditions that dominate her days: loneliness and disability. She has a well-meaning, troubled daughter in a faraway state, a caregiver who comes twice a week, a friend who checks in on her periodically, and she gets regular calls from volunteers with the Friendship Line.

It's not enough. Like most older adults, she doesn't want to be "locked up in one of those homes." What she needs is someone who is always there, who can help with everyday tasks, who will listen and smile.

What she needs is a robot caregiver.

That may sound like an oxymoron. In an ideal world, it would be: Each of us would have at least one kind and fully capable human caregiver to meet our physical and emotional needs as we age. But most of us do not live in an ideal world, and a reliable robot may be better than an unreliable or abusive person, or than no one at all. Caregiving is hard work. More often than not, it is tedious, awkwardly intimate and physically and emotionally exhausting. Sometimes it is dangerous or disgusting. Almost always it is 24/7 and unpaid or low wage, and has profound adverse health consequences for those who do it. It is women's work and immigrants' work, and it is work that many people either can't or simply won't do.

Many countries have acknowledged this reality by investing in robot development. Last year in Japan, where robots are considered "iyashi," or healing, the health ministry began a program designed to meet work-force shortages and help prevent injuries by promoting nursing-care robots that assist with lifting and moving patients. A consortium of European companies, universities and research institutions collaborated on Mobiserv, a project that developed a touch-screen-toting, humanoid-looking "social companion" robot that offers reminders about appointments and medications and encourages social activity, healthy eating and exercise. In Sweden, researchers have developed GiraffPlus, a robot that looks like a standing mirror cum vacuum cleaner, monitors health metrics like blood pressure and has a screen for virtual doctor and family visits.

Researchers in the United States are developing robot-caregiver prototypes as well, but we have been slower to move in this direction. Already, we have robots to assist in surgery and very basic "walking" robots that deliver medications and other supplies in hospitals. Robots are increasingly used in rehabilitation after debilitating events like strokes. But a robot that cleans out your arteries or carries linens isn't the same as a robot meant to be your friend and caregiver. Even within the medical community, this idea that machines could help fulfill more than just physical needs meets largely with skepticism, and occasionally with outrage.

As Jerald Winakur, a San Antonio internist and geriatrician, put it, "Just because we digitally savvy parents toss an iPad at our kids to keep them busy and out of our hair, is this the example we want to set when we, ourselves, need care and kindness?"

And yet, search YouTube and you can watch developmentally delayed children doing therapy with a cute blue-and-yellow CosmoBot that also collects information about their performance. Or you can see older Japanese people with dementia smiling and chatting happily with a robot named Paro that looks like a baby seal and responds to human speech. Sherry Turkle, an M.I.T. professor and technology skeptic, questions such artificial emotional relationships in her book "Alone Together: Why We Expect More From Technology and Less From Each Other." Yet after watching a 72-year-old woman named Miriam interact with Paro, she noted that the woman "found comfort when she confided in her Paro. Paro took care of Miriam's desire to tell her a story."

One proof of the social and emotional potential of robot caregivers is probably right in front of you. If you have walked down any street recently, or sat in a restaurant, or entered a workplace, you've probably seen numerous people oblivious to the humans with or around them, while fully engaged with the machines in their hands or on their desks. Admittedly, such people are often interacting with other humans via their machines, but the fact remains that the primary interaction is between person and machine, and despite compelling protests that such interactions do not constitute meaningful, empathic relationships, they seem to provide stimulation and satisfaction to millions, if not billions, of us. Maybe you are one of those people, reading this article on a device.

But the biggest argument for robot caregivers is that we need them. We do not have anywhere near enough human caregivers for the growing number of older Americans. Robots could help solve this work-force crisis by strategically supplementing human care. Equally important, robots could decrease high rates of neglect and abuse of older adults by assisting overwhelmed human caregivers and replacing those who are guilty of intentional negligence or mistreatment.

In the next decade, robot caregiver prototypes will become much more sophisticated. According to Jim Osborn, the executive director of the Quality of Life Technology Center at Carnegie Mellon, the current limitation is not the technology, but finding a viable business model to make it affordable. He said, "I really expect there will be a robot helping me out when I retire. I just hope I don't have to use all my retirement savings to pay for it."

In that new world, my lonely, disabled patient's life would be improved by a robot caregiver.

Imagine this: Since the robot caregiver wouldn't require sleep, it would always be alert and available in case of crisis. While my patient slept, the robot could do laundry and other household tasks. When she woke, the robot could greet her with a kind, humanlike voice, help her get out of bed safely and make sure she was clean after she used the toilet. It—she? he?—would ensure that my patient took the right medications in the right doses. At breakfast, the robot could chat with her about the weather or news.

And then, because my patient loves to read but her eyesight is failing, the caregiver robot would offer to read to her. Or maybe it would provide her with a large-print electronic display of a book, the lighting just right for her weakened eyes. After a while the robot would say, "I wonder whether we should take a break from reading now and get you dressed. Your daughter's coming to visit today."

Are there ethical issues we will need to address? Of course. But I can also imagine my patient's smile when the robot says these words, and I suspect she doesn't smile much in her current situation, when she's home alone, hour after hour and day after day.

Questions for Critical Thinking

1. What is your position on the future of robot caregivers? Had you thought about this issue before you read this argument? Did the writer sway you one way or the other?
2. If your assignment were to take issue with the writer's position, what points would you make?
3. "But the biggest argument for robot caregivers is that we need them." Write a response to this statement for the comment section of this article.

The Rhetorical Situation

Purpose: To present a clear, logical, and persuasive argument on a controversial topic.

Voice: Your voice should be authoritative but not preachy, strong but not arrogant.

Audience: Assume that your audience is unconvinced and that your job is to overcome your readers' resistance and persuade them to shift their perspectives or accept new ways of thinking.

Media and Design: Arguments appear as editorials or op-ed columns in newspapers, on blogs, in position papers, or grants for funding—just about anywhere there is more than one side of an important issue.

THE **BIG IDEA** Claim and Argumentative Thesis

Arguments begin with an informed opinion, usually a strong one, about an issue. Further developing that opinion and thinking about your reasons lead you to your *claim*, a general assertion of your position, stated or implied. Louise Aronson in "The Future of Robot Caregivers," presented earlier in this chapter, announces her claim right after the opening anecdote about her elderly patient. Referring to her patient, she writes, "What she needs is a robot caregiver." This sentence presents the beginning of her argument, her claim, but it is too broad, too nonspecific to be a thesis. She has to narrow it down, answering *why* her patient needs a robot caregiver. There could be many reasons, many arguments, but she focuses on the following statement as her argumentative thesis: "[A] reliable robot may be better than an unreliable or abusive person, or than no one at all." The argumentative thesis here gives specificity to the claim and gets us ready to hear her reasons.

Once you decide on your claim, ask yourself, "Why?" or "How?" There may be many ways to answer the question, but the one you choose points the way to your argumentative thesis. Having your claim and argumentative thesis in mind will provide a good blueprint for organizing your writing.

Claim + Why or How = Argumentative Thesis

Let's say you are interested in gender differences in learning. After doing some research, you form a claim that says something like "Separating boys and girls in

Clay Bennett © 2002 The Christian Science Monitor

PARCTICE 12.1

Crafting an Argumentative Thesis

Assume that your state legislature is considering a bill to make driving tests mandatory every time people renew their driver's licenses. According to the bill, mandatory road testing will reduce the number of accidents caused by young, inexperienced drivers and by older drivers whose eyesight and reaction time have diminished.

1. Make a list of four or five arguments on this topic, considering pro, con, and some positions in between.

2. Put the arguments in order of strength, saving the best argument for last.

3. Choose the position that you think is most compelling, and write a claim that promotes that position.

4. Edit your claim so that it is written as economically and clearly as possible. ■

What arguments do the two political cartoons make about immigration?

school is bad for both genders." This is an arguable claim, with good reasons to support it, and you can imagine a counterargument, that separating girls and boys in school has advantages for both genders. To help focus your argument, you want to think about "Why?" This is where you have to make a decision about your angle. Why is it bad? You could probably think of many reasons, but let's focus on the limitations and say something like "The current trend in separating boys and girls in school limits their futures." Then, you have to do the hard work of getting the facts, statistics, and expert opinion to support your thesis.

Other Examples:

Topic: Inequity in college acceptances
Claim: Many college applicants who were rejected were more qualified than those accepted.
Ask "Why?"
Argumentative Thesis: Students from wealthy families and legacy students took the places that students with higher GPAs should have rightfully had.

Topic: Undue pressures to get high grades in college
Claim: The emphasis on high grades has had a negative effect on today's college students.
Ask "How?"
Argumentative Thesis: The emphasis on getting the highest GPA in college has prevented students from taking challenging and difficult classes.

Taking an Arguable Position

Arguable means that good points supported by solid evidence can be made on more than one side of the issue. You could not write much of an opinion piece, for example, asserting that ethnic or gender discrimination is illegal. Who could argue with that? However, if you wrote a piece that argued that ethnic or gender discrimination exists in college admissions policies, you would certainly have an arguable position.

FACT, NOT ARGUABLE: Ethnic and gender discrimination is illegal.
ARGUABLE: Ethnic and gender discrimination exists in college admissions policies.

One way to find a specific focus for your argument is to break a topic down into its component parts. Social, political, economic, scientific, and cultural issues tend to be sprawling and multifaceted. People can spend years studying them. Find the aspect of the topic that affects you and people in your community. Stay local, and be specific. For example, assume that you have decided to write about global warming—a huge topic that interests you. As you read for background, you discover that people have focused on a number of specific solutions to global warming, including

Matt Wuerker's/The Cartoonist Group

What argument does this political cartoon make about the economy over the last few decades?

regulating automobile emissions, preserving green space, adding more-efficient mass transportation, and making buildings more energy efficient. Any one of these topics will narrow your focus. If your college or community is about to begin construction on a new building, you can further narrow your topic to that specific and local issue: persuading the builder to use solar panels or photovoltaic cells in the building, for example.

TOO GENERAL, NOT ARGUABLE: Global Warming
ARGUABLE: Regulating Automobile Emissions, One Solution to Global Warming

You will sometimes be writing a commentary on a topic for which you already have a "position and a passion," but when you write an opinion piece, you are writing about more than your personal preferences. To write knowledgeably about a public issue, you will need to be able to approach the topic in numerous ways: by examining history, reporting on current developments, citing anecdotes from a particular place or instance, noting a technological development, pointing to a change in trends, or looking through the lens of a certain discipline, such as sociology or psychology.

PERSONAL OPINION, NOT ARGUABLE: I love playing sports.
ARGUABLE: The school day should be lengthened to allow all students one hour of physical education each day.

Appealing to Your Audience

As a writer of an argument, you first have to consider your audience. Obviously, you don't want to turn off your readers by making them angry or by insulting them ("Only an idiot would vote for that candidate"). An effective argument appeals to your readers' minds or hearts or both.

The original Greek terms for argumentative appeals are *logos*, *pathos*, and *ethos*. Most arguments—whether in debates or in opinion pieces in newspapers, on radio, and on blogs—use these appeals either alone or in some combination.

Use Logical Appeals to Make a Reasonable Case

When you present a logical argument (*logos*), you appeal to the reader's intellect and sense of reason. Using logic, you create a path of evidence for your reader that inevitably leads to your conclusion. To get your reader to follow you from point to point, your argument must be clear and supported by objective evidence: facts and statistics.

For example, an editorial titled "Driving Down Childhood Obesity" asserts that even though some gains have been made for preschool children, obesity is still a significant health problem for most Americans. The writer provides evidence to

PRACTICE 12.2
Narrowing Topics

Choose one of these topics, and break it down into three or four narrower topics, as in the example on global warming. See if you can also find a local angle as you narrow the topic.

- Drug testing for athletes
- Airport security
- Film censorship
- Internet trolling
- New technologies

support this assertion by citing statistics from a report from the Centers for Disease Control and Prevention: "[O]besity rates went up for women 60 and older. A third of American adults and 17 percent of youths are obese" (*New York Times*, February 27, 2014).

Make sure that your evidence is relevant to your argument and that it directly supports the claim you are making. If the writer of the editorial on the obesity problem cited evidence from Sweden or Japan, then that evidence would not be relevant to the claim of an obesity epidemic in the United States. Be sure that your evidence is also accurate. Double-check your sources to make certain that the fact that obesity rates went up for women age 60 and older is from a reputable, impartial source and not from one that was funded by a weight-loss company, for example. (In this case, of course, a report from the Centers for Disease Control and Prevention, published in the *Journal of the American Medical Association* would pass the test.)

By making a reasoned argument and using relevant and accurate facts and statistics to support your points, you make a logical appeal to convince your readers that your views are valid.

Use Emotional Appeals to Create Empathy

Because using emotion (*pathos*) to sway opinion has often been done manipulatively, the appeal to emotion has garnered a bad reputation. Sunlit children running through fields of flowers do not make a compelling argument to vote for Candidate X. However, if you use emotion appropriately, especially in combination with a logical appeal, you can speak to readers' hearts as well as their minds, evoking anger at injustice, sadness at tragedy, or outrage at inequity.

Using emotion to support your points involves marshalling subjective evidence, such as opinions, anecdotes, and personal observations. An emotional appeal appears in "Make Chris Take His 'Meds,'" an editorial that supports legislation requiring California courts to take a person's mental illness into consideration before sentencing. To vividly illustrate the plight of mentally ill homeless people, the editorial tells the story of one man.

> Meet 22-year-old Chris Hagar, who is now locked up in the Sacramento Mental Health Treatment Center. Since age 15 Hagar has cycled in and out of six jails and mental hospitals, tormented by paranoid schizophrenia. He'd steal food from mom-and-pop grocery stores and promptly get arrested. He'd assault his parents and others. He'd break into a car to escape shadowy stalkers.
>
> —Alex Raskin and Bob Sipchen, "Make Chris Take His 'Meds'"

Even these few details of Chris's life evoke anger at the injustices he has had to face and the sadness at the tragedy of his life.

PRACTICE 12.3
Identifying Logical, Emotional, and Ethical Appeals

Read the following passages. For each, identify what type or types of appeal the writer is making—logical, emotional, ethical, or a combination of two or more of these.

1. A homeless Orlando couple with too little money to maintain a bank account must pay a fee and forfeit three percent of their meager earnings simply to cash a paycheck.
   —*Orlando Sentinel*, Editorial

2. As a professor at a liberal arts college, I must take a stand and refuse to take any more responsibility for student failure. If students plagiarize, it is not because my assignment was not creative enough.
   —Laura Tropp, Letter to the Editor

3. An average of 78 percent of the convicted felons in that program stay clean and sober for one year or longer. Re-arrest rates for those participants after release is almost two-thirds lower than for nonparticipants.
   —Jim Gogek and Ed Gogek, "Drug War Solution between Legalization, Incarceration"

The emotional appeal helps your reader connect with you and connects you with your reader. Emotion can be a way to find common ground and to say that you and your reader share a set of beliefs. In "Make Chris Take His 'Meds,'" the writer assumes the readers will be moved by Chris's story. The common ground is sympathy for a person who suffers from mental illness. In a way, the writer is complimenting the readers, saying, in effect, "We are all caring people who would want to help alleviate suffering in the world."

Courtesy of Martin C. Hansen

What type of appeal does this poster use to persuade its audience to attend the talk?

Use Ethical Appeals to Create a Trustworthy Tone

Although the word *ethics* suggests a moral code of behavior, the term *ethical appeal* (*ethos*) actually refers to the writer's credibility. To be swayed by your arguments, a reader has to trust you and know that the evidence you cite is accurate, valid, and reliable. If logic resides in the head and emotion in the heart, then perhaps *ethos* sits in your gut—your instincts about the worth of a person's character. You gain credibility in an argument, in part, through your authority and impartiality.

You do not have to be an expert yourself to establish authority in an argument. You can use authoritative sources to help support your positions. For example, your argument will be strong if you cite the surgeon general's warning about the effects of smoking rather than quote an actor who plays a doctor on a television show. Similarly, the Centers for Disease Control and Prevention is a better source for information about the latest flu epidemic than your runny-nosed roommate. You create your credibility, in good part, by clear and accurate attribution of your sources. Tell your reader who your sources are and why they are especially suited to speak to a particular subject.

Another powerful way to establish your authority and your credentials is to establish your expertise. Mark Edmundson, who wrote an editorial titled "How Teachers Can Stop Cheaters," is identified as "professor of English at the University of Virginia." The reader knows that he writes from experience. But, if Edmundson were to write about global warming, he would either have to establish himself as an expert in this field as well or rely on the expertise of environmental scientists to gain credibility.

Being impartial is another aspect of the ethical appeal. If you want your reader to trust you and even to like you, you also have to demonstrate a lack of self-interest in the outcome of the argument. In classical argumentation, this position is called *disinterested goodwill*. If you or one of your sources has a vested interest in promoting a particular cause or course of action, your reader might question your credibility.

Let's say that you read a blog that argues in favor of more extensive use of nuclear power to address issues of energy supply and global warming. If you find out that the author works for the Public Relations Department of your local nuclear power plant, you have to consider the argument in light of the plant's stakes in the outcome. Similarly, when pharmaceutical companies use pop-up ads to plug the latest cure for arthritis, depression, or high blood pressure, you know that their interest in public health is affected by their interest in making money. Having a stake in the outcome undermines the *ethos* of the argument.

On the other hand, you can enhance the ethos of your argument by speaking from an altruistic position. An altruistic person believes in the moral obligation to help others and to do good work. The ethical writer has the public interest in mind and argues from a position of what will do the most good in the world. Instead of speaking on behalf of a group, you gain credibility when you speak from the outside as an impartial but authoritative commentator. Unlike the nuclear power plant or pharmaceutical company spokespeople, scientists or medical doctors might be better suited to speak to the issues of energy and health, especially if they have public welfare in the forefront of their concerns.

These Ten Pitfalls in Logic will help you detect flaws in the logic of your own arguments—and in your opposition's.

PRACTICE 12.4

Identifying Fallacies

Identify the fallacies in these statements.

1. America—Love It or Leave It!

2. My dog was killed by a speeding car. We have to lower the speed limit in residential neighborhoods.

3. Women cannot be allowed to go to war because they are too feminine.

4. Of course, being wealthy, he would not know much about welfare reform.

5. You are either part of the problem or part of the solution.

6. Whenever I wear my lucky hat, I ace a test.

7. The company may have misrepresented its annual profits to the stockholders, but the real problem is that most companies underpay their accounting departments.

8. If we legalize medical marijuana, we will create a nation of drug addicts.

9. Our memories look more like impressionistic paintings than like TiVos.

Ten Pitfalls in Logic: Fallacies

The strength of your argument can be undercut by faulty logic. Logical errors, commonly known as *fallacies*, destroy your credibility and weaken your argument considerably. If you can detect logical pitfalls in the work of people whose views differ from yours, you can begin to deflate an opposing argument. You can sharpen your skills in logic by searching out fallacies in your own and other's thinking.

Bandwagon Appeal

If everyone else jumped off a bridge, would you? This rhetorical question, usually attributed to a parent whose child is about to make a serious mistake in judgment, is a classic example of the bandwagon appeal.

A bandwagon was a wagon big enough to hold a band and often traveled through small towns, promoting a political agenda or candidate. So jumping on the bandwagon meant that you joined the crowd that was supporting a cause or a candidate. The bandwagon appeal falsely suggests that an action is a good one because it is popular or endorsed by a popular person.

All good parents in this town support the school-budget override.

This assertion suggests that if you want to be counted among the good parents of the town, you would vote for the override. (You might also rightly ask how someone can measure who is a good parent and who is not.)

Post Hoc Fallacy

Post hoc is short for the Latin term *post hoc; ergo propter hoc,* which means "after this; therefore, because of this." Just because a result happened after an event does not mean that the event *caused* the result.

> *Because a snack-cake company advertises aggressively during Saturday morning cartoon shows, obesity rates have risen among children.*

Perhaps the obesity rate among children has risen at the same time that the advertising campaign has aired, but you cannot truly assert that the campaign caused the increase.

Ad Hominem Fallacy

Ad hominem, Latin for "to the man," means an attack that targets a person rather than that person's views or arguments—a fallacy much in vogue during political campaigns. *Ad hominem* attacks, ignores, or sidesteps the issue at hand.

> *Professor Hartley dresses like a clown. How could anyone take his economics theories seriously?*

Criticizing Professor Hartley's appearance does not build an argument that convinces your reader that his theories on economics are flawed.

Hasty Generalization

A hasty generalization is a conclusion formed from only one or two examples. Avoid falling into this trap when looking for evidence to support your position. Remember that one case does not prove a point.

> *Airbags are not worth the risk because my friend was seriously injured when an airbag opened.*

You could cite this example to illustrate the cautions that come with airbags should be taken seriously but not to argue the risks of airbags outweigh the benefits. When you also consider how many lives airbags have saved and note that injuries are much less frequent and less fatal with airbags, you avoid making this hasty generalization.

The Either-Or Fallacy

The either-or fallacy oversimplifies a complex issue. It uses language that polarizes discussion into two extreme and mutually exclusive positions, leaving no room for nuances, other options, complexities, or the existence of common ground.

(continued)

(continued)

10. Senator Wu's youthfulness makes her unable to be trusted with the serious work of the Appropriations Committee. ■

Ten Pitfalls in Logic: Fallacies *(continued)*

> *The school budget crisis can be solved either by reducing the teen center's hours of operation or by raising users' fees by $100.*

This statement suggests that the budget crisis has only two possible solutions. Many ways exist to cut costs and raise money other than these two specific suggestions.

The Red Herring

A red herring used to be dragged across a fox's trail to put hunting dogs off the scent. Similarly, the red herring fallacy diverts a reader from the path of an argument, usually by going off in a new direction.

> *Because rowdy fans turned over cars and created a public nuisance after the soccer game, it is time to examine the importance of sports in our culture.*

Instead of keeping attention on the acts of rowdy fans, this statement diverts the argument to the cultural importance of sports, which is a totally different path of inquiry.

Slippery Slope

The slippery slope fallacy assumes that once you take one step, then a series of disastrous events will inevitably follow. The conclusion is usually that the only way to avoid a catastrophe is to not take that first step. This fallacy ignores other factors that might affect the outcome.

> *If we lower the drinking age to 18, eventually 10-year-olds will be able to drink.*

This argument assumes that once you lower the drinking age to 18, then you might lower it to 17, then 16, and finally all the way down the slope to the absurdity of age 10. The argument also ignores the developmental, psychological, and societal constraints that would apply the brakes well before the enactment of any legislation allowing children to consume alcohol.

Non Sequitur

The English translation of the Latin term *non sequitur* is "it does not follow," which gives you a clear idea of this fallacy. The conclusion does not follow from the premise of the argument.

> *If 18-year-olds can fight in wars, they should also be able to drink legally.*

No logical relationship exists between fighting and drinking, so the conclusion that 18-years-olds should be able to drink legally does not follow from the fact that they are eligible to fight in wars.

Apples and Oranges

When you compare two things that have no real basis for comparison, you can be accused of comparing apples to oranges.

> *Instead of recycling, we should just consume less.*

Consuming fewer manufactured products has no real connection to the question of how we should deal with garbage, but rather that we should create less garbage. The cost—in terms of dollars and resources—of recycling compared to the cost of other methods of disposing of garbage is a more appropriate comparison.

Circular Argument

Like walking in a circle, a circular argument brings you back to the place you began—the end of the argument restates the beginning.

> *Pornography should be banned because it is obscene.*

This statement is circular, saying that pornography is pornographic.

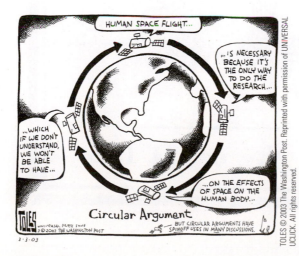

PRACTICE 12.5

Researching Other Fallacies

Select one of the following common fallacies, research its meaning, find or create examples, and present your findings to the class.

- Fourth term
- Ad populum
- Begging the question
- Poisoning the well

Visual Literacy: Seeing Arguments

THE FIRST POLITICAL CARTOON in the United States depicts the colonies as a snake divided into eight separate parts. Benjamin Franklin used the image to make the comment that without unity, the eight colonies would have no power in negotiating with the Iroquois. Franklin realized that the image would resonate with colonists, who were familiar with the belief that if sections of a snake were aligned, the snake would come back to life. The image became an important icon in the Revolution. Franklin's cartoon was an early American attempt at the art of editorial cartooning, in which a picture—with or without some text or dialogue—really does speak a thousand words of commentary. The political cartoon uses line drawings and a cartoon format to make a serious statement, usually ironic, always full of opinion. The popularity of the art form relies on the appeal of humor and the instant accessibility of a well-designed image.

- Look over the political cartoons in this chapter to see how editorial cartoonists express their opinions on contemporary issues.

- Choose an issue currently in debate and express a viewpoint by designing your own editorial cartoon.

©Everett Historical/Shutterstock.com

Research Paths: Supporting Arguments with Evidence

To argue persuasively, you must be knowledgeable about the topic that you have chosen and its background. Inform yourself by reading back issues of newspapers, magazines, and journals in libraries or online. You can also talk to expert sources—people who know your topic well. As you research, keep your audience clearly in mind. Think of your audience as made up of intelligent people whose views differ from yours, and consider their arguments respectfully and thoughtfully. Use research to find out what it means to have a different perspective on an issue about which you have strong beliefs. If you can understand other people's positions, you will be better able to argue ethically, logically, and passionately to change their minds.

- Many big-city newspapers publish indexes that organize previously printed articles by topic. Most college libraries keep at least the *New York Times Index* in their reference section and often subscribe to the *New York Times* archives online. Some of the online archives are available to nonsubscribers as well. Check your college or local library to see what indexes are readily available to you.

- Many colleges and universities subscribe to the powerful online databases LexisNexis or Factiva as resources for their students. The news section of these resources catalogs thousands of periodicals from 20 or more years ago and from all over the country. The databases retrieve information using keywords, writers' names, or article titles. The reference section gives biographical information, data from polls and surveys, quotations, and facts from the *World Almanac*.

- In addition to researching your chosen issue in newspapers and periodicals, you will likely want to go to other sources for deeper information. For example, if you are writing about a scientific breakthrough like cloning, a social issue like homelessness, or an economic issue like Social Security, you will need to read journals, books, textbooks, and public documents. You can also access a number of free databases online, including the National Archives and the archives at the New York Public Library. (For more information about consulting sources, see Chapter 15, Research.

- Another research path takes you to experts. Take advantage of your college or university community. Professors spend their lives becoming experts in their fields, and most are more than willing to pass on their knowledge and their sources of information to students. For background information on current issues in science, psychology, politics, economics, medicine, law, and a variety of other topics, you can consult your teachers. If you know other professionals or practitioners in a field related to your issue, they can also be useful sources.

PRACTICE 12.6
Brainstorming for a Topic

1. List local or global issues about which you have opinions, preferably strong ones. Look at the editorial topics in your college, community, or city newspaper for ideas. Try to generate at least 10 possible topics.

2. Choose one of the issues you listed, and make it the focal point for a freewrite. Write the topic on the top of a page and then write as many different positions on this issue as you can imagine. Do not worry about grammar at this point. Just get your ideas down on paper. Write nonstop for 10 minutes.

3. Alternatively, choose one issue that you listed, and make it the focal point of a clustering activity. Write the issue in the center of a page, circle it, and see how many points of view you can generate radiating out from this topic. (See Chapter 2, "The Writer's Process," for more information on freewriting and clustering.) ■

How Much Background Information Should You Include?

You have to decide how much background information your reader needs in order to understand your position on an issue. If your issue is current and well covered in the news, sometimes all you need is a brief reminder. However, if the issue is complicated or not well known—for example, some little-known aspect of foreign policy or local politics—you must provide enough background and context for the reader to understand the issue. Your research should help you find relevant background information, but do not try to include the complete history of the issue or a comprehensive overview. Define the out-of-the-ordinary terms, and summarize the important points for your reader. In a summary, you have to find the most concise way to put the issue in context.

Types of Evidence

As you read, collect supporting evidence—facts, statistics, public opinion polls, anecdotes, and experts' opinions—for all sides of the issue. What will convince your reader best are thoughtful, well-supported arguments. The stronger your support, the stronger your argument. Whether you search at the library, on your computer, or consult with experts, good research is key to developing your argument. The more types of support you use, the more you demonstrate the truth behind your position. To set forth a convincing argument, amass a great deal of evidence, enough to convince your most skeptical critic.

So that you can later review and document your sources, take careful notes or make photocopies of all that you read and consult. Supporting material for your arguments can come in a variety of forms:

- *Facts* state objective reality. That you have blue eyes or brown eyes is a fact. That you are attractive is an opinion based on a fact. Your factual supporting evidence should be accurate and unadulterated by opinion.
- *Statistics* are numerical data that often seem to have the weight of irrefutable analysis behind them. Statistics can be slippery, however, and can be skewed or misinterpreted to fit the desired outcome, so you have to be careful to choose reputable sources.
- *Examples* and *anecdotes* illustrate your point. An example provides a single case, and an anecdote tells a story. Be careful not to generalize from a case or story, however, and commit the hasty generalization fallacy discussed earlier. Relevant examples and anecdotes often provide vivid support for an argumentative point.
- *Testimonials*, stories of experts or witnesses, provide excellent support for arguments as long as the source is well positioned to speak to the issue.

Every print source you use needs clear attribution. Make sure to note author, title, place of publication, publisher, date, and page number for all print sources. For Internet sources, copy the URL accurately. For interviews, note the time, date, and place of your interview as well as the correctly spelled name, title, and affiliation of your source.

PRACTICE 12.7

Providing Background Information

Assume that you are writing an opinion piece about changing your college's entrance requirements. You might be advocating making entrance requirements more stringent or less stringent, or you might have a new idea about attaining gender or ethnic equity. Assume that your reader has no knowledge of the current admission standards.

1. Write as brief a paragraph as you can to provide the background information your reader will need in order to understand the issue.

2. Choose two editorials from your local paper, and identify the background information presented in them. Note how much information is provided and where it appears in the editorial. ■

Published opinion pieces in newspapers always attribute information to sources within the text, and academic papers require this information on a works cited page, so it is essential to be accurate and thorough in keeping track of all your sources. (See Chapter 16, "Documentation," for specific information on different documentation systems.)

Evaluating Evidence

If you want to argue persuasively, your evidence has to be watertight. Evidence has to pass the tests of being reliable, timely, accurate, and relevant. Here are some questions you can ask to test your evidence:

1. **Reliability** Does the evidence come from a person who is an authority in the field?

   - What are his or her credentials?
   - Is this person cited in other sources?

   Does the evidence come from a reliable study?

   - Who funded the study?
   - Was the study sponsored by a government, university, or commercial source?

2. **Timeliness** Is the information up-to-date?

   - Has it been published in the last few years?
   - Have there been more recent studies that make this one outdated?

3. **Accuracy** Is the information correct?

   - Have you found a second source to corroborate the facts and figures, especially for information found on the Web?
   - Have you double-checked your transcription of this information?

4. **Relevance** Does the information support your point?

   - Does the evidence specifically address the point you are making?
   - Have you tied this evidence clearly to the point?

Acknowledging Opposing Views and Refuting Them

To make a convincing argument, you have to acknowledge opposing views and refute them, even if only briefly. Sometimes a single sentence beginning with "Granted" or "Still" states the opposition's strongest argument with a brief refutation to disprove that argument.

Notice how Louise Aronson in "The Future of Robot Caregivers" at the beginning of this chapter disarms her opposition by stating upfront a major objection her readers might have to robot caregivers. She writes, "In an ideal world, it would be: Each of us would have at least one kind and fully capable human caregiver to meet our physical and emotional needs as we age. But most of us do not live in an ideal world."

After Aronson acknowledges that a human caregiver would be better than a robotic one, she cites a number of examples of this less than ideal world for the elderly and the ill. She is then set up to support her argument about the benefits of robot caregivers—not having dismissed but having acknowledged the validity of opposing views.

When you acknowledge your opposition's possible arguments, you enhance your credibility and build strength for your own position. Always support your counterarguments with solid research. In this way, you show that you understand and have thoughtfully considered the opposing views.

The Seven Habits of Highly Effective Arguments provides more insiders' tips on writing good arguments.

PRACTICE 12.8

Analyzing the Effectiveness of an Argument

Reread "The Future of Robot Caregivers" or choose any argumentative piece of writing in this chapter's readings. How would you rate the piece on each of the seven habits of highly effective arguments? ■

PRACTICE 12.9

Acknowledging Opposing Views

Choose one of the following opinion statements and anticipate counterarguments by creating a list of opposing views. After you have generated a list of four or five "con" arguments, arrange them so that the strongest argument is first.

■ Academic cheating can be stopped by having students endorse an honor code.

■ Pulling vending machines out of schools will not make kids eat less junk food.

■ Drivers over 70 years old should have to take a driving test every two years.

■ Drivers under age 21 should have to take a driving test every two years. ■

Seven Habits of Highly Effective Arguments

An argument should arouse curiosity, strong feelings, or both in your reader.

1. Hook your reader right away. Use a specific, personal story, or a quotation from someone you interviewed. A particularly surprising piece of data can attract attention.

2. Get to your point quickly—announce your topic clearly in the opening few sentences.

3. Keep your voice informal and engaging. Just because you are writing an argument, you do not have to sound stuffy or formal. Avoid jargon or wordiness. For example, instead of saying, "The accusation of censorship was erroneously reported in media sources," say, "The news reports got the censorship charge wrong."

4. Make sure your research is current and accurate. Use factual material from unbiased sources (for example, major newspapers or ".gov" sites).

5. Save your strongest argument for your conclusion. Leave your reader thinking about the most compelling reason to support your position.

6. Keep each paragraph to one main point. An additional or contrasting point should always begin another paragraph.

7. Leave your readers thinking about the implications of your argument. If the readers agree, what should they think or do, support or defeat?

DIY MEDIA AND DESIGN

Create a Facebook Page to Bring Attention to an Issue

SOCIAL MEDIA CAN be powerful tools for organizing social or political action. Facebook has become the go-to medium for people who want to bring attention to a cause or an issue, often by organizing events that support those causes.

Create a Facebook page to encourage conversation around an issue you support. Post links to videos and blogs that support your viewpoint.

Social media allow you to reach many people quickly, but you also have to consider how to make a brief and persuasive argument through a combination of well-chosen words and images. Post photographs and links to news and video clips that help support your position.

Facebook suggests four ways to create effective pages:

- Be personal and educational. Keep your voice conversational by using the first person and talking directly to your readers.
- Create content worth sharing.
- Join the conversation. Poll your supporters and comment on the posts.
- Use social plugins—such as the Like button, recommendations, and activity feeds—to increase the relevance of your page.

READINGS

Bren Smith, a Long Island farmer, argues that the "much-celebrated small-scale farmer can't make a living" in his op-ed piece, "Don't Let Your Children Grow Up to Be Farmers." In the Room for Debate feature in the *New York Times*, two writers respond—in very different ways—to the "War Against Online Trolls."

Don't Let Your Children Grow Up to Be Farmers
Bren Smith

Bren Smith is a shellfish and seaweed farmer. In this piece he tackles the problems of making a living as a small-scale farmer in an age when local and sustainable farming is celebrated but not necessarily lucrative.

NEW HAVEN—At a farm-to-table dinner recently, I sat huddled in a corner with some other farmers, out of earshot of the foodies happily eating kale and freshly shucked oysters. We were comparing business models and profit margins, and it quickly became clear that all of us were working in the red.

The dirty secret of the food movement is that the much-celebrated small-scale farmer isn't making a living. After the tools are put away, we head out to second and third jobs to keep our farms afloat. Ninety-one percent of all farm households rely on multiple sources of income. Health care, paying for our kids' college, preparing for retirement? Not happening. With the overwhelming majority of American farmers operating at a loss—the median farm income was negative $1,453 in 2012—farmers can barely keep the chickens fed and the lights on.

Others of us rely almost entirely on Department of Agriculture or foundation grants, not retail sales, to generate farm income. And young farmers, unable to afford land, are increasingly forced into neo-feudal relationships, working the fields of wealthy landowners. Little wonder the median age for farmers and ranchers is now 56.

My experience proves the trend. To make ends meet as a farmer over the last decade, I've hustled wooden crafts to tourists on the streets of New York, driven lumber trucks, and worked part time for any nonprofit that could stomach the stink of mud on my boots. Laden with college debt and only intermittently able to afford health care, my partner and I have acquired a favorite pastime in our house: dreaming about having kids. It's cheaper than the real thing.

12 WRITING AN ARGUMENT

But what about the thousands of high-priced community-supported agriculture programs and farmers' markets that have sprouted up around the country? Nope. These new venues were promising when they proliferated over a decade ago, but now, with so many programs to choose from, there is increasing pressure for farmers to reduce prices in cities like my hometown, New Haven [Connecticut]. And while weekend farmers' markets remain precious community spaces, sales volumes are often too low to translate into living wages for your much-loved small-scale farmer.

Especially in urban areas, supporting your local farmer may actually mean buying produce from former hedge fund managers or tax lawyers who have quit the rat race to get some dirt under their fingernails. We call it hobby farming, where recreational "farms" are allowed to sell their products at the same farmers' markets as commercial farms. It's all about property taxes, not food production. As Forbes magazine suggested to its readers in its 2012 Investment Guide, now is the time to "farm like a billionaire," because even a small amount of retail sales—as low as $500 a year in New Jersey—allows landowners to harvest more tax breaks than tomatoes.

On top of that, we're now competing with nonprofit farms. Released from the yoke of profit, farms like Growing Power in Milwaukee and Stone Barns in Pocantico Hills, N.Y., are doing some of the most innovative work in the farming sector, but neither is subject to the iron heel of the free market. Growing Power alone received over $6.8 million in grants over the last five years, and its produce is now available in Walgreens stores. Stone Barns was started with a $30 million grant

> "The food movement—led by celebrity chefs, advocacy journalists, students and NGOs—is missing, ironically, the perspective of the people doing the actual work of growing food."

from David Rockefeller. How's a young farmer to compete with that?

As one grower told me, "When these nonprofit farms want a new tractor, they ask the board of directors, but we have to go begging to the bank."

And then there are the chefs. Restaurants bait their menus with homages to local food, attracting flocks of customers willing to pay 30 bucks a plate. But running a restaurant is a low-margin, cutthroat business, and chefs have to pay the bills, too. To do so, chefs often use a rule of thumb: Keep food costs to 30 percent of the price of the meal. But organic farming is an even higher-risk, higher-cost venture, so capping the farmer's take to a small sliver of the plate ensures that working the land remains a beggar's game.

The food movement—led by celebrity chefs, advocacy journalists, students and NGOs—is missing, ironically, the perspective of the people doing the actual work of growing food. Their platform has been largely based on how to provide good, healthy food, while it has ignored the core economic inequities and contradictions embedded in our food system.

Unlike our current small-bore campaigns, previous food movements of the 1880s, 1930s and 1970s were led by highly organized farmers' organizations—like the American Agricultural Movement, National Farmers Union and Colored Farmers' National Alliance—trailblazing new paths for the economy.

They went toe to toe with Big Ag: crashing shareholder meetings; building co-ops and political parties; and lobbying for price stabilization. In the late 1970s, for example, small-scale family farmers organized a series of protests under the slogan "Parity Not Charity," demanding a moratorium on foreclosures, as well as the stabilization of crop prices to ensure that farmers could make a living wage. They mobilized thousands of fellow farmers to direct action, including the 1979 Tractorcade, where 900 tractors—some driven thousands of miles—descended on Washington to shut down the nation's capital.

It's not the food movement's fault that we've been left behind. It has turned food into one of the defining issues of our generation. But now it's time for farmers to shape our own agenda. We need to fight for loan forgiveness for college grads who pursue agriculture; programs to turn farmers from

tenants into landowners; guaranteed affordable health care; and shifting subsidies from factory farms to family farms. We need to take the lead in shaping a new food economy by building our own production hubs and distribution systems. And we need to support workers up and down the supply chain who are fighting for better wages so that their families can afford to buy the food we grow.

But none of these demands will be met until we start our own organizations—as in generations past—and shape a vision of a new food economy that ensures that growing good food also means making a good living.

Questions for Rhetorical Analysis

1. What kinds of appeals does Smith use in this piece? Identify a place where he appeals to logic, where he appeals to emotion, and where he establishes his authority.
2. In the opening paragraph, Smith distances himself—and other farmers—from "the foodies happily eating kale and freshly shucked oysters." What do these details suggest about Smith and how do they support his point of view? How effective do you find the opening paragraph?
3. What is Smith's argumentative thesis? Where does he first state it?
4. What are the main points he makes to support his thesis? How convincing is his evidence?
5. Smith provides two paragraphs of historical context about previous food movements. How important is this information in building his argument? Would you have liked him to include more information? Less?
6. Where does Smith acknowledge the opposition? Does he present a credible counterargument?
7. How effective is the conclusion? Do his suggestions for action stem clearly from his argument?

Questions for Critical Thinking

1. How has the current food movement affected you and your life? How have farmer's markets, restaurants, and college campuses responded to the food-to-table movement?
2. Would you want your children to grow up to be farmers? Why or why not?
3. Write a letter to the editor of the *New York Times*, responding to this piece. (You can read what others have written in response.)

Style Practice: Imitation

Imitate the opening paragraph where Smith distances himself and his group of farmers from the foodies at the farm-to-table dinner. Choose a topic that shows the wide gulf between people attending the same event—for example, musicians and groupies at a concert or live-tweeters and sports writers at a basketball game.

Room for Debate: The War Against Online Trolls

After actor Robin Williams's suicide in the summer of 2014, his daughter was attacked by trolls—online bullies and hecklers who anonymously tweeted hateful comments as well as disturbing images to her. This very public and upsetting event led to a great deal of debate about anonymity on the Web and prompted the *New York Times* to pose this question in their Room for Debate feature: Does anonymity on the Web give people too much license to heckle and torment others? Here are two of the responses, the first by a law professor who wrote a book about hate crimes in cyberspace and the second by a professor of communication.

Free Speech Does Not Protect Cyberharassment
Danielle Keats Citron

Danielle Keats Citron, a law professor at the University of Maryland, is the author of Hate Crimes in Cyberspace.

Trolling—like the kind of exploitative abuse spewed against Zelda Williams on Twitter after her father's death last week—is often nasty and hurtful. But it is routinely a protected expression. Internet users are free to use words and images to get a rise out of others, even at their most vulnerable. In this case, two individuals tweeted photographs of dead bodies to a young woman and wrote that her deceased father would be "ashamed" of her—forcing her to quit the service altogether. These acts are offensive, disturbing and mean-spirited, and yet, they are examples of constitutionally protected speech.

Hateful, offensive and distasteful ideas enjoy constitutional protection, so debate on public issues can be "uninhibited, robust and wide open" under the First Amendment.

Law enforcement has the tools to track down individuals that engage in cyberharassment and cyberstalking.

But there is a point when trolling escalates beyond the offensive and shocking into cyberharassment or cyberstalking—actions that are not protected.

Intermediaries—usually the websites where trolls post comments—can step in to revoke the privilege of anonymity, or even remove abusive speech that violates their community guidelines but when trolling turns into cyberharassment or cyberstalking, the law can and should intervene.

Online perpetrators can be criminally prosecuted for criminal threats, cyberstalking, cyberharassment, sexual invasions of privacy and bias intimidation. They can be sued for defamation and intentional infliction of emotional distress. In a few states, they can also be held to account for bias-motivated stalking that interferes with victims' important life opportunities, such as employment and education. Law enforcement should be able to use forensic expertise and warrants to track down individuals who engage in this conduct anonymously.

Of course, the law can only do so much: some abuse is left untouched, perpetrators can be hard to identify if they employ certain technologies and, ultimately, lawsuits require significant resources.

This is an opportune moment to educate teenagers about the suffering caused by online abuse. As parents, let's put talking about cyberharassment on par with discussions about drunk driving. And if we discover that our kids are caught up in trolling or more extreme cyberbullying, no tool is more powerful in changing teenagers' behavior than the possibility that they might lose their cellphones, computers or social network accounts. We should not squander this chance to reinforce the importance of respect as a baseline norm for online interaction.

Dialogue Is Important, Even When It's Impolite

Ryan M. Milner

Ryan M. Milner is an assistant professor of communication at the College of Charleston, where he studies participatory media and public conversation. He is on Twitter.

SOLUTIONS TO hateful speech often come down to gatekeeping. The Huffington Post, looking to "meet the needs of the grown-up Internet," only allows comments from verified Facebook accounts. Google Plus launched a real-name policy, barring anonymous or pseudonymous participation. Reddit bans users and subreddits that garner widespread negative attention.

But these restrictive practices are met with mixed responses. The Huffington Post continues to filter participants despite protests and angry readers who wanted to keep their Facebook life separate from discussions on the news website. Google Plus has softened its real-name policy to be more inclusive. Reddit still has trouble tamping down the creeps.

The problem persists despite gatekeeping measures because of hazy distinctions in communication. Zizi Papacharissi, a professor of communication at the University of Illinois at Chicago, distinguishes between "civility" and "politeness" online. Impolite communication is antagonistic, but unlike uncivil speech, it is still compatible with the democratic value of voice.

When antagonistic speech facilitates voice, satire or play, it may have civic value. The #Ask-Thicke Twitter campaign—hosted by VH1 to publicize the singer's new album—was repurposed by Twitter users to both playfully lampoon the pop star and criticize the misogyny in his lyrics.

While the #AskThicke campaign certainly became impolite, it has merit in our civil discourse.

Another example was the trending of the #YesAllWomen hashtag—cataloging the antagonisms women face daily—which became a conversation replete with impoliteness as participants debated gender inequality. However, it fostered robust conversations: uncivil perspectives were vibrantly and impolitely challenged. Voices were added to the dialogue, even when it got mean.

Ultimately, trolling blurs the line between impoliteness and incivility—it can, in its broadest definition, be either and both. And there's no algorithm for parsing impolite and uncivil speech. The categories are muddy, dependent on context and open to interpretation. For this reason, vibrant voice is essential online. Platform moderators, diverse individuals working to curate a culture of civility, can powerfully shape the online conversation. Participants on sites can, and should, do the same.

Incivility is a difficult problem for Americans, because its underlying issues are social. But restrictive gatekeeping just serves to dampen the generative value of diverse voices engaging. The impulse to silence can be just as uncivil as the trolling that inspired it.

Questions for Rhetorical Analysis

1. What is the main appeal (logic, emotion, or authority) that each of these writers uses in these two responses? Give an example to support your answer.
2. Identify the sentence in each argument that presents the writer's thesis.
3. What kind of evidence (studies, facts, statistics, anecdotes, expert opinion) does each author use to support the argument's thesis?
4. What is the main appeal of each essay? Is the appeal of the essay logical, emotional, or is the appeal based on the author's authority? Cite a sentence or two from each essay to support your answer.
5. Which of these arguments is strongest, most logical, and most convincing? Explain your reasoning.
6. The authors' voices are very different. How would you describe each? Identify a few words, phrases, or assertions in each piece that help shape these distinct voices.

Questions for Critical Thinking

1. According to Citron, what is the line between what is offensive and what is illegal online? Does this distinction make sense to you? Explain your thinking.
2. Milner asserts that "there's no algorithm for parsing impolite and uncivil speech. The categories are muddy, dependent on context and open to interpretation." Does this seem to you to be a good reason to ban any restrictions on social media? Explain your thinking with a few specific examples.
3. Weigh in on this debate. How would you answer this question: Does anonymity on the Web give people too much license to heckle and torment others?

Style Practice: Imitation

In the first two paragraphs, Citron uses a number of *triplets*, a figure of speech that uses three words or phrases, to create a pleasing sense of completeness ("These acts are offensive, disturbing and mean-spirited"; "Hateful, offensive and distasteful ideas"; "public issues can be 'uninhibited, robust and wide open'"). Write a paragraph of response to this debate, using at least three triplets.

WRITING & REVISION STRATEGIES

Gathered here are three interactive sections for you to use as you write and revise your opinion piece.

- Writer's Notebook Suggestions
- Peer Review Log
- Revision Checklist

Writer's Notebook Suggestions

Many writers informally jot down their ideas and refine their thinking in notebooks that they keep handy. This compilation of suggestions for writing and thinking can be used to generate ideas at any point as you write your opinion piece.

1. Make a list of some of the technological advances made in your lifetime. Which ones have made your life better? Which ones have made your life worse?
2. Cut out political cartoons that attract your attention, and paste them into your notebook. Write a claim for each cartoon.
3. Draw a political cartoon that presents your opinion on an issue about which you feel strongly.
4. Make a list of issues that are in the news this week. Check the blogs and news websites you frequent as well as the print newspapers in your area. Which issues pique your interest?
5. Add your voice to an online commentary, blog, editorial, or op-ed piece by contributing to the comments. Consider posting your response.
6. List policies at your college that you think should change. Choose one, and write a letter to the college president arguing against the policy or for a revised policy. Remember to consider the president's point of view.
7. You have been hired as a speechwriter for a candidate running for the student senate. The candidate has been asked to deliver a 10-minute speech on a proposed 5% tuition hike. Outline a draft of this speech for your candidate, taking a stand for or against the hike.
8. The president of your college or university has asked you to serve as student consultant for a speech that proposes a 5% tuition hike. Write an outline for the president's speech, aiming to convince students of the importance of raising tuition.
9. Make a list of issues that would be suitable for a debate, issues that have many possible positions, not just one or two. Write a thesis statement for each of three strong opinions on any one of these issues.

Peer Review Log

As you work with a writing partner or in a peer editing group, you can use these questions to give useful responses to a classmate's opinion piece and as a guide for discussion.

Writer's Name: _____

Date: _____

1. Identify the introduction. Did it get your attention? Why? What might make it stronger?
2. Underline the argumentative thesis in the paper that you are reading. Is the writer's opinion clear? Could you suggest better wording?
3. Do you understand the issue the writer is discussing? What other information might you need?
4. Put a star next to the main points of the writer's argument. Do they support the claim? Can you suggest other points the writer might consider?
5. How effectively does the writer appeal to the reader's heart or mind? Are there places that could use facts, statistics, opinions, anecdotes, or testimonials?
6. Can you identify any problems with logic? How could the writer solve those problems?
7. Does the writer effectively acknowledge opposing views? Are those opposing views refuted well?
8. Does the piece end strongly? Is there a call to action? What might make the conclusion more effective?
9. Comment on the writer's voice. Is it appropriate for this kind of opinion piece? Are there places where the writing gets bogged down? Can you suggest some places to insert stronger verbs or livelier language?

Revision Checklist

As you do your final revision, check to make sure that you

- wrote an engaging lead
- stated your argumentative thesis clearly and accurately
- provided necessary background information
- acknowledged and refuted counterarguments, if necessary
- made clear points that supported your argument
- used facts, statistics, examples, anecdotes, or testimonials to support your arguments
- appealed to your reader's intellect and emotions
- did not commit any fallacies in logic
- wrote with clarity and conviction
- concluded strongly, perhaps with a call to action

THERE'S NO BETTER FRIEND. ADOPT A DOG.
For more information about pet adoption visit www.spca.org.sg or call us at 62875355 ext 24.

Society for the Prevention of Cruelty to Animals

CREATING A VISUAL ARGUMENT
PUBLIC SERVICE MESSAGES

A writer should write with his eyes, and a painter paint with his ears.
—GERTRUDE STEIN

It is a familiar image: the room, dim, except for the television, broad-casting a sad movie. The shot even teeters on the brink of cliché, but then you look closer and see the dog is offering a tissue.

(*Insert the sound of a little chuckle.*)

Ah, that's my best friend! My dog.

Things happen when pictures tell us a story. Even more things happen when the story is a little about us—a situation we can put ourselves into, remember, re-create. The creators of this public service message have made the lonely-movie-night scenario fresh, given it a new twist, and in the process, posed a visual argument: Why not adopt a pet?

Creators of public service messages may also give us reasons, charm us, and warm our hearts. Sometimes they use images that make us cry, or make us angry, or puzzle us. Sometimes they give us something to read; other times, people who create visual arguments trust their pictures to say it all. This is what the creators know; they have a few seconds to get us interested, and maybe a few more to make their case.

They know a visual argument is an instant argument.

PROCESS PLAN

Prepare

- Choose an issue you care about, one that you want to support.

- Find an advocacy group that works on this issue.

- Research past campaigns

- Develop a fresh concept to help your argument.

Draft

- Introduction: Create a headline that generates interest, attracts readers, and announces the topic of your argument.

- Body: Create copy that intrigues and concisely explains. Create visuals that complement the copy.

- Conclusion: End with a call to action: donate money, volunteer, change behavior.

Revise

- Look for ways to strengthen the message either in words or with images.

- Check to make sure you have appealed to your target audience's minds and/or hearts.

- Be sure that you have established your authority or credibility through well-researched information.

Understanding
the Writing Project

WRITERS IN the Information Age cannot ignore the significance of the visual components of a message. In most advertisements, public service messages (PSMs) included, visuals work in conjunction with words. Building a visual argument gives you hands-on experience researching accurate and useful information, creating images to support that information, and allowing the words and images to work in concert.

Images can work on many levels, calling on associations we all share to make sense of them. It is important to understand what motivates your audience so you can choose a medium that will persuade that audience. Professionals who create public service messages are aware of not only the general reluctance of people to listen to "what is good for them" but also of the specific obstacles that lie between a message and a particular audience. Thinking about the means of delivering your message dovetails with thinking about whom you want to listen to your message.

ASSIGNMENT Find a nonprofit group or organization in your community that offers information or services that could benefit the public. This organization will be your client. Develop a portfolio of three public service messages and one "pitch letter" introducing your work to this new client. Your aim is to serve your community by raising awareness of an issue, initiating a new behavior or attitude, or changing a behavior or attitude. Choose from the following types of public service messages:

- Print advertisements for magazines, newspapers, posters, or billboards
- Storyboards and scripts for television commercials or for posting on YouTube
- Alternative media, such as messages on shopping bags, installations in public spaces, signs on buses, street performances

Later in this chapter, the DIY feature will lead you to an example of a public service message in the form of a YouTube video.

Public Service Message: You Don't Have to Be Perfect. . . .

Collect examples of public service advertisements from magazines and online and grade them using the following scorecard. Award the PSM one point for every box checked.

Public Service Message Scorecard

☐ The ad attracted my attention.

☐ The ad kept me interested; I did not stop looking at it because I was offended, confused, or bored.

☐ The ad provided information that was new to me.

☐ I believed the ad.

☐ I would read the ad again.

☐ I would read more information about the topic.

☐ I would act on the information.

☐ After reading, I remembered the message.

☐ I would tell my friends and family about the message.

_____ Total PSM score

Compare your totals with those of your classmates. Collect and examine the ads with the highest scores and the lowest scores, and decide which factors the best have in common and which factors the weakest have in common. ■

You don't have to be perfect to be a perfect parent.
There are thousands of teens in foster care who would love to put up with you.

1 888 200 4005 · adoptuskids.org

The U.S. Department of Health and Human Services and Adopt U.S. Kids

Questions for Critical Thinking

1. How does the image of the cake attract the audience's attention?
2. Explain how the headline ("You don't have to be perfect . . .") connects to the image.
3. What is the call to action? What reason is provided to support the call to action?
4. If you were to create a series of PSMs using this concept and this headline, what other images would you use?

The Rhetorical Situation

Purpose: To raise awareness of an issue, to initiate or change a behavior or attitude, to change someone's mind.

Voice: Your voice will be determined by the kind of message you're delivering. It could be playful or serious, ironic, irreverent, or sentimental.

Audience: Think about talking to one person and at the same time talking to a crowd. Each public service message is a personal appeal that just happens to be broadcast to thousands. Your target audience—that special group you want to listen to you—should be well defined in your mind.

Media and Design: Your targeted audience will determine where you decide to place your PSMs—in what publications, in which neighborhoods, on which modes of public transportation, on which websites, or at which television or radio stations.

Tips for Choosing the Best Medium for Your Message

The following basic guidelines for some of the major ways to deliver PSMs should help you think about the best medium for your message. Your call to action, for example, will vary depending on the medium you use.

- **Print** Print public service messages appear in magazines and newspapers and in the form of posters, flyers, and billboards. The way the ad looks is as important as what it says. But your call to action can be more specific in a magazine PSM than on a poster or billboard.

- **Web Pages** Websites can include "hot type," which allows your reader to immediately link to the advocacy group's web page for more information.

(continued)

PRACTICE 13.2

Finding Your Target PSM Audience

1. Generate a list of possible target groups for public service advertisements designed to solicit donations to the Every Child Is a Reader program, which gives new books to children in low-income school districts.

2. Decide where you would place the PSMs to reach each target group on your list. ■

You have been hired by Parents for Bike Safety, a group that is working to promote the use of bicycle helmets by school-age children. You have these statistics to work with: "Nearly 98 percent of bicyclists killed were not wearing a helmet at the time of injury. Helmet use is estimated to prevent 75 percent of cycling deaths." Write a memo to Parents for Bike Safety that lists three ways you might use alternative media to launch a bike-helmet safety campaign. ■

PRACTICE 13.4

How Text and Image Work Together

1. Analyze the image in one of the public service messages in this chapter.

2. What does the image tell you?

3. How does the text appeal to the audience—emotionally, intellectually, or both?

4. Using the same concept and the same text, create another image for the campaign. ■

Tips for Choosing the Best Medium for Your Message *(continued)*

- ■ **YouTube and Television** YouTube and television offer all the benefits of the medium: pictures, sound, and text. Entice your audience to view your work through Facebook or Twitter. Open your video by being immediately engaging through the use of an arresting image, language, or music.

- ■ **Alternative Media** Outside-the-box thinking has created public service campaigns that do not use mainstream media to convey messages. Buses and trains are being wrapped with messages. Video is being projected onto buildings on busy city streets, and messages are being sprayed on streets. Think about using alternative media to catch the attention of an audience overly saturated with traditional advertising.

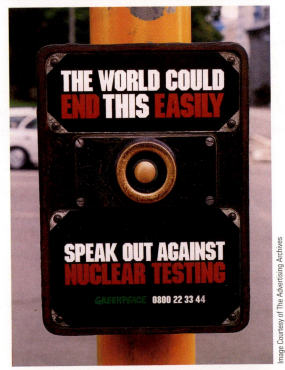

Image Courtesy of The Advertising Archives

Is this a good method for getting the message across?

Words + Images in Visual Arguments

The medium you choose will help you decide how visual and verbal elements work together in your argument. In creating an argument—any argument—your visual elements can be equal to the verbal elements. They can also be more important. In the split second it takes your retina to record a picture, you have already started to decipher the meaning and to respond both intellectually and emotionally. You see a photograph of sunglasses with one smashed lens, for example, and you think of something fragile that has broken. You may think about bad fortune or bad choices, accidents, damage, or loss. Pictures really can be worth a thousand words. When that image of broken glasses is partnered with a headline that states "Friends Don't Let Friends Drive Drunk," the image tells a terrible story and leaves a lasting impression.

Images can be photographs and illustrations, but they can also be just words. The typeface—its size and shape—becomes the image. Even the absence of a photo or an illustration delivers a powerful message. The "Mobile Madness" poster below, which uses only type, exemplifies architect Mies van der Rohe's design principal that "less is more." By making you read two sentences at once, the message itself cleverly demonstrates how hard it is for your mind to take in two things at the same time. When the type is the only image, the choices about which text type and size to choose, and how the text is arranged in the space are crucial.

PRACTICE 13.5
Typography in Visual Arguments

Typography alone can sometimes make a powerful statement. The posters below use only type to get across their messages. Write a text message to the creators of either poster and let them know whether you think it is effective here. ■

You are more
It's hard to
likely to crash your
do two things at
car while talking
the same time.
on a cell phone.

gay (gā) **1.** there once was a time when all "gay" meant was "happy." then it meant "homosexual." now, people are saying "that's so gay" to mean dumb and stupid. which is pretty insulting to gay people (and we don't mean the "happy" people).

The U.S. Department of Health and Human Services and Adopt U.S. Kids

These two posters use typography alone to get their messages across.

THE  BIG IDEA   The Concept Behind the Message

A public service message begins with the big idea—the concept behind the message. Just like the claim in a written argument, the underlying concept in a PSM begins the process of figuring out your position. Remember that to become an arguable thesis, or the specific point of your message, a big idea needs to be refined and focused.

As soon as you identify an issue you want to work on, you need to begin thinking about ways to bring your visual argument to your audience in a fresh way—a way that captures attention and brings results. Over the years, endless messages have been targeted at teens trying to persuade them not to drink. In the 1990s, a now-famous public service campaign was built around a new concept. Channeling the strong bond teens have with their friends, and recognizing that teens will probably always experiment with alcohol, the PSM shifted the topic to drinking while driving and the concept to using peer group affiliation to argue against driving while drinking. The specific message, of course, is "Friends don't let friends drive drunk."

Topic: Preventing teens from driving while drinking
Concept: Using teen's peer group affiliation (positive peer pressure)
Specific Point (tagline): "Friends don't let friends drive drunk."

Whole campaigns have been built around a single concept. The MADD (Mothers Against Drunk Driving) campaign in a later reading in this chapter offers another example of a series of PSMs built around a single concept.

Topic: Preventing teens from riding with drunk friends
Concept: Re-create a specific teen's accident through typography and imagery and install in high school corridors
Specific Point (tagline): "(Name of teen): One more reason not to ride with a drunk driver."

Visual Literacy: Text as Image

THE WORLD OF TYPOGRAPHY divides itself into two camps: *serif* typefaces and *sans serif* ("without serif") typefaces. Classical typefaces have serifs (those little lines at the feet of the letter); modern typefaces do not have those serifs. Most typefaces come in different sizes (also called *font sizes*). But new typefaces are created every day, providing more options for using typefaces and font size to enhance the meaning of words. Which type—bold or script, chunky or delicate—might be the most effective?

Angry   **ANGRY**

Designers know the power of typography, and how words can shift personality through the choice of typeface. Even without pictures and illustrations, messages can have enormous impact and eye-catching appeal. But this was new thinking in 1962, when a group of graphic designers began to explore the possibilities in text. Ivan Chermayeff, Tom Geismar, and Robert Brownjohn limited themselves to one typeface and one size to create a small booklet titled *Watching Words Move*. Their booklet caused a stir in the graphic design community and inspired designers to think about how the letters themselves could portray the meaning of a word. As simple as the concept seems, the result was revolutionary. Chermayeff and Geismar concluded that "the designer, using only the simplest means, can make certain words more evocative, and expressive of feelings, thoughts, and suggestions. In other words, words can have personality, and they don't need special typefaces or funny hats to do so."

addding

subtrcting

multimultiplying

div id ing

1. On an 8½ by 11-inch page, use layout (placement of elements on the page), typeface, type size, and color to express the meaning of one of the following words:

   Timid
   Demagogue
   Contagious
   Existential
   Committed
   Fascist
   Deception

   Heed Chermayeff's and Geismar's admonition about using novelty typefaces—letters made of bamboo or letters that seem to be dripping blood, for example—and avoid them. Also, resist the temptation to include any illustration other than the letters themselves to convey meaning.

2. On a second page, use typeface, type size, layout, and color to express the opposite of what the word means.

1. Avoid Novelty Fonts

Like this one!

OR THIS ONE. . .

Or this one. . .

Or this one. . . .

2. Use contrasting weights of a font as well as type sizes

BASKERVILLE is one of my favorites.

A good, classic sans serif. . .

Can say different things with some small modifications.

3. Combine serif and sans serif for contrast

SOME GOOD REASONS TO TAKE CARE WITH FONT
1. Your message will be clearer
2. Readers can scan for main points

4. Don't use more than 2-3 typefaces for contrast

TOO MANY FONTS

Can Make a Message

Look like a ransom note.

I'll bet that's not your goal.

Courtesy of Kate Burak

Research Paths: Finding Your Argument Strategy through the Mission Statement

Your first step in understanding how to relay a message is to interview the group for which you are designing your PSM. Understanding its mission will help you create a persuasive public service message.

Your "Client" or Advocacy Group

Start your research by contacting your "client" with a phone call or e-mail. Most websites include a contact section that offers a phone number. Contacting the group or agency that specializes in your topic could be a good way to get current information and insider sources. Explain that you are working on a project to raise awareness for a particular issue. People might be more inclined to answer your questions if they know what you want to accomplish.

The group will most likely be able to offer you the most current and relevant information you can use to become familiar with issues and previous campaigns. For example, this mission statement from Big Brothers Big Sisters of the Tri-State (West Virginia, Ohio, and Kentucky) clarifies the organization's goal.

> The mission of Big Brothers Big Sisters of the Tri-State, a nonprofit agency, is designed to provide guidance and companionship to youth from single parent homes through the provision of an adult Big Brother Big Sister volunteer. This is done through recruiting, screening, counseling, and supervision by a professional staff. The concept of our program is based on the premise that a child, in order to grow into responsible adulthood, needs a positive relationship with a mature adult figure. Where this influence is lacking, the child is handicapped in reaching his or her potential. Our clients are children needing friendship, affection, advice, and guidance. They may be emotionally deprived, in trouble at school, or just a lonely, unhappy child in need of a meaningful relationship. If the problems of the child are so severe that they require professional help exclusively, Big Brothers Big Sisters service will not be a consideration.

The mission statement informs you that Big Brothers Big Sisters' goal is to help children reach their full potential by giving them an adult mentor who will commit to a "meaningful" relationship. Knowing this information can help you design a public service message that fits them.

Searches and Sources

After you are clear regarding your client's mission, look for material that will help you understand the issues your client needs addressing. You need to include up-to-date and quality information, facts, and statistics from authoritative sources. Web searches are good starting places, but be sure to carefully evaluate your online sources. Some organizations with the intention of distorting facts might post misleading or inaccurate numbers. Look for information that comes from unbiased sources, such as universities and government agencies.

A few good Web sources are the U.S. Census Bureau, state departments of public health sites, and the U.S. government's official Web portal at www.firstgov .org. By using official statistical sources like these, you can create an argument that has authority.

Print sources help you obtain information and double-check facts and statistics you find on electronic sources. Getting information from two sources helps to verify the information, and going to the original source is the best way to get reliable information.

If you use someone else's creative work (image, photograph, music) in your PSM, you must get permission and cite the source.

The Persuasion Path

Visual arguments allow the viewer to make snap decisions about whether to engage in the message or turn away. Readers of verbal messages make the same decision, but once an argument takes a visual form and might include the layer of multimedia, the importance of the appeal factor increases exponentially. Your goal is to attract attention and keep it until you are finished making your point. These instantaneous steps viewers go through as they absorb your argument can be broken up into four parts. Think of this process as the *persuasion path*.

The Persuasion Path

1. Attract Attention and Generate Interest
   - Use both the design and the verbal elements in your argument.

2. Appeal to Hearts and Minds
   - Target your audience with your argument: choose logos, pathos, or ethos.

3. Provide Reasons
   - Make your viewers "believers" by giving them specifics.

4. Call Your Reader/Viewer to Action
   - Do not be afraid to say exactly what you want your viewer to do.

Attract Attention and Generate Interest: Headlines and Visuals

A headline, like all titles, gives readers an entry point into a public service message. The headline can be at the top or bottom, or some place in the middle. Its job is to break through all the other conversations and to get attention by creating a sense of intrigue or mystery. Sometimes you will find yourself walking the thin line between intrigue and confusion. Keep in mind that you want your viewer to be curious—but not confused.

13 CREATING A VISUAL ARGUMENT

Much headline writing involves your speaking directly to the viewer—as a friend, an expert, an authority, or a colleague—one to one. A good headline establishes the role you are playing and it does so in language that is memorable (and often quotable). Think of all the catchy slogans and zingers and memes from advertising that go "viral" with people repurposing them as punch lines or using them as inside jokes. Those headlines illustrate the way well-crafted phrases or sentences, which are ever-so-brief, make their way through the noise. Most of the time the reason the headline achieves this kind of cultural currency is because the writer understands how important the "poetry" of your language is in making something so short speak volumes.

POETRY AND ADVERTISING COPY Why do we remember so many advertising slogans through the years? Advertising copywriters often use poetic techniques to create language that stays in our minds—often pleasingly but sometimes also annoyingly. A few poetic techniques copywriters use effectively are metaphors, similes, alliteration, onomatopoeia, rhymes, hyperbole, repetition, rhythm, and parallel constructions.

> **Metaphors and Similes** Metaphors and similes compare unlike things.
> *Make your children superheroes. Teach them how to dial 911.*
>
> **Alliteration** Alliteration is the repetition of a beginning sound.
> *Hopeless, hungry, hidden*
>
> **Onomatopoeia** Onomatopoeia is the re-creation of sounds through words.
> *Every time the cash register goes ka-ching, we will donate part of the sales to helping keep the parks clean.*
>
> **Rhymes** Rhymes are words with the same end sound.
> *Imagination and inspiration in education: Art in the schools.*
>
> **Hyperbole** Hyperbole is exaggeration.
> *You can become a superhero by taking 20 minutes to become a blood donor.*
>
> **Repetition, Rhythm, and Parallel Construction** Copywriters also use repeated words or phrases and song-like rhythms created by patterns of syllables.
> *Freedom. Appreciate it. Cherish it. Protect it.*

Appeal to Hearts and Minds (Pathos, Logos, Ethos)

All arguments speak to hearts and minds, emotions and logic. In the world of classical appeals, these are called *pathos*, *logos*, and *ethos*. Many times you will find the appeals blended in PSMs.

USING PATHOS Appealing directly to the audience's emotions—pathos—in order to attract attention, is probably the most commonly used strategy in creating the images and text in public service advertisements. You can leverage emotional motivators, such as guilt, fear, outrage, joy, and pride. You can inspire your audience or make it laugh. Sometimes humor can break down barriers between the message and the audience.

Irony is one of the most commonly used forms of humor in advertising. When you use irony, you rely on parallel logic—two-track thinking that leads to a surprising or counterintuitive outcome. Jokes work in a similar way: you set up a word or a situation, then deliver the opposite of what the audience expects (the opposite of the literal meaning). Playing with your audience's expectations and assumptions can be a good way to get people interested in your message. One television ad for a fuel assistance

How effective is the visual irony in this message?

13 CREATING A VISUAL ARGUMENT

program showed a mother dressing her daughter in snow pants, mittens, and a ski hat right before tucking her into bed for the night. The ad played on the assumption that the child was going out to play in the snow, not going to an icy bed in an unheated house. In a more humorous context, jokes often twist assumptions in the same way.

Double entendre, like irony, plays with the meaning of words. When you use double entendre, your words have a second level of meaning, and the message resides in the double play of meaning. Double entendres may not be laugh-out-loud humor, but as with irony, your assumptions shift. An ad for a homeless shelter uses a play on the homonyms *grate* and *great*. The image is of a homeless man sleeping on a run-off grate, with the headline "Imagine waking up in the morning and feeling this grate." The fact that everybody understands the cliché of "feeling this great" after waking up is essential to the point. What kind of appeal does this ad make? Certainly, it rallies guilt in the audience, a put-yourself-in-somebody-else's-shoes kind of appeal.

Sometimes humor works well, and at other times it crosses the line and offends the audience. If you decide to use humor, keep in mind that offensive humor can turn off your audience, resulting not just in an ineffective ad but also in a counterproductive one.

PRACTICE 13.6
Using Humor

Use any humorous technique to create an ad that does one of the following:

- Encourages athletes to wear mouth guards to protect their teeth

- Asks people to conserve electricity by turning off lights in empty rooms

- Raises awareness about the importance of not driving when sleepy

- Encourages people to stop fertilizing their lawns to prevent groundwater pollution

- Motivates college students to vote ■

Image Courtesy of The Advertising Archives

How effective is the visual irony in this message?

USING LOGOS Another strategy is to use logic—logos. Advertisers who choose logic to attract attention often rely on statistics to make their points. Information is the focus of PSMs that use an intellectual appeal to get attention. Ads may have headlines that begin "Two out of three . . ." or sometimes use an analogy as in the Nuclear Testing PSM on page 344. The walk button on the traffic signal is visually compared to the hot button that could launch a nuclear bomb attack. The headline, "The world could end this easily" completes the comparison, appealing to your intellect as well as your emotions.

The text, known as *copy*, needs to be spare, concise, and evocative because people resist reading the messages in ads. Your job as a copywriter who is writing a public service advertisement is to compress a great deal of information into a few words to deliver your message.

In their quest to get people to read or listen to their message, advertisers realize the audience has a natural reluctance to pay attention and perhaps may even be skeptical about the information. In the headline and in the text, writers try to draw in audiences by appealing to their emotions and their intellects.

What is the main persuasive technique of this PSM that features a cancer survivor and his baby? To what else does the message appeal?

13 CREATING A VISUAL ARGUMENT

USING ETHOS When creating public service messages, your argument has extra weight with viewers because the sponsors—usually nonprofit groups—typically do not profit in a commercial sense. The groups whose argument you are positing, are looking to improve some aspect of society rather than sell a product. This fact helps your ethos, or a good reputation as a spokesperson. A PSM that encourages people to wear sunscreen to protect them from skin cancer will have more authority if "The American Academy of Dermatologists" is named as the sponsoring group in the PSM. The inclusion of this expert group gives the message a sense of trustworthiness and reliability. The group has nothing to gain from promoting the behavior. The real aim of the ad is not self-interest.

Provide Reasons in Your Argument

A visual argument can be mostly nonverbal—a message that happens in the brain, somewhere between the imagery and the viewer. Even a great image needs a few words that move beyond the showing and into the telling: a phrase, a clause, a sentence or two that explains the *why* or the *how*.

> How could somebody like me be a foster parent?
> Because "you do not have to be perfect to be a perfect parent."

> Is hunger really a problem in America?
> Yes, "12 million children are fighting hunger."

Call Your Reader to Action

The goal of a PSM is the "call to action." This is the final step in the persuasion path. If you have made your argument and persuaded your reader, it is now time to give your reader a clear course of action. Calls to action can take many forms, from asking people to get more information, to asking them to do something or to stop doing something. Some calls to action ask people to donate money; some ask them to donate their time as a volunteer or as a mentor. Some calls ask for very specific actions: use a seatbelt, vote, do not drink and drive, for example.

Presenting Your Work: The Pitch Letter

Your public service message might be useful to the group or organization whose message you are promoting; therefore, send a cover letter along with a copy of the PSM. The letter, sometimes called a *pitch letter*, should pique interest in your concept.

PRACTICE 13.7

Write a Pitch Letter

Choose any public service message in this chapter, and write a pitch letter to its sponsoring organization (see the feature called Tips for Writing Pitch Letters) persuading the organization to use the message in its new campaign. ■

Tips for Writing Pitch Letters

- Write to a specific person, usually the public relations director of the organization. Do the research to find the contact person, the correct spelling of the person's name, and the person's title.

- Keep your letter brief. One single-spaced page is ideal.

- Make sure your spelling, punctuation, and grammar are correct.

- Focus on what you can offer the organization. ("We have a fresh idea for making music piracy a thing of the past.")

- Remember that your reader is the expert in the organization. Do not tell the people in the organization things they already know, such as statistics that were generated by their organization. (Do not tell Mothers Against Drunk Driving, for example, that "drunk driving has serious consequences.")

- Use fresh, lively language and not bland, formal institutional phrasing. (*Bland:* "A group of students at our university has decided to devote time to helping to combat the enormous problem of music piracy on college campuses across this country." *Fresh:* "We want to help you help us not to steal music.")

- Be specific when you present your concept. ("Showing students where they can download free music legally will end music piracy.")

- Explain how your idea draws on your research and will bring the message to a new audience or to a traditional audience in a new way.

- Be clear about what you want the person to do if he or she likes your idea. ("Feel free to use our campaign. We consider it our contribution to helping combat drunk driving/music piracy.")

13 CREATING A VISUAL ARGUMENT

192 Freeman Street
Yardley, PA 19834
October 23, 2015

Hannah Blake, Director
MTV Think
1515 Broadway
New York, NY 10010

Dear Ms. Blake:

After spending four years at college, I have not met a single person who has been tested for HIV. I have heard many excuses from students about why they have not gotten tested, and I would like to show them the importance of testing. For a class project, three students and I created two public-service messages that we would like you to consider for your HIV testing campaign.

The current public service announcements for *Think*, MTV's HIV testing campaign, do a great job using humor to attract young people's attention. Our campaign has a serious tone that will complement your humorous approach and target the same young crowd.

Our print public service advertisement could appear in pop-culture magazines for the 18- to 24-year-old group, such as *Seventeen*, *Rolling Stone*, and *Maxim*. Our print advertisement features photos of four college students. Above each student is a speech bubble that reads, "I haven't been tested, but it's no big deal." The copy underneath the photos provides the shocking statistic that one out of every four people who are living with HIV has not had the infection diagnosed yet. The tag line of the ad reads, "That's a big deal."

We also created a radio spot that follows the same concept. Instead of photos, voices overlap saying, "I haven't been tested, but it's no big deal." After a beat of silence, an announcer reads the statistic and concludes with the tag line "That's a big deal." We conceive of this radio ad airing on national radio stations that play contemporary music, like New York's Z100.

Our goal is to encourage more young people to get tested for HIV.

Thank you for taking the time to look over these advertisements. If you would like to learn more about our campaign, you are welcome to contact us at the above address. We would be honored if you wished to use these materials to augment your current campaign.

Sincerely,
Monica Derevjanik

DIY MEDIA AND DESIGN

YouTube Advocacy Video

A video visual argument can use all the advantages of multimedia to engage the audience—sound, moving images, color, and action. This student-produced video won third place in a nationwide college PSA contest. During its National Depression Screening Day, the sponsoring organization, Screening for Mental Health (SMH), raises awareness about signs of depression. This video was selected to be screened at high schools and colleges throughout the United States. Look for other PSA contests online, and consider entering your video.

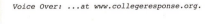

College Response National Depression Screening Day PSA

By Olga Khvan, Rachel Dushey, Kerry Aszklar, and Ephatha Park, Boston University

(Music starts -- a sad, slow tune. A shot of four fingers with faces on them wiggling, going down one by one until only the pinky is left.)

Voice Over: *One out of four young adults will experience a depressive episode by their mid-twenties.*

(Zoom in on remaining finger, fade out, zoom in on a girl's face. Hands with the symptoms written on them start moving in, pulling her hair and poking her face.)

Voice Over: *If you feel that symptoms such as anxiety, insomnia, loss of interest, and lack of appetite are messing with your head...*

(The girl shakes loose of the fingers.)

Voice Over:*...then break free.*

(Music changes to a more upbeat tune. Fade out on girl's face, fade in on her now smiling face against a new setting -- a bridge overlooking the river. Two of her friends appear and embrace her.)

Voice Over: *Take an anonymous depression screening...*

(The website is typed out letter by letter on a blank screen and the logo appears.)

Voice Over: *...at www.collegeresponse.org.*

Screening for Mental Health, Inc.

You can create your own video and post it on YouTube. Besides video images, you might use photography, typography, or animation to make your point. To get the full benefit of video, include music, sound effects, or voice-over. Make sure to get your music or images from sites such as Creative Commons that aggregate material from artists who allow their creative work to be used providing they are credited.

Choose a process you can illustrate through a visual metaphor, like the one here using hands to illustrate symptoms of depression. Try to get your point across in a concrete way and raise awareness about an issue.

READINGS

All the "readings" in this section showcase elements of contemporary public service campaigns. The first selection shows three installations created for Mothers Against Drunk Driving (MADD). The second presents a possible way to combat the problem of self-injury. The final selection shows a poster to raise awareness among teens about relationship abuse.

MADD High School Posters
Mothers Against Drunk Driving

These three photos show MADD's campaign to prevent teens from driving and drinking. The photos show actual installations in high school corridors with the accompanying informational text that was posted next to each installation.

September 5, 1997

Lisa Miller was impaled by an iron rail after the driver of the car she was riding in slammed into the side of a bridge at 70 mph. Lisa died at the scene.

LISA: One more reason not to ride with a drunk driver.

October 17, 2001

Jeff Wilson's body was crushed. The driver of the car Jeff was riding in drove into a ditch. The car flipped and Jeff's body was thrown underneath the vehicle. Jeff died at the scene.

JEFF: One more reason not to ride with a drunk driver.

May 28, 2004

Amy Roberts was hooked up to a life support machine as a result of the injuries she sustained after the driver of the car she was in hit a parked truck. Amy died four days later.

AMY: One more reason not to ride with a drunk driver.

13 CREATING A VISUAL ARGUMENT

Questions for Rhetorical Analysis

1. How does the material in the PSM appeal to the target audience?
2. What effect does the installation have on the content of the PSM? What are the potential risks of making this message large and public?
3. The appeal in the PSM is frequently made to teens. Does this PSM refresh the message? Why or why not?

Questions for Critical Thinking

1. What are the obstacles between the target audience and the message "Don't drink and drive"?
2. Are installations an effective method of raising awareness? Why or why not?

Style Practice: Imitation

You have been hired to do another in this series of PSMs to install in your former high school corridor. Create a rough draft of how you would place this message in the corridor and what the copy would say.

Girl Empowerment
NCH

NCH, The Children's Charity in Great Britain, created this poster as part of its campaign to combat self-harm among teenage girls.

Questions for Rhetorical Analysis

1. Who is the audience for this poster? How do you know?
2. What is the concept behind this campaign? Is it effective?
3. To what does this campaign appeal: *logos*, *pathos*, *ethos*, or a combination?

Questions for Critical Thinking

1. Compare this poster to the previous MADD high school posters. How are these campaigns similar? How do they differ? Which approach do you find more effective, more empowering?
2. What other approach might you take to combat self-injury among teens? How widespread is this problem?

Style Practice: Imitation

Create a rough draft of a poster for this campaign, targeting parents or teachers rather than teens.

Talk about Your Boyfriend Trouble PSM

Seth Nichols, Emily Chang, and James O'Neill

This public service message that raises awareness about relationship abuse relies on the combination of typefaces to convey its message.

HE's **MY BOY**friend.
(I fell.)
I am high maintenance. I ASKED
for too MUCH *again*
He told me not to BUT I went anyway
(And I knew he was waiting for me to CALL)
I tripped: I am *so* clumsy.
Besides, he just lost it for a second
HE LOVES ME, *really*.
(That's what it means to be A girlfriend)
He didn't mean it!!!!!!!!!
It only happened once. HE SAID
HE LOVES ME.
It only happened

Once (or twice)

Love should never physically hurt.
Visit TalkAboutYourBoyfriendTrouble@yahoo.com
if you want some anonymous advice on
what to do next.

Kate Burak

Questions for Rhetorical Analysis

1. How do these writers attempt to break down the obstacles or barriers between their message and their audience?
2. How does the variety of typefaces work in this PSM?
3. Who is the audience for the PSM?
4. What is the purpose of the PSM? What is the call to action?
5. Where would you place this PSM?

Questions for Critical Thinking

1. This PSM addresses an audience that might be reluctant to listen. What other audiences might not want to listen? Which other messages would be difficult to deliver? How have these messages been packaged in the past? For example, what kind of anti-smoking PSMs do you recall seeing?
2. Is the PSM only directed at women? Do men need to hear this message as well? Which men? Should the PSM be less gender-specific? Why or why not?

Style Practice: Imitation

Using the same technique of using "excuses" in different typefaces, create a PSM for a seatbelt campaign, a skin cancer screening campaign, or a campaign to end drunk driving.

WRITING & REVISION STRATEGIES

Gathered here are three interactive sections for you to use as you write and revise your public service message.

- Writer's Notebook Suggestions
- Peer Review Log
- Revision Checklist

Writer's Notebook Suggestions

Use these exercises to do some start-up thinking and writing for your public service message. Writers and designers say they often get the creative process started by looking at other advertisements, by looking at magazines, photography, and art books, and even by reading poetry. In the hit television series about advertising, *Mad Men*, Don Draper goes to the movies when his creativity needs a little boost. Inspiration can come to you in many ways. Try the short exercises like the ones that follow to help you get your creative process going.

1. Design a public service advertisement that will appear on the side of a bus. The topic is raising awareness about the dangers of high blood pressure. Research the topic, and define the target audience. Alert and encourage your audience.
2. Use any news story as the basis for an PSM: use the real-life testimony about the event or some aspect of it as a cautionary tale or as an example of a behavior or policy that works well.
3. Read the editorial section of a newspaper and develop a PSM (print or television) based on the premise of one editorial or column. Raise awareness or call your audience to a more specific action.
4. Design a storyboard for a television PSM. Your goal is to raise awareness about eating disorders among teens. Your audience is parents.
5. Choose a nonprofit group in your community, and design a calendar for it. The group can either sell the calendar to make money or give it away. The calendar should have a different appeal every month to remind people of the group's activities or mission.
6. Design a new logo for a group in your community.
7. Use an existing image for a cause, and rewrite the headline and copy. Use the original call to action.

Peer Review Log

As you work with a writing partner or in a peer review group, you can use these questions to give helpful responses to a classmate's public service message or as a guide for discussion.

Writer's Name: _____

Date: _____

1. Where did your eyes go first? Second? Last? Note spots with the numbers 1, 2, 3, and so on.
2. To whom does the PSM seem to address? Tell the writer to whom the PSM would appeal. Tell the writer to whom the PSM would not appeal. Who would stop reading or not be attracted at all?
3. Did you stop anywhere because you were confused?
4. Does the PSM remind you of any other ads you have seen?
5. Does the design draw you in?
6. Is the language clear?
7. Did you have to start reading from the beginning to understand the point?
8. How did the PSM make you feel? Did your feelings change as you progressed through the PSM?
9. If you saw this PSM again, would you stop to look at it or read it?

10. Tell the writer what you think the audience is called to do, and comment on this goal.
11. Is the call to action realistic?
12. Read over the pitch letter and look for
    a. Any spots that might insult the reader
    b. Any spots that assume the reader is not well informed
    c. Any places where the letter can be condensed

Revision Checklist

As you do the final revision of your public service message, check to make sure that you

- used language appropriate to your target audience
- created a headline that attracts attention
- provided compelling reasons in the body of the message
- included a clear call to action

WRITING FOR YOUR COMMUNITY
14
PROPOSALS

When you sit down to write, you must have one clear goal in your mind. What is the ONE thing you want your reader [or] funder to remember?
—*GARLAND WALLER*

Problem: Soaring student debt makes college inaccessible and unaffordable for many students.

For their capstone project at Portland State University in Oregon, a group of students proposed a way to defer tuition for students attending state or community colleges. They presented their proposal, Pay It Forward, to the Oregon State Legislature, which then passed a bill to study the proposal's feasibility.

Problem: Date rape is the most underreported crime on college campuses.

A Massachusetts high school student who was the victim of date rape proposed a campaign to bring awareness to this problem. She wrote an op-ed piece in the *Boston Globe* and proposed a public service campaign called "See It and Stop It." A local ad agency partnered with her and launched the campaign.

All over the country, students, communities, and local businesses and organizations have proposed plans to solve problems. And, like these examples of proposals (which you can read in this chapter), many of them have made positive change happen.

Chapter Objectives

craft a "big idea" that turns your concept into action
372

avoid pitfalls of past proposals
372

support your solutions with clear evidence
374

tailor your writing to a specific audience
376

find solutions to identified problems
377

PROCESS PLAN

Prepare

- Select a local or global problem to help solve.

- Figure out what background/contextual information needs to be researched.

- Come up with a solution—one that is truly feasible, targeted to a specific audience.

- Brainstorm a list of reasons that would persuade a targeted audience.

Draft

- Introduction: Clearly and briefly summarize the problem.

- Body: Amass facts, statistics, anecdotes that show the scope and seriousness of the problem.

- Provide a specific and feasible solution.

- Conclusion: Present the benefits of the solution.

Revise

- Make sure the proposal has visual as well as verbal impact.

- Check that your evidence is solid and supports your proposal well.

Understanding
the Writing Project

MOST PROPOSALS identify a problem, suggest a feasible solution, and present the benefits of the solution. The purpose of any proposal is to persuade readers to take some action: to donate time or money or to create a program, plan, or public service campaign. Proposals come in many forms: formal grant proposals, letters to agencies or funders, editorials or articles that propose solutions to problems, and public petitions that lobby for change. Many college courses also require you to use the basic proposal form—problem, solution, benefits—in papers as well as in proposals for research projects and theses. Whatever the form, a proposal has to provide readers with compelling and logical reasons that prove the benefit of taking the suggested action.

ASSIGNMENT Suggest a fresh way to help solve a local, community, or global public problem. Your proposal might take the form of a grant proposal, a letter requesting funding or other support for a program, an editorial or article that proposes a solution to a specific problem, or an Internet petition that lobbies for a specific change. Organize your proposal into three sections:

- Problem
- Solution
- Benefits

Proposals are often written by teams such as groups of citizens or staff members. You can make this a group project and experience the kind of debate and compromise that goes into the process of effecting social change. Also, PowerPoint presentations often accompany proposals as they are brought to a public audience. You can read some tips on creating effective presentations in the DIY on page 381 of this chapter.

Proposal

JESSICA HOLLANDER

Stopping Teen Dating Violence

EVERYONE WOULD like to believe that sexual assault or domestic violence happens only to someone else, somewhere else. We think of the perpetrator or even the victim as a faceless person one reads about in the papers.

Unfortunately, statistics show otherwise. One in five female high school students in Massachusetts reports being physically and/or sexually abused by a dating partner. Think of five teenagers you care about. Your daughter. Your little sister. Your best friend. Chances are they'll be affected by dating violence. It can be physical, emotional, or sexual. It starts with power and control. It starts early in our lives. And it happens everywhere.

When I was a sophomore in high school, I learned this the hard way. An old boyfriend and close friend, one whom I not only trusted but believed I loved, snuck over to my parents' house in the middle of the night. Like many young girls do too often, I sacrificed my own personal safety in the pursuit of what I thought was "romance." That night I sacrificed much more.

When other students hear my story, they are surprised because I am not how they picture a "typical" survivor. I lived in an affluent neighborhood, attended one of the best public school systems in the country, in a city that not only promotes but demands social awareness. I have a wonderful, caring, and intimate family and friends.

Because I was so convinced that I was immune to these dangers, so certain that this individual would never consider hurting me, I ignored the warning signs, my very own intuition telling me something was wrong. I learned the hard way to follow your instincts and speak up, whether it's for your own safety or the safety of a friend. My friends and his friends ignored the signs, too.

Teens need to be given more tangible tools, phrases, and words in our own language that we can use. And we need to have the confidence to know that if something in a relationship looks or feels wrong, it probably is.

The Teen Action Campaign is the long overdue vehicle to provide such tools to teens. For the past two years, I have been working with other teens from across the state to create the "See It and Stop It" campaign. We chose to launch in October for Domestic Violence Awareness month.

Because friends are such a major influence in teens' lives, the focus on bystanders is one of the main strengths of the campaign. Seeitandstopit.org asks teens to recognize the warning signs, be it jealousy, possessiveness, etc., in their friends' relationships and prevent them from escalating into a hazardous situation. The actions can be small, but can have a powerful impact.

We must all accept responsibility for the overwhelming presence of sexual assault and domestic violence in today's world. This is not just a woman's issue. Men of all ages must encourage each other not to be a man that women fear, but instead be a man that women can trust.

Those of us who helped create the "See It and Stop It" campaign are convinced that our generation has the power to speak up and change attitudes about gender violence before it becomes entrenched. But it takes resources and the support of everyone in our lives: parents, educators, faith-based leaders, philanthropists and government.

We had the help of the best experts and research in the country and the *pro bono* support of Hill Holliday Advertising, which took our ideas and made them into TV, radio, outdoor, [and] print ads; posters for schools and our website. We were supported by local philanthropists and corporations who shared our belief that we can end relationship violence as we know it. As we launch in Massachusetts, we've learned our campaign will be picked up nationally, by the Ad Council and Family Violence Prevention Fund.

After my assault, my friends and I became vigilant in our daily activities to prevent such tragedy from occurring again. Simple things, like checking in with one another at parties, staying in groups, calling one another, and saying something out loud when something didn't feel right, became automatic.

Such precautions and social awareness can make the world a safer place for all of us. Check out our campaign so [that] the next time you see it, you'll know it. You just might speak up and do something to stop it.

Questions for Critical Thinking

1. Hollander writers that domestic violence "is not just a woman's issue. Men of all ages must encourage each other not to be a man that women fear, but instead be a man that women can trust." Discuss your reactions to this statement.

2. Do you think that teens can be empowered to speak up against abusive behavior? What would stand in the way? What would pave the way?

The Rhetorical Situation

Purpose: You want to propose a feasible solution to an identified problem, either local or global.

Voice: Your voice should be confident, informed, and engaging. You want to persuade your audience to take action on your proposal.

Audience: Your audience can be an individual or an organization, whoever has the authority to grant what you are seeing.

Media and Design: There are many platforms for proposals: public petitions, letters to finders, grants, research projects, editorials, advocacy websites, PowerPoint presentations, YouTube videos, among many others.

THE BIG IDEA From Concept to Plan

PRACTICE 14.1

Choosing a Worthy Proposal Topic

Assume that your college has just received a donation from a wealthy alumnus to fund a community service project. The college president has created the President's Service Commission to decide which project should be funded. The commission has asked student groups, including yours, to come up with ideas for worthy projects. All the groups will present their ideas to the commission.

1. Create a list of at least five projects that would benefit your college or local community.

2. Choose the one project you think is most important, and prepare a brief position statement that

   - states the problem the funding will solve
   - proposes how the money will be used
   - predicts the benefits to the group and the community

3. Present your proposal to the President's Service Commission. You have only 5 minutes for your presentation. Keep in mind that the audience includes all the other groups advocating for their projects to be funded. ■

Just as the message drives a visual argument (Chapter 13) and an argumentative thesis (claim) drives an editorial, commentary, or blog (Chapter 12), the underlying concept of your proposal is the big idea that drives it. What is new or fresh in your thinking about the problem you are trying to solve?

Many proposals have been built around the concept of empowering individuals to speak out against abuse or potential threats when they observe it. No matter whether the specific issue is domestic violence or terrorism, the underlying concept is that every person should take responsibility for ensuring public safety. How can you bring this issue to your audiences in a new way—a way that will make them sit up and notice?

The specific plan emerges from this concept. In Jessica Hollander's proposal to create a public awareness campaign about date rape, her overall concept was to prevent date rape from occurring. Her specific plan was to inform students about the warning signs of overly possessive or jealous partners and to empower their friends and families to speak up. All of this is summed up in the campaign's tag line, See It and Stop It. Often, if you ask yourself how you can translate your concept into a specific action, you can come up with your plan.

CONCEPT + HOW? = PLAN

Research Paths

Troubleshooting your topic as you begin your research will save you from going down a lot of dead ends. Research past efforts, where they have succeeded and where they have failed, and then amass the evidence you need to make your proposal a stand-out.

Avoiding Pitfalls of Past Proposals

Do some research on past efforts to solve the identified problem before you propose your approach. Sometimes it is useful to interview a person in the organization, especially in the publicity department, to find out what the organization has accomplished and to see how it has targeted specific issues or particular populations. Become an expert on the group or individual who will read your proposal, and present yourself as someone who is not just knowledgeable, reasonable, and logical but also useful to the organization.

Look for places where your plan might run into problems. One student group proposed a seemingly simple solution to feeding the local homeless population: pack

Visual Literacy: Using Images in Proposals

RARELY DO PROPOSALS COME without imagery: photographs, charts, graphs, or art. For each of the images here, identify a problem the image might illustrate. Think outside the box (metaphorically or humorously). The image does not have to be a literal illustration of the issue.

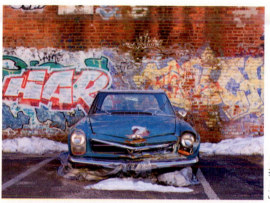

up leftover food from student dining halls and bring it to homeless shelters. However, they discovered a serious impediment to this plan when interviewing the head of food services. He told them that the college was legally responsible for the quality of the food and that anyone who might get sick after eating it could sue for damages. If the group had submitted its proposal before thoroughly researching the plan, the proposal would have been turned down immediately. Instead, the students altered their proposal to include a release form to be signed by the shelter absolving the college of legal responsibility, thus showing that their plan was fully developed down to the last detail. This kind of care in researching helps prepare you to face any hesitations your audience might have about accepting your proposal.

Using Evidence to Appeal to Your Audience

Evidence can help you appeal to your readers' logic and emotions and establish your own credibility. The original Greek terms for argumentative appeals are *logos*, *pathos*, and *ethos*, which you read about in the previous chapter.

LOGOS Appeal to the reader's intellect and sense of reason by creating a path of evidence for your reader that inevitably leads to your conclusion. To get your reader to follow you from point to point, your argument must be clear and supported by objective evidence: facts and statistics.

Facts, statistics, and studies show the seriousness and scope of your problem, make the abstractions of your ideas concrete, and give context to the issues. In Jessica Hollander's op-ed piece, "Stopping Teen Dating Violence," she opens with this sobering statistic: "One in five female high school students in Massachusetts reports being physically and/or sexually abused by a dating partner." (This statistic comes from the highly reputable *Journal of American Medical Association*.)

PATHOS The emotional appeal helps your reader connect with you and connects you with your reader. Emotion can be a way to find common ground and to say that you and your reader share a set of beliefs. Using emotion to support your points involves marshaling subjective evidence, such as opinions, anecdotes, and personal observations. In effect, pathos is evidence that presents a human face through anecdotes, quotations, and visuals.

Combining *pathos* with *logos*, emotion with logic, often provides the most compelling arguments. Notice that after she presents the statistic that one in five high school students has been the victim of abuse, Hollander puts a human face on this number as she writes, "Think of five teenagers you care about. Your daughter. Your little sister. Your best friend. Chances are they'll be affected by dating violence." Of course, her own story about being abused is at the emotional center of her proposal.

Focusing on an individual example, telling a story, or giving a voice or face to a problem helps persuade a reader already hooked by facts and statistics, or, on the

Choose one of the following proposals.

- Creating an antiviolence campaign on your campus
- Raising money for a local homeless shelter
- Advocating for 24-hour public transportation
- Lobbying against using live animals in science classrooms
- Creating a public awareness campaign about juvenile diabetes

Make a list of the kinds of research that would help you show the seriousness and scope of the problem. What facts, statistics, studies, anecdotes, quotations, and/or visuals would you want to find? First review this example:

Example: Creating a hotline for troubled teens

- Data on how many hotlines exist in nearby areas
- Anecdote about how a hotline has helped a specific teen
- Quotation from a counselor

other hand, makes the reader receptive to facts and stats to come. Logic and emotion combine to create a powerful case for any proposal.

ETHOS To be swayed by your argument, a reader has to trust you and know that the evidence you cite is accurate, valid, and reliable. You create your credibility, in good part, by clear and accurate attribution of your sources. Tell your reader who your sources are and why they are especially suited to speak to a particular subject.

In some ways, digging up statistics relies on your intuition and common sense. You can try Internet searches for organizations with expertise on the issues you are writing about, or you can enter the name of the issue into a search engine and see which groups or agencies have studied the problem. As always, make sure your sources are reputable and credible.

Finding evidence from unbiased and expert sources is one important way to create your credibility. Sometimes it is difficult to sift through all the information on a topic, especially on the hundreds of Internet sites, but it is important that you investigate the source of your information. Are the statistics about global warming that you are using to support your recycling program from a government agency, from a major research university, or from the research arm of a corporation? Who is funding the research? Answering the following five questions will help you find reliable and unbiased sources for your proposal.

(continued)

- Quotation from a teen who was helped
- Studies about the usefulness of hotlines
- Expert opinion from psychologist about effectiveness of hotlines
- Costs of operating a hotline ■

Five Questions for Determining the Credibility of Your Sources

1. What are the author's credentials and affiliations?
2. What is the author's reputation? Has the author's work been cited in many sources?
3. Is the author known as an authority in this field?
4. Has the research been published in quality publications, especially scholarly journals?
5. When was the research done? Is it current?

The Proposal Process

Not every proposal writer goes through each of these six steps in turn, but most successful proposals follow these guidelines.

Identify the Problem

Unfortunately, it is not all that difficult to identify a worthwhile issue for your proposal. Think about global problems like pollution, hunger, human rights violations, and underfunded medical research, or consider local problems like homelessness, lack of college scholarships for low-income students, and the need for bicycle lanes in your community. Find a problem that matters to you.

The problems you choose to work on are up to you. They can be local to your college campus, perhaps student safety after dark. They can involve your town or city, such as groundwater pollution caused by lawn fertilizer or rock salt de-icer. Or the problems might be global, such as hunger or disease in Third World countries. Whatever problem you choose to help solve, you will engage in a valuable process—one that helps create change in some aspect of community life, whether local or global.

Tackling a huge problem can be overwhelming, however. How can you find solutions to world hunger or war or hurricane relief when scientists and politicians around the world have failed? One way to create a manageable topic is to keep it narrow or local. Keep your goals realistic and feasible. For example, human rights violations are a vast global problem but one that you might be interested in helping to solve. To define the problem more narrowly, select a particular aspect of it or perhaps even a particular case.

One student group wanted to help eradicate human rights violations. The students began searching the Web, using the keywords *human rights violations*. They discovered countries in which people are still enslaved. As they continued their search, they found the Christian Solidarity International (CSI) organization, which is actively working to end slavery in Sudan. They decided to narrow their focus to creating a public awareness and fund-raising campaign in their communities. Helping CSI end slavery in Sudan became the focus of their community service proposal.

Identify Your Audience

Who has the authority to grant what you are seeking? This is the person or persons to whom you address your proposal. If you propose a change that requires support from the college community, find out who is the person in charge. For example, for a student volunteer program to mentor local schoolchildren, collect used books for a literacy program, or help feed the homeless people in your area, you should be able to find the person in the college administration who is responsible for that area, perhaps a dean or director.

The community group working on the skateboard proposal that is in the Readings needed to convince their town leadership to give them access to the waterfront site and to grant funds to build the ramps, pipes, and boxes needed for the park. The proposal focused on convincing the town that the skatepark benefited the entire community and would even bring in tourist revenue. The Oregon students who worked

on the "Pay It Forward" proposal presented it to a panel of legislators and persuaded one of the legislators to sponsor a bill to study their proposal.

Familiarize yourself with the group that will read your proposal. Knowing the assumptions, philosophy, and history of your audience helps you understand possible obstacles. Why would audience members resist your proposal? Why would they embrace it?

Persuading someone to say yes to a proposal also requires some understanding of an organization's work. The mission of an organization or agency is the top priority of its administrators, so you need to show how your proposal fits with that mission. Most organizations and foundations have mission statements that you can study on their websites or in their promotional materials. Before you write your proposal, make sure you have thoroughly researched the organization's mission and philosophy.

Formulate a Clear and Feasible Solution

A community service project often begins with a specific problem. After you identify a problem, you can come up with a feasible solution. To persuade readers to accept your proposal, be positive and optimistic. You are not lodging a complaint; rather, you are presenting a plan of action. In an editorial or other opinion piece, for instance, you identify a problem and write an argument to change people's minds or behaviors. But proposal writers go one step further; they present a clear and feasible solution—a plan that is doable.

No simple blueprint exists for coming up with a creative solution, although it is always useful to begin by researching the issue. Read about the issue. Find out what has been done in the past. Talk to other people about the problem and past solutions. Freewrite to discover what you think about the issue. In other words, coming up with a possible solution starts with analyzing the problem.

Let's say you read a newspaper article about the lack of interest in environmental issues, especially among low-income city youth. Being an environmental activist, you decide that you want to ensure that today's young people become educated and involved. You think the first step could be to involve urban kids in outdoor adventures. One plan is to provide city youth with outdoor experiences, taking them on biking, hiking, and camping trips. What resources would you need to implement this plan? You might come up with this list:

- Volunteers from your campus outdoor club
- Support from parents and teachers
- Donations of bikes and camping equipment from local businesses

The important question to ask is "Is this doable?" or even more importantly, "Is this doable with the resources we have?"

PRACTICE 14.4
Identifying Your Audience

Solve these research problems:

1. You want to write a proposal to post nutritional information in the student union or cafeteria. Find the name and e-mail address of the person in charge.

2. You want to send a letter supporting a proposal to create a food pantry in your hometown. Find the name and e-mail address of your local representative in the state legislature.

3. You want to locate a local environmental group. Find the names of the environmental groups active in your area. Get contact information for one group.

4. You are interested in finding out more about national service, and you know that AmeriCorps has a number of programs. Find the name and local contact information for at least one AmeriCorps program.

5. You are proposing that a local elementary school set up an e-mail pen pal program that pairs American students with kids from Europe, Asia, and Africa. Find out whether such a

(continued)

program already exists. Provide the names of existing programs and contact information.

6. Explain how you found the answers to each of these problems—whether by looking in a print source, searching online, or asking a knowledgeable person. ■

PRACTICE 14.5
Creating Feasible Solutions

Create a feasible plan to help solve one of the following problems. List some resources you might need to accomplish that plan.

■ Commuter students on your campus do not feel that they are part of campus life.

■ The arts budget has been cut in elementary schools in your community.

■ Summer residents of a beach community abandon their pets at the end of the tourist season.

■ Over the past year, on your college campus or in your town, three people have been robbed while waiting for a bus.

■ The local food pantry will run out of money next month. ■

Tips for Selling Your Solution

■ Describe your vision in clear and specific language.

■ Be positive and optimistic.

■ Show your readers exactly how your plan solves the identified problem.

■ Be brief. You are selling the concept, not describing every single detail of the plan.

■ Write concisely but with impact.

Formulating a preliminary plan on how to solve the problem helps you focus your thinking and research. You may refine or even change your approach as you gather information. But generating ideas early in the process and putting them into clear language will help you see their possibilities as well as their limitations. Once you have a plan in mind, test its feasibility by asking these questions:

■ Does this plan actually solve the identified problem?

■ Can this plan be accomplished with the resources I have or can get?

■ Can this plan be accomplished within the time that I have?

■ Has this plan been tried before?

Provide Reasons

Why should your reader accept your proposal? You have to provide compelling reasons, and you have to think about the possible downsides so as to counter possible objections. Generate as many reasons as you can—more than you will be able to use—to make sure you have considered all possibilities. Weed out the weak reasons, and select the ones that will be most persuasive.

One way to generate reasons is to analyze the problem. Break the problem down into its parts, and consider the different aspects. Working on an environmental education proposal, for example, you might think about what would compel parents, teachers, local businesses, and volunteers to support outdoor adventures for low-income city kids. Your list might be similar to this one:

1. Provides lessons in personal responsibility, achievement, and environmental awareness
2. Helps kids develop practical skills and have fun
3. Keeps low-income city kids away from gangs, drugs, and violence

4. Provides guidance from supportive adults
5. Helps kids get individualized attention
6. Boosts self-esteem while kids learn about their role in protecting the environment.

—Rachel Kleinman, "Trips for Kids Proposal"

Explain the Benefits

End your proposal by emphasizing the ways that it will benefit your readers and the general public. What is in it for them? Be persuasive and specific as you present the benefits. Also, be specific about what you want the readers to do.

- If you want readers to fund a project, make sure you have clearly presented the budget and estimated the amount of money you need.
- If you want readers to take action—support legislation or organize a charity bike ride, for example—explain exactly what steps you want them to take.
- If you want readers to use your publicity campaign, explain your materials, the concept, and the audience that you are targeting.

You might even want to create prototype materials to accompany your proposal. All these possible approaches have a common goal: to convince readers of the benefits of accepting your proposal. However you decide to end your proposal, make sure your readers know how the community would benefit from the plan. If you want readers to do something, be clear, specific, and persuasive in your call to action.

Go Public with Your Proposal

Your proposal does not have to wait to find an audience. You can find a large audience for your ideas on a website or on a blog. Your proposal site—either blog or fully developed site—can include multimedia materials that help develop your argument. Viewers can see streaming video, link to sites that support your cause, sign petitions, see design plans and blueprints, and even leave comments. The easiest way to post your proposal is on a blog dedicated to that topic, and you can even bring traffic to your blog by tweeting about it or starting a Facebook page and organizing an event that supports your proposal.

PRACTICE 14.6
Providing Reasons

1. Reread the six reasons for supporting outdoor adventures, and put them in order from strongest to weakest. Give reasons for your decisions.

2. Think of the different audiences: parents, teachers, local businesses, volunteer group leaders, and so on. Which of the six reasons would you use to persuade each of these audiences? Explain your decisions.

3. What objections might someone have to any of these reasons?

4. What other reasons can you think of to support this proposal? Try to come up with at least three more reasons. ■

Tips for Using Multimedia in Your Proposal

Use the media its fullest advantage. Posting to the Web means that you have the potential to include photography as well as video film footage and slide shows. Adding video can be as simple as linking to a YouTube video you shoot or linking to a site with its own film clip. Blog-hosting sites also allow you to post video right

(continued)

Tips for Using Multimedia in Your Proposal *(continued)*

on your blog. But remember that any material you include should fit in with your tone and be credible and of high quality. You will lose support if any of your claims are discredited or if the images and language in supporting weblinks are inappropriate.

- Carefully check all videos and links to make sure the contents are consistent with the tone of your proposal.

- Assure that the multimedia material is of high quality, both in its content and technology.

- As with all source material, be careful to attribute the source and check it for credibility and reliability.

- Avoid choosing material that includes offensive language or jokes. Your funders (and the community of viewers for your Web proposal) might not share your sense of irony.

- Be sure the material fits the assumptions of your funders. Avoid overtly partisan material. Even religious material may distract from your message (unless your funders are a religious group).

When you move from presenting your ideas to your funding organization to posting your ideas for the public, you have shifted your audience and slightly changed your goals. Going public with your proposal means that you are addressing a more varied group. Now, your readers might have different matters at stake, and your goal is not just funding but also gaining support for your cause—not necessarily a different aim but perhaps a different emphasis. Your proposal to build a skatepark in a town, for example, will be met by neighbors whose concerns primarily are noise, parking, and crowds. Your Web posting can address these concerns by linking to similar projects, possibly in nearby towns. Or you can show actual footage of an operating skatepark so that residents can get a firsthand view of one. Whatever elements you choose, keep the audience in the forefront of your planning. Posting your proposal on the Internet allows you to link to a variety of media that will help enliven and support your proposal.

DIY MEDIA AND DESIGN

PowerPoint Proposal

Create a short, 4- or 5-slide, PowerPoint presentation to present in class and perhaps even post on the Internet. Use the proposal you have written for the content, and be sure to cover the problem, solution, and benefits in your presentation. When you are designing PowerPoint presentations, consider that your audience is listening and viewing. Display part of the text on slides, and deliver a talk to accompany the slides, but provide enough information that the slides might appear without the spoken text.

PowerPoint Dos and Don'ts

1. Include powerful images that work in conjunction with your spoken text. A graph, for example, can speak a thousand words, whereas the narration points out a single conclusion.
2. Include charts that break down concepts visually (maps, pie charts, and bar graphs can visually express statistics).
3. Choose a style, vocabulary, and tone that illustrate the idea that you are "one person speaking to another person."
4. Use bulleted lists instead of blocks of text. The text on the slides is made up of titles or headlines and the main points are similar to an outline.
5. Try to limit yourself to one concept per slide.
6. Because the audience is reading while you explain further, text appearing on the slide does not need to be full sentences.
7. The text should be easily understood, brief, and concise. Slides should not be too detailed and should include illustrations the audience can read.
8. Organize your presentation so that it presents a kind of story with a beginning, middle, and end.
9. For a proposal, the structure is beginning (state the problem), middle (explain your solution), and end (state the benefits).
10. Use a "take away" or handout for details such as cost breakdowns.

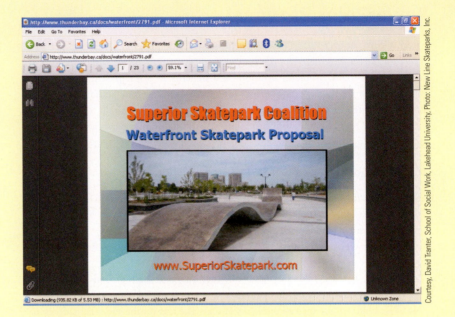

The opening screen shot from the Superior Skatepark blog is included here. To see the complete PowerPoint proposal for a skate spot sponsored by the Superior Skatepark Coalition, go to page 390 in the Readings section of this chapter. The PowerPoint proposal is posted on a blog that provides information and updates on fund-raising efforts, skating events, and links to news stories.

READINGS

Both of the readings in this section were successful in their own right. "Pay It Forward" has prompted conversation and legislation about making college more affordable and accessible not only in Oregon but in Washington, Pennsylvania, Maine, and other states across the nation. The Superior Skatepark is now part of the waterfront recreation area in Superior, Wisconsin.

Pay It Forward: A Proposal to Make College Affordable for Oregon Students

Students for Educational Debt Reform (SEDR): *Dave Coburn, Tracy Gibbs, Ariel Gruver, Nathan Hunt, Sarah Johnston, Jason Junkkarinen, Tyler McKean, Mark Miller, Kevin Rackham, Bonnie Riley, Seri Soulatha, Ruvim Tsymbal, Jianing Yu*

Students for Educational Debt Reform was founded by students participating in a Portland State University Fall 2012 Senior Capstone class titled "Student Debt: Economics, Policy, and Advocacy." It was co-taught by Barbara Dudley and Mary King and conducted with community partners Jubilee Oregon and the Working Families Organization.

I. Introduction

In a personal story posted on www.studentloanjustice .org, one distraught Oregonian stated, "I truly believed that if I got an education, I would be able to get out of poverty. With the student loan debt I will never get out of poverty." This person was the only individual from her family to graduate from high school, and desperately wanted to obtain a master's degree. Now, with a debt exceeding $80,000, she is struggling to avoid homelessness.

HIGHER EDUCATION has become an essential step to achieving the American Dream. Unfortunately, many young people are forced to finance their education using student loans. This problem is steadily growing; with $864 billion in federal loans and $150 billion in private loans, student debt in America now exceeds $1 trillion (Brown, 2012). Student debt increased nearly 50% in just four years from 2007 to 2011 (Desrochers, Lenihan and Wellman, 2010). This issue poses serious economic and social consequences that we cannot afford to overlook any longer.

The effects of student debt can be felt all over the country. According to data from 2011, two-thirds of students who earn four-year Bachelor's degrees are graduating with an average student loan debt of more than $25,000, and 1 in 10 borrowers

> "According to data from 2011, two-thirds of students who earn four-year Bachelor's degrees are graduating with an average student loan debt of more than $25,000 …"

DO YOU HAVE STUDENT DEBT REGRET?

©Dundanim/shutterstock.com
©Galina Barskaya/Shutterstock.com
©leungchopan/Shutterstock.com

S E D R
STUDENTS FOR EDUCATIONAL DEBT REFORM

Portland State
UNIVERSITY

PLEASE ATTEND OUR
LEGISLATIVE PANEL
MONDAY, 12-03-2012
2ND FLOOR GALLERY PSU URBAN CENTER
10:00AM–12:00PM

Hear about what can be done to address the growing student debt problem. Your attendance will show our panel of legislators this problem needs immediate attention.

now owe more than $54,000 in loans (Ellis, 2012). That is a tremendous financial burden to have on one's back when completing college. Particularly now, with the economy in a very slow recovery from The Great Recession, it is very hard for college graduates to find a job that allows them to earn enough to live even modestly while paying back these loans. Many graduates are taking low-paying, part time jobs and far fewer are starting their own businesses.

II. Proposal: Pay It Forward, Pay It Back

College can be made more affordable to Oregon students on every rung of the economic ladder and simultaneously maximize the likelihood that a college degree delivers on the promise of a better life. The program is called Pay It Forward.

Pay It Forward is a program that will greatly reduce and possibly eliminate the necessity for students and families to take on debt in order to secure post-secondary education. It achieves this goal through the establishment of a fund that pays the tuition and fees of all students enrolled in Oregon public community colleges and universities. In return, students make a binding commitment to pay into this fund a small fixed percentage of their income for a set number of years after leaving school.

Based on an analysis by Jason Gettel, Policy Analyst at the Oregon Center for Public Policy, graduates would pay 1.5% of their adjusted gross income for two-year Associate's degrees, 3% for Bachelor's degrees and 4% for Master's degrees. In other words, graduates would pay 0.75% of their annual adjusted gross income (AGI) for every full-time, academic year attended, based on the current level of tuition and fees in Oregon's public institutions. These payments would continue for 24 years. In this way, students who obtain a Bachelor's degree would pay, on average, $39,653 into the Pay It Forward fund, which would include $7,417 on top of the value of tuition and fees that they would otherwise have paid.

Pay It Forward is not a loan program but a system of income-based payment that operates under an economic principle akin to Social Security. Unlike Social Security, costs are incurred prior to payment into the system so the challenge lies in start-up funding. In time, however, as graduates pay into the program, the Pay It Forward fund would build a large enough surplus to pay for future students' tuition and fees without any additional money provided by the State of Oregon. The program assumes, however, that the State appropriations for higher education do not sink below their current level, adjusted for inflation. In other words, this is a program of shared responsibility.

A Sustainable, Solvent Solution

Implementing the Pay It Forward program will require a substantial start-up fund, but would lead to solvency for students and the Oregon higher educational system. At a payment rate of 3% of graduates' adjusted gross income for 24 years, the program will take in more than it spends in the 25th year, and begin to build a positive balance that will grow annually thereafter. . . . In the meanwhile, the gap would be filled either by bonding or philanthropic contributions or both. This proposal could work well in conjunction with Treasurer Wheeler's Opportunity Initiative.

A more aggressive payment plan, requiring payment of 1.25% of adjusted gross income for 24 years (i.e., 5% for a four year degree) would allow the state to recuperate costs much more quickly. Annual payments into the Pay It Forward fund are estimated by the Oregon Center for Public Policy to exceed costs in the 18th year of this program.

A Paradigm Shift

We anticipate that switching to a Pay It Forward program would encourage more people to enroll in Oregon's state universities and community colleges. Research shows that educational costs and fear of debt keeps many people out of college, particularly among low-income and minority populations. Young people in our primary and secondary schools will see their family members go to college and know that path is open to them. Many working adults who want to return to school but cannot afford to will have an opportunity to get the

education and skills that lead to careers offering living wages. Parents can save for their children's education and have confidence that it will make a significant impact on college expenses.

Upon enactment of Pay It Forward, earning a college degree with low or no debt will no longer be reserved only to the fortunate sons and daughters of the well-heeled. A clear path to higher education will be made available to everyone. In Oregon we will be able to say, "Here, the path to adulthood includes college education."

Potential Challenges and Solutions

Students for Educational Debt Reform propose that Pay It Forward should be the means by which the tuition and fees portion of college expense is paid by the entire full time, in-state student body within Oregon's community colleges and universities. However, several challenges may arise.

Part-Time Students Not everyone is a full-time student in pursuit of a degree. Students who are taking a handful of classes at the behest of an employer or for personal enjoyment could pay at the same rate as full-time students on a Pay It Forward system. Students must earn a minimum of 180 credits to obtain a Bachelor's degree at Portland State, or 45 credits a year if they were to study full-time for 4 years—and then would owe 0.75% of their adjusted gross income to the Pay It Forward fund for that year. All students could pay 1/45th of 0.75% of their income per year for each credit in which they enroll. Or it may be more practical to allow students who are enrolled with course loads below some threshold to pay tuition and fees as they do currently.

The Potential to "Freeze" Oregon's Higher Educational System at Its Current Level The reputation of our state community colleges and universities depends on providing great facilities, gathering top faculty, and attracting high quality students. Unless the state is committed to increasing its contribution to public higher education, and moving back toward per-student funding levels available 20 years ago, the quality of Oregon's institutions of higher education is at risk of falling further behind those institutions elsewhere.

Would Pay It Forward Provide an Incentive for Low Work Effort? Objections may be raised based on the possibility that some graduates may choose to earn relatively little, thus minimizing their payments. However few people go to college in preparation for future unemployment. Certainly, unwanted unemployment is its own punishment. One possibility is that people be expected to pay for 288 months (24 years), which ideally would be consecutive but could be deferred on the basis of unemployment. [However,]. . . the risk of unemployment is much greater for those with less education.

If graduates decide to take some time out of the labor force to care for young children, or elderly parents, society as a whole is benefited. And the analysis of the costs and structure of Pay It Forward are based on the earnings histories of college graduates on average in the U.S., which incorporate the fact that a certain proportion of people work part-time or not at all for periods of their lives, for a variety of reasons. If people return to full-time work after a period of part-time or no paid work, they are likely to earn more with more education.

We see no reason to expect that a payment as low as 3% of income would reduce work effort, given the much greater gains available in terms of promotion and career development to those who obtain more education and build on it in the work force.

Is a Shift to Pay It Forward Too Ambitious?

Perhaps the most obvious criticism likely to be leveled at Pay It Forward will be that it is simply too ambitious and the money cannot be made available. To this we say that the current level of student debt is at a crisis level and must be addressed.

Second, a Pay It Forward program could be launched on a partial or pilot basis that is less daunting than immediate statewide implementation. One possibility for partial implementation is through designation of pilot institutions, perhaps one university and one community college. If begun on a pilot basis, we anticipate that the Pay It Forward program will be highly sought after by the majority of Oregon's college students.

III. Conclusion

Student debt is a heavy burden on Oregon's younger generations and a drain on Oregon's economy. Parents, guidance counselors, and the State's elected leaders tell students that they need a college education to succeed in today's economy, and yet the State's commitment to funding higher education has been lagging for decades. Thus tuition keeps rising, leaving students with no choice but to borrow significant sums of money before they even know what their future employment prospects will be. The result is that students graduate from Oregon's public colleges and universities into an uncertain job market burdened with high levels of debt. This is not a recipe for success either for the individual or for our state.

A number of proposals are being considered on a federal level that would alleviate the burden of already existing student debt, through Income Based Repayment plans, loan forgiveness after a certain number of years, a cap on interest rates, and reinstatement of the ability to discharge student debt in bankruptcy. All of these are worthy of support, and our elected leaders should work actively toward their passage.

But for future students, Students for Educational Debt Reform (SEDR) proposes a dramatically different approach, one that demonstrates shared responsibility, a commitment to future generations, and a seriousness about the value of higher education. Pay It Forward represents a social commitment, not a debt. The State will maintain at least its current level funding of higher education, and the students will contribute a small fixed percentage of their actual earnings for a set number of years after graduation.

We have the opportunity to make a dramatic impact on one of society's most urgent and pressing problems and to fulfill a promise to those students who work hard, graduate from high school and look to our public colleges and universities as a pathway to a better future. We owe them nothing less.

Summary: Pay It Forward for Oregon's Future

Debt-Free Public Higher Education in Oregon

- No tuition or fees for instate students.
- Upon entering university or community college, students sign a binding contract to pay a low percentage of their incomes for a set number of years to an Oregon Higher Ed Fund.
- 3% of an individual's income for 24 years is estimated to cover 4 years of tuition and fees and pay an additional $7,400 (on average) to build the Oregon Higher Ed Fund.
- The State of Oregon will contribute to public higher education at least at the per student level of 2009/2010; preferably at the higher level of earlier years.
- Start-up costs to be paid by bonding and philanthropy.

- Pay It Forward could be started on a pilot basis at a few institutions or for Oregon Opportunity Grant recipients.
- Pay It Forward is under discussion in California, Washington, Vermont and Pennsylvania.

References

Ash, Michael, and Shantel Palacio. 2012. "Economic Impact of Investment in Public Higher Education in Massachusetts: Short-Run Employment Stimulus, Long-Run Public Returns." http://umassmsp.org/sites/umassmsp.org/files/Ash%20&%20Palacio%20Report%205-4-12.pdf

Brown, Meta. 2012. "Grading Student Loans" (Federal Reserve Bank of New York), March 5, 2012.

Collinge, Alan. 2009. *The Student Loan Scam: The Most Oppressive Debt in U.S. History, and How We Can Fight Back*. Boston, MA: Beacon.

Consumer Financial Protection Bureau. "Consumer Financial Protection Bureau Report Finds Private Student Loan Borrowers Face Roadblocks to Repayment." *Consumer Financial Protection Bureau*. Consumer Financial Protection Bureau, 16 Oct. 2012. Web. 25 Nov. 2012. http://www.consumerfinance.gov/pressreleases/consumer-financial-protection-bureau-report-finds-private-student-loan-borrowers-face-roadblocks-to-repayment.

Cortright, Joe. 2010. "The Fiscal Return on Education: How Educational Attainment Drives Public Finance in Oregon." Report to OBC/E.

Desrochers, Donna M., Colleen M. Lenihan, and Jane V. Wellman. 2010. *Trends In College Spending, 1998–2008: Where does the money come from? Where does it go? What does it buy?*

Delta Project on Postsecondary Education Costs, Productivity and Accountability. www.deltacostproject.org/.../Trends-in-College-Spending-98-08.pdf

Draut, Tamara, Robert Hiltonsmith, Catherine Ruetschlin, Aaron Smith, Rory O'Sullivan, and Jennifer Mishory. 2011. *The State of Young America: Economic Barriers to the American Dream—The DataBook*. Demos and The Young Invincibles. http://www.demos.org/sites/default/files/publications/SOYA_The-Databook_2.pdf

Ellis, Blake. "Private Student Loan Debt Reaches $150 Billion," CNN, July 20, 2012.

Elwell, Craig K. 2006. "Long-Term Growth of the U.S. Economy: Significance, Determinants, and Policy." *Congressional Research Service Report for Congress*, RL 32987. http://fpc.state.gov/documents/organization/68789.pdf

Goldin, Claudia, and Lawrence Katz. 2007. "Long-run Changes in the Wage Structure: Narrowing, Widening, Polarizing." *Brookings Papers on Economic Activity*, Issue 2, pp 135–165. http://www.brookings.edu/~/media/Projects/BPEA/Fall%202007/2007b_bpea_goldin.PDF

Institute of International Education. 2012. Open Doors. http://www.iie.org/Research-and-Publications/Open-Doors/Data/International-Students/Leading-Places-of-Origin/2010-12

Moretti, Enrico J. 2005. "Social Returns to Human Capital." *NBER Reporter: Research Summary*. National Bureau of Economic Research: Boston, MA. http://www.nber.org/reporter/spring05/moretti.html

Oregon Community Colleges (OCC). 2011. http://www.oregon.gov/ccwd/pdf/Enrollment/2010-2011FinalAuditedTotalFTE.pdf

Oregon State Treasury. 2012. "The Opportunity Initiative." http://buyoregonbonds.com/treasury/AboutTreasury/Pages/Opportunity-Initiative.aspx.

Oregon University System (OUS) Factbook 2010. http://www.ous.edu/factreport/factbook/2010

Oregon University System. 2011a. "A Report on Strategies to Meet Oregon's 40-40-20 Education Goals." http://www.oregon.gov/gov/oeib/docs/nnousreport.pdf

Oregon University System. 2011b. Legislative Brief Higher Education." http://www.ous.edu/sites/default/files/dept/govrel/files/2011IB40-40-20.pdf

Oregon University System. 2011c. OUS 2011 Facts and Figures. http://www.ous.edu/factreport/factbook/2011

Quinterno, John. 2012. *The Great Cost Shift: How Higher Education Cuts Undermine the Future Middle Class*. Demos. April 3. http://www.demos.org/publication/great-cost-shift-how-higher-education-cuts-undermine-future-middle-class

Sabatier, Julie. 2011. "Restructuring Higher Education." Oregon Public Broadcasting, Jan 3. http://www.opb.org/thinkoutloud/shows/restructuring-higher-education/

Schiavelli, Mel. 2011. "STEM Jobs Outlook Strong, But Collaboration Needed to Fill Jobs," *US News & World Report*, Nov. 3. http://www.usnews.com/news/blogs/stem-education/2011/11/03/stem-jobs-outlook-strong-but-collaboration-needed-to-fill-jobs

State House News Service. 2012. "Study: Higher Ed Investment Returns Exceed Casinos, Tax Cuts." *Worcester Business Journal Online*. http://www.wbjournal.com/apps/pbcs.dll/article?AID=/20120511/NEWS01/120519991/1040

U.S. Bureau of Labor Statistics. 2012. Employment Projections. http://www.bls.gov/emp/ep_chart_001.htm

U.S. Dept. of Education. 2012. "Many Non-U.S. Citizens Qualify for Student Aid." http://studentaid.ed.gov/eligibility/non-us-citizens

U.S. Senate Health, Education, Labor and Pensions Committee. 2010. "Emerging Risk? An Overview of Growth, Spending, Student Debt and Unanswered Questions in For-Profit Higher Education." June 24. http://www.help.senate.gov/newsroom/press/release/?id=2a870217-b476-492b-aace-d015d22bd13d&groups=Chair

Wendler, C., B. Bridgeman, R. Markle, F. Cline, N. Bell, P. McAllister, and J. Kent. (2012). *Pathways Through Graduate School and Into Careers*. Princeton, NJ: Educational Testing Service.

Questions for Rhetorical Analysis

1. Summarize the problem, solution, and benefits that the students present in this proposal.
2. Who is the audience for this proposal? How do you know? Pay attention to the voice of the collective proposal writers.
3. Consider the research that supports this proposal, and think about the intended audience. How solid is the research? What other kind of research might help convince this audience?
4. How do the students use persuasion in this proposal? Identify places where they appeal to logic, emotion, and authority.

5. What do the writers say in the conclusion to persuade the reader that this proposal is a feasible solution to the problem of student debt? Are you convinced?

Questions for Critical Thinking

1. What are some of the advantages of this proposed way to repay student loans over traditional private loans or loans by the federal government?
2. If you oppose this proposal, what reasons might you find to defeat it?
3. What might be some other ways to solve the problem of soaring student debt?

Style Practice: Imitation

This proposal opens with a quote from a student who couldn't afford college. Craft a different opening for this proposal, using a story or getting a quote from someone you know who would benefit from deferring tuition payment.

Waterfront Skatepark Proposal

Superior Skatepark Coalition

THE FOLLOWING proposal is for a skatepark that would be part of a waterfront development plan. The proposal is a series of PowerPoint slides that include the elements of a good proposal. The Superior Skatepark Coalition has to sell the community on an activity that is growing in popularity but has some critics. Note how the group addresses the concerns of many constituencies within the community and makes a case for supporting the skatepark cause.

Courtesy, David Tranter, School of Social Work, Lakehead University. Photo: New Line Skateparks, Inc.

Courtesy, David Tranter, School of Social Work, Lakehead University. Photo: New Line Skateparks, Inc.

Who Are We?

Since we began almost two years ago, our focus has been:

1. Positive participation in alternative sports through mutual support and respect.
2. Planning, fundraising and building a new, all-concrete, professionally-designed and built skate/BMX park for everyone.

Coalition Halloween Bash

Courtesy, David Tranter, School of Social Work, Lakehead University. Photo: New Line Skateparks, Inc.

Our Activities:

➤ Biweekly planning meetings
➤ Skatepark design sessions
➤ Proposal writing
➤ Meeting with stakeholders
➤ Skateboarding Days
➤ Yard Sales
➤ BBQs
➤ Fun Skateboarding Competitions
➤ Skateboarding video nights
➤ Halloween Party
➤ T-shirt sales
➤ Video games competitions
➤ Skatepark clean-ups
➤ Road trips to visit other parks (Fort Frances, Kenora, Winnipeg, Dryden, Superior, Duluth, Terrace Bay)

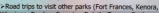

Park Design Meeting

Courtesy, David Tranter, School of Social Work, Lakehead University. Photo: New Line Skateparks, Inc.

Why We Need a New Park

1. Our current parks don't support the demand.
2. Our current parks don't support the skill level of our skateboarders and BMXers
3. Our current parks are on the fringes of our community.
4. Our current parks don't capitalize on what a modern skatepark can do for a community.
5. Our current parks aren't appealing enough to draw skateboarders away from skating the streets.
6. Our current parks aren't as safe as modern ones.
7. We can learn from the experience of other cities.

Winnipeg Forks

Courtesy, David Tranter, School of Social Work, Lakehead University. Photo: New Line Skateparks, Inc.

The Old

Old Design: Linear flow, asphalt, small, placed on unwanted property, bleak, unwelcoming, single use (designed only for skateboarders).

West Thunder Skatepark

Courtesy, David Tranter, School of Social Work, Lakehead University. Photo: New Line Skateparks, Inc.

The New

New Design: Plaza style, larger, multiple use, blends with setting, thematic, open flow, smooth concrete, central, space for spectators, welcoming, a gathering place, landscaped, clean and bright.

Kettering, Ohio

Courtesy, David Tranter, School of Social Work, Lakehead University. Photo: New Line Skateparks, Inc.

The New

The new "plaza" design parks are among the centrepieces of modern public spaces where everyone is welcome. Below is the new Winnipeg Forks Skatepark:

Winnipeg Forks Skatepark

Courtesy, David Tranter, School of Social Work, Lakehead University. Photo: New Line Skateparks, Inc.

Why a Park is Good for the Whole Community

1. Skateboarding is the fastest growing sport in North America.

- Skateboarding has become more popular than basketball, baseball and even hockey in North America.
- There are over 1000 active skateboarders in Thunder Bay.
- Skateboarding clothing and shoes top all clothing sales.
- Skateboarding videos games are among the bestsellers of all time.
- Skateboarding is no longer a fad, it is the single fastest growing athletic activity on the continent and shows no sign of slowing down.

Burnaby, BC

Courtesy, David Tranter, School of Social Work, Lakehead University. Photo: New Line Skateparks, Inc.

Why a Park is Good for the Whole Community

2. Skateboarding is also the most popular activity among kids who aren't in mainstream sports.

- Not only has skateboarding surpassed mainstream sports, it is also the sport of choice for non-mainstream athletes.
- Youth who might not otherwise play organized sports (or exercise at all) get involved in skateboarding.
- Skateboarding breaks down barriers between sports and encourages youth of all ages, abilities and backgrounds to participate on their own terms.

Winnipeg Forks

Courtesy, David Tranter, School of Social Work, Lakehead University. Photo: New Line Skateparks, Inc.

Why a Park is Good for the Whole Community

3. Skateboarding is inexpensive, non-competitive and teaches skills for life.

- Skateboarding requires inexpensive equipment and emphasizes personal creativity and development, rather than "beating the other team".
- Skateboarding also requires extraordinary dedication and tenacity.
- Youth learn to compete against themselves instead of others, and focus on building personal skills rather than winning at all costs.

Courtesy, David Tranter, School of Social Work, Lakehead University. Photo: New Line Skateparks, Inc.

Why a Park is Good for the Whole Community

4. Skateboarding is not dangerous when done properly.

- Contrary to its reputation as being an "extreme sport", the rate of injury is well below other mainstream sports.
- When injuries do occur in skateboarding, it's usually a result of skateboarding at a poorly designed park or on private property.
- Skateboarding injuries are especially rare in well-designed, supervised skateparks.

Vancouver Skateplaza

Courtesy, David Tranter, School of Social Work, Lakehead University. Photo: New Line Skateparks, Inc.

Why a Park is Good for the Whole Community

5. If the city doesn't have a skatepark, then it will become a skatepark.

- The growth in popularity of skating has led to a growth in skating everywhere including on private property.
- The only way to draw skaters away from turning Thunder Bay's private and business property into skate spots is to give them a better alternative.

Winnipeg Forks

Courtesy, David Tranter, School of Social Work, Lakehead University. Photo: New Line Skateparks, Inc.

Why a Park is Good for the Whole Community

6. It's not just a skatepark, it's an accessible, supervised and safe outdoor youth centre for all.

- Unlike our current small skateparks that are exclusively for skaters and built on the fringes of the community, today's new skateparks are open and welcoming recreation centres for all youth and are easily accessible and situated in highly visible locations.
- They are built to rigorous safety standards and are usually supervised by a staff of volunteers.
- Thunder Bay's youth deserve a safe and accessible place to be.

Squamish, BC

Courtesy, David Tranter, School of Social Work, Lakehead University. Photo: New Line Skateparks, Inc.

Why a Park is Good for the Whole Community

7. Today's skateparks support urban renewal.

- The new skateparks are professionally designed to be aesthetically pleasing and complimentary to the surrounding landscape.
- They quickly become the centrepiece of a recreation area and draw skaters as well as many spectators.
- A new park will revitalize an underused part of Thunder Bay's community.

Winnipeg Forks

Courtesy, David Tranter, School of Social Work, Lakehead University. Photo: New Line Skateparks, Inc.

Why a Park is Good for the Whole Community

8. Today's destination skateparks create tourism.

- Skateboarding is a multi-million dollar industry and skateboarders are a dedicated group.
- They travel hundreds of kilometres just to skate a park.
- Thunder Bay's skateboarders regularly travel four hours to Superior, Wisconsin just to skateboard the park there.
- More parents are planning their family vacations around visiting popular skateparks.
- Also, families who are considering moving to a new city are increasingly investigating the availability of skateparks in the area.
- If you build it, they will come. If you don't, they won't!

Courtesy, David Tranter, School of Social Work, Lakehead University. Photo: New Line Skateparks, Inc.

Why a Park is Good for the Whole Community

9. The park planning and organization process teaches kids to be leaders in their community.

- The skatepark planning, designing and building process helps to teach Thunder Bay's youth the skills associated with project management, budgeting, fundraising, dealing with municipal government, grant proposal writing, public presentations, and working together to make our community stronger.

Courtesy, David Tranter, School of Social Work, Lakehead University. Photo: New Line Skateparks, Inc.

Why a Park is Good for the Whole Community

10. Invest in our youth to keep our youth in the community.

- Youth out-migration is at a critical level in Thunder Bay.
- If we want to keep our youth here, we need to show them that we are willing to invest in them and provide them with facilities that will make our city attractive to them.

Courtesy, David Tranter, School of Social Work, Lakehead University. Photo: New Line Skateparks, Inc.

Our Recommendations

- View it as a youth (and family) outdoor recreation plaza.
- View it as a tourist attraction.
- Pro-designed and pro-built.
- Break ground in the Fall of 2006.
- Do it right: Budget of around $400,000.
- We will continue to fundraise (and build public support) and help in whatever way we can!

Winnipeg Skatepark
Opening Day (10,000 people showed up!)

Courtesy, David Tranter, School of Social Work, Lakehead University. Photo: New Line Skateparks, Inc.

The End

Courtesy, David Tranter, School of Social Work, Lakehead University. Photo: New Line Skateparks, Inc.

Questions for Rhetorical Analysis

1. Who is the audience for this proposal? How do you know?
2. What sort of image does the proposing group seem to have? Who is in the group?
3. How does the group address the criticisms of both the sport and the skatepark?
4. Does the plan adequately address all counterarguments?
5. What kind of research has the group done? What does the information about sales of clothing and computer games add to the argument?
6. Who, aside from the skaters, would benefit from the proposed park? In what way does this information augment the proposal?
7. Does the plan's lack of financial details detract from the proposal? Why or why not?

Questions for Critical Thinking

1. What events could the group plan that might show civic leaders that this is a good and worthwhile proposal for them to consider?
2. In what other ways, besides a PowerPoint presentation, could the group present this proposal?
3. Would you support this proposal for a skatepark? Why or why not?

Style Practice: Imitation

Using three of the PowerPoint slides as models, design three slides for a proposal to create a dog park in your town or a community garden at your college.

WRITING & REVISION STRATEGIES

Gathered here are three interactive sections for you to use as you write and revise your proposal:

- Writer's Notebook Suggestions
- Peer Review Log
- Revision Checklist

Writer's Notebook Suggestions

You can use these exercises to do some start-up thinking and writing for your proposal.

1. Write a one-page proposal aimed at the U.S. Postal Service recommending a commemorative stamp design. Choose a person or event you think worthy of a stamp, and make an argument for it.
2. You want to organize a fund-raising barbecue to support a homeless shelter if your local chapter of the Salvation Army will sponsor it. Write a brief letter to the Salvation Army proposing this idea.
3. Talking with friends, you realize that each of you knows someone battling smoking or who has a smoking-related disease. You are irate that cigarette company advertisements target young people and poor people. Write a short e-mail to the American Cancer Society, proposing that it pitch its next efforts to keep junior high kids from smoking.
4. Choose an editorial from your local paper. Write a letter to the editor, proposing a solution to the problem discussed in the editorial.
5. Write an e-mail to your boss or former boss, proposing improvements in the workplace. Consider your audience carefully.
6. You learn that your college is trying to recruit students from abroad to help create a more international student body. You decide to write and shoot a short promotional video to help recruitment efforts. Write a one-page proposal, pitching your ideas to your college president and asking for funding for your project.
7. Write an e-mail message to a former professor, proposing a feasible change to the course syllabus.
8. Valentine's Day is approaching. Write a proposal to your sweetheart.

Peer Review Log

As you work with a writing partner or in a peer review group, you can use these questions to give helpful responses to a classmate's proposal or as a guide for discussion.

Writer's Name: _____

Date: _____

1. Who is the specific audience for this proposal? What do you know about this audience? Can you make any suggestions on how the writer can more effectively tailor the proposal to this audience?
2. Bracket the introductory section. Does the introduction hook the reader? Can you suggest ways to strengthen this section?

3. Underline the problem statement. Can this statement be clarified? Does it need more support?
4. Underline the solution presented in the body of the paper. Is the solution feasible? What might make it more appealing or more doable?
5. Point out places where the writer has considered possible objections to the proposal. Can you suggest other points the writer might consider?
6. Mark places where research appeals to logic (facts, statistics, studies, graphics) and emotion (anecdotes, quotations, visuals). Are the sources credible? Does the proposal need more or different kinds of support?
7. Bracket the conclusion. Underline sentences that explain the benefits of the proposal. Are these benefits clearly stated? Can you suggest other possible benefits?
8. Look at the overall design of the proposal. Could the writer use white space, headings, or different typefaces to help organize the proposal and make it more visually appealing?
9. Put a wavy line under writing that could be more concise, clear, positive, or specific. Can you make suggestions to strengthen the writing?
10. Does the proposal persuade you? If not, what else might the writer do to win you over?

Revision Checklist

As you do your final revision for your proposal, check to make sure that you

- chose a specific audience for your proposal and tailored your writing to that audience
- wrote an introduction that engages your reader
- stated the problem clearly in the introduction
- provided some background or contextual information
- included research that shows the scope and seriousness of the problem
- attributed your research clearly to credible sources
- presented a clear solution to the problem
- provided the necessary details to show the feasibility of your solution
- explained the benefits of your solution to your audience
- designed the proposal visually so that it is clear and easy to read
- wrote with language that is concise, clear, positive, and specific

RESEARCH AND DOCUMENTATION

"On the Internet, nobody knows you're a dog."

RESEARCH

Research is formalized curiosity. It is poking and prying with a purpose.
—ZORA NEALE HURSTON

You are a student at the University of Nebraska at Lincoln. At lunch one day, your friends observe that, based on conversations they have had with other students, crime on campus seems to be rising.

Because you have a trend article due soon, you decide to look into the question of whether the crime rate at the university is rising, and you wonder how this shift may or may not compare with the crime rate at other four-year colleges in Lincoln and what all of this says about student safety on campus. You do a quick Internet search and you find crime rates for Lincoln, but your subject is so specific that you have trouble finding information on the topic of crime at colleges in Lincoln. Data must be compiled somewhere, you think.

Since you are walking by the library, you get the idea that you could ask a librarian for some advice. Why not? So you say, "I want some really quick, but reliable information." The librarian says, "It's simple. Just add an extra word to your search."

So you go to a computer and type in "campus crime statistics," and you include the word "database." You also ask yourself, "Why didn't I think of that?"

Just a second later, you have a source: The United States Department of Education collection of data on crime at colleges. Rejoicing, you think, "High-quality source number one!"

Your research has begun.

Chapter Objectives

find a method to overcome the madness of information overload
404

take your first step: asking a tough question
405

keep track of sources
408

avoid plagiarism
409

the bias detective: evaluating sources
412

create an annotated bibliography
419

Understanding Research

More people than ever are incorporating research into their everyday lives, using the Internet for comparison shopping and finding out about medical conditions, and consulting experts through e-mail. The Internet makes it possible to research quickly and well, so long as you know the variety of tools available online.

Still, some inquiries need other approaches. Complex questions such as "What were the effects of the Industrial Revolution on women?" might be best answered in a book or in a specialized database available at the library. Research for some projects may even take the form of interviewing experts or hunting through archives and public documents, such as birth and death records in the county courthouse.

Formulating a valid research question is the first step. Locating high-quality sources is the next. But the ocean of sources available to you through the Internet—including libraries, databases, journals, video, and audio files—can be overwhelming. A huge array of research tools—books, websites, directories of experts, and public documents, to name just a few—is available through your Internet connection and at your school or public library. There are so many tools, in fact, choosing the right ones can be a researcher's most baffling problem. How do you find the best books among the stacks at the library? Why use a book if you have an Internet connection? Dealing with so many sources may lead researchers into winding paths that consume lots of time and sometimes yield very few quality results.

Of course, you want your work to be as efficient as possible, making your research path as methodical as it is creative is essential. A good method involves

- refining a question
- knowing where to find sources
- knowing how to evaluate good sources quickly

In this chapter, you will learn to research more efficiently and effectively, following a research path that ends in high-quality information.

No single tool can do every research task. A good researcher knows how to use a variety of search tools—including talking to experts, such as librarians. As you will see in this chapter, the best research uses a combination of approaches. You will also learn some ways to make your writing more creative through research.

Brainstorming: Researching to Discover Topics

Many people in creative professions—designers, architects, and film producers, to name a few—use research to jump-start new projects and get ideas flowing. Some people in technical and scientific fields say that even before they have a topic firmly fixed, they first brainstorm by doing a quick electronic keyword search. Many

professionals report browsing "bricks and mortar" bookstores or even electronic bookstores like Amazon.com for inspiration.

Researchers who use this browsing method say they:

- look for unusual twists on familiar subjects by reading through titles and leafing through books, noting chapter titles and authors
- look at current journals that reflect recent topics and trends in specific fields of study

Browsing through journals and magazines at the library or bookstore might even be easier and more useful than surfing the Internet with keywords. Current professional and scholarly journals and other periodicals reflect the most up-to-date thinking, and it may be easier to evaluate the credibility of sources in the library than online. Later in this chapter you will see how important evaluating credibility is and why the publications you find in bookstores and libraries, which have been reviewed and selected, might be more reliable than Internet sources.

Wikipedia

Wikipedia, a "collaborative" website that lets users contribute and edit material anonymously, is often criticized as being an unreliable source for facts. You might use Wikipedia to discover topics, but remember most teachers forbid citations that refer to Wikipedia. Yet, it is a good place to get an initial overview of a topic.

Virtual Library: The Online Subject Catalog

You can browse the "virtual shelves" at the library by beginning with a hunt through the online subject catalog. Libraries own a great variety of encyclopedias, guides, dictionaries, bibliographies, and other general reference works that can give you an overview of a subject you might not know much about. You can find these sources in the library catalog or with the help of librarians.

Online encyclopedias, such as *Britannica Online*, provide broad background information. For example, the following entry shows the result of a keyword search for "carbon dating" to research the way archeologists use carbon dating on digs.

Carbon-14 Dating and Other Cosmogenic Methods, from *Dating*

The occurrence of natural radioactive carbon in the atmosphere provides a unique opportunity to date organic materials as old as 50,000 years. Unlike most isotopic dating methods, the conventional. . . .

Radiocarbon Dating

Scientists in the fields of geology, climatology, anthropology, and archaeology can answer many questions about the past through a technique called radiocarbon, or carbon-14, dating. One key to understanding

PRACTICE 15.1

Brainstorming through Research

Before you assign yourself a type of writing project (editorial, review, profile, short essay, trend analysis), identify a subject area you want to know more about.

Are you interested in green technologies or the history of the circus? Do you want to know more about a process or about the origins of something?

1. Divide a sheet of paper into six sections. Give each section a general subject (for example, circuses, solar energy, the sport of lacrosse, and others).

2. Write five questions in each section (Where was the first recorded circus? Where does the name "lacrosse" come from?).

3. Next, do a quick Internet search to answer your question. If you end up using Wikipedia, also visit the footnoted links. ■

Boston University Libraries

Telnet to Catalog   **Web Catalog**

Search
Author
Title or Journal Title
Word
Author / Title
Subject Headings
Call Numbers
ISBN, OCLC
Gov. Doc. Numbers

Reserve Services
By Course Number
By Professor's Name

Help and Renewal
Library Information
Borrowing Record
Book Renewal
Library Purchase Request

BU Library Web Sites
Boston University Libraries [▼] [Go]

Boston Library Consortium
BLC Gateway‖ Virtual Catalog ‖

Boston University
Page designed by the Web Catalog Committee.
http://library.bu.edu/

Boston University - Mugar Memorial Library

You can search the library holdings from anywhere–but searches will be more efficient if they are limited by your use of good keywords.

how and why something happened is to pinpoint when it happened. (See also Anthropology. . . .)

Carbon
Without the element carbon, life as we know it would not exist. Carbon provides the framework for all tissues of plants and animals. These tissues are built of elements grouped around chains or rings made of carbon atoms. Carbon also provides common fuels—coal, coke, oil, gasoline, and natural. . . .

You can also search the *Britannica Elementary Encyclopedia* for articles about carbon dating.

Carbon Dating
Introduction to this technique. Contains information on its accuracy, applicability, and related theory.

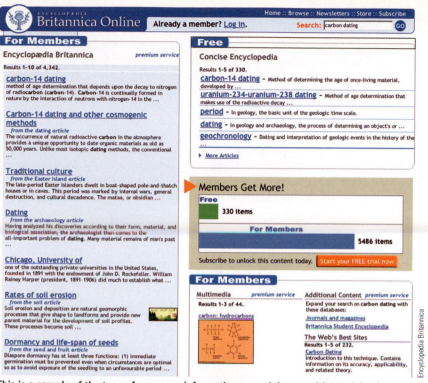

This is a sample of the type of summary information you might get with good databases available through your school or public library. These "for members" sections require a password, so your membership through school or your community helps you get access to more and different information than you would find on a basic web search.

Archaeology and Ancient History: Archaeology

British Broadcasting Corporation

Resource on various aspects of this study of the material remains of the past human activities. Includes illustrated articles on marine and virtual archaeology, carbon dating, and the Piltdown man. Also contains reports on the British sites, and game.

Learning from the Fossil Record

University of California, Berkeley

Educational reference on paleontology, for students. Includes classroom activities and projects on plate tectonics, dinosaurs, carbon dating, fossils, and climate change. Provides access to related educational resources.

Prehistory
Teacher Net

Collection of resources on evolution, agriculture, tools, weapons, art, the major civilizations, and archaeology of this period of ancient history. Facilitates access to picture galleries, guided tours, interactive maps, timelines, and online books. Includes sections on dinosaurs and carbon dating techniques.

You can see the usefulness of this site for beginning your research path. Each of the headings provides a snippet of information that you can explore in more depth if it is pertinent to your project. If you were researching a coastal dig, for example, "Learning from the Fossil Record" promises material that deals with marine archeology. The website also provides links to other sources and other websites, giving you many avenues to follow.

Primary Sources

Library and Internet research can lead you to primary sources that are original or firsthand documents that detail data.

Primary Sources

- Interviews (with experts, practitioners, and witnesses)
- Public documents (tax records, police reports, government studies, census data, minutes from meetings with public officials—anything available through the Freedom of Information Act)
- E-mail
- Diaries, letters, and journals
- Manuscripts, music, films, speeches, and works of art
- Experiments and observations
- Surveys and polls
- Autobiographies
- Journals

Using or consulting primary sources will tend to make your writing more credible and original, and less derivative. Sometimes, however, primary sources may be unavailable or not appropriate for your assignment.

Secondary Sources

In the course of your research, you may also want to read what other people have thought or figured out about a topic. Secondary sources analyze and interpret original sources.

Secondary Sources

- Analytical books
- Commentaries in magazines and journals
- Newspaper articles
- News broadcasts
- Reviews
- Online discussions, bulletin boards, and listservs
- Biographies

Remember always to give credit to the writer responsible for the research and ideas. See Chapter 16 on how to cite and attribute sources.

Narrowing Your Topic and Formulating a Specific Research Question

For each type of writing assignment you research, you will have to do some preliminary reading to help you narrow your topic. Assume you choose to look at new trends in the social life of college students. You do some preliminary reading on blogs and websites in current newspapers and magazines to see what trends are in the news.

After you have narrowed your topic, you can formulate a *research question*. Having a specific research question helps make your research efficient. It also allows you to enter into research with an open mind, genuinely seeking answers to a question you find interesting. A good research question might be "Why is crime rising at college campuses?" or "Are colleges required to report crimes in a different way than they did in years past?" If you begin to research without a question, you might spend a lot of time going in too many different directions. Even with a question in mind, you might start with one idea, begin reading and researching, and find that it is not

PRACTICE 15.2

Narrowing a Search Question

Using your questions from Practice 15.1, decide on a genre of writing. For example, you may have asked how solar panels are manufactured. Maybe you found yourself wondering about the cost of installing solar heaters. Why is it so expensive? How could the government help make it more affordable? This is a good question to investigate, especially if you are interested in writing an editorial.

1. Make a list of writing projects that correspond with the questions you started researching.

2. When you have identified your writing project, write a one-sentence summary—a "pitch" or abstract—in which you tell your teacher/publisher/ blog reader what the question in your piece is. ■

interesting to you. You can always go back to your preliminary brainstorming and narrow your search to another branch of the topic and another question.

A good research question is thorough enough to help you formulate a thesis—the main argument or point of your paper—yet narrow enough to fit the parameters of your assignment. Your thesis probably will not be fully refined until you do your research and see where you want to go with an idea. Although following a single research question helps lead you to information, you should always be flexible in your researching. If you bump into another interesting trail of information, follow it. A solid thesis might occur to you after you follow different research paths and try several times to formulate a research question.

Your library may offer a number of good ways to help you begin your reading and formulate your research question. Most libraries have research tools ranging from online catalogs to special databases available through computer terminals at the library or through "proxy" or home computer connections. Your library may pay fees to link to these databases. Most will provide citations for articles. You can track down the articles on microfilm or microfiche or even in back copies of journals at the library. Others provide full text of sources. (See the box titled Databases for places to go to help you hone your research question.)

Databases

Some common databases are Ebscohost, CQ Researcher, and Twayne Series. Here are some others that will help in refining your research topic.

Worldcat

WorldCat lists and describes books and holdings from libraries in 45 countries. The database includes journals, musical scores, video recordings, maps, magazines, newspapers, computer programs, manuscripts, sound recordings, visual materials, and websites.

Infotrac and Gale

InfoTrac and Gale are searchable online libraries that contain full-length articles, abstracts, and bibliographic citations from scholarly and popular periodicals, including a broad range of journals, magazines, encyclopedias, and newsletters.

LexisNexis

LexisNexis provides legal, news, public record, and business information, including tax and regulatory publications in online or print formats. The database is searchable by field of interest, such as news, business, medicine, and law.

Readers' Guide Full Text

Readers' Guide Full Text, produced by the H. W. Wilson Company, offers index listings—with full citations—and abstracts of the most popular general-interest periodicals published in the United States and Canada. You can get the full text for articles written after 1994. Some libraries also have Readers' Guide Full Text available in bound book.

ISI Web of Science

The ISI Web of Science links to the Science Citation Index Expanded, Social Sciences Citation Index, and Arts and Humanities Citation Index. It provides access to multidisciplinary information from research journals, including full-text articles.

Proquest

Proquest provides the full text of current periodicals and newspapers and is updated daily, dating back to 1986. You can also link to e-journals and get information about dissertations. "Back files of record" pages from Proquest Historical Newspaper Collection show the pages exactly as they appeared to the original readers.

Creating a Working Bibliography

Keep track of all your sources, even if you are not certain you will use them in your writing. Careful record keeping will ensure that citations and quotations are accurate. Noting the title, author, publisher, date of publication, volume and page numbers, and web page addresses while you are researching will make it unnecessary to retrace your steps after you decide which sources to include.

One useful way to create your working bibliography is to write all the information for each source on a separate index card. Using the correct documentation style

when you write the information (see Chapter 16) will make it easy to type the *Works Cited* page when you have completed your paper: simply alphabetize the cards and copy the information. You might also want to make notes on the cards about the usefulness of the source or about what information it covers. Then, when you review your sources, you will know which source to consult for which information.

Another time-saving strategy researchers use is to give each source a code letter. If you put the letter on each note card you make from the source, you will not have to write all the bibliographic information on each card, but you will still keep your material organized efficiently.

A card might look like this:

(continued)

8. For a trend article about compulsive gambling: Why can you gamble on Indian reservations?

9. For an explanation of a trend: Are teens smoking more now than they were 10 years ago?

10. For an editorial on schoolyard bullies: Find an expert to interview.

11. For a proposal: Get statistics on the number of dogs euthanized in your state last year.

12. For a proposal involving conserving fossil fuels: What was the top-selling car in the United States last year, and what kind of gas mileage does it get? ■

> **A**
>
> Kauffman
> Kauffman, Stanley. <u>Regarding Film.</u> Baltimore: Johns Hopkins University Press, 2001.
> Compilation of his reviews from <u>The New Republic,</u> 1993-2000.

©Cengage Learning®

Reading with Focus: Taking Useful Notes and Avoiding Plagiarism

Accuracy is essential when taking notes—and so is focus. As you read through your sources, look for ideas that support or refute your thesis. If you encounter ideas you have not considered, do not ignore them; read them and allow them to refine or qualify your original thinking. However, do not feel that you need to write down every fact, every example, or every quotation you find. Keep focused on your topic, and skip sections in your sources that are tangential or irrelevant to your concerns.

The most useful note cards tell you three things at a glance:

1. They tell you the source from which you got the information by including the code letter of the source or the last name of the author.
2. They tell you the page number(s) for a written source, the URL of an electronic source, or the date and time when an interview was conducted.
3. They tell you the general topic of the information on the card.

Try to create topic headings that are consistent. For example, do not write *film reviews* on one card and *movie criticism* on another.

The information you write on a card should be one of the following:

- A summary
- A paraphrase of the material
- A direct quotation

Tips for Avoiding Plagiarism

- Take the time to put quotation marks around every phrase or sentence as you take it from a source so that you will not have to rely on your memory to determine which words are yours and which come from the source.

- Using more than three words from a source without quotation marks or attribution is considered *plagiarism*. Passing off a source's original thinking as your own is also considered plagiarism. When you are working on a long-term project, even if you have the best of intentions, you will not remember whose words you are copying by the time you write the first draft. Most unintentional plagiarism can be avoided by being careful and accurate at this point in the research project.

Sample Notecard

A note card might look like this:

Kauffman   Themes   A
Review of <u>Eyes Wide Shut</u>, August 16, 1999
—"Every married person has within himself or herself a secret cosmos of sexual imaginings, longings, fantasies, and perhaps extramarital actions."
—Original story written in 1926 by Arthur Schnitzler

p. 145

Taking notes on cards is a good way to organize your material, but many people use photocopies to keep track of their sources. They print out copies of citations and full-text articles, and even e-mail themselves notes and copies or take photos with their phones. Whichever method you use, make sure to keep track of the origin of the ideas. Tracking down a source again to get the publication date or correct spelling of the author's name can waste a lot of your time. Making a quick notation of the full source as you read will save you time later.

Tips for Avoiding Plagiarism of Internet Sources

Plagiarism is defined as "the use of a source without giving credit to the author."

- Online plagiarism includes cutting and pasting sections, paragraphs, and even phrases from online sources *without* using quotation marks or other indications that the material was written by someone else.

- Plagiarism also includes taking ideas from sources without noting the original source of the ideas.

- Even if you rephrase an idea or put it into your own words, always cite the source.

You can find more on how to attribute Internet sources in Chapter 16, "Documentation."

The Rhetorical Situation: Evaluating Your Sources

Libraries all over the world share so much information that finding the few sources that are just right for your inquiry may be a daunting task. One online search for "the space program in the 1960s" returned 58,260 results, or "hits." A library search was equally comprehensive, linking to sources covering rocket science and planet exploration, among others. Knowing how to evaluate your sources will save you time and will help you eliminate irrelevant information and focus on the information most useful to your research project.

A Note about Wikis, Blogs, and Message Boards

Blogs can offer some of the best writing on the Web—insightful, well-researched, and current—and tools like wikis, blogs, and message boards can be useful in getting yourself educated about a subject. You can use blogs to link to studies, background news stories, and other commentary. Wikipedia also lists links and footnotes of some sources you might not otherwise think of using. Message and bulletin boards can give you ideas that you might not get anywhere else. Still, you must be careful when using wikis, blogs, and message boards as sources of factual material. Remember, also, most teachers forbid citations that refer to Wikipedia.

Evaluating sources involves critical thinking and a system or set of criteria for judging their usefulness. Whatever you read, evaluate it in terms of its authorship, scholarship, bias, and currency. These criteria can assist you in deciding what is useful and reliable; they can also help you narrow and refine your search when selecting certain material. Remember that Web material, for the most part, is unevaluated.

Criteria for Evaluating Sources

Authorship: Who wrote the article and why?

Scholarship: Is the information credible and reliable?

Bias: What is the purpose of the work?

Currency: When was the work published or posted? Is it up-to-date?

Authority

Finding out about the person who researched and wrote the information is key in evaluating books, articles, and Web material. What are the author's credentials? For example, has the author shown up in bibliographic lists you have found at the ends of articles or in textbooks or other books? Has the author written other books on the subject? Is the author connected with a school or organization? Connections to advocacy groups—groups that take positions on issues—can shape an author's point

of view and make it closer to opinion than fact. Other questions will assist you in judging the authority of an author or company:

- Is there a clear statement of whose site it is and who is responsible for the content? Have you heard of the organization before? Are the articles signed? Is there a print version?
- Does the homepage include a phone number or postal address that indicates the company is legitimate?
- Can you find a link to information about the identity of the company, such as "About Us"?
- Is the formality of the writing or graphics appropriate to the subject matter?
- Is the material being provided as a public service?

Scholarship

Quoting from works with good research makes your writing credible. Does the writing refer to other sources? Does it offer depth, or is it an overview? Are claims explained and documented? Does the work include a list of sources, links, or a bibliography that leads to other information? Is it well written and free of typographical, spelling, grammatical, or other mistakes that bring its accuracy into question? Remember that what looks like a fact on a web page might not be. Here are more questions to help you assess your research:

- Does the website include sources to document claims?
- Does any material that seems like a claim have a citation so you can check the source directly? Does the site link to sources?
- If the site includes excerpts from other published sources, are the sources complete? Have they been altered or shortened?
- Can you find errors in grammar or spelling that indicate there also may be incorrect information?
- Does the site include a bibliography?

Bias

What is the purpose of your writing: to argue, to report, to sell, to entertain? Who is the audience? Is the audience a specialized group with shared values? Is the audience general? How do the credentials of the authors you are citing imply a possible point of view in the writing? Is bias apparent? A source with a clear bias can be useful when you want a strong position on an issue rather than a balanced view. However, a researcher must understand the bias of a source in order to use the source well. In general, sources with the least amount of bias offer more reliable and factual information than do biased sources. Quoting facts from sources that argue for a special point of view can make you seem like a spokesperson for the viewpoint rather than an objective writer.

Some websites conceal their purpose. Some might seem to be offering information but instead make sales pitches or arguments. Others lure you in with the promise of one thing and then switch to another topic or to a specific view of a topic. Expect promotional sites to present only one side. Noncommercial sites might also be posted by advocacy agencies, so be aware of the purpose of the site.

- Is the purpose of the site to sell or promote a product or service?
- Is the information aimed at promotion of a specific point of view?
- Does the site link to other sites that espouse a distinct point of view?

Currency

When was the book published, and by whom? Has the material been updated? Asking these questions is particularly important with sources that report new information—scientific publications, for example. Your research is fundamental to making your writing credible. Quoting outdated sources may show your reader that you do not understand the subject you are writing about.

Check posting dates and most recent updates when researching on the Web. It is especially important to do this with news sites, the best of which are updated frequently, sometimes hourly.

- Do the links work?
- Are the links current?

Quick Evaluation for Websites

Use the type of domain in the domain name to help you evaluate Web sources and their likely usefulness.

.com	business or marketing site, news site
.gov	government site
.edu	educational site
.mil	military site
.org	noncommercial site

Answering the questions on authorship, scholarship, bias, and currency can help you understand whether you want to use the source in your writing, but your answers don't necessarily eliminate a source. At times, you may want to show an extreme viewpoint, when making a counterargument in an editorial, for example. Perhaps you want a historical perspective that you can get only from information that is clearly out of date to show the context of a social movement. For instance, the following book, published in 1953, might be useful to a researcher looking at women and society, even though the thinking about women and sexual behavior has changed since the book's publication date. Starting with an outdated notion that was considered state-of-the-art thinking in 1953 might make a really interesting—and creative—opening

for an argument. Likewise, citing a well-accepted theory about women and behavior that has not changed since the 1950s might also make a thought-provoking opening.

> *Author:* Kinsey, Alfred C. (Alfred Charles), 1894–1956
> *Title: Sexual Behavior in the Human Female,* by the Staff of the Institute for Sex Research, Indiana University: Alfred C. Kinsey [and others]

The Search: Secondary Sources

The best researchers use multiple avenues of investigation. They consult a range of already published sources (secondary sources) and conduct surveys, polls, and interviews (primary sources).

Using Books

Books are edited, reviewed, and selected by librarians for inclusion on the shelves. Most material on the Web, on the other hand, has not been screened. Anyone can post anything, so web material ranges from worthless to exceptionally valuable. Sometimes the Web can be the place to find facts fast or to do general reading. At other times, books are the right place to go for research. For example, if you are researching the life of a slave in Georgia in 1860, books would probably offer more depth than web pages.

HOW TO FIND BOOKS ON YOUR SUBJECT All libraries have catalogs, which today are mostly online catalogs rather than drawers of cards.

Catalog entries list author, title, publisher, and call number. Other information that might be helpful in assessing the source are the number of pages, the presence of a bibliography and index, and a list of subjects related to the material in the publication.

WHAT A CATALOG TELLS YOU You get a great deal of information from a catalog entry, including basics such as author and title. The following entry came up in a keyword search on "children and television viewing."

> *Author:* Anderson, Daniel R., 1944–
>
> *Title:* Early childhood television viewing and adolescent behavior: the re-contact study/Daniel R. Anderson . . . [et al.]; with commentary by Reed Larson.

You find out who published the work and what type of source it is—a book, a study, a thesis, or a dissertation, for example.

> *Imprint:* Boston: Blackwell Publishers, 2001.

You get information about the location of the book—in which library, where it is shelved, and whether the book has been checked out.

PRACTICE 15.5

Reading a Catalog Entry

Compare the following entry with the one at the top of this page (Author: Kinsey, etc). How are these sources different? How are they alike?

Author: Menzigian, Margaret H.

Title: A study of the leisure-time activities, television viewing habits, and the expressed interests of a selected population of fifth-grade children in connection with their studying of natural science by television, by Margaret H. Menzigian [and] Ellen Marion Shepherd

Imprint: 1960

Location: Mugar

Call No.: EdM 1960 me

Status: Available

Descript: v, 65 p., 66 folded insert, 67–72 p. illus. 30 cm

Note: Thesis (M.A.)—Boston University, 1960

Alt author: Shepherd, Ellen Marion, joint author ■

Location: Mugar

Call No.: LB1103. F35 v. 66 no. 1

Status: Available

The catalog entry will contain other information—length of publication, a brief description of the publication (sometimes with chapter headings or section titles), and subject headings covered in the publication.

EVALUATING BOOKS Use the questions about authorship, scholarship, bias, and currency to help you narrow your book choices (see the box titled Criteria for Evaluating Sources on p. 411). Look at the title, author, and date of publication. The title could provide a good sense of whether the source is right for your purpose.

Using Periodicals: Academic Journals, Trade Journals, and Popular Magazines

Periodicals of all types are available both online and in print. You can find journal articles by searching through indexes on library databases such as the *Readers' Guide to Periodical Literature*. Academic journals like the *Journal of Finance, Social Work: The Journal of the National Association of Social Workers, American Literature*, and *Circulation: The Journal of the American Heart Association* announce and explain new findings in their specialty fields. They are usually not written for the average reader but rather for people with special training or interest in the field. Nevertheless, they can be useful to you because they are reliable and current. Journal articles are juried— that is, they are reviewed and chosen by scholars or experts in the field. Therefore, the articles are usually in-depth, with footnotes and detailed bibliographies. In other words, the conclusions the authors have reached are clearly documented.

Trade journals, too, have specialized audiences, but they can be useful in your research. These periodicals help professionals in specific fields keep up with current trends, new products, and other up-to-date information. Article authors are practitioners in specialty fields, and they are writing for other experts. They are often writing to report trends and new findings—just the information you may be looking for. Studies in the *Journal of the American Medical Association*, for example, often announce new theories or counter conventional medical thinking. Other useful trade and professional publications include *WWD: Women's Wear Daily, Nutrition Today, Adweek*, and *Editor and Publisher*.

Although some popular magazines, such as *Time, Scientific American, Discover*, and *Smithsonian*, might not have the authority and depth of academic journals, they are usually reliable, cover a wide range of topics, and are highly readable because they are written for a general audience. Although they quote sources, they do not include bibliographies. They can be good sources for up-to-date news and current reporting on trends and events.

Be especially alert for bias in periodicals because it can be difficult—especially when you search electronically and do not see all the articles in a particular publication—to judge whether an article is fair and reasonably objective. Since popular magazines do not include bibliographic citations or footnotes, you must look carefully at the way the writers cite sources within the text. Their sources might be worth checking. For example, if you find census data that reveal a significant population decrease in a particular state, you might go directly to the most recent census data—through either an online or a library search of government documents—to confirm those figures for yourself before you cite them as factual in your paper.

Using Surveys and Polls

Sometimes you will consult periodicals that have a distinct point of view. Trade journals, for example, report news from within a certain industry. You will not find criticism of the industry in such publications, but you will find a particular perspective. Being aware of bias proves to your readers that your research is thorough and your writing is trustworthy.

Using Newspapers

You can search most large daily newspapers through their online archives by going directly to their websites, but the online archives probably will not date back much farther than 1975.

In evaluating news sources, ask:

- Is the news source a well-known paper with an established record of reliability?
- Are the opinion pieces labeled and separated from the news stories, and is advertising set apart from news articles by appearance and by content?
- Does the writer provide attribution following quotations or make clear references to the source in the text ("according to a report released by the NRA today," "according to a company statement released today")?

The Search: Primary Sources

Data gathered from surveys and polls can be useful to writers, especially writers trying to prove a trend in behavior or establish a new wave of current thinking about an issue. In general, though, you should be wary of citing surveys and polls. If you do cite one, carefully evaluate the origin of the study. The U.S. Census Bureau, for example, is a good source. But a quick newspaper opinion poll might not reveal much about public opinion. A poll conducted by a company might be designed to solicit attention for a product rather than to provide information.

Conducting objective and reliable surveys and polls is a job for trained professionals—people who know how to write questions and how to combine them so that the survey solicits clear, valid data from which one can extract meaning. These professionals also know how to administer a survey to a wide variety of people so that the answers represent a cross section of the group. If a survey or poll is not conducted according to rigorous standards, results can be invalid or twisted to "prove" the point that someone wants to advance.

In evaluating polls and surveys, ask:

- What are the sources of polling and survey data?
- Were the questions written to solicit a certain response? For example, you might ask people on your street if they watch Home Box Office (HBO) at least once a week. Negative replies do not necessarily mean that people do not like the network. What if cable is not available in the area, or if the cost of a premium channel is prohibitive?
- Do the survey responses represent a cross section of the population?
- Did the survey ask enough questions?

Using Interviews

Many researchers in academia, in the media, and in business do field research. They interview experts for background information and current thinking. Using quotations from these primary sources enlivens writing and makes it convincing and professional. Consider using interviews for news and technical reports, editorials and speeches, proposals, profiles, trend stories, and academic papers.

You may decide to conduct informal interviews, collecting background material to help you understand topics before you start to write about them. You may also conduct more formal interviews, collecting quotations from people who are experts on subjects that you are writing about.

Tips for Conducting Interviews

- **Make a Contact List.** Figure out who the main sources might be: names of experts, organizers, advocates, witnesses, and people central to your writing project.

- **Get Advance Materials before the Interview.** Read widely so that you are well informed about the issues your interview subject represents. Find out if your source has been quoted in writing before, if your source is an expert, or whether he or she has written books or articles. Read all you can to prepare.

(continued)

The art and craft of interviewing consists of two parts: asking good questions and listening carefully to the answers. Most people enjoy being interviewed. They like to talk about their work, research, and fields of expertise, and they enjoy expressing their opinions.

Creating an Annotated Bibliography

While gathering your sources for other research projects, you will find it extremely helpful to create an annotated bibliography, which is an alphabetized list of your sources, put into the documentation style you will be using (MLA, APA, or another; see Chapter 16 on documentation styles). Include in your bibliography notations with summary, evaluation, and/or commentary. Teachers sometimes assign the annotated bibliography as a stand-alone project for the purpose of students becoming knowledgeable about the research in a particular field of study. Professional scholars and researchers often publish annotated bibliographies

as major pieces of research, collecting and disseminating the scholarship in a particular field. However, a less formal type of annotated bibliography has also found its way into popular culture and onto many websites. The "Top 10 . . ." or "The Best of . . ." lists of restaurants, music videos, websites, films, and books are variations of the annotated bibliography. The "Top 10" or the "Best" choices in these fields are listed, summarized, evaluated, and often include interesting and quirky personal commentary.

The annotated bibliography can help you with your research in a number of ways:

1. It helps you read carefully and critically.
2. It helps you sort through the available information and select the material relevant to your topic.
3. It familiarizes you with the issues and perspectives that are being discussed in the area of your research.
4. It helps you develop your line of reasoning and craft your argument.

Kinds of Annotations

Depending on the class and the assignment, you may be asked to provide different kinds of annotations. It is important, as always, to check with your professors about what kind of annotations they want you to do. Most annotations fall into these three categories, and you may be asked to do one or more.

- **Summary** Write a brief overview of the material. (For more on how to write a summary, see Chapter 4, "Reading, Thinking, and Writing Critically.") What are the key points? What other topics does it cover?
- **Evaluation** Comment on the strengths and weaknesses of this material. How useful is it in your research? How credible is the source?
- **Personal Commentary** Note how this material fits into your thinking about the topic. How can you use this material in your argument? Does it support or refute your thesis? Does it open up another topic you might explore?

Organizing Your Annotated Bibliography

The best way to keep track of all your source material is to annotate it as you read it. Annotating will help you remember the key points of each source and not get confused later as to which source made what point. This kind of sequential organization allows you to build your knowledge and understanding of a topic. You will also be able to determine who the experts are in the field by noting which names are cited most often.

The most common organization for an annotated bibliography follows this sequence:

- A statement of intent: What are the parameters of your bibliography? What topics will you be covering?

- A list of all your sources, alphabetized by last name, and in correct MLA or APA style. (See Chapter 16 for correct documentation style guidelines.)
- A concise summary of the material.
- An evaluation of the strengths and weaknesses of the material.
- Your personal commentary on the usefulness of this material to your research.

Tips for Reading Sources and Writing Annotated Bibliographies

- Read your sources carefully to identify their central arguments. You can often find the writer's thesis stated in the introduction and summarized in the conclusion.

- Look at the headings and the topic sentences of paragraphs to understand the scope of the material.

- Write clearly and economically.

- Be consistent in using the correct bibliographic format (MLA, APA, or another format) for all your sources.

- Be consistent in the format for the annotations. You can use phrases, sentences, or even bullet points, but be sure to use them consistently for each entry.

- Avoid unintentional plagiarism by putting quotation marks around all words you take directly from sources.

- Use the personal commentary section to make connections to your argument but also to raise questions, suggest new paths of inquiry, or clarify your thinking.

Assignment

Create your own annotated bibliography. Imagine you have been given the task of writing an entry for a "Top 10" website. Choose an area that interests you (films, books, music videos, restaurants). Or choose a trend you have observed in health, culture, science, technology, politics, entertainment, or consumer habits.

1. You will need to write an entry that summarizes, evaluates, and comments on your choice for the "best" in that Top 10 category, or create an entry on the trend you have selected.

2. Use the example from "The Future of Robot Caregivers" (facing page) as a model for each entry and create an annotated bibliography with several entries on your "Top 10" or on the trend you have selected. Be sure to include summary, evaluation, and personal commentary.

ANATOMY OF AN ANNOTATED BIBLIOGRAPHIC ENTRY

This example of an entry for an Annotated Bibliography uses MLA style. (You can read "The Future of Robot Caregivers" in Chapter 12.)

Aronson, Louise. "The Future of Robot Caregivers." *New York Times*. NewYork Times, 20 July, 2014. Web 19 July, 2014.

Author's Last Name, First Name. "Title of Article." *Title of Newspaper*. Publisher, Day Month Year. Medium. Day Month Year of access.

summary

The article presents an optimistic view of using robots as caregivers, especially for the elderly and for children with disabilities. Aronson concedes that in an "ideal world" we would each have humans to care for us, but she says that "most of us do not live in an ideal world, and a reliable robot may be better than an unreliable or abusive person, or than no one at all." Japan, Sweden, and many European countries have developed robot caregivers that are "social companions" or that help with dispensing medicines or doing routine medical tasks like monitoring blood pressure.

— thesis of article
— quotation marks around words from article

evaluation

Aronson is a professor of geriatrics and an MD. Her anecdotes come from her practice, and she cites other doctors like Jerald Winakur and Sherry Turkle, an MIT professor, to support her views. However, Turkle in a letter to the editor of the *New York Times* (July 25, 2014) says she is not a supporter of robot caregivers because ". . . robots proposed as 'caring machines' fool us into thinking they care about us."

— has authority and cites credible sources
— cites bibliographic information for another source
— one source disagrees with how she's been cited

commentary

Aronson's argument is persuasive on the surface, and she does a good job of showing some of the positive ways robots can be used to help the elderly and children with disabilities. But she too thinks that human caregivers are preferable. I don't agree with her position that robots are the next best things to human caregivers. She really doesn't address the economic issues of robots outsourcing people in these jobs. I can use this controversy in my section on economics and work (IIIA).

— writer's position
— keys this article to topic in outline

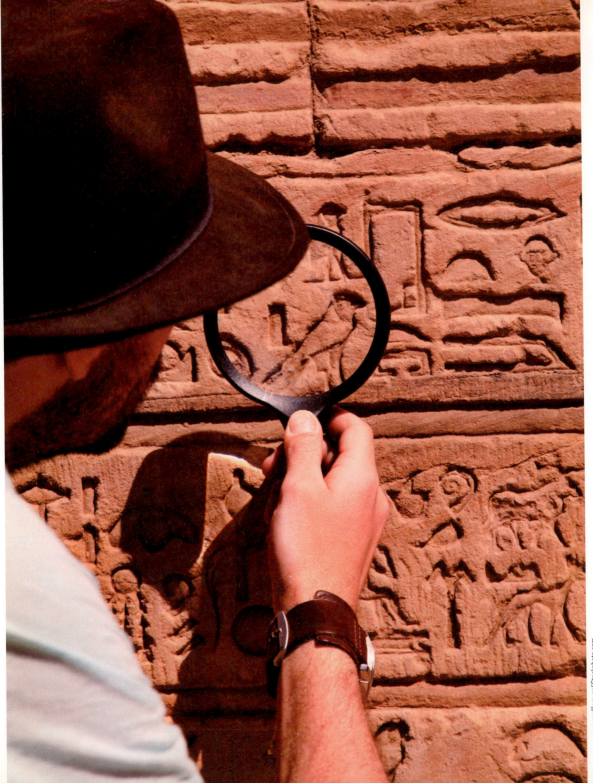

Heinz Koenig/
Shutterstock.com

DOCUMENTATION

The outer surface of truth is not smooth, welling and gathering from paragraph to shapely paragraph, but is encrusted with a rough protective bark of citations.

—NICHOLSON BAKER

Documentation

Many of the writing assignments you do in college and at work require you to become knowledgeable about topics that are new to you. Becoming expert enough to write with some authority about a historical era, a scientific discovery, a film theory, or a leading philosopher is one reward of research. To be a credible and reliable researcher, trusted by your readers, you must clearly document all the sources you consulted. The conventions of research writing are specific, and it is important to attend carefully to all the details.

Attributing Sources

Attributing your sources—an essential part of research writing—means honestly acknowledging the books, periodicals, experts, and websites you consulted. Attributing sources gives you credibility. If your points are backed up by reliable and valid research or acknowledged experts in a field, your reader will trust what you have written. Clear attribution also allows readers to find your source and read in more depth about your topic. For each source that you use in your paper, even one you do not quote directly from, you need to provide information that will allow a reader to find and examine the same material that you did.

423

You have to be scrupulously honest about acknowledging your sources, whether you are using other writers' language or ideas in your work. You must give them credit; if you do not, you have, in effect, plagiarized—stolen from them. The consequences of plagiarism, as you probably know, are serious. Students and professors found guilty of plagiarism are often suspended or dismissed from an institution. In the professional world, people who plagiarize often lose their jobs. However, most plagiarism in student papers is unintentional, due to lack of knowledge or information rather than a result of dishonesty.

Avoiding Plagiarism

The best way to avoid plagiarism is to keep careful notes as you do your research. Immediately put quotation marks around any words you take from a source, and write down the name of the author, the title of the source, and other publication information. Here is the essential information you need for citing books, articles, and websites:

Books	Articles	Websites
Author(s) or editor(s)	Authors(s)	Authors(s)
Title	Title	Title
Edition	Periodical	Publisher
Place and date of publication	Volume and issue	Date of electronic publication
Name of publisher	Date	Date you accessed the source
Page numbers	Page numbers	URL (Internet address)

The ease of cutting and pasting information from websites into your notes makes it especially important to be careful when you use online sources. As you write your notes, be sure to indicate any direct information you have pasted in from websites, either by highlighting the information in another color or by inserting quotation marks around it. Follow the material immediately with the information given in the list above.

The ethics of research demand absolute honesty in reporting information from your sources. As careful as you are in documenting sources, be equally careful not to twist someone's theories or ideas to fit your thesis. Even adding a word to a quotation without noting that you have added it violates the unspoken contract you have made with your reader to be a reliable and credible researcher.

What to Document

Just as a car or a cell phone belongs to you, so does your original thinking. If an author has developed a theory or an insight after studying a subject, that theory or insight is his or her intellectual property, and you cannot use it without giving credit

to the source. This rule applies to words, speech, visuals, music, computer programming code, and mathematical notations. If you use someone's original thinking, you have to attribute it to that person by means of a clear citation.

However, you do not have to give a citation for a fact or observation that is general knowledge. If you read in three or four sources that Barack Obama was first elected president in 2008, you do not have to provide citations stating where you read that fact. It is considered common knowledge. Common knowledge includes the following:

- Historical facts that you can find in many reference books (George Washington was the first president of the United States)
- Commonly accepted opinions (children should be protected from viewing extreme violence or explicit sex)
- Information that appears in many reference books (the boiling point of water, the colors of the rainbow)
- Commonly known proverbs or quotations (idle hands are the devil's workshop)

On the other hand, if you read a political analyst's theory about the impact of the fall of communism in 1989, you have to attribute that theory to the analyst, even if you do not quote his or her exact words. If you were writing for a history course and using Modern Language Association, or MLA style, you would cite the author's name in the text, giving a brief explanation of his or her expertise.

MLA STYLE

Historian and scholar Timothy Garton Ash, after witnessing the collapse of communism in Eastern Europe, believes that the free market of capitalism will be embraced by Eastern Europeans and regarded as a panacea for economic ills (152).

This in-text reference tells the reader to search under "Ash" to find the full citation on the Works Cited page.

MLA STYLE

Ash, Timothy Garton. *The Magic Lantern: The Revolution of 89.* New York: Random House, 1990. Print.

Integrating Sources: Quoting, Paraphrasing, and Summarizing

When you take material directly from a source, you have three possible ways of using it in your paper: you can quote it, paraphrase it, or summarize it. As you write your paper, you have to make decisions about which and how much material you will use. Too many citations or many long citations make a reader feel as though you have done no original thinking about the topic but have merely strung together the work of others. Choose your quotations on the basis of how authoritative they are and how well they are phrased, and use them to support or illustrate *your* points. Likewise, use summaries sparingly to condense important information, but be assured that your reader does not want to read a whole paper of summaries of other people's ideas. (See Chapter 4 for more discussion of this topic.)

Quoting

When you quote directly, you copy the words you are citing—carefully and accurately—into your text, and you enclose them in quotation marks. If you are using MLA documentation style and if the material is four or fewer typed lines, enclose it in quotation marks. Be sure to introduce the quotation clearly, attributing the words to the writer. If you quote a passage of five lines or more, indent the material farther than the paragraph indentation (usually another half inch), and omit the quotation marks. The indentation and this block format, as well as the page reference at the end, inform your reader that it is quoted material.

In-Text Citation

Notice that when your in-text citation (298) is given, the period belongs *after* the citation number. Here is an example of an in-text citation using MLA style:

> In her interview with Christopher Scanlan, Dianne Donovan says, "For an editorial writer, reading is just extremely important because you have to know about so many things" (298).

Block Form

Different style manuals have different requirements for the amount of space to indent and the number of lines to include in a block quotation. See pages 459–463 for guidelines for quoting material using American Psychological Association style. Notice that when you are using the block form, the citation number goes after the final punctuation mark. Here is an example in MLA style:

> In her interview with Christopher Scanlan, editorial writer Dianne Donovan says,
>
>> For an editorial writer, reading is extremely important because you have to know about so many things. You have to have a breadth of knowledge, if not of experience, which most of us don't. That allows you to be able to see a lot of different viewpoints and also to be able to come up with a lot of different things to write about. (298)

Paraphrasing

When you paraphrase material, you put it into your own words, but you cover all the same material as the original. The length of your paraphrase should be roughly the same as that of the original. Even though you are using your own phrasing and wording, the ideas are not yours, so you still must attribute the passage to the author. You might paraphrase the Christopher Scanlan interview this way:

> In her interview with Christopher Scanlan, Donovan says that because editorial writers have many different topics to write about, they have to read widely and deeply. Most editorial writers cannot know everything about the topics they have to write about, and they have to come up with new topics and be able to see them from multiple perspectives (298).

USING ELLIPSES, BRACKETS, AND SINGLE QUOTATION MARKS

IF YOU INTENTIONALLY leave out some words in a quotation, use ellipses (. . .) to indicate the omission.

> As Dianne Donovan says, "You have to have a breadth of knowledge . . . which most of us don't."

If you add a clarifying word or phrase, put it in brackets to show that it is your language.

> Dianne Donovan says, "[Editorial writers] have to have a breadth of knowledge, if not experience, which most of us don't."

If you incorporate a quotation within your quotation, use single quotation marks to set off the incorporated quotation.

> Discussing how the editorial conference works, Donovan says, "I'll pitch something. 'Here's the issue and here's what I think we should say about it,' and you make your argument."

Summarizing

Summarizing is a way to condense lengthy material. In summarizing, you convey the highlights of someone's ideas, but you do not usually include the details or illustrative examples. One trick in summarizing a long section is to look for the topic sentence in each paragraph. If you put these topic sentences in your own words, you can usually accurately summarize a long piece of writing. Again, if you are summarizing or paraphrasing someone else's ideas, you have to give the person credit in the form of a clear citation.

The first three pages of Dianne Donovan's interview with Christopher Scanlan might be summarized this way:

> In her interview with Christopher Scanlan, Dianne Donovan talks about her craft as an editorial writer. She has always enjoyed writing and began writing editorials in high school. She believes that a good editorial writer has to read widely and deeply. She also believes that writing editorials is a craft, not an art. Her beat originally was family issues, but soon she became interested in welfare reform and juvenile justice. She has written fourteen or fifteen editorials about the juvenile justice system in Chicago (298–312).

Documentation Guidelines: MLA and APA Styles

Different fields of knowledge have developed different conventions and rules for citing sources within a paper and at the end of a paper in a Works Cited or a References section. Documentation styles vary in terms of where you place the date of publication within a citation, whether to use a comma after the name of an author, and so on. The differences might seem arbitrary, but they provide important information to readers and signal that you have been careful with details. No one expects you to memorize these conventions, but you are expected to consult the appropriate style manual when citing sources and to apply the guidelines accurately.

The two most common documentation styles in academic writing are MLA style and APA style. Modern Language Association (MLA) style is used primarily for writing in the humanities and is described fully in the *MLA Handbook for Writers of Research Papers*, now in its seventh edition (New York: Modern Language Association, 2009). American Psychological Association (APA) style is used primarily for writing in the natural and social sciences and is described fully in *Publication Manual of the American Psychological Association*, currently in its sixth edition (Washington, DC: American Psychological Association, 2009) and updated in the *APA Guidelines to Electronic References*. Some specialized fields use their own documentation forms. A few of these other forms are listed here.

> *The Associated Press Stylebook and Briefing on Media Law*, ed. Norm Goldstein (New York: Associated Press, 2007). [Note: This is also referred to as "AP style."]
>
> *The Chicago Manual of Style*, 16th ed. (Chicago: University of Chicago Press, 2010). [Note: This is also referred to as "Chicago style."]
>
> *The Columbia Guide to Online Style*, 2nd ed., Janice Walker and Todd Taylor (New York: Columbia University Press, 2006). [Note: This is also referred to as "CGOS style."
>
> *Scientific Style and Format: The CSE Manual for Authors, Editors, and Publishers*, 8th ed. (New York: Cambridge University Press, 2014).

Ask your instructor or editor what style you should use, and then stick to those conventions. Many websites, especially sites of university writing centers, contain guides to the major documentation forms. And, of course, each of the listed groups publishes its own manual that gives complete, specific, and clear rules for creating in-text citations and Works Cited or References pages. The following overviews of MLA and APA style will give you the information you need for most of your academic writing assignments.

Overview of MLA Style

The *MLA Handbook for Writers of Research Papers* is the authoritative source for documenting research papers in English and the humanities. You can consult the handbook or the Modern Language Association website at www.mla.org for more detailed information. The following overview provides information on:

- formatting the manuscript
- citing sources in the text
- creating a Works Cited list

At the end of this section is a student paper in MLA style that you can use as a model.

Formatting the Manuscript (MLA)

Presentation is important, and the *MLA Handbook* specifies these conventions for preparing a paper for submission. Also see the model paper on pages 453–457.

PAPER Use good-quality $8\frac{1}{2}$ by 11-inch paper. Fasten the pages with paper clips; avoid staples and binders, both of which make it harder for your professor to read and comment on your work.

TITLE PAGE Title pages are not required in the MLA format, although your professor might require one. If you do not use a title page, set up the first page with your name, the professor's name, the course name and number, and the date in the upper left corner, with all lines double-spaced. Leave a 1-inch margin from the top and the left side. Double-space, center the title, double-space again, and begin typing your paper.

MARGINS, SPACING, FONT, AND INDENTING Leave 1-inch margins on all four sides, and double-space the entire paper. Use an easy-to-read font—12-point Times and Times New Roman are the most commonly used. Indent ½ inch at the beginning of each paragraph. When you use a quotation of more than four lines of prose or three lines of poetry, indent 1 inch, and do not use quotation marks around the indented quotation. Double-space within the quotation.

PAGING Put your last name and consecutive page numbers in the upper right corner of the paper, about ½ inch from the top. Use Arabic numerals (1, 2, 3) for page numbers, and do not use punctuation, the word *page*, or its abbreviation.

HEADINGS Headings are optional in MLA-formatted papers, and MLA does not specify any format in text. However, if the material is complicated and would benefit from being subdivided, create headings that are brief and parallel in phrasing, and be consistent in the font you use for them.

VISUALS If you include graphs, tables, maps, charts, illustrations, or photographs, place them as close as possible to your first discussion of them in the text, preferably after they are introduced. Identify a table with a table number and title above the table (Table 1 Album Titles and Release Dates). Label each figure with a number and a caption below the visual (Fig. 1. Album revenues). Cite the source underneath the table or visual.

WORKS CITED The final section of your paper is titled Works Cited. Begin a new page and center the title 1 inch from the top. Use regular type for the title, avoiding quotation marks, boldface, italics, and so on. Alphabetically list all works you cited in the text. Runover lines should be indented ½ inch (word processing software calls this a *hanging indent*).

Citing Sources in the Text

The MLA format requires citing sources in the text, usually by placing the author's last name and the page number in parentheses after the quoted or paraphrased material. The citation should be brief but complete enough to lead your reader to the full citation in the Works Cited section at the end of the paper. For example, if you mention the author's name in the sentence, you can simply enclose the page number(s) in parentheses after the quotation. The following list shows how to cite sources in the text of your paper.*

DIRECTORY TO IN-TEXT CITATIONS

1. One author: a complete work
2. One author: part of a work
3. Two or more works by the same author(s)
4. Works by authors with the same last name
5. A work by two or three authors
6. A work by four or more authors
7. A work authored by an organization
8. An anonymous work
9. Two or more works included in one citation
10. A series of citations from a single work
11. A work referred to in another work
12. A one-page work
13. A work without page numbers
14. A work in an anthology or a collection
15. An item from a reference work
16. A part of a multivolume work
17. A sacred text or famous literary work
18. Quoting verse
19. Quoting prose

1. **One Author: A Complete Work** You do not need an in-text citation if you identify the author in your text. (See the first entry.) However, you must give the author's last name in an in-text citation if it is not mentioned in the text. (See the second entry.) When a source is listed in your Works Cited page with an editor, a translator, a speaker, or an artist instead of the author, then use that person's name in your citation.

    ### WITH AUTHOR IN TEXT (preferred for citing a complete work)

    In *No Need for Hunger*, Robert Spitzer recommends that the U.S. government develop a new foreign policy to help Third World countries overcome poverty and hunger.

    ### WITHOUT AUTHOR IN TEXT

    Do not offer page numbers when citing complete works, articles in alphabetized encyclopedias, one-page articles, or unpaginated sources.

* *Reprinted with permission from* The College Writer's Handbook *by Randall VanderMey, Verne Meyer, John Van Rys, and Pat Sebranek (2006).*

No Need for Hunger recommends that the U.S. government develop a new foreign policy to help Third World countries overcome poverty and hunger (Spitzer).

2. **One Author: Part of a Work** List the necessary page numbers in parentheses if you borrow words or ideas from a particular source. Leave a space between the author's last name and the page reference. No abbreviation or punctuation is needed.

> **WITH AUTHOR IN TEXT**
>
> Bullough writes that genetic engineering was dubbed "eugenics" in 1885 by a cousin of Darwin's, Sir Francis Galton (5).
>
> **WITHOUT AUTHOR IN TEXT**
>
> Genetic engineering was dubbed "eugenics" in 1885 by a cousin of Darwin's, Sir Francis Galton (Bullough 5).

3. **Two or More Works by the Same Author(s)** In addition to the author's last name(s) and page number(s), include a short version of the title of the work when you are citing two or more works by the same author(s). In parentheses, authors and titles are separated by a comma, as in the second example.

> **WITH AUTHOR IN TEXT**
>
> Wallerstein and Blakeslee claim that divorce creates an enduring identity for children of the marriage (*Unexpected Legacy* 62).
>
> **WITHOUT AUTHOR IN TEXT**
>
> They are intensely lonely despite active social lives (Wallerstein and Blakeslee, *Second Chances* 51).

4. **Works by Authors with the Same Last Name** When citing different sources by authors with the same last name, it is best to use the authors' full names in the text so as to avoid confusion. However, if circumstances call for parenthetical references, add each author's first initial. If first initials are the same, use each author's full name.

> Some critics think *Titus Andronicus* too abysmally melodramatic to be a work of Shakespeare (A. Parker 73). Others suggest that Shakespeare meant it as black comedy (D. Parker 486).

5. **A Work by Two or Three Authors** Give the last names of every author in the same order in which they appear in the Works Cited section. (The correct order of the authors' names can be found on the title page of the book.)

> Students learned more than a full year's Spanish in ten days using the complete supermemory method (Ostrander and Schroeder 51).

6. **A Work by Four or More Authors** Give the first author's last name as it appears in the Works Cited section followed by *et al.* (meaning "and others").

> Communication on the job is more than talking; it is "inseparable from your total behavior" (Culligan et al. 111).

7. **A Work Authored by an Organization** If a book or other work was written by an organization such as an agency, a committee, or a task force, it is said to have a corporate author. If the corporate name is long, include it in the text (rather than in parentheses) to avoid disrupting the flow of your writing. After the full name has been used at least once, use a shortened form of the name (common abbreviations are acceptable) in subsequent references. For example, *Task Force* may be used for *Task Force on Education for Economic Growth*.

> The Task Force on Education for Economic Growth details a strong connection between education and the depth and breadth of the workforce (105).
> The thesis of the report is that economic success depends on our ability to improve large-scale education and training as quickly as possible (Task Force 113–114).

8. **An Anonymous Work** When there is no author listed, give the title or a shortened version of the title as it appears in the Works Cited section.

> Statistics indicate that drinking tap water can account for up to 20 percent of a person's total exposure to lead (*Information* 572).

9. **Two or More Works Included in One Citation** To cite multiple works within a single parenthetical reference, list them in alphabetical order and separate the references with a semicolon.

> In Medieval Europe, Latin translations of the works of Rhazes, a Persian scholar, were a primary source of medical knowledge (Albe 22; Lewis 266).

10. **A Series of Citations from a Single Work** If no confusion is possible, it is not necessary to name a source repeatedly when making multiple parenthetical references to that source in a single paragraph. If all references are to the same page, identify that page in a parenthetical note after the last reference. If the references are to different pages within the same work, you need identify the work only once, and then use a parenthetical note with the page number alone for the subsequent references.

> Domesticating science meant not only spreading scientific knowledge but also promoting it as a topic of public conversation (Heilbron 2). One way to enhance its charm was by depicting cherubic putti as "angelic research assistants" in book illustrations (5).

11. **A Work Referred to in Another Work** If you must cite an indirect source—that is, information from a source that is quoted from another source—use the abbreviation *qtd. in* (quoted in) before the indirect source in your reference.

> Paton improved the conditions in Diepkloof (a prison) by "removing all the more obvious aids to detention. The dormitories [were] open at night: the great barred gate [was] gone" (qtd. in Callan xviii).

12. **A One-Page Work** Cite a one-page work just as you would a complete work.

> As S. Adams argues in her editorial, it is time for NASA "to fully reevaluate the Space Shuttle's long-term viability for sending humans into space."

13. **A Work without Page Numbers** If a work has no page numbers or other reference numbers, treat it as you would a complete work. This is commonly the case with electronic resources, for example. Do not count pages to create reference numbers of your own; however, if possible, refer to stable divisions within the document, such as sections or paragraphs.

> Antibiotics become ineffective against such organisms through two natural processes: first, genetic mutation; and second, the subsequent transfer of this mutated genetic material to other organisms, which appears to be the main way that bacteria attain a state of resistance (Davies par. 5).

14. **A Work in an Anthology or a Collection** When citing the entirety of a work that is part of an anthology or a collection, if it is identified by the author in your list of Works Cited, treat the citation as you would one for any other complete work.

> In "The Canadian Postmodern," Linda Hutcheon offers a clear analysis of the self-reflexive nature of contemporary Canadian fiction.

Similarly, if you are citing particular pages of such a work, follow the directions for citing part of a work.

> According to Hutcheon, "postmodernism seems to designate cultural practices that are fundamentally self-reflexive, in other words, art that is self-consciously artifice" (18).

15. **An Item from a Reference Work** An entry from a reference work, such as an encyclopedia or a dictionary, should be cited similarly to a work from an anthology or a collection. For a dictionary definition, include the abbreviation *def.* followed by the particular entry designation.

> This message of moral superiority becomes a juggernaut in the truest sense, a belief that "elicits blind devotion or sacrifice" ("Juggernaut," def. 1).

Although many such entries are identified only by title (previous entry), some reference works include an author's name for each entry (next entry). Others may identify the author by initials, with a list of full names elsewhere in the work.

> The decisions of the International Court of Justice are "based on principles of international law and cannot be appealed" (Pranger).

16. **A Part of a Multivolume Work** When citing only one volume of a multivolume work, if you identify the volume number in the Works Cited list, there is no need to include it in your in-text citation. However, if you cite more than one volume of a work, then each in-text reference must identify the appropriate volume. Give the volume number followed by page number, separated by a colon and a space.

> "A human being asleep," says Spengler, ". . . is leading only a plant-like existence" (2: 4).

When citing a whole volume, however, either identify the volume number in parentheses with the abbreviation *vol.* (using a comma to separate it from the author's name) or use the full word *volume* in your text.

> The land of Wisconsin has shaped its many inhabitants more significantly than they ever shaped that land (Stephens, vol. 1).

17. **A Sacred Text or Famous Literary Work** Because sacred texts and famous literary works are published in many editions, include sections, parts, or chapters. If using page numbers, list them first, followed by an abbreviation for the type of division and the division number.

> The more important a person's role in society—the more apparent power an individual has—the more that person is a slave to the forces of history (Tolstoy 690; bk. 9, ch. 1).

Books of the Bible and well-known works may be abbreviated.

> "A generation goes, and a generation comes, but the earth remains forever" (*The New Oxford Annotated Bible*, Eccles. 1.4)

> Hamlet observes, "One may smile . . . and be a villain" (Ham.1.5.104).

18. **Quoting Verse** Cite classic verse plays and poems by division (act, scene, canto, book, part) and line, using Arabic numerals for the various divisions unless your instructor prefers roman numerals. Use periods to separate the various numbers.

NOTE: A slash, with a space on each side, shows where each new line of verse begins. If you are citing lines only, use the word *line* or *lines* in your first reference and numbers only in additional references.

In the first act of the play, Hamlet comments, "How weary, stale, flat and unprofitable, / Seem to me all the uses of this world" (1.2.133–134).

In book five of Homer's *Iliad*, the Trojans' fear is evident: "The Trojans were scared when they saw the two sons of Dares, one of them in fright and the other lying dead by his chariot" (lines 22–24).

19. **Quoting Prose** To cite prose from fiction, list more than the page number if the work is available in several editions. Give the page reference first, and then add a chapter or section, if appropriate, in abbreviated form after a semicolon.

In *The House of the Spirits*, Isabel describes Marcos, "dressed in mechanic's overalls, with huge racer's goggles and an explorer's helmet" (13; ch. 1).

When you are quoting any sort of prose that takes more than four typed lines, indent each line of the quotation 1 inch and double-space it; do not add quotation marks. In this case, you put the parenthetical citation (the pages and chapter numbers) outside the end punctuation mark.

Allende describes the flying machine that Marcos has assembled:
The contraption lay with its stomach on terra firma, heavy and sluggish, looking more like a wounded duck than like one of those newfangled airplanes they were starting to produce in the United States. There was nothing in its appearance to suggest that it could move, much less take flight. (12; ch. 1)

Placement and Punctuation of Parenthetical Documentation

Present and punctuate citations according to these rules:*

- Place the parenthetical reference after the source material.
- Within the parentheses, normally give the author's last name only.
- Do not put a comma between the author's last name and the page reference.
- Cite the page number as a numeral, not a word.
- Don't use the abbreviations *p.*, *pp.*, or *page(s)* before page number(s).
- Place any sentence punctuation after the ending parenthesis.

NOTE: For many of these rules, exceptions exist. For example, classic literary texts could be cited by chapters, books, act, scenes, or lines. Moreover, many electronic sources have no stated authors and no pagination.

* *Reprinted with permission from* The College Writer's Handbook *by Randall VanderMey, Verne Meyer, John Van Rys, and Pat Sebranek (2006).*

Creating a Works Cited List

The last page of your paper will be titled Works Cited. All the parenthetical citations you inserted in your paper refer your reader to the complete entries in this final list. Include each work you have cited in your paper, but do not include works you read but did not cite. Alphabetize your list by the last name of the author or, in the case of an entry without an identified author, the first word of the title, excluding the articles *A*, *An*, and *The*.

DIRECTORY TO MLA WORKS CITED ENTRIES

Books and Other Documents

1. A book by one author
2. Two or more books by the same author
3. A work by two or three authors
4. A work by four or more authors
5. A work by a corporate author (an agency, a committee, or other organization)
6. An anonymous book
7. A single work from an anthology
8. A complete anthology
9. Two or more works from the same anthology or collection
10. One volume of a multivolume work
11. An introduction, a preface, a foreword, or an afterword
12. A republished book (reprint)
13. A book with multiple publishers
14. Second and subsequent editions
15. An edition with an author and an editor
16. A translation
17. An article in a familiar reference book
18. An article in an unfamiliar reference book
19. A government publication
20. A book in a series
21. A book with a title within its title
22. A sacred text
23. The published proceedings of a conference
24. A published dissertation
25. A pamphlet, brochure, manual, or other workplace document

Periodicals

26. An article in a weekly or biweekly magazine
27. An article in a monthly or bimonthly magazine
28. An article in a scholarly journal paginated by issue

67. An advertisement (in print)
68. A lecture, a speech, an address, or a reading
69. A legal or historical document
70. A map or chart

WORKS CITED ENTRIES: BOOKS AND OTHER DOCUMENTS

The entries that follow illustrate the information needed to cite books, sections of a book, pamphlets, and government publications. The possible components of these entries are listed in this order:

- Author's name
- Title of a part of the book (an article in the book or a foreword)
- Title of the book
- Name of editor or translator
- Edition
- Volume number
- Series name
- Place of publication, publisher, year of publication
- Page numbers, if citation is to only a part (For page spans, use a hyphen or an en dash. If clarity is maintained, you may also drop a digit from the second number: 141–43, but 201–334.)
- Medium of publication (print, Web, MP3; additional media types are listed.)

List only the city for the place of publication if the city is in the United States. For cities outside the United States, add an abbreviation for the country if necessary for clarity. If several cities are listed, give only the first. Publishers' names should be shortened by omitting articles (*a, an, the*), business abbreviations (*Co., Inc.*), and descriptive words (*Books, Press*). Abbreviate University Press as UP. Also use standard abbreviations whenever possible.

NOTE: In general, if any of these components do not apply, they are not included in the Works Cited entry. However, in the rare instance that a book does not state publication information, use the following abbreviations in place of information you cannot supply:

n.p.	No place of publication given
n.p.	No publisher given
n.d.	No date of publication given
n. pag.	No pagination given

1. **A Book by One Author**

    Jacob, Mira. *The Sleepwalker's Guide to Dancing*. New York: Random, 2014. Print.

2. **Two or More Books by the Same Author** List the books alphabetically according to title. After the first entry, substitute three hyphens for the author's name.

> Link, Kelly. *Get in Trouble: Stories*. New York: Random, 2015. Print.
> – – –. *Pretty Monsters*. New York: Viking, 2008. Print.

3. **A Work by Two or Three Authors**

> Bornstein, Kate, and S. Bear Bergman. *Gender Outlaws: The Next Generation*. Berkeley: Seal P, 2010. Print.

NOTE: List the authors in the same order as they appear on the title page. Reverse only the name of the first author.

4. **A Work by Four or More Authors**

> Miller, Korina, et al. *Lonely Planet Greece (Travel Guide)*. Victoria, Austral.: Lonely Planet, 2014. Print.

NOTE: You may also choose to give all names in full in the order used on the title page.

5. **A Work by a Corporate Author**

> World Service Office. *Narcotics Anonymous*. Baltimore: World Service, 2008. Print.

6. **An Anonymous Book**

> *Chase's Calendar of Events 2014*. Chicago: Contemporary, 2014. Print.

7. **A Single Work from an Anthology**

> Means, David. "The Secret Goldfish." *The Best American Short Stories: 2005*. Ed. Michael Chabon. Boston: Houghton, 2005. 288–297. Print.

8. **A Complete Anthology** If you cite a complete anthology, begin the entry with the editor(s).

> Chabon, Michael, ed. *The Best American Short Stories: 2005*. New York: Library of America, 2000.
> Cain, William E, et al., eds. *American Literature*. Boston: Pearson, 2014. Print.

9. **Two or More Works from the Same Anthology or Collection** To avoid unnecessary repetition when citing two or more entries from a larger collection, you may cite the collection once with complete publication information (see the following *Forbes* entry). The individual entries (see the following *Joseph* and *MacNeice* entries) can then be cross referenced by listing the author, title of the piece, editor of the collection, and page numbers.

> Forbes, Peter, ed. *Scanning the Century*. London: Penguin, 2000. Print.
> Joseph, Jenny. "Warning." Forbes 335–36.
> MacNeice, Louis. "Star-Gazer." Forbes 504.

10. **One Volume of a Multivolume Work**

> Greenblatt, Stephen, ed. *The Norton Anthology of English Literature*. Vol. A. New York: Norton, 2012. Print.

NOTE: If you cite two or more volumes in a multivolume work, give the total number of volumes after each title. Offer specific references to volume and page numbers in the parenthetical reference in your text, like this: (8: 112–114).

> Salzman, Jack, David Lionel Smith, and Cornel West. *Encyclopedia of African-American Culture and History*. 5 vols. New York: Simon, 1996. Print.

11. **An Introduction, a Preface, a Foreword, or an Afterword** To cite the introduction, preface, foreword, or afterword of a book, list the author of the part first. Then identify the part by type, with no quotation marks or italicizing, followed by the title of the book. Next, identify the author of the work, using the word *By*. (However, if the book author and the part's author are the same person, give just the last name after *By*.) For a book that gives cover credit to an editor instead of an author, identify the editor as usual. Finally, list any page numbers for the part being cited.

> Simon Schama Center for European Studies. Afterword. *After the Victorians: Private Conscience and Public Duty in Modern Britain*. Eds. Peter Mandler and Susan Pedersen. New York: Routledge, 2014. Print.
>
> Locher, Dick. Foreword. *Chester Gould: A Daughter's Biography of the Creator of Dick Tracy*. By Jean Gould O'Connell. Jefferson: McFarland, 2012. ix. Print.

12. **A Republished Book (Reprint)** Give the original publication date after the title.

> Atwood, Margaret. *Surfacing*. 1972. New York: Doubleday, 1998. Print.

NOTE: New material added to the reprint, such as an introduction, should be cited after the original publication facts: Introd. C. Becker.

13. **A Book with Multiple Publishers** When a book lists more than one publisher (not just different offices of the same publisher), include all of them in the order given on the book's title page, separated by a semicolon.

> Wells, H. G. *The Complete Short Stories of H. G. Wells*. New York: St. Martin's; London: A. & C. Black, 1987. Print.

14. **Second and Subsequent Editions** An edition refers to the particular publication you are citing.

> Dean, Ceri B., et al. *Classroom Instruction That Works: Research-Based Strategies for Increasing Student Achievement*. 2nd ed. Alexandria: Association for Supervision and Curriculum Development, 2012. Print.

15. **An Edition with an Author and an Editor** The term *edition* also refers to the work of one person that is prepared by another person, an editor.

> Brontë, Charlotte. *Jane Eyre*. Ed. Barnita Bagchi. London: Anthem, 2016. Print.

16. **A Translation**

> Sappho. *A New Translation of the Complete Works*. Trans. Diane Rayor. New York: Cambridge UP, 2014. Print.

17. **An Article in a Familiar Reference Book** It is not necessary to give full publication information for familiar reference works (encyclopedias and dictionaries). For these titles, list only the edition (if available) and the publication year. If an article is initialed, check the index of authors (in the opening section of each volume) for the author's full name.

> Lum, P. Andrea. "Computed Tomography." *World Book*. 2000 ed.

18. **An Article in an Unfamiliar Reference Book** Give full publication information as for any other sort of book.

> "S Corporation." *The Portable MBA Desk Reference*. Ed. Paul A. Argenti. New York: Wiley, 1998. Print.

19. **A Government Publication** State the name of the government (country, state, and so on) followed by the name of the agency. Most U.S. federal publications are published by the Government Printing Office (GPO).

> United States. Dept. of Labor. Bureau of Labor Statistics. *Occupational Outlook Handbook* 2014–2015. Washington: GPO, 2014. Print.

When citing the *Congressional Record*, list only the date and page numbers.

> Cong. Rec. 5 Feb. 2014: S311–15. Print.

20. **A Book in a Series** Give the series name and number (if any) before the publication information.

> Paradis, Adrian A. *Opportunities in Military Careers*. VGM Opportunities Series. Lincolnwood: VGM Career Horizons, 2005. Print.

21. **A Book with a Title within Its Title** If the title contains a title normally in quotation marks, keep the quotation marks and italicize the entire title.

> Ishiguro, Tatsuaki. *"Biogenesis" and Other Stories*. New York: Vertical, 2015. Print.

If the title contains a title that is normally italicized, do not italicize that title in your entry:

> Beckwith, Charles E. *Twentieth Century Interpretations of* A Tale of Two Cities: *A Collection of Critical Essays*. Upper Saddle River: Prentice, 1972. Print.

22. **A Sacred Text** The Bible and other such sacred texts are treated as anonymous books. Documentation should read exactly as it is printed on the title page.

> *The Jerusalem Bible*. Garden City: Doubleday, 1966. Print.

23. **The Published Proceedings of a Conference** The published proceedings of a conference are treated like a book. However, if the title of the publication does not identify the conference by title, date, and location, add the appropriate information immediately after the title.

> McIlwaine, la C., ed. *Advances in Knowledge Organization*. Vol. 14. Proc. of Eighth Intl. ISKO Conf., 13–16 July 2014, Krakow. Wurzburg: Ergon-Verlag, 2014. Print.

24. **A Published Dissertation** An entry for a published dissertation contains the same information as a book entry, with a few added details. Add the abbreviation *Diss.* and the name of the degree-granting institution before the publication facts.

> Jansen, James Richard. *Images of Dostoevsky in German Literary Expressionism*. Diss. U of Utah, 2003. Ann Arbor: UMI, 2003. Print.

25. **A Pamphlet, Brochure, Manual, or Other Workplace Document** Treat any such publication as you would a book.

> Planned Parenthood. *What Is a Negative Body Image?* New York: Planned Parenthood Federation of America, 2015. Print.

If publication information is missing, list the country of publication [in brackets] if known. Use the abbreviation *n.p.* (no place) if the country or the publisher is unknown and the abbreviation *n.d.* if the date is unknown.

> *Pedestrian Safety*. [United States]: n.p., n.d. Print.

WORKS-CITED ENTRIES: PERIODICALS The possible components of these entries are listed in order:

- Author's name, last name first
- Title of article, in quotation marks
- Name of periodical, italicized
- Series number or name, if relevant (not preceded by a period or comma)
- Volume number (for a journal)
- Issue number, separated from volume with a period but no space
- Date of publication (abbreviate all months except May, June, and July)
- Page numbers, preceded by a colon, without *p.* or *pp.*
- Medium of publication consulted
- Supplementary information

NOTE: If any of the preceding components do not apply, they are not listed. The entries that follow illustrate the information needed to cite periodicals.

26. **An Article in a Weekly or Biweekly Magazine** List the author (if identified), article title (in quotation marks), publication title (italicized), full date of publication, and page numbers for the article. Do not include volume and issue numbers.

    > Weiner, Jonah. "Kim Gordon's New Noise." *Rolling Stone* 12 Mar. 2015: 18. Print.

27. **An Article in a Monthly or Bimonthly Magazine** As for a weekly or biweekly magazine, list the author (if identified), article title (in quotation marks), and publication title (italicized). Then identify the month(s) and year of the issue, followed by page numbers for the article. Do not give volume and issue numbers.

    > Jacobson, Roni. "The Persistence of Memory." *Scientific American* Apr. 2015: 14–16. Print.

28. **An Article in a Scholarly Journal Paginated by Issue** Rather than month or full date of publication, scholarly journals are usually identified by volume number. If there is also an issue number, include that immediately following the volume number, separated by a period. List the year of publication in parentheses, the page numbers of the article, and the medium of publication.

    > Kelley-Woolfitt, William. "'Oh, Catfish and Turnip Greens': Black Oral Traditions in the Poetry of Marilyn Nelson." *African American Review* 47.2 (2014): 231–46. Print.

29. **An Article in a Scholarly Journal with Continuous Pagination** *MLA* no longer makes a distinction between separately and continuously paginated journals, so include both journal and issue number in your citation.

    > Moorley, Calvin, and Teresa Chinn. "Using Social Media for Continuous Professional Development." *Journal of Advanced Nursing* 71.4 (2015): 713–17. Print.

30. **A Printed Interview** Begin with the name of the person interviewed when that is whom you are quoting.

    > Hilary Mantel. "The Art of Fiction No. 226." Interview by Mona Simpson. *Paris Review* Spring 2015: 36-71. Print.

    If the interview is untitled and the interviewer is not identified, the word *Interview* (no italics) and a period follow the interviewee's name.

31. **A Newspaper Article** A signed newspaper article follows the form below:

> Hughey, Matthew W. "Fraternities Can't Fix Themselves." *New York Times* 14 March 2015, late ed.: A19. Print.

An unsigned newspaper article follows the same format:

> "Sports Briefs." *Charleston Gazette* 11 Mar. 2015: B4. Print.

NOTE: Cite the edition of a major daily newspaper (if given) after the date (1 May 2014, Midwest ed.: 1). If a local paper's name does not include the city of publication, add it in brackets (not italicized) after the name. To cite an article in a lettered section of the newspaper, list the section and the page number. (For example, A4 would refer to page 4 in section A of the newspaper.) If the sections are numbered, however, use a comma after the year (or the edition). Then indicate sec. 1, 2, 3, and so on, followed by a colon and the page number (sec. 1: 20).

32. **A Newspaper Editorial** Put *Editorial* (no italics) and a period after the title.

> Shibley, Robert. "Censorship Can't Cure Oklahoma Frat Racism; A Marketplace of Ideas is the Answer." Editorial. *USA Today* 12 Mar. 2015: A7. Print.

33. **A Letter to the Editor** Put *Letter* (no italics) and a period after the author's name.

> Pender, Vivian B. Letter. *New York Times* Mar. 13, 2015, late ed.: A28. Print.

34. **A Review** Begin with the author (if identified) and title of the review. Use the notation *Rev. of* (no italics) between the title of the review and that of the original work. Identify the author of the original work with the word *by* (no italics). Then follow with publication data for the review.

> D'addario, Daniel. "Literary Hack." Rev. of *Amnesia*, by Peter Carey. *Time* 23 Feb. 2015: 104. Print.

35. **An Abstract** To cite an abstract, first give the publication information for the original work (if any); then list the publication information for the abstract itself. Add the term *Abstract* and a period between them if the journal title does not include that word. If the journal identifies abstracts by item number, include the word *item* followed by the number. (Add the section identifier [A, B, or C] for those volumes that have one.) If no item number exists, list the page number(s).

> Faber, A. J. "Examining Remarried Couples through a Bowenian Family System Lens." *Journal of Divorce and Remarriage* 40.3/4 (2004): 121–133. Social Work Abstracts 40 (2004): item 1298. Print.

36. **An Unsigned Article in a Periodical** If no author is identified for an article, list the entry alphabetically by title among your works cited (ignoring any initial *A, An,* or *The*).

> "Arts & Entertainment: Quick Reviews." *Pittsburgh Post-Gazette.* 19 Mar. 2015, sooner ed.: WE16. Print.

37. **An Article with a Title or Quotation within Its Title** Use single quotation marks around the shorter title if it is normally punctuated with quotation marks, or if the source publication formats this title in quotation marks.

> McNulty, Charles. "Theater: 'Hamilton' Is Nearly Set to Make History." *Los Angeles Times* 8 Mar. 2015, home ed.: F1. Print.

38. **An Article Reprinted in a Loose-Leaf Collection** The entry begins with original publication information and ends with the name of the loose-leaf volume (*Youth*), editor, volume number, publication information including the name of the information service (SIRS), the article number, and the medium of publication.

> O'Connell, Loraine. "Busy Teens Feel the Beep." *Orlando Sentinel* 7 Jan. 1993: N. pag. *Youth.* Ed. Eleanor Goldstein. Vol. 4. Boca Raton: SIRS, 1993. Art. 41. Print.

39. **An Article with Pagination That Is Not Continuous** For articles that are continued on a nonconsecutive page, whatever the publication type, add a plus sign (+) after the first page number.

> Sylvester, Rachel. "Criminal Cartels Run Thousands of Slaves in Britain." *London Times* 7 Mar. 2015, natl. ed.: N4+. Print.

WORKS CITED ENTRIES: ONLINE AND ELECTRONIC SOURCES

Citations for online sources follow the strategies used for print sources, with a few additions to reflect the changeable nature of the Internet. After the author's name and the title of the document, include any print publication information; then list the electronic publication details and access information.

- Author's name
- Title of article or web page (italicized)
- Original/print publication information (if not exclusively online)
- Title of website (italicized)
- Site sponsor or publisher
- Version (volume and issue) number
- Date of electronic publication
- Medium (usually *Web*)
- Date of access

If any of these components do not apply, they are not listed. For documents with no listed date of electronic publication, use the site's posting date, date of update, or copyright date if available. Date of access means the most recent date on which you viewed the document online. URLs, if needed, are enclosed in angle brackets and should identify the complete address, including the access-mode identifier (http, ftp, telnet, and so on).

40. **An Entire Website** Most websites have sponsors or publishers, not a named author, so unless there is one, begin with the site title (italicized), followed by a period. Then provide the name of the site sponsor, the date of publication or update of the site, and the medium of publication (Web), followed by your date of access.

> *Foreign Languages and Literatures.* Marquette University, 2015. Web. 10 Mar. 2015.
>
> *The Millions.* The Millions, *2015.* Web. 10 Mar. 2015.
>
> Strickland, Ron. *Shakespeare on Stage.* Dept. of English, Illinois State U., 2014. Web. 5 Mar. 2015.

For personal websites, since it might be difficult for the reader to locate the site without an address, consider including the URL in angle brackets. A description such as *Home page* (not italicized) can substitute for a site name.

> Abbott, Debbie. Home page. Lucas College of Business, San Jose State University. Web. 30 Sept. 2014. <http://www.cob. sjsu.edu/abbott_d/>.

NOTE: If the URL is necessary and you must include a line break in it, do so only after a slash (see shown in the sample entry), and do not add a hyphen to indicate the break. For a URL that is long and complicated enough to invite errors in transcription, give the URL of the site's search page instead.

41. **A Scholarly Project or Information Database** The title of the site is listed first, then the name of the editor (if given). Follow this information with the version number (if relevant), date of publication or update (if available), name of the sponsor, medium of publication, and the date of access.

> *Women Writers Project.* Ed. Julia Flanders. Northeastern University, Oct. 2014. Web. 10 Mar. 2015.

If you are citing a book that is part of an online scholarly project, first list information about the printed book, followed by publication information for the project.

> Astell, Mary. *Reflections on Marriage.* London: Wilkin, 1706. *Women Writers Project.* Providence: Brown UP, 1999. Web. 7 Mar. 2015.

42. **A Specific Page or Document (Such as a Poem) on a Site** List the name of the document's or work's author (if given), the title of the shorter document or work (in quotation marks), and the name of the site where found (in italics).

"Poetry Near You." *Poets.org*. Academy of American Poets, 2015. 5 Mar. 2015.

If relevant, provide print publication information before electronic publication details.

Nemerov, Howard. "Found Poem." *War Stories*. By Nemerov. Chicago: U of Chicago P, 1987. Poets.org. Academy of American Poets. Web. 5 Mar. 2015.

43. **An Article in an Online Periodical** Begin with the author's name; the article title in quotation marks; the italicized name of the periodical, including the volume or issue number for scholarly journals; and the date of publication. Close with the medium of publication and the access date.

Williams, Mary Elizabeth. "I Gave Up Social Media for Lent." *Salon*. Salon Media Group, 18 Feb. 2015. Web. 9 Mar. 2015.

44. **An Article Accessed through a Subscription Database** Add the name of the database, italicized, after original publication information and before the medium.

Talib, Adam. "Sound and Sense in Classical Arabic Poetry." *Journal of Arabic Literature* 45.1 (2014): 129–32. *Academic Search Complete*. Web. 11 Mar. 2015.

45. **A Blog Post or Article**

Treat a blog post like any other periodical article. If there is no title for the post, use *Web log post* (using no quotation marks or italics) in place of it.

Sullivan, Andrew. "As the World Turns." *The Daily Dish*. 6 Feb. 2015. Web. 15 Mar. 2015.

46. **Comment on a Blog or Article, or Post to an Online Form**

Describe postings to online forums as *Online posting* (no italics). If a comment attached to an article does not have its own title, add *Comment* on (no italics) before naming the piece itself. Follow with the subject of the conversation or title of the piece.

Cubby, J. "Re: Connecting Playwrights and Theatre Companies." Online posting. 27 May 2004. AACT Online Forums: Playwriting & Playwrights. Web. 12 Jan. 2015.

Novak, Eric. Comment on "Pesticides and Bees: It's Complex." *Wired*. 18 Mar. 2015. Web. 19 Mar. 2015.

47. **A Post on Social Media (Facebook, Twitter, etc.)**

Goodwin, Megan. "Today's Portland Summary . . ." 18 Mar. 2015. Facebook post.

Parker, Alex (@Alex_Parker). "A writer's false name is a nom de plume. A chicken is a plume de nom. MyFrenchProbablyNeedsWork." 19 Mar. 2015. Tweet.

48. **A Podcast**

> Abumrad, Jad, host. "The Trust Engineers." *Radiolab*. WNYC, 9 Feb. 2015. Web. 10 Mar. 2015.

49. **An Online Video (YouTube)**

> Pollen, George. "Virginia Woolf's House." Online video clip. *YouTube*, 14 Feb. 2011. Web. 10 Mar. 2015.

50. **An Online Image** After the usual information for the type of work (painting, photograph, cartoon) being cited, add electronic publication information, including, in this instance, the URL.

> Goya, Francisco de. *Saturn Devouring His Children*. 1819–1823. Painting. Museo del Prado, Madrid. Web. 13 Mar. 2015. <http://www.usc.edu/ schools/annenberg/asc/projects/comm544/library/>.

51. **An Online Transcript of a Broadcast** Give the original publication information for the broadcast. Then add the description *Transcript* (no italics), followed by a period, the medium of publication, and the date of access.

> Lehrer, Jim. "Character above All." *The NewsHour with Jim Lehrer* 29 May 1996. Transcript. Web. 12 Mar. 2015.

52. **A Book Accessed Online or by e-Reader** In general, follow the format for printed books. Include publication information for the original print version if available. Follow the date of publication with the medium of publication (Web.) and the access date.

> Anderson, Sherwood. *Winesburg, Ohio*. New York: B. W. Huebsch, 1919. *Bartleby.com*. Web. 9 Mar. 2015.

When citing part of an online book, the title (or name of the part, such as *Foreword*) follows the author's name; the title of the book (italicized) is followed by its author's name if it is different from the first name listed.

> Untermeyer, Louis. "Author's Apology." *The Donkey of God*. iUniverse, 1999. Web. 7 Mar. 2015.

When citing an edition of a book accessed through an e-reader (such as a Kindle), note the type of e-reader as the medium:

> Ortberg, Mallory. *Texts from Jane Eyre*. New York: Macmillian, 2014. Kindle.

53. **An Article in an Online Reference Work** Unless the author of the entry is identified, begin with the entry name in quotation marks. Follow with the usual online publication information.

"Eakins, Thomas." *Britannica Concise Encyclopaedia* 2004. Encyclopaedia Britannica. Web. 26 Feb. 2015.

54. **An Online Government Publication** As with a government publication in print, begin with the name of the government (country, state, and so on), followed by the name of the agency. After the publication title, add the electronic publication information. (When citing the *Congressional Record*, the date and page numbers are all that are required.)

    United States. Dept. of Labor. Women's Bureau. *WB: An Overview*. Web. 12 Aug. 2014.

55. **A Publication in More Than One Medium** For a work that consists of more than one type of medium, either list all the media that make up the work or cite only the medium that contains the specific material cited in your paper.

    CultureGrams. Lindon: Axiom, 2002. Print, CD-ROM.

WORKS CITED ENTRIES: OTHER SOURCES: PRIMARY, PERSONAL, AND MULTIMEDIA

56. **A Periodically Published Database on CD-ROM or DVD-ROM** Materials published on CD-ROM or DVD-ROM are becoming rarer, but they still may be relevant to your research. Cite these like print sources, with these added considerations: (1) The contents of a work may vary from one medium to another; therefore, the citation must always identify the medium. (2) The publisher and vendor of the publication may be different, in which case both must be identified. (3) Multiple versions of the same database may exist, a situation that calls for citation of both the date of the document cited and the date of the database itself.

    Ackley, Patricia. "Jobs of the Twenty-First Century." *New Rochelle Informer* 15 Apr. 1994: A4. *New Rochelle Informer Ondisc*. CD-ROM. Info-Line. Oct. 1994.

57. **Computer Software or Apps** If you use a reference book recorded on CD-ROM, use the following format. If available, include publication information for the printed source.

    The American Heritage Dictionary of the English Language. 3rd ed. Boston: Houghton, 1992. Cambridge: Softkey Intl., 1994. CD-ROM.

    When citing a source accessed through applications on your phone or tablet, or an app itself, treat it like software. Be sure to include the version number.

    Byword. Vers. 2.3. Metaclassy, 2015. iPhone App.

58. **A Television or Radio Program**

> "The Ultimate Road Trip: Traveling in Cyberspace." *48 Hours*. CBS. WBBM, Chicago. 13 Apr. 1995. Television.

59. **A Film** The director, distributor, and year of release follow the title. Other information may be included if pertinent.

> *Eternal Sunshine of the Spotless Mind*. Dir. Michel Gondry. Perf. Jim Carey, Kate Winslet. Focus Features, 2004. Film.

60. **A Film or Television Program on DVD or Blu-Ray, or Streaming** Be sure to note the medium.

> *The Impressionists: Monet*. Kultur, 2006. DVD.

> Franklin, Carl, dir. "Chapter 14." Perf. Kevin Spacey. Perf. Robin Wright. *House of Cards*. Netflix, 14 Feb. 2014. Netflix Streaming Video. 12 Feb. 2015.

61. **An Audio Recording** Indicate *CD, LP,* or *MP3* (or similar), followed by a period. If you are citing a specific song on a musical recording, place its title in quotation marks before the title of the recording.

> Fey, Tina. *Bossypants*. Hachette Audio, 2011. MP3.
> Malloy, Dave. "Starchild." *Ghost Quartet*. Ghost Quartet, 2014. CD.

62. **A Performance** Treat this entry similarly to a film entry, adding the location and date of the performance.

> *Chanticleer: An Orchestra of Voices*. Young Auditorium, Whitewater, Wisc. 23 Feb. 2003. Performance.

63. **An Artwork on Display**

> Titian. *The Entombment*. 1602–1603. Oil on canvas. The Louvre, Paris.

64. **A Letter or e-Mail Received by the Author (You)** Here, TS following the date refers to "typescript" and MS refers to a handwritten letter ("manuscript").

> Thomas, Bob. Letter to the author. 10 Jan. 2015. TS.
> Selfon, Amanda. "Re: Middle English." 5 Mar. 2015. Email.

65. **An Interview by the Author (You)**

> Brooks, Sarah. Personal interview. 15 Oct. 2004.

66. **A Cartoon or Comic Strip (in print)**

> Luckovich, Mike. "The Drawing Board." Cartoon. *Time* 17 Sept. 2001: 18. Print.

67. **An Advertisement (in print)** List the subject of the advertisement (product, company, organization, or such), followed by *Advertisement* (no italics) and a period. Then give the usual publication information.

> Vaio Professional notebooks. Advertisement. *Campus Technology* Oct. 2014: 45. Print.

68. **A Lecture, a Speech, an Address, or a Reading** If there is a title, include it. Conclude with the descriptive label (for example, *Lecture*).

> Annan, Kofi. Acceptance of Nobel Peace Prize. Oslo City Hall, Oslo, Norway. 10 Dec. 2001. Lecture.

69. **A legal or historical document** Familiar historical documents such as the U.S. Constitution are typically not included in a Works Cited list because they can so easily be abbreviated in a parenthetical note within the text of your paper: "(US Const., art. 4, sec. 1)," for example. (Note that such documents are not italicized.)

> To list a legislative act in your works cited, begin with its name, then give its public law number, its date of enactment, and its Statutes-at-Large number.

> Do-Not-Call Implementation Act. Pub. L. 108-010. 11 Mar. 2003. Stat. 117–557. Print.

> Abbreviate the names of law cases (spelling out the first important word of each party's name). Do not italicize the name in your works cited (although it should be italicized within the body of your paper). Follow with the case number, the name of the court, and the date of decision.

> Missouri v. Seibert. No. 02-1371. Supreme Court of the US. 28 June 2004. Print.

70. **A Map or Chart** Follow the format for an anonymous book, adding the word *Map* or *Chart* (no italics), followed by a period, to conclude the entry.

> *Wisconsin Territory*. Madison: Wisconsin Trails, 2013. Map.

Model of Student Paper in MLA Style

Cassandra Lane's paper "Paper or Bioplastics?" uses the MLA documentation style that is the preferred style for English courses.

Cassandra Lane
Professor Davis
ENG 201
25 April 2008

Identifying information should be flush left and double-spaced.

Paper or Bioplastic?

The title is centered and double-spaced with no extra space above or below.

A plastic bag dances in circles, twirling and twisting with the dead leaves on the sidewalk in front of a red brick wall. It is so light that the wind picks it up and tosses it, as if it were one of the leaves.

The text begins two lines (one double-space) below the title and is double-spaced.

This bag is the epitome of beauty for Wes Bentley's character Ricky Fitts in *American Beauty*. The Internet Movie Data Base (IMDb.com) cites a similarly drifting paper bag as screenwriter Alan Ball's inspiration to write the film in the late 1990s. Although many Americans took the film's tagline "look closer . . ." (*American Beauty*) to heart and saw the bag as a symbol for all the little things we miss on a daily basis, isn't it just garbage? After a while, the bag begins to look like a blemish rather than the idyllic image Fitts saw.

Spell out the name of the organization and give the abbreviation in parentheses.

Italicize names of films.

That bag will take up to 1,000 years to break down into small pieces in landfills, and it will never biodegrade. Since plastic bags are polyethylene, a synthetic polymer that comes from petroleum, the microorganisms that consume biodegradable materials do not recognize plastic bags as food. Thus, plastic—a crude-oil-based product—has no place in the natural food chain. In brief, those bags are going to be with us for a long, long time, and the problems that they cause will also be with us. Not only do plastic bags create much of the bulk in landfills, but they also choke wildlife and act as blemishes on the face of otherwise beautiful landscapes. With environmental concerns growing rapidly around the world and movies like Al Gore's *An Inconvenient Truth* winning Oscars, a campaign

This information is general knowledge and requires no citation.

against that little plastic bag has retailers and consumers changing their behavior, signaling one way that the green movement has real roots.

The writer's last name appears in every header and is followed by the page number (without a comma).

The writer gives the author's credentials. Citation information appears on the Works Cited page.

Online source requires no page number.

Name the author and source for an author with more than one work cited.

Still, about 80 percent of customers choose plastic, according to a May 2007 article by Michael Milstein in *The Oregonian*. He argues that the plastic bags "are often more -convenient when walking and sturdier—especially in the rain" than paper alternatives. Michael Jessen, founder of Zero Waste Solutions (a small company in British Columbia that helps corporations reduce overall waste), disagrees. "This is one product that actually does more harm than good. Imagining our lives without plastic bags should be possible," said Jessen ("Bag Beast"). A world without plastic is possible and could become a reality.

The international community has already been paying increasing attention to the "floating dump of plastic bigger than the state of Texas in the North Pacific" (Jessen, e-mail). The Environmental Protection Agency says that more than 380 billion plastic bags are used in the United States every year, approximately 100 billion of which are plastic shopping bags (West). Some governments are playing an important role in decreasing the use of the plastic bag. For example, in March 2002, the Irish government levied a fifteen-cent tax on every plastic shopping bag (Jessen, "Bag Beast"). In the first year after the implementation of this Irish "PlusTax," consumption of plastic bags dropped almost instantly, resulting in a nearly five-billion-gallon reduction in the use of crude oil. Government officials and business owners were also pleased: the government gained $9.6 million in revenue, and retailers now were selling reusable totes as well as saving the approximately $50 million per year they were spending on plastic prior to the tax (Jessen, "Bag Beast").

In the United States, the movement is also catching on. The San Francisco Board of Supervisors voted in March 2007 to place an outright ban on plastic bags from large supermarkets and pharmacies, starting discussions of similar bans in many U.S. cities, including Phoenix; Santa Cruz, California; and Portland, Oregon (Viser).

Bans like the one in San Francisco made businesses and consumers look beyond the convenience of plastic, opening the door to viable alternatives. Many are turning to reusable cloth totes, but some (like the small, specialty grocery chain Trader Joe's) have started to use bags made of bioplastics—a compostable cousin to the old classic that is made out of renewable products such as corn or potato starch rather than crude oil (Cody).

Governments are not the only bodies capable of changing the way the world sees the plastic bag; individual firms and consumers are jumping on the green train as well. For example, Texas-based grocery chain Whole Foods recently promised on its website to rid itself of plastic bags by Earth Day 2008, turning instead to paper bags and reusable cloth totes that sell for 99 cents at most stores.

Some people are even starting to question the viability of the recyclable paper bag. Although some customers might balk at the idea of paying for their grocery bags, paper bags, although they are biodegradable and made from renewable resources, have a relatively short useful life. Cloth bags trump paper bags because their lives are long. Jessen argues that "paper cannot compete [with reusable cloth bags] when life-cycle costs are entered into the equation. The solution is to make people aware that we need to choose the option that can be continued as far as we can see into the future. Whatever choice we make must be viable at least seven generations into the future."

Firms such as Whole Foods and Trader Joe's have picked up on that idea and are trying to discourage the use of paper in their stores, offering incentives to every customer who brings his or her own bags when grocery shopping. The Whole Foods website offers "a refund of at least 5 cents per bag," and the San Francisco area Trader Joe's stores entered their environmentally friendly consumers in a raffle to win $25 worth of groceries.

This information is from an online posting.

But waste-reduction efforts across the United States are not all moving at the same pace. In Boston, companies such as CVS Pharmacies still offer only plastic bags. Although Matt Viser described a plastic ban in Boston that would mirror the ban in San Francisco in a *Boston Globe* article in April of 2007, there has been no successful legislation to date limiting Boston's plastic use. In the article, Viser quoted Christopher Flynn, president of the Massachusetts Food Association and an opponent to the proposed legislation, who claimed that legislators were "making the plastic bags a scapegoat for litter and environmental issues, which is not the ultimate problem. The problem is individuals and their own behavior."

The writer cites a work in which a quotation appears.

Actions taken by stores throughout Boston have successfully created change, though. Several local grocery store chains (including Shaw's and Trader Joe's) are starting to move in similar directions as their West Coast counterparts, away from plastic bags. Colorful signs reminding customers to "Make Beantown a

Greentown" hang from cash registers, shelves, and the ceiling throughout the Trader Joe's on Boylston Street in Boston, reminding every person who walks through the sliding doors to use reusable shopping bags. The store sells a variety of bags ranging from simple cloth bags to insulated bags for perishable groceries. For the customers who prefer to stick with single-use bags, Trader Joe's does have plastic bags, but unlike at CVS, the default bag is recyclable paper.

Grocery shopping is not the only place where consumers and suppliers are cutting out plastic: some retailers are also going green. Swedish home decoration store Ikea promises to "bag the plastic bag" in its stores by October 2008, according to an April 2008 article on *The Corporate Social Responsibility Newswire*. Ikea sells cloth bags for fifty-nine cents each and even assigns a five-cent price tag to plastic bags, with the proceeds going to the nonprofit conservation company, American Forests. The success of this experiment led to the proposed plastic bag ban by October 2008.

Raising awareness about banning plastic bags has become popular with fashion designers as well. "High-profile designers have already brought the plastic bag issue needed attention," wrote Michael Jessen in an e-mail to the author. Designers Marc Jacobs and Steve Madden replaced their disposable shopping bags with cloth bags that are reminiscent of the bags on sale in Shaw's and Trader Joe's. Making a fashion statement out of alternatives to single-use plastic bags can also mean profits: "Designers can charge something extra for their bags if they do so in conjunction with an initiative to encourage a ban on plastic," according to Jessen.

Though the movement to rid the world of plastic shopping bags is still in its infancy, the acceptance of the argument in favor of alternatives is growing in popularity and effectiveness. Whether this movement follows the failed path of a similar movement to reduce disposable diaper use remains an open question, but the support of government, retailers, and consumers is beginning to add up to less.

The writer cites an e-mail written to her.

Works Cited

American Beauty. Dir. Sam Mendes. Perf. Kevin Spacey and Annette Bening. Dreamworks SKG, 1999. Film.

"American Beauty (1999)." Internet Movie Database. Web. 22 Apr. 2008. Cody. Telephone interview. 29 Apr. 2008.

Jessen, Michael. "Re: Plastic Bag article." Message to the author. 21 Apr. 2008. E-mail.

Jessen, Michael. "The Bag Beast." *Environmentally Speaking: Michael Jessen Speaks Up for the Environment*. Web. 19 Apr. 2008.

Milstein, Michael. "Which Bag Is Best: Paper or Plastic?" *Oregonian* 17 May 2007. Web. 24 Apr. 2008.

"The Results Are in . . . Over 92% of IKEA Customers Bagged the Plastic Bag!" *Corporate Social Responsibility Newswire*. Online posting. 2 Apr. 2008. Web. 24 Apr. 2008.

Viser, Matt. "Plastic Bags May Be Banned in Boston." *Boston Globe* 26 Apr. 2007. Web. 24 Apr. 2008.

"We're going all out for reusable!" Online posting. Web. 26 Apr. 2008.

West, Larry. "Paper, Plastic, or Something Better?" *About.com: Environmental Issues*. Web. 24 Apr. 2008.

The header is centered.

Indent the second line of each entry five spaces or ½ inch.

Overview of APA Style

The *Publication Manual of the American Psychological Association* is the authoritative source for documenting research papers in the sciences and social sciences. You can consult the handbook or the website at www.apastyle.org for more detailed information. Here, you will get an overview of

- formatting the manuscript
- citing sources in the text
- creating a References page

At the end of this section is a portion of a student paper in APA style that you can use as a model.

Formatting the Manuscript (APA)

APA style has somewhat different requirements for formatting than MLA style, but presentation is just as important.

PAPER Use good-quality 8½ by 11-inch paper. Fasten your manuscript with paper clips; avoid staples and binders, both of which make it harder for your professor to read and comment on your work.

TITLE PAGE APA style calls for a separate title page, numbered as page 1. A title—or a shortened title if yours is long—and page number go against the right margin, about half an inch from the top of the paper. This running head should appear on all the pages of your paper.

Although APA does not specify how to format the title page, the usual format is to center your title about a third of the way down the page. Use regular type and the same font as in the rest of the manuscript (do not use all capital letters, italics, boldface, or the like). Double-space the title if it is longer than one line. Double-spaced and centered under the title, type your name. Double-spaced under your name, type your course number; then, after another double space, type the date.

ABSTRACT The second page of your paper is the abstract, a brief (no more than 120 words) summary of your paper. Center the word *Abstract* about 1 inch from the top of the page, and double-space the text.

MARGINS, SPACING, FONT, AND INDENTING Leave 1-inch margins on all four sides. Double-space your entire manuscript. Use easy-to-read fonts; 10-point to 14-point Times and Times New Roman are most commonly used. Indent a half inch at the beginning of each paragraph. For quotations of more than 40 words, indent a half inch, and do not use quotation marks. (Some professors will ask you to indent 1 inch in academic papers.) Double-space within the quotation.

PAGING Begin your paper on page 3.

HEADINGS Headings are encouraged in APA-formatted papers. If your material is complicated and would benefit from being subdivided, create headings that are brief, parallel in phrasing, and consistent in the font you use. Use no more than two levels of headings, if possible.

VISUALS If you include graphs, tables, maps, charts, illustrations, or photographs, place them directly after you introduce them in the text. Label the table at the *top* with the table number and title (Table 1. Album Titles and Release Dates). Label each figure *below* the image with a number and a caption that identifies it (Figure 1. Album revenues). Cite the source underneath the visual.

REFERENCES The final page of your paper is called References. Center the title about 1 inch from the top of the page. Do not add quotation marks, boldface, italics, and so on. Alphabetically list all works you referred to in the text of your paper, double-spaced with a hanging indent.

Citing Sources in the Text

The APA format requires you to cite at least the author and the date in the parenthetical citations within the text of your paper. Sometimes you will add the page reference as well. A citation should be brief but complete enough to lead your reader to the full citation in the References list at the end of the paper. The following list shows how to cite sources in the text of your paper.*

DIRECTORY TO IN-TEXT CITATIONS

1. One author: a complete work
2. One author: part of a work
3. One author: more than one publication in the same year
4. Works by authors with the same last name
5. Two to five authors
6. Six or more authors
7. A work authored by a committee or other organization
8. A work with no author indicated
9. A work referred to in another work
10. A work in an anthology
11. An electronic or other Internet source
12. An entire website
13. Two or more works in a parenthetical reference
14. A sacred text or famous literary work
15. A personal communication

SAMPLE IN-TEXT CITATIONS

1. **One Author: A Complete Work** The correct form for a parenthetical reference to a single source by a single author is opening parenthesis, last name, comma, space, publication year, closing parenthesis. Also note that final punctuation should be placed outside the parentheses.

   > The great majority of Venezuelans live near the Caribbean coast (Anderson, 2001).

2. **One Author: Part of a Work** When you cite a specific part of a source, give the page number, chapter, or section, using the appropriate abbreviations (*p.* or *pp.*, *chap.*, or *sec.*). Always give the page number for a direct quotation.

   > Bush's 2002 budget, passed by Congress, was based on revenue estimates that "now appear to have been far too optimistic" (Lemann, 2003, p. 48).

---

* Reprinted with permission from The College Writer's Handbook *by Randall VanderMey, Verne Meyer, John Van Rys, and Pat Sebranek (2006).*

3. **One Author: More Than One Publication in the Same Year** If the same author has published two or more articles in the same year, avoid confusion by placing a small letter *a* after the first work listed in the references list, *b* after the next one, and so on. The order of such works is determined alphabetically by title.

Parenthetical Citation

Coral reefs harbor life forms heretofore unknown (Milius, 2001a, 2001b).

References

Milius, D. (2001a). Another world hides inside coral reefs. *Science News*, 160 (16), 244.

Milius, D. (2001b). Unknown squids—with elbows—tease science. *Science News*, 160 (24), 390.

4. **Works by Authors with the Same Last Name** When citing different sources by authors with the same last name, it is best to add the authors' initials to avoid confusion, even if the publication dates are different. When possible, mention the author's name in the text the first time material is used. Afterward, including the name in parentheses is appropriate.

Although J. D. Wallace (2005) argued that privatizing Social Security would benefit only the wealthiest citizens, others such as E. S. Wallace (2006) supported the movement toward greater control for individuals.

5. **Two to Five Authors** In APA style, all authors—up to as many as five—must be mentioned in the first text citation, like this:

Love changes not just who we are, but who we can become, as well (Lewis, Amini, & Lannon, 2000).

NOTE: The last two authors' names are always separated by a comma and an ampersand (&) when enclosed in parentheses.

After the first mention, use only the name of the first author followed by *et al.* (the Latin abbreviation for *et alii*, meaning "and others"), like this:

These discoveries lead to the hypothesis that love actually alters the brain's structure (Lewis et al., 2000).

6. **Six or More Authors** If your source has six or more authors, refer to the work by the first author's name followed by *et al.*, (no italics) for both the first reference in the text and all references after that. However, in your references list, be sure to list the first six authors; any additional authors can be shortened to *et al.*

According to a recent study, post-traumatic stress disorder (PTSD) continues to dominate the lives of Vietnam veterans, though in modified forms (Trembley et al., 2005).

7. **A Work Authored by a Committee or Other Organization** Treat the name of the group as if it were the last name of the author. If the name is long and easily abbreviated, provide the abbreviation in square brackets. Use the abbreviation without brackets in subsequent references, as follows:

First Text Citation

A continuing problem for many veterans is heightened sensitivity to noise (National Institute of Mental Health [NIMH], 2005).

Subsequent Citations

In addition, veterans suffering from PTSD continue to have difficulty discussing their experiences and sharing suicidal thoughts with family members or mental health professionals (NIMH, 2005).

8. **A Work with No Author Indicated** If your source lists no author, treat the first two or three words of the title as you would an author's last name. A title of an article or a chapter belongs in quotation marks, whereas the titles of books or reports should be italicized:

One key to avoiding serious back injuries and long-term back pain is adopting low-stress postures especially in the workplace ("Diagnosing Back," 2001).

9. **A Work Referred to in Another Work** If you need to cite a source that you have found referred to in another source, mention the original source in your text. Then, in your parenthetical citation, cite the secondary source, using the words *as cited in*, like this:

A key development in the research on bipolarity was the theorem given by Richards (as cited in McDonald, 1998).

NOTE: In your references list at the end of the paper, you would write out a full citation for McDonald, not Richards.

10. **A Work in an Anthology** When citing an article or a chapter in an anthology or a collection, use the names of the authors of the specific article, not the names of the anthology's editors. (The article should also be listed by its authors' names in the References section.)

Phonological changes can be understood from a variationist perspective (Guy, 2005).

11. **An Electronic or Other Internet Source** As with print sources, cite an electronic source by the author (or by a shortened title if the author is unknown) and the publication date (not the date that you accessed the source). If citing a specific part of the source, use an appropriate abbreviation: *p.* (page), *chap.* (chapter), or *para.* (paragraph).

> One study compared and contrasted the use of Web and touch screen transaction log files in a hospital setting (Nicholas, Huntington, & Williams, 2001).

12. **An Entire Website** Whenever possible, cite a website by its author and posting date. In addition, refer to a specific page or document rather than to a home page or a menu page. However, if you are referring to a specific part of a Web page that does not have page numbers, direct your reader, if possible, with a section heading and a paragraph number.

> According to the National Multiple Sclerosis Society (2003, "Complexities" section, para. 2), understanding of MS could not start to take shape until the 1920s, when scientists began to research nerve transmission.

13. **Two or More Works in a Parenthetical Reference** Sometimes it is necessary to provide several citations in one parenthetical reference. In that case, cite the sources as you usually would, separating the citations with semicolons. Place the citations in alphabetical order, just as they would be ordered in the References list:

> These near-death experiences are reported with conviction (Rommer, 2000; Sabom, 1998).

14. **A Sacred Text or Famous Literary Work** Sacred texts and famous literary works are published in many different editions. For that reason, the original date of publication may be unavailable or not pertinent. In these cases, use your edition's year of translation (*trans. 2003*) or indicate your edition's year of publication (*2003 version*). When you are referring to specific sections of the work, it is best to identify parts, chapters, or other divisions instead of your version's page numbers.

> An interesting literary case of such dysfunctional family behavior can be found in Franz Kafka's *The Metamorphosis*, where it becomes the commandment of family duty for Gregor's parents and sister to swallow their disgust and endure him, endure him and nothing more (trans. 1972, part 3).

Books of the Bible and other well-known literary works may be abbreviated if no misunderstanding is possible.

> "Generations come and generations go, but the earth remains forever" (*The New International Version Study Bible*, 1985 version, Eccles. 1.4).

15. **A Personal Communication** Personal communications may include personal letters, phone calls, memos, e-mail messages, and so forth. Because they are not published in a permanent form, APA style does not place them among the citations in your references list. Instead, cite them only in the text of your paper in parentheses, like this:

> The manifestation of such kleptomania late in life can be explained by the disintegration of certain inhibitions, according to M. T. Cann (personal communication, April 1, 2005). However, such criminal trespasses are minor compared with the more serious breakdown of mental processes through dementia (M. T. Cann, personal communication, April 1, 2005).

NOTE: For more information about APA style, check out www.apastyle.org. There you can find a list of answers to frequently asked questions, the most recent details for citing electronic sources, and advice for avoiding bias about gender, race, sexuality, and disabilities in your writing.

Creating a References Page

The last page of your paper will be titled *References*. All the parenthetical citations that you inserted in your paper refer your reader to the complete entry in this final list. Include each work you cited in your paper but not works that you read but did not cite. Alphabetize your list by last name of the author or, in the case of an entry without an identified author, by the first word of the title, excluding the articles *A*, *An*, and *The*.

DIRECTORY TO APA REFERENCES ENTRIES

Books and Other Documents

1. A book by one author

2. A book by two or more authors

3. An anonymous book

4. A chapter from a book

5. A single work from an anthology

6. One volume of a multivolume edited work

7. A separately titled volume in a multivolume work

8. A group author as publisher

9. An edition other than the first

10. Two or more books by the same author

11. An English translation

12. An article in a reference book

13. A reprint, different form

14. A technical or research report

15. A government publication

Periodicals

16. An article in a scholarly journal, consecutively paginated

17. An abstract of a scholarly article (from a secondary source)

18. A journal article, paginated by issue

19. A journal article, more than seven authors

20. A review

21. A magazine article

22. A newspaper article

23. A newsletter article

Online Sources

24. A periodical accessed online (with DOI)

25. A periodical accessed online (no DOI)

26. A multipage document created by a private organization

27. An article accessed through a subscription database

28. A nonperiodical online document

29. A document or an abstract available on a university website

30. A report from a university, available on a private organization's website

31. A U.S. government report available on a government agency website

32. A paper presented at a symposium or other event, abstract retrieved from a university site

33. An e-mail message

34. Electronic book (e-book)

Reference Material

35. Online encyclopedia

36. Online dictionary

37. Wiki

Other Sources

38. Audio podcast

39. Weblog (blog) post

40. Message posted to a newsgroup, online forum, or discussion group, or comment on a blog or article

41. Specialized computer software with limited distribution

42. An application (app)

43. A television or radio broadcast

44. A television or radio program (episode in a series)

45. Online video (YouTube or similar)

46. An audio recording

47. A music recording

48. A motion picture

49. A published interview, titled, single author

50. An unpublished paper presented at a meeting

51. Social media post (Facebook, Twitter, etc.)

APA REFERENCE ENTRIES: BOOKS AND OTHER DOCUMENTS

The general APA form for a book or brochure entry is this:

Author, A. (year). *Title*. Location: Publisher.

- Author's last name and initial(s) followed by a period
- Year of publication in parentheses followed by a period
- Title lowercased in italics, with only the first word and any proper nouns capitalized, followed by a period
- Publication city (and state, province, or country if the city is not well known for publishing) followed by a colon
- Publisher name followed by a period

1. **A Book by One Author**

    Miller, K. R. (2013). *Coming clean*. New York, NY: New Harvest Press.

2. **A Book by Two or More Authors** Follow the first author name (or names) with a comma; then join the last and next-to-last names with an ampersand (&) rather than with the word *and*. List up to six authors; abbreviate subsequent authors as *et al.*

Lynn, J., & Harrold, J. (1999). *Handbook for mortals: Guidance for people facing serious illness*. New York: Oxford University Press.

3. **An Anonymous Book** If an author is listed as *Anonymous*, treat that word as the author's name. Otherwise, follow this format:

   American Psychological Association. (2009). *The publication manual of the American Psychological Association* (6th ed.). Washington: Author.

   NOTE: In this title, the words *American Psychological Association* are capitalized because they are a proper name. The words publication manual are not capitalized.

4. **A Chapter from a Book** List the chapter title after the date of publication, followed by a period or appropriate end punctuation. Use the word *In* before the book title, and follow the book title with the inclusive page numbers of the chapter.

   Tattersall, I. (2002). How did we achieve humanity? In *The monkey in the mirror* (pp. 138–68). New York: Harcourt.

5. **A Single Work from an Anthology** Start with information about the individual work, followed by details about the collection in which it appears, including the page span. When editors' names come in the middle of an entry, follow the usual order: initial first, surname last. Note the placement of the word *Eds.* in parentheses.

   Guy, G. R. (2005). Variationist approaches to phonological change. In B. D. Joseph & R. D. Janda (Eds.), *The handbook of historical linguistics* (pp. 369–400). Malden, MA: Blackwell.

6. **One Volume of a Multivolume Edited Work** Indicate the volume in parentheses after the work's title.

   Holmes, P., Sternberg, & Farnfield, S. (Eds.). (2014). *The Routledge handbook of attachment: Theory* (Vol. 3). New York, NY: Simon & Schuster.

7. **A Separately Titled Volume in a Multivolume Work** When a work is part of a larger series or collection, as with this example, make a two-part title consisting of the series and the particular volume you are citing.

   The Associated Press. (1995). *Twentieth-century America: Vol. 8. The crisis of national confidence: 1974–1980*. Danbury, CT: Grolier.

8. **A Group Author as Publisher** When the author is also the publisher, simply put the word *Author* in the place where you would list the publisher's name.

   Amnesty International. (2011). *Freedom: Stories celebrating the universal declaration of human rights*. New York, NY: Random House.

9. **An Edition Other Than the First** Indicate a second or subsequent edition with that edition's publication date (not the first edition's) plus the edition number in parentheses after the title. Writers accustomed to MLA citations must remember that APA references capitalize only the first word and any proper nouns in a title.

> Macionis J. J. (2014). *Society: The basics* (13th ed.). New York, NY: Pearson.

10. **Two or More Books by the Same Author** When you are listing multiple works by the same author, arrange them by the year of publication, earliest first.

> Gladwell, M. (2013). *David and Goliath: Underdogs, misfits, and the art of battling giants*. New York, NY: Little, Brown.

> _____. (2008). *Outliers: The story of success*. New York, NY: Little, Brown.

11. **An English Translation**

> Setha, R. (1998). *Unarmed* (R. Narasimhan, Trans.). Chennai, India: Macmillan. (Original work published 1995)

12. **An Article in a Reference Book** Start the entry with the author of the article, if identified. If no author is listed, begin the entry with the title of the article.

> Lewer, N. (1999). Non-lethal weapons. In *World encyclopedia of peace* (pp. 279–280). Oxford: Pergamon Press.

NOTE: If you use the original work, cite the original version; the non-English title is followed by its English translation, not italicized, in square brackets.

13. **A Reprint, Different Form**

> Albanov, V. (2000). *In the land of white death: An epic story of survival in the Siberian Arctic*. New York: Modern Library. (Original work published 1917)

NOTE: This work was originally published in Russia in 1917; the 2000 reprint is the first English version. If you are citing a reprint from another source, the parentheses would contain "reprinted from *Title*, pp. 000, by A. Author, year, Location: Publisher."

14. **A Technical or Research Report**

> Green, M., Travis, J., & Downs, R. (2001). *ADAM preliminary 2000 findings on drug use and drug markets: Adult male arrestees*. Washington: National Institute of Justice.

15. **A Government Publication** Generally, refer to the government agency as the author. When possible, provide an identification number for the document after the title in parentheses.

National Institute of Justice. (2012). *National Institute of Justice Annual Report 2012* (NIJ Publication No. 12-244249.). Washington, DC: Office of Justice Programs, U.S. Department of Justice.

APA REFERENCE ENTRIES: PERIODICALS The general form for a periodical entry is this:

> **Author, A. (year). Article title. *Periodical Title, Volume Number*, page numbers.**

- Last name and initial(s) as for a book reference
- Year of publication in parentheses and followed by a period
- Title of article in lowercase, except for the first word and any proper nouns (not italicized or in quotations), followed by a period
- Title and volume number of periodical italicized and capitalized, each followed by a comma
- Inclusive page numbers, with all digits repeated, separated by a dash
- DOI, if provided (See page 470 for more on digital object identifiers, now used along with citations for both print and online sources.)

Include some other designation with the year (such as a month or season, spelled out in full) if a periodical does not use volume numbers. The entries that follow illustrate the information and arrangement needed to cite periodicals.

16. **An Article in a Scholarly Journal, Consecutively Paginated** Pay attention to the features of this basic reference to a scholarly journal:

> Burger, J. M. (2014). Situational features in Milgram's experiment that kept his patients shocking. *Journal of Social Issues, 70*, 489–500. doi:10.111/josi.12073

17. **An Abstract of a Scholarly Article (from a secondary source)** When referencing an abstract published separately from an article, provide publication details of the article followed by information about where the abstract was published.

> Shlipak, M. G., Simon, J. A., Grady, O., Lin, F., Wenger, N. K., & Furberg, C. D. (2001, September). Renal insufficiency and cardiovascular events in postmenopausal women with coronary heart disease. *Journal of the American College of Cardiology, 38*, 705–711. Abstract obtained from *Geriatrics*, 2001, *56*(12), Abstract No. 5645351.

When the dates of the article and the secondary source abstract differ, the reference in your text would cite both dates, the original first, separated by a slash (2001/2002). When the abstract is obtained from the original source, the word *Abstract* is placed in brackets following the title (but before the period).

NOTE: When the page numbering of the issue starts with page 1, the issue number (not italicized) is placed in parentheses after the volume number.

18. **A Journal Article, Paginated by Issue**

Dougherty, L. R., Leppert, K. A., Merwin, S. M., Smith, V. C., Bufferd, S. J., & Kushner, M.R. (2015). Advances and directions in preschool mental health research. *Child Development Perspectives, 9*(1), 14–19. doi:10.1111/cdep.12099

19. **A Journal Article, More Than Seven Authors**

Talih, S., Balhas, Z., Eissenberg, T., Salman, R., Karaoghlanian, N., Hellani, A. E., Baalbaki, R., . . . Shihadeh, A. (2015). Effects of user puff topography, device voltage, and liquid nicotine concentration on electronic cigarette nicotine yield: Measurements and model predictions. *Nicotine and Tobacco Research, 17,* 150-157. doi:10.1093/ntr/ntu174

20. **A Review** To reference a book review or a review of another medium (film, exhibit, and so on), indicate the review and the medium in brackets, along with the title of the work being reviewed by the author listed.

Updike, J. (2001, December 24). Survivor/believer [Review of the book *New and Collected Poems 1931–2001*]. *The New Yorker*, 118–122.

21. **A Magazine Article**

Rettew, D. (2014, January). Do you have a disorder or just a trait? Rethinking the idea that psychiatric "illness" is easily defined. *Psychology Today*, 42.

NOTE: If the article is unsigned, begin the entry with the title of the article:

The myth of cool. (2014, November). *Psychology Today*, 23.

22. **A Newspaper Article** For newspaper articles, include the full publication date, the year followed by a comma, the month (spelled out), and the day. Identify the article's location in the newspaper using page numbers and section letters, as appropriate. If the article is a letter to the editor, identify it as such in brackets following the title. For newspapers, use *p.* or *pp.* before the page numbers; if the article is not on continuous pages, give all the page numbers, separated by commas.

Accusations of sexual abuse against U.N. workers are cited. (2015, March 17). *The New York Times*, pp. A11, A13.

Isherwood, C. (2015, March 10). Slaves in need of a very special ship. *The New York Times*, p. C1.

23. **A Newsletter Article** Newsletter article entries are very similar to newspaper article entries; only a volume number is added, in italics.

Teaching mainstreamed special education students. (2002, February). *The Council Chronicle, 11*, 6–8.

APA REFERENCE ENTRIES: ONLINE SOURCES The 2007 *APA Guidelines to Electronic References* present a few changes to references to materials retrieved electronically. They include the following:

- *For journal articles*: Include both journal issue number and volume number for all journals, whether the pagination is separate for each issue or continuous in the volume.
- *Retrieval date*: Include the retrieval date for undated or changeable content retrieved from Web sources, especially from the open Web. Do not include the retrieval date for material with fixed publication dates, such as a journal article or a book.
- *The Digital Object Identifier (DOI)*: The Digital Object Identifier (DOI) is a string of numbers and letters often published on the first page of an article. (Sometimes the DOI may be under a button for "article," "Cross-Ref.," or the vendor's name.) When activated, it will link to the content you are referencing. Whenever this DOI is available, substitute it for the URL in the reference.
- *Reference books*: Include the home page or menu page URL for dictionaries and encyclopedias.

24. **A Periodical Accessed Online (with DOI)**

    Author, A., & Author, B. (year). Title of article. *Title of Periodical, volume* (issue), inclusive page numbers (if available). doi: letters and numbers (no period)

    Nelson, G., Aubry, T., & Lafrance, A. (2007). A review of the literature on the effectiveness of housing and support, assertive community treatment, and intensive case management interventions for persons with mental illness who have been homeless. *American Journal of Orthopsychiatry, 77*(3), 350–361. doi: 10:1037/0002–9432.77.3.350

25. **A Periodical Accessed Online (no DOI)**

    Author, A., & Author, B. (year). Title of article. *Title of Periodical, volume* (issue), inclusive page numbers (if available). Retrieved from electronic address (no period)

    Dyer, J., & Beck, N. (2007). Psychocardiology: Advancing the assessment and treatment of heart patients. *E-Journal of Applied Psychology, 3*(2), 3–12. Retrieved from http://ojs.lib.swin.edu.au/index.php/ejap/ issue/view/13

NOTE: Include an issue number in parentheses following the volume number if each issue of a journal begins on page 1. Use the abbreviation *pp.* (page numbers) in newspapers. Page numbers are often not relevant for online sources. End the citation with a period unless it ends with the electronic address.

26. **A Multipage Document Created by a Private Organization**

> National Multiple Sclerosis Society. (n.d.) *About MS: For the newly diagnosed.* Retrieved March 15, 2015, from http://www.nationalmssociety.org

NOTE: Use *n.d.* ("no date") if a date is unavailable. Provide the URL of the home page for an Internet document when its pages have different URLs.

27. **An Article Accessed through a Subscription Database** If an article has an assigned DOI, there is no need to reference the database where you found it; treat it just like a print source, and include the DOI. However, if there is no DOI, list the database as shown here.

> **Author, A., & Author, B. (year). Title of article or webpage. *Title of Perodical, volume number*, inclusive page numbers. Retrieved Month day, year, from name of database.**
>
> Moksnes, U. K., Espnes, G. A., & Haugan, G. (2014). Stress, sense of coherence, and emotional symptoms in adolescents. *Psychology & Health*, 29(1), 32–49. Retrieved March 15, 2015, from Academic Search Complete.

NOTE: If the document cited is an abstract, include *Abstract* before the *Retrieved from* statement. The item or accession numbers are optional.

28. **Nonperiodical Online Document**

> **Author, A., & Author, B. (year, Month day). *Title of work.* Retrieved Month day, year, from electronic address**
>
> Boyles, S. (2015). *Wireless medicine.* Retrieved March 19, 2015, from http://webmd.com/new/future-of-health/#wireless-medicine
>
> Catholic Near East Welfare Association. (2002). Threats to personal security. In *Report on Christian emigration: Palestine* (sect. 5). Retrieved March 19, 2015, from http://www.cnewa.org/news-christemigrat-part1.htm

NOTE: To cite only a chapter or section of an online document, follow the title of the chapter with "In *Title of document* (chap. number)." If the author is not identified, begin with the title of the document. If a date is not identified, put *n.d.* in parentheses following the title.

29. **A Document or an Abstract Available on a University Website**

> **Author, A., & Author, B. (year). *Title of work.* Retrieved Month day, year, from name of host: electronic address**

Magill, G. (2001). *Ethics of stem cell research*. Retrieved March 15, 2015, from St. Louis University, Center for Health Care Ethics website: http://www.slu.edu/centers/chce/drummond/magill.html

NOTE: Name the university or government agency (and the department or division, if it is named), followed by a colon and the URL.

30. **A Report from a University, Available on a Private Organization's Website**
List the university and the institute as authors, followed by the publication date, the report's title, and retrieval information.

> **University, Institute. (year, Month).** *Title of work.* **Retrieved Month day, year, from electronic address**

> University of Wisconsin, Sonderegger Research Center and Kaiser Family Foundation. (2014, July). *Prescription drug trends*. Retrieved March 15, 2015, from http://www.kff.org/content/2014/3019/

NOTE: If the private organization is not listed as an author, identify it in the "retrieved from" statement.

31. **A U.S. Government Report Available on a Government Agency Website**
> **Name of government agency. (year, Month day).** *Title of report.* **Retrieved Month day, year, from electronic address**

> United States Department of Commerce, Economics and Statistics Administration. (2015, February). *Indicators*. Retrieved March 19, 2015, from http://www.esa.doc.gov/content/indicators

NOTE: If no publication date is indicated, use *n.d.* in parentheses following the agency name.

32. **A Paper Presented at a Symposium or Other Event, Abstract Retrieved from a University Website**
> **Author, A. (year, Month day).** *Title of paper.* **Paper presented at name of event. Abstract retrieved Month day, year, from electronic address**

> Dolakova, V., Voracek, J, & Zelena, V. (2013, February 7). *Corporate language culture as a promising performance driver*. Paper presented at International Conference on Management, Leadership and Governance, Bangkok University, Thailand. Abstract retrieved March 19, 2015, from http://academic-conferences.org/pdfs/icmlg_2013-abstract-booklet.html

NOTE: To cite a virtual conference, do not use *Abstract* before the *retrieved from* statement.

33. **An e-Mail Message** An e-mail is cited only in the text of the paper, not in the References list.

34. **Electronic Book (e-book)** Use "available from" when the URL leads you to information about how to access the book online. Use "retrieved from" when the URL leads directly to the book.

> Galsworthy, John. (n.d.). *The forsyte saga*. Retrieved from http://www.gutenberg.org/catalog/world/readfile?fk_files=101684

When you access an e-book through a device like a Kindle, do not provide a URL or access date; just treat the book like a print text, citing the publication date of the Kindle edition.

APA REFERENCE MATERIAL

35. **Online Encyclopedia** If no author appears in the article, begin with the title. Include the retrieval date and the home or index page URL.

> Forging, in criminal law. In *The Columbia encyclopedia*. Retrieved May 12, 2015, from http://www.bartleby.com/65/.

36. **Online Dictionary**

> Forgery. (n.d.). In *The free dictionary*. Retrieved March 13, 2015, from http://www.thefreedictionary.com/forgery

37. **Wiki** Like *Wikipedia*, all wikis are open to anyone who wishes to write, edit, or change the entry.

> Schizophrenia—Developmental factors. (n.d.). Retrieved May 14, 2008, from *The Psychology Wiki*: http://psychology.wikia.com/wiki/Schizophrenia_Developmental_factors

APA REFERENCE ENTRIES: OTHER SOURCES

38. **Audio Podcast** Include all the information you can find, including date, title, and identifier.

> Adams, B. (2007, November 12). *The theory of social revolutions* [Audio podcast]. LibriVox. Retrieved from details http://www.archive.org/revolutions_librivox

39. **Weblog (blog) Post**

> Lee, K. (2015, March 16). How to create shareworthy Twitter images: 10 ways to maximize engagement on your tweets [Web log post]. On *Buffer*. Retrieved from https://blog.bufferapp.com/social-media-report

40. **Message Posted to a Newsgroup, an Online Forum, a Discussion Group or a Comment on a Blog or Article** If the author's name is not available, use the screen name. Include the date of posting.

> Howarth, D. (2005, June 6). Intellectual property rights [Meg 6]. Message posted to the information forum, archived at http://www.wipo.int/roller/comments/ipisforum/Weblog/theme_seven_how_is_intellectual#comment6

41. **Specialized Computer Software with Limited Distribution** Standard, non-specialized computer software does not require a reference entry. Treat software as an unauthored work unless an individual has property rights to it. Indicate the software version in parentheses after the title, and note the medium in brackets.

> Carreau, S. (2001). Champfoot (Version 3.3) [Computer software]. Saint Mandé, France: Author.

42. **An Application (app)**

> Handup. (2014). *Handup vote* (Version 2.0.1) [Mobile application software]. Retrieved from http://itunes.apple.com

43. **A Television or Radio Broadcast** List a broadcast by the show's producer or executive producer, and identify the type of broadcast in brackets after the show's title.

> Crystal, L. (Executive Producer). (2011, February 11). *The NewsHour with Jim Lehrer* [Television broadcast]. New York, NY, and Washington, D.C.: Public Broadcasting Service.

> Bianculli, D. (Host). (2013, June 27). "Americanah" author explains "learning" to be black in the U.S. *Fresh Air* [Radio broadcast]. Washington, D.C.: National Public Radio. Retrieved from http://www.npr.org/2014/03/07/286903648/americanah-author-explains-learning-to-be-black-in-the-u-s

44. **A Television or Radio Program (episode in a series)** When identifying a specific episode in a television or radio series, identify the episode by its writers, if possible. Then follow with the airing date, the episode title, the type of series in brackets, and details about the series itself.

> Tambor, J. (Performer). (2014, September 26). Moppa [Television series episode]. In J. Solloway (Producer), *Transparent*. Seattle, WA: Amazon.

45. **An Online Video (YouTube or similar)**

> Playbill Video. (2014, March 21). Life with Laura: Laura Benanti teaches a master class for young actors [Video file]. Retrieved from https://www.youtube.com/watch?v=E94FUhkO5H8

46. **An Audio Recording** Begin the entry with the speaker's or writer's name, not the producer's. Indicate the type of recording in brackets.

> Offerman, Nick. (2014). *Paddle Your Own Canoe: One Man's Fundamentals for Delicious Living* [CD]. New York, NY: Penguin Audio.

47. **A Music Recording** Give the name and function of the originators or primary contributors. Indicate the recording medium (CD, record, cassette, and so on) in brackets, immediately following the title.

> Mike Noordzy Quintet. (2013). *Oo-chee-wa-wa* [MP3]. Edison, NJ: Nacht Records.

48. **A Motion Picture** Give the name and function of the director, producer, or both. If its circulation was limited, provide the distributor's name and complete address in parentheses.

> Anestis, P. (Director). (2013). *Galileo: Fighting in the dawn of modern science* [Motion picture]. Greece: Eugenides Foundation.

49. **A Published Interview, Titled, Single Author** Start the entry with the interviewer's name, followed by the date and the title. Place the interviewee's name in brackets before other publication details.

> Brockes, Emma. (2014, March 21). Don't we all write about love? [Interview with Chimamanda Ngozi Adichie]. *The Guardian*. Retrieved from http://www.theguardian.com/books/2014/mar/21/chimamanda -ngozi-adichie-interview

50. **An Unpublished Paper Presented at a Meeting** Indicate when the paper was presented, at what meeting, in what location.

> Clark, A. (2015, March). *Gender parity*. Paper presented at the meeting of Voices of the Middle West: Midwestern Gothic, Ann Arbor, Michigan.

51. **Social Media Post (Facebook, Twitter, etc.)**

> Loewy, D. (2015, February 2). I was curious about the reasons social justice workers run so many marathons . . . [Facebook status update]. Retrieved from https://www.facebook.com/david.loewy.5?fref=ts

> Whitburne, S. K. (@swhitbo). (16 March 2015). Crossing the street may be the very essence of #neurosis, even when the light says "walk" #psych#mental #health http://ow.ly/KoBmC [Tweet]. Retrieved from https://twitter.com/swhitbo/status/577500903265140738

NOTE: Use the abbreviations below in all APA reference entries. With author's names, shorten first and middle names to initials, leaving a space after the period. For a work with more than one author, use an ampersand (*&*) before the last author's name.

For publisher locations, use the full city name plus the two-letter U.S. Postal Service abbreviation for the state. For international publishers, include a province and country name; for well-known publishing cities such as Boston, you may offer the city only.

Spell out *Press* in full, but for other publishing information, use these abbreviations:

chap.	Chapter	n.d.	No date
ed.	Edition	No.	Number
Ed.	Editor	Pt.	Part
Eds.	Editors	p. (pp.)	Page (pages)
Rev. ed.	Revised edition	Vol.	Volume
2nd ed.	Second edition	Vols.	Volumes
Trans.	Translator(s)		

Model of a Student Paper in APA Style

THIS VERSION of Eóin O'Carroll's paper, "Unchained Melodies," uses the APA documentation style that is appropriate for a communication or sociology course. The title page, the abstract, the first page of text, and the References page that are reprinted here illustrate the main points of the APA style of documentation.

The title of the paper appears in the header, followed by five spaces and the page number.

Unchained Melodies: Music and Innovation in the Digital Age

Eóin O'Carroll

ENG 201

The title, writer's name, and class go in the center of the title page, double-spaced.

Reprinted by permission of Eóin O'Carroll.

APA

The abstract should be single-spaced and no more than 120 words. It should outline the paper. (See more about writing abstracts on the Writing in the Works Website.)

Abstract

Record companies are claiming that free mp3 downloads are killing music, but it is really the labels, not the consumers, that are killing music. Even if digital music is hurting album sales—and experts disagree over whether they do—many recording artists are embracing free mp3s for the increased exposure they offer. At the same time, recording artists are complaining that they are being harmed by the labels' business practices. Digital music potentially allows the musician to make a fair wage while providing a broader range of music to the consumer for less money. And they do not need the record labels to do it.

The paper begins on page 3.

Unchained Melodies: Music and Innovation in the Digital Age

The title is centered and double-spaced.

In the early eighties, the record industry was experiencing a sharp decline in sales. Falling revenues, they claimed, were the fault of the blank audiocassette. "Home taping is killing music" was the industry slogan at the time. Today, with sales slumping again, the record industry is making the same dire predictions. The bugbear of the Recording Industry Association of America (RIAA) this time is not audiocassettes and home tapes, but peer-to-peer networks and mp3 file sharers. On September 8, 2003, the day that the RIAA launched its first round of lawsuits against file sharers, the association issued a press release quoting president Cary Sherman: "We simply cannot allow online piracy to continue destroying the livelihoods of artists, musicians, songwriters, retailers, and everyone in the music industry" (RIAA, 2003, p. 4).

The text begins two lines below the title and is double-spaced.

Eóin spells out the name of the organization and gives the abbreviation in parentheses.

This press release is from a Web page and doesn't have a page number. When citing quotations or facts from Web pages without page numbers in APA style, give the paragraph number.

It is hard to say, however, to what extent digital music is responsible. If file sharing is cutting into album sales, it is not necessarily a bad thing—after all, people who make CD burners have livelihoods, too. Moreover, cutting into album sales is not necessarily the same thing as "killing music." Rather, many of the record industry's practices are killing music. Digital music is more likely to rescue it.

To review some background to present events, in the late 1970s, the record industry saw a looming crisis. After hitting an all-time high in 1978, album sales were declining precipitously. Between 1978 and 1982, sales dropped more than forty percent, with revenues falling from $6 billion to about $3.5 billion (Liebowitz, 2003, p. 7).

This internal text citation gives the author's last name, the year, and the page number. The citation is surrounded by parentheses and followed by a period. Note the p. before the page number.

APA

APA

References

Alderman, J. (2001). *Sonic boom: Napster, MP3, and the new pioneers of music.* Cambridge: Perseus.

Berman, D. (2000). Lars Ulrich vs. Chuck D: Facing off over Napster. *Business Week*. May 25, 2000. Retrieved March 11, 2004, from http://www.business-week.com/ebiz/0005/0525ulrich.htm

Brown, D. (2003). Home taping did not kill music. CBC News Viewpoint. October 23, 2003. Retrieved March 11, 2004, from Canadian Broadcasting Company website: http://www.cbc.ca/ news/viewpoint/vp_browndan/ 20031023.html

Electronic Frontier Foundation. Making P2P pay artists. (n.d.). Retrieved March 11, 2004, from http://www.eff.org/share/compensation.php

Ian, J. (2002). The Internet debacle: An alternative view. Retrieved March 10, 2004, from http://www.janisian.com/article-internet_debacle.html

Jenkins, M. (2002). Hit charade: The music industry's self-inflicted wounds. *Slate*. August 20, 2002. Retrieved March 11, 2004, from http://slate.msn. com/?id=2069732

Lessig, L. (2001). *The future of ideas*. New York: Random House.

Liebowitz, S. (2003). Will MP3 downloads annihilate the record industry? The evidence so far. Retrieved March 9, 2004, from University of Texas at Dallas website: http://www.pub.utdallas.edu/~liebowit/intprop/records.pdf

Love, C. (2000). Courtney Love does the math. *Salon*. June 14, 2000. Retrieved March 2, 2004, from http://archive.salon.com/tech/feature/2000/06/ 14/love

Recording Industry Association of America. (2003). Recording industry begins suing P2P file sharers who illegally offer copyrighted music online. Retrieved March 9, 2004, from the RIAA website: http://www.riaa.com/news/newsletter/090803.asp

Straziuso, J. (2004). Music piracy activity slows. *Detroit Free Press*. February 23, 2004. Retrieved on March 13, 2004, from *Detroit Free Press* website: http:// www.freep.com/money/business/bnews23_20040223.htm

Heading is centered.

Indent the second line of the citation five spaces.

No posting date was available on this site.

If you must break a Web address into two lines, put the break after a period or slash. Never hyphenate a Web URL.

If a page is part of a large and complex website, such as that for a university or a government agency, identify the host organization before the URL. Precede the URL with a colon.

16 DOCUMENTATION

Figure Captions
Figure 1 Album sales over the past three decades
(Liebowitz, 2003, p. 7)

Figure 1

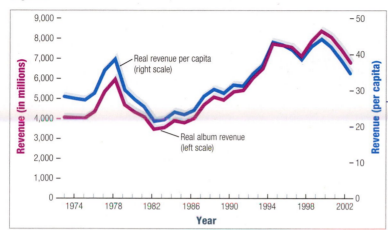

When appropriate, use figures to illustrate your argument.

GRAMMAR HANDBOOK

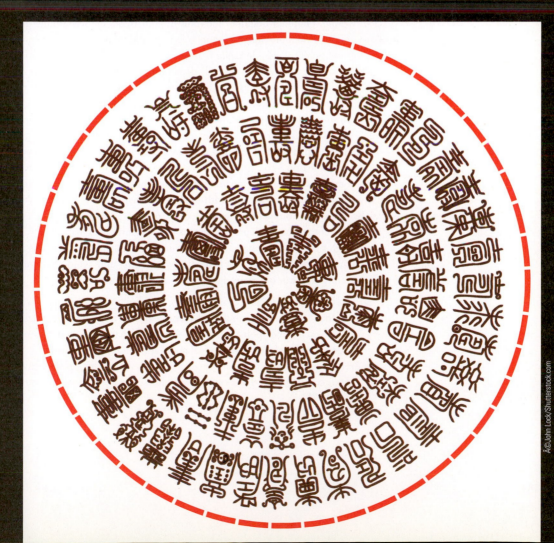

Why Study Grammar?

Grammar enables us to practice the three behaviors that mark us as literate human beings: it helps us write with power, read with a critical eye, and talk about how meaning is made.

—ROY PETER CLARK

Some people believe that grammar is a set of ironclad rules they must memorize. Others believe that grammar describes a constantly shifting system of conventions, ways to communicate clearly and predictably within a community of people who speak and write in that language. Our view is this: rules exist. Some may seem confusing at first, but the purpose of learning grammar is to understand the basic patterns of the language in which you are writing. In a very real sense, when you are engaged in the act of writing, grammar describes the tools of your trade. Understanding grammar allows you to write more precisely, more elegantly, and even more creatively.

On the practical side, in college, at work, and in your community, your ideas will be considered more or less seriously depending on how well you use the conventions of standard, written grammar. Poor grammar creates a kind of static between you and your reader, making it hard for the reader to "hear" what you are saying. Good grammar skills give you another real-world advantage. You can accomplish the basic work of writers: refining, editing, and proofreading your own writing so that you can say exactly what you mean to say the way you mean to say it. When you learn grammar for a reason—to edit your own work, to write with clarity, to improve your style—it may make new sense to you, perhaps in a way it never has before. To ensure that your good ideas will be read with the interest they deserve, learn the rules and play by them. Later on, perhaps, you can break them.

The next three chapters provide an overview of grammar. Chapter 17 will guide you through a review of the basic vocabulary of grammar, and Chapter 18 is a review of punctuation rules. Chapter 19 will help you identify and avoid common grammatical errors. You can use these chapters in a number of ways.

- You can read each chapter sequentially, first building a grammar vocabulary, and then using that vocabulary to identify and correct common errors. At the end of each major point is a practice exercise that you can use to test your understanding of that grammatical point and reinforce its concept.
- You can use the chapters as a reference handbook, looking up the conventions of punctuation (18b–f, for example), or the rules governing subject-verb agreement (19b–1).

- Each topic is keyed to one of the numbers and letters in the outline printed at the beginning of each chapter as well as in the index.
- You can use the practices to test your skills in identifying and fixing errors in a text and then to review the points you do not understand.
- You can keep a grammar log of the errors you make in your papers and key them to the sections that address those issues.

GRAMMAR REFRESHER

©Andriy Zholudyev/
Shutterstock.com

487

17a Parts of Speech

Knowing the basic parts of speech gives you the vocabulary to talk about grammar and gives you an important understanding of how each part of speech functions. The following is a brief overview of the eight parts of speech.

17a-1 Nouns

Nouns name people, places, things, or abstract concepts: *daughter, city, pencil, hope.*

■ **Countable Nouns** **Countable nouns** name countable things and have a plural form: *book (books), child (children), friend (friends).*

■ **Noncountable Nouns** **Noncountable nouns** name things that you cannot count, so they do not have a plural form: *courage, advice, information* (see 20a).

■ **Proper Nouns** **Proper nouns** name specific persons, places, organizations, months, and days of the week. Proper nouns are capitalized: *Mother Jones, Central College, TGI Fridays.*

■ **Common Nouns** **Common nouns** name general persons, places, things, or abstract concepts: *parent, school, weekdays.*

■ **Collective Nouns** **Collective nouns** name groups but are usually referred to as single entities: *a committee, an audience, a community.*

17a-2 Pronouns

Pronouns substitute for or refer to nouns, noun phrases, or other pronouns. The noun that the pronoun refers to is its **antecedent**.

> *Professor Garcia* read from *her* new book. [*Professor Garcia* is the antecedent of *her.*]

> *Travel* is *its* own reward. [*Travel* is the antecedent of *its.*]

■ **Personal Pronouns** **Personal pronouns** refer to specific persons, places, or things. Personal pronouns can be subdivided by their function in a sentence, whether they substitute for nouns that function as subjects (see 17b-1), substitute for nouns that function as objects (see 17b-2), or show ownership or possession (see 18e-1).

Subject Pronouns (SP)	Object Pronouns (OP)	Possessive Pronouns (PP)
I	*me*	*my, mine*
you	*you*	*your, yours*
he, she, it	*him, her, it*	*his, her, hers, its*
we	*us*	*our, ours*
they	*them*	*their, theirs*
who/whoever	*whom/whomever*	*whose*

She talked about *her* travels in Asia.
^{SP}   ^{PP}

We gave *her* a standing ovation.
^{SP}   ^{OP}

■ **Indefinite Pronouns** **Indefinite pronouns** refer to nonspecific persons, places, or things and do not need antecedents: *all, any, anybody, anyone, anything, both, every, everybody, everyone, everything, few, many, most, none, no one, nothing, somebody, someone, something, several, some.*

> *Everyone* was fascinated by Professor Garcia's adventures.
>
> *No one* stirred as she talked.

■ **Reflexive Pronouns** **Reflexive pronouns** refer back to the subject or to another noun or pronoun in the sentence.

Singular	Plural
myself	*ourselves*
yourself	*yourselves*
himself	
herself	*themselves*
itself	

> Megan traveled for six months by *herself*.
>
> Megan saw the other students starting off by *themselves*.

■ **Intensive Pronouns** **Intensive pronouns** emphasize nouns and use the same forms as reflexive pronouns.

> Megan *herself* made all the arrangements.
>
> We *ourselves* decided it was the right time to travel.

■ **Relative Pronouns** **Relative pronouns** introduce dependent clauses (see 17b-4): *who, whom, whose, whoever, whomever, whichever, whatever, that, which, what.*

> Professor Garcia was the professor *who* influenced me the most.
>
> Biology class was the one class *that* I never missed.

■ **Interrogative Pronouns** **Interrogative pronouns** begin questions: *who, whom, which, what, whose.*

> *Who* went with you?
>
> *Whose* car did you take?

■ **Demonstrative Pronouns** **Demonstrative pronouns** point back to their antecedent nouns, noun phrases, or clauses: *this, that, these, those.*

> Amy got an interview with the lead singer of her favorite band.

PRACTICE 17.2

Pronouns

Identify the boldfaced words in the following sentences as personal pronouns (PP), indefinite pronouns (IP), reflexive pronouns (REF), intensive pronouns (INT), relative pronouns (REL), interrogative pronouns (INTER), or demonstrative pronouns (DP).

1. Colonel Mustard **himself** put the coded message in **its** secret hiding place.

2. **Anyone** can collect stamps by ordering **them** on the Internet. **Who** wants to order stamps?

3. The architect **who** put the Arts and Crafts detail on **your** front door was a genius.

4. Give the mitten to **whoever** needs warm clothing for the camping trip.

5. Five years ago, **someone** left a mysterious message on **my** phone. **That** was weird. ■

That was the highlight of her year.

She wrote these two articles for her school paper. *This* is better than *that*.

17a-3 Verbs

Verbs express action (*read, love, study*) or a state of being (*is, seem, appear*).

■ **Auxiliary Verbs** Some auxiliary verbs are forms of *to be, to do,* and *to have* that help the main verbs.

> Frida *was* painting in her studio. *(be, am, is, are, was, being, been)*
>
> Frida *does* paint well. *(do, does, did)*
>
> Frida *has* painted beautiful landscapes. *(have, has, had)*

Other auxiliary verbs, called **modals**, express probability, such as *may/might, can/could, will/would, shall/should, must, ought to,* and *have to.*

> Frida *ought to* contact a gallery.
>
> She *might* become as famous as her namesake, Frida Kahlo.

■ **Transitive Verbs** Transitive verbs (**VT**) show action and transfer that action from the subject to the receiver of the action, which is called the **direct object (DO)**. The direct object answers the question *what?* or *whom?* after the verb.

> Frida *paints* abstract *landscapes.*
>
> She *loved* Maria.

■ **Intransitive Verbs** Intransitive verbs (**VI**) may express an action, but there is no receiver of that action, no direct object. Common intransitive verbs are *lie, sit, sleep, occur, die, fall, walk, go,* and *come.*

> Frida *sat* on a stool while she painted.
>
> When she finished her work, Frida *slept* soundly.

■ **Linking Verbs** Linking verbs (**LV**), also known as state-of-being verbs, link the subject to a word after the verb. The word can either describe the subject (an adjective) or rename the subject (a noun). The most common linking verb is the verb *to be* in any of its forms: *am, are, is, was, were.*

> Frida *is* lovely. [*Lovely* describes Frida.]
>
> Frida *is* my cousin. [*Cousin* renames Frida.]

Other linking verbs that can express a state of being are *feel, seem, look, taste, smell,* and *appear,* depending on how they are used in the sentence. The verb *feel,* for example, can be either a transitive verb, taking a direct object, or a linking verb, connecting an adjective to the subject.

I *feel* the material between my thumb and index finger. [*Feel* is transitive; it takes the direct object *material*.]

I *feel* sad today. [*Feel* is a linking verb, expressing a state of being and linking the adjective *sad* to the subject *I*.]

■ **Verb Tenses** Verb tenses change to indicate the time of an action or process, often relative to the time of the writing.

	Present	Past	Future
Simple	*I paint*	*I painted*	*I will paint*
Progressive	*I am painting*	*I was painting*	*I will be painting*
Perfect	*I have painted*	*I had painted*	*I will have painted*

Verbs in the **progressive tense** use a form of *to be* plus the *-ing* form of the verb to show actions that continue for a while.

This morning I *am painting* the third in my landscape series.

Yesterday I *was painting* my second landscape.

Verbs in the **perfect tense** express actions completed by the present, past, or future time.

I *have painted* my series, and I am ready for the show.

I *had painted* my second landscape before I fell asleep.

I *will have painted* the entire series when the show opens.

■ **Verb Moods** Verbs express three **moods**. Verbs in the **indicative** mood make statements or ask questions.

I *will paint* today.

Will you *join* me?

Verbs in the **imperative** mood issue commands.

Come in here!

Do not make a mess.

Verbs in the **subjunctive** mood express wishes in conditional terms or hypothetical conditions.

I wish I *were* as good a painter as Frida.

If I *had taken* lessons when I was young, I *might be* an artist today.

17a-4 Adjectives

Adjectives modify, describe, identify, or give information about nouns and pronouns. Adjectives can be placed before the nouns or pronouns they modify or after linking verbs. Adjectives placed after linking verbs are called **predicate adjectives**. (*Predicate*

PRACTICE 17.3

Verbs

Identify the verbs in the following sentences as transitive verbs (VT), intransitive verbs (VI), or linking verbs (LV).

1. The night sky **seemed** luminous.

2. Joe **slept** past noon every day on his vacation.

3. Leah **ran** the marathon in record time.

4. We **felt** the first stirrings of love that night.

5. Ethan **felt** strong after his workout.

Choose the correct verb tense or mood in the following sentences.

1. Before Zachary (**made/had made**) plans, he (**checked/ had checked**) online for the movie times.

2. When Kayla (**ran/ is running**) fast, she always wins the race.

3. If Mac (**was/were**) in charge, things would be different around here.

4. Yoshi made the changes to the proposal that she and Mac (**discussed/had discussed**).

5. When Ben (**was/were**) younger, he was always in trouble. ■

The *fresh* breeze blew past Joel's head. [*Fresh* modifies *breeze*.]

The breeze felt *fresh*. [*Fresh* is a predicate adjective and modifies *breeze*.]

Adjectives show degree or intensity. The suffix *-er* or the use of the adverb *more* makes an adjective comparative, and the suffix *-est* or the use of the adverb *most* makes the adjective superlative.

Positive	Comparative	Superlative
fresh	*fresher*	*freshest*
independent	*more independent*	*most independent*

■ **Articles** *A*, *an*, and *the* are types of adjectives that are called **articles**. (See also 20a.) *A* and *an* are **indefinite articles** because they describe one of a number of things.

Give Becca *a* book to read, and she is happy.

***A* library can be *a* sanctuary.**

The is a **definite article** because it describes only one thing or class of things.

Give me *the* book on the shelf.

***The* local library is her sanctuary.**

17a-5 Adverbs

Adverbs modify or give information about verbs, adjectives, other adverbs, or entire clauses or sentences. They often explain *how, when, where, why,* or *to what extent* something happens. They convey manner, time, frequency, place, direction, and degree.

The thief ran *quickly* down the alley. [The adverb *quickly* modifies the verb *ran*.]

The *very* fast thief jumped the fence. [The adverb *very* modifies the adjective *fast*.]

The thief climbed the ladder *extremely quickly*. [The adverb *extremely* modifies the adverb *quickly*.]

***Unfortunately*, the thief escaped.** [The adverb *unfortunately* modifies the entire sentence.]

■ **Conjunctive Adverbs** **Conjunctive adverbs** modify clauses or sentences while helping to connect a clause or sentence to the previous one. Some conjunctive adverbs are *consequently, however, moreover, therefore, thus,* and *for example.*

> The thief escaped. *However,* he turned himself in the next day.

> He was filled with remorse; *moreover,* he returned the money he stole.

17a-6 Prepositions and Prepositional Phrases

Prepositions are often short words like *of, by, for, to, in,* and *around* that begin prepositional phrases. They often show relationships of time and space. Some common prepositions are *about, above, across, after, along, around, before, behind, below, beneath, beside, between, by, except, for, from, in, into, like, near, of, on, through, to, under,* and *with.*

> *Around* the block

> *In* the air

> *Down* the street

> *Across* the avenue

> *To* the meeting

> *At* one o'clock

A **prepositional phrase** is made up of the preposition and the words that follow it. The noun or pronoun after the preposition is called the *object of the preposition.*

PREPOSITIONAL PHRASE	PREPOSITIONAL PHRASE
PREP. OBJECT	PREP. OBJECT

Ben went *around the neighborhood on his new bicycle.*

PREP. PHRASE	PREPOSITIONAL PHRASE
PREP. OBJ.	PREP. OBJ.

At dusk he went *into his house.*

17a-7 Conjunctions

Conjunctions join two or more similar sentence parts, such as words, phrases, and clauses.

■ **Coordinating Conjunctions** **Coordinating conjunctions (CC)** link two or more parallel words, phrases, or clauses. The seven coordinating conjunctions are *and, but, for, or, nor, so,* and *yet.*

> The baker made tarts *and* pies. [The coordinating conjunction *and* connects the two words *tarts* and *pies.*]

> He couldn't decide whether to make a crust *or* to buy one. [The coordinating conjunction *or* connects the two phrases *to make a crust* and *to buy one.*]

> He made the pie crust, *but* he bought the tart shell. [The coordinating conjunction *but* connects the two clauses *He made the pie crust* and *he bought the tart shell.*]

PRACTICE 17.5

Prepositions, Conjunctions, Interjections, and Expletives

Identify the boldfaced words in the following sentences as prepositions (P), coordinating conjunctions (CC), subordinating conjunctions (SC), correlative conjunctions (COR), interjections (I), or expletives (EX).

1. The Industrial Revolution began **when** steam-powered machines started spinning cotton thread.

2. The construction crew identified contaminated soil yet failed **to** report it **to** the Environmental Protection Agency.

3. **"Never!"** we answered **after** Coach asked when we would be willing to give up.

4. **Either** I will major in math, **or** I will go into engineering.

5. Bats are scorned and treated as pests, **but** they are useful in controlling mosquito populations.

6. **There** are compelling reasons to study biology, **and there** are equally good ones to specialize in mammals. ■

■ **Subordinating Conjunctions** Subordinating conjunctions (SC) introduce dependent clauses and connect them with independent clauses (see 17b-4). A subordinating conjunction establishes a relationship between dependent and independent clauses, usually telling *when, why,* or *under what conditions*. Some of the many subordinating conjunctions are *after, as, as soon as, because, before, even if, if, since, unless, when, while,* and *why.*

DEPENDENT CLAUSE
SC
When he ran out of cherries, the baker started making apple pies. [*When he ran out of cherries* is a dependent clause. *When* is the subordinating conjunction.]

DEPENDENT CLAUSE
SC
Our mouths watered *while* the pies cooled. [*While the pies cooled* is a dependent clause. *While* is the subordinating conjunction.]

■ **Correlative Conjunctions** Correlative conjunctions (COR) appear in different parts of the sentence but work together to join the two sentence parts. Common correlative conjunctions are *both/and, just as/so, either/or, neither/nor, not only/but also,* and *whether/or.*

Either cherry pie ***or*** apple pie is fine with me.

Not only does he love baking them, ***but*** he ***also*** loves eating them.

17a-8 Interjections and Expletives

Interjections are emotional exclamations and are often punctuated by the exclamation mark if they stand alone.

Eureka!

Ouch!

Wow!

Interjections can also be incorporated into sentences.

I smiled at him, but, *oh*, he made me mad.

***Darn*, he missed the bus.**

Expletives are words that are place markers. Since they are introductory words and are often followed by a form of *to be*, they are often mistaken for subjects of sentences. Expletives never function as subjects.

***There* are**

***Here* is**

Expletives tend to be overused and can cause confusion with subject-verb agreement. When possible, limit your use of expletives.

USE OF EXPLETIVES: ***There* are two reasons for us to go: economy and efficiency.** [The subject is *reasons.*]

OMITTED EXPLETIVE: Two reasons for us to go are cost and efficiency.

17b Parts of Sentences

17b-1 Subjects and Predicates

Sentences have two parts: subjects and predicates. The **simple subject** is the agent of the action, *who* or *what* the sentence is about, and the **simple predicate** expresses the action or, in the case of linking verbs, the state of being. (See also 20c.)

SUBJECT PREDICATE
The *senator voted.* [*Senator* is the subject; *voted* is the predicate.]

SUBJECT PREDICATE
The *bill passed.* [*Bill* is the subject; *passed* is the predicate.]

Most sentences are more complicated than a simple subject and predicate and include other words, phrases, and clauses that modify or complement the subject and predicate, forming the complete subject or the complete predicate.

SUBJECT PREDICATE
The angry senator in the first row voted vehemently against the motion. [The complete subject is *The angry senator in the first row*, and the complete predicate is *voted vehemently against the motion.*]

SUBJECT PREDICATE
The appropriation bill passed by a slim margin. [*The appropriation bill* is the complete subject, and the complete predicate is *passed by a slim margin.*]

17b-2 Complements

A word or group of words that completes a predicate is called a **complement**. Complements can be direct objects, indirect objects, object complements, and subject complements. Four common sentence patterns show how these complements are used. (See also 20c-1.)

- Subject + Transitive Verb + **Direct Object** (S + VT + DO): The **direct object** answers the question *what?* or *whom?* after a transitive verb.

SUBJECT PREDICATE
VT DO
The senators passed *the bill.*

SUBJECT PREDICATE
VT DO
The bill gave *more money* to schools.

- Subject + Transitive Verb + **Indirect Object** + Direct Object (S + VT + IO + DO): The **indirect object** answers the question *to whom?* or *to what?* after a transitive verb.

SUBJECT PREDICATE
VT IO DO
The senators handed *the clerk* the signed bill.

VT IO DO
The bill gave *the teachers* a pay raise.

PRACTICE 17.6
Parts of Speech

In the passage below, identify each boldfaced word as a noun (N), pronoun (P), verb (V), adjective (ADJ), adverb (ADV), preposition (PR), conjunction (C), interjection (I), or expletive (EX).

Watching a **film** is an experience like no other **that** I have had. **When** the **velvety darkness surrounds** me, I am **literally** transported **to** another **world**. Nothing exists **except** the screen and **me**. The **music** begins, the credits **roll, and I am completely hooked. Anyone who** knows me well **knows neither** to offer me a handful of popcorn **nor** to talk to me. I am by **myself in** my own world, apart from **everyday** reality. **Hush! It** is magic. ■

■ Subject + Transitive Verb + Direct Object + **Object Complement** (S + VT + DO + OC): The **object complement** describes (adjective) or renames (noun) the direct object.

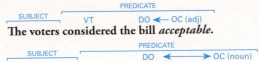

The voters considered the bill *acceptable.*

Illinois voters elected the clerk their *state senator.*

■ Subject + Linking Verb + **Subject Complement** (S + LV + SC): The **subject complement** describes or renames the subject after a linking verb (*be, become, appear, feel, seem*). (See 17a-3.)

A complement that describes the subject is called a **predicate adjective (PA).**

A complement that renames the subject is called a **predicate noun (PN).**

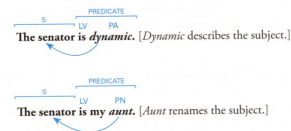

The senator is *dynamic.* [*Dynamic* describes the subject.]

The senator is my *aunt.* [*Aunt* renames the subject.]

USAGE TIP When you substitute a pronoun for a predicate noun, use the subject form of the pronoun: **The senator is *she.* It is *I.***

17b-3 Phrases

A **phrase** is a group of words that lacks a subject or a verb; it never expresses a complete thought by itself but instead modifies a noun or a verb. Four categories of phrases are prepositional phrases, verbal phrases, appositive phrases, and absolute phrases.

■ **Prepositional Phrases** A **prepositional phrase** contains a preposition with its object, which is the noun or pronoun in the phrase.

Over the river and *through* the woods, *to* grandmother's house we go.

■ **Verbal Phrases** Verbal phrases are formed from verbs but function as nouns or modifiers. Three types of verbal phrases are infinitives, gerunds, and participles.

■ **Infinitives** Infinitives are formed by adding to in front of the verb (*to pass, to run, to love*). An infinitive phrase includes the infinitive and its modifiers.

PRACTICE 17.7

Subjects and Predicates

Identify the complete subject and the complete predicate in the following sentences.

1. Life is good.

2. Our lives are sometimes easy and sometimes difficult.

3. I spent an exciting three weeks trekking through the rain forests of Costa Rica.

4. I hiked up mountains and through forests thick with vegetation.

5. Six of us who had taken a course in rock climbing went on a separate adventure. ■

PRACTICE 17.8

Complements

Show your understanding of complements by writing sentences in the following patterns.

1. Write a sentence with a transitive verb and a direct object.

2. Write a sentence with a transitive verb, an indirect object, and a direct object.

3. Write a sentence with a linking verb and a predicate adjective.

Jon gave himself a huge party *to celebrate his birthday.* [infinitive phrase]

He invited all his family, friends, and colleagues *to dance at a club.* [infinitive phrase]

- **Gerunds** A **gerund** is formed by adding *-ing* to a verb, and it functions as a noun in sentences. For example, a gerund could be the subject of a sentence or its direct object. A gerund phrase includes its modifiers.

GERUND AS SUBJECT

Passing the age of twenty **made Jon feel old.** [gerund phrase as subject]

GERUND AS DIRECT OBJECT

He loved *celebrating with his friends.* [gerund phrase as direct object]

- **Participles** **Participles** are formed by adding *-ing* in present tense or *-ed* in past tense to verbs, and they function as adjectives that modify nouns or pronouns. A participial phrase includes its modifiers.

The boy, *passing Micha on the street,* **broke into a run.** [present participle modifying the noun *boy*]

Running fast, **he looked back over his shoulder.** [present participle modifying the pronoun *he*]

Exhausted, **Ed slowed to a walk.** [past participle modifying the noun *Ed*]

- **Appositive Phrases** **Appositive phrases** modify the nouns or pronouns they follow by describing them in different words. An appositive phrase consists of the appositive (the word that describes the noun or pronoun) and its modifiers.

Jack, *my best friend from high school,* **broke into a run.** [appositive phrase describes *Jack*]

The appositive, *the word that describes the noun or pronoun,* **often appears between commas.** [appositive phrase describes *appositive*]

- **Absolute Phrases** An **absolute phrase** modifies a whole sentence or clause and consists of a noun plus a participle with its modifiers or complements. Absolute phrases can be placed anywhere in the sentence.

Noah tiptoed into the room, *his eyes squinting in the sudden light.*

Noah, *his eyes squinting in the sudden light,* **tiptoed into the room.**

His eyes squinting in the sudden light, **Noah tiptoed into the room.**

(continued)

4. Write a sentence with a linking verb and a predicate noun.

5. Write a sentence with a transitive verb, a direct object, and an object complement. ■

PRACTICE 17.9

Phrases

Identify the boldfaced phrases as prepositional (P), infinitive (I), gerund (G), participial (PL), appositive (APP), or absolute (ABS).

1. **Shooting a film** is Emma's ambition, but, *Finding Remo,* **her student film,** was terrible.

2. The animation came out jumpy, and no one wanted **to sit through the hour-long film.**

3. **Shooting their film,** Emma and Jesse felt totally confident.

4. **Sweat running down her face,** Jesse yelled, "It's a wrap."

5. **Making films** is truly all they want **to do.**

17b-4 Clauses

A **clause** is a group of words that includes both a subject and a verb. Clauses may be **independent clauses** or **dependent (subordinate) clauses**.

■ **Independent Clauses** Independent clauses (IC) express complete ideas. They can stand alone as complete sentences or be part of longer sentences.

INDEPENDENT CLAUSE
The film was tasteless.

INDEPENDENT CLAUSE
The film was tasteless **because it showed violence only to gross out the viewer.**

■ **Dependent Clauses** Dependent clauses (DC) (also called *subordinate clauses*) cannot stand alone. As all clauses do, a dependent clause has a subject and a verb, but it does not express a complete thought by itself. A dependent clause has to be linked to an independent clause for the meaning to be clear. The signal of a dependent clause is that it begins with a subordinating conjunction (SC), such as *if, when, because,* or *while,* or a relative pronoun (RP), such as *who, whom, which,* or *that.* (See 17a-7.)

INDEPENDENT CLAUSE — DEPENDENT CLAUSE
SC
The film was tasteless *because it showed violence only to gross out the viewer.*

DEPENDENT CLAUSE — INDEPENDENT CLAUSE
SC
If I could have gotten my money back, **I would have left in the middle.**

IC — DEPENDENT CLAUSE — IC
RP
My friends, *who do not usually mind violence,* **had to cover their eyes.**

■ **Noun Clauses** Dependent clauses can function in sentences as nouns, adjectives, or adverbs. **Noun clauses** function as subjects, objects, complements, or appositives, and they begin with relative pronouns such as *that, who, whom,* or *whoever* or with subordinating conjunctions such as *how, why,* or *whatever.*

SUBJECT
Whatever Jay decides to do **will make him successful.** [noun clause functions as subject]

DIRECT OBJECT
We know *why he works so hard.* [noun clause functions as direct object]

■ **Adjective Clauses** Adjective clauses, sometimes called *relative clauses,* modify nouns or pronouns, and they begin with relative pronouns such as *who, whose, whom, which,* or *that* or subordinating conjunctions such as *how, when,* or *where.*

His father, *whom Jay greatly admires,* **set the standard.** [adjective clause modifies *father*]

PRACTICE 17.10
Clauses

Identify the boldfaced clauses as either dependent or independent. Identify each dependent clause as a noun clause (NC), adjective clause (ADJ), or adverb clause (ADV).

1. Anne Bradstreet was a remarkable poet **who wrote in the seventeenth century.**

2. She came to America **when she was only sixteen.**

3. Even though she was so young, **she was already married to Simon Bradstreet.**

4. **Simon Bradstreet became governor** soon after they arrived from England.

5. **Anne, however, retired to the wilds of Andover and wrote poetry.** ■

The day *when his father retired* was the day Jay took over the business. [adjective clause modifies *day*]

■ **Adverb Clauses** Adverb clauses modify verbs, adjectives, other adverbs, or whole clauses, and they begin with subordinating conjunctions such as *before, because, if, when,* and *while.*

DEPENDENT CLAUSE   INDEPENDENT CLAUSE
SC
When he took over the business, Jay wrote a note to his father. [adverb clause modifies the independent clause]

INDEPENDENT CLAUSE   DEPENDENT CLAUSE
SC
Jay kept all his father's traditional values *as he updated the business.* [adverb clause modifies the independent clause]

17c Sentence Types

With an understanding of phrases and clauses, you can build interesting and varied sentences. The three essential types of sentences are simple, compound, and complex. These three types are the patterns on which all sentences are built.

17c-1 Simple Sentences

A **simple sentence** has one independent clause (IC). It can be a two-word sentence, with one subject and one verb, or it can be longer, including many modifiers and phrases but no other clauses. Both of the following sentences are simple sentences.

INDEPENDENT CLAUSE
SUBJECT   VERB
Kim studied.

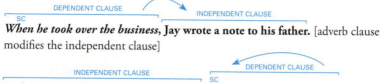

PREP. PHRASE   PREP. PHRASE   SUBJECT   PARTICIPLE PHRASE
On Tuesday evening between ten and midnight, *Kim,* **hoping to ace the**

VERB   PREP. PHRASE   PREP. PHRASE   PREP. PHRASE
course, *studied* **hard for her midterm exam in history on the causes of the**
PREP. PHRASE
Vietnam War.

A simple sentence can have great power. After a long, explanatory paragraph, a simple sentence can emphasize or clarify a point.

> At that moment I saw my father for what seemed like the first time. He was insecure, jealous, vulnerable, and weary. He was also kind, honest, hardworking, and brilliant. He was a perfect human being.

PRACTICE 17.11

Phrases and Clauses

Show your understanding of phrases and clauses by writing the following sentences. Identify each of the elements with a label.

1. Write a sentence that includes a prepositional phrase and an infinitive phrase.

2. Write a sentence that includes a gerund phrase.

3. Write a sentence that includes a participial phrase.

4. Write a sentence that has a subordinate clause that functions as a noun.

5. Write a sentence that has a subordinate clause that functions as an adjective.

6. Write a sentence that has a subordinate clause that functions as an adverb.

7. Write a sentence that has an infinitive phrase, a prepositional phrase, and a subordinate clause. Label each phrase or clause. ■

17c-2 Compound Sentences and Coordination

A **compound sentence** has at least two independent clauses connected by a coordinating conjunction (CC) (*and, but, for, or, nor, so,* or *yet*) that is preceded by a comma. Two independent clauses may also be connected by a semicolon.

INDEPENDENT CLAUSE   CC   INDEPENDENT CLAUSE
Kim studied for the exam, **and** *then she slept soundly.*

INDEPENDENT CLAUSE   INDEPENDENT CLAUSE
Kim studied for the exam; *then she slept soundly.*

INDEPENDENT CLAUSE   CC   INDEPENDENT CLAUSE   CC   INDEPENDENT CLAUSE
Kim studied for the exam, **and** *then she went to bed,* **but** *she slept fitfully.*

Too many compound sentences can create the rhythm of the breathless narratives of unsophisticated writing (*And then I went to the store, and I saw this man, and he had a big moustache, and I asked him if he saw my pet frog*).

Avoid too many compound sentences in a row, but a few well-constructed ones can be used to good effect to create a sense of **coordination**. Since compound sentences have independent clauses on either side of the conjunction, they can be used effectively to create a sense of balance in your writing. If you want to show two equally attractive alternatives or give equal emphasis to two ideas, the compound sentence is a good stylistic choice.

> We had not spoken a word to each other but I knew we were thinking the same thing. Her wide eyes stared into mine, and I could read what was behind them, a plan for her future, exactly what I prayed for, too.

17c-3 Complex Sentences and Subordination

A **complex sentence** has one independent clause and at least one dependent clause (DC). The dependent clause begins with a subordinating conjunction such as *although, because, if,* or *when* or a relative pronoun such as *which, who,* or *that*.

DEPENDENT CLAUSE   INDEPENDENT CLAUSE
SC
Although Kim studied hard, she slept fitfully.

DEPENDENT CLAUSE   INDEPENDENT CLAUSE   DEPENDENT CLAUSE
SC   SC
Although Kim studied hard, she slept fitfully because she was nervous.

The idea of one clause being dependent or subordinate should give you a clue about how to use the complex sentence most effectively in your writing. When one idea is less important than another or when one idea depends on another, you can use the structure of the complex sentence to subtly suggest this sense of **subordination**.

> **"Later that evening,** *when Thelma insists on stopping at a honky-tonk bar despite Louise's protestations,* **the gun comes in handy."**

—Janet Maslin, "On the Run with Two Buddies and a Gun"

PRACTICE 17.12
Sentence Types

Test your understanding of sentence types by identifying the sentences below as simple, compound, or complex.

1. When the stock market crashed, I thought I would not be affected.

2. I knew a few families that had invested their life savings.

3. They had worked hard, and they felt safe.

4. They had made some bad choices, but it was not out of ignorance or greed.

5. Everyone at that time was in the same situation.

6. When classes were over for the semester, Jeff went straight to bed.

7. He slept for two days in a state of complete exhaustion.

8. Jeff had hoped to spend the rest of the break relaxing; however, his empty bank account suggested otherwise.

9. Within a week he had one part-time job at the mall and one at a restaurant.

10. Jeff will finally be able to relax when classes begin again. ■

PUNCTUATION 18

501

Punctuation is a set of conventions used to clarify your meaning. Punctuation marks have two main purposes: to end sentences and to show grammatical relationships within sentences.

18a Proofreading Symbols

Copyeditors, writers, and writing teachers often use a shorthand method to indicate corrections they make while proofreading. Most proofreading symbols are easy to understand, and they give you a convenient way to make corrections when you proofread your own work or a writing partner's work during peer revision. The most common proofreading symbols are in the following chart.

Symbol	Example (change marked)	Example (change made)
^o	Correct a typo.	Correct a typo.
-r/ m-/ ^o	Correct more than one typo.	Correct more than one typo.
t	Insert a leter.	Insert a letter.
ɤ	Make a deletion.	Make a deletion.
Ɛ	Delete and close up space.	Delete and close up space.
#	Insertproper spacing.	Insert proper spacing.
# / ⌒	Inserts pace and close up.	Insert space and close up.
tr	Transpose letters indicated.	Transpose letters indicated.
tr	Transpose as words indicated.	Transpose words as indicated.
tr	Reorder shown as words several.	Reorder several words as shown.
⊏	Move text to left.	Move text to left.
⊐	Move text to right.	Move text to right.
₢	Indent for paragraph.	Indent for paragraph.
no ₢	No paragraph indent.	No paragraph indent.
run in	Run back turnover lines.	Run back turnover lines.
∫	Break line when it runs far too long.	Break line when it runs far too long.
⊙	Insert period here.	Insert period here.
⸝	Commas commas everywhere.	Commas, commas everywhere.
∨	Its in need of an apostrophe.	It's in need of an apostrophe.
∜ / ∜	Add quotation marks, he begged.	"Add quotation marks," he begged.
;	Add a semicolon don't hesitate.	Add a semicolon; don't hesitate.
:	She advised "You need a colon."	She advised: "You need a colon."
?	How about a question mark	How about a question mark?
ˆ=ˆ	Add a hyphen to a bill like receipt.	Add a hyphen to a bill-like receipt.
(/)	Add parentheses as they say	Add parentheses (as they say).
lc	Sometimes you want Lowercase.	Sometimes you want lowercase.
caps	Sometimes you want upperCASE.	Sometimes you want UPPERCASE.
ital	Add italics instantly.	Add italics *instantly*.
rom	But use *roman* in the main.	But use roman in the main.
bf	Add boldface if necessary.	Add **boldface** if necessary.

18b Periods, Question Marks, and Exclamation Marks

18b-1 Periods

Periods (.) are used at the ends of sentences; in abbreviations, decimals, and initials; and inside Internet addresses.

- **Sentences** A period is placed at the end of a declarative sentence or a mild command or request.

  The latest virus disabled my computer.

  Show me your paper.

- **Abbreviations** Periods are also used after most abbreviations: **Dr., Ms., Ph.D., a.m.**

  Mr. Carter won the Nobel Peace Prize in 2002.

  I will get my B.A. in three years.

Exceptions to this rule are names of organizations, countries, agencies, and U.S. Postal Service abbreviations of state names.

  CBS, USA, FBI, ME (Maine)

USAGE TIP If you end a sentence with an abbreviation that has a final period, do not add an end period: **In three years I will get my B.A.**

- **Decimals** Periods are used in decimals and fractional amounts of money.

  My GPA is 3.5.

  You owe me $3.50.

- **Initials and Internet Addresses** Periods are used with initials and computer addresses.

  You can buy F. Scott Fitzgerald's books on Amazon.com.

18b-2 Question Marks

A question mark (**?**) ends an interrogative sentence.

- **Direct Questions** Place a question mark after a direct question.

  Is this lecture confusing?

- **Direct Quotations** When used in direct quotations, question marks go inside the quotation marks when the quotation asks the question, and outside the quotation marks when the full sentence poses the question.

  Who said "Two paths diverged in a yellow wood"?

  I asked him, "Who wrote the poem?"

Madame Helen—does anyone remember her?—will be available for consultations after nine o'clock.

Do you believe in psychic occurrences? Extrasensory perception? Unidentified flying objects?

18b-3 Exclamation Marks

An **exclamation mark** (**!**) ends an urgent sentence or a sentence that shows emotion or excitement.

Bring me a bandage immediately!

I won!

USAGE TIP Limit your use of exclamation marks in formal writing. Try to find a verb that expresses excitement or emphasis rather than using punctuation to signal excitement. *Okay:* Schuyler was curious! *Better:* Schuyler bombarded me with questions.

18c Semicolons and Colons

18c-1 Semicolons

A **semicolon** (**;**) joins elements in a sentence in specific ways.

■ **Independent Clauses without Conjunctions** Use a semicolon to join two independent clauses that are not joined by coordinating conjunctions. Using a semicolon instead of a period is a stylistic decision that conveys that the ideas in the clauses are closely related.

Zoe laughed at his joke; she did not think it was funny. [closely related]

Zoe laughed at his joke. Conversation shifted to a new topic. [not closely related]

■ **Independent Clauses with Conjunctive Adverbs** Use a semicolon to connect independent clauses when the second begins with a conjunctive adverb such as *however, nevertheless, moreover, therefore,* or *thus,* or a transitional phrase such as *for example.* The conjunctive adverb or transitional phrase is followed by a comma.

Zoe laughed at his joke; however, she was offended.

She tried to change the subject; for example, she asked him where he went to school.

■ **Items in Subdivided Lists** Use a semicolon to separate items in a list, to avoid confusion if some items in the list are already separated by commas.

Tamar was at the party with her oldest friends, Marlene and Doug; her twin brothers, Caleb and Jacob; and Cindy and Peter, her coworkers.

PRACTICE 18.1

Periods, Question Marks, and Exclamation Marks

Proofread the following short passage. Add periods, question marks, and exclamation marks where necessary. Practice using the appropriate proofreading symbols from the proofreading chart.

Yesterday morning around five a m, two masked men robbed a jewelry store at 51 Main St in St Paul, MN and shot a bystander C B S and N B C had camera crews on the spot within the hour One eyewitness, Maria L Gonzalez, M D, asked the police how she could feel safe going on calls at night knowing she might bump into a thief She exclaimed, "I'm terrified" Then she asked, "How can I protect myself" You can follow the story on CNN com ■

18c-2 Colons

A **colon** (**:**) presents specific details.

■ **Before a List, Series, or Quotation** Use a colon to introduce a list, a series, or a formal or long quotation.

> **I did all my work: a history report, an article about cloning, a take-home exam, and math homework.**

> **All term my professor repeated this message: "If you manage your time well, you will be able to do all your work and have some time to relax."**

■ **Between Independent Clauses** Use a colon to connect two independent clauses when the second one illustrates or explains the first.

> **Ellen completed her work early and could do the one thing she had wanted to do all term: She slept for twelve hours straight.**

■ **Before an Example** Use a colon after a clause to provide a one-word example.

> **I completed my work early and could do the one thing I have wanted to do all term: sleep.**

■ **Other Uses** Some other common uses of the colon are as follows.

    ■ After a salutation in a formal letter or memorandum

> **Dear Professor:**

> **To: Ben Gould**

    ■ In a book title, to separate the subtitle from the title

> ***The Fourth Genre: Contemporary Writers of/on Creative Nonfiction***

    ■ In citations from the Bible or in bibliographic sources

> **Judges 11:3**

> **Trimmer, Joseph F. *The River Reader*. 12th ed. Boston: Houghton, 2003.**

    ■ In divisions of time

> **I get up at 6:05 every day.**

18d Commas, Dashes, and Parentheses

18d-1 Commas

A **comma** (**,**) clarifies relationships within a sentence.

■ **Lists** Use commas between items in a list.

> **Mia's progress has been slow, steady, and significant.**

PRACCTICE 18.2

Semicolons and Colons

Proofread the following short passage, and add semicolons and colons where necessary. Practice using the appropriate proofreading symbols from the proofreading chart shown earlier.

Dear Town Official

At 530 yesterday evening, I went to return *The Flight of the Iguana A Sidelong View of Science and Nature* to the library on Main Street however, I was unable to cross the street. The traffic was so fierce that I waited for a solid forty minutes then I returned to my home. It is time for this town to take its head out of the sand and install that new-fangled modern convenience a traffic light. ■

USAGE TIP Academic writers use a comma before the conjunction in a list; writers in journalism and media often omit the last comma before the conjunction. Whichever style you choose, be consistent.

- **Coordinate Adjectives** Use a comma between coordinate adjectives. (Coordinate adjectives each modify the same noun.)

Mia has shown a slow, steady improvement.

- **Introductory Phrases or Clauses** Use a comma after an introductory phrase or a dependent clause.

To improve over such a short time, **Mia had to have worked hard.**
[introductory phrase]

Since she had worked so hard, **Mia improved significantly.** [introductory dependent clause]

If the independent clause comes before the dependent clause, do not use a comma.

Mia improved significantly since she had worked so hard.

- **Coordinating Conjunctions** Use a comma before a coordinating conjunction (*and, but, or, for, nor, so, yet*) in a compound sentence.

Mia's improvement was significant, but she was still not happy.

If the conjunction is not followed by an independent clause, do not put a comma before the conjunction.

Mia's improvement was significant but *unsatisfying to her.*

(The expression *unsatisfying to her* is a predicate adjective and a prepositional phrase, not an independent clause.)

- **Inessential Clauses** Use commas around inessential (nonrestrictive) dependent clauses. Do not put commas around essential (restrictive) clauses.

A clause is **inessential** or **nonrestrictive** if it can be taken out of the sentence without changing the basic meaning of the sentence. Commas around the clause signal that the enclosed idea is additional information, not essential to the meaning of the sentence.

An **essential** or **restrictive** clause cannot be taken out of the sentence without altering the meaning of the sentence. The lack of commas signals that the clause is essential to the meaning of the sentence.

Mia, *who is almost twenty,* improved significantly in her work. [provides additional but not essential information]

The student *who worked so hard* is named Mia. [provides essential information]

PRACTICE 18.3

Commas, Dashes, and Parentheses

Proofread the following passage, adding commas, dashes, or parentheses where necessary. Practice using the appropriate proofreading symbols from the proofreading chart.

The term film noir pronounced nwah which translates from French as "black film" was first used by film critics to refer to the dark themes of many American films that were released during and after WWII. Film noir is not a distinct genre of film but it is defined by the bleak world view the despair and even the paranoia of the post-war period. The hard-boiled detective such as Humphrey Bogart in *The Maltese Falcon* adapted from the novel by Dashiell Hammett was often the anti-hero of these films. Female leads were often tough brassy characters. One of the best known and earliest of these films was *Citizen Kane* 1941. Although less well known *Double Indemnity* 1944 *Spellbound* 1945 and *Murder, My Sweet* 1944 are also good examples of film noir. ∎

USAGE TIP The relative pronoun *which* always introduces an inessential clause, so commas always go around a *which* clause. The relative pronoun *that* always introduces an essential clause, so commas never go around *that* clauses.

The exam**,** *which I found challenging***,** was the final graduation requirement. [provides additional but not essential information]

The exam *that I passed* allowed me to graduate. [provides essential information]

- **Participial and Appositive Phrases** Use commas around participial phrases (verbal phrases that function like adjectives) and appositive phrases (noun phrases that modify nouns or pronouns by describing them in different words). (See 17b-3.)

Modifies

Mia**,** *having worked as hard as she could***,** took a break. [participial phrase]

Renames

Mia**,** *the most diligent student in the class***,** finally earned her A. [appositive phrase]

- **Attributions and Interrupters** Use commas around attributions in quotations and around phrases that interrupt a sentence.

"I am proud of Mia**,**" *he said***,** as he looked over her work. [attribution]

Other teachers**,** *however kind they may be***,** do not see her improvement. [interrupter]

Show me her scores**,** *please*. [interrupter]

- **Clarity** Use commas to help your reader avoid confusion.

To Mia**,** Anne was the role model of a hard worker.

- **Other Uses Commas** are also used in the following situations.

  - In addresses and names of geographical places

    Becca lives at 81 Main Street**,** Madison**,** Wisconsin.

    Last year she traveled to Florence**,** Italy.

  - In openings and closings of letters

    Dear Professor Lopez**,**

    Sincerely**,**

  - In direct address

    Michael**,** do you hear me?

  - In inverted names in bibliographies, indexes, and other reference lists

    Lazlo**,** Ernestine

  - To separate a name from a title or degree and with *Jr.* and *Sr.*

    My internist is Ernestine Lazlo**,** M.D.

    Frank Sinatra**,** Jr.**,** was never as famous as his dad.

- In dates

  October 22, 1968

- With figures that have more than four digits

  $1,250

  1,000,000 burgers sold

18d-2 Dashes

Dashes (— or - -) are used in certain situations instead of commas. A dash creates a less formal tone in a piece of writing.

- **Surprise and Irony** Use a dash to create a sense of surprise or to signal an ironic comment.

  Professor Tsao told us to read all of Chapter 8, to write out four exercises, to complete our research papers—and to have a good weekend. [sets off an ironic comment]

- **Parenthetical Comments** Use dashes to set off a parenthetical comment in a sentence.

  Professor Tsao—a teacher who loves to challenge students—told us to read all of Chapter 8, to write out four exercises, and to complete our research papers by Monday morning. [sets off a parenthetical comment]

- **Lists and Explanations** Use a dash to introduce a list or explanation at the beginning or end of a sentence.

  Tonight I have a huge amount of homework—all of Chapter 8, four exercises, and a research paper.

18d-3 Parentheses

Parentheses ( ) are used in the following cases.

- **Asides** Use parentheses around asides or incidental information.

  Professor Tsao (*my workaholic economics teacher*) piled on the homework.

- **Explanatory Material** Use parentheses around explanatory material.

  I finished all the work (*Chapter 8, four exercises, the research paper*) at midnight on Sunday.

- **Lists within Sentences** Use parentheses around letters or numbers in a list within a sentence.

  I finished the three assignments: (*1*) Chapter 8, (*2*) the exercises, and (*3*) the research paper.

18e Apostrophes and Hyphens

18e-1 Apostrophes

Apostrophes (') are used in possessives and contractions.

- **Possessives** Use an apostrophe to indicate that a noun or an indefinite pronoun is possessive.

  Singular Nouns Use **'s** with singular nouns or pronouns.

  *Professor Johnson***'s** class is hard but interesting.

  *Everyone***'s** workload is lighter than mine.

Use **'s** with most singular nouns ending in *s*. If the noun ends with a *z* or *eez* sound, use the apostrophe alone.

  The *dress***'s** hem was dragging on the ground.

  *Ray Charles***'** performance was mesmerizing. [noun ends with a *z* sound]

- **Plural Nouns** Use **s'** with plural nouns that form the plural by adding an *s*.

  I attended both *professors***'** classes.

  My workload is heavier than all the *bosses***'** workloads put together.

  Use **'s** with irregular plural nouns that do not use *s* to form the plural.

  Put the cheese next to all the *mice***'s** holes.

  *Children***'s** games are often more fun than *adults***'** games.

- **Compound Nouns** Use **'s** on the last word of a compound noun.

  My *sister-in-law***'s** mother visited yesterday.

- **Two or More Nouns** Use **'s** on each noun to show individual ownership, but only on the last noun to show joint ownership.

  *John and Susan***'s** new house required a huge mortgage. [joint ownership]

  *John***'s** *and Susan***'s** studios needed serious renovations. [individual ownership]

USAGE TIP Since possessive pronouns already show possession, they never use apostrophes: *his, hers, its, yours, theirs, whose*: **The line snaked *its* way around the block.**

- **Contractions** Use an apostrophe to replace the letter or letters deleted in a contraction.

do not	don't
that is	that's
Madam	Ma'am
forecastle	fo'c's'le
it is or it has	it's

18e-2 Hyphens

Hyphens (-) are used as follows.

- **Compound Modifiers** Use a hyphen to punctuate compound modifiers that work together to modify nouns.

    The election was a *hard-fought* battle. [*Hard* modifies *fought*, not *battle*; together *hard* and *fought* modify *battle*.]

    Hannah is a *three-year-old* terror. [The words *three*, *year*, and *old* work together to modify *terror*.]

Generally, when the modifier follows the noun, do not hyphenate it.

The battle was *hard fought*.

When the modifier is preceded by an adverb that ends in *-ly* or by the adverb *very*, omit the hyphen.

Kristen is an *extremely bright* child.

Greg is a *very kindhearted* guy.

- **Compound Words** Use the hyphen to form a compound word—a word made up of more than one word that functions as a single word.

    My *brother-in-law* is a *happy-go-lucky* guy.

Make a compound noun plural by putting *s* at the end of the main noun.

I have two accomplished *brothers-in-law*.

Since conventions vary widely about using compound modifiers, it is a good idea to check your dictionary.

- **Prefixes and Suffixes** Use the hyphen to link some prefixes and suffixes to words. The most commonly hyphenated prefixes are *ex-*, *pro-*, *self-*, and *neo-*, and a common suffix is *-elect*. Do not use a hyphen with the common prefixes *anti*, *co*, *non*, *post*, *pre*, and *un*.

    The *governor-elect* tried to be both *pro-choice* and *pro-life*.

Check a dictionary or style guide to determine whether to hyphenate a word with a prefix or suffix.

- **Other Uses** Following are additional uses of hyphens.

    - At the end of a line to divide a word between syllables
    - In written fractions

        one-tenth

    - In numbers from *twenty-one* to *ninety-nine*
    - In numbers and dates that indicate a span

        1979-2015

18f Ellipses, Brackets, and Quotation Marks

18f-1 Ellipses

Ellipses (**. . .**) have the following uses.

■ **Intentional Omissions** Use ellipses to tell your reader that you have intentionally omitted a word or phrase in quoted material.

> In despair Hamlet cries, "O that this too, too sullied flesh would melt **. . .** How weary, stale, flat, and unprofitable seem to me all the uses of this world!" [The writer has omitted three lines of Hamlet's speech that are not pertinent to her point.]

■ **Hesitancy** Use ellipses to indicate a speaker's hesitation or uncertainty.

> Veronica said, "I cannot quite remember **. . .** well **. . .** maybe a few lines from *Hamlet* have stayed in my head."

If the ellipses end the sentence, add the period to make four dots.

> Veronica said, "I just cannot remember**. . . .**"

18f-2 Brackets

Square brackets (**[ ]**) and angle brackets (**< >**) are used in these situations.

■ **Quotations** Use square brackets to indicate that you have added clarifying material to quoted passages.

> The governor said, "I will be glad to give her **[***his opponent, Senator Reo***]** a chance to debate me in a public forum."

Use square brackets to insert words that are necessary to make a quotation grammatical or comprehensible.

> The governor said he would be glad to "debate **[***Senator Reo***]** in a public forum."

■ **Internet Addresses** Some teachers may ask you to use angle brackets in e-mail addresses and Web URLs.

> You can find the news at **<www.cnn.com>**or by e-mailing me at **<kbaruk@ hotmail.com>.**

18f-3 Quotation Marks

Quotation marks (**" "**) have the following uses.

■ **Direct Quotations** Use quotation marks around all material that is directly quoted from other sources or to indicate someone's spoken words in dialogue.

Hamlet's most famous speech begins, "*To be or not to be—that is the question.*" [quotation from other source]

Senator Reo replied, "*I would love to debate the governor.*" [dialogue]

Do not use quotation marks around indirect quotations.

Senator Reo replied that she would love to debate the governor.

USAGE TIP In a quoted sentence within a sentence, do not use a period: **The line "Show me the money" became popular last year.**

■ **Titles** Use quotation marks to set off titles of magazine articles, television episodes, poems, short stories, songs, and other short works. Titles of longer works such as newspapers, magazines, novels, films, television shows, and anthologies are italicized.

I read "The Good Doctor" in the *New Yorker*.

"The Pine Barrens" was my favorite episode of *The Sopranos*.

■ **Single Quotation Marks** Use **single quotation marks (' ')** to set off quotations inside quotations.

The governor announced, "Senator Reo said, 'I accept,' so the debate is on."

■ **Other Punctuation** Follow these rules for using quotation marks with other punctuation marks.

  ■ **Commas and Periods** Commas and periods always go inside quotation marks.

  "Well, then, it is all set," said the governor, "and I am happy."

  ■ **Question Marks and Exclamation Marks** Question marks and exclamation marks go inside the quotation marks when the quoted material is a question or an exclamation, and outside the quotation marks when the whole sentence is a question or an exclamation.

  Who said, "I accept"? [whole sentence is the question]

  The senator asked, "When do you want to debate?" [quoted material is the question]

  He said, "Eureka!" [quoted material is the exclamation]

PRACTICE 18.5

Quotation Marks and Accompanying Punctuation

Proofread the following dialogue, adding all necessary commas, periods, question marks, exclamation marks, and quotation marks. Practice using the appropriate proofreading symbols from the proofreading chart.

1. Quiet she commanded

2. What is wrong he asked Do you hear something

3. What I hear is you talking she answered so stop talking

4. I am scared he cried

5. Then go home she growled You asked Can I come and I said Yes you can

6. Well you should have said No way he said and ran home. ■

18g Capital Letters, Numbers, and Italics

18g-1 Capital Letters

Capital letters are used at the beginning of sentences, in titles, for proper nouns, and for adjectives derived from proper nouns.

- **Proper Nouns** Use capital letters to begin specific names of people, races, titles, geographical locations, regions, historical eras, months, seasons, organizations, and institutions, but not general names of the same.

  > **Georgetown High School** [specific name] **was the best** *high school* [general name] **in the area.**

  > **I shook** *President Zeroff's* [specific title and name] **hand; she was the fifth** *president* [general title] **of** *Central College* [specific institution].

- **Adjectives from Proper Nouns** Use capital letters to begin adjectives made from proper nouns.

  > **The best ethnic food in London is** *Indian* **food.**

  > **Most Londoners prefer crumpets to** *English muffins.*

- **Sentences and Quotations** Use capital letters to begin sentences and quotations. Do not use a capital letter if the quotation is the continuation of a sentence or an excerpt that is a word, phrase, or dependent clause.

  > **"I tried to run," she said, "but my feet would not move."** [quotation is continuation of a sentence]

  > **She felt "awkward, clumsy, and stupid," but it turns out that she was suffering from hypothermia.** [quotation is an excerpt]

- **Titles** Use capital letters to begin all words in titles except for articles (*the/a*), short prepositions, and conjunctions, unless they are the first word in the title: of a book, film, television episode, but do not capitalize for magazines, journals, and newspapers.

  > **"The Pine Barrens" is my favorite episode of** *The Sopranos.*

  > **"The Good Doctor" was first published in the** *New Yorker.*

- **Other Uses** Other examples of the use of capital letters include the following.
  - Nations: *England, Turkey, Japan*
  - Planets: *Mercury, Mars, Venus*
  - Stars: *Perseus, Sirius*
  - Public places: *Times Square, Fisherman's Wharf, the Chicago Loop*
  - Names of streets: *Beacon Street, Oak Lane, Allen Road*
  - Days of the week and month: *Friday, November*
  - Holidays: *Thanksgiving, Bastille Day, Fourth of July*
  - Religions, deities, sacred texts: *Buddhism, Zeus, The Upanishads*
  - Languages: *Hindi, Swedish, Vietnamese*
  - Names of ships and aircraft: *Queen Mary, Enola Gay*
  - The first-person pronoun: *I*

Check a dictionary if you are not sure whether a word or phrase should have an initial capital letter.

18g-2 Numbers

Numbers can appear as numerals or as words.

- **Academic Writing** Spell out numbers from *one* through *ninety-nine* in academic writing.

  It rained for forty days and forty nights.

Use numerals for 100 and higher.

  Archeologists discovered 5,000 bones at the site.

- **Media Writing** Spell out numbers from *one* through *ten* for media writing.

  The census showed ten single-parent households in this village.

Use numerals for *11* and higher.

  The police counted ten members of the clergy and 120 protesters at the sit-in.

- **Beginning Sentences** Spell out numbers that begin sentences.

  Two hundred people attended the council meeting.

- **Page and Chapter Numbers** Use numerals for page and chapter numbers.

  Read pages 3–30 in Chapter 9.

- **Fractions and Percentages** Use numerals for percentages.

  The polls showed a 75 percent approval rating.

- **Addresses and Dates** Use numerals for addresses and dates.

  On January 5, 2006, I will move to 29 Packard Road.

18g-3 Italics

Italics (*italics*) or underlining (<u>underlining</u>) are used in the following situations.

- **Titles** Use italics (on the computer) or underlining (in handwriting) to set off titles of long works such as books, newspapers, magazines, journals, movies, and plays.

  I read a review of *The Taming of the Shrew* in *Entertainment Magazine*.

  I read a review of <u>The Taming of the Shrew</u> in <u>Entertainment Magazine</u>.

- **Foreign Words** Use italics (on the computer) or underlining (in handwriting) to set off foreign words.

  Jacques called his grandmother "*grand-mére*."

- **Words, Letters, Numbers** Use italics (on the computer) or underlining (in handwriting) to set off words, letters, and numbers when referring to them.

  How many *3*s are in *9*?

  Spell *quick* with a *q* not a *kw*.

PRACTICE 18.6

Capital Letters, Numbers, and Italics

Proofread the following passage, adding capital letters, numbers in their correct form, and italics where necessary. Practice using the appropriate proofreading symbols from the proofreading chart.

4 years ago I had no idea that college was even in my future. I lived in a small town, population twenty thousand, in the southwest. Only fifty percent of our graduating class went on to college. One day in english class I read a novel by the portuguese writer Jose Saramago. The novel was called blindness, and it is about White Blindness that causes everyone in an unnamed european City to go blind. We discussed the Novel in class, and I realized that I loved talking and thinking about Books and Movies. It was then that I decided that College was indeed what I wanted, and I went to my Guidance Counselor that very day. ■

©Shawn Hempel/
Shutterstock.com

COMMON ERRORS

Once you understand the parts of speech, parts of sentences, and sentence types reviewed in Chapter 17, you know the basic concepts that will allow you to make sense of grammatical rules. In this section, you will learn to identify and avoid making errors in

- sentence structure
- agreement
- verb tense
- parallelism
- modification
- frequently confused words

19a Sentence Structure Errors

19a-1 Fragments

A sentence written in standard English has a subject and a complete predicate (a verb and its modifiers or complements). (See 17b.) A **fragment** is missing one of its parts, either the subject or the verb. Sometimes writers use fragments intentionally for emphasis or to dramatize thinking that is confused.

I love you. *A lot.* [emphasis]

She ran through the corridors. *Where to go? In a room? In a closet?* [confusion]

Using intentional fragments is a stylistic choice. When fragments are unintentional, they are considered sentence structure errors. Learn to identify and correct the following kinds of fragments.

■ **Omitting the Verb** A fragment may be caused by the omission of a verb.

FRAGMENT: *Isabel running down the corridor into rooms and closets.* [*Running* (a participle) describes Isabel, and the subject *Isabel* has no true verb.]

COMPLETE SENTENCE: Isabel ran down the corridor into rooms and closets. [*Ran* is the verb.]

■ **Omitting the Subject** Not including a subject also causes a fragment.

FRAGMENT: Isabel ran down the corridor. *And looked into rooms and closets.* [The verb *looked* has no subject.]

COMPLETE SENTENCE: Isabel ran down the corridor and looked into rooms and closets. [*Isabel* is the subject; *ran* and *looked* are compound verbs describing what she did.]

COMPLETE SENTENCE: Isabel ran down the corridor. She looked into rooms and closets. [*She* is the subject of the second sentence.]

■ **Using Dependent Clauses Alone** A **dependent (subordinate) clause** contains a subject and a verb, but it cannot stand alone. It must be connected to an independent clause to form a complete sentence.

Dependent clauses begin with subordinating conjunctions such as *although*, *because*, *if*, and *when* or relative pronouns such as *who*, *which*, or *that*. (See 17b-4.)

FRAGMENT: ***Although she was initially scared and confused.*** [Even though this group of words has a subject *she* and a verb *was*, it is a dependent clause and a fragment. It does not express a complete thought and cannot stand alone.]

COMPLETE SENTENCE: Although she was initially scared and confused, Isabel finally figured out where she was. [The dependent clause *Although she was initially scared and confused* is now connected to the independent clause *Isabel finally figured out where she was.*]

COMPLETE SENTENCE: She was initially scared and confused. [Dropping the subordinating conjunction *although* makes this a complete sentence.]

19a-2 Fused Sentences and Comma Splice Errors

Fused sentences and **comma splice errors** occur when two complete sentences are run together. A fused sentence has no punctuation between the two complete sentences.

FUSED: ***Isabel ran down the corridor she did not know where she was going.*** A comma splice error has a comma between the two complete sentences.

COMMA SPLICE: ***Isabel ran down the corridor, she did not know where she was going.*** To correct the errors, first identify the two complete sentences. Then you can fix them in one of four ways.

1. Add a period.

    Isabel ran down the corridor. She did not know where she was going.

2. Add a semicolon.

    Isabel ran down the corridor; she did not know where she was going.

3. Add a comma and a coordinating conjunction.

    Isabel ran down the corridor, but she did not know where she was going.

4. Add a subordinating conjunction to one sentence.

    Although Isabel ran down the corridor, she did not know where she was going. [If you introduce the sentence with a dependent clause, put a comma after the introductory clause.]

19b Agreement Errors

In English grammar, subjects agree with their verbs and pronouns with their antecedents.

PRACTICE 19.1

Fragments, Fused Sentences, and Comma Splice Errors

Identify and correct the sentence structure errors in the following passage. Mark all fragments (frag), fused sentences (FS), and comma splice errors (CS).

Isabel never forgot her car keys, they were always clipped securely to her belt. Always handy. She was surprised and annoyed that she had lost them, moreover, she was late for her practice. Isabel, not believing she was in such a crunch. She checked the ground near her car, then she bolted for the building. As she ran down the corridor, checking the floors and looking into classrooms. She heard the clanking of metal on metal. In front of her was her little sister Molly, Molly had a grin on her face as she jangled the keys. "I guess you can give me that ride now," Molly said, "Let's go, you don't want to be late for practice." ∎

19b-1 Subject-Verb Agreement

Subjects and verbs agree in number; a singular subject takes a singular verb, and a plural subject takes a plural verb.

SINGULAR SUBJECT AND VERB: *Chris runs* **three campaigns at the same time.**

A verb agrees with the subject of the sentence, not with the noun in an intervening prepositional phrase.

One **of the boys** *runs* **the antismoking campaign.** [The subject is *one*, not the noun *boys* in the prepositional phrase *of the boys*.]

PLURAL SUBJECT AND VERB: *Chris and Jason run* **three campaigns together.**

■ **Compound Subject** A verb that agrees with a **compound subject** joined by *and* is usually plural.

Christopher and Jason run **the campaign.** [The compound subject is *Christopher and Jason*.]

A verb agreeing with a compound subject that is preceded by *each* or *every* is singular.

Each **boy and girl** *is* **a good organizer.**

When a compound subject is joined by *or* or *nor*, the verb agrees with the subject closest to it.

Neither **Christopher** *nor* **the other** *boys run* **the campaign in a vacuum.** [*Boys* is the subject closest to the verb, so the verb is plural.]

■ **Collective Noun** A verb agreeing with a **collective noun** (a noun that represents a group but functions as a single entity) is singular. Some examples of collective nouns are *audience, committee, jury, family*, and *group*.

The antismoking *committee runs* **a fundraiser each year.**

■ **Indefinite Pronoun** Agreement of verbs with **indefinite pronouns** can be confusing. These three rules govern the agreement of indefinite pronouns and verbs.

1. Some indefinite pronouns always take singular verbs; *each, everyone, everybody, everything, either, neither, anyone, anybody, anything, one, no one, nobody, nothing, someone, somebody*, and *something* act as third-person singular pronouns.

Someone has **to run this campaign.**

One **of the boys** *is* **going to be the high school liaison.**

2. Some indefinite pronouns always take plural verbs; *many, most, both, few,* and *several* are plural in meaning and thus take plural verbs.

Many *are* go-getters, but *few are* as enthusiastic as they.

Several *are* extraordinarily talented.

3. Some indefinite pronouns can be either singular or plural, depending on the context. These indefinite pronouns include *all, any, none,* and *some.*

All the boys *are* qualified to run the campaign. [In this case, *all* refers to *boys,* which is plural.]

All the pie *has* been eaten. [In this case, *all* refers to *pie,* which is singular.]

19b-2 Pronoun-Antecedent Agreement

Pronouns must agree in person (first, second, third), gender (male, female), and number (singular, plural) with the nouns or other pronouns they refer to in the sentence. (In pronoun use, **person** refers to the use of I or *we* for first person, *you* for second person, and *he, she, it,* or *they* for third person.)

The nouns or pronouns that pronouns refer to are called their **antecedents**. The general rule is that pronouns refer to the closest already-named noun. As a writer, you have to be sure that the pronoun reference is both unambiguous and in agreement.

■ **Ambiguous Pronoun** An **ambiguous pronoun reference** confuses the reader as to whom or what the pronoun refers.

AMBIGUOUS: When Christopher asked Jason to run the campaign, *he* **blushed**. [Since *he* could refer to either man, it is not clear who blushed.]

CLEAR: When Christopher asked Jason to run the campaign, *Jason* **blushed**.

Ambiguity also occurs when pronouns do not refer to anything that has been named in the sentence. Usually the ambiguous pronouns are *it, this, that,* or *which.* In these cases, substitute clear nouns for the ambiguous pronouns.

AMBIGUOUS: The campaign was funny and irreverent. *They* **hung** *it* **in the student union and put** *it* **on the campus radio station.**

CLEAR: The campaign was funny and irreverent. *The committee members* **hung** *a poster* **in the student union and put** *an ad* **on the campus radio station.**

■ **Agreement in Person** Make sure the pronoun agrees in person (first, second, or third) with its antecedent. Do not, for example, mix a third-person antecedent with a second-person pronoun.

INCORRECT: *Students* **should bring** *your* **good ideas to the meeting.**

CORRECT: *Students* **should bring** *their* **good ideas to the meeting.**

DO NOT ENTER
WRONG WAY

PRACTICE 19.2

Agreement

Identify and correct the agreement errors in the following passage. Mark and correct all errors in subject-verb agreement (s-v agr) and pronoun-antecedent agreement (p-a agr).

Today, a collegewide coalition of student activists meet to launch their antismoking campaign. The two organizers, one a sophomore and one a junior, speaks at noon. The event is open to anyone who are students at this college.

Each committee member have created a public awareness poster or radio spot that best expresses his position on the anti-smoking issue. It should be relevant and appeal to students. Some students have written radio spots; others have drawn posters; someone have even created a television storyboard.

After the presentation, they will vote for the best one. Either one student or two has a chance to win a $50 prize. The best reward, of course, is a heightened awareness of its dangers. ■

■ **Agreement in Gender and Gender-Equal Pronouns** Pronouns and their antecedents have conventionally agreed in gender. Male antecedents have required *his* as the pronoun referent; female antecedents have required *her*. This rule does not usually pose a problem unless you get into the tricky area of deciding whether to refer to a mixed-gender group as male or female. Since you want to be both clear and accurate, the most sensible way to solve this problem is either to change the pronoun and its antecedent to their plural forms or to use the slightly longer, but equally acceptable, *his or her*. Rules about gender specificity are changing, however, and these rules are evolving to allow the gender non-specific pronoun "their" and "they" with a singular antecedent.

PLURAL: *People brought **their** best ideas.*

GENDER EQUAL: *Each person brought **his or her** best idea.*

GENDER NON-SPECIFIC: *Each person brought **their** best idea.*

■ **Agreement in Number** Make sure a singular pronoun agrees with a singular antecedent and a plural pronoun with a plural antecedent. If the antecedent is a compound subject joined by *and*, the pronoun will be plural.

*Christopher and Jason did **their** work well.*

If the antecedent is a compound subject joined by *or*, the pronoun will agree with the antecedent closest to the pronoun.

*Either Christopher or Jason did all **his** work.*

If the antecedent is an indefinite pronoun, the pronoun is usually singular. (See the rules for subject-verb agreement in 19b-1 for indefinite pronouns that are singular, plural, or both.)

*Either can do the work as long as **he** is willing.*

*Ask both to bring **their** best ideas.*

19c Pronoun Case Errors

Pronouns change forms depending on whether they are used as subjects or objects in a sentence, or show possession.

Subject Pronouns (SP)	Object Pronouns (OP)	Possessive Pronouns (PP)
I	me	my, mine
you	you	your, yours
he, she, it	him, her, it	his, her, hers, its
we	us	our, ours
they	them	their, theirs
who/whoever	whom/whomever	whose

19c-1 Subject Pronouns

Subject pronouns (also known as **nominative pronouns**) substitute for nouns that are subjects in clauses and sentences, are appositives of words in the subject case (17b-3), or are subject complements (nouns that come after linking verbs and rename the subjects). (See 17b-2.) A pronoun can be the subject of the sentence.

>*He* **plays lead guitar in the band.** [*He* is the subject of the verb *plays.*]

>*They* **are booked for the next three weekends.** [*They* is the subject of the verb *are.*]

The pronoun can serve as an appositive.

>*We* **fans go to all of the shows.** [*We* is the appositive of the subject noun *fans.*]

The pronoun can be used as a predicate noun.

>**The most ardent fan is** *she.* [*She* is the subject complement of the noun *fan.*]

>**It was** *they* **who began the new sound in popular music.** [*They* is the subject complement of the pronoun *it.*]

19c-2 Object Pronouns

Object pronouns substitute for nouns that are direct or indirect objects, the objects of prepositions, or appositives of nouns in the objective case. Pronouns can be direct or indirect objects.

>**The usher gave** *us* **our programs.** [*Us* is the indirect object.]

>**The usher gave** *it* **to us.** [*It* is the direct object.]

A pronoun can serve as the object of a preposition.

>**My little sister sat** *between* **my friend and** *me.* [*Me* is the object of the preposition *between.*]

An object pronoun can be an appositive.

>**The lead guitarist sang directly to** *us* **fans.** [*Us* is the appositive of the noun *fans.*]

19c-3 Who and Whom/Whoever and Whomever

Knowing that the pronouns *who* and *whoever* are subject pronouns and *whom* and *whomever* are object pronouns should help you figure out how to use these pronouns correctly.

>**Greg is the drummer** *who* **plays with the band.** [*Who* is the subject of the verb *plays.*]

>**The manager hires** *whoever* **has talent and drive.** [*Whoever* is the subject of the verb *has.*]

>**Greg is the drummer** *whom* **Tess loves.** [*Whom* is the direct object of the verb *loves.*]

Greg is the drummer to *whom* Tess wrote a fan letter. [*Whom* is the object of the preposition *to*.]

Tess contacts *whomever* she admires. [*Whomever* is the direct object of the verb *admires*.]

Sometimes the choice between *who* and *whom* can be confusing when words or phrases come between the subject pronoun *who* and its verb.

PARENTHETICAL

Tess is the fan *who* we all agree is most knowledgeable about the music. [The words *we all agree* form a parenthetical expression that interrupts the sentence. *Who* is the subject of the verb *is*.]

Choosing between *who/whoever* and *whom/whomever* in prepositional phrases can also be tricky. Most of the time, a pronoun in a prepositional phrase takes the object form.

To *whom* should Tess give the tickets? [*Whom* is the object of the preposition *to*.]

However, when the prepositional phrase includes a clause, the rule changes. The pronoun after the preposition becomes the subject of the dependent clause, and the entire clause functions as the object of the preposition. The correct pronoun form should be *who* or *whoever*.

OBJECT OF PREPOSITION
PREP. | S | V

Tess wanted to speak with *whoever* could get her an autograph. [*Whoever* becomes the subject of the verb phrase *could get*. The entire noun dependent clause *whoever could get her an autograph* becomes the object of the preposition *with*.]

OBJECT OF PREPOSITION
PREP. | S | V

The band gave autographs to *whoever* waited at the stage door. [*Whoever* becomes the subject of the verb *waited*. The entire noun dependent clause *whoever waited at the stage door* becomes the object of the preposition *to*.]

19c-4 Possessive Pronouns

Possessive pronouns, like possessive nouns, show ownership.

Coach *Brown's* team was not ready for the game. [*Brown's* is a possessive noun.]

***His* team was dispirited because of *its* losses.** [*His* and *its* are possessive pronouns.]

When they show possession, personal pronouns and the relative pronoun *who* do not use apostrophes. *My, mine, our, ours, your, yours, his, her, hers, its, their, theirs,* and *whose* are already in the possessive form. (See 18e-1 for apostrophe use with possessive nouns and indefinite pronouns.) Be careful not to mix up the possessive form of these pronouns with contractions of pronouns and verbs:

it + is = it's   *you + are = you're*

who + is = who's   *they + are = they're*

Choose the correct pronoun case from the boldfaced words in the following sentences.

1. **(We/Us)** students decided to hike for a week during the break.

2. The seniors gave the job of organizing the equipment to **(we/us)** sophomores.

3. Graham gave us a lecture about **(his/him)** hiking.

4. The most enthusiastic hiker is **(he/him)**.

5. The student **(who/whom)** was the most experienced will be the leader for the first day.

6. Most of us will follow **(whoever/whomever)** we respect.

7. The job of cook will go to **(whoever/whomever)** can boil water.

8. Hikers **(who/whom)** Graham says are fit can begin **(their/they're/there)** trek tomorrow.

9. Helena will be one of the hikers **(who/whom)** Graham will train tonight.

10. **("Your/ "You're)** ready to start whenever **(your/ you're)** group is ready," he said. ■

POSSESSIVE PRONOUN: Give the team *its* due.

PRONOUN-VERB CONTRACTION: *It's* time to look at the bright side.

POSSESSIVE PRONOUN: This is the team *whose* efforts have been greatest.

PRONOUN-VERB CONTRACTION: Jake is the player *who's* most improved.

POSSESSIVE PRONOUN: *Your* hard work has paid off.

PRONOUN-VERB CONTRACTION: *You're* to be congratulated.

POSSESSIVE PRONOUN: *Their* teamwork has been exemplary.

PRONOUN-VERB CONTRACTION: *They're* proud of all the players this season.

USAGE TIP Be careful not to confuse *their* and *they're* with the expletive *there*:

> *There* are many reasons that *they're* proud of *their* efforts.

Use the possessive case when a pronoun modifies a gerund (a verbal formed by adding *ing* to a verb that functions as a noun). (See 17b-3.)

> *Their* running has been superb. [*Their* modifies the gerund *running.*]

> No one can fault *his* coaching. [*His* modifies the gerund *coaching.*]

19d Verb Tense Errors

Sometimes verbs can trip you up if you are not careful about the time relationships among events in your writing. Two problem areas are maintaining the correct verb tense progression and using the correct verb tense consistently.

19d-1 Verb Tense Progression

Verbs change tense in order to show time relationships among events. The principal verb tenses are listed on this chart.

	Present	**Past**	**Future**
Simple	*I run*	*I ran*	*I will run*
Progressive	*I am running*	*I was running*	*I will be running*
Perfect	*I have run*	*I had run*	*I will have run*

Simple tenses show events occurring in the present, the past, and the future.

PRESENT: Chris *runs* a good campaign.

PAST: Chris *ran* a good campaign.

FUTURE: Chris *will run* a good campaign.

PRACTICE 19.4

Verb Tense Progression

Choose the correct verb tense for each sentence below.

1. After the success of the campaign, Chris **(will run/will have run)** for office in his public relations organization.

2. Jason **(was/had been)** an officer the year before they mounted the campaign.

3. Right now, Chris and Jason **(are speaking/speak)** to students in the Student Union.

4. In high school Chris and Jason **(belonged/had belonged)** to a PR club.

5. Before they **(graduated/had graduated/were graduating)**, they **(had won/won/were winning)** a prize for creativity. ■

Progressive tenses show an action in progress.

PRESENT: Chris *is running* a good campaign.

PAST: Chris *was running* a good campaign.

FUTURE: Chris *will be running* a good campaign.

Perfect tenses show an action completed prior to another action.

PRESENT: Chris *has run* a good campaign until today.

PAST: Chris *had run* a good campaign until he hit a snag yesterday.

FUTURE: Chris *will have run* a good campaign when he finally wins an election.

19d-2 Verb Tense Consistency

To maintain verb tense consistency, do not shift verbs from one tense to another unless you are indicating a time change. Once you choose a verb tense in which to report an event or tell a story, be consistent.

INCORRECT: When the campaign *was* over, they *feel* satisfied.

CORRECT: When the campaign *is* over, they will *feel* satisfied.

CORRECT: When the campaign *was* over, they *felt* satisfied.

Three conventions of verb tense use are as follows.

1. In discussing literary works, use present tense.

   Jonathan Franzen *writes* about the Midwest state of mind.

2. In reporting a story for a newspaper, use past tense.

   Jonathan Franzen *explained* his perspective in a reading last night.

3. In making a generalization, use present tense.

   Jonathan Franzen *writes* postmodern fiction.

19e Parallelism

To maintain parallelism or parallel structure in your writing, keep words, phrases, and clauses in the same grammatical form when they are in a series or connected by a coordinating conjunction.

PARALLEL NOUNS: Dana does not eat *candy*, *cake*, or *pasta*.

PARALLEL ADJECTIVES: Dana is *strong*, *healthy*, and *athletic*.

PARALLEL VERBS: Dana *rides* horses, *plays* basketball, and *swims*.

PARALLEL PHRASES: Dana loves *riding horses*, *playing basketball*, and *swimming laps in the pool*. [parallel gerund phrases]

PARALLEL CLAUSES: *Dana loves to ride horses*, and *she loves to play basketball*. [parallel independent clauses]

PRACTICE 19.5
Verb Tense Consistency

Choose the correct verb tense for the boldfaced verbs in the following sentences.

1. Three students (**worked/ work**) for Habitat for Humanity over spring break, according to the Office of Student Services.

2. Community service (**is/ was**) an important part of an education at our college.

3. Erica (**teaches/had taught/ taught**) school kids in Ecuador last year.

4. The plot of the book (**centers/centered**) around three students who wander into the rain forest.

5. When they returned from spring break, they (**write/ wrote**) a report to put on file. ■

FAULTY PARALLELISM: Dana loves *to ride*, *play*, and *swimming*. [*to ride* and *play* are infinitives; *swimming* is a gerund]

Maintain parallel structure in comparisons using *as* or *than*.

NONPARALLEL STRUCTURE: *Eating healthfully* is as important as *to play sports*.

PARALLEL STRUCTURE: *Eating healthfully* is as important as *playing sports*.

NONPARALLEL STRUCTURE: Dana's *sports equipment* is better than *Louise*. [comparing sports equipment to Louise]

PARALLEL STRUCTURE: Dana's *sports equipment* is better than *Louise's*. [correctly comparing Dana's equipment to Louise's equipment]

Maintain parallel structure with correlative conjunctions (see 17a-7).

NONPARALLEL STRUCTURE: *Not only* does Dana love to swim *but* she *also* is running every day.

PARALLEL STRUCTURE: *Not only* does Dana love to swim *but* she *also* runs every day.

USAGE TIP Use parallel structure to achieve a sense of balance and elegance in your writing. Many memorable lines in literature or speech use this kind of parallel structure or balance: *"Ask not what your country can do for you; ask what you can do for your country."*—John F. Kennedy. *"I have nothing to offer but blood, toil, tears and sweat."*—Winston Churchill.

19f Modification Errors

Modifiers are words, phrases, or clauses that qualify or limit. Modifiers function as adjectives or adverbs (see 17a-4 and 17a-5). Errors occur when modifiers are misplaced or positioned so that they do not clearly refer to the word or phrase they modify.

19f-1 Misplaced Modifiers

Modifiers should appear next to the word(s) they modify. Misplaced modifiers often create confusion and sometimes even unintentional humor.

MISPLACED: I rented a movie at the video store *starring Tom Hanks*. [*starring Tom Hanks* incorrectly refers to the video store, not the movie]

CORRECTLY PLACED: At the video store, I rented a movie *starring Tom Hanks*.

MISPLACED: My friend gave me four dollars to rent the movie *in quarters*. [*in quarters* incorrectly refers to the movie, not the four dollars]

CORRECTLY PLACED: My friend gave me four dollars *in quarters* **to rent the movie**.

Modifiers like *only*, *frequently*, and *sometimes* can be confusing if they are placed in the middle of a sentence; such placement can cause confusion about whether these adverbs are modifying the words that precede them or follow them.

AMBIGUOUS: Tom Hanks plays roles *frequently* **portraying a hero**. [*Frequently* can refer to how often Hanks plays roles or to how often he portrays a hero.]

CLEAR: Tom Hanks *frequently* **plays roles portraying a hero**.

CLEAR: Tom Hanks plays many roles; he portrays a hero *frequently*.

19f-2 Dangling Modifiers

Dangling modifiers dangle because they have nothing in the sentence to modify. Often, dangling modifiers are introductory participial phrases like *seeing the movie* or infinitive phrases like *to see the movie*. Grammatically, the phrase should modify the noun or pronoun that immediately follows it.

DANGLING MODIFIER: *Seeing the movie,* **Tom Hanks was extraordinary.** [*Seeing the movie* dangles. This phrase incorrectly modifies *Tom Hanks*.]

CLEAR: *Seeing the movie,* **Gus thought Tom Hanks was extraordinary.** [*Seeing the movie* modifies *Gus*.]

DANGLING MODIFIER: *To see the movie clearly,* **glasses had to be worn.** [*To see the movie clearly* dangles. The phrase incorrectly modifies *glasses*.]

CLEAR: *To see the movie clearly,* **Gus had to wear his glasses.** [*To see the movie clearly* modifies *Gus*.]

19g Frequently Confused Words

Some pairs of words sound enough alike or have such similar spellings or meanings that they may be confusing. This list explains some word pairs that are frequently confused.

■ **advice, advise** *Advice* is a noun, and *advise* is a verb.

   My counselor *advised* me to listen to his good *advice*.

■ **affect, effect** Most of the time *affect* is a verb meaning "to influence."

   How much will that C *affect* my final grade?

Rewrite the following sentences, identifying and fixing the dangling modifiers (DM) and misplaced modifiers (MM).

1. Seeing the film for the first time, Tom Hanks was perfect in the role.

2. When finding himself alone, a soccer ball became his surrogate friend.

3. Hanks's character dined on fish and coconut milk that he speared in the ocean.

4. After being rescued, raw fish turned his stomach.

5. The camera focused on the lavish buffet of lobster, crabs, and sushi in a tight shot.

6. I eat fish frequently getting an allergic reaction. ■

Most of the time *effect* is a noun meaning "the result."

What is the *effect* of that C on my final grade?

Used as a verb, *affect* means "to put on a false show."

He *affected* an air of boredom.

Effect can be also a verb, meaning "to cause."

He *effected* the change of mood by laughing loudly.

■ **among, between** Generally, use *among* when referring to many things and *between* when referring to two things.

Kenza divided the candy *between* the two kids; they divvied it up *among* their friends.

■ **anxious, eager** Use *anxious* to suggest worry and *eager* to suggest anticipation.

Isabella is *eager* to start her new job but *anxious* about making a mistake.

■ **as, like** *As* is a subordinating conjunction. It introduces a subordinate clause.

Jose looks as *if* he saw a ghost.

Like is a preposition. It is followed by the object of a preposition.

He looks *like* a ghost.

■ **bad, badly** *Bad* is an adjective, and *badly* is an adverb. Use the adjective form *bad* after a linking verb.

Scott felt *bad* because he had the flu. [*Bad* describes his state of being.]

Scott played the piano *badly*. [*Badly* describes how he *played* the piano.]

■ **beside, besides** *Beside* means "next to." *Besides* means "also" or "other than."

I put my book *beside* the table.

***Besides*, I wanted to read it before I went to sleep.**

Nothing *besides* a nap would do.

■ **censor, censure** Both words can be nouns or verbs. As a noun, *censor* names the person who deletes objectionable material, and as a verb *censor* is the act of deleting that material.

The *censor censored* my mail.

As a noun, *censure* means "disapproval," and as a verb it means "to disapprove."

The student body *censured* Gene for plagiarism.

Gene took the *censure* seriously.

■ **continual, continuous** *Continual* means "repeated often," while *continuous* means "ongoing."

Shane had *continual* run-ins with his professor.

Their *continuous* argument about grades gave us all headaches.

■ **different from, different than** Generally speaking, use *different from*.

> This movie is significantly *different from* the book.

■ **disinterested, uninterested** A *disinterested* person is impartial; an *uninterested* person is bored.

> Fatima was *uninterested* in the lecture, but she wanted a *disinterested* person to judge whether the professor was boring.

■ **elicit, illicit** *Elicit* is a verb that means "to draw out"; *illicit* is an adjective that means "illegal."

> The detective *elicited* a confession from the crook, but since his words were recorded on an *illicit* wiretap, the confession was inadmissible in court.

■ **farther, further** In formal writing, use *farther* to suggest distance and *further* to suggest degree.

> Augie lives *farther* from school than you.

> Callie has *further* research to do on her paper.

■ **fewer, less** Use *fewer* with countable items and *less* with quantities or amounts.

> The store sold *fewer* quarts of milk this week.

> They now have *less* milk in stock.

■ **good, well** Generally speaking, *good* is an adjective and *well* is an adverb.

> Lila had a *good* plan that she executed *well*. [*Good* modifies the noun *plan*; *well* modifies the infinitive (a verb form) *executed*.]

After a linking verb, use the predicate adjective *good*.

> Although I have attended only one lecture, Professor Bloom seems *good*.

When referring to health, *well* functions as an adjective.

> Although she was ill for a while, now Professor Bloom seems *well*.

■ **hanged, hung** Use *hanged* with bodies (executions) and *hung* with objects (curtains).

> In old westerns, murderers were *hanged* at dawn.

> We *hung* our clothes in the closet.

■ **imply, infer** Both words are verbs, but *imply* means "to suggest" and *infer* means "to deduce" or "to draw a conclusion."

> I *implied* that we should be friends, but he *inferred* that I never wanted to see him again.

■ **irregardless, regardless** *Irregardless* is considered nonstandard usage in all situations. Always use *regardless*.

> I want to see you *regardless* of the consequences.

528

- **its, it's** *Its* is a possessive pronoun, and *it's* is a contraction of *it* and *is*.

    The clock had a smudge on *its* face.

    ***It's* time to go.**

- **lay, lie** *Lay* is a transitive verb that takes a direct object. It means "to put something down." *Lie* is an intransitive verb that means "to recline."

    I *lay* the book on the table.

    When I am tired, I *lie* down.

The two verbs use the following forms (see 19d-1).

Present	Past	Perfect	Progressive
lay	*laid*	*laid*	*laying*
lie	*lay*	*lain*	*lying*

- **lend, loan** Use *lend* as a verb and *loan* as a noun.

    Jacob had to take out a *loan* because Tony would not *lend* him a dime.

- **media, medium** *Media* is the plural form of *medium*.

    The film *medium* is the most dynamic, but all the visual *media* interest Vassili.

- **prejudice, prejudiced** *Prejudice* is a noun; *prejudiced* is an adjective.

    Jonah had a great deal of *prejudice* against *prejudiced* people.

- **principal, principle** Use *principal* for a person who is the head of an organization, such as the principal of a school. When used as an adjective, *principal* also means the main or most important element. *Principle* is a truth, a tenet, or a belief.

    Mr. Leavy is the *principal* of my sister's high school. [head of school]

    The *principal* crop is wheat. [main]

    The university's hiring policy is based on the *principles* of diversity and equality. [tenets]

- **proved, proven** Use *proved* as the past participle form of *prove* and *proven* as the adjective form.

    His *proven* [adjective] record of support for tax cuts *has proved* [past participle] that he is the best candidate for mayor.

- **quote, quotation** *Quote* is a verb, *quotation* a noun.

    Always *quote* accurately from all *quotations*.

Media writers sometimes use *quote* as a noun.

    The reporter got some good *quotes* for her article.

PRACTICE 19.8
Frequently Confused Words

To review confusing word pairs, choose the correct word in the following sentences.

1. (To/Too/Two) often we are so (eager/anxious) to begin a new adventure that we forget to (sit/set) for a while and think about (its/it's) possible outcomes.

2. (There/Their/They're) are many questions to (rise/raise) before (your/you're) able to choose wisely.

■ **raise, rise** *Raise* is a transitive verb, so it always takes a direct object. It means "to cause something to move upward" or "to bring up." *Rise* is an intransitive verb that means "to move upward."

Mama *raised* her kids to *rise* when grownups entered the room.

■ **sit, set** *Sit* is an intransitive verb meaning "to take a seat." *Set* is a transitive verb that takes a direct object and means "to put something down."

When you *sit* on your chair, please *set* the teacup on the table.

■ **than, then** Use *than* with comparisons and *then* to indicate time.

She is taller *than* her mother.

She grew as tall as her mother, and *then* she grew taller.

■ **their/there/they're** Each of these homonyms has a different meaning. *Their* is a pronoun that indicates possession. *There* is an adverb that indicates place. *They're* is a contraction of *they* and *are*.

The children have *their* father's eyes.

Put the book down *there*.

They're free to leave whenever they desire.

■ **to, too, two** Each of these homonyms has a different meaning. *To* is a preposition (to the store). *Too* is an adverb meaning "also" or "many." *Two* is the number after *one*.

We went *to* the all-you-can-eat buffet.

We ate *too* much.

Two of us had to lie down for an hour.

■ **who, whom** Use *who* or *whom* when referring to people; use *that* or *which* when referring to objects.

Who functions as a subject in a sentence or clause, and *whom* functions as an object in a sentence or clause.

Who is this masked man? [*Who* is the subject of the sentence.]

He is the masked man *who* saved your life. [*Who* is the subject of the dependent clause.]

Whom do you trust? [*Whom* is the direct object.]

He is the man *whom* I trust with my life. [*Whom* is the direct object in the dependent clause.]

■ **who's, whose** *Who's* is a contraction of *who is*, and *whose* is a possessive pronoun.

Whose turn is it to see the man *who's* so ill?

■ **your, you're** *Your* is a possessive pronoun; *you're* is a contraction of *you are*.

You're a person who likes *your* food prepared well.

(continued)

3. For example, (who/whom) do you want to accompany you when you (sit/set) off?

4. (Who/Whom) is your choice of companion when you feel (bad/badly) or when things don't go (well/ good)?

5. I would want to be with someone with a (proved, proven) track record, someone (who/whom/that/ which) would rather be safe (than/then) take risks (regardless/irregardless) of the consequences.

6. I don't mean to (imply/infer) that I am (prejudice/preju- diced) against risk-takers. I just feel (like/as if) I want to have a cool head around me when I'm about to (lay/ lie) my life on the line.

7. My (principal, principle) goals are to experience life, to go (further, farther) than people expect, and to make (fewer/less) mistakes than those who have gone before me. ■

19 COMMON ERRORS

INDEX

PUBLISHING *WRITING IN THE WORKS* WRITING PROJECTS

Few things are more satisfying—or more affirming—for a writer than seeing your work in print. If you are lucky, you may even get paid for it. Publishing your work is possible if you research the markets that exist for the writing assignments you have done.

MEMOIRS

Think about the stakeholders in your story. Is your story about alcoholism, anorexia, or another "overcoming-odds" subject? If so, health magazines might be a good market. If your memoir focuses on a particular ethnic or religious community (growing up African-American, Italian, Catholic, or Jewish), look for magazines such as *African-American Heritage, The American Citizen Italian Press, The B'nai B'rith International, Jewish Monthly, and American Dane*. A great resource for the professional writer is *Writer's Market*, an annual catalog of American and Canadian publications that lists publications by areas of interest. You can get information on what type of articles the publication buys, the address for sending a manuscript or query letter, and how long it will take to get a response.

PROFILES

If you are going to try to publish any of your writing, this genre is the best choice. Because so many businesses, clubs, churches, and civic groups have national magazines and newsletters that include interesting profiles of members or people involved in activities related to the group, you have an excellent chance at publishing almost any profile. Your college newspaper or alumni magazine (if there is one) would also be a good place to publish a profile about a current student, a graduate, a professor, an administrator, or an employee. Large metropolitan papers have special sections for specific geographical areas. These special sections are always looking for profiles, especially if they have some connection to a news event or some recent issue. Your local daily newspaper and specialty magazines are obvious places to start. Investigate whether the publication has recently published similar profiles and if the tone, style, and topic of your profile fits with the profiles previously published. Many publications have Web sites that list publication guidelines and give information on submitting articles.

SHORT ARTICLES AND REPORTS

The Internet is a great venue for "going public" with your writing. On Web sites the skill of compressing many words to few is especially important because of the way people use the Web as an information source. Some online magazines, like the online *Smithsonian*, post abstracts of longer articles, which function essentially as short essays. Web technology in general, with its hot buttons and links, has made it easy for writers to add interesting asides to their articles. Read several issues before querying a particular publication about your piece, and find out who is supposed to receive such queries by looking at the Web site or phoning the publication. You can call or e-mail a query. Keep your pitch short: One paragraph is best. Explain why your piece would interest the audience of the publication. Indicate whether the piece is time-sensitive. Because of security and virus concerns, put the information (including your contact information) in the body of your e-mail message.